What are "emotions"? Drawing together the threads of current research on the nature and functions of emotional expression, of physiological reactions, and of emotional experience, this book offers a balanced survey of facts and theory. Nico Frijda discusses the motivational and neurophysiological preconditions for emotions, and the ways in which emotions are regulated by the individual.

Considering the kinds of events that elicit emotions, he argues that emotions arise because events are appraised by people as favorable or harmful to their own interests. He takes an information-processing perspective: Emotions are viewed as outcomes of the process of assessing the world in terms of one's own concerns, which, in turn, modify action readiness. This analysis leads him to address such fundamental issues as the place of emotion in motivation generally and the discrepancy between the functions of the emotions and their often irrational and disruptive character.

An important contribution to recent debates, *The Emotions* does not presuppose extensive prior knowledge.

Studies in Emotion and Social Interaction

Paul Ekman
University of California, San Francisco

Klaus R. Scherer
Justus-Liebig-Universität Giessen

General Editors

The emotions

Studies in Emotion and Social Interaction

This series is jointly published by the Cambridge University Press and the Editions de la Maison des Sciences de l'Homme, as part of the joint publishing agreement established in 1977 between the Fondation de la Maison des Sciences de l'Homme and the Syndics of the Cambridge University Press.

Cette collection est publiée en co-édition par Cambridge University Press et les Editions de la Maison des Sciences de l'Homme. Elle s'intègre dans le programme de co-édition établi en 1977 par la Fondation de la Maison des Sciences de l'Homme et les Syndics de Cambridge University Press.

The emotions

NICO H. FRIJDA

Universiteit van Amsterdam

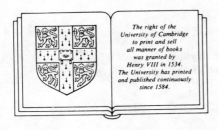

The right of the
University of Cambridge
to print and sell
all manner of books
was granted by
Henry VIII in 1534.
The University has printed
and published continuously
since 1584.

CAMBRIDGE UNIVERSITY PRESS

Cambridge
London   New York   New Rochelle
Melbourne   Sydney

EDITIONS DE LA MAISON DES SCIENCES DE L'HOMME

Paris

Published by the Press Syndicate of the University of Cambridge
The Pitt Building, Trumpington Street, Cambridge CB2 1RP
32 East 57th Street, New York, NY 10022, USA
10 Stamford Road, Oakleigh, Melbourne 3166, Australia
and
Editions de la Maison des Sciences de l'Homme
54 Boulevard Raspail, 75270 Paris Cedex 06, France

First published 1986

Printed in the United States of America

Library of Congress Cataloging-in-Publication Data
Frijda, Nico H.
The emotions.
(Studies in emotion and social interaction)
Bibliography: p.
Includes indexes.
1. Emotions. I. Title. II. Series. [DNLM:
1. Emotions.   BF 531 F912e]
BF531.F75 1986   152.4   86–17522

British Library Cataloguing in Publication Data
Frijda, Nico H.
The emotions. – (Studies in emotion
and social interaction).
1. Emotions
I. Title   II. Series
152.4   BF531

ISBN 0 521 30155 6 hard covers
ISBN 0 521 31600 6 paperback
       2 735 10173 8 hard covers (France only)
       2 735 10174 6 paperback (France only)

To
Merlijn
Michael
and Miranda

Contents

Preface   *page* xi

1 **Introduction**   1
   1. 1   Emotional phenomena   1
   1. 2   Overview of the present approach   4

PART I   ANALYSIS

2 **Emotional behavior**   9
   2. 1   Expressive behavior and its explanation   9
   2. 2   Relational interpretation of expressions   14
   2. 3   Variants of relational behavior   24
   2. 4   Behavior intensity, activation, and inhibition   32
   2. 5   Smiling, laughing, and weeping   47
   2. 6   Expression, emotion, communication, and mood   55
   2. 7   Emotional expression as unlearned response   62
   2. 8   Action tendencies and activation modes   69
   2. 9   Emotional behavior generally   94
   2.10   Emotions as intentional structures   98
   2.11   The provenance of emotional behavior   103
   2.12   Behavioral consequences of emotion   109

3 **Physiology of emotion**   124
   3. 1   Introduction   124
   3. 2   Autonomic variables related to emotions   126
   3. 3   Temporal characteristics of autonomic responses   141
   3. 4   The nature and function of autonomic responses   143
   3. 5   Hormonal changes   146
   3. 6   Electrocortical changes   152
   3. 7   Muscle tension and tremor   153

3. 8   Physiological response patterns   155
3. 9   Arousal, emotion, and physiological change   168
3.10   Consequences of physiological response   174

4   Emotional experience   176
4. 1   Theoretical viewpoints   176
4. 2   The investigation of emotional experience   178
4. 3   The nature of "experience": reflexive and irreflexive
       consciousness   186
4. 4   Emotional experience as experience of the situation   193
4. 5   Emotional experience as experience of autonomic
       arousal   221
4. 6   Emotional experience as awareness of action and
       action tendency   231
4. 7   Hedonic quality   242
4. 8   The significance of emotion   245
4. 9   Intensity of emotional experience   247
4.10   Emotional experience: its structure and varieties   249
4.11   Definition of emotion and kinds of emotion   256

PART II   ANTECEDENTS

5   Emotional stimuli, or situational antecedents   263
5. 1   Theoretical viewpoints   263
5. 2   "Stimuli," events, and cognitive processes   267
5. 3   Unlearned emotional stimuli   271
5. 4   The elicitation of emotion   277
5. 5   The description of emotional stimuli   285
5. 6   Factors affecting emotional intensity   290
5. 7   Acquisition of emotion   303
5. 8   Loss and persistence of emotions   312
5. 9   The stimulus reception process   324

6   Concerns and other dispositional antecedents   333
6. 1   Dispositional sources of emotion   333
6. 2   Concerns   335
6. 3   Discussion of some source concerns   344
6. 4   The structure of concerns, pleasure and pain,
       and the problem of circularity   359
6. 5   The function of emotions and "feelings"   371
6. 6   Other dispositional antecedents   374

7 Neurophysiological conditions   379
   7. 1   Brain structures involved in emotion   379
   7. 2   Elicited behavior   381
   7. 3   Activating mechanisms   386
   7. 4   Evaluation functions   389
   7. 5   Inhibitory and regulatory functions   391
   7. 6   "Feeling" and mood   395
   7. 7   Hemispheric differences   399

8 Regulation   401
   8. 1   Regulation phenomena   401
   8. 2   Instigation of regulation   408
   8. 3   Major regulatory mechanisms   414
   8. 4   Input regulation and intrapsychic coping   418
   8. 5   Regulation of emotional impulse and response   440
   8. 6   External regulation   445

PART III   SYNTHESIS

9 Theory of emotion   453
   9. 1   The emotion process   453
   9. 2   Emotional experience   463
   9. 3   Psychological theory of emotion   465
   9. 4   The concept of "emotion"   473

References   481
Author index   527
Subject index   538

Preface

This book was written because I wanted to put the various bits and pieces that I encountered in the literature on emotion in some sort of order. And because I wanted to understand what they had to do with emotions as they fill one's daily life. The connections were, when I began, not always obvious.

When I began the book, to give a representative account of work on emotion appeared to be a feasible task. I am not so sure now that I have succeeded, considering the upsurge of interest in emotion during the last several years. In any case, work on the book ended in early 1985.

I profited much from conversations, comments, and other contributions. I wish to thank the members of our group on emotions with whom I discussed this work for their stimulating remarks and cooperation: Bob Nieuwenhuyse, whom we had to lose; Bob Bermond, Gerbrand Bovenkerk, Rita Dapper, Huib van Dis, Hetty Rombouts; and also Martijn den Uyl.

I thank my mother for her warm support and unceasing readiness to meet succorance needs.

I wish to thank my good friend Louis Tas for persistent interest, comments, and ideas; and my late friend Johan Barendregt for what I owe him.

I am grateful to several other people who read parts of the manuscript and helpfully commented upon them: John Dorling, Paul Ekman, Richard Lazarus, Avishai Margalit, Co Orlebeke, Nanne van de Poll, Karl Pribram, Klaus Scherer, and Paul Voorhoeve.

Many thanks go to Molly Veenman and Andries Denys for their enthusiastic work in preparing the text; to Andries also for his careful and intelligent editing of the final version; and particularly to Willy Krijnen for untiring work on many previous versions; and to Hansje Ehbets for so much help. Anjo Anjewierden I thank for his time and energy generously spent in adapting text-processing facilities to suit my purposes, and Beulah MacNab and Cambridge University Press's copy editor Bill Green for doing the same in shaping up my English. My good friend Jan Bons did me the kindness of designing the expression of expression on the dust jacket.

I wish to thank Yolande Waldeck and Roos Kroon for their inspiration and friendship.

I give the book to my children. It is the best I have to offer.

N.H.F.

Amsterdam, March 1986

1. Introduction

The aim of this book is to present a survey of data theories on emotion. This book considers the primary questions concerning emotions: (1) What is the nature of the phenomena called "emotions" or "emotional"? (2) Which conditions – stimuli, dispositions, activities – give rise to these phenomena? (3) What functions, if any, do these phenomena serve? and (4) By what processes and through what mechanisms do the conditions lead to these phenomena? Part I, "Analysis," is concerned with question 1; Part II, "Antecedents," discusses questions 2 and 3; Part III, "Synthesis," which comprises the last chapter, is devoted to question 4. In discussing the above questions, a coherent theoretical framework will be developed into which phenomena concerning emotion can be ordered.

1.1. Emotional phenomena

Any study must begin by defining the subject of investigation. One must know, and let be known, what one is talking about. In the case of emotion this is a difficult matter. The phenomena to which the label *emotion* or *emotional* is attached appear to be diverse. Also, there is no agreement about which phenomena these are. Some people, laymen as well as scientists, consider "hunger" an emotion; others do not. Some talk about the "sex emotion"; in many treatises on emotion such a concept or phenomenon is, however, absent. To include a particular phenomenon under the label *emotion* is to see similarity; to exclude to see difference. Seeing and emphasizing similarities or differences are matters of theoretical outlook. In other words: A definition of *emotion* can only be a product of theory; it thus can be reached only at the end of the investigation.

Yet investigation must start somewhere. We propose to derive a rough indication of the field of inquiry, a "working definition," from an in-

1

vestigation of the phenomena that motivate the use of the label *emotion* or constituent labels like *fear, joy,* or *anger.* To investigate the nature and conditions of these phenomena will then be the goal of inquiry.

We thus ask: For what reasons do we use words like *emotion* or *emotional, anger* or *fear?* Three major classes of phenomena appear to lead to the use of such words: phenomena of behavior, of physiological response, and of subjective experience.

Phenomena of behavior

Emotion terms are almost unavoidable when describing the behavior of people and even of animals. Evidently, there is behavior that invites one to use such terms. Why does certain behavior do that, and which is the behavior that does so?

It appears to be this: At some moments when observing behavior, that behavior seems to come to a stop. Effective interaction with the environment halts and is replaced by behavior that is centered, as it were, around the person himself, as in a fit of weeping or laughter, anger or fear. Or interaction with the environment may go on but seems peculiarly ineffective. When someone smashes the dinner plates, the broken plates would hardly seem to be the end result the person had in mind. Other behavior that invites emotion words seems to contain a surplus that is not needed for the end results: superfluous emphasis in speed and scope of movement, or hesitation and undue toning-down, or a smile that, in someone who is stroking a child, does not add to the tenderness of the touch. The surplus can reside also in nonresponse: A dog walks up to another dog, stops two feet away, and turns its head away without moving and without looking at anything in particular.

What leads to the use of emotion words, then, appears to be superfluousness or disruption or ineffectuality with respect to instrumental purpose or coherence of interaction. *Emotion* thus appears to be a hypothesis to explain behavior that has neither sufficient nor adequate external purpose or reason; the explanation, then, is sought "within" the subject. This behavior, with the characteristics mentioned, offers a starting point for the investigation of emotion. *Emotion* can be provisionally defined as the inner determinant of noninstrumental behavior and noninstrumental aspects of behavior. *Emotional behavior* can provisionally be defined as that behavior itself. The definition needs further specification, for as it stands it applies also to behavior that does not strike one as emotional: mannerisms, play, mistakes. The specification will come from consideration of the stimuli eliciting the behavior, to be discussed below.

Characterization of emotion through noninstrumental attributes of behavior has found its way into psychological theory. Emotion has often been defined as disturbance – for instance, by Munn (1946), Young (1943), and Hebb (1949). The characterization is meant here, however, not as a theoretical interpretation but as an impressionistic account and a provisional, heuristic designation. It may be possible, and will in fact turn out to be possible, to replace its negative nature (as signaled by the "non" of *noninstrumental* and the "dis" of *disturbance*) with something more positive. By itself, the characterization serves merely as a starting point; but one which indicates the behavioral phenomena to be studied.

Physiological manifestations

There exists physiological upheaval that, on the face of it, does not appear to have a sufficient cause in physical events, either to the subject himself or to an outside observer: sweating or trembling without heat or cold or physical exertion; blushing; palpitations; butterflies in the stomach and weakness in the legs. Such changes tend to follow psychological causes: sudden events or psychologically significant ones. These changes, too, ask for explanation; the notion of emotion is one kind of explanation and, we may assume, invented or at least employed for that purpose.

Characterization of emotion through physically unexplained physiological upset has also found its way into psychological theory. Emotional experience has been identified with such upset, particularly in attribution theory approaches (e.g., Schachter 1970). Again, this is not what is meant here. The constellation of physically unexplained physiological change does, however, describe one of the conditions that engenders the use of emotion words. It thus provides a second starting point for investigation of emotion.

Experience

Subjective experience is another source of the use of emotion words. People use expressions like "I feel sad" and "I feel happy." Presumably, something is special about the experiences referred to by these expressions. Two features of the expressions serve to roughly identify the experiences involved. The first is evaluative connotation. When emotion words are judged by means of semantic differential rating scales such as *good–bad* or *weak–strong*, the largest amount of variance by far is taken up by the evaluative dimension (e.g., Block 1957). The second feature is subjective reference: "I feel . . . ," "I am in the state of . . . "

The "stimulus"

The phenomena of behavior, bodily response, and experience that lead to the use of "emotion" or related notions all tend to involve the idea of response to some event. Emotions are elicited. The eliciting events appear to fulfil a special role; they are not just stimuli. They appear to act through their significance, their meaning, their rewarding or aversive nature.

Working definition of emotion and the emotional

The provisional or working definition of *emotional phenomena* thus becomes the following: *Emotional phenomena* are noninstrumental behaviors and noninstrumental features of behavior, physiological changes, and evaluative, subject-related experiences, as evoked by external or mental events, and primarily by the significance of such events. An *emotion* is either an occurrence of phenomena of these three kinds or the inner determinant of such phenomena; the choice will be made later. This defines the present domain of investigation.

1.2. Overview of the present approach

By a closer investigation of the phenomena mentioned we hope to arrive at a substantive definition of emotion instead of the negatively phrased and imprecise working definition given. A definition of emotion, however, is not our primary concern. We will proceed as if we do not know what emotion is. We will try to understand the phenomena indicated – their nature, their function, their interrelations, the conditions of their occurrence. That is the aim of this study. Whatever turns out to define them, as a class or as classes of phenomena, will then constitute a definition or set of definitions of emotion.

The study that follows manifests some orienting principles of a not entirely empirical kind. Whereas these principles may in part be considered generalizations from the data and interpretations to be discussed, at the same time they have given direction to interpretation and ordering. These orienting principles are:

1. Emotions have a biological basis. This is meant in two senses. First, emotions are, or can be, matters of the body: of the heart, the stomach, and intestines, of bodily activity and impulse. They are of the flesh and sear the flesh. Also, they are of the brain and the veins. Second, emotions occur in animals, and some occur in animals in ways highly similar to humans. In emotion, we are each other's next of kin: we share the emotions of fear, anger, dejection, and attachment as well as sexual desire and curiosity. We are, to quite some extent, cousins in emotion; the study of human emotion can therefore profit from the study of animal emotion. A corollary of the biological principle is the functional point of view. If emotions are, wholly or in part, biological phenomena, they must serve a purpose for survival. The search for functional significance is one of the heuristics in the study of emotion.

2. Emotions in humans are human phenomena; that is, human emotions may be expected to present typically human aspects. They may be expected to be related to norms and values, to human modes of interaction, and to human cognitive possibilities – in particular, those of reflective awareness and intentional activity.

3. Both animals and humans not only are subject to emotional impulses, they also endeavor to cope with them. Inhibition and control are to be found even in animals, and efforts to cope with the emotional experience as such, in humans. *Regulation*, as it will be called here, is an integral part of emotion.

The reader who is familiar with the literature will recognize that these principles lead to a theoretical orientation concerning emotion closely akin to that of Freud (e.g., 1926) and, more specifically, to that of Lazarus (1966; Lazarus & Folkman 1984). The theory developed toward the end of this book can, in fact, be considered a variant of the latter's theory, and indebtedness to his formulations should be acknowledged at this point.

The approach taken in this book – if one wishes to oppose cognitive and behavioral formulations – is a cognitive one. But this does not do justice to the present orientation. A better designation is *affective* or *conative*. What is interesting about emotion is the emotional. Feeling is not cognition, it is feeling – it is responding "yes" or "no." Striving is not behavior, it is tending-toward, trying to reach or to avoid.

In the survey to be presented, a theoretical view of emotion will be developed. Emotions will be considered as changes in action readiness.

Such changes have a quantitative aspect called "activation" and a qualitative aspect called "action tendency"; they tend to be accompanied by autonomic changes. Emotions differ in terms of mode of activation, in terms of kind of action tendency, and in terms of autonomic response. Manifest behavior is realization of action tendency and manifestation of activation mode, as modified by regulatory processes.

Different emotions – that is, different action tendencies or activation modes – are evoked by different stimulus constellations, as these are appraised by the subject. Relevant variables in those constellations regard both what the stimulus event may do to the subject (relevance evaluation) and what the subject may do to the event or is (or is not) allowed to do by the entire situation concerned (context evaluation).

Emotions are elicited by significant events. Events are significant when they touch upon one or more of the concerns of the subject. Emotions thus result from the interaction of an event's actual or anticipated consequences and the subject's concerns.

Emergence of emotion thus depends upon occurrence of events, presence of concerns for which these events are relevant, and cognitive processes by means of which event consequences are or are not recognized. In addition, emotions are shaped by regulatory processes that are elicited by properties of the event and propensities of the subject.

The emotion process as sketched is subject to regulatory processes in each of its components. Those regulatory processes range from involuntary inhibitory processes over cognitive transformations to voluntary suppression and input regulation.

PART I

Analysis

2. Emotional behavior

2.1. Expressive behavior and its explanation

There exist behaviors that distinctly justify the provisional definition of emotion given in the previous chapter – the behaviors usually called "expressive." These behaviors characteristically are evoked by events that an observer, or the subject, understands as aversive or desirable or exciting. They serve no obvious purpose in the same sense that instrumental and consummatory behaviors do. They are called "expressive" because they make the observer attribute emotional states to the person or animal concerned. They do so even when no eliciting event can be perceived by the observer: They make a mother look for the undone safety pin in the baby's diaper, or cause a child to be frightened of the dog someone else is frightened of.

Expressive behavior therefore serves as an appropriate entry point to the study of emotion. Why does it exist? There are several interrelated questions. First question: Why do expressive behaviors accompany the various emotions? That is, why do they follow events called "astonishing" or "amusing" or "fearful," and why do they accompany subjective experiences called "astonishment" or "amusement" or "fear"? Second question: Why do the various expressive behaviors have the form they have? Why is the response to certain grieving events, and the response accompanying certain feelings of grief, that of weeping, tears, sobs, drawn mouth and so on; and similarly for the other expressions? Third question: What is their nature? Do they fulfill some sort of function, or do they just happen to be there for accidental reasons?

Darwin and others

Darwin (1872) explained expression in terms of three principles that still dominate theorizing in this domain. The first of these principles, that

9

of "serviceable associated habits," has found widest popularity and indeed has the largest explanatory power:

> Certain complex actions are of direct or indirect service under certain states of mind, in order to relieve or gratify certain sensations, desires etc.; and whenever the same state of mind is induced, however feebly, there is a tendency through the force of habit and association for the same movements to be performed, though they may not then be of the lease use. (1872 [1965, p. 28]).*

The principle is usually taken to show that Darwin considered expressions to be mere hereditary remnants. Several things should be noted, however. First, according to the principle, expressions are actions that are of service at least under some conditions. Second, their occurrence under conditions where they are not of service is explained by habit and association; these latter are supposed to have become hereditary. Threat evokes both useful crying and feelings of fear in the helpless infant; henceforth, fear evokes crying under every circumstance, and the linkage becomes fixed in evolution. Interestingly, Darwin invoked evolutionary principles primarily to explain the reflex-like, involuntary occurrence of behavior that he assumed to have originated as voluntary behavior in human infants. Derivation from phylogenetic ancestors he employed only occasionally, as for instance to explain pouting, or bared teeth in the expression of anger.

The Lamarckian twist – habits that become hereditary dispositions – may well be superfluous and at any rate is not of primary interest here. What is of interest is that many expressions have actual functional significance, in humans, even for Darwin, even if only under some conditions or if only for infants. Even to Darwin, they were not "mere remnants of communicative acts," as, for instance, Mandler (1975, p. 146) asserted them to be.

The kinds of functional significance invoked were several. From Bell (1844) Darwin borrowed the emphasis upon respiratory activity and its consequences for facial activity; respiratory activity is needed for the utterance of useful cries. From Engel (1785) and Gratiolet (1865) he took the importance of sensory functioning or nonfunctioning – taking in or warding off impressions, facilitation of unhampered perception, and the like – and that of preparation for muscular exertion.

Others than Darwin still more explicitly discussed actual functional

* There is a second half to this principle, which concerns suppression of actions associated through habit and failure of suppression of muscles that are least under separate control of the will. Expressive movements are the result of this latter condition.

aspects of expression. Piderit (1867) emphasized sensory functioning and sensory readiness; his viewpoints have recently been taken up by Peiper (1963). The prime example is the expression of disgust; it reduces sensory contact with distasteful substances in the mouth cavity and tends toward expelling those substances. Bühler (1934) in his "action theory of expression," pointed to the fact that many expressions can be considered preparations for effective action or initial stages of such actions. The expression of determination consists of the mobilization of muscular force, either for possible future action or in order to brace for attack or for overcoming resistance. Expressions of eagerness, desire, and reluctance are incipient actions of approach and shrinking back.

Actual functional significance thus explains much of expression. The question is whether it can explain all of expression. According to Darwin, it cannot. First, there is generalization toward nonfunctional situations, which Darwin explains by habit and association and others by imagination (Piderit) or similarity between sensory sensations and emotional qualities (Wundt 1903; Chiva 1985). Then there are expressions that resist even such interpretation. Darwin needed three principles. The second and third will be discussed later (sections 2.3 and 2.4). For the moment, we will focus upon expressions that do appear to be of actual use.

Expression as behavior

Some expressions, then, have actual functional significance. That is to say: These "expressive" movements produce actual effects in the interaction with the environment by helping to protect, to discern, and the like; or at least they serve subjectively to facilitate or hinder information intake, readiness for further action, and so on. This implies that expressions are not mere movements, but forms of behavior: modes of interaction with the environment. In fact, many facial expressions are but part of global action patterns, the behavioral nature of which is more evident. The *startle pattern*, the reflex-like response to sudden intense stimuli such as a pistol shot, provides an example. In this response, the eyes are forcefully closed, the eyebrows drawn together producing a frown, and the lips are compressed; in addition, the head bends forward, shoulders are hunched, and the knees are drawn up (Landis & Hunt 1939). Likewise with other expressions. A tight, angry facial expression tends to go together with general tenseness, solid stance, and clenched fists, all preparations for vigorous activity. A fearful facial expression tends to extend into hunched shoulders and crouching attitude, producing a global protective response. The surprised face, when spontaneous, is part of the total *orientation response*, which includes behavioral interruption and changes in blood flow, respiration, and EEG pattern. Laughter and weeping, too, are generalized reaction patterns: The person who laughs or weeps is *doing* something, albeit involuntarily, and often is doing that to the exclusion of doing anything else.

A thin line divides expression from true emotional actions, largely innate, like flight or freezing or attack, or like embracing, cuddling, and care giving. A thin line, too, divides expressions from what Lewin (1927) called *field actions* and that indeed also strike one as expressive behaviors: emotionally motivated actions, the properties of which are determined primarily by the properties of the actual situation – for instance, hiding under the table, clinging to the mother, crouching in a corner, covering one's eyes, all of which are protective behaviors occurring in both human and monkey infants (Suomi & Harlow 1976). The behavioral and functional nature of movements called expressive is particularly evident in gaze modalities. The dynamics of looking, looking away, and not looking, the fullness or partial reserve with which each segment is performed, the temporal aspects of gaze change and stationary gazing constitute modulations of contact and contact readiness. These gaze modalities are highly expressive; yet they do not express mode of contact. They *are* modes of contact.

The fact that expressive movement can be interpreted as behavior with functional significance in the subject's interaction with his environment is of central importance for clarifying the relation between expression and emotion; or for clarifying what is meant by *emotion*, for that matter. Expression suggests that emotions are tendencies toward given modes of interaction. If this is so, expression is merely those tendencies' embodiment, the manner (or a manner) in which the tendencies are effectuated. These two points indeed form the major thesis of the present chapter. They form the reason to discuss expressive behavior in some more detail. If the thesis is to be tenable, all of expression should be amenable to functional interpretation, and it should be so in a plausible way, considering the conditions under which each expressive movement feature arises.

Expression as relational behavior

The "serviceable habits" in Darwin's first principle concern vocal activities that exist for the purpose of communication and actions that serve observation, protection, or attack. Piderit added that certain expressive movements serve regulation of sensory input generally. Bühler, in pointing to action preparation as one of the components of expression, revived Engel's (1785) "action principle of expression," according to which desire tends to approach its object and aversion tends to draw back from it. From all this, one principle can be derived that appears to cover the various functions: the principle of relational activity. *Relational activity* means activity that establishes or modifies a relationship between the subject and some object or the environment at large. The term refers to activity that establishes or modifies such a relationship by modifying the relationship rather than the environment. This, indeed, can be considered the most general characteristic of expressive behavior, which sets it apart from other kinds of behavior, manipulatory and consummatory behavior. It is the positive counterpart of the negative characteristic contained in the working definition of chapter 1. Expressive behavior is behavior that establishes or enhances, weakens or breaks, some form of contact with some aspect of the environment or that aims at doing so or is accessory in doing so. This statement has to be restricted somewhat in view of other principles of expression to be discussed later, but it applies to those expressions that have functional significance.

Expressive behavior can establish or modify relationships in various modes: bodily by means of locomotion; visually; aurally (in animals, by pricking up the ears); and with the sensory surfaces of the body (as in someone abandoning himself to sunshine, wind, or glances). In every mode it can do so either partially or fully.

Relational activity also has a general intensive dimension. There can be more or less of it. Disinterest and apathy represent the low end of this dimension. We will, for that low end, utilize the expression of *null state* of relational activity. This somewhat paradoxical turn of phrase intends to stress that lack of relational activity is itself a relational mode, on a par with turning toward, turning away from, and turning against.

The sense of expressions

Relational activity establishes or modifies relationships; and it does so mainly not by modifying the environment, but by modifying the location, accessibility, and sensory and locomotor readiness of the subject. It does so by endeavoring to achieve certain useful effects: Hiding and crouching diminish chances of being hurt or seen, flight increases distance to danger, disgust movement ejects distasteful substances, and so forth.

However, there is another side to functional significance. Whatever its ultimate useful effects, eye closure does shut off visual stimuli. Exposure of the body does expose oneself to sense impressions and other people's glances, whether or not this fulfills some purpose. Muscle tenseness does increase resistance against physical impacts, whether this does or does not help in the given circumstances. This is what we call the *sense* of expressive behavior: its functional nature of establishing or allowing, breaking or barring, modes of contact, or of being a state of readiness or unreadiness for action, regardless of the usefulness of that contact mode or state of readiness. The sense of full body exposure – body straight, arms and hands hanging, turned toward a source of stimulation – is unrestrained openness for stimulation; the sense of taking to one's bed, covers over the head, is passive withdrawal from every form of contact, even when the disagreeable events are not thereby abolished. The sense of weeping is interruption of effective commerce with the environment and surrender to one's distress. These descriptions of *sense* can hardly be called interpretations of the behaviors concerned. They are descriptions of factual states of affairs, facts of receptivity or nonreceptivity or preparedness, and which states of affairs the subject himself can be aware of.

This notion of sense will appear helpful in understanding the occurrence of expressions under circumstances in which "usefulness" becomes a tricky explanatory concept. It is helpful, for instance, for characterizing relational null states. These consist of nonbehavior rather than behavior; yet their sense is definite and to be characterized positively. Disinterest negates a relationship – as everyone knows who ever tried to draw the attention of a disinterested person. It negates in a specific fashion, different, for instance, from that of disgust. Drooping eyelids may be useful in sleepiness to keep stimulation out, but they are not in disinterest. They are, however, meaningful in both cases because of their sense, which is simply: having nothing to do with external stimulation.

2.2. Relational interpretation of expressions

This section discusses expressive behavior that corresponds to some of the major emotions; it discusses primarily those emotions of which Ekman and Friesen (1975) extensively analyzed the characteristic facial expressions. We try to show that these expressive behaviors can be functionally interpreted as relational activities. We also try to show that the "meaning" of these expressions, their relational intent, is appropriate in view of the emotional conditions under which the expressions can be assumed to occur.

Interpretation of expression, functional or otherwise, should proceed by way of careful description and distinction of patterns and subsequent analysis of stimuli that elicit them or of experiences that accompany them. Description of patterns traditionally has been based upon informal observation; observation was supported by study of facial movements induced by electrical stimulation of facial nerves (Duchenne 1876; Dumas 1933) and neuropathologically caused paralyses and contractures (Dumas 1933). Only recently have techniques for systematic analysis been developed (see Ekman 1982b), notably the Facial Action Coding System (FACS) for analyzing facial expression (Ekman & Friesen 1978) and the Bern system for studying nonverbal interaction (Von Cranach & Kalbermatten 1982). In the FACS system, expression photographs are coded by way of the correspondence of each of their parts (lip position, eyebrows, etc.) with one of a set of standards; the standards differ in the action of one or a few muscles. Only such systematic techniques permit going beyond gross codings such as "smile" or "frown," or "angry face" and thus to distinguish between similar expressions, for instance, different smiles or frowns (e.g., Blurton-Jones 1972b; Oster & Ekman 1978). Analyses using these techniques for describing human expression are as yet few (see section 2.7). In ethology, careful descriptions of behaviors have been made of some species. Social behavior patterns in chimpanzees, for instance, have been classified in detail by Van Lawick-Goodall (1968) and Van Hooff (1973).

Little exists in the way of systematic study in humans of the conditions under which the various patterns appear. Of course, a vast descriptive literature exists, from the general studies of Bell (1844), Darwin (1872), and Dumas (1933, 1948a) to the more specialized surveys of Strehle (1954) on gesturing, Kietz (1956) on gait, Kiener (1962) on movement generally, Schänzle (1939) on facial expressions during thinking, and Benesch (1960) on expressions when failing during problem solving. Many of these studies, particularly the older ones, contain charming descriptions of eliciting conditions and often are quite convincing in showing that the expressions represent the emotions they are supposed to represent; yet observation and analysis again are informal. Ethology once again fares somewhat better, particularly through methods of sequential analysis (see Van Hooff 1982). Van Hooff (1972), in observing a group of free-moving chimpanzees, recorded for each behavior pattern which, if any, preceded and which, if any, followed it. Analysis of the matrix of transition frequencies yielded identification of behavior systems, which in turn assisted in the interpretation of separate patterns. In a different study, sequential analysis was made of the expressions manifested by the different animals engaged in a given interaction, with the similar aim of interpreting each pattern (Van Hooff 1972).

As said, for human expressions little of this sort exists. The analyses that follow are largely based upon information of the informal variety.

Fear

In the preceding section we described the startle pattern: forceful eye closure, frowning by drawing the eyebrows together, bending the head, hunching the shoulders, bending the trunk and knees. Several animal species show a startle response similar to that in humans, with the addition of flattening the ears. Landis and Hunt (1939) interpret the response as a preparation for jumping, which is unlikely considering the animal counterparts. It should rather be considered a protective response (Young 1943; Andrew 1972). A response similar in form but less reflex-like is produced under conditions of danger of actual physical harm.

This protective response can be understood in various ways: as protection of the vulnerable vital organs, including the eyes (Andrew 1963); as decrease in visibility as a target; or as a way of shutting off external stimulation – in fact, a variant of the first explanation. Most likely, the first explanation applies to the startle response, whereas in the slower danger response the other two functions participate. Whatever its precise nature, the protective function explains the details of the response. It is similar in intent to the flinch and shrink movements found in both humans and chimpanzees (Van Lawick-Goodall 1968; Van Hooff 1973). The functional interpretation fits Darwin's explanation of the oblique eyebrows and resulting vertical frown, which are part of the expression universally recognized as one of fear (Ekman & Friesen 1975, fig. 12): They may well result from an impulse to protectively close the eyes while simultaneously forcing oneself to keep them open, in order to keep track of the fearful object. A feature that does not fit this interpretation so easily is retraction of the corners of the mouth (see Ekman & Friesen 1975), which in animals can be particularly pronounced (Andrew 1972). It could be part of a backward movement of retreat; it also could, however, in humans be a true remnant of the "fear grimace" that in rhesus monkeys occurs uniquely in social fear situations (Suomi & Harlow 1976) and is probably a social signal.

Quite apart from their useful effects as protection responses, the above behaviors manifest the sense of diminishing contact with external stimulation. Startle halts and fear reverses the direction of locomotion. The subject adopts an attitude that conflicts with action toward the environment and with the reception of stimulation. Aspects of this attitude are embodied also in the position of someone in deep misery: sitting with knees drawn up, arms around oneself, head bent deeply, hunched shoulders, and, if possible, curtains closed and no one around. The difference between this attitude and the above one of fear is instructive. Fear shrinks; misery closes off, and it does so diffusely.

Variations of facial fear expressions depend, among other things, upon concurrent visual attention. As said, eyes may be closed or be kept open with obliquely contracted eyebrows. Another expression has eyes widely opened, without eyebrows raised, or with the eyebrows raised as in surprise. It could be argued that the latter represent expressions of a mixture of fear and interest or of fear and surprise. However, it seems more appropriate to say that more active or more passive forms have occurred together.

The relationship between withdrawal or protection and fear is obvious: A fearful situation is one with which commerce is not desired, or not altogether. Withdrawal of some sort, or readiness for it, can be expected wherever diminished commerce with the environment seems called for: in fear, in timidity, in shyness, in caution. The emotion names in part refer to properties of the eliciting situations: *Shyness*, for instance, primarily refers to response to other people. In part, the names refer to differences in intensity and generality of the withdrawal tendency and the degree to which approach and exposure are still tolerated. There exist continuous variations and mixtures of protection, withdrawal, wary readiness for withdrawal, and cautious restriction of action in view of the risks of exposure that action entails. Hence all the varieties of expression in which withdrawal, protection, caution, and attenuation of action are involved: the fearful face with oblique eyebrows; the fearful face with widely opened eyes; the averted face in which the body remains exposed but the glance breaks contact; the hesitance and awkwardness of movement.

The fearful expressions discussed are interpreted as protective or withdrawal responses. Other fear responses can be seen as implementing the relational aim of reducing risks in a different fashion. Outright flight and freezing, for instance, endeavor to avert the dangerous event rather than attenuate its harmful outcomes; the social fear grimace would seem to try to prevent it. Finally, there exists behavior in response to danger with the relational sense of letting the harmful events come as they may. That is, there exists fear that only shows in limpness and a bland expression. It will do so when counteraction appears meaningless or impossible: Extreme fear is expressionless.

Withdrawal tendency occurs outside fear; that is to say, it occurs outside situations of danger and without readiness for escape or further physical protection. Deep concentration is an example, and, indeed, some expressions of deep concentration are sometimes mistaken for fear expressions (Frijda 1953).

Amazement, surprise, and wonder

A response to sudden stimuli that differs from the startle reflex consists of widening of the eyes, brief suspension of breathing, and general loss of muscle tone. The loss of muscle tone causes the mouth to fall open, and may make the subject stagger or force him to sit down. This response, too, is present in animals: cats, dogs, and monkeys (Andrew 1972). Immobilization in response to unexpected stimuli, with widely opened eyes and open mouth, occurs in infants at around five months (Malrieu 1960). Dumas (1933) interprets the expression as general inhibitory reaction. The eyebrows are not raised in this primitive surprised response.

Again, the response is similar to a more active one, into which it may change: the true expression of surprise or amazement (Ekman & Friesen 1975). In that expression the eyebrows are raised; a sound like "oh!" may be emitted, even by Tahitians when the *Beagle* fired some rockets (Darwin 1872). The eyebrow raising, says Dumas, is a combination of arrest of movement and "open attention." Raising the eyebrows facilitates lifting the upper eyelid, and together they are supposed to facilitate rapid eye movements and enlarge the field of peripheral vision (Darwin 1872; Dumas 1933). The sense of the expression is a passive, receptive mode of attention. It is passive both in the arrest of locomotion and instrumental action, and in that the direction of visual attention is not fixed but, instead, set for peripheral stimuli wherever these may come from. In its several variants, the attitude involved may impress as one of stupidity (Darwin 1872), of innocence and defenseless impressionability, or of relaxed sensuality – all probably with right. Open attention, with the forgetful relaxation of the rest of the body, is equally used to represent religious devotion and admiration generally; these representations may correspond to factual occurrences, considering the appropriateness of the attitude involved under the given conditions. With slight admixtures of withdrawal activity, the expression turns into one of fear, as just discussed, or (mouth closed) into one of wary readiness for action (as when walking in the dark or being ready to respond to attack).

Anger

Most animals can manifest unambiguous readiness for attack, which at any moment may change into overt attack: body tense, teeth bared or bill ready for striking. There are other expressions, in cats, dogs, chimpanzees, and other animals (Darwin 1872; Andrew 1972; Van Hooff 1973), often accompanied by vocalizations, that perhaps more properly can be termed "angry," since they represent irritable excitement rather than the initial stage of attack, and that will be discussed in the next section as instances of "interactive expressions."

Human anger has a large variety of manifestations. Most characteristic is the fierce glance: fixed stare, eyes slightly widened, eyebrows contracted (Darwin 1872; Ekman & Friesen 1975). The eyes, however, can also be narrowed; widening the eyes is probably restricted to face-to-face situations. Muscular tension is generally increased, sometimes with clenched fists. Lips are often compressed, teeth may be clenched, and movements are vigorous and brisk. The mouth can be contorted, and the voice is usually loud, up to shouting. The facial features generally resemble those of muscular effort and appear to have the same significance of readiness for forceful movements or actual exertion of force. Only the widened eyes are clearly special. Widening the eyes without raising the eyebrows, or without raising them strongly, has been met already in discussing the expressions of fear. In anger it can be argued to have the same meaning: that of wary, alert observation of the environment within an active, action-ready framework. The action-ready framework, however, is different here; it appears geared to forward movement rather than retreat. The widened eyes may also be given the entirely different interpretation of a threatening stare, which also will be discussed as an interactive expression.

Drawing the eyebrows together is a regular, though not necessary, component of angry expressions and does not depend upon general forceful contortion of the face. Darwin noticed its presence in many situations where an obstacle has to be overcome, such as in concentrated attention. We will further discuss it in that connection (next subsection) and regard it here as restricted actional readiness, linked to either visual attention or forward movement.

The mouth, as noted, can have various positions. Sometimes, it is said, teeth are bared in anger; it is interpreted as an atavistic remnant of readiness to bite, inherited from our forebears (Darwin 1872; Izard 1971). The expression, when it occurs, probably is not an atavism at all, since some people, particularly children, actually bite in anger. Or more precisely: Atavistic it may be called, though as a desire, not as expression.

The sense of angry expressions, in all varieties, is that of an active stance, manifest in mobilization of muscular force and focused attention, directed toward overcoming resistance or resisting outside forces. The expressions are not primarily preparations for attack, although mobilization of force may serve that purpose. Dumas (1933), indeed, is careful to distinguish between the expression of anger as manifestation of an attitude of "revolt," and manifestations of aggressive intent; and I think he is right.

Variations in angry expressions can be understood as variations in the kind of forceful action one is ready for. Widely opened eyes, with eyebrows both raised and contracted are described in Chinese literature (see Averill 1982) and appear in Japanese theater (Eibl-Eibesfeldt 1974). They can be observed in Western countries, too, in people full of stern indignation, acting as if preparing to rise to full height and start on a harangue. They would seem to represent readiness for frontal and erect antagonistic approach. The narrowed eyes of the more common expressions of anger suggest a different mode of approach: less frontal, less from above, with more self-protective readiness.

Other expressions of anger represent different forms of action control. An angry person may fall silent, compress his lips, narrow his eyes and remain rigid until he either quits or snaps at the opponent or explodes (or recovers from his anger); the expression represents inhibitory withdrawal to choose one's tack, the better to jump at the opponent at a later moment. Which of these many expressions of anger are to be considered elementary, or elements of an innate anger program, and which are to be considered derived, or acquired, is at present hard to say. The fact that the "characteristic" expression with the fierce glance and contracted eyebrows is generally and universally recognized as one of anger (Ekman, Friesen, & Ellsworth 1972; Izard 1971) does not seem to be sufficient argument to consider it the major or only original anger expression. Anger may well manifest itself equally naturally in any of the above.

Concentrated attention

As just said, the horizontal frown occurs in mental concentration as well as in anger. According to Darwin, the frown appears during mental activity "when a difficulty is encountered or when the person is interrupted by some disturbance." It occurs when someone is puzzled, and Darwin cites relevant observations from peoples like the "Australians," Malays, Kafirs, and Guaranis. Stammerers, notices Piderit (1867), frown in speaking. According to Darwin, the frown also occurs during crying and in pain; that frown, however, probably is different.

What, then, of the frown in mental concentration and anger? The same frown, it would seem, is shown in a different circumstance: that of focused visual attention under unfavorable conditions. One frowns when trying to read small print while on a vibrating boat or rattling train, and when trying to discriminate distant detail under glaring light. In both kinds of circumstance, frowning appears useful: for steadying the glance in the first, and for shielding the eyes from overhead glare in the second (Darwin, in fact, gives similar interpretations, next to one involving support of eye closure).

Still, concentrated visual attention is not concentrated thought, although the words indicate commonalities. The curious fact is that frowning when meeting an obstacle in thinking is not in any way a means of expressing concentration but a means of maintaining it. That is how it feels, but that is also why it occurs. Weber (1929) observed that subjects try to ward off auditory distractors by increasing muscular tension and defensive movements like head shakes, shoulder shrugs, and "emphatic focusing of the task materials." Frowning seems of quite similar service for maintaining concentration as increasing muscle force when typing and repeating out loud materials to be studied; both the latter activities appear to effectively decrease the effects of distractors (Morgan 1916; Ford 1929). All this leads Schänzle to conclude: "The thought process should be regarded as purposive action; the accompanying expressive behavior as an (objectively) appropriate realization of such action" (Schänzle 1939, p. 102).

But why? It may not be as mysterious as it seems. On the one hand, the frown might be just a manifestation of muscular readiness for action in a specific direction; this readiness might be showing in the frown only because of muscular mechanics (which is, in fact, Dumas's point of view) or because looking generally fixes the goal point of action, as during locomotion. On the other hand, horizontal frowning might serve to prevent attention to be drawn elsewhere and action preparation to develop in the wrong direction. Such function, in a less emphatic way, determines the sideways, downward glance in reflective thinking (Day 1964; Duke 1968), which presumably serves both to look at nothing in particular and to avoid glancing in the primary direction of action. Such a control function satisfies the condition for the frown in anger, in stammering, and in muscular effort, as well as in thought and puzzlement: That condition consists of presence of a requirement for subject-determined control of both action and information intake. The attitude involved stands in clear opposition to the passive–receptive one discussed in connection with surprise and wonder.

Sadness

There are many ways to be sad, as there are many ways to be angry. We will focus first on silent, passive sadness. The prominent features, including that of depressed corners of the mouth, are consequences of lowered muscle tone rather than of active muscle contraction. Dumas (1933, 1948) presents photographs of patients suffering from one-sided facial paralysis due to hemiplegia: The stricken side shows a passively sad expression.

The expression and attitude, the passivity, downcast eyes, and so forth are easily understood as consequences of lack of activity and, more particularly, absence of interest. The response is obviously meaningful, given its eliciting conditions such as loss of objects of interest. At the same time, it cannot be said to possess functional significance; it has none. This does not contradict the hypothesis that expressions are functional responses, because, properly speaking, passive sadness is not a response: It is nonbehavior. Nor does it conflict with the view that expressions are relational activities. The sense of passive sadness is explicit absence of relational activity. The expression represents a relational null state.

Variants of sadness are primarily such as to turn this null state into withdrawal, or nonbehavior into behavior. Withdrawal involves rejection of stimuli reminding one of the lost object or calling for action. The expression of eyebrows drawn downward, the "clouded brow," implements turning inward and closing off, in the same sense as the actions of deep misery mentioned earlier: closing the curtains, taking to one's bed, and pulling up the covers.

Frequent in expressions of grief are the oblique eyebrows discussed before. Darwin, as noted, explained them from simultaneous efforts to close the eyes and keep them open to watch what is going on. In passive sadness they rather result from counteracting the hypotonic downward sag of eyebrows and head in efforts to maintain a somewhat vigilant posture. Other features of grief are expressive of pain. Facial expressions of pain can be understood in part as consequences of general muscular activation (Dumas 1948a); these, in turn, can be understood from efforts to suppress the pain or distract oneself away from it. In part facial expressions of pain are aspects of vain efforts to escape from stimulation that cannot be escaped from.

Weeping will be discussed in a later section.

Grief and depression quite often are characterized by agitation and restlessness, rather than by apathy. Grief and sadness being in large part reactions to loss, agitation and restlessness are meaningfully interpreted as futile search for the lost object (Bowlby 1969) and as efforts to protest, resist, escape, or cope.

Gaze modalities

Reference has been made already to gaze modalities as clearly illustrating the relational activity nature of expressive behavior. The various spatial and temporal patterns such as looking askance, the stolid glance, the furtive glance, the cursory glance, looking with downcast eyes are all highly expressive. Many of the expressions just discussed center around attentional activity and thus, the gaze: the downward glance in sadness and reflexive thought, and the activities of keeping track and gaze aversion in fear, for instance.

There is abundant research showing the significance of gaze dynamics (see Exline & Fehr 1982). Looking at a person who has just treated you badly decreases in frequency or duration (Exline & Winters 1965); preferences for a person (a confederate in an experiment), expressed after a meeting, correlated .40 with amount of eye contact (Kleck et al. 1976). An infant placed apart from its mother looks at her almost constantly, if it can (Ainsworth 1967). Amount of eye contact depends upon status relations and sex factors (Mehrabian 1972): A longer look between sexes can be felt as too intimate, given the relationship, or too imposing. As implied by Argyle and Dean's (1965) equilibrium model, when pressures toward intimacy increase (for instance, when the other person comes closer), gaze breaking occurs. It also does when the topic of conversation increases in intimacy (Exline, Gray, & Schuette 1965; Schulze & Barefoot 1974); gaze breaking then corresponds to embarrassment, shyness, or timidity (Modigliani 1971). The words *embarrassment, shyness,* and *timidity* do not do justice to the fluctuations in balance between contact-restricting and contact-maintaining tendencies as these occur in interaction situations and are manifest in gaze and eye contact interplay.

2.3. Variants of relational behavior

Relational behavior modalities

Much of expressive behavior can be understood as relational behavior; that is what the preceding tries to illustrate.

The expressive behavior concerned can be understood as relational behavior. This fact is of interest by itself, quite independently of the questions of whether that behavior is to be considered "expression of emotion" and what that phrase could mean. Expressive behavior has its inherent significance, as relational activity, as the manner in which the subject positions himself with respect to the environment. Also, a given item of expressive behavior can occur in different emotional contexts and fulfill roughly the same function in each. Weeping occurs in different emotions; it can be considered to have the same meaning in each, as we hope to show later. It is a specific manner to relate (or not relate) to the environment, and can be understood as such, regardless of its motive, its inner determinant.

The notion of relational behavior easily applies to variations in attitude for which appropriate emotion words are often hard to find, but which continuously modulate social interactions: variations in acceptance, interest, reticence, bashfulness, and the like. The terms themselves refer to variations in approach and sensory reception activities and their being toned down by simultaneous withdrawal or unreadiness features. The notion of relational behavior also applies to instrumental and consummatory behaviors when these are viewed from a relational angle – that is, as behaviors that seek to establish contact of some sort as well as aiming at their instrumental and consummatory goals. Tender movements, for instance, aim at soft touching and soft caring; a tender look is a way of looking that implies unobtrusive, nonanalytic, and accepting interest and a willingness for further tender approach.

Relational behavior as discussed so far consists of behavior that establishes, maintains, or disrupts the relationship with the environment by changing spatial relationships and sensory and actional readiness. The relational sense is visible, open to inspection. Relational change can also be effected in a different way, however: namely, by influencing the response of other individuals.

Interactive expressions

Several expressions cannot be understood as modes of approach or avoidance or as sensory or actional readiness: for instance, foot stamping in anger, attitudes of shame, or vocal expressions. Many of these expressions, however, can be understood from their effects upon other people or animals. They will be called *interactive expressions*: expressions the primary function of which appears to be to influence the behavior of others. Many of the expressions discussed before also, on occasion, influence others; but such influence does not appear to be their primary function, nor does such influence explain that they occur under the conditions under which they in fact happen to occur. The expressions to be discussed now, by contrast, appear to be shown for the sake of influencing others, appear to have developed for, or because of, such effect, and occur under eliciting conditions in which influencing others in that particular way appears to be of distinct instrumental value.

The term *interactive expressions* should not be misunderstood. It is used here to refer to behaviors that are triggered by emotional situations in exactly the same fashion as the expressions discussed so far. Both kinds of expression serve the same general purpose of establishing or changing a relationship between subject and environment. They merely do so by different means: the relational expressions directly, the "interactive" ones indirectly, by modifying the behavior of others. All serve the same general relational purpose of having some source of discomfort or annoyance removed.

Vocal expressions provide the clearest examples of interactive expressions as meant here. Shrieks are to startle, as in warning calls, or to chase away, as do the dog's bark, the cat's hiss, and shouts of anger. Distress calls in the young of higher animals lead to rapid maternal approach; infant crying is its human version: Both presumably exist for that purpose even if not made consciously or intentionally for that purpose.

There also exist facial and body expressions that have strong effects upon others and that, too, presumably exist for that purpose. As said, this particularly applies to expressions that are difficult to explain relationally. Many human manifestations of anger are not easily understood as preparations for attack or for bracing oneself against oncoming attack. These manifestations are strikingly similar, however, to threat displays and bluffing behavior in animals. They are intimidating demonstrations of power. Stamping one's foot is an unlearned anger expression; it has been observed even in a blind and deaf idiot (Eibl-Eibesfeldt 1973). It is closely akin to a chimpanzee behavior pattern that, according to sequential analysis, belongs to the bluffing behavior system (Van Hooff 1973). Destruction of inanimate objects, too – smashing the dinner plates – may well be a show of force rather than "redirected aggression": This behavior also occurs in the chimpanzee and goes together with production of loud sounds and apparent increase of body size through bristling hairs. All this effectively intimidates others. The sight of a Chinese quail, height 10 centimeters, with its feathers fluffed, advancing to defend its minuscule chicks, is enough to make one start; and so is the hissing of a two-week-old kitten. True, some threat and dominance behaviors are functional also in the direct relational way. Mobilization of force and stretching to full height are advantageous in the control of behavior of others. The interactive and the directly relational are mutually reinforcing.

Eye widening in anger similarly seems to serve threat and intimidation purposes rather than deserving the more relational interpretation given earlier. Staring as agonistic behavior is, again, common in animals (Andrew 1963), and many animals react aggressively or frightened when stared at. Exline and Yellin (1969) had human experimenters stare at male rhesus monkeys: In 47% of the trials the stared-at monkey attacked, and in an additional 29% they showed threat behavior. Staring someone down and stern looking as a form of disciplining occur in humans. It therefore is likely that the fierce look is shown in anger primarily because of its intimidation value. In rhesus monkeys, aggressive facial expressions belong to the unlearned distress stimuli (Sackett 1966). Alerting effects of being gazed at are biologically extremely widespread (Argyle & Cook 1976). The threat value of looking-at is reckoned with in the interactive behavior of looking-away. Dogs when meeting for the first time appear careful not to look at each other, presumably in order not to incite attack; the same sort of thing occurs in rats and birds (Chance 1962) and submissive primates (Hall & DeVore 1965).

Submissive behavior is in the first place behavior that placates more dominant individuals. It should therefore have characteristics opposite to those of aggressive, dominant, or angry behavior, and it does. Expressions of submission in animals are clear demonstrations of lesser power, smaller size, and less readiness for action. The dog flattens against the ground or rolls on its back (Darwin 1872); the submissive chimpanzee crouches, shrinks, or approaches hesitantly (Van Hooff 1973). In humans, submissiveness is manifest in glance aversion, general unobtrusive behavior, and conventional bowing. The "expressions of shame" described in the literature, or those of guilt (Tomkins 1962; Izard 1971), are best (and easily) understood as submission behaviors: head bent, glance downward, (or upward from the bent head), hands hanging in explicit inaction. They are not specific for shame or guilt.

Unobtrusiveness is interactive in the present sense since it presupposes the perceptual activity of others and aims at influencing it, albeit negatively. Unobtrusiveness is emphasized not merely in submission, but everywhere where being seen might involve risks: in social fear, shyness, and timidity, for instance. Shy constriction of movement and the timid soft voice are functionally similar.

As there is unobtrusiveness behavior, there is conspicuousness behavior. Angry and bluffing behaviors and helpless crying are in part to be viewed from this angle; so are all forms of drawing attention as these occur in animal and human courting and in responses of enhanced self-feeling in proudness and triumph. Joyful behavior in general can profitably be considered as conspicuousness behavior. Conspicuousness reliably results in exuberance, and exuberance may therefore well serve that purpose. Being seen – and being seen nonaggressively – enhances bonds with other individuals and tends to elicit bond-strenghtening behavior from their side: attention, and in particular, participation. Participation, indeed, is a solid effect of joyful exuberance. Put otherwise: Joyful behavior entraps the other in an interaction. The dog jumps and wags his tail when its owner comes home who is thus easily enticed to play with it or at least stroke it; tail wagging in fact has been interpreted as social-contact-soliciting behavior (Panksepp 1982). The child who has been promised an outing draws the parents into his anticipations and preparations; he does so by both his antics and his talk and makes it more difficult for the adult to take the promise lightly.

The interactive effects of most of the expressions just discussed can be understood from their perceptual characteristics: their auditory and visual conspicuousness or inconspicuousness. Other interactive expression effects presuppose specific sensitivities in the recipient: the effects of looking-at, staring, and aggressive grimaces; and, perhaps, the effects of smiling.

Smiling serves as a sign of friendliness and inoffensiveness. As such, it might be a conventional sign, but this is not likely: The smile's "friendliness" function appears to be universal. Moreover, a morphologically similar expression in chimpanzees, the "silent bared-teeth display," appears to have a similar function. It participates in the "affinitive behavior system" (Van Hooff 1972); one of its varieties (the horizontal bared-teeth display) is preceded and followed by submissive behavior in the subject and appeases aggressive behavior in a dominant interaction partner; other varieties elicit affinitive behavior. How does the smile achieve that? It might be because the smile (or the silent bared-teeth display) is explicitly nonaggressive and clearly not fear (it is supposed to derive, phylogenetically, from a vocalized fear response). In fact, the smile is behavior that explicitly occurs in a plane orthogonal to the direction of approach, attack, and flight and may be intelligible as "friendly" for that reason.

Laughter also produces interactive effects, which may well be one of its major functions. Its chimpanzee homolog, the "play face" (Van Lawick-Goodall 1968) or vocalized "relaxed open mouth display" (Van Hooff 1972), appears to indicate that fighting or romping is not meant seriously; it serves as a gloss to such seemingly aggressive behavior. In Van Hooff's (1972) study, it was followed, in 88% of its occurrences, by the interaction partner showing play behavior.

Interactive expressions, in the sense meant here, can be considered means of communication. It should be clear, however, that they do not primarily communicate feelings. What they communicate are behavioral intentions or requests for action. Interactive expressions are social imperatives. At the same time, their motives are the same desires and urges that motivate direct relational behavior: desire for the removal of discomfort (as in crying), for the disappearance of frustrating obstacles (as in angry threat), for nonaggression in others, for participation by others, and so on. They thus are truly "emotional expressions," that is, movements not intentionally produced because of their effects (Frijda 1982). They should not be confused with facial or other "gestures" that indeed are produced with a view to their effects (see section 2.6). Interactive expressions can be copied to symbolize attitudes or to intentionally communicate feelings; but that is not their original nature.

Darwin's second principle

Interactive expressions constitute the proper domain of Darwin's second principle of expression, the principle of antithesis:

> Certain states of mind lead to certain habitual actions, which are of service, as under our first principle. Now when a directly opposite state of mind is induced, there is a strong and involuntary tendency to the performance of movements of a directly opposite nature, though these are of no use; and such movements are in some cases highly expressive. (Darwin 1872, [1965, p. 28])

It is not that opposite feelings engender opposite behavior, but that opposite interactional effects are obtained by opposite means; and the more surely so, the more distinctly opposite the behaviors; that is, the more unambiguous the signals. Submissive behavior forms the clearest example.

Transferred expressions

In his first principle, Darwin was concerned with the problem that expressions occur under conditions where they "may not then be of the least use." Tendency to close the eyes occurs in fright when there is nothing to harm the eyes; crying and weeping occur when there is nobody around to help; a disgusted face occurs in response to a disgusting story. Generally speaking, expression occurs in response to emotions and not merely in response to events requiring the actions involved – hence Darwin's hypothesis concerning the hereditary association between the emotions and those actions.

The problem, as faced by Darwin, is to a large extent the product of an inappropriate conceptualization of emotion. Emotion is viewed as mere inner feeling. If, however, emotions are not conceived of as mere feelings but as states involving tendencies toward relational behavior, and expression as one form of such behavior, the problem is greatly simplified. Disgust evoked by morally repulsive events just involves the same relational tendency of desiring to reject as that evoked by sensorily repulsive events; fright evoked by seeing a suspense movie involves the same relational tendency of shielding against the event as that evoked by physical dangers.

The problem then reduces to one of explaining why behavior that is appropriate to the relational tendency is shown under circumstances where it cannot be effective. There are two possible answers; they are complementary. The first: Something akin to stimulus generalization is involved. Piderit (1867) supposed transferred expressions to consist of behavior in relation to "imaginary objects"; Wundt (1903) pointed to a "similarity" between, for instance, sensory and moral revoltingness, or between sweetness and pleasingness in general. The notion finds support in observations on development of expression in infants: Expressions of affective appreciation grow out of the sensory ones at a very early age (Chiva 1985).

The second kind of answer: Expression forms a primitive behavior system that operates on the principle "shoot first, ask questions later." Only part of the stimulus array is responded to, namely, its repulsive, or frightening, or pleasant (etc.) aspect, without regard to further details, consideration of which would have proven the response useless. Such a principle would not be implausible considering that emotions are elicited by serious events urgently demanding response. The problem really is not that expressions are "transferred" to conditions where they are useless, but that there exist "transferred emotions": physically shrinking from morally repulsive events, and the like. In fact, a morally repulsive story can actually induce vomiting and not merely elicit a facial expression of disgust; fright induced by shocking news can send one running, hands before the eyes.

In addition, as Dumas (1933, 1948a) argued, the importance of transferred expressions may have been grossly overestimated by both Darwin and Piderit. Many or most transferred expressions are not emotional expressions at all, but *"mimiques,"* facial gestures. The problem, in Dumas's view, does not exist. "Bitter" and "sour" expressions in response to other than gustatory stimuli are voluntary copies of truly emotional – that is, involuntary – expressions, albeit on a basis of similarity between the attitudes giving rise to them and those involved in the rejection of bitter- and sour-tasting substances.

The primitivity and flexibility of expressive behavior

Transferred expression suggests that expression be considered part of a primitive response system. The primitivity resides in the behavior being largely innate, prewired, preprogrammed, as will be more extensively argued in section 2.4. It is manifest primarily, however, in the crudeness of discrimination with respect to appropriate eliciting stimuli. Expressive behavior is elicited even when finer cognitive analysis would have shown the behaviors to be objectively useless. Blinking upon sudden noise, crying when alone, and nausea upon morally shocking events are like stooping when hearing a bullet whiz by: It is stupid, but not stooping would be even more stupid. Emotion, we argue, functions at that level.

Yet cognitive control of expressive behavior is not entirely absent. Expressive behavior does not consist of fixed response patterns that run off in stereotyped fashion and that would do so independently of the nature of the given stimulus situation. Properties of the specific stimulus situation shape expressive behavior in two different ways. First, expressive response patterns tend to be adjusted to those properties in direction and intensity. They are directed toward or away from the location of relevant objects, and they are adjusted to the apparent strength or resistance of these objects. Coherence with the situation shows clearest in expressions of anger. Angry actions usually are directed toward the offender or toward objects that are likely as offenders. Even defensive aggressive actions elicited by electrical stimulation of the hypothalamus are directed at persons or animals nearby, and not at a block of wood or the experimental apparatus (see chapter 7.)

Second, the expressive pattern shown varies with the circumstances. The variety of facial and other expressions of anger has been discussed in a previous section. The varieties appeared to depend upon whether the object of anger is or is not physically present and upon the kind of angry action put in readiness; the latter, again, would seem to be a function of the nature and behavior of the opponent.

Similar variety was noted among expressions of fear. Eyes are either open or closed, depending upon what makes most sense in the given circumstances. The same in animals. The rat, for instance, has a repertory of defensive reactions: freezing, running, jumping, fighting. Which reaction is shown depends primarily upon what is appropriate under the kind of circumstance: freezing in the open field, running in alleys with exits, fighting when another rat is around. Rate of conditioning of either of these reactions to a warning signal strongly depends upon the kind of circumstance in which conditioning takes place: A rat easily learns to run in the activity wheel and to freeze in the open field (Bolles 1970).

In all, undue emphasis has often been placed upon fixedness of fixed action patterns that correspond to given emotions. A measure of flexibility appears to be the rule.

2.4. Behavior intensity, activation, and inhibition

Expressive behavior varies in intensity. Fearful withdrawal may be manifest as outright flight or as a face full of terror, or it may be merely alluded to in rigidity of posture, or a slight frown, slight narrowing of the eyes, and a tremble around the lips; and so for any other relational activity. The intensity aspect forms a major dimension in the description of emotional behavior and in judgments of expression. It is easy to order expression photographs on a continuum such as "sleep–tension" (Schlosberg 1954). In experiments in which observers have to rate expressions on a set of bipolar scales ("pleasant–unpleasant," "active–passive," "strong–weak," etc.), intensity invariably appears as one of the major underlying factors; scales like "active–passive" and "uncontrolled–controlled" show the highest loadings on that factor (Osgood 1955; Frijda 1969). Multidimensional scaling of similarity judgments of expression photographs yields intensity as the major dimension (Abelson & Sermat 1962). Substantial correlations have been found between factor scores on the intensity dimension and the amount of facial change involved in the expressions ($r = .71$ in one study, $r = .52$ in another; Frijda 1969).

Intensity is not a simple concept, though. For one thing, it can be used to apply to amount of muscular change from a normal or resting position, irrespective of whether that change is due to muscular activity or to loss of muscle tone. It obviously functioned in this manner in the above judgment experiments: Deep passive sadness is a more intense expression than a neutral face. Apart from that, intensity refers to a number of different behavior parameters: scope or amplitude of active movement; expression extent – the extent to which the body as a whole participates in the expression (just the eyes, or just the face, or the entire body); duration of response, given a certain stimulus duration; speed and force of movement, if applicable; and amount of muscular tension involved.

These parameters may or may not be correlated. The question of correlation of parameters is of some importance. It is customary in the literature to refer to behavioral intensity, or to its underlying disposition, as "activation." A person is said to be in a lesser or higher state of activation, or to show a lesser or higher "level of activation." If, however, different parameters of behavior intensity do not correlate highly and may even manifest opposite signs, "level of activation" (or behavior intensity, for that matter) is not meaningfully employed as a unitary concept. Some of the relevant points are the following.

Movement scope and expression extent can be expected to be solidly correlated in emotional expression, provided voluntary suppression or enhancement are discounted. In spontaneous emotional behavior, scope of movement in different body parts can be expected to follow certain rules and to be in some form of harmony. There are two kinds of evidence. The first again stems from judgments of expression. Disagreements among expression components evoke the impression of artificiality, unnaturalness, or willfulness. Surprise expressed by widely opened eyes but closed mouth, or by outspoken facial expression but with body motionless and arms just hanging, does not impress as natural surprise; it is the kind of surprise seen on the amateur stage. Similar disagreements differentiate facial gestures from true expressions: Conversational communication of surprise – of the message "You don't say!" – consists of widening the eyes, eyebrows up, and nothing else. Asymmetry generally suggests gesturing rather than expression; Ekman, Hager, and Friesen (1981) demonstrated this to apply to smiling. The second kind of evidence comes from animal behavior, where intentional modifications of movement are supposedly absent and where, presumably, the movements of the various body parts partake in some general degree of activity, with a gradient from the snarling mouth to the tail and over general posture. Hence the "natural grace" of animal movements. These same considerations lead to the hypothesis of positive correlations between movement scope and its time course, and particularly between scope and the time it takes for affective expressions to fade away.

Movement scope, expression extent, and time parameters probably correlate with another intensity parameter, muscular tension, and in particular with simultaneous tension of agonistic and antagonistic muscles. Harmonious covariation of these four variables might account for the impressions of "passionate" or "driven" movements. Such movements are of theoretical importance: They seem to correspond with active, spontaneous, vigilant, motivated behavior as distinguished from reactive response. They suggest different dimensions of activation, one dimension underlying the former kind of behavior, the other the latter.

Scope, extent, and duration of expression, regardless of whether that expression is active, reactive or hypotonic, can be assumed to be related to emotional intensity, if the latter is defined by external criteria like subjective report or severity of eliciting conditions. The correlation cannot be perfect, obviously, because of the possibilities of inhibition and voluntary enhancement.

Movement scope and extent must necessarily show a moderate or weak correlation with muscular tension. There exist states of rigid immobility and tense, inhibited movements as well as relaxed immobility and unrestrained movement. There is evidence that these parameters indeed are to some extent independent. The evidence is indirect, coming not from behavior intensity measurements but from self-ratings of mood states. Thayer (1967, 1978a, 1978b) repeatedly found two separate factors in factor-analytic studies of his "Activation–Deactivation Adjective Check List"; these factors recur in other studies using similar self-rating scales. The first of these factors, called Activation A by Thayer, represents the opposition between feelings of energy and vigor on the one hand and tiredness and drowsiness on the other. One can assume this to be related to movement scope and extent. The second factor, Thayer's Activation B, represents the dimension tension–calmness; it is presumably related to muscular tension, considering the adjectives with high loadings: *tense, jittery, clutched-up* versus *at rest, still, calm, placid*.*

We will refer to these latter manifestations as *tenseness*. We refer to the behavioral intensity parameters generally as *activation manifestations* and will distinguish between several varieties. The variety discussed so far – extent and scope of relational or instrumental behavior – will be called manifestation of *bound* activation: It is bound to effort for achievement of some relational or other goal.

Activation manifestations; Darwin's third principle

Not all expressive behavior is relational in the direct or interactive sense. Excited jumping, random excited movements, restlessness, and the grimaces of muscular effort cannot be so understood. They are the movements that Darwin sought to account for in his third principle, that of "direct action of the nervous system," and that led Spencer (1870) to his closely related principle of irradiation or diffuse discharge of nervous energy. Darwin's third principle was phrased as follows:

* To be precise, Thayer found four factors, acting in pairs: General Activation ("lively," "active," "peppy," "vigorous") correlated negatively with Deactivation–Sleep ("sleepy," "tired," "drowsy"); High Activation ("jittery" etc.) correlated negatively with General Deactivation ("at rest" etc.). Thayer's factors have been shown to dissolve into combinations of activation per se and the pleasantness continuum (Russell 1980). This does not alter the present argument, however.

When the sensorium is strongly excited, nerve-force is generated in excess, and is transmitted in certain directions, depending on the connection of the nerve-cells, and partly on habit: or the supply of nerve-force may, as it appears, be interrupted. Effects are thus produced which we recognize as expressive. (Darwin 1872 [1965, p.29])

According to Spencer's theory, every emotional state has a general and diffuse activating effect upon the motor system. The effect is proportional to the intensity of the emotional state and independent of its pleasant or unpleasant character. It is manifest in general activity or general muscle tension. For Spencer, even the expressions that Darwin explained by his first principle merely result from local distributions of general muscular activation. Dumas (1933, 1948) revived Spencer's principle and demonstrated its usefulness in explaining expressions that resist functional interpretation, particularly when complemented by inhibitory mechanisms of a similar diffuse and general nature.

Excitement and joy

Excited behavior is partly relational. When I put on my coat and say, "Yes," my dog jumps up and runs toward the door, looks at me, jumps around me, runs back toward the door, going on until we leave. In addition, however, there is excess of movement in other directions: He meaninglessly runs to and fro, jumps up and down, and wags his tail; near the door he is in continuous action. This excess of movement is no different from excited behavior in humans: that of a child impatiently claiming his turn in a game or that of an upset person who briskly paces up and down his room.

Excited behavior impresses as superfluous excess because of the high frequency of unfounded and goalless changes in direction and the preponderance of movements orthogonal to the direction of locomotion: jumping, sideways swaggers, pacing, movements to and fro. The "excitement" behavior system identified by Van Hooff (1972) in chimpanzee social behavior similarly consists of items like "squat bobbing," "vertical head shake," and "rapid oh-oh vocalization." The same features of frequency of change and absence of direction are present in excited scribblings (see the zigzagging lines by which subjects represent excitement; Krauss 1930, Clynes 1980); in excited chatter; in fidgetings ("autistic gestures") such as nose scratching, hair pulling, tie straightening, and lip sucking (Krout 1935); and in the pitch peaks of excited voice intonation (Bezooijen 1984).

Much excited behavior can be understood as blocked locomotion: relational activity blocked in proceeding toward its object. The dog bounds off when the door is opened; the child runs toward his place in the game when his turn has come. Andrew (1972) interprets animal excitement – tail wagging, the erected tail of a cat, impatient stamping of a horse – in a similar fashion. The relational origin may still show in the points around which the behavior is centered (the door, the game) and in the nature of superfluous movement. Both Darwin and Andrew interpret the foot stamping of impatient horses as the closest substitute to the blocked intended behavior. Often there is no true blocking, but action cannot be accomplished as rapidly as desired: Amorous possession, mental as well as physical, cannot be achieved in a jiffy, and hence may lead to antics; this interpretation of joyful excitement is Sartre's (1934).

Under other conditions, there exists a motive or desire for relational activity, but no appropriate action is possible under the circumstances. This is illustrated by restlessness under suspense: The event toward which activity has to be deployed has not yet materialized.

In some respect, then, excited behavior can be understood in the same way as relational activity: Its origin is readiness for such activity. In another respect, however, it poses a problem. Why doesn't the person or animal whose action is blocked sit still? Evidently, the incitement to relational activity has properties that cause undirected activity to take place when its proper realization is held up. There is activity flowing from sources that do not prepare just that activity; there is a source of activity that remains in effect, irrespective of the kind of activity it was to mobilize. There is a "need" to do something when the proper thing cannot be done. Also, such a need appears when there is no proper thing to do, as when excitement bursts out after suspense is over: after the missed field goal in a football game, or after the scored run. There apparently exists activation that is relatively unspecific in its manifestation, though still tied to its origins. To the notion of activation we will return later; the manifestation can be called *derived* activation manifestation.

Joyful behavior shares in the characteristics of excited behavior; in fact, there is no dividing line between the two, since there exists joyful excitement. Joyful behavior, too, tends to center around the joy-producing object: the door if the dog perceives signs that we are going out, the object newly acquired, the friend who is hugged and kissed. Joyful behavior is relational insofar as it constitutes increased commerce with the object of joy: through delighted gazing at the object and through the game of encounters and reencounters that render the object more vividly present and more acutely obtained. It is interactional in the sense defined earlier insofar as it invites or entices the object to participate. But again it contains movement components that go beyond the relational and the interactive. Movements orthogonal to the direction of locomotion are as conspicuous in joyful behavior as in excited behavior. Among the items in the chimpanzee "play" behavior system are "gymnastics": "a variety of exuberant locomotor patterns like climbing, swinging, dangling from arms or feet, pivoting, rolling over, turning somersaults etc." (Van Hooff 1973, p. 90). When such behaviors occur during social interaction they tend to go together with the "relaxed open-mouth face," to be discussed shortly. The joyful behaviors in humans are of a similar nature: See the behavior in the football stadium after a score or among winners of television quiz games. And the nondirectional pattern of laughter is the human equivalent of the chimpanzee relaxed open-mouth face. The exuberance of joyful moods is underscored by the shouting, whistling, and singing that accompany them; Darwin at least said so, and who would deny it?

There is one important difference between joyful behavior and the kinds of excitement sketched earlier. Joyful behavior is not (except in the transitional case of happy suspense) tied to some blocked behavior tendency; that is to say, it does not change into other behavior if circumstances permit. Joyful behavior often is shown after a happy event and then does not contribute to that event's occurrence – as when one goes home whistling, and with a hop or two, after a gratifying amorous encounter. Joyful behavior can therefore be considered pure superfluousness: manifestation of free activation.

The word *free* as used here has two connotations. The first concerns the fact that the activity in joy (or in sheer vitality, which amounts to the same) is not focused upon any specific object or goal, or not entirely so – hence, as just argued, the impression of surplus. The second connotation is that in joyful behavior the available activation resources are not, at that moment, wholly absorbed by vital interests. That fact sets them apart from bound activation manifestations and from the derived activation manifestations of excitement and tenseness. Joyful behavior implies a measure of freedom from such vital interests. This last use of the word *freedom* can refer to the fact that such interests do not, for the moment, preoccupy the subject in a marked way: There is freedom from fear and want. Alternatively, it can refer to the fact that the subject has managed to maintain a certain distance from such interests even when they are present and making themselves felt – such distance as also enables him to joke about his condition or to take time off for play. Both constellations exist, and to both the notion of free activation applies.

According to the preceding analysis, joyful behavior has no function, in the sense that angry or fearful behavior has. It has no purpose, it is just there. The relational aspects, as well as the possible interactive aspects mentioned in section 2.3, are, we think, secondary. Of course, some explanation will have to be sought for the increase of free activation under the conditions indicated. The increase of drive or energy and of interest may be useful, given the circumstances, and the issue will be returned to; but the behavior per se does not appear to be functional.

In the preceding, the word *activity* has repeatedly been used. This might be misleading. It might suggest that excited and joyful behavior represent increase or surplus of mere movement. The notions of "direct action of the nervous system" and of "discharge of nervous tension" also might contain that suggestion. However, to consider the manifestations of derived activation in excitement and of free activation in joy as mere increases of movement does not do justice to the facts. What we see are increases in behavior in the strict sense of that word: increases in activities implying some relationship between organism and environment. One might say, borrowing from philosophy, that joy involves increased intentionality, meaning by *intentionality* not the presence of intentions but the orientation toward objects or goals of activity as such, in which sense even just looking is an intentional act (Brentano 1874; Dennett 1969). In joy, intentionality is free, available to attach to whatever goal or object appears; or intentionality may involve relating to the environment as a whole; or it may consist of orientation toward specific objects, in mere recognition of their presence, in the manner of "disinterested interest." Joyful behavior can be said to be stimulus seeking and relational for the sake of being relational.

All this is not merely words. What is meant is that the somersaults in joy, the whistling and singing, however useless and however purposelessly produced, still are products – modes of behavior. What is meant also is that joyful behavior, while not relational activity, still has positive relational sense, however fleeting and noncommittal the relatings may be. In joyful exuberance there is explicit readiness to indulge in relational activity. This is so perceptually, in the subject's gathering of impressions; it is so interpersonally, in embracings, touchings, slapping shoulders, or volatile conversations.

The connection between joy, increased activity, and intentionality is particularly clear in manic states. These show both increased motor activity and increased interest, even if the latter is capricious. The manic patient hardly sleeps. He talks incessantly, but his logorrhea is at the same time flight of ideas – insights, theories, judgments. He tends to make grandiose plans and executes parts of them. Increased intentionality is as marked as increase in mood or movement.

Deactivation states

Behavior in passive sadness can be understood as deactivation. Coupled to a relational null state is absence of intentional directedness. Just as a manic state entails increase in interest and the making of plans, so depression tends to entail loss of interest in any object, relation, or purpose whatever. Man delights him not, nor woman for that matter. There often is, in depression, true apathy, pale indifference, and emotional emptiness.* Behaviorally, it is the lack of attentional responsivity that differentiates depressed mood from calm and relaxedness, which latter we will call "inactivity states."

Deactivation, too, exists in different varieties, both behaviorally and with respect to eliciting conditions or to stimuli capable of lifting the state. *Fatigue, boredom, listlessness,* and *spleen* are names of deactivation states differing in these regards.

As said before in connection with the expression of sadness, deactivated behavior is no behavior, properly speaking, but absence of behavior. Its mode of appearance, therefore, does not require further explanation. However, some of its major occurrences present a puzzle. Why should various conditions leading to such states indeed do so; that is, why should personal loss, and even absence of interesting stimuli, as in boredom, lead to a decrease in activation below normal, average levels? Why does sadness become hypotonic? The puzzle is similar to that presented by joyful behavior: Why jump and shout after a happy event? In both cases, several explanations have been brought forward, some functional and others not; we will return to them.

---

* What is meant is depressed mood or depressed emotional response; in clinical depression, of course, there is much more, or something other, than apathy.

Tenseness

Tenseness is here defined as generalized muscular tension, wholly or partly independent of overt movement. It can be outwardly visible in rigid posture, jerky movements, or movements of more restricted scope than would be natural; in addition, it can be manifest in secondary effects like tremors.

Tenseness is measured by action potentials of muscle groups not involved in overt movement under the conditions at hand; chin and forehead muscles are the most popular candidates, since they show high loadings on a general factor in tenseness studies (Goldstein 1972).

Tenseness increases under a variety of conditions and for a variety of reasons. It can represent a state of readiness for overt action, as in cats before jumping or in a motorist ready to brake. It can serve the precise control of delicate movement as when threading a needle. It is a regular accompaniment of enhanced attention, presumably in order not to be disturbed or distracted by one's own involuntary movements. It also serves to increase solidity of stance when bracing for some physical impact. In most of these conditions, tenseness results from "sympathetic tensing": tensing of muscles that are not needed in some activity along with others that are. With increased proficiency, such sympathetic tension becomes restricted in measure and extent; with experience, the tongue does not protrude when the needle is threaded. This change with experience suggests that general bodily tenseness results from a primitive mode of action preparation and action control, which tends to become differentiated by learning but recurs under emotional conditions. Tenseness in attention and mental concentration can perhaps be understood by similar reference to that primitive provision. Muscle tension increases when listening to a story (Smith, Malmo, & Shagass 1954) and during problem solving to a degree that tends to correspond with problem difficulty (Davis 1938; Shaw & Kline 1947). It actually is of service: Increase in muscle tension reduces reaction times (Malmo 1959). Tenseness in anger, fear, and apprehension probably derives from the same functions of attention control, action readiness, and bracing for physical resistance, with the above feature of lack of differentiation. Tenseness increases in motorists when passing or in airplane pilots during difficult maneuvers like taking off and landing (Williams, MacMillan, & Jenkins 1947).

Much tenseness under emotional conditions probably results from the control of action tendencies that are undesirable or impossible to obey:

There is action readiness, but the action itself is suppressed. One may tense up under unwanted caresses, suppressing the impulse to withdraw or strike out. Sometimes it appears to serve simple control of sensory as well as motor response to sensory stimuli. Muscular tension can raise pain thresholds (Bills 1927, 1937). Tenseness increases under sensory stimulation, more or less proportionally to stimulus intensity (Davis 1953); under exhaustion, responses to simple stimuli can be strongly enhanced, presumably because the control by tensing is weakened.

The reason for enumerating these different sources of tenseness is to stress the functional role of tenseness under emotional conditions. This, in turn, is to argue that tenseness is not a ubiquitous concomitant of emotion as such. Tenseness, it is true, is intimately related to emotion. It is somewhat in the nature of emotions to emerge when the situation cannot be resolved as smoothly and effectively as seems called for. Hence, there is action readiness in excess of behavior fulfilling it. At the same time, this relation between emotion and tenseness predicts that not all emotions involve tenseness: not those in which action and urge correspond, nor those in which there is deactivation rather than activation, nor those in which there is free activation freely given vent. Tenseness can be supposed to occur in emotion mainly when action falls short of action tendency.

Time course: phasic and tonic, reactive and active responses

Hardly any research has been done on the temporal aspects of expressive behavior: the rate at which expressions come and go, their duration, the gradients of onset and decline, their temporal coherence with eliciting events. Yet temporal aspects show up theoretically fundamental issues, such as the distinction between emotions proper, or reactive emotional responses, and other emotional responses that are of a more spontaneous or more motivational nature.

Emotional responses typically are phasic responses: They have a more or less well-defined onset and termination. Onset and, to some extent, termination of response depend upon onset and termination of the eliciting events; the events qualify as eliciting for that reason and the emotions, by consequence, as "reactive" ones. Of course, phasic responses are not necessarily single behavioral items – expressions that come, reach their peak, and go – but usually consist of response complexes developing in coherence with the development of the eliciting event or one's awareness of it. Laughter develops as the amusing story develops and continues with successive jokes or punchlines.

By contrast, many other emotional behaviors are of a more tonic nature; or they appear to emerge spontaneously, not elicited by given stimuli, but rather emerging from previously existing readiness, motives, or interests of the subject. Interest (in the sense of an emotion of interest), vigilant attention, concentration are examples. Quite different, but also of a tonic nature, are behaviors that appear to be released rather than elicited by external events: increase in activity evoked by seeing others enjoy themselves and joining in the fun; and the behavior released by lively music. Activation induced by lively music is not a response to that music in the same sense that enjoyment of that music is. You like it because it activates, and not vice versa. And it activates because (and when) there is readiness to be activated, as such readiness varies from moment to moment, and from person to person, and is marked particularly in younger people.

Of a different nature again are patterns of expression that persist for an indefinite period and do not show a particular change over time: ways of moving, for instance, or facial expressions that linger and last and may even be habitual. Due to their time course they are considered indicative of moods and, in the event, of personality traits. Upon these more or less persisting patterns of expression, phasic ones, and tonic ones of definite duration, may be superimposed. What is of importance here is to note that time course and temporal coherence with events lead to categorizations of theoretical consequence: they lead to the distinction of "emotions proper," the reactive variety of phasic reactions (see section 2.8 for further discussion), motivational acts, and moods or habitual emotional attitudes.

Gradients of onset and offset of expressions and patterns of temporal development vary. Descriptions in the literature of gradients and patterns are few. Impressionistic classifications and interpretations are given by Strehle (1954) and Kietz (1956). Clynes (1977, 1980) produces some evidence of differences between emotions in temporal activation pattern. The evidence was obtained by having subjects imagine a given emotion and press a button upon a signal; horizontal and vertical pressures over time are recorded. Older studies report systematic differences between simple lines drawn by subjects when requested to depict various emotions. Anger usually shows powerful lines, often with sharp changes in direction, sadness thin lines sloping downward, joy stronger lines sloping upward, and so on (Poffenberger & Barrows 1924; Krauss 1930).

Generally, brisk onset of expressive movement and of facial expression appears to be characteristic of either reactive and reflex-like or voluntary response; more gradual onset appears to be characteristic of what one would call emotional impulse or true action tendency. Of particular interest is slow onset – a delay in response after advent of the stimulus, but a rise to a peak in intensity thereafter. It gives the impression of passionate, internally driven behavior (see Clynes 1980): impulse that gradually gathers strength to overcome control or deliberation.

Offset, too, can be either brisk or gradual. Brisk offset suggests voluntary action or suppression; a spontaneous smile fades away whereas a polite smile betrays itself by falling off one's face. Gradual offset, like delayed onset, is of theoretical interest, since it suggests something "behind" the overt movement pattern: an impulse, an inner activation state that presses for response but exists independently of it. A fit of anger does not always end upon an apology or upon retreat of the offender; it may rage on for quite a while. Panicky flight outlasts actual pursuit. Laughter and weeping follow their own course. Laughter may continue even when the funny event does not appear so very funny any longer, and a fit of weeping may end without the cause of sorrow having ended. It is as if these response patterns, once evoked, are self-sustaining until they are "spent."

The self-sustaining character of some reaction patterns is particularly evident in what can be called a "point of no return" in violent emotional responses. Expressions of fear and anger, and of laughing and weeping, can often be voluntarily controlled; if, however, control is abandoned to some small extent, response often cannot be further restrained. If someone suppresses his anger but then allows himself just one stinging remark, he may explode beyond what he intended. When one sob is permitted to come through, one may be unable to further hold back the tears. It is easier not to start running in fear than to stop once started, before the impetus is spent. Similarly with laughter; similarly with cravings or desires: It is sometimes less difficult not to touch at all than to touch and stroke just a little. All these examples point to a relative independence of the completion of response patterns from their eliciting conditions. Once triggered, they tend to run off on their own accord. We will try to draw the theoretical conclusions later.

Impulsiveness

Emotional behavior often shows the characteristics of impulsiveness: brief latency, sudden onset (brief rise time), vigor, and weakness of stimulus control. Weakness of stimulus control refers to disregard for control-relevant features of the situation and for features that would render lesser response intensity more appropriate. Under strong excitement, movements have more power and are less well aimed, voices are louder than circumstances warrant. Kicking, in violent rage, is vicious, regardless of consequences for either subject or victim. Violent anger, violent fear, and violent desire are blind. The blindness also involves deficiencies in timing (responding too soon) and continuation of action beyond the point where its effects have been achieved: continuing to run or hide when danger is over, or kicking and hitting the victim when he is down. Action runs its entire course, as discussed above. These characteristics contrast with those of deliberate, voluntary behavior and may intrude upon the latter, as when anger at a stubborn bolt makes equipment break.

Inhibition and control

Tendencies toward movement can be voluntarily suppressed, in self-control, or checked involuntarily, in inhibition. The notion of inhibition, as applied to behavior obviously involves inference since it assumes readiness for a response that is not shown. Cues for assuming inhibition are movement rigidity, tenseness, or discrepancies of various sorts, as will be discussed more fully in chapter 8.

Inhibition can be an aspect of any kind of behavior. It is explicit in some expressive patterns, notably those of rigid anxiety and what in animals is called freezing, and in movement interruption. The startle reaction in which the mouth falls open and the eyes are opened wide is interpreted by Dumas (1933) as an inhibitory response.

Inhibitory responses have distinct relational sense in that they go counter the risks involved in action: risks of exposure to physical hazards as well as to interactional ones. To the latter belongs conspicuousness; in fact, freezing can be interpreted as a specific kind of unconspicuousness behavior – a German term was the "keeping dead reflex" (*Totstell-reflex*). In humans, conspicuousness hazards extend to social criticism, to doing the wrong thing socially, or to eliciting social response and requests for further interaction that then in turn have to be responded to: the conditions for social shyness. Inhibition is furthermore the means for controlling action in progress and attuning it to goals at hand: Attack has to wait for the appropriate moment in order not to miss its target; flight has to reckon with the movements of the pursuer and the nature of the environment. Emotional action has to be geared to the cues that are missed in unrestrained impulsive action. Inhibition finally may serve to safeguard against the general risk of emotional responding – that of getting carried away and of passing the point of no return mentioned, beyond which voluntary control appears to lose its power.

The above functions of inhibition can be subsumed under the general function of caution; inhibitory response is cautionary response. This can be extended to anxiety and its subspecies such as shyness, timidity, embarrassment. Anxiety – the rigid, inhibited variety – can be understood as hypertrophy of the caution system. This is compatible with the view of Gray (1971, 1982), who interprets anxiety as inhibitory response. It is also compatible with interpreting anxiety as incompetence response: Rigid anxiety can be seen as the response in which every action is inhibited because no action appears feasible or uncharged with unacceptable risks.

Inhibition in anxiety extends to all kinds of response: to thought processes as well as to overt movement. Just as there is inability to move or awkwardness of movement, there is inability to concentrate and to think straight. These cognitive disturbances, in true terror as well as in common social anxiety, are inhibitory reactions. Inhibition manifests the same primitive lack of differentiation as activation, as discussed earlier.

The above description and interpretation of anxiety does not, to all likelihood, apply to panic attacks. Panic attacks can be characterized as "catastrophe reactions" (Goldstein 1939) and appear to represent helplessness reactions – more specifically, responses of separation distress (Klein 1981). Their structure in terms of activation, inhibition, or relational activity is unclear; they may consist of extreme undirected, disorganized activation states (Van Dis 1986).

Inhibition results in response suppression and immobility only under certain circumstances. Ordinary caution, reserve, wariness, and reticence merely tone down responses or perhaps cause expression extent in excess of expression scope. A measure of caution, of inhibition, is ubiquitous in normal emotional behavior (see chapter 8). That measure varies. The balance between impulse and inhibition (or voluntary control) shifts continuously. It shifts, presumably, as a function of actual need for caution and control and of the subject's daring, sense of competence, desire to hold himself in hand, and similar variables. There is a continuously changing balance in emotional behavior between letting go and restraint, between reacting and acting on one's initiative, between taking control and being controlled, in response to what happens outside as well as in response to internal variations in propensity. Such a changing balance is visible particularly in the representation of emotional behavior in music and dancing. Flach (1928), in her descriptive and introspective study of expressive behavior, speaks about the flow of tension and countertension, of binding and loosening, Kreitler and Kreitler (1972), in their study of art, use the same terms.

Emotional responding and transaction

The main purpose of the present exposition has so far been to describe expressive behavior, in order to understand its form and function. As a consequence, that behavior has mainly been treated as if it consisted of relatively brief single expressive reactions. However, emotional responding usually is made up of a sequence of reactions that shows change and development in time. Emotions are responses to events that rarely fall upon a person unexpectedly: There is a period during which the event gradually reveals its impact or comes closer; emotional responding grows accordingly. Once the event is truly there, it may last for some shorter or longer time or persist indefinitely, as do the burdens of oppression or the satisfactions of a love affair. In emotional responding to enduring events, different responses succeed one another. Grief may travel from stupefaction over weeping to silent dejection; silent dejection may permeate daily doings that still are pursued, or take over and make the person sit down motionless and staring. Behavior at different times shows different degrees of response suppression or inhibition, according to the degree to which the subject wants to keep himself in hand, or can do so, or must do so.

Even relatively incidental events, such as a slighting, a physical threat, or the appearance of a desirable object, give rise to a sequence of behaviors. Anger, for instance, can show the development of tensing up, then taking a resisting stance, which may turn into protest and outright retaliation, first vocal, then physical, during which various forms of threat and aggression succeed one another.

Emotional responding, the sequence of emotional response to a given event and its aftermath, shows the four features of succession of "different" emotions, succession of different behaviors apparently expressive of the "same" emotion, variation in activation, and variation in inhibitory control.

The reason that responding to a given event shows these successions is, of course, that a given event consists of a succession of part-events and of ways the subject perceives and experiences what happens or has happened; and that emotional response affects the situation at hand. Fearful withdrawal may make the situation be felt as less threatening; anger may make the offender step back. More important, perhaps, is the fact that the environment reacts to the way it is affected by the subject's behavior and so creates a new emotional situation. Others may take advantage of your fear; or, conversely, that fear may stir them into being more considerate. Psychologically, subjectively, environmental "reaction" goes further: Fate does not listen to protests and so reveals itself as immovable, and so on. For these reasons, Lazarus and coworkers (e.g., Lazarus & Folkman 1984) describe emotional responding as a "transaction" between subject and environment, a transaction that is characterized by "flux" – continuous change, in the manner indicated.

2.5. Smiling, laughing, and weeping

There are three major human expressive patterns that have not yet been discussed. All three have so far resisted satisfactory functional interpretation. They have something more in common than just being puzzling. All three should be classed among the interactive emotions (section 2.3.); at least, all three show strong interactive effects. Smiling appeases, laughter invites participation, and weeping enjoins succorance. Yet all three appear to be more than interaction signals because of the conditions that evoke them and because of their particular activation course.

Smiling

Smiling has been considered (e.g., Darwin 1872; Spencer 1870) as beginning laughter or a weak form of it. Although some smiles may be just that, it is unlikely that all smiles are. One argument for the distinction is that smiling and laughter appear to belong to different behavior systems, that is, they occur in different contexts, in both humans and chimpanzees. The chimpanzee smile homolog belongs to the affinitive behavior system; the laughter homolog of chimpanzees and laughter in preschool children form part of the play behavior system (Van Hooff 1972; Blurton-Jones 1972b). In adults, smiling and laughter appear to correspond to the overlapping though distinct domains of friendliness and amusement, respectively (Van Hooff 1972).

In essence, three interpretations of the smile have been advanced. The first, and most traditional, considers the smile an expression of positive mood, of happiness or joy. Of course, the smile occurs in conditions of pleasure; however, it does not occur in every condition of pleasure: Who smiles during sexual pleasure, for instance? The major conditions for such smiling as will not continue into laughter appear to be those of satisfaction and contentment (Dumas 1948b). The condition of satisfaction may be defined as one in which strong involvements are momentarily at rest. One does not usually smile when in suspense or truly fascinated, however pleasurable the situation. A certain measure of distance from or command over the situation appears to be a prerequisite.

The second interpretation considers the smile as an expression of mastery or competence rather than one of happiness or satisfaction as such. Goldstein (1939) labeled the smile a "reaction of adequacy." The mastery or competence interpretation has obtained support from the important studies on infant smiling and laughter by Sroufe and his associates (Sroufe, Waters, & Matas 1974; Sroufe & Waters 1976). Infants smile particularly in response to stimuli that challenge, but still are just within reach of, their cognitive capacities (Sroufe did not distinguish between smiling and laughter). The interpretation accords with the infant smile in response to the human face or to facelike stimuli (Spitz 1965; Ahrens 1954): There is cognitive mastery over those stimuli (both of the other theories explain these smiles equally well, though). The interpretation also accords with smiling in embarrassment, condescending or derisive smiles, and noncommittal and defensive smiles, such as when refusing to respond to accusations or probing personal questions.

In the third interpretation, the smile is primarily seen as a social response. In one version of this interpretation, the smile is a signal to appease or reassure the interaction partner. The chimpanzee "smile" clearly has such effects, considering subsequent behavior of interaction partners (Van Hooff 1972). The ritualized use of smiling in human greeting, which appears to be universal (Eibl-Eibesfeldt 1973), and in encouragement and recognition can also easily be seen as signaling nonaggressive intent. Such appeasement function, however, does not apply easily to infant smiles, nor does it fit well with the bond-strenghtening effects of these smiles upon the mother (Vine 1973). Hence a second version, in which the smile is considered a response of affection: of acceptance or the desire to be accepted. The smile can be said to be elicited by affiliative stimuli. The two versions are compatible: What is friendliness for the subject may be appeasing or reassuring to his interaction partner.

The smile as a motor pattern has been explained in various ways. Darwin (1872) sees it as weak laughter; the facial features of laughter are derived from eye closure to protect the eyes during shouting; the derivation is rather implausible. Van Hooff (1972) and others see the origin of smiling in the defensive grin of lower mammals, the face of hissing; the smile (or the chimpanzee silent, bared-teeth face) has acquired opposite meaning by dropping the vocalization; I do not know whether the muscles involved in the defensive grin or the "silent, open-mouth display" are the same as those involved in the human smile (zygomatic and risorius muscles in particular). Dumas's (1933, 1948b) explanation is quite different, and quite simple: The smile is the result of global moderate contraction of the facial musculature. This mechanical explanation is based upon electrical stimulation of the facial muscles by Duchenne (1876) and of the facial nerve itself (Dumas 1933). The global innervation itself is but part of a general increase in muscle tone and is notable in the face merely because of muscle dynamics, according to Spencer's principle of least effort (section 2.3.).

It is not easy to combine the preceding hypotheses; nor to choose from among them. It is, in fact, possible that several different smiles exist that each have a distinctly different meaning. Young and Decarie (1977) describe seven different smile patterns in 8- to 12-month-old infants. Van Hooff (1972) distinguishes two variations of the chimpanzee "smile," the one more submissive, the other more friendly. Ekman, Friesen, and Ancoli (1980) found evidence that only a certain kind of smile corresponds to feelings of happiness. However, some common core would be a more satisfying assumption, as in fact is the case with the chimpanzee variations.

A common element can indeed be found in the three kinds of interpretation of human smiling. It consists of a combination of interest and absence of vital concerns like hunger, desire, or safety. The smile might be seen as a mode of free activation, of active, attentive rest, and of dispassionate concern, either just as an outflow of the subject's general condition (as Dumas has it) or as a social, affinitive bonding response: nonagonistic, nonwithdrawing, nonpossessive, and evident as such to interaction partners.

Laughing

Laughter is different from smiling, apart from manifesting more pronounced facial change, by its vocalized expirations. It shares certain features with smiling, though, which make laughter, too, a free activation manifestation: It is active, but nonrelational, in the sense employed in this study. "Laughter neither shrinks nor advances," says Gregory (1924), and "an Irishman might say of laughter that it does something without doing anything" (Gregory 1924, p. 26).

Dumas (1933, 1948a), like Darwin, views the facial pattern of laughing as being nothing more than the intensification of the smiling patterns (except, of course, for the widely opened mouth, linked to the vocalized breathing). He accordingly considered it the product of more intense general innervation of the facial nerve. Quite different explanations have, again, been brought forward by ethologists. According to Andrew (1963) and Van Hooff (1972), laughter, too, derives from the defensive grin, by way of the chimpanzee's vocalized "play face." Ambrose (1963) sees the facial pattern as a cross-breed of those of smiling and crying, Morris (1967) as one of approach and defense. Neither of these explanations is convincing, one of the reasons being that neural centers involved in laughter appear to be quite different from those involved in defensive behavior or in crying (see chapter 7).

The vocalizations demand separate explanation. Darwin (1872) viewed them as communicative cries, as different as possible from distress calls, in line with the principle of antithesis. Ambrose (1963) sees them as crying toned down by the inspiratory components of enjoyment responses: Laughter would result from near-simultaneous activity of diaphragm-effected expirations and abdominally effected inspirations (Lloyd 1938). Andrew (1963) interprets them as the result of defensive constriction of the glottal aperture plus excited expiration. Dumas (1933) explains the convulsions of laughter as a kind of seizure, resulting from irradiation of nervous excitation in that thalamic region where tumors cause compulsive laughter.

A true fit of laughter manifests a characteristic time course. It continues beyond the eliciting event till it is spent, often ending with a few residual chuckles more widely separated in time. This time course differs from that of crying (not from sobbing), which make theories like Ambrose's unlikely, since they see laughter as derived from distress calls. After a fit of laughter is over, the person tends to be relaxed and sometimes is exhausted. Laughter shares with weeping (and with vomiting, which it resembles) the peculiar feature that Plessner (1941) has called "surrender": The subject abandons himself to his bodily response; the body takes over. Time course, quieted end-state, surrender, and the convulsiveness of peals of laughter are the features that have led to considering laughter a process of "tension release" (Freud 1905; Gregory 1924) or of "discharge of nervous excitation" (Spencer 1870; Dumas 1933).

The notion of tension release applies to the psychological context of laughter as well as to its form and time course. This, of course, is evident in laughter of relief (Gregory 1924) and in laughter about a joke or remark that breaks the tension in conflict or suspense. Resolution of tension fairly literally describes what happens in occasions for infant laughter. Rothbart (1973) reports on studies in which stimuli that are, in themselves, fearful or at least potentially threatening (sudden appearance, poking, bouncing, tickling) give rise to laughter when the children have reached a certain age or are in the right mood; the same stimuli evoke crying when the children are younger or tired or wary. Sroufe (Sroufe & Waters 1976), as said, came to similar conclusions, emphasizing mastery over cognitive challenge and adding that laughter often terminates wary or attentive inhibition of movement.

In some sense, either a literal or a more figurative one, the notion "resolution of tension" can be fitted to all, or most, conditions for laughter (Gregory 1924). *Tension* here means activation as defined earlier: readiness to respond emotionally or attentionally. The conditions can be described as presentation of stimuli that induce arousal of activation, which activation is then permitted to drop immediately after. Berlyne (1960, 1969) called the result an "arousal jag": increase of activation followed by more or less sudden decrease. The word *decrease* perhaps does not do full justice to the situation that permits the activation drop: That situation appears to be one in which the subject actually can relax or which has turned out to his advantage. Rothbart (1973) describes her theory of laughter as an "arousal-safety theory." The conditions for laughter mentioned – relief, breaking tension, mastery over challenging situations, threatening situations that turn out to be harmless – all fit that pattern. The pattern can be considered also to fit the conditions for sense of the ludicrous and those for amusement, at least as these are phrased in several humor theories. These theories, in one way or another, see the core element of humor to be the presentation of some opposition, contradiction, or difficulty that is subsequently resolved: something incongruous that can yet be grasped, something serious that turns out really to be something innocent or unimportant or of lesser value, in such a way that it benefits the subject. A good representative of such theories is that of Freud (1905). A joke alludes to problematical wishes or desires, which allusion elicits defensive action; the punchline, however, proves this defense to have been unnecessary.

Paradoxical laughter, too, fits the pattern: laughter upon tragic news taken seriously by the subject, or nervous fits of giggling unaccountable to the subject himself. Such laughter can be seen as defensive action to postpone the helplessness involved in full realization of the event and to do so by escaping from commitment to the situation involved.

One of the most elementary manifestations of laughter is that in play, particularly rough-and-tumble play. There it clearly flows from a keyed-up level of activation, together with the nonseriousness of the entire context. The specific eliciting events within play that elicit laughter appear to be mock aggressions (Gregory 1924): victories, defeats, and performances that are not taken seriously but that still, as victories, defeats, and performances, constitute arousal-mastery sequences.

Laughter, then, appears to fulfill some sort of release function. The phenomena suggest an accumulation of activation, which activation is subsequently drained by laughter: If laughter does not do that, why does not the subject just relax when tension is over? Such an accumulation-and-release hypothesis has been rejected by Berlyne (1969) on the grounds that it would seem to imply some mysterious "mental energy." However, keyed-up activation, keyed-up alertness, or readiness for defensive or coping action is real enough, and actual tenseness is manifest in many situations leading to laughter.

Even so, tension release does not fully describe or explain laughter. As noted, the situation of tension decrease in laughter is one that is distinctly to the subject's advantage: It is one of mastery, or one in which failure or defeat is recognized but explicitly taken lightly. In other words, there is detachment from previously mobilized concern. Laughter involves an annulment of seriousness. A shift occurs from bound activation to free activation. Perhaps it is this shift and detachment that are effected by laughter and sought in joking that breaks tension. Perhaps that laughter can be considered a mechanism for detachment rather than merely one for tension release.

The above interpretations lack reference to the social, interactive sides of laughter. Laughter can be called a social response. It is incomparably more frequent, and stronger, when in company than when alone; so much so that the social aspect would appear to be primary. The interactive effects of laughter upon the behavior of others are evident. First, it is contagious: You tend to laugh even when you don't know what other are laughing about. Second, it blocks aggression. This is so with the chimpanzee homolog, of which signaling nonaggression intent appears to be the function (Van Hooff 1972b); and it is so with humans.

Laughter can make an attacker stop in midair, so to speak, when responded to in that manner rather than with fear or counterattack; I have observed this to happen, and have received accounts of it from others, in truly serious attack situations.

As with smiling, the social aspect and that of activation manifestation and detachment are not easily combined. Laughter will have to be left at that, but not without suggesting that, perhaps, laughter should be considered a form of bond-strengthening behavior: behavior that one can perform together with others (like singing, or weeping) and that might exist for that purpose.

Weeping

Weeping is considered the expression of sorrow, as laughter is considered that of joy; but just as laughter is not uniquely an expression of joy, weeping is not uniquely one of sorrow.

Weeping and laughter have much in common. Their facial features resemble one another. Both tend to be true behaviors, implicating the entire body and replacing or interrupting other behavior. Both are primarily nonrelational: they neither shrink nor advance. They differ in vocalization and in the tendency toward extensor activity in laughing and flexor activity in weeping. Their sense differs accordingly. The sense of weeping can be said to be helplessness. In weeping, the person abandons his efforts for coping; he breaks down. Weeping implies surrender in the face of persisting reasons for activation: persisting threat, deprivation, or frustration.

Interpretation as helplessness response fits the different occurrences of weeping. One weeps in grief, but not in all grief. One weeps when loss has been recognized as final and irrevocable. This, it seems, is why weeping may offer relief and is welcomed as the solution to pent-up grief: Hope, protest, or coping efforts are relinquished and the finality of loss is accepted not merely intellectually, but on the plane of action tendency. Weeping is the bodily recognition of helplessness. One weeps in impotent anger and impotent frustration. The weeping of infants is obviously helpless. Weeping, however, should be distinguished from crying. Crying, as the human distress call, is effective action in a context of helplessness; it is active sound production in contrast to the unintentional vocalizations of sobbing and even wailing.

Weeping in happiness is usually interpreted as resulting from previous misery or suspense. It occurs when the subject can allow himself the recognition of the earlier distress and helplessness; as in weeping from grief, it is a form of unbending. Alternatively, weeping in happiness can be seen as the manifestation of powerlessness to absorb and integrate the new, overwhelming situation; that situation is too much to be grasped and adjusted to. Weeping in happiness does not seem to be very different from that in grief: It reflects inability to cope and surrender to such inability. At any rate, it would be entirely wrong to say that weeping can on occasion be an "expression of happiness." To be precise, it is neither an expression of happiness nor of grief: It is the expression of surrender to helplessness.

Like laughing, weeping can be called a mechanism for or mode of tension release: All weeping is preceded by increased activation or, at least, emotional upset, and it usually ends in increased quietness and relaxation. Whereas in laughing the initial activation turns out to be unnecessary, here, in weeping, that activation turns out to be pointless: No effective coping with the situation is possible. Like laughing, weeping can be considered a "detachment response," a means to get rid of active emotional involvement. As noted before, weeping shares with laughter its social character: People can weep together. There is a strong consolation effect in shared weeping. The widespread institution of professional mourners or wailing women probably is no arbitrary cultural convention but more likely based upon the relief from isolation that communal weeping provides. The interactive effects of weeping are more extensive than this. Seeing tears tends to elicit tears. Weeping evokes sympathy and compassion, or it evokes irritation because of the pressures toward sympathy exerted. All this suggests some basic social function of weeping, too; weeping also might be bond-strengthening behavior, in distress this time.

Why weeping – why sobbing and shedding tears? No useful hypotheses exist. Usually, the emphasis in explaining weeping is put upon the aspect of crying or the distress call; this still leaves those two features of sobs and tears.

Sobbing and laughing appear related; their sounds are often confused. Dumas (1933), indeed, considers them as due to the same mechanism: thalamic convulsions that discharge some state of excitation. Compulsive laughter and weeping occur, according to Dumas, in the same neurological patients, and they may in fact easily switch over from one into the other. Poeck (1969) does not confirm this opinion.

Tears remain a complete mystery. Darwin (1872) explains them by the forceful closure of the eyes during screaming. The explanation does not convince; nor did Darwin himself sound convinced. An amusing hypothesis is that of Morgan (1972): Tears come from the necessity of keeping the eyes clear in emergencies, and they serve such purpose in aquatic animals like crocodiles or whales – or humans, descended from sea apes, as Morgan supposes them to be. Recently, suggestions have been advanced as to possible metabolic advantages of the shedding of tears.

The puzzles of smiling, laughing, and weeping

In all, the origins and functions of smiling, laughing, and weeping are not really transparent. However, whether viewed as tension release and detachment mechanisms, as bonding behaviors, or as social signals, laughing and weeping are to be considered meaningful, and not mere odd movements. When viewed as activation modes, they still are meaningful; that is, they are states of readiness and, again, not just movements. Under all interpretations they – at least, laughing and weeping – are behaviors interrupting other behavior.

2.6. Expression, emotion, communication, and mood

Principles of expression

Darwin proposed three principles of expression: that of associated serviceable habits; that of antithesis; and that of direct action of the nervous system. These principles served to explain both the formal properties of expressions and their occurrence under the conditions that elicit them. As will be recalled, other writers introduced additional principles.

From the preceding analyses, four principles have emerged that, to a large extent, are similar to those of Darwin and others, but different in emphasis and theoretical phrasing. These principles are:

1.   *The principle of relational activity.* Some expressive behavior can be understood as relational activity: activity that establishes, weakens, and negates the physical and cognitive relations of the subject with the environment, by means of locomotion and modifications of bodily and sensory exposure. Some expressive behavior has relational significance without properly being relational activity: relational null states.

2.   *The principle of interactive effectiveness.* Some expressive behavior can be understood as action that aims at modifying the relation

of the subject to the environment, through influencing the behavior of other individuals.

3. *The principle of activation.* Some expressive behavior can be understood as the manifestation of behavior activation as such, or of decrease in behavior activation. By *activation* is meant intentional
directedness – readiness for attention, striving, and responding.

4. *The principle of inhibition.* Some expressive behavior can be understood as the result of inhibition of behavior. Some of this behavior
results from inhibition of expressive behavior falling under the
previous principles.

Together, these principles are supposed to explain the nature of expressive behavior – both its form and its occurrence. Admittedly, some
expressive behavior is resistant to explanation in terms of these principles: weeping and the peals of laughter in particular. In this respect,
however, the present formulations are not worse off than previous ones,
since extant explanations are unsatisfactory.

In intent, the present first principle corresponds to Darwin's first and
to those of Piderit and Bühler; Darwin's notion of association and Piderit's of "imaginary objects" are here covered by the added notions of
generalization and cognitive primitivity. The present second principle
covers some of Darwin's "serviceable habits" and, in particular, accom-
modates applications of Darwin's principle of antithesis. The third principle corresponds with Darwin's third and with Spencer's and Dumas's
principle of excitation. The fourth principle mirrors the last part of Darwin's first principle (see the footnote in section 2.1) and Dumas's notion
of inhibition.

The major feature of the present formulations (and, in fact, their intent)
is to provide for a direct link between emotion and expression. As already
mentioned, and to be elaborated in section 2.8, emotion can be interpreted as the instigation to relational activity: Expression is part of the
relational activity instigated. The link between emotion and expression
thus is an intrinsic one. It is that between a plan and its execution, or
between an intention and the behavior that realizes that intention. This
holds even for, for instance, the apathy of sadness: Loss of intent turns
into loss of action and hypotonia.

The present analysis of expression, in fact, strongly suggests the above
interpretation of what we mean by *emotion*. It also suggests hypotheses
concerning the structure of the different emotions. The different emotions can be analyzed, and to a large extent characterized, in terms of
the specific mode of relational intent manifest in the corresponding ex-

pressive behavior. This, too, will be elaborated further down (section 2.8 and chapter 4).

This view, furthermore, leads to satisfactory explanation of the variable relationships between emotion and expression, the intrinsic nature of their relationship notwithstanding.

Different emotions can share a given expression because mode of relational intent is only one of the aspects that define a given emotion; the point will also be clarified shortly. Some emotions are not expressed in any specific or constant fashion at all because relational intent can be quite variable under given eliciting conditions, whereas these conditions, on occasion, define the emotion; shame, jealousy, and regret are examples. Expressions of a given emotion can be variable also because a given relational intent is not necessarily always implemented by the same kind of relational activity: Several kinds of activity may serve one kind of intent under different conditions.

Finally, the present formulations explain the perception of emotion in others; they explain recognition of expression (see Frijda 1969). Recognizing expression consists of recognizing relational tendency, activation state, and inhibitory control in the expressive movement patterns. It is not surprising that the presence of the former can, with reasonable accuracy, be ascertained on the basis of the latter. On the other hand, to the extent that emotions share the same relational activity, errors in recognition are to be expected, as in fact is found to be the case (see section 2.7).

Activation modes, relational modes, and inhibition modes

Activation manifestation can vary continuously, from apathy to high vigor and free activity, from placidity to intense tenseness. Inhibition can vary from high control to absence of restraint. Relational activity can also vary continuously along its major dimensions: from openness and turning toward the outside world to closure and turning inward, from approach to withdrawal. These continuous variations are determined by the meanings and impacts of outside events as well as by thoughts and by the flow of free activation or vitality.

The more pronounced reactions are indicated by the emotion names; these names are usually not used for the passing hesitations, withdrawals, and turnings-toward, which are of the same relational or activation nature. Even the more pronounced emotional response patterns that we call "emotions" categorize into discrete classes what are, in fact, intensity continua. Rage, anger, irritation, being bothered, and being irked are but intensity bands on one of these continua. Many of the intensity variations do not have names, particularly the many activation modes, where "I feel light/lighter/lightest" or "I feel strong/stronger/strongest" are the most one can say when increased vitality does not seem to have a sufficiently articulate cause or object to call it "joy" or "happiness"; feeling "heavy" or "in low spirits" indicate deactivation that is not sufficiently definite to call it sadness or sorrow.

It is not only weaker states that have no names; no names are usually attached to those states that are not solidly anchored in eliciting events – in which activation, relational readiness, reticence, or unwillingness are fleeting and tentative and depend as much upon what occurs within the subject as what confronts him from the outside. A remark may lead to withdrawal and wariness that would be called "fear" if truly fixed upon the object, but that will not receive that name when abandoned immediately after, because of some different perspective adopted. Yet this play of opening up and closing, reserve and letting go, strength and stance moving up and down forms the emotional warp and woof of daily human interaction – much more so than the full-fledged action patterns receiving emotion names. The full significance of these variations in relational readiness, activation, and control does not reside merely in the actions shown (or not shown) per se. It also resides in the coherence, or noncoherence, between action and ongoing events. That is to say: Expressive behavior consists as much of nonresponse to significant events, and of response in the absence of events, as of responding in a strict sense of that word. Nonresponse manifests control, or turning-inward, or postponement; response in the absence of events is, or manifests, spontaneity: stimulus seeking, contact seeking, generalized eagerness for impressions, and the like. The significance of expressive behavior, further, resides in its temporal dynamics, its relationships with what went before or after. Some response is abandonment of previous control, or regained equilibrium, or courageous overcoming of hesitation and reserve. All these variations can be understood from the few principles mentioned above; they belong to the domain of emotion because they are manifestations of changes in action readiness, without necessarily representing states that should be called "emotions."

The same variations in action readiness as occur in response to specific events can occur spontaneously, without such events, as manifestations of relational readiness and activation "à vide" – directed toward, or away from, the external world as a whole. They then occur as generalized readiness or unreadiness, or as generalized desire for relational commerce. The continuous variations of such play à vide, of opening up and closing, reserve and letting go, are, it would seem, the fabric that music and dance are made of, emotionally. Music and dance can with right be called emotional because they consist of the same type of actions (or their audible results) as emotional responses; the actions have the same sense and, perhaps, intent. They only represent states of readiness or states of being per se, rather than modes of interaction with specific external occurrences. Assessing the sense of these actions or their results – that play of opening, control, reequilibration, abandonment, increase and decrease in vitality – may well be considered to constitute a major source of the pleasure provided by the perception of music and dancing. Playing that play may be considered a major source of the pleasure provided by the acts of performing music and dance.

Mood

Emotional activity discussed so far is phasic and centered around the location of the eliciting object or event. When activation states, relational preparedness, or unwillingness and inhibitory states are tonic and not centered around an object or event, they are called "moods." Mood, according to Nowliss, is the "effect upon the person of his own configuration of activity," which "configurations may be conceptualized as fundamental patterns of general functioning and orientation, such as level of activation, level of control, level of concentration, direction of social orientation, and positive (pleasant) or negative (unpleasant) general appraisal" (Nowliss 1966, p. 353). Mood applies equally to these configurations of activity themselves, or rather to their instigations in corresponding tendencies or states of readiness. These configurations are continuous, not necessarily when there are continuous events that entertain them (as in continuous fear), but more often without such actual events. Behaviorally, moods are configurations of activity that are not centered around an object or event, but that in a fleeting manner attach now to this object, then to that; or similar configurations of activity easily evoked by a multitude of relatively insignificant events. Moods thus fit harmoniously into the present perspective on emotional behavior: They are manifestations of the same sort as those called emotions, but at the same time distinguished by the characteristic just mentioned. In fact, the characteristic is not clear-cut. Centering can be more or less pronounced; but the distinction between moods and emotions, as these words are usually used, is equally unsharp.

Expression and communication

Expressive behavior, facial expression in particular, is often considered to exist for the purposes of communication: It is there to communicate the subject's state of mind to one's fellow humans or animals. This is, perhaps, the implication of Darwin's work, and it is explicit in the considerations of Tomkins (1962) and Izard (1971).

It follows from the preceding analyses, if these are convincing, that this is not so. Expressive behavior is functional, relational activity, and activation or inhibition manifestation; it is to be considered part and parcel of the emotion process, serving to implement or modify the subject's relation to the environment. Obviously, expressive behavior does serve communication. It permits others to make inferences concerning the subject's state of mind, and these inferences are often correct. However, it does not exist for that purpose. It is not produced for that purpose nor, we may assume, did evolution maintain or develop it for its communicative value.

There is one important qualification: There exists the class of interactive expressions. They communicate. As said, however, their function is not to communicate states of mind. They communicate requests and intentions. They are there to influence the behavior of others, and not to promote understanding. Or, to put it differently, they do not communicate anything, they *are* forms of communication (Frijda, 1982).

That is not to deny that communication and social mechanisms do play an important role in expression. For instance, communication intent and social mechanisms can make for important discrepancies between expressive behavior and underlying relational action tendencies and activation states. Expressions can, as said earlier, be attenuated, put on, or enhanced in view of their effects upon others. One may not want to expose oneself by showing one's emotions, or one may withhold from the other the satisfaction of appearing hurt, vulnerable, or dependent; one can coerce others by angry bullying or by manifestly being hurt or vulnerable or dependent. One can also emphatically show anger or sadness just to let the other know or participate, or to indicate the presence of maddening or saddening events. Perhaps these motives play almost always some role in social situations since almost always the options are available of considerate, modest, or self-protective attenuation as well as of coercive enhancement.

Intentional production or suppression of expression, performed for social or communicative reasons, thus may modify such expression, or fake it, or just occur as a mode of behavior in its own right. The distinction between true expression on the one hand and willful modification or communicative production on the other is often available to naive impression. Faking and dissimulation and the mere politeness of a polite smile are often detected. That fact suggests that differences exist between the patterns of true expressions and voluntary ones. Ekman and Friesen (1969a) have discussed "leakage" through "clues to deception"; these clues mostly consist of discrepancies in the expressive pattern, as was discussed before: asymmetries (e.g., Ekman, Hager, & Friesen 1981), or appearance of hand, foot, and body movements when the more readily controlled facial expression is absent, etc.

Intentionally produced expression-like behaviors are called *gestures* or *emblems* (Ekman & Friesen 1969b; *vocal emblems* for vocal expression – Scherer 1979). The distinction implies that true expressions are not intentionally produced and form a separate class of responses. The distinction between expressions and gestures is, apart from the evident difference between faking or dissimulation and spontaneous expression, based upon observations of blind subjects, of consequences of certain neurological disturbances, and of differences between expression-like behavior which does and that which does not show cross-cultural differences in pattern.

The range of expressions of blind-born children is more restricted than that of seeing ones (Fraiberg 1971); the expressions that blind-born children do show tend to be more extreme and thus less controlled (Fulcher 1942); and blind-born children appear incapable of producing facial expressions upon request, whereas seeing children of comparable age do this without difficulty (Dumas 1932; Fulcher 1942). As regards neuropathological observations: Pyramidal lesions may grossly impair voluntary movement, without affecting spontaneous, emotionally elicited expressions (see section 7.2).

Among the facial "gestures," Dumas (1933) distinguishes "facial gestures of imitation," "transferred facial gestures," and "metaphorical facial gestures"; Ekman and Friesen (1969b) make similar as well as additional distinctions. The first of Dumas's categories consists of gestures that copy spontaneous expressions, produced in order to show the presence of the corresponding feelings and attitudes. They have just been discussed. Imitative gesturing can go far: Professional mourners may shed real tears. "Transferred facial gestures" are similar to the "transferred expressions" discussed earlier (section 2.4), except that they are conversational or social signs rather than true emotional responses. Smiles of disdain, contempt and mockery are by Dumas considered to be of such gestural nature, and he may be right; study of the blind would decide the issue. "Metaphorical gestures" are truly symbolical, in that they form part of (or replace part of) verbal communications. Ekman and Friesen (1969b) distinguish "emblems," "speech illustrators," and "speech regulators." Similar distinctions probably apply to vocal emblems. Metaphorical gestures represent intellectual attitudes such as doubt, disbelief, and agreement, and they steer conversation: "How funny," "Go on," "Shut up." Most notable among the metaphorical gestures are those of affirmation and negation, the movements of "yes" and "no."

Cultural conventions are important with respect to both amount and kind of these gestures; "yes" and "no" are signaled differently around the Mediterranean and in Western Europe or North America. Cultural differences in expressions of which so much has sometimes been made (Labarre 1947), are largely restricted to transferred and metaphorical facial gestures (Ekman 1973). The Japanese are said to smile when reprimanded (Labarre 1947); instead of concluding that smiling can be an expression of distress, such smiles should be seen as the social signal saying, "Thank you, Master, for putting me right."

This is not to deny that the cultural environment does have powerful effects upon true emotional expression. One learns when to manifest expressions, and to what extent. Ekman and Friesen (1972, 1973) extensively discuss culturally defined "display rules." They distinguish four mechanisms that we have already met: intensification, deintensification, neutralizing, and masking. Cultural definitions can be highly differentiated. Traditional Chinese codices, for example, prescribe the amount of weeping at a funeral proper to the different kinship relations (Granet 1922; see also Gordon 1981). Within a given culture, different display rules again exist for what is appropriate in public, in intimate relationships, or with priest or psychotherapist. In fine, as Ekman and Friesen conclude, culture defines not what emotional expressions to make, but when to make them, and how strongly.

2.7. Emotional expression as unlearned response

In the preceding we argued that expression is intrinsically related to emotion. Expression has served as the entry point to the study of emotion, and its analysis has suggested the conception of emotion to be presented in the next sections. The argument requires that expression be related in systematic fashion to whatever other cues for emotion exist; and it requires that expression not be linked to emotion (that is, to whatever other cues for emotion exist) in a haphazard way or in one primarily determined by the conventions of a given culture. The evidence favors the conclusion that this is in fact the case. That evidence consists of indications for the existence of systematic relationships between expressions and emotions and for the unlearned nature of emotional expression, facial expression in particular. A repertory of expressive behaviors belongs to the biological disposition of humans as well as of other higher animals.

Systematic relationships between expression and emotion

People ascribe emotions to others, and they do so largely on the basis of those others' facial or other expressions. Such ascription, on the whole, is not fancy. The reasonable success of social interaction attests to this. In addition, there is considerable experimental evidence on consensus with respect to ascription and some evidence on the ascription's correctness.

In these experiments, observers are asked to assign emotion labels or more extensive interpretative descriptions to photographs or films showing facial expressions or other expressive behavior. Usually, agreement among observers is fair to high. Amount of agreement varies with the kind of expression, being high with outspoken expressions and lower or low with more subtle or subdued ones. It also varies with the way in which agreement is defined. If each different emotion word used by the observers is considered a different interpretation, agreement is low. If similarity between words or interpretations is taken into account – for instance, by lumping words with similar meanings together – or if observers can only choose from among restricted sets of labels, agreement often is considerable (see Fridja 1969; Ekman, Friesen, & Ellsworth 1972; and Ekman 1982b for reviews and methodological discussion).

It has proved feasible to select sets of facial photographs that produce very high degrees of agreement when observers are to choose from a restricted set of labels and when the labels each refer to a major emotion class. In experiments by Ekman and Friesen, subjects had to select, for each of 30 photographs, one of the following labels: happiness, surprise, fear, sadness, anger, or disgust. With American subjects, percentage agreement ranged from 97% (for "happiness"; that is, laughter or smiling) to 69% (for the "anger" photographs). Comparable results were obtained with Latin American and Japanese subjects (see Ekman, Friesen, & Ellsworth 1972). Similar scores, with a similar technique, were obtained by Izard (1969) with subjects from various European countries and Japan; results from subjects referred to as "African" were appreciably lower, although still far above chance levels (these subjects did not, however, receive the instructions and emotion names in their native language).

Most of these emotion recognition experiments used posed expressions. The few experiments that used spontaneous expressions support the conclusion that people agree reasonably well in interpreting emotional expressions. These experiments also show interpretations to be reasonably correct: Reasonable agreement has been found between interpretations and emotional state as reported by the persons photographed or as judged by observers with full knowledge of both the eliciting events and the complete response. This is the case even when expressive reactions are unselected with respect to salience, intensity, or distinctness (Ekman & Bressler, and Ekman & Rose, who sampled during psychiatric interviews; both quoted in Ekman, Friesen, & Ellsworth 1972; Frijda 1953; Lanzetta & Kleck 1970). In one such experiment (Frijda 1953), for instance, subjects had to provide free descriptions of emotional state for each of 68 brief film sequences. Correctness (agreement with presumed "true" emotional state) was scored on a 5-point scale. Average correctness score, for 30 subjects, was 43.2% of the possible maximum; 32% of the responses obtained scores of full or fair agreement on the 5-point scale.

Vocal expression (intonation patterns) also produce emotion judgments that tend to show interobserver agreement and to correspond with what the speakers intended to convey (e.g., Scherer, Koivumaki, & Rosenthal 1972; Bezooyen 1984; see Scherer 1981 and Bezooyen 1984 for reviews). Accuracy percentages, when restricted label sets are employed, tend to rival those obtained with facial expressions. Experiments with bodily expressions suggest that these add to accuracy gained from facial expression, intonation patterns, and/or content of verbal messages (e.g., Kline & Johannsen 1935; Ekman, Friesen, O'Sullivan, & Scherer 1980).

Some – but only a few – studies have systematically investigated which expressive patterns correspond with which emotion ascriptions. Ekman and Friesen (1975) carefully described the features of those facial expression photographs consistently judged as falling in one of the six emotion classes just mentioned; the descriptions have been used in an earlier section. Frijda (1969) found correlations between facial expression features as dimensions of emotion ascription. Scherer (see Scherer 1981) and Bezooyen (1984) studied the cues responsible for emotion attribution to auditory cues (clipped speech, normal speech, and/or synthesized auditory stimuli) and found systematic relationships, both with emotion classes and with emotion dimensions.

Studies of recognition accuracy can give only global and indirect information concerning the relation between expression and emotion. They give no information about how close the relationship is, nor do they answer the question of which expressive patterns actually correspond to which emotions.

There are a few studies describing the expressions actually occurring under specified conditions. The informal studies have been mentioned earlier (section 2.2). The new techniques, like ethological behavior classification and Ekman and Friesen's FACS, mentioned earlier, have as yet been used only in very limited measure. FACS's predecessor was used to show the similarity in facial expressions of American and Japanese subjects viewing stressful films (Ekman 1972). Oster and Ekman (1978) used FACS in the description of infant facial expressions; they also ascertained that facial signs presumably indicative of negative affect indeed correspond to such affect, as assessed from subjective report. "Happiness" has been shown to correspond to a specific kind of smile and not to just any smile (Ekman, Friesen, & Ancoli 1980); unnatural smiles were shown to be more asymmetric than natural ones (Ekman, Hager, & Friesen 1981); a few more studies of similar nature exist.

Taking together the recognition studies, the impressionistic studies, and the few more systematic ones and adding the information on innateness of expressions to be discussed presently, the conclusion can be drawn that expressive behaviors indeed are indicative of emotional states. The available evidence is sufficient to discard the view that emotion and expression are not systematically related. That view has become widespread mainly because Landis (1924) found wide variability of expression with identical eliciting conditions and poor recognition of these expressions; it was based also upon observations of cross-cultural variability in expressive, or expression-like behavior. The experiment and conclusions by Landis have been effectively criticized (Davis 1934; Ekman, Friesen, & Ellsworth 1972; Izard 1971). The issue of cross-cultural variability has been lucidly discussed by Ekman (1972; 1973) and was shown, in the preceding section, to have been clouded by confusion of emotions and gestures and neglect of display rules.

Yet, important qualifications are in order. Although the relationship between expression and emotion is an intrinsic one, the nature and closeness of the relationship still have to be specified. This is so first of all, of course, because so far the notion of emotion has hardly been elucidated; it has figured in the preceding discussions primarily as a reference to the use of emotion labels in observing expressions or to the occurrence of emotionally significant events, as elicitors of expressions. Secondly, all the above evidence leaves open whether the relationship between emotion and expression is a necessary one or else fails to specify the system in the systematic relationship.

The relationship, in fact, is not simple. A given emotion does not invariably manifest itself in a given expression; we saw this in the preceding, where different manifestations of fear, anger and joy were discussed. Also, a given expression does not invariably manifest a given emotion. Weeping occurs in anger, frustration, and happiness as well as in grief and distress; laughter may spring from nervousness as well as from joy, and smiling from embarrassment as well as from amusement or friendliness. It is true that in different circumstances different patterns of weeping, laughter, or smiling might be involved; we mentioned the evidence with respect to smiling (Ekman, Friesen, & Ancoli 1980); but this merely complicates the issue and does not clarify it.

Furthermore, whereas recognition accuracy, in expression recognition experiments, usually is far above chance, it also usually is far from perfect; and the same holds for consensus among observers. Differentiation between emotions on the basis of expressions alone, and when unselected samples of expressions are used, appears to be rather crude and unstable. There is, moreover, an experimental finding not mentioned so far. If subjects are given large sets of labels to choose from (or are left free to choose their own labels), the range of interpretations given to any one expression almost always is very large. The majority of subjects may agree upon one interpretation, but the remainder still contain quite a variety. Most of these interpretations are quite plausible, given the expression concerned; that expression, it often seems, could very well have been an expression of every one of the states mentioned by the subjects (see Frijda 1953).

These various inconsistencies do not argue against the hypothesis of an intrinsic relationship between expression and emotion. On the contrary. They point to the concept of "relational activity" as the proper significance of expression. A given form of relational activity can be the common content of different expressions: Different expressions may be different forms of withdrawal or deployment of force. The inconsistencies point to the hypothesis that a given mode of relational activity can be a common feature of widely different emotions, thereby causing these widely different emotions to have a similar expression: Weeping was an example. They also point to the fact that the tendency toward a given mode of relational activity may fulfill a different role, have a different place, in different emotions: Shutting off from external stimuli is almost definitory for fear and somewhat peripheral in mental concentration, both of which may show closed eyes and a knit brow. Most importantly, they are among the reasons to interpret emotions as relational action tendencies or, more generally, as changes in action readiness, as will be discussed in the next section.

The innateness of expression

The conclusion that expressive movement is largely unlearned follows from several lines of evidence. First, there is the universality of expressions. Many facial expressions, including the facial–vocal patterns of laughter and weeping and the expression of surprise ("Oh!") occur throughout the world in every human race and culture. The expressions appear to represent, in every culture, the same emotions. This at least is the conclusion that best fits the available evidence. Darwin (1872) sent a questionnaire to 36 observers – mostly government officials and missionaries – in various parts of the world, inquiring whether given emotions were expressed by the peoples concerned (Maoris, Dayaks, Fuegians – from Tierra del Fuego – Abyssinians, etc.) in ways specified in the questionnaire: "astonishment by eyes and mouth being opened wide and by the eyebrows being raised" etc. He found impressive agreement. True enough, his survey method was crude; the descriptions and examples added by his respondents, however, give considerable strength to the global conclusion. It has frequently been objected that contact with Westerners was not controlled in these observations; the expressions could have been derived from prestigious Western influence. But why should all these "aborigines" have imitated the few white people present at that time rather than each other? The supposition grossly overestimates intercultural learning in relation to intracultural learning or innateness.

More recent observations confirm Darwin's conclusions. Expressions of fear and surprise, laughter, smiling and weeping, and looking puzzled are among those occurring universally and under similar conditions (e.g., Eibl-Eibesfeldt 1973, 1974). The conclusions are supported by the findings on cross-cultural agreement in the recognition of facial expression photographs. The two major studies, by Izard (1969, 1971) and by Ekman and his colleagues (Ekman, Friesen, & Ellsworth 1972; Ekman 1982b) have been described already; they concern Western cultures, Japan, and an African group. Comparable agreement was found in several preliterate cultures who had no contact with Western mass media: the South Fore in New Guinea and the Dani in Iran (reported by Ekman 1973; see also Ekman & Oster 1979; Ekman 1982b). Ekman and Oster (1979) conclude that facial expressions of anger, disgust, happiness, sadness or distress, fear, and surprise are universal. By inference, there is good, albeit not compelling, reason to consider them innate. Izard (1977) adds interest, shame, guilt, and contempt to the list of universal expressions. With respect to interest, there is ample evidence; the evidence for shame, guilt, and contempt is unconvincing.

There is some evidence on cross-cultural generality of vocal expression of emotion in intonation patterns; the evidence comes from recognition-of-emotion studies. Bezooyen (1984) presents a review and some novel evidence, using Dutch, Japanese, and Taiwanese subjects and Dutch speech material. Generally (in her results as well as in those of others), cross-cultural recognition accuracy is substantially lower than intra-cultural accuracy, but still decidedly above chance. It cannot be concluded, though, that specific emotions can avail themselves of distinct intonational patterns; rather, dimensions or aspects of activation that correlate with different emotions would appear to account for the results (Bezooyen 1984).

The second kind of evidence on innateness concerns the occurrence of expressions in human subjects who could not have learned: infants and the congenitally blind. Babies under the age of 3 months show a variety of expressions, and they do this under circumstances similar to that under which adults show them (Malrieu 1960; Charlesworth & Kreutzer 1973). They do so when imitation of behavior is, at most, fleeting and unstable (Guernsey 1928; Meltzoff & Moore 1979). Infants, of course, cry when hungry or hindered. They smile after one to two months, in response to social stimuli (Wolff 1963). They show startle. They produce expressions of disgust and other, differentiated, gustatory reactions (Peiper 1963; Chiva 1985). They show a relaxed, "contented" expression when comfortable and just fed. They show attention or wariness. Their expressive repertory soon extends beyond this: manifesting "anger" or impatience by cries and violent movements (5 months); "surprise" by attentively looking, widely opening the eyes, and raising the eyebrows or by compressing the lips (4 months); and true vocalized laughter (4 months) (Malrieu 1960; Blurton-Jones 1972a). Eliciting stimuli are such as to warrant use of the above emotion labels (see, for instance, Sroufe & Waters 1976; Malrieu 1960; Chiva 1985), although systematic evidence is admittedly meagre (Ekman & Oster 1979).

It is generally concluded that facial expressivity of the congenitally blind is poorer than that of normal people; still, they do spontaneously show the usual expressive patterns on appropriate occasions (Thompson 1941; Dumas 1932;). The same is true for children born blind and deaf (Goodenough 1932; Eibl-Eibesfeldt 1973; see Charlesworth & Kreutzer 1973 for a review). Surprise, laughter, smiling, pouting, frowning when faced with some difficulty, crying, and angry foot stamping, as well as angry facial expression, were observed in these subjects; they were observed even in an idiotic child studied by Eibl-Eibesfeldt (1973).

The third line of evidence: phylogenetic continuity. Most of the behavior patterns and facial expressions discussed – with the exception of weeping – find clearly similar counterparts in animal behavior. Darwin (1872) again gave the first extensive comparative illustrations; more recent ethological research adds abundant and systematic material (e.g., Andrew 1972; Van Hooff 1973; Suomi & Harlow 1976; see Chevalier-Skolnikoff 1973). Examples were given in section 2.4. The similarities should not be underrated: apathic, "depressive" response to personal loss can be observed in dogs and in chimpanzees (Van Lawick-Goodall 1972; Hamburg, Hamburg, & Barchas 1975). Some evidence on continuity with respect to vocal expression also exists (see Malatesta 1981); distress calls tend to be understood across species.

Finally, the fourth kind of evidence: The expressive behavior described, at least some of it, is regulated by the more primitive neural regions – limbic system, hypothalamus, brainstem – and relatively independent of the higher cortical centers that govern voluntary behavior. The evidence will be presented in chapter 7.

2.8. Action tendencies and activation modes

Action readiness and emotion

Expressive behavior can be suppressed and it can be held in abeyance. It springs forth when suppression is lifted or when the appropriate moment for execution has come; it springs forth when inhibition has become insufficient to restrain it. It may not become manifest at all when suppression is maintained or when the situation resolves itself before the behavior is let loose.

One must therefore conclude that there exist tendencies to execute expressive behavior, which tendencies are present prior to execution and independently of execution. We call such tendencies, with Arnold (1960), *action tendencies*.

Readiness to execute action can exist also with respect to other types of behavior, having a sense or intent similar to that of expressive behavior. These types include full-fledged actions like flight or attack, of which what we call expression often is a part; and more or less instrumental actions like crying out, "mama!" when faced by danger, uttering insults when being slighted, or constantly thinking of the other person when seriously in love. These actions, too, can be checked or held in abeyance and thus flow from some readiness or tendency.

The readiness from which behavior flows is not merely the readiness to execute that behavior; it is the readiness or unreadiness to achieve a given kind of end result. Such readiness often is apparent from the expressive behavior itself. Some of that behavior, as we have seen, represents preparatory stages for other action, to be executed when need be or when opportunity arises; other forms represent readiness or unreadiness to accept stimulation. Action tendency, then, appears to be the core concept toward which expressive behavior is pointing.

Action tendencies are states of readiness to execute a given kind of action. A "given kind of action," and thus an action tendency, is defined by its end result aimed at or achieved. That end result can be inferred from behavior; the basis of inference is the behavior's flexibility. As was discussed earlier (section 2.3), expressive behavior shows a measure of flexibility. A given expressive pattern may manifest variation, to fit the circumstances; and different expressions exist, which all impress as angry or fearful and so forth and which all are shown in response to apparently angering or fearful events. These different variations and expressions have something in common: their relational sense. They share the sense of withdrawal or protection seeking, of deployment of force and seeking freedom of action, and so on. They share this sense with field actions and with the more or less instrumental actions mentioned above. The various expressions that succeed one another in emotional responding also largely share the same sense, while successively adapting to variations in circumstances, ebb and flow of control, and the increase and decrease of situational urgency.

Action tendency is readiness for different actions having the same intent. One action tendency is readiness for attacking, spitting, insulting, turning one's back, or slandering, whichever of these appears possible or appropriate at a given moment; a different action tendency is readiness to approach and embrace, fondle, look at avidly, or say sweet things, again according to what the circumstances favor.

Action tendencies are hypothesized at this point of the discussion for theoretical reasons: to account for latent readiness and to account for behavior flexibility. Note that daily interaction makes the same assumption, and for similar reasons: to explain behavior equifinality and to predict what will happen next. An expressive cue signals a tendency to behavior that might appear. A twitch around the mouth suggests withdrawal tendency, a readiness to close; outright withdrawal or rejection of the event is expected to ensue might the event continue or become more pressing.

It will be clear that "action tendency" and "emotion" are one and the same thing. Emotion, too, refers to some inner state that predicts forthcoming behavior: if he is angry, better beware! Emotion, it is true, can be said to refer to inner experience; but such experience, as will be argued in chapter 4, is to a large extent awareness of action tendency – of desire to strike or to flee, to investigate or to be with. Emotion, said Arnold (1960), is felt action tendency.

We may say: Emotions are action tendencies. More fully: Emotions are tendencies to establish, maintain, or disrupt a relationship with the environment.

This definition of emotion is not quite adequate. It applies only to some emotions. Not all emotions are action tendencies, since not all expressions are relational activities, although all have relational sense. Some forms of expressive behavior, we argued, represent relational null states and activation modes; others manifest disruption of relational tendency or vain desire. Apathy, disinterest, excitement, confusion, behavioral interruption, and inhibition were instances mentioned. However, null states, activation modes, and action tendencies proper, all are modifications of action tendency in a general sense: They all represent modes of readiness, unreadiness included, for relational action. Interruption is such a mode, free activation is such a mode, and activation loss or disinterest is such a mode. These latter, as well as action tendencies, constitute modes of response to significant events. *Emotions, then, can be defined as modes of relational action readiness, either in the form of tendencies to establish, maintain, or disrupt a relationship with the environment or in the form of mode of relational readiness as such.*

Since there exist different kinds of relational activity and different activation manifestations, there exist different modes of action readiness. We can thus say: Different action tendency or activation modes correspond to different emotions. Inversely, different emotions, as language distinguishes them, correspond, by and large, to different modes of action readiness. "By and large" is a necessary qualification, since language distinguishes emotions on more grounds than that of action readiness mode.

Definitions of emotions; "basic emotions"

Emotions are identified with action readiness change. Different modes of action readiness correspond to different emotions, and many emotions can be defined by such mode. Anger is the urge to attack or, more properly, the urge to regain freedom of action and control. Fear is the urge to separate oneself from aversive events, and so forth. Many emotions can be characterized more or less unambiguously by their action tendency or activation mode; that is to say that many emotion names are names for the action readiness modes concerned. Many emotions map neatly onto action readiness modes.

Emotions that can be characterized in terms of action readiness mode correspond to what are often called "elementary," "primary," "basic," or "fundamental" emotions. Emotions so considered are, in fact, distinct and elementary forms of action readiness. McDougall (1923) indeed defined elementary emotions as those corresponding to those elementary action instigations that he called "instincts" – instincts for pugnacity, protection, and so on. Both Arnold (1960) and Plutchik (1980) explicitly link basic emotions to distinct action tendencies or elementary behavior modes. Ekman and Friesen (1975), Tomkins (1962), and Izard (1977) consider elementary those emotions that are manifested by unambiguously specific facial expressions, as determined by high recognition accuracy (see section 2.6). For Ekman and Friesen, these emotions are happiness, surprise, anger, fear, sadness, and disgust. Izard (1977), as said, adds distress, interest, contempt, guilt and shame; the evidence for considering the last three basic, as also said earlier, is weak.

Emotions not considered basic or fundamental are often considered to be mixtures or blends. Of course, blends exist. The emotion called wariness can be said to consist simultaneously of interest and moderate fear. However, most important nonbasic emotions cannot be so defined. Jealousy is not a mixture of anger and grief, as Arnold (1960) has proposed. It is not a mixture at all. The emotion of jealousy consists of action readiness change – any action readiness change implying non-acceptance – elicited by a specific constellation of events, a specific "story," as Ekman phrases it. That story defines the emotion: It is that someone else enjoys something I have a claim to enjoyment upon, and which event is felt to interfere with satisfaction of this claim. Many different forms of action readiness change can spring from this constellation: mere upset, or excitement, or stupefaction; or the apathy of grief; or the impulse to undo the event, the impulse of anger.

Generally speaking, emotions may be defined either by mode of action readiness change or by the nature of the emotional object – that is, by the nature of the object or event that the relational action readiness change is relational to. There exist two different principles of categorization. They are independent, and they may be at variance. The action readiness change of jealousy may be that of hatred, and then aim at the destruction or removal of either of the participants in the enjoyment; or that of grief, and then be that of helplessness and abandonment of striving; or that or mere suffering, and then be that of mere desire for the situation to end. The simultaneous application of two emotion terms (jealousy and hatred, or jealousy and grief) does not refer to mixtures, but to two different levels of analysis.

Jealousy is but one example of an emotion defined by its object. Contempt presents an other example: It can be said to be the rejection of, or an attitude of indifference toward, something or someone esteemed to be of low value. The rejection and indifference as such do not differ from rejection or indifference toward any other kind of object; it is the object that provides the specificity of contempt. Similarly for shame. Shame implies that one is to blame, and mostly in relation to moral standards; action readiness can be one that corresponds to mere suffering, or to trying to escape from suffering, or to submission to those who blame.

As a consequence of this dual principle of categorization, emotions defined primarily by their object cannot be specified by action tendency or activation mode. This implies that they have no characteristic facial expression and that their presence cannot be recognized by means of expressive behavior alone. Wrath, jealousy, shame, contempt, guilt, nostalgia, cannot be recognized from expression alone (Frijda 1953, 1969); contrary evidence for contempt, shame, and guilt (Izard 1971), to repeat, is unconvincing (see also Ekman & Oster 1979).

It is obvious that categorization by object is highly dependent upon which objects – sorts of events – are being distinguished and considered important by the environment providing the categorization. Emotion taxonomies show marked differences from one culture to another; emotion vocabularies differ (Hothschild 1979; Gordon 1981). Village Eskimos among whom regulation of hostility appears to be important, are reported to have many subtly different anger and hostility terms (Briggs 1970); distinctions among feelings associated with respectful behavior are said to be fine in Java, where interpersonal respect rules are highly differentiated (Geertz 1959).

The dual principle of categorization is not applicable to so-called complex emotion concepts only. The words *fear* and *anger* are applied to action readiness changes, whatever their nature, in response to respectively threat and offense. *Fear* is applied to freezing or nervously pacing up and down, as well as to flight or protective response or mere excitement, provided any of these responses occurs in the face of threat. Even anger when it is defensive anger can be and is called a fear response: *anger* referring to action tendency, *fear* to the object. In fact, many emotion words, fear included, are often used merely to refer to the presence of cognitive constellations similar to those eliciting emotion (that is, eliciting action readiness change), even when these constellations do not elicit any emotion: "We fear potato crops will be smaller than last year, although we hope they do not, current disappointments notwithstanding" is not a report on emotion. Words like *hope, fear,* or *anger* do not refer to unitary psychological phenomena. Even when referring to emotional states (that is, to changes in action readiness), each word tends to cut out several different, though overlapping, subdomains, because of this dual principle of emotion categorization.

It should be noted that the two principles touch at various points. Categorization by object still implies *some* action readiness change; otherwise, the notion of emotion loses its sense or boundary. Moreover, the object of fear implicitly points to fear action tendency, and that of anger to anger action tendency, in the sense that these tendencies are the most "logical," most natural answers to the presence of the respective objects; the point will be elaborated in chapter 4. Furthermore, definition of action tendency itself implies reference to a corresponding object. The withdrawal or protection tendency of fear implies reference to some threat; the action tendency of anger implies reference to something that blocks freedom of action or control; and the action tendency of surprise implies reference to something unassimilable. It is such reference to a corresponding object that, for instance, sets off the action tendency of anger from that of aggressive desire: The end states differ because the objects differ.

The nature of action tendencies

To the extent that action readiness changes involve action tendency, emotions are to be considered intention-like events; and to the extent that they involve activation mode, emotions are modifications of relational tendency, or intentionality, as such.

Action tendencies are intention-like events because, on the one hand, they consist of a readiness to execute action; they involve activation of a class of responses from among the subject's response repertoire. On the other hand, they consist of readiness to achieve a given relational change or to maintain a given relation; they thus involve orientation toward a given state, either a forthcoming one or one actually present. The classes of responses involved can only be defined by their aims: They are protective, obstacle-removing, contact enhancing, and so on.

Yet emotional action is not intentional action, in the more restricted sense of *intentional*; it is not usually guided by a prior goal representation. Emotional action tendencies are felt as impulses, urges. How to account for them? What do we mean by "impulse" or "urge"? We will try to sketch what could be the structure of action tendencies; we will phrase this sketch in information-processing terms because of the functionalist perspective that entails.

Emotional action tendencies, as said, are states of readiness to achieve or maintain a given kind of relationship with the environment. They can be conceived of as plans or programs to achieve such ends, which are put in a state of readiness.

The kind of program put in readiness at a given moment can vary. It can be the program for a behavioral system, such as the set of threat diminishing, or of angry, or enjoying behaviors: fear, anger, or joy. It also can merely be unspecified readiness to call up behavior systems as soon as clarification of the situation allows this: mere excitement. Or, still more elementary in the hierarchy of action control, it may consist only of being set to achieve a given end by whatever program may turn out to be feasible and appropriate, *when* action turns out to be feasible and appropriate. Such emotions merely consist of the urgent desire to have the situation change, the object obtained, or the intrusion removed, and they tend to be called by names like *distress*, *desire*, or *aversion*.

Form or degree of readiness also can vary. There can be actual readiness for execution of behavior: motor preparation, with muscles tensed. Action may even be under way, in which readiness is for its completion, its end state only. But there also exists readiness that consists merely of "being set," in the way just indicated: We have the set of programs ready for choosing among them and for execution when circumstances permit; no muscular tension needs to betray it, although autonomic arousal may. And there exists readiness that consists in blocking access to information-processing and action systems for programs not serving the urgent purpose at hand; that is the structure of behavioral interruption and wary attention.

Action tendency is not necessarily readiness for overt action. Action tendency can actualize in mental actions having similar intent to overt ones: turning toward an object in thought, or away from it; disengaging emotionally from it; turning toward or away from the thoughts themselves. Worrying is equivalent to wary visual attention, ruminations to exploration, and intellectualization to overt avoidance. Such equivalence is quite clear in being in love or infatuation. Being in love can be considered one of the forms of the action tendency of maintaining proximity or being with; and the desire to maintain proximity manifests itself, apart from kissing and touching and gazing and holding hands, in incessant preoccupation with the love object, in wearing her or his shirts, and driving past her or his house, even when it is known that she or he is out of town (Rombouts, 1983). Activation states can also be manifest merely on the mental plane. Nostalgia is awareness that something past, while desired, cannot be regained, except by maintaining proximity in thought. If search tendency nevertheless gets the upper hand, it turns into recurring grief; if impotence with respect to desire is added, it turns into belated painful suffering.

What kind of programs in readiness are action tendencies? As said, many action tendencies can be considered tendencies toward change: change from an actual situation as perceived (the eliciting event in its context) to a desired situation as somehow represented in or by the subject. There is a discrepancy or mismatch that initiates the program; decrease in this discrepancy guides and terminates the behavior (other sources of termination aside). This description fits approach as well as avoidance (and aggressive) tendencies: In the first, the discrepancy is between an available object not yet in possession or a situation not yet mastered and an object in possession or a situation controlled; in the second, it is between a desired situation and an actual situation incompatible with the former's achievement or conservation. Tendencies toward maintaining a given relationship (watchfulness, staying close to the mother, etc.) can easily be accommodated within the same framework.* The description also fits intentional or goal-directed behavior generally (see Miller, Galanter, & Pribram 1960), and it fits motivation. It thus, as it stands, is too general. The generality is not quite as bad as it seems, though. As regards motivation, a sharp distinction between emotion and motivation cannot be made. They are overlapping concepts; notice the fact that many authors discuss an emotion of desire. The issue will be taken up again in chapter 6 (section 6.4 in particular) and chapter 9 (section 9.1). The major specification needed concerns distinction of the emotions proper like fear, anger, and joy. They are marked by the fact that their action tendencies are of a relational kind; they concern being with or without. The point will be elaborated toward the end of this section. As regards intentional behavior, the distinction with emotion will be discussed in the subsection on "action tendency, intention and passivity," further down.

Discrepancy or mismatch generates impetus for change; different kinds of mismatch generate impetus for different kinds of change, and thus different action tendencies. Kinds of mismatch correspond to what is perceived as relevant in the actual situation, and as constituting the source of mismatch. They correspond to what is seen as responsible for the fact that mismatch exists or that complete match appears possible. If, for instance, the situation is seen as an unfamiliar one, action tendency is generated for actions removing that unfamiliarity: alertness, scanning the environment. If the situation is seen as one that blocks freedom of action, action tendency emerges that aims toward removing that obstruction: anger. If mismatch consists of something desirable not possessed, action tendency is toward possession: craving or desire.

The structure of action tendencies; control precedence

Action tendencies, in this view, originate in discrepancies: in mismatch or in perception of potential match. Action tendencies terminate in unresolvable mismatch or in match.

Mismatch, potential match, and match must be assumed to give rise to signals indicating that action is called for, is likely to succeed, or can

*Actually, not all emotional behavior can be accommodated in this framework. Behavior that does not will be discussed in connection with activation and the model encompassing it in chapter 6.

terminate. We may identify these signals with the feelings of pain and pleasure and desire. These are the signals that initiate, maintain, and terminate action tendency. They constitute the direct source of "being set" for change or continuation of the given situation. At the same time, they confer an "aim" upon action tendency: They provide such tendency with an end point, the functional equivalent of a goal. Action tendency continues until the mismatch signals that initiated and maintain it die down; action tendency remains aligned when potential match signals resound, and terminates when match signals indicate success.

The most important characteristic of action tendencies is a consequence of the kind of signals they respond to. It also is their most distinctive characteristic. The characteristic is the place of action tendencies in the general action control structure.

Action tendencies have the character of urges or impulses. Action tendencies – and action readiness changes generally – clamor for attention and for execution. They lie in waiting for signs that they can or may be executed; they, and their execution, tend to persist in the face of interruptions; they tend to interrupt other ongoing programs and actions; and they tend to preempt the information-processing facilities. Evidence for all this has been discussed in section 2.3; further evidence will be discussed in connection with the disrupting effects of emotion (section 2.12). Evidently, then, action tendencies are programs that have a place of precedence in the control of action and of information processing. We therefore say: Action tendencies – action readiness changes generally – have the feature of *control precedence*.

The system constituting emotion is constructed, it appears, so as to allow for control precedence.There would seem to be two ways to account for this feature. The first: There exist certain action programs that in reflex-like fashion are linked to the mismatch (and potential match) signals under concern; these links might provide for built-in control precedence. In other words: In this view, emotional response is seen as based upon innately (and perhaps upon acquired) highly dominant stimulus–response links. This is the traditional behaviorist conception. The second: match and mismatch signals are responsible. The signals involved are highly persistent; they are loud and claim attention; and the system recognizes their claim upon control and their nature as calling for change or for continuing along present lines. Control precedence, in other words, could be due to the properties of pleasure and pain, their seductiveness and intolerableness. The two conceptions are not very different. Both necessitate assumptions regarding some function that maps degrees of mismatch (or promised match) upon degrees of control precedence. Both require threshold notions: Not all events are so urgent as to require or elicit response. They do differ in one important regard. The second account – the one giving the central role to pleasure and pain – much better allows for a flexible action control structure. It can smoothly accommodate readiness of a behavioral system of functionally equivalent actions (as in anger or fear), as well as the readiness of merely being set to achieve change (as in mere upset or excitement) and other, more cognitively indicated forms of readiness to be discussed presently.

We have shifted discussion from the nature of action tendency – its being readiness, its nature as a program, its aim – to the control structure within which it operates. Because action tendencies are programs set for execution, it is in their nature also to be subject to control: to prior feasibility tests and to monitoring of progress. That is to say: Whether action tendency does arise and, if so, which action tendency can be expected to depend upon more than mismatch and its "kind." It can be expected to depend also upon whether or not the situation offers cues for the selection of specific actions or types of action, as situations often do not, in conditions of uncertainty or upon sudden events that have not yet been explored. Indeed, fear (that is, response to threat), jealousy (that is, response to the contingency described earlier), shock (that is, response to something sudden), all, under certain circumstances, consist of mere excitement, mere upset. Whether action tendency arises furthermore depends upon estimated success of action; such estimate may flow from efforts spent so far, from previous successes and failures, from the apparent overpowering nature of the present situation, and the like. Helplessness, apathy, and impotent rage illustrate contingencies where action tendency suffers peculiar fates: There is no action tendency, although mismatch is evident; action tendency "knows" it is blocked in impotent rage, and it cannot even be envisaged in despair. By contrast, foreseeing free and easy accomplishment is the mode of action readiness that constitutes joy: Many joys consist of approach and enjoyment action tendencies that are sure, in their execution, that the goal can be reached or has been reached. Finally, emergence of action tendency depends upon the availability of resources for program execution. In exhaustion, such resources are absent; in vitality, and upon success, they tend to be available. All this can be phrased in terms of feasibility tests and monitoring of progress. The influence of resources, of previous failure and success, and of uncertainty upon the nature of emotional response is well known. The present formulation, however, allows both the emotional responses consisting of action tendencies and those consisting of action readiness change only, apathy included, to be subsumed under a coherent action-tendency-cum-control analysis.

Action control procedures – testing what can be done and what has been achieved – show in subjective awareness in one's sense of competence or impotence. They show behaviorally in persistence or nonpersistence of vigilant readiness and, for instance, in the neglect of opportunities after failure that constitutes learned helplessness (Seligman 1975); they also show behaviorally in presence or absence of "free activation" manifestations: self-assuredness and luxury of movement. They also show in the central role of estimates of "difficulty" in the emergence of behavioral features important in emotion theory: activation manifestations (activated movement, activated readiness) and autonomic arousal. Emotion can be, and has been, defined by activation and arousal. We did not do so: It is being defined by action readiness change as anchored in expression and behavioral persistence, as well as in activation and arousal. However, the latter two can be considered immediate responses to estimates of difficulty in envisaged response success; such estimate is not identical with, but will be correlated with, the occurrence of mismatch or potential match that generates action readiness change generally.

Action tendency, intention, and passivity

Action tendencies were defined by their aims. What, then, is the difference between action tendencies and intentions? Action tendencies can be said to differ from intentions, first, in that the desired, to-be-achieved, to-be-maintained, or to-be-regained situation is not a true goal. It is not an anticipated future state to be achieved, but one that should obtain *now*, according to standards that are laid down in the system and that exist within that system prior to a call for action: freedom from pain, presence of a given person, unhampered achievement of a goal one is set for, to name a few. We call these standards *concerns*; they will be discussed in chapter 6. Action tendencies differ from intentions, second, in that their aim is not given as the representation of a future state but is implicit in the mismatch or promised match signal, elicited by the current situation. As a result, action tendency does not aim at achieving a future state, but at achieving change (or at maintaining the status quo) with respect to the actual situation. Action tendency generated by an event that blocks freedom of action aims at removing the obstacle rather than achieving regained freedom. Panicky flight is directed, not toward a place of safety, but away from the place of danger. Desire pushes away from the state of not-yet-possessing, rather than toward that of possessing; it aims at crossing the distance to the object, rather than being guided by the prospect of the achieved embrace, at least in a naive subject. Intention, by contrast, does strive toward regained freedom, a place of safety, or the prospect of possessing. Action tendencies are pushed by the feelings of pain, current pleasure or desire, and the control precedence they impose; intentions are pulled by goal anticipations without such imposed control precedence.

Of course, intentional behavior is involved in emotion, and in humans no doubt it more often is than it is not. Most flight is toward safety; desires are propelled by the prospect of being in each other's arms. Intention and action tendency, in fact, do not exclude one another. Intentions can be in the service of action tendency: Setting up an intention can be the first action that action tendency instigates, and it can be the last resort when ready-made behavior sequences fail. Intentions are "emotional" when they originate in action tendency and when the latter's aim is, by the subject's taking cognizance of it, transformed into a true goal.

The major feature, then, that sets emotion off from intention is control precedence, induced by match or mismatch signals. It is that feature that confers upon action tendency the characteristic of urge or impulse, upon the behavior the characteristic of being involuntary, and upon the subject the sense of passivity, of being overcome by one's impulse and responsible neither for having it nor for acting upon it.

Because passivity, the urge quality, and the compellingness of emotion are dependent upon control precedence of action programs, they do not, therefore, derive from some property of the action programs themselves. They derive from the mismatch and potential match signals being produced, unasked for, by the events, and from the fact that the properties of these signals dictate control precedence. They derive from the unbearableness of sufferings, the irresistibility of attractions, and the alluringness of achievements. The compellingness does not reside in the biological, innately prepared nature of emotional responses. The facts favoring the second conception of what determines control precedence, discussed above, underline this. Mere preoccupations, and plans fed by action tendency, are as compelling as is arousal of primitive behavior modes. It is the pain, the pleasure, and the desire that compel; that is, it is the biologically prepared connection between certain matches and mismatches and their signals, and between such signals and control of the action system. That connection, obviously, remains the same, whether the actions for which control is claimed are primitive, innate ones, or are acquired and are organized by some intention.

The primary compellingness of the intolerableness of pain and the irresistibility of attraction is complemented by the prospects of future escape from pain and future advent of pleasures. These expected profits of the actions one is set for add to the measure to which one is set for them. The compellingness of emotion, therefore, in part derives from the fact one wants to be compelled, is enticed by the lure of escape from threat or of possession of the desired object. These lures are not easily let go of; compellingness of emotion is in part the force of seduction one has shed responsibility for.

A reservation, or addition, must be made to the preceding. We encountered, in section 2.4, evidence for self-sustaining activation of response programs: Under conditions that are not very clear, anger attacks, panic, fits of laughter and crying, once triggered, continue on their own until spent; and there appears to be a point of no return beyond which intense responses cannot be controlled. It might be that activation states of specific action programs are, on occasion, sufficient to maintain control precedence. The issue is not easy to decide, since response in progress changes the psychological situation (anger, for instance, provokes response), which in turn modifies pleasure and pain as instigators.

The concept of emotion

There are in principle two ways in which action programs can be related to their aims. They can be reflexly linked to given stimulus conditions – to kinds of mismatch or promised match, in the present case – and so made as to happen to affect the stimulus conditions; their aim is implicit in that latter fact. Alternatively, they can be organized in terms of means–ends relations: Behaviors are selected because of their proven, or expected, outcomes; the aim is present explicitly as a wish or goal – a representation of a desired situation. Even when reflexly linked to stimulus conditions, organization can be rigid; or response provisions are true programs, where execution adapts flexibly to variation in conditions; the aim forms part of the program's sensitivity to feedback. Most defense and attack behavior systems in higher animals are of this latter sort; so are the more elementary human action tendencies.

To the extent that action programs are fixed and rigid, the concept of action tendency loses much of its meaning. The situation merely elicits action; action readiness only exists to the extent that inhibition can block action execution. To the extent that the program is flexible, however, action tendency, and action readiness generally, become meaningful concepts. Flexible programs are those that are composed of alternative courses of action, that allow for variations in circumstances and for feedback from actions executed. In such programs, wishes, intentions, and aims have become independent of the particular actions. Action tendency acquires the properties of a plan (see Schank & Abelson 1977; Wilensky 1983) or, more precisely, as a plan placed into readiness by the initiating signals. With such a structure, it is meaningful to speak of emotion.

Desires, enjoyments, and emotions proper

So far, emotion and action tendency have been identified with readiness for relational activity. There is no need to so restrict both concepts. There exist action readiness states and action tendencies that have other than relational aims. There are tendencies to execute consummatory behavior and states of readiness to receive the corresponding satisfactions: tendencies to engage in eating, sexual intercourse, contemplating beautiful objects, possessing things of value, inflicting harm, excercising power, and so forth.

Many emotion words refer to such tendencies: hunger; desire or excitement; admiration; greed; cruelty; arrogance. Other words refer to the action readiness changes and actions involved in enjoyment of outcomes: sexual climax; lust; relish; enthusiasm. Others again embrace both: love, hate, tenderness. Tenderness can be regarded as the impulse toward tender – that is, care-giving – behavior; or else as the acute act of recognition of an object as a fit object for such behavior. Love and affection refer, among other things, to that urge toward proximity seeking in which proximity as such is the satisfaction; or else they refer to the act of stopping to note some object as fit for being-with. Hunger and appetite refer to the urge toward food consumption, or else to recognition of a control-precedence shift toward the corresponding behavior. Delight refers to the activity of enjoyment of any kind of satisfaction object, admiration to the specific form of delight produced by acts of contemplation of objects of value and so on.*

The above terms are of a distinct motivational nature. At the same time, what they refer to conforms to the definition of emotion: The states referred to imply action readiness change; they manifest themselves in control-precedence claims and persistence; and they become manifest in activated behavior and arousal when meeting with difficulty. Many authors indeed have classified them as emotions.

There is no contradiction here, nor any place for a conflict of opinions. Emotion and motivation are not coordinate concepts. If emotions are defined as changes in action readiness, action tendency included, the states referred to are emotions. At the same time, they are motivational states, or they reflect motivational states, depending upon definitions of the latter term: They specify the satisfactions that action tendency and behavior seek to obtain. We call these emotions *enjoyments*: states of readiness to engage in given kinds of consummatory behavior and of readiness to be engaged in enjoyment of such behavior's outcomes.

Related to enjoyments are desires. *Desire* refers to readiness to approach or bring about situations of satisfaction; at least, it refers to giving control precedence to readiness for accepting such situations. Similar meanings attach to the several variants of desire, such as longing, craving, and eagerness. Desire is notably absent in current basic emotion lists. Yet it is one of Spinoza's three elementary emotions; in being a state of action readiness, it is rightly so classified, its motivational nature notwithstanding.

Enjoyments and desires do, however, form a class of emotions distinct from that to which fear, anger, joy, sorrow, and the like belong. Emotions in that latter class will be called *emotions proper*. Emotions proper are variants of relational action tendency and of activation modes having relational significance. They are reactive emotions: as said earlier (section 2.4), they tend to be phasic reactions to events, aiming at dealing with these events, with the help of general, relation-modifying actions. Desires and enjoyments tend to be tonic reactions; their action tendencies aim at achieving satisfaction states and their behaviors are tailored to the specific purposes of eating, sexual intercourse, social interaction and the like.

Still, the two classes of emotion hang closely together. Desire itself is

---

*Most of the terms used are employed also to refer to dispositional rather than actual states: He who admires Shakespeare is not constantly filled with admiration. It is the terms' usage in their actual sense that is being discussed here.

an emotion proper: It is the tendency to bring nearer whatever the desire is for. Joy (some joy) is the impetus to bring the final goal, the enjoyment, nearer by energizing action to use the opportunity when it has been obtained. Love, by contrast (it is a desire, or an enjoyment) is relational as well as consummatory: it is the tendency to be with for the sake of being with.

Varieties of action tendency

Basic emotions were identified, above, with distinguishable varieties of relational action tendency. Which varieties can be distinguished?

There is no consensus with respect to which emotions are to be considered basic emotions, or how many. Ekman and Friesen (1975), as said, distinguished 6, Izard (1977) 11. Plutchik (1980) names 8, which do not form a subset of Izard's 11. The 6 of Ekman and Friesen – happiness, fear, sadness, surprise, anger and disgust – are included by nearly every author, under some name or other; then agreement stops.

The point is that no satisfactory principle exists upon which derivation of basic emotions can be based or, in the present perspective, from which a list of distinct action tendencies can be derived. Several different principles have been proposed. Arnold (1960) employed a set of dimensions along which action tendency can vary; combination of values on those dimensions yields basic emotions. The dimensions are based upon major properties of emotion-eliciting situations; the main distinction is that of approach and avoidance. The scheme will be further detailed in chapter 4. It does not satisfy, because approach and avoidance do not cover all action tendencies and, as said, the dimensions do not refer primarily to properties of action tendency but to properties of the emotional objects. The same can be said with respect to the interesting scheme advanced by De Rivera (1977), which, although concerned with "impulses," has most of its major dimensions in the domain of what the impulse does with, or wants from, the object. De Rivera's scheme will also be returned to in chapter 4.

A second principle is that of deriving emotions from presumably basic biological functions. McDougall (1923), as said, based his emotion list upon a list of instincts; instincts, to him, were biological purposes coupled to modes of behavior. Plutchik's (1980) approach is not unlike McDougall's. Basic emotions are considered to correspond to basic biological functions that are general throughout the animal world; each of these functions is served by a specific behavior mode. The functions

– protection, rejection, acceptance, and the like – are phrased in terms of goals or end states. Functions, emotions, and behavior modes are but three languages describing the same biological phenomena; however behavior modes serving a given function may differ from one animal species to another. The functions are derived, with adaptations and deletions, from a listing of general behavioral systems by Scott (1958, 1980), who incidentally shares the general approach. The functions are protection, destruction, reproduction, reintegration, incorporation, rejection, exploration, and orientation. The corresponding eight basic emotions are fear, anger, joy, sadness, acceptance, disgust, expectancy, and surprise.

The endeavor to link the major emotions to adaptive functions does not impress as successful, since several of these links look rather strained. Why, for instance, should joy be uniquely linked to reproduction? Also, the evolutionary viewpoint, searching for generality from worms to humans, is debatable; evolution may well have yielded new emotions, as it has yielded new functions and behavior modes. It does not, in fact, appear appropriate to directly link basic adaptive functions like food search or reproduction to specific emotions, except for the enjoyments and desires. On the contrary. Emotions proper serve whatever basic function is, at a given moment, to be safeguarded. Anger defends the territory, the self, the food, the young, and the mate, and joy confirms success on any of those counts. Still, Plutchik's proposal is suggestive, in that it links emotions, behavior systems, and end states or functions of these systems.

Another approach to identification of basic emotions, or action tendencies, is to look for discriminable species-specific behavior patterns or behavior systems. Earlier in this chapter we described the ethological approach, in which behavior systems were distinguished by analysis of cooccurrence, common conditions, or sequential coherence of behavior patterns. Different behavior systems correspond to distinct action tendencies at some level of analysis of the latter. The way in which Tomkins (1962), Izard (1971), and Ekman and Friesen (1975) arrived at their sets of basic emotions is somewhat comparable. Basic emotions are those emotions that correspond to a uniquely characteristic, and presumably species-specific, "innate" behavior mode. The authors mentioned selected facial expression as the behavior mode, but of course there is no reason why this approach should be restricted to facial expression.

Finally, basic emotions can be distinguished and defined on the basis of behavior modes being differentially influenced by neurophysiological manipulations: lesions, electrical brain stimulation, biochemical treatments. Panksepp (1982), for instance, argues that four basic neural circuits can be identified, suggesting four basic emotions: expectancy or desire, fear, rage, panic or distress. Gray (1982) marshals evidence for a distinction between anxiety and fear and proposes fear and anger to be manifestations of one underlying mechanism – to constitute one basic emotion, responsive to one general class of events, namely unconditioned aversive stimuli. So far, this approach, too, has not produced consensus; further results are reviewed in chapter 7.

Obviously, different approaches – and different levels of analysis within a given approach – will yield different sets of basic emotions; here, too, there is room for needless disagreement. In line with the approach of the present chapter, it is considered profitable to distinguish forms of emotion in terms of distinctly different forms of action readiness. A list of such forms is given in Table 2.1. The intent of that table is not to present one more list of basic emotions. Rather, it lists action tendencies and activation modes that appear to be elementary, not composites. Each of these is conceptually distinct, in terms of a particular relational aim or sense. Each of these can be distinguished behaviorally by at least one behavioral manifestation consisting of some facial expression or of some more elaborate behavioral pattern. Each of these appears to correspond with a species-specific behavior mode or system, in humans and other higher animals, or otherwise with explicit nonoccurrence of a particular behavior mode. The forms of action readiness may be considered to define basic emotions, except that basic emotions could equally well be defined from a totally different angle (that of objects). Also, they map reasonably well upon what usually are counted among the basic emotions – as they should, since those latter may be held to correspond to the basic level of categorization of daily interaction, in Rosch's (1978) sense. Whether each of these modes corresponds to a relatively independent behavior system or neurophysiological substrate remains open.

The emotion names in Table 2.1 were chosen because the corresponding emotions paradigmatically, "prototypically"(again in Rosch's sense) appear to contain that action tendency or activation mode. The names emphatically do not imply that a given emotion always contains the corresponding action tendency or activation mode, as may be clear from what has been said on the definition of emotions; nor do they imply that occurrence of a given action tendency always defines the corresponding emotion, for reasons also indicated in earlier sections.

Table 2.1. *Relational action tendencies, activation modes, and inhibition*

Action tendency	End state	Function	Emotion
1. Approach	Access	Producing situation permitting consummatory activity	Desire
2. Avoidance	Own inaccessibility	Protection	Fear
3. Being-with	Contact, interaction	Permitting consummatory activity	Enjoyment, confidence
4. Attending (opening)	Identification	Orientation	Interest
5. Rejecting (closing)	Removal of object	Protection	Disgust
6. Nonattending	No information or contact	Selection	Indifference
7. Agnostic	Removal of obstruction	Regaining control	Anger
8. Interrupting	Reorientation	Reorientation	Shock, surprise
9. Dominating	Retained control	Generalized control	Arrogance
10. Submitting	Deflected pressure	Secondary control	Humility, resignation
11. Deactivation	—	(Recuperation?)	Sorrow
12. Bound activation	Action tendency's end state	Aim achievement	Effort
13. Excitement	—	Readiness	Excitement
14. Free activation	—	Generalized readiness	Joy
15. Inactivity	—	Recuperation	Contentment
16. Inhibition	Absence of response	Caution	Anxiety
17. Surrender	Activation decrease?	Activation decrease or social cohesion?	(Laughter, weeping)

The entries listed in the table fall into certain groups. Items 1 through 10 are action tendencies or (6 and 8) major complements of action tendency; items 12 through 16 are activation modes. Items 1 through 5 are the straightforward modes of tendency toward relational change or no change. Most of the items need brief comment. "Approach" and "avoidance" are meant to include whatever other action aims at establishing or decreasing interaction. "Being-with" refers to occasion for sustained interaction – that which is sought in approach and left in avoidance.

"Agonistic" covers attack and threat. The action tendency of anger is interpreted as tendency to regain control or freedom of action – generally to remove obstruction. "Removal of obstruction" can serve as a termination signal for aggressive behavior, even in animals, and thus is more plausible as the action tendency's aim than would be hurting or killing the opponent (what is "death" to an animal?). "Removal of obstruction" includes removal of power, or prestige, or existence-for-me of antagonists in more symbolic instances of being robbed of control. Insult and derision thus can be seen to imply this same action tendency.

"Dominating" is given a separate entry, since bluffing and subduing actions appear sufficiently distinct from truly aggressive ones; at least in the chimpanzee they form a distinct subsystem (Van Hooff 1973). Traditional facial expressions of pride, contempt, or scorn typically exemplify size increase and actions from above. "Submitting" is the obvious opposite. Humility, shame, guilt and remorse, and devotion (in both the religious and interpersonal sense) are usually depicted as involving size decrease and avoiding looking straight at the other. Submission in the social sense can be seen as being merely an instance of submitting to the forces that be and as serving the same general purpose of "secondary control" (Rothbaum et al. 1982): saving fruitless efforts and obtaining secondary gains.

The activation modes and inhibition have been discussed previously. We may add that free activation, the action tendency of joy, is in part aimless, unasked-for readiness to engage in whatever interaction presents itself and in part readiness to engage in enjoyments. As said, the action tendency of joy is characterized by its particular activity-monitoring features (mastery, freedom), as well as by its particular aims of sustaining coping endeavors (Lazarus et al. 1980).

"Surrender" is added because of the separate status of laughter and weeping; because they are behavior patterns and not emotions, they are put in parentheses in the table. The entry summarizes what has been suggested in the discussion of these behavior patterns.

The entries of Table 2.1 do not exhaust the variety of action tendencies. That variety encompasses, in addition, the desires and enjoyments. One cannot, therefore, consider each emotion to consist of one, or a blend of several, of the basic elements from a limited set like the above (as, for instance, Plutchik's theory argues). One can, however, see the emotions proper, the reactive emotions, in that way. Every emotional reaction to events can be analyzed in terms of one or more of the above plus, of course, the object characteristics mentioned in a previous subsection. Similarly, every emotion, regardless of the class it belongs to, can be analyzed in terms of one or more kinds of action readiness mode plus, again, the nature of the object concerned; in that vein, nostalgia and tenderness were tentatively analyzed as we did above. But to reiterate, action readiness, in these instances, is not characteristic, not specific, for these emotions. It merely stamps them as "emotions."

The concept of activation

Activation is a core concept in the theory of emotion, mainly due to Duffy's (1941, 1962, 1972) work focusing on muscle tension, and that of Lindsley (1951) on EEG arousal. Activation, in Duffy's sense, is equivalent to energy mobilization (a term she also used); level of activation is defined as "the extent of release of potential energy, stored in the tissues of the organism, as this is shown in activity or response" (Duffy 1962, p. 171). What we call emotions, says Duffy, are the more extreme states of activation, both in the sense of high and of low levels; emotions are to be identified with such extreme states of activation. In Lindsley's view, behavioral activation – wakefulness, alertness, and emotion – corresponds to intensity of organized cortical activity, and is a consequence of it. The two views are obviously compatible; essential in both is the notion of a central energizing state that can vary continuously and which is the major variable, or one of the major variables, underlying emotional phenomena.

For a long time the concept of activation has been treated as identical to that of *arousal;* that is to say that both words have generally been used interchangeably, and that readiness for overt behavior and deployment of energy, attentional arousal, autonomic activity, and EEG arousal have all been considered to represent one dimension of variation. The issue of unidimensionality will be discussed in chapter 3; we will not go into it here. In the present context, the term *activation* is taken to refer to an organism's state of readiness for action; that is, as the construct necessary to account for the phenomena of behavioral activation as described in sections 2.4 and 2.5. Its meaning and intent are highly similar to that of the notion of activation that Pribram and McGuinness (1975) have split off from the blanket term *arousal;* the relationship to other constructs will concern us in the next chapter.

From the perspective of the description of behavior an activation concept is needed for referring to a variable state of readiness that underlies variations in behavioral intensity. Such a concept is needed because of the nature of those variations. As we saw in section 2.4, variations in mood and in intensity of emotional response concern not scope or power of motor activity per se, but of "interestedness," of intentionality in the wide sense; both these terms refer to a motivation for behavior rather than to behavior itself. Some central, underlying state of readiness is further suggested by the aspects of emotional behavior that made us introduce the notion of activated behavior. As argued in section 2.4: Activity sometimes does, and sometimes does not, spread over the entire organism; when it does, as in unhampered emotional response, there appears to exist a correlation between behavior scope and extent. Presence of physiological arousal underscores this "organismic" aspect of the behavior concerned. That aspect necessitates the assumption of an underlying process that simultaneously activates (or leaves unactivated) the various muscle groups relevant to a given response according to a distribution that, presumably, is specific for that response. The extension of the startle response, from eye closure to knee flexion, as it spreads both in space and time, is an example. The characteristics of activated behavior are present not merely in unhampered emotional response. They are distinctive of the overall movement pattern in vitality; degree of vitality, indeed, appears equivalent to tonic level of activation.

Both features, intentionality and activated behavior, indicate that more is involved in the moment to moment intensity variations than degree of energy mobilization. As said, what is involved is a state of readiness; and a state of readiness that appears to have a number of properties. In fact, a concept of activation of the nature meant is called for on different counts; some of these are presented by the activation manifestations discussed in sections 2.4 and 2.5. These counts, in turn, are among the reasons to introduce the concept.

First, there exists readiness for action that does not show in muscle tension or any other way. Muscle tension and action readiness can be uncoupled, as in kung fu or jiu-jitsu fighting; readiness only shows, after the fact, in brief movement latency and movement precision, and in vigor and scope.

Second, autonomous dynamics of activation states are suggested by the particular time courses of expressive behavior, described in section 2.4. Single responses, of startle, say, have their proper times for rise and decay. Complex patterns such as those of rage, panic, laughter, and weeping appear in many instances to pass a "point of no return" and tend to run their course until they are "spent." These phenomena appear to ask for an activation notion that is compatible with the image of "tension" seeking "release" and "relief." Several other phenomena point in the same direction: the derived activation manifestations of excitement, the relief produced by laughter and weeping, and the conditions of emergence of these responses. Something, it seems, is pent up prior to them, and released in them. That which is pent up does not appear to be physical readiness as such, or autonomic arousal; it probably can even be demonstrated that laughter and weeping may occur, and give relief, without previous autonomic arousal or muscular tenseness.

Third, activation, state of readiness, can exist as subthreshold readiness for particular types of response; that subthreshold readiness again appears to possess its particular autonomous decay time. Subsided anger remains for a while as excitability or irritability; this is so even for defensive attack evoked by electrical brain stimulation: irritability remains for some time after stimulation has ended (Hess 1957; see chapter 7).

Fourth, a central state of readiness with its own dynamics of persistence and decay is also suggested by joyful behavior. As noted, joyful behavior elicited by success tends to outlast achievement of that success and, thus, to be pointless. To be sure, joyful behavior may well be functional (see Lazarus et al. 1980), and we will return to that issue; but its functions do not appear to reside in dealing with the event which elicited it. One explanation of such behavior, then, is that of activation for relational activity set free and seeking to have its way.

Finally, activated behavior in the sense meant above, vivid emotional response included, appears to depend upon background variables manifest in prevailing level of vitality, and suggestive of variable, limited activation resources. Evidence for this suggestion is admittedly weak; yet we mention it. Occurrence of activated behavior and vivid emotional response appear to depend upon physical fitness and to be undermined by exhaustion; but physical fitness per se does not seem to be the major variable. More purely psychological conditions may act likewise; witness emotional indifference under severe psychological adversity, as in post-traumatic numbness (see section 8.3) and apathetic helplessness under inescapable suffering. If there is exhaustion under these conditions, it is central rather than peripheral. Resources as mentioned particularly seem to affect spontaneous, self-initiated behavior of which the prime instance, being interested in one's surroundings, does not seem to require much physical energy.

Activation as defined here represents a dimension of variation behind behavior called emotional. Variation of activation often appears as the major emotional aspect involved, as in apathy or vitality and joy; and they also stamp the specific behaviors discussed earlier as resulting from action tendency rather than being voluntary behaviors.

Activation has been defined above as readiness for action, or intentional readiness. *Emotion*, in turn, may be defined as change in activation in this wide sense of the concept. The change may be in intensity, both up and down, and in quality. Change in quality is identical to elicitation of action tendency, just as relational null states imply decrease in quantity. In fact, the present definition is not really different from the definition of emotion given before (section 2.7). Only the emphasis differs: It is on the qualitative, directional aspect there, and on the quantitative aspect here. Activation, of course, is activation of something: of the behavior systems or plans involved in action tendency.

The notion of activation as advanced is close to that of "drive" in the old Hullian sense, and Duffy (1962) explicitly identified the two. It presents dilemmas and puzzles similar to those raised by drive (see Bolles 1975). Like drive, activation may be thought to refer either to some sort of generalized state of readiness potentiating whatever action program happens to be elicited, or only to the state of readiness of specific action programs, with the dynamic properties that such a state of readiness may be assumed to have and that were hinted at in the preceding. As with drive, the crucial information relevant to distinguishing the two conceptions concerns whether activation of one program affects activation of a different program. That is to say: Does activation of tendency X also activate tendency Y, or can action Y drain activation from action X? There are some suggestions that it can. Sexual excitement increases propensity for aggression (e.g., Cantor, Zillmann & Bryant 1975); aggression against superiors can be "redirected" toward inferiors. But, then, the two programs or actions, in these observations, may well have common components; a link between sex and aggression, at least in males, has been made before, and on grounds other than those of energy metaphors (or of attributional hypotheses, for that matter). For instance, both sexual and aggressive behavior are facilitated by the hypothalamus–hypophyseal–gonadal system (Beach & Holtz 1946; Bermond 1982; Poshivalov 1982); and sexual stimuli such as the sight of a female or pornographic movies have been shown to result in activation of that system (e.g., Laferla et al. 1978). For the moment, it appears most adequate to consider activation to involve readiness of specific action systems or plans (including such global plans as those of readiness "to have a given situation changed" or "to exert power and assert dominance"); with the qualification that such readiness is facilitated by general resources, as suggested, and that one such action system is general-purpose readiness, alertness. It may be added that the various pieces of evidence reviewed – particularly those pertaining to time course parameters – suggest hormonal and neuropeptide mechanisms to be among the major mediators of activation states and dynamics; which possibility in turn gives some more body to the activation concept itself.

2.9. Emotional behavior generally

Characteristics of emotional behavior

So far, the discussion of emotional behavior has focused upon expressive behavior. The reason for this restriction is clear: Expressive behavior corresponds to the initial working definition of emotional behavior, in its apparent uselessness or superfluousness.

However, once emotional behavior is defined as behavior stemming from action tendency and its initiating conditions, expressions turn out to form only a subset of such behavior, and certainly not the most important subset. If much of emotional behavior aims at the achievement of desired changes or at maintaining desired states, expression only does so transiently, not very effectively, and merely by changing the subject's relationship to the environment. Closing one's eyes in fright does not abolish the danger, nor does it bring one out of danger's reach. Flight, however, does the latter. Fighting does the former. The construction of shelter may do both. Looking at someone and tenderly bending over brings him or her nearer; it does so not as much and not as solidly as taking his or her arm, as offering dinner, or a wedding ring.

There exists, in other words, an infinity of ways in which a given relational aim may be realized. Some of these ways are primitive; others are learned. Some of these are direct; others are more indirect and involve producing intermediate effects for the achievement of the final aim, as bribing may help in damaging an offender. Most importantly: Most of these ways consist of instrumental activity. In contrast to expression, instrumental activity produces relational change by effectively changing the world. It changes the world's objective state, as when constructing shelter or killing a rival; or its subjective state, as when deprecating a rival's worth in one's mind; or its subjective state in someone else's mind, as by the promise or presentation of a wedding ring. Or instrumental activity can change the subject's relation with the emotional event by instrumental means, as by boarding a ship to flee danger.

If, as was just done, the term *emotional behavior* is considered to apply to behavior motivated by relational action tendency, then most human emotional behavior consists of intentional behavior in the restricted, voluntary sense. It is behavior prompted by outcome expectancies and, to a large extent, by conscious anticipations of those outcomes.

Such behavior is not unambiguously emotional, as expression is. It does not strike an observer as superfluous; it is not evidently, perceptually, relational behavior; and it may not show the characteristics of activated behavior. It is similar in outward appearance to nonemotional behavior. It is held, however, to be emotional when it is assumed to spring from action tendency and therefore to serve an ultimate relational purpose of setting right mismatch or achieving completed match. It is held to be emotional *because* it is assumed to spring from such tendency and to serve such purpose. Of course, one may err in such attribution.

It is the relational aim that binds together the various behaviors that spring from a given emotion: attack, threatening, shouting, making deprecatory remarks, withholding alimony, slandering, and withdrawing from contact, all of which may fulfill the same action tendency of anger; or stroking, kissing, gazing, paying full attention to the other's words, buying presents she likes, putting up candles and turning down the lights, all of which serve the aim of "maintaining intimate proximity." Clearly, and as emphasized already, the relation involved can be a symbolic rather than a physical one, and the behavior can be likewise symbolic. Not listening to discourse, disregarding implications of what is said, or breaking emotional contact are forms of advoidance; thinking of her and thinking like her are forms of contact; deprecating the other's worth is increasing one's own control; gaining self-esteem or self-confidence is as much a mode of approach as gaining physical possessions; and so forth.

Levels of response

In emotional behavior, different levels of response can be distinguished, corresponding to different levels in processing mechanisms. Leventhal (1979) distinguishes (1) expressive motor mechanisms; (2) schematic processing mechanisms; and (3) conceptual mechanisms. The first corresponds with most of the behaviors discussed so far; the second corresponds with response complexes as discussed under the heading of emotional responding, in which complexes' acquired responses as well as more elementary expressive ones take part in overall response programs; and the third corresponds with voluntary, instrumental behavior, intentional behavior in particular. The three levels also correspond with levels in the processing of emotional stimuli, to which we will turn in chapter 5.

Emotional behavior as a mode of coping

The major characteristic of instrumental emotional behavior, apart from having its source in action tendency, is that it represents coping activity. Lazarus (1966) introduced the notion of coping in this connection: Emotional behavior aims at coping with the emotion-eliciting event. It represents "primary coping" activity, as distinct from "secondary coping activity," which endeavors to cope with the emotional response and experience (chapter 8). To consider emotional behaviors as modes of coping gives these behaviors a functional interpretation. Such interpretation is fairly obvious for the examples of instrumental behavior cited so far, and was likewise applied to much of expression. For much of emotional behavior, the functional kind of interpretation is perhaps not so obvious. The coping viewpoint, however, serves as a heuristic. It leads to the endeavor to give functional interpretation to emotional manifestations, or else to clear recognition of where the limits of functional interpretation lie and what behavior beyond this limits consist of.

Indeed, not all behavior elicited by emotional events can be considered coping activity. When discussing expression, we noted inability consequences, particularly apathy and mere suffering. Instrumental behavior, too, shows dysfunctional or nonfunctional features, among them sheer disturbance manifestations like decreased precision of skilled movements, or the primitivization of language production; or just sitting there and staring out the window. Other behaviors are mere activation manifestations: increased zest at work under the prospect of a pleasant evening, for instance, or the activation increase after success, mentioned earlier.

However, the limits of what can be interpreted to be coping activity are flexible; they are a function of increased theoretical insight or plausible hypothesis. Freud (1915) interpreted the continuous painful preoccupation with incurred loss in bereavement as a mode of coming to grips with that loss; it constitutes a "work of grief." Janis (1958), in a similar vein, described the "work of worry" as useful adjustment effort toward anticipated hardships.

Inactivity and apathy can be interpreted as the results of depletion of resources, but also as forms of adjustment to uncontrollable conditions and of avoidance of vain efforts. Rothbaum et al. (1982) have so reinterpreted passivity as a mode of "secondary control," and depressive apathy has been tentatively interpreted as help-soliciting action, as an energy-conserving behavior mode, or as behavior serving disengagement from concerns (Klinger 1975). Numbness after disaster or trauma (Janis 1971; Parkes 1972; Horowitz 1976), has been viewed as a form of defense against immediate realization of the incurred losses, and thus a form of "secondary coping." Sartre (1934) even interpreted fainting in emotional shock as an act of defensive denial. He may not have been entirely wrong: Bettelheim (1943) noted the low incidence of fainting when, in the concentration camp, such response was blatantly dysfunctional. In similar vein, activation increase after success can be seen as response to an ecology that has proved conquerable. Nearly all emotional behavior presents the alternative possibilities of functional interpretations (let us say, the type of approach of Darwin) or of viewing it as mere contingency, due to the way the nervous system is built and to its limits in adequately handling "excitations" (Spencer's viewpoint).

Emotional behavior, from a coping viewpoint, is seen as behavior that endeavors to achieve an action tendency's aim. There is other behavior more remote from actually fulfilling an action tendency while still connected to it. Behavior can be motivated by anticipation of emotion that could or will occur. Passive avoidance and well-established active avoidance are examples. No emotion, at least no autonomic arousal response, occurs in an animal that has learned to smoothly escape upon a signal, before the shock signaled by that signal comes on (Solomon, Kamin, & Wynne 1953). Many forms of behavior regulation can be understood as anticipatory endeavors geared to having or not having certain emotions (chapter 8). They, too, are in some sense emotional behaviors. They are motivated by the prospect of emotions that could or will occur. Their structure is different from that of the behaviors discussed before, though. Including them under the heading "emotional behavior" unduly stretches that concept, because it can be argued that *all* behavior either anticipates or forestalls some emotion or other. Yet the dividing line between emotional behavior and behavior motivated by emotion anticipation appears blurred.

2.10. Emotions as intentional structures

Much of emotional behavior is intentional behavior, albeit motivated by action tendency. Many emotions can be defined by an intentional structure: that of maintaining or changing a given kind of situation, and doing that in certain ways, with respect to certain aspects of the given situation and with regard to given kinds of object in those situations. They can often be more closely, more appropriately, and more specifically defined in this manner than in any other. In other words: Many emotion names refer to intentional structures engendered as part of the plan to fulfill a given action tendency; these names refer to intentional structures and not merely to the action tendency underlying them. An example, again, is love. *Love* was defined earlier as tendency toward maintaining proximity, for the sake of such proximity, and such tendency appears to explain relational behavior and the intentional acts to which love gives rise. It explains the feeling or upsurge of love, which can be considered to be awareness of the desire to join, as an end in itself. However, it does not exhaust the description of love. It does not specify what the proximity is for, nor how it is to be consummated. It thus does not differentiate between kinds of love, which is important since every love is some kind of love; love in the abstract does not exist. A given love aims at bodily proximity and skin contact; a different one is the "desire towards increased value of the object" (Scheler 1923).

Obviously, defining different emotions as different intentional structures (different intentional structures all springing from some change in action readiness) is defining those emotions at a different plane from that adopted hitherto. Up to now, the focus has mainly been upon single events. It now shifts to longer-lasting, or at least more elaborate, response patterns, in which anticipations play a more important role. This focus is upon a class of psychological events that takes emotions as discussed so far to be its constituents, its atoms.

It might appear appropriate to introduce a different name to refer to those psychological events. Apart from hurting common usage with respect to the word *emotion*, there are other reasons for not doing so. One is that emotions that take the shape of intentional structures are still changes in action readiness; the intentional structures are rooted in action tendency – they are motivated by the signals pressing for change or continuation, and they claim control precedence. Another reason is that changes in action readiness in humans tend to develop into intentional structures. Very brief and sudden emotions are rare: Most jealousy goes beyond mere pangs; most flashes of anger go beyond impulse to strike, and extend into intention to hit, and to hit well, and again to-morrow. It appears more appropriate to consider extension of action readiness into intentional structure a continuous dimension of variation within emotions. A third reason, and most important in this connection, is: Many emotions (that is, many emotion concepts) can only be defined adequately by intentional structures, namely, those emotions that were said to be defined by their objects. Definition by objects, the making of distinctions among emotions on that basis, is psychologically relevant precisely because it refers to different complexes of intentions for coming to grips with those particular kinds of object.

Take the various forms of love; or take again jealousy. It has been remarked quite correctly that jealousy is not a "thing" like fear, nor a string of "things," but a structure (White 1981). Perceiving the other's enjoyment (or its likelihood) not merely leads to the action tendency of hatred or to the action tendency states of helpless grief or mere suffering. It leads to a variety of urges to disturb the fact of that enjoyment. Ob-struction of the rival's actions, threatening him, chasing him away, com-prise one way to accomplish this. Blocking access to the envied object is a second: guarding her, overseeing her every movement, preventing the other from seeing her or talking to her, or worse. Still another is deprecation of the enjoyment involved: subjectively decreasing her value or his pleasure, as one imagines that pleasure to be. Instrumental to these actions is certainty concerning the facts: hence spying upon her, cross-examining her, perusing her mail or her purse or her traffic tickets. Or intentions may follow a different tack: obtaining control by partici-pation in the enjoyment, in imagination or by wanting to know its every detail. Intentions further vary according to whom is considered the prime enjoyer, she or he; and according to the concern that makes that enjoyment painful: the attachment to the other or one's safety, self-esteem, or honor (see White 1981; Buunk 1980), or sheer envy regarding the enjoyment as such (Freud 1922). None of these intentions, inciden-tally, needs to lead to overt action; action often remains restricted to ruminations, or the intentions merely lead to the agitation of being subject to their call.

Or consider guilt feeling. Is it merely a pain, or a pain with special qualities due to the nature of its cause? Nonsense. Guilt feeling is shrink-ing from facing the fact and facing others, but knowing you have to face it and them, and trying to do that, too; it is knowing one cannot claim to be what one would like to be and, consequently, it is trying to be less arrogant, more modest, seeing life events more from two sides.

In a sense, jealousy *is* the intentional structure corresponding to what was just described; and guilt feeling *is* that shrinking and trying and knowing with its consequences – provided, in both instances, that the intentional structures are instigated by pain, impetus for change, and control precedence for the intentions that that impetus entails. No doubt, the simple pang of jealousy or guilt is an emotion, too. The pangs are called "jealousy" or "guilt" because of the object of thought in the event that elicited them, but they are worth being called so because the features of that object of thought are such as to call for, or cry out for, intentional structures as described.

Characterizing an emotion by an intentional structure does not merely apply to so-called complex emotions. Different fears require different behaviors, and they differ in the intentional structure underlying those latter. In social anxiety, the action tendency to diminish danger, common to all fears, is implemented by such specific actions as remaining un-obtrusive, speaking softly, running to fetch the teapot to be of help, humoring other people. Fear of heights requires different behaviors, and fear of failure requires different behaviors again. Intentional structures, in fact, are what makes one fear different from any other and the action tendency of withdrawal or protectiveness only a thin thread stringing them together.

There is good reason to discuss intentional structures in emotion at some length. They provide a parameter of emotional intensity quite separate from the parameters that were discussed before (section 2.4) and that characterize intensity of momentary response. Emotions differ in the scope of their intentional structures, the duration with which these latter may outlive the precipitating event, and the persistence over time with which they govern action. Emotions may be said to be more intense the more persistent the intentions, the longer these remain, and the more varied the structures are. It is this kind of intensity that is of social relevance, rather than the intensity of momentary response, the loudness of the voice, the number of tears spent. Who – to paraphrase Kenny (1963), to whom the point is due – is more afraid of nuclear war: he whose heart beats violently upon some news item, or bites his lips and reads with a contorted face, or he who, when considering the risks of nuclear war, modifies his life plans, enters politics, or loses his interest in life? The same for other emotions. It is likely that response intensity, as evident from activation manifestations, specific expressions, and autonomic response, and intensity of intentional structure are positively correlated, although only weakly so; but it is mostly the latter that is of consequence to the individual and his environment.

Passions and sentiments

With the discussion of intentional structures, emotions shade over into more persistent psychological events likewise characterized by intentional structure and likewise instigated by some congruence or discrepancy between desired and actual state, but not as such leading to change in action readiness. We call such psychological events "passions" and "sentiments," the latter in accordance with Shand (1896), McDougall (1923), and Arnold (1960), among others.

There exists fears that dominate behavior, yet without necessarily giving rise to a fast-beating heart. Fear of nuclear war that motivates political action or causes loss of one's sense of the meaning of life is an example; so is a well-arranged phobia that consists of incessant careful avoidance of confrontations with the phobic object. No emotion of fear is present, perhaps, yet the threat makes itself constantly felt and guides behavior. So for some griefs. They may lead to tears and to despair, but in between, life is filled with other things: actions to fill the emptiness or seek contact with the lost person by arranging flowers before her portrait or dusting his clothes in the closet. Evidently, the absence is continuously present and reacted to; there is continuous grief, but in some other sense than that of action readiness change. Other emotions than grief can take on similar shape – in fact, all emotions that in some way imply a judgment of an object or kind of event. So, for instance, indignation: There exists indignation that leads to protracted personal or political action, indignation aroused by perceived injustice or oppression, for instance. Another example is love, which persists when the lover is asleep, shows itself when time off from work is given or taken, and bursts out in true emotion when the beloved is met, or ill, or departed.

The word *emotion* earlier in the preceding paragraph is used confusingly, and for convenience. The phenomena under discussion are those that we choose to call *passions*. The structure of these passions, these fears and griefs, indignations and loves, does not seem to be very different from that of the corresponding emotions. The object, or that which initiates the response, is similar or may even be the same: some mismatch, be it threat, loss or offense; or some actual or promised match. Actions in passions follow the same pattern as do those stemming from action tendency: protection seeking, removal of offense or offender, and so on. The only difference is that in the structures we call passions, actions are undertaken spontaneously, that is, not necessarily elicited by actual confrontations with relevant events. They follow from a previously established plan. In what we call passions, actions flow from goals, which goals have high priority for control over action in the individual's goal hierarchy. Emotions are action tendencies, passions are goals; emotions imply action control precedence, passions imply high priority in the goal stack.

The goals called passions persist, as dispositions, both when at a given moment they do not occupy the top priority position and when they actually instigate and guide action. That is to say: passions are emotions turned into concerns, which we define as dispositions to prefer occurrence of a given state of affairs over its nonoccurrence (see chapter 6). They are emotions turned into concerns because a given kind of situation, a given kind of mismatch, which is of a nature to elicit emotion, persists for the subject's mind, and has become a persistent source of striving. An emotion of indignation is replaced by knowledge of an indignity, et cetera.

Passions as well as many emotions derive from more or less enduring appraisals of the objects concerned. To be filled with the goal of achieving proximity or possession of a given person, that person must have been appraised as desirable, as uniquely fit to satisfy the concerns involved. These appraisals, of course, are structurally identical to those underlying emotions generally, which we phrased as appraisals of mismatch or match or potential match between an event and some concern or between the potentials of an object and some concern. However, the more or less enduring appraisals – likes and dislikes, appetites and aversions – are dispositional entities. They are there, presumably, even while asleep. They are there when they do not manifest themselves in joys, sorrows, or angers, although one can know about them when taking stock of one's likes and dislikes, while quietly lying in bed.

These appraisals are called *sentiments*. The use of this term in the work of Shand and Arnold is slightly ambiguous: Sometimes it appears to refer to awareness of one's attitude – to how one feels about an object or issue – and other times to the disposition of which the feelings are the expression. We will use the term *concerns* (more particularly, *surface concerns* – see chapter 6) for the dispositions.

One may quarrel with the above definitions of *passion* and *sentiment* or with the analysis given of the phenomena to which the terms are applied. The major point, here, concerns not the precise definitions or analyses. It is that emotion words like *fear, anger, grief, love,* or *hate* are applied indiscriminately to emotions, passions, and sentiments – that is, to momentary responses, to goals persisting over protracted periods, and to attitudes or modes of appraisal. The word *emotion* itself is sometimes used to refer to all three indiscriminately. Love, hatred, and being in love refer more often to sentiments and passions than to emotions; for words like *grief* and *fear* the balance may lie differently; but with each one, now this, then that is meant. Hence all sorts of confusions and unnecessary differences of opinions.

Hence also apparent paradoxes. One can be indifferent to everything because of grief; jealousy may make one angry; love may make one unhappy and nervous. The paradoxes – emotions causing emotions – may be interpreted as reflecting emotion mixtures or blends. Jealousy, as we saw before (section 2.8), may be thought to contain anger as one of its components, and so on. Nothing mixes or blends, however, in these examples, but statements involving two different kinds of entity– more or less enduring or dispositional ones, passions, sentiments, or concerns; and more or less incidental ones, emotions. That each passion, sentiment, or concern can generate a variety of emotions need not surprise, since "the particular organization into which all emotions are growing is one in which they are to occur as modes or phases in the life-history of the sentiments" (Shand 1896, p. 217) – a central point for emotion theory, to which we will turn in chapter 6.

2.11. The provenance of emotional behavior

Where does emotional behavior come from? The question contains two quite different ones, which should be kept separate. First question: How does it come about that certain stimuli are capable of eliciting emotional response? Second question: How have the responses come to be part of the subject's behavior repertoire and to be responses to the kind of stimuli they are responses to? The present section briefly discusses the second question; treatment of the first question will be kept until chapter 5.

Species-specific behavior

Species-specific behavior refers to behavior that belongs to the innate endowment of the species; that endowment enables the animal to show the behavior without the benefit of learning or, at least, to quickly learn it when others set the example. Walking upright, in humans, is an example of the latter contingency.

Evidence for the innateness (in the above sense) of expressive behavior and many elementary emotional behaviors such as flight, freezing, and attack has been presented in section 2.6. As argued, expression forms part of behavioral systems, together with the more full-fledged behaviors. To the innate endowment further belong the activation modes as well as deactivation patterns and inhibitory behavioral response; and the autonomic arousal patterns to be discussed in the following chapter.

Animals, of course, have at their disposition a number of behavior programs subserving the desires and enjoyments: predatory behavior modes, sexual behavior modes, courtship behaviors included, social behaviors of various sorts. Unlearned responses other than facial expressions are generally considered unimportant in humans. Their importance may have been somewhat underrated; various types of behavior tend to show up under conditions of loss of inhibition or occur nearly universally. Biting as angry behavior is seen, for instance, in rage attacks of neurologically disturbed patients (see Poeck 1969). Kissing, caressing, and giving presents, to children and to partners in love, would seem to be part of a biologically prepared care-giving behavioral system, considering their very widespread occurrence cross-culturally. Showing off bodily force, in males, and making erotically suggestive body movements to potential erotic partners, in females, both cross-culturally also quite general, would seem to be part of an innate courting pattern. Other near-universal behavior patterns include social greeting by means of hand signals (waving, handshaking; Eibl-Eibesfeldt 1974), smiling as a social acceptance signal, perhaps giving food to nonhostile visitors; and vocal or visual greeting of strangers met on the way.

Insight

There exist behaviors that cannot properly be considered innate, nor can they be considered learned, in the sense that proven success in performance leads to their repetition on subsequent occasions. These behaviors flow naturally from the situation in which they arise; they seem the logical thing to do, and their success appears not after but during execution. The most notable examples are approach, as the action proper for getting something you want, and avoidance (physical retreat), as the action proper for not being bothered by what you don't want.

The problem posed by these behaviors was pointed out earlier by Köhler (in his *Gestaltpsychology* [1929], I think, though I have not been able to retrace the source): Why should the action toward something attractive be approach, and why should approach tend to follow a straight line? Evidently, approach and the straight line follow from the dynamics of the situation; approach, evidently, is the action that decreases the mismatch that motivates it, and the straight line does so in the best manner.

We will call this mode of behavior generation, and this kind of link between stimulus and response, *intuitive*, quite in line with the perceptual ring of "insight." It is immaterial whether insightful problem solutions and intuitive generation of behaviors derive from learning; they probably indeed go back upon that mode of learning called "acquisition of learning sets" (Harlow 1949); and avoidance indeed appears to be absent when experience with harmful events is absent (Melzack & Scott 1957). What is of importance, is that approach is not learned as a response to wanting to get closer, and neither is it an innate response to such desire or to an attractive stimulus; the same holds for avoidance in the strict spatial sense. And approach and avoidance do not strike us as the least prominent of emotional behaviors and of action tendencies.

Intuitive links are probably of much more pervasive importance in the development of emotional behavior. It has been pointed out (Testa 1974) that animals have great difficulty in acquiring behaviors when act and consequence do not follow each other closely in time (as in "delay of reinforcement") or when the location of act and consequence do not coincide in space (for instance, when pressing a pedal abolishes shock presentations at the other end of the cage) – in short, when the cues for the perception of causality (Michotte 1950) are violated.

Learning

Acquisition of emotional behavior is traditionally seen to proceed along the lines of instrumental learning, or outcome learning, as Irwin (1971) called it. Outcome learning is exemplified by learning to run a maze for food reward or by the avoidance learning paradigm, in which the animal learns to execute a response upon presentation of a signal when executing that response happens to forestall an aversive stimulus that otherwise would have followed. Behavior is learned as response to a stimulus when and because it produces rewarding outcomes in the presence of the stimulus. According to theory and experiment, the outcomes need not have been experienced directly: There exists so-called symbolic learning, in which reasoning and being told inform about outcomes; and there is observational learning, learning by seeing others achieve rewarding outcomes by given means (Bandura 1977a).

It is unclear to what extent acquisition of emotional behavior corresponds to the description of instrumental or outcome learning. Avoidance learning, that original paradigm, at any rate does not. Avoidance learning in animals, according to Bolles (1970), consists of selectively learning which of the available unlearned responses to frightening stimuli is most profitably made in response to the present ones. The responses of jumping, freezing, and running, "acquired" in response to the shock signal, are not just arbitrary responses in the animal's repertoire: They are "species specific defense responses" (Bolles 1970). Teaching the animal to make an arbitrary response in order to avoid shock – licking its paw, for instance – proves extremely hard, if not impossible (Bolles 1972). It is like teaching a human to relax rather than to tense up when he is falling or to act with deliberation rather than to run or jump or grab when in an emergency.

Restrictions granted, a large measure of emotional behavior, particularly in humans, is acquired by individual experience, by observational learning or by being told; or by reasoning. Note that the desirable outcomes are often inherent in the actions and not dependent upon external reinforcements. Threatening behavior, whether innate or copied from others, effectively intimidates others; daydreaming effectively brings the love object near, be it in imagination, or it effectively replaces worrisome thoughts in one's mind. Note also that learning about the outcomes of emotional actions is occurring outside as well as within emotional conditions. What serves to produce proximity, or removal of obstructions, or protection from unwanted influence under one condition may also serve under other conditions.

A rich source of emotional behaviors, as said, is observation of examples presented by others. Modes of physical and verbal aggression are rapidly adopted by children when such behavior is observed (and observed as being successful or approved) either in vivo or through the mass media (Bandura 1973). Passive modes of behavior are likewise amenable to adoption when seen in others – thus, for instance, crying to invoke help or attention, behaving submissively to avoid trouble or gain subtle control, or sulking as a mode of passive resistance.

As said, many modes of emotional behavior are modeled upon examples the environment offers. The social environment, including cultural tradition, thus has a strong formative influence upon the individual's behavior. It has such influence by offering instrumental means for implementing the aims of action tendencies, such as in providing the use of weapons or insults and the forms each of these can take. It also, on a more basically emotional level, provides modes of expression that can give shape to otherwise unstructured excitements. Beating one's breast, tearing one's clothes, pulling one's hair, and heaping ashes upon one's head probably are purely cultural inventions, without which there would merely be cries and contortions. Averill (1982) has described cultural patterns of frenzied aggressive behavior, such as amok in Java or "being a wild man" in New Guinea. These behavior modes are considered cultural patterns because the syndromes appear to differ from culture to culture, are culturally accepted and labeled, and presumably are adopted by the individual because he has seen them in other members of the tribe. Yet some caution is in order when evaluating the role of culture in these and similar syndromes. The syndromes merely give shape to action readiness, to disturbance, which was there anyway. Also, it is unclear how far the formative influence of culture really goes. Amok, the wild man syndrome, and the related syndromes, although different in many respects, appear to be essentially similar. Another cultural syndrome, *latah*, on Java, a compulsion-like tendency to imitate others, occurs during what impress as states of clouded consciousness, and therefore may be not dissimilar to responses that occur under hypnosis in our culture. Which rather makes one wonder whether culture really provides the modes for emotional manifestations or rather permits as well as necessitates universal modes of response to appear in a thin culture-specific disguise.

Behavior frequency

Learning affects behavior not merely in the appearance of new modes of behavior, but also in the readiness with which behavior modes are displayed. Behavior frequency, given conditions for its occurrence, is a function of expected outcome of that behavior; and that, in turn, is a function of previous reinforcements. If, as we saw, running during fear is rewarded, it tends to increase. The same holds for aggression. Success in fighting, in rats, produces animals that are more aggressive, whereas a history of defeats rather tends to induce subsequent submissiveness (Scott & Marston 1953). When aggressive behavior in pigeons is rewarded with food, such behavior sharply increases in frequency (Azrin & Hutchinson 1967). Similar effects hold for humans. When the environment bows to outbursts of anger, such anger will tend to show upon slight provocation. For instance, in an experiment by Cowan and Walters (1963), rewarding aggressive behavior in boys strengthened such behavior, and aggression tended to remain increased, even after rewards were withdrawn. "Vicarious reinforcement," observing that certain behavior meets with success in others, again tends to increase propensity to act likewise (Bandura 1973). Again, the parameters of reinforcement effects are relatively obscure. There are always those who do not become more aggressive, even when encouraged. To take another example: Responding to infant crying with attention or food, contrary to what is generally assumed, does not appear to increase such crying (Murray 1979).

Behavior is strengthened not only by success with respect to the goals that that behavior ostensibly serves. Behavior tendencies are also enhanced by side effects such as approval or encouragement, or being socially accepted, or by the mere feeling of coming closer to other people or to one's standards of self-esteem by showing the behavior concerned. These are the "reinforcers" that explain the powerful effects of the social environment upon behavior. Enhancement of aggression by social approval provides examples of these effects (see Bandura 1973); so does collective anger or enthusiasm in mass behavior; so do the fears, indignations, and delights particular to specific cultures and thrown into relief by intercultural comparison (see Gordon 1981). With respect to maladjustive behavior such side effects of emotion are often referred to as "secondary gains," which tend to perpetuate the maladjustive behavior. Bandura (1977a), for instance, quotes a study by Harris, Wolfe, and Baer (1964) that demonstrated how withdrawn behavior of certain children in the classroom varied as a function of the amount of attention the teacher gave those children when showing the withdrawn behavior. If attention was given to the subjects only when showing initiative, withdrawn behavior decreased. In a similar vein, fearful behavior in phobics is said to be sustained by the attention and succorance that behavior elicits in their partners. Rewards often are more subtle still. Unhappy, helpless, victim-like behavior produces the benefit of instilling guilt feelings in one's interaction partner.

Anger, in addition to intimidating others, tends to enhance feelings that one is in control and that the frustrating situation is one which can be modified. Depressed and helpless nonbehavior discharges the subject from the obligation to try to undertake efforts. Passive and avoidant behavior generally obviate necessities for coping. Self-punishment, in guilt, enhances one's self-esteem as a moral person over and beyond constituting an effort to even off the guilt.

Whether the behavior reinforcement model implied in the above is the most appropriate model to account for secondary-gains effects, and for behavior enhancement generally, is not so certain. In the examples just given, it would seem that it is not the behavior per se that is strengthened, but the emotion; that is, the instigation for the behavior, the action tendency or activation state, the urge to do something about the situation or the perceived inability to do so.

2.12. Behavioral consequences of emotion

Emotions have consequences for other behavior, including cognitive behavior. These consequences form the substance of one of the basic controversies regarding the nature of emotion: Is emotion to be viewed as a disturbance of the organism's proper functioning or as an adaptive and energizing mechanism?

Young (1961), for instance, considered the disruption of effective adaptive behavior the distinguishing feature of emotion, and the only feature by which emotion can be defined as distinct from other psychological phenomena. Hebb (1949), too, considered disorganization the major aspect of emotion, that is, as the major behavioral datum requiring special explanation. The emotion-as-disturbance view has met with vehement opposition from, for instance, Leeper (1948) and Arnold (1960, 1970). The opposition stresses the motivating power of emotions such as fear, anger, or joy; the constructiveness of the behaviors that can ensue from curiosity and love; and the adaptive nature of the action tendencies involved, geared as these are to protecting or satisfying the organism.

Both sides of course have arguments to support their interpretation of emotion. The controversy boils down to the questions of the extent to which emotion decreases or increases behavior effectiveness; of the conditions under which either the one or the other occurs; and of explaining decrement or increment when it occurs. When, in other words, does emotion disorganize and when does it organize and motivate, and why?

Not all consequences of emotion can be described as either disturbing or energizing and adaptive: Some consequences just exist. This particularly applies to the influences of emotion upon the organization of memory and the contents of thinking. These influences will be briefly discussed toward the end of this section.

Behavioral disturbance

Deleterious effects of emotional events upon cognitive and psychomotor functioning have been described on the basis of observation as well as experiment. Only some 20% of the infantrymen engaged in combat are reported to fire their rifles; and only a fraction of those take aim carefully (Marshall 1947, quoted by Hebb 1970): whether it is emotion that is to blame is, of course, an open question. Victims of natural disasters and bombings are often seen to wander aimlessly among the ruins instead of taking those steps towards survival that are still possible. Fugitives from floods or fires tend to take futile belongings rather than valuables or necessities. Some 15% of disaster victims shows total behavior inefficiency (e.g., Tyhurst 1951). Lindemann (1944) and Parkes (1972) describe similar gross collapse of coordinated activity after the death of a husband or wife. The subject may be unable to take care of his or her daily needs or personal appearance; time is filled with trivial undertakings such as watering the plants for the third time in a row; the subject may feel, and be, incapable of fulfilling his or her professional or parental obligations. In emergencies, people are often reported unable to concentrate upon necessary actions and to be preoccupied by recurrent, stereotyped thoughts or by irrelevant, unimportant details of the situation.

Behavioral disturbances caused by trauma such as disaster, personal loss, or severe illness can to a large extent be brought under two headings: those of numbness or "denial state" and of "intrusion state" (Horowitz 1976, 1982). Numbness will be further discussed in chapter 7. We follow the description of intrusion states by Horowitz. Intrusion states are characterized by enhanced startle reactions, sleep and dream disturbances, and intrusive thoughts – constant thoughts and ruminations about the event, the ruminations turning again and again to the same issues – and unbidden images – perceptual illusions, believing one sees the lost person, and pseudohallucinations, particularly when the subject is lying down to sleep. There is "hypervigilance": the response pattern consisting of excessive alertness, constant scanning of the environment, continual readiness to interpret new stimuli as announcing new stressful events; everything is perceived in the light of what has happened. In regard to other topics there is inability to concentrate and confusion of thought.

This pattern, to some degree or other, is not confined to the aftermath of trauma. Hypervigilance, including preoccupation and rumination, is a marked feature of the stress and threat of having to make important personal decisions (Janis & Mann 1977).

Of probably somewhat different nature are the paralyzing and thought-restricting consequences of anxiety, as evident in danger-induced panic, stage fright, social embarrassment. Thought is blocked and the mind goes blank or focuses on one single issue, one perceptual object, one course of action that is blindly followed.

Much of ordinary emotional behavior is dysfunctional to some extent, even if its adaptive sense can be recognized, along the lines sketched earlier in this chapter. Not only is it in some measure dysfunctional, but the subject may well know this and still be unable to desist. Stage fright may be understood as meaningful withdrawal in the face of threat; it still blocks the performance one has set out to give. Shyness, anger, and desire make one say things one knows one should not say while saying them. Outbursts of jealousy, while understandable as recuperative behavior, seldom bring one's partner back and more seldom still make her or him love you more. Anger, when not checked, may deteriorate the quality of attack.

Some deleterious effects of emotions have been studied experimentally. Psychomotor coordination was found impaired by nervousness ([*sic!*] Luria 1932), in students coming up for political screening in the Soviet Union in the 1920s, and in anxious subjects as compared with nonanxious ones (as defined by Manifest Anxiety Scale scores; Farber & Spence 1953). Other examples of disturbance are found in more cognitively determined activities. "Roughness of speech," as defined by hesitations, repetitions, and decrease in syntactic well-formedness, was shown to increase during stressful parts of psychiatric interviews (Mahl 1959; Dittman 1962). When asked to learn lists of words, anxious subjects made more errors or were slower in learning than less anxious subjects (e.g., Montague 1953; Jensen 1962). Subjects made more errors in a visual detection task when they were given electric shocks (Wachtel 1968). Performance decrements like those mentioned do not invariably accompany increase in emotion or anxiety, however, as we will further discuss below. It must be added that the data cited are such as are usually cited in the present connection, although the relevance of comparing different groups of subjects, such as anxious with nonanxious ones, may well be contested; no evidence exists that emotion at the time of testing parallels the group difference.

Response suppression

Emotional response frequently interferes with other ongoing activity or with tasks that have to be performed; interference results from preoccupation or from freezing or paralysis in anxiety. Interference of emotion with ongoing activity is investigated in animals by means of the *conditioned emotional response* (CER) paradigm (Brady & Hunt 1955). In this experimental arrangement, the subject first learns an instrumental response, such as bar pressing for a food reward; the response is then maintained at a steady rate by some partial reinforcement schedule. The subject also learns that a certain signal (e.g., a light going on) is followed by electric shock; the signal thus presumably induces fear. Presentation of the signal during responding interrupts the latter or slows down its rate. Degree of response suppression has been shown to relate to variables like previous shock intensity and administration of tranquilizing drugs (Brady 1970).

The inverted U-curve

Emotion, as said, not always disturbs. It may energize, pushing the subject to peaks of courage or performance. This holds for positive emotions in particular. Lazarus et al. (1980) have described a number of different positive consequences of positive emotions: positive emotions may provide impetus as well as distractions and periods of rest under stress. Not only positive emotions can have positive consequences. Anger may induce vigorous action to redress injustice and defamity, and it is probably is a major stimulus in social protest (Tavris 1982). Positive effects of negative emotions are also present in everyday settings. Anxiety motivates careful preparations, for examinations or social interactions. Experimental manipulations of anxiety do not always induce poorer performance; highly anxious subjects sometimes perform better in laboratory tasks than do less anxious ones (Spence & Spence 1966).

It is generally assumed that the relationship between emotion and performance follows the so-called Yerkes–Dodson law. According to this "law," the relation between motivation and performance can be represented by an inverted U-curve. Increase in emotional intensity (or in motivation) from some zero point upward is supposed to produce increase in the quality of performance, up to an optimal point. Further increase in intensity then leads to performance deterioration and, finally, to disorganization (Broadhurst 1957; Hebb 1970). The optimal point is reached sooner, that is to say, at lower intensities, the less well-learned or more complex is the performance; increase in emotional intensity supposedly affects finer skills, finer discriminations, complex reasoning tasks, and recently acquired skills more readily than routine activities. Evidence for the inverted U-curve relationship and for the Yerkes–Dodson law in its entirety exists, but is far from convincing. An experimental example is presented by Broadhurst (1957, 1959). Mice had to perform either an easy or a difficult brightness discrimination task under high or low stress; the stress consisted of having to swim under water for a longer or shorter time. The number of errors in the discrimination task showed the expected interaction between stress and task difficulty.

Spence (1956) and Spence and Spence (1966) investigated the influence of degree of learning in cognitive tasks in human subjects. Anxious subjects tended to do better than nonanxious subjects in verbal paired-associates tasks when the pairs were not yet well learned; with extended training, the difference disappeared or was even reversed. High-anxious subjects performed better in lists with low response competition between items on the list and worse with high intralist competition. Also, anxious subjects tended to do worse than nonanxious ones when the paired-associates learning task was made more difficult by increasing the rate of presentation of the word pairs (Spence 1956; Jensen 1962); the problems connected with comparing anxious and nonanxious subjects to study effects of emotion or motivation were pointed out earlier in this section.

The issue of emotion being an energizer or a disturbance may thus be seen as relating to either the upward or the downward branch of the inverted U-curve. However attractive the inverted U-curve relationship, evidence for that relationship, and for the full Yerkes–Dodson law, is actually quite weak. The evidence does not warrant it to be considered a law, contrary to what one might think in view of the frequency with which it is referred to in the literature (Brown 1961; Bartoshuk 1971; Näätänen 1973). In the first place, no experiment known to the present author has investigated more than two points on the curve, or three if a control condition ("no shock" or "no motivation") is included; this may be considered weak evidence for establishing a curve. In the second place, experimental evidence concerning the effects of the major varia-bles is very limited. Few kinds of tasks have been studied. The range of variation in task difficulty has been small; so usually is the range of emotional or motivational intensities. And so is the range of emotions investigated; on positive emotional arousal there is hardly anything in this connection. In the third place, the independent variable, emotional intensity (or "arousal" or "strength of motivation") is not a simple con-cept that could be measured in an unambiguous way – least of all arousal, to which the law is usually linked (see chapter 3). Furthermore, it has proven difficult to obtain independent estimates of task complexity and of degree of prior learning, particularly in ecologically relevant situations; a priori predictions often fail (Brown 1961). In fact, whether behavior improves or deteriorates under the influence of emotion depends very much upon the relevance of the behavior for the situation at hand. If the task is such that an SSDR, a species-specific defense reaction, will help, emotion may well improve performance; if it is such that an SSDR will hinder because some other action is required, emotion will disturb. Amsel (1958) has noticed that frustrative nonreward, which is highly emotion-arousing, can have either facilitating or depressing effects, de-pending upon whether it evokes interfering responses or potentiates desired response. The so-called frustration effect, increase in running speed, consists precisely of such potentiation of the running response; running, of course, is an appropriate thing for a rat in search of a desired object to do. Human behavior, too, would seem to improve under com-patibility between task and behavior. It is part of soccer lore that the coach should make his players angry at the opposing team; this lore may have a basis in fact, since running and kicking with force are ag-gressive acts and may even belong to human aggressive species-specific responses. In a similar way, a speech meant to be inciting may well be more effective if the speaker is indignant: Turns of phrase and tone of voice come naturally in that mood, whereas these have to be constructed with effort when one is cool.

In fact, authors who stress the organizing and energizing influence of emotion usually illustrate their argument with examples of situations in which the emotionally motivated behavior is task-relevant, or at least task-compatible. By contrast, authors who stress the disorganizing nature of emotion tend to point to effects upon behavior that serves goals foreign to the emotional concerns of the moment: upon food-getting behavior when a subject is submitted to electric shocks (the CER), or upon word list learning when suffering from test anxiety.

Still, it is true that behavior directly relevant to dealing with the emotional situation is often also disrupted. Examples have already been mentioned from combat and disaster studies. Anecdotes abound about being unable to move or think when confronted with danger, or about ineffectual fumbling with oxygen masks and escape hatches, or about the last match extinguished by the trembling of one's fingers. Too much anger in a soccer player gains him a penalty rather than a goal. Task complexity and degree of prior learning no doubt make their contributions independently of situational compatibility.

Explanations of emotional disturbance and energizing

Whether or not the Yerkes–Dodson law is valid or useful, it at best is a descriptive law only. To explain emotional performance decrements and increments, a large number of hypotheses have been advanced. They will be briefly reviewed.

a. The response competition hypothesis. Emotional responses interfere with task performance to the extent that the two are incompatible, as inhibition is with motor performance, or withdrawal with stage performance. Said otherwise, the subject may feel impelled to more urgent actions than those involved in the task at hand. Emotional responses facilitate if they coincide with task-relevant ones, as in the soccer example given above. More precisely and generally: More dominant responses interfere with less dominant ones (or they interfere more effectively than vice versa). More dominant responses are those that are unlearned as responses to the given situation, or better practiced, or more strongly motivated under the given conditions. Increase in motivation increases response tendency; therefore, as mentioned, mild emotion and even mild anxiety actually improve performance (Spence 1956). Increase in motivation increases response tendency in proportion to dominance of the response (motivation discounted); therefore, emotional responses tend to interfere more the stronger the emotion, once their threshold has been surpassed. Also, the stronger the emotions, the more un-learned or other simple responses will gain over complex, more delib-erate, and more rational ones.

b. The attentional capacity hypothesis. Stimuli elicit or increase attentional arousal, and they do so in proportion to their significance, up to some upper limit (Lindsley 1951). This accounts for performance increment. Decrement occurs when, and because, the subject has other things to attend to than those relevant to the task at hand or is so preoccupied as not to have attentional capacity to devote to construction of deliberate action, as opposed to simple, unlearned response.

Easterbrook (1959) advanced the hypothesis that emotion restricts the range of cue utilization: Fewer cues are attended to. Restriction can be supposed primarily to affect cues that are relatively peripheral to the sub-ject's focus of interest. Indeed, when a subject is rewarded for correct performance on a pursuit-rotor task (keeping track of a moving point on a rotating disk) and simultaneously has to perform a (not-rewarded) vis-ual detection task, administration of electric shocks decreases scores on the peripheral detection task without affecting the pursuit-rotor scores (Wachtel 1968). Performance on the central task may also decrease, though less so than on the peripheral one, unless the latter is very easy (Bacon 1974). The net reduction of attentional capacity may be due to one of the reasons given above: readiness for coping response toward shock, or distraction from autonomic cues, for instance (Mandler 1975).

True overall reduction of attentional capacity is an additional possi-bility. Enduring stress, since it makes you tired, may well exhaust the "effort reservoir" needed for voluntary attention (Kahneman 1973). The hypothesis has been advanced by Cohen (1978), who found that enduring stress, in addition to causing performance decrements, de-creases interpersonal sensitivity.

c. The overflow hypothesis. Strong neuronal impulses due to emotional stimuli may disturb other functions. The disorganizing effects of high levels of (cortical) arousal have been so explained (the suggestion, at least, is present in Lindsley 1951). Some form of cortical overflow hypoth-esis was popular in the neuropsychological theories of the last century: Spencer's irradiation theory and Bekhterev's explanation of weeping and laughter are examples. Peripheral deregulations could also occur. Arnold (1960) discusses disturbances in oxygen metabolism due to high epineph-rine secretion under emotion, which in turn (by way of disturbance of acid–glycogen resynthesis) may result in more rapid muscular fatigue; there is some experimental support for the hypothesized cycle (e.g., Cohen & White 1951). More conspicuous are disturbances of motor co-ordination by trembling and speech difficulties due to a dry mouth.

d. The disorganization hypothesis. Emotion can be said to be disorganizing by nature and necessity, to the extent that it results from the incompatibility of required and available responses or of information presented and available dispositions to process it. There is inability for organized response, both at the neural and overt level. As Hebb (1949) puts it: Emotion results from desynchronization of neural timing due to the incompatibilities mentioned.

The disorganization hypothesis can be given a different slant by assuming that behavioral inhibition is involved. Inability to envisage appropriate response due to high uncertainty or danger may mobilize the "behavioral inhibition system" (Gray 1982), which blocks the execution of action, including thought.

e. The regression hypothesis. Emotion can be seen as a form of regression, that is, as regression toward a more primitive mode of functioning. Darrow (1939) called emotions (or at least the more vehement ones) states of "functional decortication." Decortication might be caused in various ways: because lower centers overrule the higher ones (Darrow 1950) or because higher centers are unable to devise ways of coping (hypothesis d). In addition, regression itself can be considered a response mode available when all else fails: taking recourse to childish passivity, dependent attitude, magical thought, or calling for help; or, for that matter, taking recourse to elementary preprogrammed behaviors that require little organizing effort such as shouting and footstamping. Falling back upon simple strategies such as stubbornly persisting in behavior one is used to ("fixation"; Maier 1949) can in a similar vein be considered a regressive response mode that interferes with optimal response.

The various hypotheses do not exclude one another. They may all be true, each for certain phenomena. In fact, it can hardly be otherwise, considering the fact that the disturbance phenomena are so complex: true disorganization next to primitive response modes that are merely inappropriate or suboptimal and disruption of task accomplishment next to inability to respond at all. It is unlikely that all these phenomena can be explained by one simple principle. On the other hand, all the explanatory hypotheses reviewed are compatible with the general notion that emotion involves control precedence for the action tendency evoked; this control precedence affects action planning as well as utilization of information-processing resources for such planning and for action execution. Perhaps the hypothesis may be added to those mentioned that emotional disturbance and maybe even the inverted U-curve are a necessary consequence of that control precedence arrangement.

Irrational thought and action

The previous discussion hardly touched upon one important feature of so much of emotional behavior, both in thought and in overt action: its irrationality.

Irrationality in thought is evident, particularly, in changes in probability and credibility estimates. Under appropriate conditions, implausible stories are considered possible or likely if they foster hope or hate; dubious sources of information are believed. The hopes engendered by fear can have the slenderest of bases, without the slenderness being noticed by the subject. Apprehension may alert to possible dangers, but it also tends to create belief for unbelievable stories. Wartime rumors offer striking examples. They concern successes of one's own side as well as evils perpetrated by the enemy: numbers of victims or cities already occupied.

Emotions can cause some measure of belief in the efficacy of actions one would not believe in under other conditions. One may speak of an increase in regressive modes of thinking under the pressures of emotions. There is an upsurge of superstitions under fear or uncertainty. People make vows about actions they will undertake if only they can pass an examination or be accepted for some job, if the object of their infatuation will respond or if some beloved person recovers from his sickness; they make vows to stop smoking, to give donations, to never quarrel again, as if the vow could influence the outcome. Moreover, people tend, at least for a certain time, to keep these vows when dangers are over, perhaps because the tables may as yet be turned if the vows are broken. It is said that the last war and the occupation in Western Europe increased religious activities: church attendance and even belief.

Then there is emotion-instigated fantasy behavior. Fantasy behavior can in part be viewed as any kind of emotional behavior producing some sort of satisfaction and consisting of imagined approach, avoidance, agonistic tendencies, and so on, contributing to their planning. Still, the satisfactions are neither real nor lasting, and yet the fantasies may occur over and over again. They can even be enacted at the level of overt behavior. A widow may, for years, brush her deceased husband's clothes, set the table for two, and be ready for his homecoming at six o'clock (Parkes 1972).

More empathically striking as irrational are painful fantasies that, however painful, are yet sought by the subject himself. After personal loss, one may dwell tearfully on comforts irretrievably lost. When suffering pain of unknown origin, one may imagine the most serious incurable illness. Fear often paints the bleakest prospects. Jealousy is notorious for such self-torture. Afflicted with jealousy, people are often plagued with vivid fantasies; Iago is not an evil stranger but part of Othello himself. The jealous person can suffer from self-invented events that, in his lucid moments, he knows did not occur, do not occur, and could not occur. Self-torture is not restricted to fantasy: Partners are interrogated and details are requested.

Irrationality goes into the heart of emotional behavior: into many elementary overt actions themselves. I do not mean irrational fears or likes or dislikes; they can, probably, be explained through the subject's expectations, and those expectations by his history. I mean useless or even dysfunctional actions: anger at some deed that cannot be undone by the angry aggression, nor its recurrence prevented; desirous pursuit of someone whom one knows does not want to be pursued, calling by phone a loved one that one knows is not home – all those actions, in fact, that led Sartre (1934) to interpret emotion as magical transformation of reality.

Many of the above irrationalities are irrational only in appearance; they can be given plausible functional interpretations that remove the irrationality. Many painful fantasies can be understood as means for coming to grips with the loss or anticipated threat involved: They are part of the "grief work" and "work of worry" already referred to. Jealous fantasies can be understood as ambivalent participations in the joys, particularly from a homosexual perspective (Freud 1922). Other painful fantasies try to reduce uncertainty and so produce relief a well as distress. Hope, even irrational hope, generates grounds for persisting in coping efforts. Hopes should well be sought to combat the paralysis of despair. Positively pleasurable fantasies offer some actual satisfaction, and they can do so particularly since so much satisfaction is merely cognitive anyway: that of closeness, that of possession, that of self-esteem. Even if these satisfactions derive from ultimate, more tangible rewards (protection, utilization, social acceptance), they function independently for long periods, perhaps even indefinitely.

More essentially, irrationality is apparent rather than real when, and because, emotional reaction is a last resource; the point was raised earlier. Strong concerns are involved that happen to conflict with pursuit of actions relevant to more rational choices: The irrationality resides in the concerns, the preference, rather than in the emotions per se. And behavior is irrational primarily when compared to the more effective, more rational behavior that is excluded by the situation (cf. R. C. Solomon 1976, 1980).

But much true irrationality remains. Hopes can be flatly unjustified and detract from one's taking realistic measures. Pleasurable fantasies can hinder actual endeavors. Many angers are just "expressive"; they serve no regulatory purpose. Two kinds of explanation can be advanced that are advanced for unrealistic behavior generally, the one motivational, the other in terms of general strategic principles. Nisbett and Ross (1980) extensively discuss these altenative explanatory views in connection with social judgment.

The motivational view extends the interpretations given in the paragraph before last. People often tend to construct their environment to conform to their wishes. They create or cling to illusions when these satisfy or when these relieve pain, even if only for the moment. They are often willing to trade long-term efforts for short-term pleasures and buy present hope for later disappointment; or they find difficulty in resisting that temptation. The fact is indisputable, and in part merely illustrates how difficult it is to foresake short-term satisfactions. The view does not apply only to unfounded beliefs, magical practice, and fantasies; it also applies to urbane acts. Calling the absent friend brings her for a moment within illusory reach. Getting angry at unalterable events creates the illusion of being able to change or undo. The same is true for many feelings of guilt; both anger and guilt may give a momentary sense of control. These motivational hypotheses help explain why sometimes anger or guilt feeling is "chosen" rather than sorrow or distress, as a response to loss or other unalterable mishap; the point will recur later (chapters 4 and 8).

In the strategic view, people generally act from limited rationality, and there is little else they can reasonably do; under emotional conditions they only do somewhat more so, because of the urgencies involved. They tend to act upon, or base their judgments upon, easily available information and upon "representative" – that is, somehow typical – information. In judgment formation, these information utilization principles are called the availability and representativeness heuristics (Kahneman & Tversky 1973; Tversky & Kahneman 1974; see Nisbett & Ross 1980). In using these heuristics, aspects of reality are disregarded. For instance, judgment is usually based only upon the "present–present" cell of the 2 × 2 table, the other three being disregarded. Emotion may well enhance utilization of these heuristics, in view of the desirability of rapid action or, more generally, the restriction of range of cue utilization.

In some contexts, this merely means that people do what they want to do, irrespective of how realistic it is. Anger is evoked by, roughly, what should elicit anger: situations of willful harm or obstruction; or: when you want to call the friend, you call the friend, period. In other contexts this amounts to acting and judging upon slender probabilities without taking their slenderness into account.

There is, as Nisbett and Ross emphasize, no reason to choose between the alternative views. Both kinds of mechanism no doubt apply. But of course it will have to be decided which of the two is more likely to be operative in a given situation.

Influences upon memory and thought content

It has often been asserted that memory for unpleasant events is worse than that for pleasant events. Extensive review of the evidence does not support this generalization (Rapaport 1950). Neither is there a general tendency to make unpleasant events look rosier than they really are: People do show avoidant thinking and denial of unfavorable aspects of events (see chapter 8), but they also manifest hypervigilance and anticipatory worry (Janis 1958; Janis & Mann 1977; see chapter 5).

Of more interest is the evidence on differential influences of moods or emotions upon the organization of memory and retrieval. Two sets of phenomena in particular have recently attracted experimental attention: mood-state-dependent retrieval and mood congruity effects.

Mood-state-dependent retrieval is illustrated by an experiment by Bower, Monteiro, and Gilligan (1978). Subjects were hypnotized and then brought into either a happy or sad mood by asking them to recollect a happy or a sad event; each subject was brought first into one mood and then into the other. They were taught to free-recall two 16-word lists, one while happy, the other while sad. Later they were asked to recall both lists when rehypnotized and brought into one mood or the other. Recall was significantly better when occurring under the same mood as that of learning than when under the different mood; the effect was similar whether the moods were happy or sad. The type of effect is strong and has been replicated under varying conditions and by various investigators (e.g., Clark & Isen 1982; Snyder & White 1982); it is also observed as a function of spontaneous moods in clinical groups (Weingartner et al. 1977). The effect, however, only shows up when other, factual retrieval cues are weak: It shows up in free recall but not, for instance, in recognition tasks (Bower & Cohen 1982).

Mood congruity effect refers to increased salience in perceiving and remembering information consistent with the subject's prevailing mood. When the subject is happy, more happy event features are noticed or retained; when sad, more sad features; when angry, more obnoxious features. For instance, subjects hypnotized and brought into a sad or happy mood were given a story to read. Later recall under neutral mood contained more sad facts when the subject had been sad, more happy facts when he had been happy (Bower & Cohen 1982).

A number of cognitive production tasks show mood congruity effects. Free associations differ when the subject is happy or when angry; so does fantasy content; so do snap judgments about people and objects (Bower & Cohen 1982). Johnson and Tversky (1983) made subjects read either a neutral story or a tragic story; the tragic story described a cause of death, which could be either illness, murder, or accident. Subjects were next asked to indicate degree of risk and their own degree of worry about a number of possible causes of death, as well as a likelihood estimate of each type of cause. A depressed mood induced by the story enhanced all risk and likelihood estimates, and it did so regardless of the specific cause mentioned in the mood-inducing story.

Bower and Cohen (1982) have sketched a theory to account for the various results; the theory is an extension of general semantic network theory. In their theory, each distinct emotion is represented by a separate node in the memory network; all information associated with a given emotion or mood is assumed to be linked to such a memory node. Actual mood then serves as a retrieval cue and as an activated node to which congruent information is more easily attached during learning. The theory does not impress as altogether plausible since it treats emotions or moods in the way words are treated – as distinct and discrete entities. The influence of mood is more appropriately viewed as the actualization of information-processing procedures – coding strategies and retrieval strategies. In positive moods, processing concerning success of concern-related events is facilitated; in negative moods, processing of information relevant to failure is facilitated (Den Uyl & Frijda 1984). This view is more consistent than that of Bower with the purportive cognitive structure of moods and emotions and with the results of Johnson and Tversky's experiment. Spiro (1981; Spiro et al. 1982) has advanced similar notions.

3. Physiology of emotion

3.1. Introduction

Emotional responses have both physiological conditions and physiological response components. Certain parts of the brain are indispensible for the manifestations of emotion, and certain hormones are necessary or facilitative for the readiness with which emotions, or certain emotions, are evoked; these brain structures and hormones can thus be regarded as conditions for the occurrence of emotions. This chapter will discuss only the physiological response components, reserving discussion of conditions for chapter 7.

Three major groups of physiological response components can be distinguished: those mediated by the autonomic nervous system, primarily involving changes in functioning of the smooth muscles and other internal organs, which will be collectively referred to as *autonomic responses*; changes in hormone secretions; and neural responses such as those reflected in changes in the EEG. In addition, there exist changes in chemical composition of body fluids (saliva, blood) and changes in the activity of the skeletal muscles involved in respiration, muscle tension, and overt movement; the last have been treated in the preceding chapter. Responses of the different physiological response component groups are not independent of one another. Activity of the sympathetic part of the autonomic nervous system, for instance, liberates the hormones epinephrine and norepinephrine, which in turn stimulate activity of various internal organs. Still, the different response groups and the different responses within each group can be described separately.

Description of physiological response is of course a relevant part of the description of emotional response. In addition, it is relevant for two theoretical issues. The first concerns the function of those physiological response components. What are they for, and what is their relationship to the behavioral and experiential components? The second issue con-

124

cerns the nature of emotion in general and the nature of the difference between different emotions.

It can be argued that emotion and physiological arousal are one and the same thing. Emotion could be defined by the occurrence of physiological arousal: no arousal, no emotion, by definition (e.g., Wenger 1950; Schachter 1964). It is no use quarreling with definitions. What this kind of definition really intends, however, is to assert that whenever there is evidence of emotion – the subject says so, or manifests overt behavior as discussed previously – there is arousal (or dearousal, in some variants): no arousal, no emotion, as an empirical statement. Such is the view of several theorists. The views of these various theorists differ in that for some (notably Schachter 1964; Mandler 1975, 1984), arousal is a necessary but not a sufficient condition for emotion: Cognitions of given sorts are also necessary. For all, however, physiological response is an essential, indispensable component and forms the core of emotional response as a whole.

This interpretation of emotion, as said, requires that whenever there is emotion, on some criterion, there is arousal or marked dearousal. A similar interpretation can be advanced with respect to what makes one emotion different from another. Lange (1885) and James (1884) argued that different emotions are reflected in different patterns of physiological response. They argued that the different emotional experiences – of anger, or fear, or joy, and so on – are nothing but awareness of different physiological response patterns: the James–Lange theory of emotion.

Emotional experience will concern us in the next chapter. The basic requirement of the theory, however, will concern us here: the requirement that the physiological response patterns corresponding with the different emotions indeed be different. They should be so much and so reliably different that the different emotional feelings can in fact be based upon them.

The James–Lange theory has received powerful criticism from Cannon (1927, 1929); the James–Cannon debate has long been one of the fundamental issues in emotion theory and still to some extent is. Cannon countered the James–Lange theory by stressing the similarity of physiological response patterns in the different emotions and the similarity between these patterns and those occurring under less emotional conditions, like those of hunger or cold. Cannon's position has further implications for emotion theory and for the theory of emotional experience: If emotions do not differ in their physiological response and feedback, what else do the differences between emotions consist of?

The importance assigned to cognitive and behavioral aspects depends upon the answer to the question of physiological specificity.

We will first review the evidence concerning physiological changes in emotions generally; next that relating to different response patterns and to differences between emotions; finally we will discuss the concept of arousal, as it is central to various emotion theories.

In discussing physiological variables, no details on measurement techniques and problems of parameter definition will be given. Such details can be found in Greenfield and Sternbach (1972), Martin and Venables (1980), and Obrist (1981), and in the references given by Grings and Dawson (1978).

3.2. Autonomic variables related to emotions

Heart rate

Heart rate (HR) is expressed as (average) number of beats per minute or, equivalently, as (average) time interval between successive beats. HR sensitively responds to the appearance of intense, novel, or interesting stimuli, to mental and bodily activities, and to emotional strain.

HR increases not only during muscular activity (Obrist 1981) but also when preparing for such activity, in animals (Black & deToledo 1972) and in experienced athletes. It can thus increase before actual oxygen shortage can have triggered it (Cannon 1929). It increases in response to loud noises, such as a pistol shot (Landis & Hunt 1939; Sternbach 1960a), during mental concentration, as in counting backwards or performing mental calculations (Lacey & Lacey 1970), and when tensing up for risky, complicated, or delicate psychomotor performance. HR, for instance, rises in motorists when passing other cars, in physicians during the more difficult of their daily tasks (Ira, Whalen, & Bogdanoff 1963), and in airplane pilots, even experienced ones, during takeoff and landing (Smith 1967). In fact, in bomber pilots HR goes up more during those activities than during the bombing raid itself (Roman, Older, & Jones 1967, quoted in Gunn et al. 1972).

HR is often increased under true emotional strain, both during unpleasant events and upon their anticipation – for example, upon electric shock and upon a warning signal that shock will be administered (Blatz 1925; Epstein 1973). HR goes up in cats when facing a barking dog (Cannon 1929) and in humans when viewing a gruesome film (Lazarus & Opton 1966). High HR levels may persist as long as the threat persists and remains alive to the subject. The magnitude of those levels varies with the nature and closeness of threat. Epstein and Fenz (1965) describe HR changes in novice parachutists on jump days. HR begins to rise in the morning, steadily rises further as starting time approaches, increases steeply while waiting for the airplane take off, and reaches a peak during the fall. In experienced parachutists there is some rise at the beginning of the day, which then declines, a steep rise and peak just before jumping, and a rebound after hitting the ground. Ursin et al. (1978) likewise note very high HR levels just before, during, and after jumping, recording rates of 140–180 beats per minute even in experienced jumpers.

HR is high not only in unpleasant emotions and threatening events, but also during joyful expectation and pleasant excitement. It is sometimes (though often not) found to be elevated when viewing sexually arousing images (Bernick, Kling, & Borowitz 1971). It steeply increases during sexual intercourse and orgasm (Boas & Goldschmidt 1932; Masters & Johnson 1966), reaching levels comparable to those of parachutists, up to 180 bpm. Whether these high heart rates are due to sexual excitement, the process of orgasm as such, or the pleasurable sensations is unclear: In any event, sheer physical activity probably plays a minor role, since the same levels obtain during masturbation (Masters & Johnson 1966). Boredom (lengthy vigilance with few signals) also induces HR increase (London et al. 1972).

As suggested by the steady rise during jump day in the novice parachutists, HR tends to parallel stimulus intensity or the seriousness of the threat or challenge involved in the stimulus event. Such parallelism has also been found in other contexts. DiMascio, Boyd, and Greenblatt (1957), for instance, found a rank order correlation of .69 between HR and tenseness of patients, as judged by a therapist over the course of 11 psychotherapy sessions.

As said, HR increases in excitement, in mental concentration, and upon the presentation of intense sensory stimuli. HR tends to decrease under a number of conditions. An extensive review is given by Van der Molen et al. (1985). HR decrease is observed during attentive visual and auditory observation (Lacey & Lacey 1970) and in some form of emotional strain, namely anticipation of aversive stimuli (Obrist 1981). Phasic HR deceleration is a component of the orienting response, the regular response to nonthreatening novel stimuli; HR acceleration is considered part of a defensive response (Graham 1979) and generally a response upon stimuli with negative personal significance. Whether HR deceleration is due to the suppression of movement during attention (Obrist

1981), to some special attention regulation mechanism (Lacey & Lacey 1970), or some other mechanism is a matter of debate, to which we will return.

Tonic HR deceleration has been noted in subjects when angry (Ax 1953). Low HR levels are found during rest and peaceful relaxation and when receiving pleasant sensory stimulation (Lehmann 1914).

HR increase under mental and moderate physical effort is functionally different from that under strenuous effort and emotional excitement. Heart rate is controlled by the parasympathetic division of the autonomous nervous system (vagus nerve) and the sympathetic division: Excitation of the first slows heart rate down; excitation of the second speeds it up. Heart rate, at any moment, is a function of both parasympathetic and sympathetic control, which may act antagonistically as well as synergistically. Heart rate decrease when one is waiting for aversive stimuli is a consequence of increased vagal (parasympathetic) tone. HR increase under mental effort and moderate exercise is due to loss of vagal tone. HR increase in strenuous effort and excitement is due to sympathetic influence (Obrist 1981).

An obvious function of HR increase is to augment oxygen supply to muscles and brain. In emotion, sympathetic innervation supposedly serves that function in "emergency" fashion, anticipatorily, before energetic movement actually requires it (Cannon 1929). Vagal restraint may be a consequence of control processes. Emotional excitement sometimes does not show in HR until that inhibitory vagal increase is abandoned. This is Fenz and Epstein's (1968) explanation for prejump HR deceleration and postjump HR rebound in experienced parachutists. In fact, Ursin et al. (1978) found that HR remained stable in their parachutists until just before the jump.

Blood pressure and blood flow distribution

Blood pressure increases during physical exercise (Obrist 1981); it increases particularly when the exercise involves static, isometric effort rather than true movement (Zanchetti & Bartorelli 1977). Blood pressure also increases upon loud noise (Steinman et al. 1955), under stress such as prior to examinations (Tigerstedt 1926; Brown & Van Gelder 1938), while discussing delicate or disturbing topics during psychiatric interviews (see McGinn et al. 1964 for a review of these and other studies on correlates of blood pressure), and during other kinds of personal strain, such as having your blood pressure taken! (Van Montfrans 1984) or harsh questioning of false witnesses during a staged courtroom trial (Marston 1917). Schneider (1968) reports on a stockbroker whose blood pressure was elevated during the opening hours of the stock market. Blood pressure rise, as in these last instances, is not due to the intellectual activities of lying or evaluating stock prices per se, since no increase is observed in purely intellectual tasks such as making up a story (Marston 1917); it is observed during distinct mental effort, though (see Obrist 1981).

Blood pressure decreases during relaxation (e.g., Schwartz et al. 1981), in relaxed intellectual activities like relating the events of the day (Marston 1923), and while listening to soothing music (Steinman et al. 1955). Increase does not result only from unpleasant stimuli. It follows excitements of various sorts, even if excitement is merely enacted (Bogdanoff et al. 1959) or imagined (Schwartz et al. 1981). It also is elicited by stirring music like jazz or rock (Steinman et al. 1955). Sharp rises in blood pressure are observed upon first meeting "an attractive member of the opposite sex" (Marston 1923). Scott (1930) found rise in blood pressure in nearly all of his 100 male subjects when shown "a film containing a love scene" (anno 1930); 88 of these subjects reported a "sex emotion" of at least moderate intensity. Pictures of nude women also increase blood pressure in men (Davis & Buchwald 1957), as do erotic prose materials subsequently rated as arousing (Wenger et al. 1968). Such increases are comparable in magnitude to those evoked by disgusting or horrifying materials (see Zuckerman 1973). Blood pressure is very much elevated during actual sexual stimulation and intercourse (Kinsey et al. 1953); during orgasm, systolic pressure (pressure during the heart's contraction) reaches peaks in both sexes (Masters & Johnson 1966).

Emotions proper have differential effects upon blood pressure and upon systolic pressure as compared with diastolic pressure (pressure during the interval between heartbeats). Anger has been repeatedly found to produce marked increase in diastolic pressure (Ax 1953; Schachter 1957; Schwartz et al. 1981). This appears to hold in particular for anger overtly expressed, or "anger out" as opposed to "anger in" – anger that is not expressed in violent response but kept inside or suppressed (Funkenstein, King, & Drolette 1957). This latter finding is contradicted by the higher habitual diastolic pressure levels of black male subjects whose coping style is that of suppressed hostility ("anger in" plus guilt feelings about anger; Harburg et al. 1973) and by recovery rate data to be mentioned below. Systolic pressure is elevated in both outwardly expressed and suppressed anger; it has also been found to be elevated during fear (being faced with malfunctioning electrical equipment; Ax 1953; Schachter 1957), when reliving a fearful experience in imagination (Schwartz et al. 1981; Ekman et al. 1983), and in cats when barked at by a dog (Cannon 1929). Results during positive emotion are quite variable and depend (among other things) upon whether the subject is moving or not (Schwartz et al. 1981). Obrist (1981) offers the generalization that blood pressure increase is contingent upon conditions for "active coping" (see section 3.8).

Under most conditions, blood pressure rapidly returns to base level after the emotional events have terminated. However, intense and prolonged emotional stress can lead to level increases that far outlast stimulation and eventually lead to tonically increased levels of indefinite duration (see Harrell 1980 for a review). When anger is suppressed or when expression of anger evokes fear of retaliation, return to normal levels is considerably delayed (Hokanson 1961; Hokanson & Burgess 1962; see Geen & Quanty 1977 for a review). Graham (1945) found increased diastolic pressure in battle tank crews several months after battle; Ruskin et al. (1948) recorded elevated diastolic levels in survivors of an explosion one to two weeks after the disaster. Repeated stresses appear to accumulate with respect to blood pressure. In rhesus monkeys tied to a restraining chair and subjected to a continuous avoidance procedure (electric shock every 10 seconds, unless a button was pushed), blood pressure gradually built up to hypertensive levels (Forsyth 1969; Herd et al. 1969). Suggestion of accumulation was found in the Harburg et al. (1973) study: anger-coping mode, socioecological stress, and skin color (that is, the consequences of black skin color) appear to add up in determining diastolic level. There are indications that suppressed hostility, as a personality trait, is an etiological factor in essential hypertension (see Diamond 1982 for a review of the evidence).

Emotional events can, on occasion, lead to sharp drops in blood pressure rather than to rises; it has been observed in the restraining chair experiments (see Brady 1970). Fainting can result. Becoming deadly pale in emotional shock, as for instance upon hearing tragic news, probably results from such blood pressure decrease together with peripheral and cerebral vasoconstriction (Cannon 1942). The precise conditions for such fall in blood pressure are unknown.

Changes in blood flow distribution are caused by differential vasoconstriction and vasodilatation over various parts of the body. Blushing and pallor are the results of widening and narrowing, respectively, of the facial skin blood vessels.

In pain, hunger, fear, and rage, peripheral and gastrointestinal blood flow is usually decreased, with simultaneous increased flow toward the muscles; presumably, this is to maximize energy supply where, in those circumstances, it is needed (Cannon 1929). Startle usually leads to pallor, and so does anxiety (Neumann, Lhamon, & Cohn 1944). Both physical exercise and sexual excitement lead to reddening, the latter probably independently of the physical exercise involved. General peripheral vasodilatation, according to Kinsey et al. (1953; also Masters & Johnson 1966; Wenger et al. 1968), is the most marked feature of sexual arousal, apart of course from the obvious vasodilatation in the genital organs and some less obvious local changes like increased flow in the breasts (Masters & Johnson 1966). Penile and vaginal blood flow tend to increase with the arousal value of the stimulating materials or fantasies, as rated by the subjects. Quiet relaxation also tends to lead to peripheral vasodilatation (contented rosiness), which then shows large pressure fluctuations. Pronounced vasodilatation restricted to the face (or sometimes neck, shoulders, and upper chest as well) occurs in shame and embarrassment: true blushing.

Blood flow changes generally tend to follow changes in local energy needs: increased flow to the stomach during eating and digestion, genitals during sexual excitement, the muscles during physical exercise. Peripheral vasoconstriction occurs quite often during anger and probably is the cause of the rise in diastolic blood pressure discussed above; peripheral vasoconstriction appears to be advantageous for isometric as opposed to isotonic muscular effort and thus, perhaps, for self-control and/or for bracing for assault rather than for actual fighting; this might explain why, and predict when, white rather than red anger occurs.

Both thinking and dreaming cause increase in brain blood volume; this was observed in patients in whom part of the skull had been surgically removed for medical reasons and where the scalp (Hammond 1883) or the membranes covering the brain (Shephard 1906) could be seen to rise and fall. Increase in cerebral blood flow during mental effort has since been confirmed by means of more generally applicable methods (Risberg & Ingvar 1968). As said, startle or, in general, apprehension and alarm reactions decrease peripheral blood flow. The orienting reaction (OR) in response to novel or unexpected stimuli consists in part of decreased blood flow in the extremities – at least in the fingers – together with increased blood flow in the forehead (Sokolov 1963). This latter distribution change probably is indicative, according to Sokolov, of the increased cerebral blood flow mentioned.

Findings on blood flow distribution are not all consistent. As said, Cannon (1929) observed peripheral vasoconstriction in animal "rage"; Schwartz et al. (1981) obtained supporting evidence with respect to anger in humans reliving experiences of the emotion. Ekman et al. (1983), by contrast, found significantly increased finger temperature in anger (insofar as aroused by imagination or by adopting angry facial expression) as compared to the other emotions they studied.

Respiration

Respiration varies along a number of dimensions, the most important being respiration rate (number of inspiration–expiration cycles per second), depth (volume of air per cycle), regularity (variance of depth and/or cycle time), and relative duration of inspiration in the respiration cycle (I-fraction; Woodworth 1938). Another important variable related to respiration is CO_2 level (arterial, or in the expired air), which is an inverse function of both respiration rate and depth. Respiration and heart rate are to some extent dependent upon one another, since the muscular activity of stronger respiration tends to speed up HR.

Physical effort generally leads to both faster and deeper respiration; the same holds for emotional excitement, pleasant as well as unpleasant (Lehmann 1914; Rehwoldt 1911). Faster respiration has been found in startle, anxious anticipation, acute fear, depression, and surprise (Oken et al. 1962; Mora et al. 1980; Skaggs 1930). Emotional experiences may also lead to slower and to more superficial respiration; increases are, however, more frequent than decreases (Woodworth 1938). Peaceful rest and relaxation lead to slower and shallower respiration.

Sudden intense stimuli tend to cause brief inhibition of respiration – a brief gasp and the need to catch one's breath. This inhibition is a standard component of the orientation reaction. In startle the brief suspension is followed by compensatory deeper and faster breathing (Sternbach 1960b). Concentrated attention, particularly in attempts to see or hear, also suppresses or suspends breathing, presumably to suppress distracting movements and body sensations (Suter 1912). Protracted mental concentration can make breathing faster and shallower. Negative emotional reactions not only speed up respiration, they also tend to make it uneven (Skaggs 1930; Cohen et al. 1975); the unevenness probably corresponds to tenseness or tension in these states. Negative reactions (fear, suspense, depression) also generally tend to lead to lowered CO_2 levels at the end of expiration (e.g., Suess et al. 1980).

The I-fraction is low during mental activities such as mental arithmetic (Suter 1912), during feelings of tenseness (Drozýnski 1911), and pronouncedly so during laughter: Laughter consists of sharp inspirations and extended, spasmodic expirations (Féléky 1916). The ratio is high in excitement (Rehwoldt 1911). It is very high during startle and loss of balance (Blatz 1925), presumably due to holding one's breath.

Respiration is both under sympathetic and parasympathetic control, and thus subject to general and specific autonomic excitation. It is also under the control of the skeletal musculature and thus subject to voluntary interference and to general, voluntary, and involuntary inhibitions of movement, as these may occur during tenseness, anxiety, and sensory attention. The dual control is reflected, at least in part, by the balance between thoracic and abdominal respiration. Abdominal respiration dominates in relaxation and pleasant mood; thoracic respiration during tense, unpleasant states such as disgust or apprehension (e.g., Ancoli, Kamiya, & Ekman 1980).

Respiration patterns and mechanisms possess more dimensions of variation, related to emotional response, than enumerated above; sighing is one. They rarely have been subjects of investigation. Subjective experience reports feelings of a lump in one's throat, of "being oppressed," of pressure upon the chest, which may point to respiration variables not usually recorded in psychophysiological investigations.

Electrodermal activity and sweating

The skin possesses electrical conductance that manifests gradual and relatively long-lasting changes in level, called tonic changes, as well as phasic changes elicited by stimuli and by activities of the subject. Tonic and phasic changes are not essentially different phenomena: Both are caused by similar activity changes of the sweat glands (Edelberg 1972). Tonic level is usually called skin conductance level (SC). Phasic responses are usually referred to as electrodermal response (EDR), galvanic skin response (GSR), psychogalvanic response (PGR), or skin resistance response (SRR). The magnitude of both level and response are expressed in terms of the skin's electrical conductance, the inverse of the resistance (and measured in terms of mhos, the reciprocal of ohms). An EDR (a phasic response) consists of a drop in the skin's resistance (and thus a rise in its conductance), which occurs with a latency of 1.5–4 seconds after stimulus onset, reaching a peak shortly after and then returning to a resting level. Tonic changes occur either spontaneously – that is, without discernible stimulus – or in response to changes in condition of the subject. EDRs are most readily detected on the palms of the hands or the soles of the feet, those surfaces having the highest density of sweat glands (Venables & Martin 1967). Electrodermal responses from different body surfaces do not always behave in identical fashion and can therefore not be considered equivalent (Tursky 1974).

Three kinds of variables are of interest with respect to electrodermal manifestations of emotional response: occurrence and amplitude of EDRs in response to stimuli; frequency of EDRs during a specified period or under specified conditions; and skin conductance level (SC) during a given period or under specified conditions.

EDRs are evoked by alerting stimuli: sudden noise or flashes (Landis & Hunt 1939; Sternbach 1960b) and novel (Furedy 1968), unexpected (Epstein 1973), or interesting (Berlyne 1960) stimuli; questions put to the subject; unpleasant stimuli, such as ice-cold water or electric shocks (e.g., Tursky 1974); and signals announcing the probable or possible advent of such unpleasant stimuli (Van Olst 1971; Epstein 1973). EDRs also occur in response to emotionally significant events, such as one's name being called out or being shown anxiety-provoking images. In a study by Smith (1922), the emotional value of words, as judged by a group of subjects, correlated with the magnitude of the EDRs evoked by those words in an association test. Phobic patients manifest EDRs when shown pictures of their phobic objects (e.g., Wilson 1967), the subjectively more anxiety-provoking images eliciting larger responses (Klorman 1974). Both fear and anger are accompanied by EDRs or by increased SC; response magnitude tends to be larger in fear (Ax 1953). Erotic materials (nude pictures, erotic stories) evoke EDRs in both men and women (see Zuckerman 1971 for a review). EDR thus appears to correspond to interest or excitement rather than to either pleasant or unpleasant affect. EDR magnitude tends to correlate with stimulus intensity or subjectively rated affective value – for instance, with subjectively rated pain intensity (Tursky 1974); many studies do not obtain such correlation, however.

EDRs elicited by simple or novel stimuli show rapid habituation upon repeated stimulus presentation. Much slower habituation occurs in response to painful stimuli or to emotionally significant stimuli such as signals for coming electric shock (Epstein 1971; Van Olst 1971) or pictures of phobic (Klorman 1974) or potentially phobic (Öhman & Dimberg 1978) objects. On occasion there is no habituation at all – for instance, when the stimuli are particularly intense (Klorman 1974).

Increased SC is observed in excitement or under acute stress, as when viewing a gruesome film (Lazarus & Opton 1966); levels may also increase, however, under more neutral interesting conditions such as viewing an innocuous film (Lazarus, Tomita, Opton, & Kodama 1966 – a study using Japanese subjects). SC is also elevated during physical exercise (mostly nonpalmar SC); during sleep deprivation when subjects are trying to stay awake (Malmo 1959); and during the execution of difficult mental tasks. SC has been shown to be correlated with task difficulty (Stennett 1957).

In depressed patients, markedly decreased SC and EDRs have sometimes been found.

Skin conductance and EDR are not the same as sweating; still, they tend to be strongly correlated (Edelberg 1972). Vigorous perspiration in the face (forehead, upper lip), armpits, and palms can be observed in fear and, it would seem, particularly in social fears: embarrassment, shame, fear of failure. Whether it indeed occurs more frequently under those latter states than under other emotions and, if so, why, has not been subjected to systematic investigation.

In the view of Dumas (1933), who here follows Darwin (1872), sweating in emotion occurs particularly under conditions where overt motor activity is inhibited. Social fears clearly belong to those conditions, and so does controlled anger. Dumas interprets profuse sweating as a direct consequence of this inhibition of movement impulse.

Electrodermal activity is determined by sympathetic activity. It is, however, subject to complex cortical regulations and therefore not a simple index of cortical or subcortical arousal (Edelberg 1972). The functions of sweating upon which electrodermal activity depends are complex. The primary function, or one of the primary functions, is thermoregulatory: Sweating produces heat loss through evaporation. However, palmar and plantar perspiration (perspiration on palms and soles), which are particularly responsive to emotional stimuli, appear to contribute little to such thermoregulation. Other functions of these latter have therefore been suggested. Sweating in palms and soles (particularly moderate sweating) renders the skin more supple and more resistant to abrasion; it also permits a stronger grip upon ground and objects and possibly increases tactile sensitivity (see Edelberg 1972). Palmar and plantar sweating thus might serve defensive coping purposes. Furthermore, since sweat has a distinct smell, it might serve as a pheromone, a communicative smell signal. Sweating might help in being identified (by one's fellows), and plantar sweating in particular may leave identifiable tracks (Edelberg 1972). It should be noted that thermoregulatory and manipulatory functions make sweating similar to the relational expressions discussed in the previous chapter; pheromone function relates it to the interactive expressions. Of course, giving off smell signals is extremely common in animals, and the triggers and mechanisms that produce these smells may properly be considered "emotional": Significant stimuli are the triggers, and specifically changed action readiness is the mechanism.

Gastrointestinal and urinary activity

Gastrointestinal functioning and its psychophysiological aspects have been reviewed by Wolf and Welsh (1972), and the summary that follows is largely drawn from that review.

Gastrointestinal activity tends to be inhibited under the influence of pain and stress. Gastric and intestinal contractions and the secretion of gastric juices decrease or stop. Pavlov, for instance, observed the disappearance of conditioned gastric responses in dogs disturbed by upsetting events. Cannon (1929) described arrest of gastric responses in cats when manifesting fearful withdrawal or defensive anger upon confronting a barking dog. Similar observations have been made on human patients with gastric or colonic fistulae. Wolf and Wolff (1943) report extensively upon a male patient, Tom, whose stomach became pale when frightened or depressed or when he felt overwhelmed. Spastic movement disturbances in the duodenum and gallbladder and contractions of the cardiac sphincter (preventing the entrance of food into the stomach) have been observed in response to emotional upset. Prolonged decrease of gastric activity probably is accompanied by loss of appetite – hence, at least in part, the weight loss during depression and grief. Depressed patients have been found to have low levels of gastric acid secretion (Farr & Lueders 1923).

Increases in gastric activity occur when smelling, seeing, and thinking of food; also when angry, resentful, or impatient. When Tom was frustrated and angered, the gastric mucosa became filled with blood and turned deep red (Wolf & Wolff 1943); similar observations have been made on other patients (Wolf & Welsh 1972). High degrees of gastric acid secretion have been found in hypomanic patients (Farr & Lueders 1923). Increased gastric acid secretion can irritate the stomach wall and cause bleedings or gastric ulcers; there thus might exist a connection of those latter with high incidence of states of anger.

Stomach contractions increase when one is hungry; hunger pangs are their subjective counterpart (Cannon 1929). Stomach contractions also might increase in states of nervousness, if such is a correct interpretation of the sensation of "butterflies in the stomach."

Reversal of the usual direction of stomach and esophagus contractions produces nausea and vomiting. Nausea and vomiting occur as responses of disgust, but may also be caused by nervous trepidation and anxiety. Why this should be so is unclear; neural overexcitation and its irradiation have been advanced as an explanation, analogous to the nausea that accompanies concussions (Dumas 1933).

The colon, according to Wolf and Welsh (1972), can show two kinds of movement: transport movements, which propel the bowel contents to their exit, and static contractions serving to dry these contents. Transport movements can be increased in sudden fright and "petulant hostility" (Wolf & Welsh 1972, p. 451); such enhanced, exaggerated transport movements become outwardly manifest in diarrhea. Increased defecation is a manifestation of fear in rodents; number of fecal boluses is sometimes used as a measure of the rat's "emotionality." Such defecation and excitement diarrhea do not appear to be the same. Sustained hyperfunction of the colon may lead to colonic ulcers. Colonic ulcers, it is said, occur particularly in subjects who markedly restrain pronounced tendencies toward anger and resentment.

Exaggerated nonpropulsive drying contractions are manifest in constipation. Constipation is said to be shown particularly by individuals who outwardly function normally and efficiently with "grim persistence," but inwardly are subject to feelings of sadness, discouragement, pessimism, and mild depression.

Finally, intestinal tone may be decreased, the colon being inactive, relaxed, and delayed, which results in a different form of constipation. Wolf and Welsh suggest that this may occur in depressed subjects.

Urinary secretion is frequently inhibited under fear and stress. Enhanced urination, however, is frequent also in emotional excitement in humans as well as among many animals. Enhanced urination urge also occurs in laughter. Whether these enhancements are due to loss of sphincter control, to increased secretion, or to rebound from preceding inhibition is unknown to this author. In many animal species urination is a consequence of specific excitements, such as sexual excitement, and appears to serve interactive signaling purposes such as territorial marking.

The functions of gastrointestinal activity changes in emotion or under stress appear to be complex. Inhibition of secretions, blood flow, and motility are interpreted by Cannon as regulations with the purpose of maximizing energy supply elsewhere. However, many changes do not fit this interpretation, and in fact the hypothesis of general visceral inhibition in pain, hunger, fear, and rage (see section 3.8) is flatly contradicted by the observations on gastrointestinal activity in anger and sometimes in excitement or fear. It is unclear whether the conditions for this enhanced gastrointestinal activity differ from those for inhibition; nor is it clear why they occur. Rebound has been mentioned as a possibility, as have signaling functions, of which evolutionary remnants might exist in humans; such functions are not likely for diarrhea in excitement, though. Enhancement of gastric activity in anger is interpreted by Wolf and Wolff (1943) as preparation for eating the object of angry attack. The interpretation is unlikely in view of the psychological and neurological differences between angry and predatory attack (Moyer 1971; see chapter 7). Interpretative endeavors are hampered by the fact that neural control of intestinal activity is ill understood. On the whole, activity is maintained by parasympathetic excitation; however, according to Wolf and Welsh, its precise operation in the various movements and the sources of inhibitions of movement are still rather obscure.

Secretory functions

Emotions can cause changes in secretory functions: Activity of the lacrymal glands in weeping is the most obvious instance.

Excitement, nervousness, anger, fear, and severe grief all tend to decrease saliva flow, which results in dryness of the mouth; perhaps all excited emotional states entail this change. Seeing, smelling, and otherwise anticipating appetizing food lead to increased salivation; so does sexual arousal.

Perspiration and urine secretion have been discussed. Sexual arousal by visual stimuli, prose materials, or fantasy, as well as by direct stimulation, causes vaginal lubrication in women; degree of flow appears to be more or less proportional to intensity or directness of stimulation. Anxiety and tenseness inhibit such secretions (Masters & Johnson 1966). Anger is said to increase nasal, vaginal, and intestinal secretions (Wolff 1950).

Pupillary response

The pupils of the eyes not only react to changes in illumination but also to attentional or motivational variables. They dilate upon presentation of novel or interesting stimuli (Sokolov 1963); they also dilate when the subject is paying attention, is concentrating, or otherwise spends mental effort (Bumke 1911). Degree of dilation tends to correspond with degree of interest. Hess and Polt (1960) found the pupils of women, but not of men, to dilate when looking at the photograph of a baby; men show enlarged pupils when looking at a female nude, whereas women do not, or less so. The relationship between mental effort and pupil size can be close. In a study by Kahneman and Beatty (1966) subjects were instructed to remember a string of digits: Pupil size increased with each subsequent digit presented.

Pupils also enlarge in pain, fear, and defensive anger (Cannon 1929). Angry cats show large pupils, as do cats manifesting uncontrolled rage after brain surgery (Bard 1928).

Dilatory responses can probably best be understood as response to alerting stimuli generally (Janisse 1977). Whereas alerting stimuli cause pupil dilation, drowsiness leads to constricted pupils. Tonic pupil size (given constant illumination) is considered to be a sensitive index of alertness or drowsiness (Janisse 1977). Shape and magnitude of pupillary responses – to light flashes, for instance – vary as a function of fatigue (Lowenstein & Lowenfeld 1951).

Pupillary constriction has sometimes been reported as response to unpleasant stimuli: Hess (1972) hypothesized, and found, that pupils constrict upon seeing unpleasant, aversive stimuli (e.g., photographs of skin disease) and dilate when seeing pleasant ones (the babies or nudes mentioned). Pupil size would thus be an index of emotional attitude, in line with tendencies to reject or accept the stimulus. However, differences in pupillary response to pleasant and to unpleasant stimuli have, with few exceptions, not been observed by other investigators; where they have been found, this can be explained by changes in base level (Janisse 1977). Under all alerting and arousing conditions, whether pleasant or unpleasant, the pupillary response appears to be one of dilation (Goldwater 1972; Janisse 1977).

Trembling

Trembling consists of spontaneous oscillatory movements of the limbs and other body parts, leading to chattering teeth, knees shaking or knocking together, shivering movements of the trunk, and severe disturbances in the execution of coordinated movements. It occurs after strenuous physical exercise and in overt excitement; but also in states where tendency toward restless movement is not conspicuous: dejection, grief, passive fear (fear not marked by tendencies for flight), suspense (Luria 1932). It occurs in angry or fearful as well in joyful excitement: Darwin reports his observation of a boy whose hands trembled violently after having shot his first pheasant. Trembling also is a common aftereffect of excitements: After anger, startle, or fear have died down, trembling may persist, forcing the subject to sit down.

The occurrence of trembling under such diverse emotional conditions is unexplained; it probably has several causes. It may sometimes be triggered, as in cold, by extreme peripheral vasoconstriction and then presumably serves to generate heat. It may result from central cerebral interference in motor control, in the manner in which it occurs in neurological disturbances (e.g., cerebellar affections, Parkinsonism; Dumas 1933). Arnold suggests that it may be a by-product of elevated epinephrine secretions; indeed, trembling is one of the consequences of epinephrine injections.

Miscellaneous

Emotional upset can lead to a host of other bodily responses – for instance, to changes in composition of blood and saliva.

A noteworthy response, common throughout the animal world, is that of piloerection: erection of hairs, feathers, or quills, with its human variants of gooseflesh, having one's "hair stand on end," and having one's "skin crawl." Darwin (1872) listed observations on erected hair, in different animal species, in situations of anger and fear. Dumas (1933) noted its presence in extreme terror, illustrating such presence with a photograph of a Chinese criminal being tortured to death. Besides such vivid emotions, gooseflesh can be evoked, for unknown reasons, by such strident noises as chalk dragged across a slate or a fork over a plate. As Dumas remarks, all occurrences of piloerection in humans can be found in excitatory conditions – those that in general tend to evoke sympathetically controlled reactions (to which class of reactions piloerection belongs).

In animals, piloerection has thermoregulatory and interactive functions. As for the latter, piloerection here forms a part of dominance and threat patterns: It increases the apparent size of the animal. Perhaps gooseflesh, in humans, is an evolutionary remnant of such dominance or threat response, although this would not easily explain its evocation by strident sounds, unless such sounds can be interpreted as similar to some primitive warning calls.

3.3. Temporal characteristics of autonomic responses

Little reference has been made so far to temporal characteristics of the autonomic response: temporal stability, response latency, and recovery time.

Temporal stability

Responses may habituate: Response magnitude may decrease upon repeated or continuous presentation of the eliciting stimulus. By contrast, responses may remain stable or even increase in magnitude with repetition or over time. Examples were encountered in the preceding: habituation of components of the orienting reaction; increase in response to repeated presentations of very aversive stimuli; gradual buildup of blood pressure under continued stress.

Within continuous response, fluctuations may occur. Sinus arrhythmia (fluctuation in heart rate) is an example: It is manifest during rest and tends to diminish or disappear under attention and mental effort (Mulder 1980). The same applies to respiration rate. Another example is peripheral vasodilatation, which shows large fluctuations during relaxation, as opposed to dilatation with small fluctuations during movement and constriction with small fluctuations often seen in anxiety (Neumann, et al. 1944).

Response latency

Autonomic variables in general have a relatively long latency, typically on the order of 2 seconds. The various variables possess different characteristic response latencies, in part because some are neurally and others hormonally controlled, and control of yet others is mixed; also, negative feedback plays various roles. Latency is of importance for the phenomenology of emotional experience and is relevant in discussions on the theory of emotion. Emotional experience sometimes has distinctly shorter latency than autonomic response – notably, sensations of the pleasantness or unpleasantness of sensory stimuli (Lehmann 1914). Also, some somatomotor responses are faster than autonomic ones (e.g., the eyelid reflex in startle, perhaps some aggressive responses). Autonomic responses thus cannot be the primary source of emotional experience or the cause of emotional somatomotor response (Cannon 1927).

Of special interest are very long latencies, which sometimes take the form of rebounds. We mentioned the example of steep rise in heart rate in experienced parachutists after touchdown (Epstein & Fenz 1965). Of the same nature, perhaps, are the violent autonomic reactions that surge up after the stimulus event has passed and an appropriate response has been given: the fright and trembling after one has slammed on the brakes or brought the car out of a skid. Such long latencies or rebounds, as said before, suggest the operation of self-controlling, inhibitory processes (Epstein & Fenz 1965; Fenz & Epstein 1968; Ursin et al. 1978).

Recovery rate

The time it takes for a physiological response (EDR, heart rate increase or decrease, etc.) to return to base level is called the *recovery rate*. Freeman and Katzoff (1942) introduced the concept of the "recovery quotient": peak response divided by residual response after a prescribed period of time. Both recovery rate and recovery quotient can be used as measures of response intensity; they probably correlate with peak intensity, but can be expected to have their particular sources of variance.

Recovery rates of given responses vary. Mention was made of very slow blood pressure restabilization after severe stress. Slow recovery merges into persistent, nonreversible changes, like the increased diastolic pressure levels that form part of the "general adaptation syndrome" shown after prolonged stress (Selye 1956).

Slow recovery or a persistently high level can result from high peak intensity and from prolonged stimulation and stimulus-bound increased level; both may result in a resetting of the organism's regulatory mechanisms (Harrell 1980). It may also be caused by inhibition of overt response and/or persistence of threats as appreciated by the subject. We already mentioned the substantial evidence linking diastolic blood pressure increase with "anger in" or suppressed hostility. Mention was also made of Hokanson's studies, in which diastolic pressure recovery rate after harassment was shown to be considerably slower when the subject had no opportunity to retaliate than when he had. Recovery rate was still slow when such opportunity did exist and was used, but high status of the antagonist represented chances of retaliation from the latter's side (Hokanson & Burgess 1962).

Qualitative changes

A response may change over time in quality as well as in intensity. Heart rate deceleration after unexpected stimuli often changes into acceleration: Heart rate response to unexpected stimuli is often biphasic (Graham & Clifton 1966; Graham 1979). Compensatory rebounds, such as faster respiration to make up for having to hold one's breath, provide other examples. Qualitative changes often are produced by the effects of the response itself upon the organism – for instance, by depleting of resources.

3.4. The nature and function of autonomic responses

In section 3.2 a survey was given of the various autonomic changes that can be observed under "emotional" circumstances. The findings reviewed need several qualifications.

Most findings were reported in a form such as "increase in heart rate is observed in fear." Statements like this mean only what they explicitly say: In the given experiments, or under the conditions mentioned, a response is observed to occur in a given emotional condition or under a given type of stimulation. Such statements do *not* mean a number of things they might suggest or seem to imply.

When a given response is found to occur when a given emotion is evoked (presumably, or as somehow verified), this does not imply that that response is invariably related to occurrence of that given emotion. First, the response may or may not occur with that "same" emotion when it is evoked by, or observed in, different conditions. Wolf and Wolff (1943) found enhanced gastrointestinal activity in anger in humans; Cannon (1929) found gastrointestinal inhibition in his enraged cats. Evidently, the anger of a patient treated rudely is not the same anger as that of a cat barked at by a dog. Second, the response of concern may or may not occur in all subjects. Most of the investigations referred to report only average response scores; rarely are data available on the number of subjects who did and who did not show the given response. Some subjects may have shown no response or a response in the opposite direction – something that usually cannot be deduced from variance data. In fact, it sometimes is clear that a given significant average change is produced by just 25% or so of the participating subjects (Plutchik & Ax 1967). Third, the response may be and quite often is common to a wide range of emotional and nonemotional conditions in addition to those studied and reported. A response found to occur in, say, sadness, may not at all be specific to sadness, or even to negative, violent, or emotional reactions. It may be specific to movement, or to attention, or to restraint.

It can be, of course, that no single physiological response is characteristic of a specific emotion, but that patterns of responses are. Patterns indeed exist, and will be discussed in section 3.9. The issue of specificity will be taken up there.

The occurrence of different responses in the "same" emotion can often be understood as the result of different overt response modes (expressed versus suppressed anger, for instance), different response phases (for instance, immediate response versus rebound), and in particular different autonomic response functions. The relationships between autonomic responses and emotional states must necessarily be complex, considering the functional diversity among these responses.

The preceding sections mentioned several different kinds of function that autonomic responses in emotion fulfill or are supposed to fulfill. The first kind of function corresponds to their primary physiological functions: muscular energy supply, metabolism, thermoregulation, energy conservation. Many autonomic responses in emotion can be regarded as part of an "emergency response" to prepare for flight or fight (Cannon 1929). The second kind of function is regulatory with respect to the individual's responses, overt as well as physiological. Restabilization rebounds can be grouped here, but also the autonomic reactions contingent upon efforts toward response suppression and response control. Also, many autonomic responses are contingent upon dealing with the stress rather than with the stressful situation: efforts to continue as usual, anxiety notwithstanding, and the like. Many autonomic responses under, for instance, anxiety probably result from efforts toward such "secondary coping," rather than being part of anxiety response itself. High diastolic pressure in anger likewise may be not an anger response proper, but a suppression response or a being-hemmed-in response, a response to energy mobilization that cannot be discharged. All this, of course, confounds a simple relationship between given emotions and given autonomic responses or response patterns.

The third kind of function pertains to regulation of specific cognitive or motor activities, as distinct from general energy mobilization. Palmar sweating was tentatively explained as serving grasping, climbing, or manipulation; and heart rate deceleration will be discussed as possibly sustaining arousal and attention (section 3.9).

The fourth type of function is interactive, communicative. Reference has been made to possible pheromonal, smell signal, functions in sweating, urination, and defecation and to piloerection as a threat signal. Blushing in particular is a candidate for interactive interpretation; we will return to it. Interactive interpretations of human autonomic responses are distinctly speculative; but, after all, we are animals like others.

The final, fifth, type of function is not a function at all: It is dysfunction. Some autonomic responses may just reflect dysregulation. Persistent high blood pressure after stress is an example.

The autonomy of autonomic variables

Autonomic systems primarily respond in reflex-like fashion to physiological and emotional conditions. They nevertheless are not independent of learned influences and, more specifically, of voluntary control.

Learned influences are manifest most distinctly in conditioning of autonomic responses and particularly in "interoceptive conditioning." In the latter, the conditional stimulus is an internal stimulus – for instance, increase in bladder pressure. If bladder pressure is artificially increased while at the same time peripheral blood flow is increased by immersing the feet in cold water, the first may come to elicit the second (see Razran 1961). By the same means, the subject may come to control some of his autonomic responses: If artificial increase in bladder pressure is preceded by a manometer reading, the manometer reading (and even setting the manometer) may cause such increase.

Operant conditioning of autonomic responses has also been demonstrated. Subjects – rats as well as humans – can learn to increase or decrease their heart rate or the temperature of their left or right hand (that is, increase or decrease of the skin blood flow). They can learn this when such increases or decreases are rewarded or punished – in rats by brain stimulation or shock, in humans by producing feedback on whether the intended change was achieved (*biofeedback*).

Such changes are largely, or entirely, due to skeletal muscular activity: to overt movement or its inhibition, isometric tension or relaxation, breathing control, and the like (Roberts 1978). Skeletal muscular activity can effect these changes, since autonomic variables respond to it: Heart rate increases in response to muscular effort, blood pressure to isometric tension. Isometric tension itself decreases with slow and even respiration. The scope and stability of autonomic changes effected by biofeedback are relatively small and modest (Blanchard & Young 1973). The point in the present context, however, is that such dependence of autonomic responses upon skeletal activity exists and that it constitutes a mechanism of self-control, as well as of suppression or involuntary inhibition of excitement. It must be added that demonstrations of direct operant control of visceral activity (that is, not by way of skeletal activity, or by cognitive means; see chapter 8) as these were reported by Miller and DiCara (1967; Miller 1969) have not withstood efforts at replication and methodological criticism (Roberts 1978).

3.5. Hormonal changes

The sympathetic–adrenomedullary axis: epinephrine and norepinephrine

The catecholamine hormones epinephrine and norepinephrine are secreted into the bloodstream by the adrenal medulla upon sympathetic stimulation. Their actions upon various visceral organs resemble the effects of direct sympathetic action; in fact, impulse transmission from sympathetic nerve to target organ is, for the most part, ensured by norepinephrine.

The effects of epinephrine and norepinephrine are somewhat different from one another. Epinephrine causes increase in heart rate and heart stroke volume and constriction of peripheral blood vessels. Norepinephrine causes decrease in heart rate and stroke volume and vasoconstriction in the muscles. Both produce bronchial dilatation, some increase in respiration rate, a decrease in stomach motility, and (each for a different reason) increase in blood pressure (Wenger et al. 1960). Epinephrine also causes trembling, feelings of being stirred up, and jumpiness (Marañon 1924).

Catecholamine secretion often increases under the influence of stressors: when confronted with taxing mental or physical demands, under threat, and in anger like that of a cat barked at by a dog and hissing in return (Cannon 1929). Catecholamine increase has been observed in subjects receiving electric shocks during vigilance tasks (see Frankenhauser 1975) and in novice as well as experienced parachutists just before jumping (Ursin et al. 1978). As with autonomic variables, catecholamine increase is not linked to unpleasant experiences only. Levi (1972) observed epinephrine and norepinephrine increase in subjects viewing amusing and suspenseful movies; similar findings were reported by

Pátkai (1971) and Trap-Jensen et al. (1982). Catecholamine increase thus appears to be a function of alertness and emotional arousal rather than of quality of emotion. In line with this, catecholamine level decreases in rest and tranquility. It rises with general activity and physical effort, roughly proportionally to the amount of effort involved (Frankenhauser 1975). It may rise to fivefold the resting level or more in states of excitement (this figure applies to epinephrine increase).

Conditions for epinephrine and norepinephrine increase are not the same. Physical effort elevates the level of both, but that of norepinephrine more than that of epinephrine (Elmadjian et al. 1957; see Frankenhauser 1975). On the other hand, excitement tends to have a greater effect upon epinephrine secretion: Whereas hockey players show rise in both catecholamines during play, they show increase only in epinephrine when watching others play. Rise in norepinephrine level without concomitant epinephrine increase was observed in rhesus monkeys put in a restraining chair and subjected to the continuous avoidance task mentioned earlier (Brady 1970; Mason 1975), as well as during conditioned emotional response sessions (unavoidable shock following a warning signal; Brady & Hunt 1955; Mason, Brady, & Tolson 1966). Ursin et al. (1978) observed in their parachutist trainees that norepinephrine rose earlier, in anticipation of jumping, than did epinephrine; also, norepinephrine rise did not diminish with experience, as did increase of epinephrine. Trap-Jensen et al. (1982) found that pleasant excitement (playing a video game) raised norepinephrine but not epinephrine.

These findings suggest that epinephrine increase results from response to uncertainty and from not knowing what to do about the situation; whereas norepinephrine increase corresponds with the mere presence of emotional strain or requirements for alertness, irrespective of hedonic tone or possible coping actions. Ursin et al. (1978) apply Obrist's (1981) distinction between "active coping" and "passive coping" (see section 3.8). Epinephrine might have more to do with the former and norepinephrine with the latter. This hypothesis is supported by the results of experiments in which both uncertainty and possibility of coping action were varied (see Frankenhauser 1975). Frankenhauser and Rissler (1970), for instance, submitted their subjects to four conditions: unpredictable electric shock; shocks some of which could be avoided by the subject's own action; shocks that could all be so avoided; and a control condition in which the subject could relax. Epinephrine level decreased over conditions in the order mentioned: Under unpredictable and uncontrollable shock it was three times as high as in relaxation.

Uncertainty and absence of control are both clearly critical variables. Norepinephrine levels, in contrast, were high during all three shock sessions and remained fairly high in the relaxation condition. It should be added, though, that subjective stress decreased in the same order over conditions as did epinephrine level. On the other hand, consonant with the hypothesis is the fact, reported by Frankenhauser (1975), that men show more elevated epinephrine response to stress than do women; that difference accords with other evidence concerning stronger inclinations toward active coping in men.

It has been suggested that fear engenders an epinephrine pattern of autonomic changes, and anger a mixed epinephrine–norepinephrine pattern (Ax 1953). Funkenstein (1956) hypothesized a difference between overtly expressed anger as primarily a norepinephrine response and "anger in," as well as fear, as primarily epinephrine responses; the hypothesis was based upon individual differences in blood pressure response to mecholyl and epinephrine injections. Some investigators (e.g., Silverman & Cohen 1960) found catecholamine excretion data consistent with this hypothesis. Later studies, however, failed to obtain supporting evidence. Patients with affective disorders do not show differences as expected from Funkenstein's hypotheses (see Mason 1972 for a review). Differences in epinephrine–norepinephrine relationships, as found and as surveyed above, cut across distinctions like that between fear and anger, or between anger overtly expressed versus anger turned inwardly or suppressed. Frankenhauser (1975) doubts that hormonal pattern between emotional states can be distinguished along the lines suggested by Ax and Funkenstein. Differences in catecholamine response pattern rather correspond to variables like active versus passive coping, to uncertainty and to being capable of exerting control. Findings like those of Woodman et al. (1978) have been quoted as supporting the Funkenstein and Ax hypothesis; Woodman et al. found considerably higher norepinephrine response in anticipation of shock in violent criminals than in controls. Obviously, the finding can easily be accommodated by an active coping interpretation.

The pituitary–adrenocortical axis: ACTH and corticosteroids

In response to certain bodily needs, to physical activity, and to stressors of various sorts, the pituitary gland releases ACTH, adrenocorticotropic hormone. ACTH, in turn, stimulates the adrenal cortex to increase its secretion of corticosteroid hormones, among them cortisol. Cortisol, among other things, subserves the liberation of glucose into the blood-stream, and in its turn it inhibits ACTH release. Because of its responsiveness to stressors and its important function in mobilizing energy resources with which to resist stress, ACTH has been called the stress hormone (Selye 1956).

Increase in cortisol secretion, increase in its metabolites such as 17-OH–CS in urine or plasma, and other evidence of enhanced adrenocortical activity have been observed under numerous stressful conditions. Mason (1972) presented an extensive survey of research up to that time. Rats manifest increased adrenocortical activity when their legs are tied together or wrapped in a towel (Selye 1956). In mice, rats, and other animals, adrenocortical hypertrophy results from overcrowding. In mice with experience of defeat in fighting, the 17-OH–CS level increases when they are confronted with other mice. Animals of various kinds manifest such increase when put in new environments, when handled, or when placed in an open field. Rhesus monkeys produce increased plasma 17-OH–CS levels when put in a restraining chair and when exposed to the conditioned emotional response and continuous avoidance schedules. Pharmacological agents that tend to diminish distress, such as reserpine or meprobromate, also lower the cortisol levels under the stressful conditions mentioned (Mason & Brady 1956; Makela, Näätänen, & Rinne 1959).

In humans, similar increases are observed in airline pilots, in soldiers in anticipation of exhausting exercise (Mason et al. 1973), and in bomber crews and parachutists (Basowitz et al. 1955; Ursin et al. 1978). Rise in cortisol level tends to be higher in anticipation of those dangers than in the actual confrontations. Cortisol increase has also been recorded, more or less regularly, in patients upon hospital admission and just before an operation, in students just before a major examination (see Mason 1972), and in parents of children suffering from leukemia (Wolff et al. 1964).

In neurotic and psychotic patients, cortisol levels show strong increase in periods of acute anxiety, distress, or depression; levels tend to correlate with intensity of distress rather than with degree of disturbance or confusion (e.g., Sachar et al. 1963; Board, Persky, & Hamburg 1956). In depression, elevated levels were found particularly in patients who appeared to be more acutely aware of, and more engaged in struggling with, their illness (Bunney, Mason, & Hamburg 1965). Sometimes, though not always, correlations were found between day-to-day changes in severity of depression and cortisol levels (see Mason 1972).

Mason (1972) concludes that cortisol increase is the general and relatively unspecific response to emotional arousal, both of the moderate kind as contingent upon daily events and of the more dramatic kind as exemplified in several of the studies mentioned. Several factors might particularly contribute to intensity of response: novelty and uncertainty on the stimulus side and "involvement" and actively trying to cope as subject variables. In addition, intensity of distress and breakdown are distinctly related to cortisol response intensity.

There are a number of physical influences, such as cold, extreme heat, toxic influences, and surgery, that lead to enhanced ACTH–corticosteroid activity. Selye (1956) considers the ACTH–corticosteroid response to be the general, unspecific reaction to any influence that taxes the organism. Mason (1972, 1975) and Lazarus (1975) argue that hormonal response follows the emotional impact of such influences rather than the influences as such. The physical stressors observed as effective by Selye hardly ever are without emotional meaning. Mason points to the studies of the parents of fatally ill leukemic children to illustrate the importance of psychological factors. Parents who manifested defensive coping styles and who tended to deny the seriousness of their children's condition or its impact upon them responded with 17-OH–CS decrease to acutely distressing information; in this they contrasted with those parents who allowed themselves to be upset. When psychological defenses were taken into account (as assessed by MMPI profiles), correlations between gravity of presented information and corticosteroid level increased considerably (Wolff et al. 1964; Rose, Poe, & Mason 1968).

Two important features of adrenocortical response should be mentioned; both are illustrated in the study just referred to. First, individual differences in both base levels and response amplitude are considerable: some subjects may even respond to stress with corticosteroid decrease. Second, it appears that corticosteroid level and responses can be suppressed and even inhibited in overcompensatory fashion: Decremental response seems to be contingent upon lower-than-average base levels. Individual differences of this nature were observed in helicopter crews during the Vietnam War (Bourne, Rose, & Mason 1967). Inhibition of corticosteroid response is also suggested, according to Mason, by the lower-than-baseline responses that monkeys show after very long series of weekly 72-hour avoidance sessions. After 6 weeks of such sessions, 17-OH–CS excretions during avoidance activity are far below the base levels at the beginning of the experiments and even slightly lower than the levels after the end of the avoidance sessions (see Mason 1972).

Table 3.1. *Hormonal stress pattern*

17-OH–CS increase	Insulin decrease
Epinephrine increase	Testosterone decrease
Norepinephrine increase	Estrone decrease
BEI (thyroid) increase	
Growth hormone increase	

Source: After Mason 1975.

Patterns of hormonal response

Emotional conditions can lead to a host of other hormonal changes: changes in thyroid and gonadal hormones, in growth hormone, in insulin, and in vasopressin (see Mason 1972). For instance, sexual arousal in human males has been found to increase luteinizing hormone and testosterone production (e.g., Laferla et al. 1978). Stress and worry tend to depress the gonadal hormones testosterone, androsterone, and estrone secretions. Outbreaks of hyperthyroidism have often been observed following major life crises or traumatic incidents (see Mason 1972, p. 42). Mason (1975) presents the pattern of Table 3.1, regularly found under adverse conditions, in male monkeys as well as men.

The pattern is interpreted as increase in catabolic (metabolism-enhancing) hormones and decrease in anabolic (energy-restoring) hormones, in line with Cannon's view of the emergency (fight- and flight-supporting) function of bodily changes in emotion. Anabolic hormones tend to show a restorative rebound after the stressful events are over.

Mason gives the above interpretation as tentative. Much is as yet unclear, and complexities arise that perhaps are due to the interactions between the various hormonal responses. In addition, there exist deviations from the pattern. Deviations with respect to epinephrine change have been discussed previously. Gonadal hormones may be increased rather than decreased: There are indications that this is so under conditions provoking anger or otherwise requiring aggressive or competitive response (Mason 1975).

The gross opposition, suggested by Mason, between catabolic emergency response with anabolic depression and anabolic restoration with catabolic depression leads that author to a hypothesis of reciprocal inhibition of endocrine responses.

The above pattern notwithstanding, there is evidence for a functional differentiation of the system involving the catecholamines, epinephrine, and norepinephrine and that involving cortisol. The first generally appears to respond to phasic stressors and efforts, the latter to more tonic ones (e.g., Ursin et al. 1978). The issue is important in that it suggests a differentiation between arousal and activation systems; the point will be taken up further down (section 3.9).

3.6. Electrocortical changes

The electroencephalogram (EEG) of humans and animals at rest shows, at least in its parietal and occipital derivations, the alpha rhythm: relatively regular voltage fluctuations with frequencies between 8 and 13 cycles per second. Under the influence of sensory stimuli (light flashes, buzzers, pinpricks, electric shocks) and upon mental activity requiring attention, alpha blocking occurs. The EEG then shows desynchronization: low voltage, fast and irregular activity, sometimes referred to as beta rhythm. Alpha blocking in response to sensory stimuli starts about 4 seconds after the onset of stimulation, lasts 1–2 seconds if the stimuli are brief, and shows habituation if simple stimuli are repeated. Alpha blocking generally occurs in response to the stimulus variables that elicit the orienting response: novelty, complexity, unexpectedness (Berlyne 1960). In fact, alpha blocking is a regular component of the orienting response.

Alpha blocking is also called the cortical arousal response (Lindsley 1951): It occurs upon stimulation of the brain stem reticular formation. It also occurs in emotional excitement. Startle caused by a sudden loud stimulus leads to desynchronization lasting longer than 2 seconds. The EEG also tends to be desynchronized when the subject is tense and anxious: During medical EEG examinations, alpha only appears when the patient has relaxed. Desynchronization has been observed in various states of excitement: in cats perceiving a mouse, in human subjects when embarrassed (Williams 1939), in children when frustrated by the experimenter (Jost 1941). Desynchronization disappears, and alpha returns, during relaxation (Lindsley 1951) and meditation (e.g., Anand, Chhina, & Singh 1961; Wallace 1970), and under the influence of barbiturates. In ecstatic meditation states, alpha has been observed while the subject had his eyes open; during such states, sensory stimuli may fail to cause alpha blocking.

3.7. Muscle tension and tremor

Muscle tension has already been discussed in the previous chapter (section 2.4). It will be briefly taken up again because it usually is treated along with other psychophysiological parameters and is relevant to the concept of arousal, which will be the concern of a subsequent section.

Muscle tension obviously is involved in the preparation and execution of overt movement; in activities such as resisting upcoming physical impact; and when suppressing unwanted movements or sensations. Tension involved in the preparation and execution of movement generalizes beyond the organs of execution; often, unintended synergistic movements occur, as for instance clenching one's jaws when using scissors. One has to learn to abandon unnecessary tension in dancing, playing tennis, and other activities; one of the effects of learning sensorimotor skills is that tensions in irrelevant muscle groups gradually drop out (e.g., Meyer 1949).

Generalized muscle tension is theoretically important since it has been assumed to be an essential component of "activation" (Duffy 1962, 1972; see section 2.8). It has in fact been proposed as one of the major indices of such activation. The questions thus arise whether a dimension of general muscle tension can be meaningfully distinguished; if so, whether it can be reliably measured; and whether such tension varies systematically with the occurrence of emotionally significant stimuli.

Study of intercorrelations of electromyogram (EMG) measurements, and of such measurements with stimulus variables, has led to various suggestions as to the muscle group yielding the most valid index of generalized tension and thus of activation. Malmo (1959) proposed the frontalis muscle. Eason and Branks (1963) favored the neck muscles since tension in that group covaried with task load even when muscle tension is not needed for the task. Laville and Wisner (1965) found that neck muscle EMG increased progressively during work on a 2-hour precision task in which the neck itself presumably was not involved. Other authors again preferred the chin muscles. Factor analysis of concurrent muscle tension measurements yielded a general factor in which tension in the extremities (e.g., the forearm flexors) showed the highest loadings (Goldstein 1972). The extremities therefore qualify as candidates for producing the best general tension measure.

Measuring generalized tension by means of one or a few measures necessarily is of limited value, since there exist indications of individual response specificity. Different individuals tend to tense up by way of different muscle groups. For instance, subjects with head and neck complaints showed greater EMG increases in head and neck muscles in response to painful stimuli than did control subjects (Malmo & Shagass 1949). Patients suffering from backache show EMG increases in the back region (trapezius and lumbar sacrospinalis, as well as hamstring muscles) in response to a variety of stressors (Holmes & Wolff 1950).

Even if we disregard such complications and assume the presence of a general muscle tension factor and reasonably valid measurement procedures, there remain problems in referring muscle tension to some underlying construct of activation. There exist "dissociations" between different activities that are difficult to reconcile with such a notion. During REM sleep, for instance, lowered muscle tone is accompanied by rapid eye movements – although, granted, this discrepancy may rightly be considered a special case. More important, perhaps, is the consideration that generalized tenseness of muscles that are not engaged in the task at hand is not necessarily nonspecific. Such tenseness may have a well-defined function, more specific than that of manifesting energy mobilization or general readiness for action, as implied in Duffy's activation concept. The frontalis muscle is among those involved in frowning; and frowning, as we have seen, is linked to concentration or mental effort. The neck muscles, as perhaps also those of the chin and forearm, are involved in movement control, suppression of involuntary or impulsive movements, protective crouching, and bracing for upcoming outside forces. "Generalized tension," then, may be indicative of such actions rather than of general, unspecific action readiness.

If generalized tension reflects "activation" (or, at least, somatomotor activation), it should vary meaningfully with stimulus conditions and with other indices of emotion. Indeed, it does. As mentioned, muscle tension varies with mental load and thus, presumably, with mental effort, though not necessarily with performance (Eason 1963). After successful performance, tension tends to drop; after error, tension either drops or remains high for some time (see Goldstein 1972 for a review). Stressful conditions frequently lead to tension increase, as reviewed in the previous chapter. Tension increase is to some extent a function of the subjective amount of stress: anxious subjects tense up more than controls under the same kind of stressful stimulation (see Goldstein 1972).

Tremors are phenomena in their own right; some tremors are produced by autonomic influences or are themselves autonomic responses.

Their increase under conditions of apprehension or, perhaps, excitement generally (Luria 1932) has been touched upon in chapter 2.

3.8. Physiological response patterns

Sympathetic arousal: the emergency reaction

Of the physiological changes discussed before, those elicited by activity of the sympathetic nervous system tend to occur together. The pattern of these changes has been called by Cannon (1929) the "emergency reaction" since the responses concerned can all be considered to serve mobilization of energy for physical activity. They do so either directly or by inhibiting physiological activity that does not contribute to energy mobilization; or else the changes serve optimal sensory functioning.

The responses contributing to the pattern are the following: increase in heart rate and heart stroke volume; increase in muscular blood flow; bronchial dilation; increase in activity of the sweat glands that results in the psychogalvanic skin response; increase in blood glucose level; constriction of the blood vessels in the skin, stomach, intestines, and sexual organs; decrease of gastric and intestinal motility; decrease of saliva flow; contraction of anal and urinary sphincters; pupillary dilation; increase in epinephrine secretion, which in turn triggers a number of the responses just mentioned. In addition, deeper and faster respiration serves to meet increased oxygen requirements. The emergency pattern is also being referred to as "sympathetic arousal" (or, incorrectly, "autonomic arousal"). Sympathetic arousal is supplemented by the pattern of hormonal changes described in section 3.5. The emergency pattern is interpreted as preparation for fight or flight or, in general, for vigorous response to emergency situations. It does so anticipatorily, in view of possible energy requirements to come (Cannon 1929).

The sympathetic arousal pattern has been observed to occur in all forms of excitement: in "pain, hunger, fear, and rage," in which Cannon described it, as well as in sexual excitement and in merriment.

Cannon's interpretation has not gone unchallenged; it should be considered an interpretation rather than a statement of fact. The usefulness of some components of the emergency response can be questioned. Arnold (1960), for instance, argues that epinephrine secretion, by causing trembling and distracting palpitations, harms motor coordination as much as it might improve muscular force or endurance. Also, it is hard to see the advantages of decrease in saliva flow and the resultant dry mouth and speech impediment.

Sympathetic arousal thus is a conspicuous aspect of many emotional responses; and it plays such a central role in much emotion theorizing that, as said, it has been identified with the concept of emotion.

There are two major problems with this identification. The first is the question mentioned before of the covariation of sympathetic arousal and other criteria for emotion; this question will concern us later. The second concerns the meaningfulness of the concept of sympathetic arousal itself, considering the fact that the various parameters mentioned do not always covary together.

Although the sympathetic nervous system tends to respond in diffuse or global fashion, by no means do the various components making up the emergency response always vary together in magnitude or even direction. Correlations between the various response magnitudes tend to be low; a measure of degree of sympathetic arousal based upon any of these therefore necessarily has low reliability; and, moreover, one is at a loss to decide which one to take as a measure. A few examples of these intercorrelations will be mentioned. Ax (1953) obtained average intercorrelations of only .157 between the autonomic response measures in one of his experimental conditions and of only .09 in the other. Sternbach (1960a) found very modest intercorrelations in a variety of situations. Morrow and Labrum (1978) report an average intercorrelation of .15 between six autonomic measures in heart patients with varying degrees of acute anxiety and worry. Eason, Harter, and Storm (1964) obtain nonsignificant correlations between SC, HR, and muscle tension during a combination of mental and bodily effort. It is true that considerable correlations are obtained when intraindividual instead of interindividual correlations are studied – that is, correlations between concurrent measures within the same individual at different moments, rather than the concurrent scores of different individuals (Duffy 1972). Lazarus, Speisman, and Mordkoff (1963) thus found a correlation of .54 between SC and HR in a group of subjects at different moments of viewing a stressful film. Lader (1975) reports intraindividual correlations of .90 between HR and forearm blood flow and of .72 between that bloodflow and EDR. Even so, however, high correlations rarely or never extend over the entire domain of sympathetic variables. Consequently, it is unclear how – by what parameter or parameters – degree of sympathetic arousal should be measured; and thus the meaningfulness of the concept of arousal becomes a matter of dispute.

Several reasons can be advanced to explain the low intercorrelations, while maintaining the assumption of a dimension of general sympathetic arousal. First, the different response systems all have their individual properties. The various responses reach their respective ceilings at different rates and with different stimulus intensities, and they start with different latencies (Davis, Buchwald, & Frankmann 1955). It might therefore be inadequate to measure them all at the same time rather than, for instance, picking the peak of each (Duffy 1972). The various responses may also have different elicitation thresholds and habituation rates (Lazarus, Averill, & Opton 1970).

Second, autonomic variables have their regular physiological functions, which they continue to accomplish when also responding to emotional conditions. Requirements of actual muscular activity, heat regulation, and metabolism may preempt some variables – and may preempt them differentially – according to the circumstances. Moreover, they are not independent but may react to each other's activity; HR, for instance, may tend to slow down as compensation for increases in blood pressure (Duffy 1972).

Third, there exists "individual response stereotypy" or individual response specificity (Lacey & Lacey 1958): Individuals differ in the sensitivity and responsiveness of the various autonomic (and hormonal and somatic) variables. Some individuals appear to respond to any stimulus with blood pressure increase and others with gastrointestinal inhibition (Lacey & Lacey 1958; Engel 1960). Stability over time of such response preferences has sometimes been found, but has not been convincingly established (see Roessler & Engel 1977).

Finally, sympathetic arousal may be overlaid or modified by other psychologically relevant response modes. There may exist "dissociations between systems" or "directional fractionation" (Lacey & Lacey 1970); these will be discussed presently. It is largely a matter of taste whether such directional fractionations are taken to represent variations upon a basic "autonomic arousal pattern" or rather different autonomic response patterns.

The best conclusion appears to be to retain sympathetic arousal as a meaningful concept, referring to the pattern as described by Cannon; which concept, however, is of limited practical value because of the technical problems of measurement. Suggestions exist in the literature for overcoming these technical problems. One could take a weighted sum of the various responses as the arousal index (Wenger & Cullen 1972); or one could take the single maximal deviation from base values:

High arousal is indicated *either* by elevated blood pressure *or* by HR increase, and so on. The value of such solutions is still unclear (cf. Duffy 1972). In view of all this, considering emotion equivalent to sympathetic arousal would appear to be unjustified, and considering sympathetic arousal *the* physiological response in emotional excitement a gross simplification.

There is one sense in which the notion of sympathetic arousal must be confusing, whatever its functional merits. The pattern of manifest autonomic activity never reflects the degree of sympathetic activity per se, but reflects balance between the reciprocally inhibiting sympathetic and parasympathetic systems.

Autonomic balance and parasympathetic responses

The autonomic response pattern shown at a given moment is the re-sultant of simultaneous sympathetic and parasympathetic activity; it can be considered the individual's momentary deviation from "autonomic balance" (Wenger & Cullen 1972). In fact, stimuli that increase sympa-thetic activity tend also to increase parasympathetic activity, only less so. As Sherrington showed, sounds cause HR increase in dogs; upon transsection of the spinal cord, which abolishes sympathetic innervation but leaves parasympathetic innervation intact, sounds cause HR de-crease (after Gellhorn & Loofburrow 1963). Similarly, sham rage causes increase of blood sugar level in cats; transsection of the spinal cord leads to a drop in that level; subsequent cutting of the vagal nerve again abolishes this drop, which demonstrates that it had been a parasym-pathetic response ordinarily masked by the sympathetic one (Gellhorn, Cortell, & Feldman 1941; see Obrist 1981). The interplay between sym-pathetic and parasympathetic excitation is complex, since response changes may result either from excitation of the one or from inhibition of the other. As said, HR increase in tense anticipation results from parasympathetic inhibition; only in true excitement does the sympathetic come in. Vasodilation in the skin, due to elevated temperature or to effort, results from inhibition in sympathetic tone only.

The sympathetic system can be characterized as geared to energy mobilization and to effective dealing with the environment; the para-sympathetic system can be seen as geared to establishing and conserving energy reserves. The systems have been opposed, or juxtaposed, as "ergotropic' and "trophotropic" systems, respectively (Hess 1957; Gell-horn & Loofburrow 1963). From moment to moment there is a shift in dominance by either one or the other, or they may perfectly balance each other; individuals tend to differ in habitual dominance of one of the systems (Wenger & Cullen 1972).

Parasympathetic dominance is found under conditions of rest, relaxation, and calm pleasure and happiness. Early research found pleasurable sensations – pleasant smells, classical music – to be accompanied by vasodilation in the skin, HR decrease, and a slowing down of respiration (e.g., Alechsieff 1907). People are said to be or feel "rosy" from contentment. After orgasm, respiration rate, HR and blood pressure drop steeply (Masters & Johnson 1966). Bagchi and Wenger (1957) found lowered skin conductance levels in yogis during meditation; Wallace (1970) observed decrease in heart rate and respiration rate and increased SC during transcendental meditation; the same was observed for ananda yoga exercises (Ellson, Henry, & Cunis 1977). All this was accompanied by increases in cortical alpha rhythms. Relaxation exercises usually lead to the same changes (Simpson, Dansereau, & Giles 1971); ordinary muscular relaxation does not always produce these results (Ellson et al. 1977).

The preceding observations have led to a hypothesis concerning a difference in response to pleasant and unpleasant emotions. According to this hypothesis, unpleasant emotions lead to sympathetic dominance and pleasant emotions to parasympathetic dominance (Arnold 1970; Gellhorn & Loofburrow 1963). This cannot be correct. For one thing, there exists sympathetic arousal in pleasant excitement: in amusement (see the Levi 1972 and Pátkai 1971 studies with amusing films; section 3.5) and during sexual arousal (Masters & Johnson 1966). For another thing, a variety of parasympathetic responses are manifest under decidedly unpleasant conditions. They have been discussed in preceding sections: increased gastrointestinal activity in anger; increased defecation, up to diarrhea, in fear; falls in blood pressure in startle, fear, dejection, and depression, with voodoo death as an extreme consequence (Cannon 1942). In addition, there exists sympathetic inhibition in unpleasant emotions: blind red anger and angry flushes, blushing in embarrassment and shame.

Parasympathetic response patterns appear, in part, to correspond with passivity: absence of muscular activity, abandoning readiness for such activity, relinquishing focused attention. Such passivity is, of course, noticeable in the calm pleasant emotions, but the connection is not an exclusive one. One would expect sullen resignation to be equally parasympathetic. The sympathetic–parasympathetic opposition corresponds, not to opposition in hedonic quality, but more likely to oppositions in activity or action readiness. Parasympathetic dominance, then, reflects energy conservation, either in pleasantness and rest or in sitting it out under adverse conditions until things have blown over.

Little is known about parasympathetic dominance in violent emotions: fainting from fear or from being startled, vomiting in emotional upset, increased gastrointestinal activity in fear or nervousness. Some of this may be rebound, but not all of it seems to be: not the vomiting, not butterflies in the stomach. They all appear to occur under conditions in which coping action is impossible or unavailable. Such impossibility is paramount during weeping, a parasympathetic response that was interpreted (section 2.5) as the response of acknowledged helplessness. Stomach ulcers that are produced by excessive gastric secretory activity are generated in rats or monkeys receiving uncontrollable shocks, but much less so in rats or monkeys receiving as many shocks but actively engaged in controlling these (Weiss 1971a, 1971b); rats exposed to uncontrollable shocks also defecate more. Uncontrollable situations like random presentation of unavoidable, very unpleasant white noise lead to decreased EDR in human subjects (Gatchel & Procter 1976). Monkeys in the restraining chair show depressed HR and blood pressure during the first 10 trials (Brady 1970). There seems to be a relationship, then, between parasympathetic dominance and inability to respond. Such a relationship is suggested also by the finding that parasympathetic innervation may lead to motor inhibition (Gellhorn 1964): Stimulation of cut vagal nerve is reported to lead to suppression of knee tendon reflex and to outright paralysis. What the relationship means is unclear. Of course, parasympathetic responses also occur in settings that have very little of either passivity or inability to act: sexual response, for instance, erection, and vaginal flow.

Whatever the interpretation of these latter responses, it is probably justified to make a distinction between patterns of parasympathetic dominance as seen in rosy contentment, meditation, or flat despair and the parasympathetic uproars in weeping, fears, angers, and sexual arousal. The first consist of anabolic activities, the second do not. Moreover, it would seem that the latter usually occur within syndromes of sympathetic dominance.

It is the latter type of response that might render a concept of autonomic arousal appropriate and useful. A subject who is shivering and manifesting increased gastrointestinal activity is as clearly in a state of bodily uproar as one who shows purely sympathetic response. *Autonomic arousal* then refers to both sympathetic and parasympathetic deviations from some baseline – perhaps from that presented by balanced para-sympathetic dominance or "peacefulness."

Different emotions, different patterns?

Low intercorrelations between autonomic measures may be due to the fact that different emotions correspond to different autonomic or physiological response patterns.

The issue touches the basic controversy in emotion theory, mentioned earlier. According to Cannon, physiological response in all excited emotions consists of the emergency pattern. He thereby contested the James–Lange theory, which argued that every emotion has its own distinctive pattern. What is the evidence?

It has been found that physiological response is more varied than just degree of sympathetic arousal. It varies with different emotionally significant stimulus conditions; the fact has been referred to as "situational response specificity." Davis (1957) identified different patterns in response to simple sensory stimuli, tactile pressure, warmth and cold, female nude pictures (male subjects), and mild physical exercise. EDR and muscle tension increased in all conditions; HR, peripheral blood flow, and respiration rate differentiated. Wenger and Cullen (1958) recorded 9 autonomic variables under 14 conditions, among them anticipation of electric shock, actual shock, receiving an injection, and cold pressor test (feet in ice-cold water for 1 minute). Each condition produced a different pattern.

However, different response patterns with different stimulus conditions does not necessarily mean that these patterns will generally occur with those conditions – that they represent responses to simple sensory stimuli in general, or to receiving injections in general, for example. More importantly: Different stimulus conditions are not necessarily different emotions.

Few studies have explicitly compared different response patterns in different emotions. Numerous studies, it is true, have investigated physiological response in anxiety, depression, anticipatory fear, or bodily discomfort. However, these studies generally compared the emotional condition with a neutral control, or they compared stimulus intensity levels or levels of experienced intensity. They thus confounded the concomitants of emotional arousal as such, or of intensity as such, with those of the specific emotion under concern. Also, even when different emotions are compared with one another, effects of emotions as such are confounded with those of other variables present, such as degree of attention, anticipation, stimulus unfamiliarity, or bodily movement. Respiration patterns found under amusement may not characterize amusement per se, but laughter, et cetera. Few if any of the studies did investigate more than one condition eliciting a given emotion – fear, or anger, or mirth – so that the various possible response determinants could have been separated out.

Moreover, many studies purportedly studying psychophysiological aspects of emotions have not distinguished between actual presence of a given emotion (say, anxiety) and presence of mere propensity for such emotion in the subjects (say, "anxiety trait"); or they just employed subjects diagnosed as, say, "depressive." Often no effort has been made to ascertain the emotional state at the time of testing when studying anxious or depressive patients or when investigating the effects of supposedly painful, or amusing, or exciting stimuli.

For whatever they are worth, studies that did compare different emotions tended to demonstrate different response patterns in those different emotions; a few of such differences were found consistently. The evidence distinctly contradicts Cannon. It does not necessarily support James and Lange, though. That is to say: Judging from the available evidence, different emotions tend to differ in their physiological response patterns; they do not differ, however, to such a degree and with such consistency that the response patterns could serve to define or identify the respective emotions; nor are the patterns always there when the given emotions can be assumed to be there or are felt by the subject. This applies even to basic emotions (and not only to complex ones like envy or pride), which in fact are about the only ones investigated and to which this survey is therefore confined.

Anger predominantly shows the sympathetic arousal pattern. Repeatedly, however, increased diastolic blood pressure has been found as a distinguishing feature in comparison to, for instance, fear (Ax 1953; and other studies mentioned in the section on blood pressure). A few studies failed to replicate this finding (Lacey & Lacey 1958; Kahn 1966), perhaps because it only characterizes either outwardly expressed anger (Funkenstein et al. 1957) or suppressed anger (Hokanson 1961; Harburg et al. 1973). Schwartz et al. (1981) found increased blood pressure in subjects recollecting angering events when sitting still, but not when moving about. Ax (1953) further found anger, as compared to fear, to manifest a greater number of HR decreases, EDRs, and muscle tension increases. Data on gastrointestinal responses are contradictory (Cannon 1929; Wolf & Wolff 1943). Ekman et al. (1983) found high skin temperature and thus enhanced peripheral vasodilation in anger but not in any of the other five emotions they studied. HR did not differ from that in either fear or sadness.

Fear, when compared to anger, showed greater average SC, more muscle tension peaks, higher HR, and faster respiration in Ax's study, where "fear" means anticipatory fear. Schachter (1957) and Lewinsohn (1956) replicated these findings. Low skin temperature was the only distinctive feature of fear in the Ekman et al. (1983) study; imaginal reliving and adopting fearful posture were the conditions there. True fear often causes enhanced gastrointestinal activity. Tremors were reported by Luria (1932), although they were found to be stronger in pain by Schachter (1957). Increased HR was found in several other studies, together with increased systolic blood pressure, elevated EDR, and decreased saliva flow – the usual sympathetic pattern. However, many studies on anticipatory fear (that is, response to conditioned stimuli signaling aversive stimulation) show decreased rather than increased heart rate (Obrist 1981). Patients with anxiety symptoms sometimes manifest an array of sympathetic responses and muscle tension and sometimes do not (Lader & Wing 1966). Degree of experienced anxiety, in anxious patients, does not correlate with response magnitudes (Morrow & Labrum 1978), or only moderately so (Tyrer & Lader 1976). Startle was found to present the same general picture as anticipatory fear (Sternbach 1960b).

Sadness and *grief* tend to be accompanied by enhanced sympathetic responses (Averill 1969; Schwartz et al. 1981; Ekman et al. 1983; all three studies with imagined sadness or sadness induced by films). Strongly increased SC distinguished imagined sadness from anger and fear in the Ekman et al. (1983) study, and increased blood pressure (*not* SC) distinguished imagined sadness from mirth in the study of Averill (1969), but not in that of Schwartz et al. (1981).

Disgust (imagined or induced by posing the expression) lowered HR in the Ekman et al. (1983) study. Lowered HR distinguished disgust from all other emotions in that study, but, as said, decrease in heart rate is frequent during sensory intake and anticipatory fear under natural conditions.

Distress may, in this connection, perhaps be equated with response to pain. Pain has been observed to increase diastolic blood pressure, as does anger (Schachter 1957), but it often does not elevate HR, as Cannon said it should (Schachter 1957; Lewinsohn 1956), and it may induce tremors and salivation (Sternbach 1968).

Boredom increased HR, EDR, and SC (London et al. 1972).

Happiness, mirth, and *pleasure*: One must agree with Stern et al. (1975), who in their review on "pleasure" complained of the dearth of studies of positive emotions. Whatever there was was nearly all about sex; the situation has not drastically changed.

Averill (1969) and Levi (1972) studied responses of subjects viewing a funny movie, Trap-Jensen et al. (1983) the responses of subjects playing a video game, and Schwartz et al. (1981) and Ekman et al. (1983) the responses of subjects reliving happy experiences. The conditions varied, as did the responses. Averill and Schwartz et al. report considerable HR increase; Ekman et al. low HR. Averill reports elevated skin conductance, both level and response, in mirth as much as in sadness; Ekman et al. differentiate sadness by that variable. Averill also mentions irregular respiration rate resulting from laughter (Ekman's subjects presumably only smiled); respiration might not be too different in crying. Levi finds elevated norepinephrine secretion and further sympathetic signs.

Much of course depends upon what "happiness" refers to: mirth or calm delight. Older studies generally reported parasympathetic dominance in response to pleasurable stimuli (e.g., Alechsieff 1907; Lehmann 1914; also De Jong 1981); so do studies of pleasurable and contented relaxation states (e.g., Brown 1971; Nowlis & Kamyia 1970). Exciting music elevates blood pressure (Steinman et al. 1955).

Sexual arousal patterns are fairly specific in their mixture of sympathetic arousal (EDR, HR) and parasympathetic or sympathetic inhibition symptoms: vasodilation in the skin, increased saliva flow, genital blood-flow, and genital secretions (Wenger et al. 1968; Masters & Johnson 1966).

One may conclude: responses differ. Differentiation is not as consistent or sharp as one might wish, though. No doubt this is due to the relatively small number of physiological parameters used in any one study. But the variability within any one given emotion shows that this cannot be the major cause. Responses may differ sharply from one study to another, or from one kind of "fear" or "pleasure" to another. This need not surprise us. Attention mode may be drastically different in anticipatory fear and diffuse anxiety; activity or activity urge differs drastically in mirth and in calm pleasure. Parameters such as these may be expected to strongly influence, or even determine, physiological response.

Functional variations in physiological response

Considering the information from the preceding subsections altogether, it becomes apparent that physiological response patterns correspond to the functional requirements of dealing with the environment rather than to different emotions. This is only to be expected. Physiological response in emotion, in Cannon's view, is functional for preparation of active, energy-requiring response. Other modes of dealing with the environment – other modes of activity or activity control, or of coping response – can be expected to correspond to other physiological response patterns, or to variations within some given pattern. In other words, physiological response can be expected to show directional fractionation systematically related to stimulus and action requirement variables. To the extent that such variables are correlated with given emotions, physiological response is correlated to those emotions; but many of these variables may be expected to cut across emotion classifications. There is calm joy and active joy, there is rigid and mobile fear, there is active and blocked or inner-directed anger, and so forth.

A major example of a functionally specific and directionally fractionated response pattern is the orienting response, the response to the collative stimulus variables novelty, unexpectedness, and complexity. The orienting response consists of several of the usual sympathetic components – galvanic skin response, peripheral vasoconstriction, pupil dilation – together with some specific features: vasodilation in the forehead, brief suspension of breathing, and turning the eyes and head toward the source of stimulation (Sokolov 1963). In addition, HR decelerates unless "defensive" HR acceleration overrides it or cuts it short (Graham 1979).

Lacey and Lacey (1970) observed HR deceleration as part of the response to tasks requiring attention to external stimuli: detection, vigilance, and reaction time tasks. Tasks involving mental effort (e.g., mental calculation), by contrast, induce strong HR acceleration. Attention to external stimuli thus produces directional fractionation. Lacey and Lacey interpret the HR deceleration in terms of an "intake-rejection" hypothesis: The organism seeks to facilitate intake of stimuli when the stimuli prompt it or the task requires it, and it seeks to reject unpleasant or (in the case of mental effort) distracting stimuli. HR is supposedly involved in such intake-rejection regulation: It is supposed to influence cortical arousal, by way of HR effects upon activity of the brain stem's reticular formation; high HR might dampen it, and low HR facilitate it (heart rate might do so because it influences carotid artery pressure, which has been shown to influence reticular activity in the directions indicated; see Lacey & Lacey 1970).

Whatever the mechanism, Lacey's hypothesis is interesting for several reasons. First, it brings the functional viewpoint to directional fractionation: Variations in physiological response reflect variations in coping requirements. Second, the content of the hypothesis relates HR change to a general functional process, that of attention regulation (Lacey & Lacey 1978).

Whether the particular hypothesis is correct is another matter; evidence is conflicting (e.g., Cacioppo 1979; Carroll & Anastasiades 1978; Elliott 1974). Obrist (1981) has produced evidence that HR decrease, in attention to external stimuli as well as in anticipatory fear, is linked to suppression of somatic responses such as eye movements. It is part of a response mode that he refers to as "passive coping": waiting for and enduring and attending to stimuli. The HR decrease results from parasympathetic vagal activity. The pattern is different from the response mode that constitutes readiness for physical activity or actual activity itself and in which parasympathetic activity is suspended, with moderate HR increase as a result. It is different again from the response mode of active coping which shows sympathetically controlled heart rate increase not coupled to somatic activity. By *active coping* Obrist means tonic readiness to act upon an event. For instance, sympathetically elevated HR is observed when a subject can sometimes avoid an aversive stimulus; it is not observed when he never can or always can; it is also observed in mental concentration. Whether HR in a given situation is sympathetically controlled or not can be inferred from whether beta-blocking agents do or do not decrease it. Active coping evidently is the action readiness condition of Cannon's emergency response.

The main point in the preceding is: There exist different physiological response patterns; these patterns are tied to the functional requirements of action readiness mode and/or attention regulation. There are of course more of such patterns than those mentioned, and quite obvious ones. That of actual physical effort is one, in which peripheral vasodilation is coupled to HR increase and thus keeps blood pressure within bounds; others are those of sexual excitement in its various phases.

Blushing

A few words may be devoted to blushing, since it is both a conspicuous and frequent and an ill-understood pattern.

Blushing as it occurs in embarrassment probably is caused both by inhibition of sympathetically controlled vasoconstriction and the release, by the sweat glands, of a substance called bradykinin, which has strong vasodilatory effects (Folkow & Neil 1971). Oddly enough, blushing appears to be confined to a limited skin area: the face, sometimes the neck and shoulders, in rare instances the upper chest. It has been asserted, in fact, that blushing is confined to exposed body surfaces; the blush may spread if the chemise is removed; experimental controls have been lacking.

Blushing is sensitive to self-awareness of the response or to its anticipation to an extent unknown in other autonomic responses: Fear of blushing considerably enhances it, as do remarks by other people. "You blush?" often makes a blusher blush.

Because of the restricted localization, blushing cannot be regarded simply as vasodilatory response, as, for instance, Dumas (1933) does. Also, its occurrence is very much confined to social situations. Blushing occurs in shame and embarrassment and, in general, when caught in some act the outside world might think reprehensible. It also occurs upon becoming the focus of attention, particularly when this gives rise to ambivalence: when one is the object of erotic attention to which one is not entirely indifferent; in timidity; when one is surprised by some friendly gesture or when receiving praise; in former times, in modesty. True enough, one may blush in solitude. "Several ladies, who are great blushers, are unanimous in regard to solitude; and some of them believe that they have blushed in the dark" (Darwin 1872 [1965, p. 335]). Even then, however, judgment of oneself by oneself or by others seems invariably to be involved (Darwin 1872). Perhaps not all occasions of blushing are of this judgmental nature; there exist angry flushes. Such flushing, however, may not be the same thing as blushing; perhaps angry flushes are just vasodilation, and perhaps they do not spread in the way blushes do. Also, it is possible that the angry flush occurs when some judgment is involved: perhaps flushing from anger is contingent upon insults or slightings.

In view of the importance of the social, judgmental factor in eliciting blushing, one might be tempted to view blushing as an interactive signal: The blushing person indeed becomes more conspicuous. Blushing might, for instance, be an appeasement or endearment signal – hence its occurrence in coyness as well as shame. Darwin observed that dark races also blush. The blushing of blacks, I am being assured, is hardly noticeable even to other black people, and no great fear of blushing is said to exist among them. This might be considered an objection to interactive explanations, at least those that consider blushing a visual signal (it might still be an olfactory one).

Darwin's own explanation is that attention directed at autonomic changes enhances those changes. Blushing, presumably, is originally elicited by worry concerning one's outward appearance; the usual evolutionary mechanisms, generalization and the change from effects of attention to automatism, explain its occurrence under judgments of various sorts. The explanation is not convincing because it involves too many speculative steps; also, it does not explain why judgment by others is so potent a triggering circumstance.

Perhaps a clue is provided by the ambivalence mentioned above, which seems to be present in many blushing situations. The person who blushes when being flirted with does not respond in kind; nor does she or he become angry, though: She or he is not even indifferent. Similarly for blushing when receiving praise: One enjoys it, but does not consider it deserved; or one is annoyed, but still not angry. "Modesty" has the same structure: There is attention received and humility that keeps the attention at some distance.

Shame and embarrassment may not be states of ambivalence; still, they do have something in common with ambivalence. Shame is caused by some act that should have been left undone (or done so as not to be noticed). The same holds for embarrassment. In all instances of blushing, then, there seems to be an action tendency that is stopped, blocked, or suppressed. Blushing thus could be a response of sudden inhibition of some tendency to act. Why this should become manifest in vasodilation, however, remains obscure.

3.9. Arousal, emotion, and physiological change

The concept of arousal

In the literature on emotion one frequently encounters the concepts of arousal and of activation, in a sense that embraces the three response systems: autonomic arousal, electrocortical arousal, and behavioral activation. Arousal is treated as a unitary dimension along which the state of the organism varies, from deep sleep over wakefulness via alert attention to high level of excitement. The three systems supposedly participate about equally in intensity variation along this dimension. On this supposition it is meaningful to talk about *the* level of arousal (or activation) of the organism at a given moment. Level of activation, in this sense, has been considered a major dimension of emotion (Woodworth & Schlosberg 1954), an essential constituent of emotion (Mandler 1984), or the principal aspect of what is meant by emotion (Duffy 1962, 1972).

The notion of general arousal or activation hinges upon the degree of covariation of the three systems, just as the notion of autonomic arousal hinges upon intercorrelation between autonomic variables and that of somatomotor activation upon intercorrelation of muscle tension measures. The key questions are, therefore: Can the three systems be regarded as one system, and can the state of this system be measured meaningfully?

About a certain interrelatedness of the three systems there can be no doubt. Stimulation of the reticular formation usually produces EEG desynchronization as well as behavioral activation: lifting the head, pricking up the ears, pupillary dilation, and eye movements. Increase in muscle tension usually goes hand in hand with increased skin conductance level (Freeman 1948). Emotional excitement usually, or often, is manifest in desynchronization, autonomic arousal, and behavioral activation (expression, activated behavior, increased muscle tension). Yet, the dissociations that occur are considerable. EEG arousal and autonomic responsiveness can be uncoupled. Sternbach (1960a), for instance, found no correlation between the Wenger index of autonomic (sympathetic) activity and percentage alpha activity in resting subjects. Duffy (1972) concludes that the relationship between arousal pattern as indicated by EEG and by autonomic measures or somatic response is a gross one.

Dissociations between various autonomic measures and somatomotor activation are frequent. Lader (1975), while finding high intraindividual correlations between autonomic variables (.70–.90), observes low correlations only between EMG on the one hand and blood pressure, blood flow, HR, and EDR on the other (.13–.40). Obrist (1981) extensively discusses "cardiac–somatic uncoupling": high HR with no muscle movement in "active coping."

At the level of individual differences there even exist inverse relationships between somatic and autonomic activity. High sympathetically reactive children, for instance, tend to be overtly, emotionally, under-reactive (see Hare 1976 for a review).

In the same way as explanations could be found for dissociations between autonomic variables, explanations can be found for dissociations between the systems under discussion. For instance, inhibition of overt movement sometimes slows down recovery from autonomic excitation; we encountered this kind of interaction in connection with anger expression and blood pressure, and we will encounter it again in inverse relations between autonomic response and facial expression (section 4.6). Also, motor restlessness may be triggered by low cortical arousal in order to elevate the latter, such as might be the case with hyperactive children (see Venables 1976); this, too, complicates correlation between the three systems. Further, inhibition and self-control evidently upset such correlation, even if the three systems are functionally tied together.

However, the source of dissociations seems to be a more profound one. For one thing, the concept of general arousal or activation is hazy because it fails to specify the processing stage at which it should be assessed. That is to say: What exists as activation, as excitation, at one level need not be manifest as activation or activity at another level. HR decrease can be due to enhanced vagal activity; habituation of attentional arousal probably is due to active suppression of reticular activation by hippocampal activity (Lindsley & Wilson 1975; see chapter 7), to give two illustrations.

The major reason for dissociations, however, is simply that there are functionally distinct systems. Cortical arousal is one thing, with its own function and its own regulation; behavioral activation another; autonomic response another, or set of others, again. Within overt behavior and autonomic response, there are different subsystems that need not be completely interdependent. There can be behavioral urge with great power but without much excitement, as in psychopathic impulses; Mailer's (1979) reconstruction of Gary Gilmore's murders provides a convincing illustration of murders committed in a fashion that was bland, with feelings that were bland, but where the source of behavior was clearly emotional, namely, the murderer's girlfriend having said she was going to leave him. At the other end, there can be overt movement or autonomic arousal without action tendency, impulse, or activation, as when lifting a heavy stone.

Descriptively, then, postulating a unitary dimension of arousal does not appear to be justified. Labeling a subject "aroused" is ambiguous. Descriptively, at least four kinds of "arousal," of sources of activity of some sort, should be kept separate: sympathetic (or autonomic) arousal; attentional arousal or "increased capacity for perceptual analysis" (Broadbent 1971); behavioral activation; and electrocortical arousal. Functionally, too, assumption of a single arousal continuum appears unjustified. A distinction between phasic and tonic response mechanisms is suggested by physiological (HR, hormonal) and behavioral data. A further distinction between phasic arousal, tonic activation, and voluntary effort appears necessary on neurophysiological grounds (Pribram & McGuiness 1975). Evidence for several distinct neurophysiological mechanisms underlying phenomena of behavioral, autonomic, and cortical intensity will be discussed in chapter 7.

Emotions and physiological parameters

As to the relationship between emotions and physiological parameters, it has become clear that the terms *arousal* and *sympathetic arousal* insufficiently characterize patterns of autonomic response, respiration, and hormonal response. It has also become clear that different emotions are not systematically related to different physiological response patterns. Rather, physiological response patterns are modes of physical action preparation and action control, which are related in somewhat loose fashion to the action readiness modes that define the emotions (see section 2.8).

Physiological response patterns are energetic and regulatory aspects of the way in which action readiness as defined in chapter 2 translates into actual physical readiness. They thus are correlated with, but not specifically linked to, the various action tendencies – to protective tendency, opposing tendency, antagonistic tendency, and so on. They are of a different functional kind, and a different level of generality. Anger, for instance, is defined by antagonistic, obstacle-removing action tendency. That action tendency usually involves enhanced activation and readiness for overt action; it more often than not involves active coping, in Obrist's sense. But it can exist without them; and neither activation nor readiness for overt action defines angry action tendency or is specific for it.

Various physical readiness and control modes have come under discussion in the preceding: sensory attentional arousal; defensive or expectant readiness, passive coping; active coping, readiness for action deployment; behavioral inhibition and voluntary forms of behavioral control; consequences of interruption; deactivation. Each of those appears to correspond to a distinct physiological pattern or parameter. Each of those, also, might be systematically related to stimulus or task parameters, to what we will call, in the next chapter, "situational meaning components": novelty, for instance, or controllability, or uncontrollability, or uncertainty about response consequences. To repeat: They will not be systematically related to the various action tendencies that define the basic emotions; nor even to the activation modes, since the activation modes are defined more at the level of relational intent, whereas the action readiness modes meant here are defined more at the level of plans for actual behavioral implementation.

Emotion and autonomic arousal

The fact that emotionally significant events – events relevant to the individual's welfare – elicit physiological responses of course is one of the major facets of emotion, and it is one of the main reasons for emergence of the emotion concept.

A large number of these responses can be subsumed under the heading of "autonomic arousal," meaning that they constitute departures of responses over some baseline. The heading is meaningful as long as it is realized that it refers to some crudely computed rough total of autonomic changes – to the rough fact that at some moments the body hums and buzzes and at some other moments it does not, or less so.

One might define emotion by such autonomic arousal; as said, this was done by Wenger, Schachter, and Mandler. We chose not to do so, because behavior suggestive of action readiness change, as well as experience involving such change, appear to come closer to the reasons for using the word *emotion* and its variants. Of course, it is not very important which set of phenomena is called *emotion*. What is of importance is to determine the relationship between occurrence of autonomic arousal, occurrence of action readiness changes as manifest in behavior and in subjective awareness, and occurrence of stimuli eliciting the latter.

The evidence favors the view that responses accompanied by autonomic arousal form a subset of the responses consisting of some mode of action readiness change. There is a definitional side to this statement, since calm happiness and peaceful relaxation are here included among the modes of action readiness changes. There is also a more empirical side to it, however. Sometimes, to all evidence, there are no signs of autonomic arousal while subjects say they are, or feel, happy or anxious or angry. It is as well to take such subjects at their word, as long as their behavior does not contradict them. Emotion can be there, it appears, without physiological upset of any note, according to the criteria of subjective experience and expressive behavior. The major argument, in this regard, consists of the merely moderate correlations between autonomic indices and behavioral ones reported in this chapter and those between autonomic indices and subjective experience to be mentioned in the next.

It can nevertheless be argued that emotional responses accompanied by autonomic arousal differ drastically and are of a different class from emotional responses not so accompanied. This, of course, is true; but it merely says that there exist excited emotions and calmer ones.

At the same time, the distinction between excited and calmer emotions points to a satisfying formulation of the relation between emotion and autonomic response. Excited emotions, emotions showing marked autonomic response, are emotions contingent upon some situation with the features of difficulty or urgency: difficulty in achieving or escaping, urgency to do something about what happens.

That is to say: Autonomic response accompanies those changes in action readiness in which actual response preparation is involved – changes in action readiness that go beyond mere tendency, mere plan invested with control precedence, or mere behavioral interruption. And it accompanies such action readiness changes only when action is not expected to run off smoothly or with plenty of time. Autonomic response, in other words, is part of action readiness change at some stage of actual execution or preparation of actual overt (or cognitive) response, under conditions that such response is felt to need extra resources or adjustments.

The above constellation is perhaps illustrated most clearly in those emotions that might be viewed as problems for the present conception: the conception that emotions are changes in action readiness. Meant here are emotions like mere upset, mere nervousness or excitement, which show little or no overt behavior or few or no signs of being set for such behavior. As argued earlier (section 2.8), such emotional states are characterized precisely by presence of action readiness but inability to actually plan coping action. There is urgency but considerable difficulty. These emotions represent states of passive coping, which are states with distinct relational sense. They consist of alertness and mere nonspecific readiness to act if the situation might change, both of which possess pronounced action control precedence.

We thus conclude: physiological response, autonomic arousal included, is part of action readiness mode. It can be considered as offering logistic support for the actions that that readiness is readiness for; or, in the event, it embodies withdrawal of such logistic support. It is thus one of the major aspects of emotion, but it does not define emotion. That of which it is part, action readiness, does. It is a part that on occasion may be absent or negligible.

3.10. Consequences of physiological response

The physiological aspects of emotional response have behavioral consequences. The most noticeable of those are the discomforts produced by autonomic upset – palpitations, sweating, dry mouth, being out of breath – and the disturbances caused by that upset – disturbances of thought by being distracted or too hot; or motor behavior by trembling and sticky clothes, and so forth.

Of often longer duration is fatigue. Autonomic response and, in particular, hormonal response are highly energy-consuming. Hormonal response may last considerably beyond termination of emotional stimulation and of overt, or direct autonomic, response; hormonal response, much more than energy expenditure by physical exercise, accounts for the exhaustion after violent or protracted emotional interactions.

Prolonged emotional impact tends to produce widespread and persisting physiological changes that may even be irreversible. Protracted consequences can result from brief but very intense events, as well as from prolonged stresses. They are consequences both of the emotional response itself and of the subject's efforts to control his emotional response while coping with the events.

The physiological consequences of severe stress have been described by Selye (1956) as the "general adaptation syndrome." Three phases are distinguished in the development of the syndrome: alarm phase, resistance phase, and exhaustion phase. The alarm phase corresponds with sympathetic arousal; Selye's description emphasizes release of ACTH and corticosteroids. Enduring and very intense stresses may cause such response to persist for an indefinite period after cessation of the eliciting events. Also, they may disrupt physiological regulation and induce a state of shock: severe fall in blood pressure and in heart rate.

The effects of persistent autonomic arousal, hormonal activation, and dysregulation include weight loss and loss of resistance against infectious and other disease, loss of appetite with further weakening consequences, development of gastric and peptic ulcers (e.g., Brady et al. 1958), enlargement of the adrenal cortex, and degenerative processes in the spleen, pineal gland, and lymph glands (Selye 1956).

The resistance stage, according to Selye, consists of stabilization at increased physiological levels. High blood pressure can develop into hypertension (Harrell 1980), with concomitant risks for further cardio-vascular disturbances. Cortisol production remains at some higher level, while appetite and body weight may return to normal. In the meantime, however, resources may be depleted and permanent organ changes produced.

Psychologically, brief intense trauma and prolonged stress can both produce the syndrome of "nervous exhaustion," formerly called the "hyperesthetic–emotional syndrome" or "neurasthenic syndrome" and forming part of what Horowitz (1976) described as "intrusion states." Notable features are sleep disturbance, irritability, loss of concentration up to an inability to concentrate for more than a few minutes, restlessness, trembling with concomitant difficulty in motor coordination, fatigue, jumpiness, low startle threshold, vulnerability to anxiety attacks, depressed mood, and weeping spells. To what extent these psychological changes and the physiological changes of the exhaustion stage are coordinated in time, and which are their causal relations, is unknown to the present author.

4. Emotional experience

4.1. Theoretical viewpoints

What does emotional experience consist of? There are two main questions. First: What in general, is the nature of emotional experience; what distinguishes it from other modes of experience and enables the subject to identify his or her experience as "emotional"? Second: What, specifically, is the nature of the different emotional experiences; what distinguishes the experience of one emotion from that of another and enables the subject to identify his or her experience as one of anger, sadness, and so forth?

Three types of theory have been advanced to answer these questions. They have been called central, peripheral, and cognitive theories, respectively. They correspond to three ways in which the nature of emotional experience can be viewed.

Central theory

Emotional experience can be considered a distinct kind of subjective awareness; different emotions correspond to different varieties of this kind of awareness. Although sensations other than those specifically affective ones may participate in emotional experience (for instance, body sensations), the specific subjective emotional feeling forms the core. By being irreducible to sensations, such experience must be a direct outcome of corresponding brain processes; it must be of "central" origin.

The viewpoint was the current one in the "psychology of mental content" dominant around the turn of the century, and its main proponents were Wundt (1903) and Titchener (1908). The viewpoint was essentially shared by Cannon (1927), as it probably is today by many neurophysiologists: Emotional feeling, that particular glow and warmth, is added to mere perception by the activity of the brain.

176

In the central view, overt response follows upon brain activity that produces experience; response thus follows upon experience (see Fehr & Sterns 1970). For most theorists, response was considered not only to follow upon, but also to be elicited by, that experience. This, at least, was how Wundt and his contemporaries saw it, as common sense still does. Emotional experience is, in the central view, assigned a causal role with respect to response: We run and tremble because we feel afraid.

Peripheral theory

Alternatively, emotional experience can be considered to consist of body sensations; it can be considered to consist of the feedback from autonomic and behavioral responses made. Emotional experience, in this view, comes from the periphery and from response. We are afraid because we run and tremble, as the catch phrase ran that summarized the theories of James (1884) and Lange (1885). Emotional experience is relegated to the role of mere epiphenomenon: Since it follows response, it cannot have caused that response. Response itself, according to James, follows directly the "perception of the exciting fact."

Emotional experience thus is considered to correspond to body sensations; different emotional experiences correspond to different patterns of such sensations. True enough, for James emotional experience never was entirely peripheral. The awareness of pleasantness and unpleasantness was for him as irreducible and central as it was for Wundt (Lehmann 1914). The point has faded into the background in most discussions, as has the entire notion of hedonic quality in more recent versions of peripheral theory.

Cognitive theory

Emotional experience can also be considered to consist of cognitions or to contain cognitions as an essential ingredient. Experience of fear may be considered to consist of the awareness of a frightening or threatening event; experience of anger may consist primarily of awareness of an offense. Cognitions may explain the difference between the different emotional experiences.

Of course, emotional experience cannot consist of cognitions only. Additional constituents must be assumed. The additional constituent might consist of peripheral feedback. Such indeed is the conception of Schachter (1964) and of Mandler (1975, 1984), for whom that peripheral feedback comes from autonomic arousal response. I feel afraid because I feel bodily upset and attribute this to some frightening event. In other variants of cognitive theory, cognition is not about events but about one's own behavior. According to "self-perception theory" (Bem 1972): I feel afraid because I feel aroused and happen to behave in fearful fashion.

Cognitive theories of this kind are curiously incomplete. They beg the question of what emotional experience consists of, since emotion words recur in the explanation. The theories do not specify what "frightening" events or "angry" behaviors are. In fact, the theories do not endeavor to explain experience, but merely the labeling of one's own state or response.

Other kinds of cognitive theory diverge from the above in two ways: first, by including the "central" experiences of pleasure and pain, or of well- being, in the analysis and second, by endeavoring to specify what makes the cognitions emotional (that is to say, angering, frightening, etc.) cognitions. The theories of Lazarus (1966) and Arnold (1960) and many other current approaches, including the present one, go in that direction; so did the classical approaches of Descartes (1647) and Spinoza (1677).

4.2. The investigation of emotional experience

Methods of investigation

The only direct approach to experience is that of introspection or, more generally, self-observation; the reasons for the distinction will become clear presently. Self-observation has been developed into systematic procedure by controlled stimulus presentation and standardized report instructions. Report can be standardized by means of questionnaires, checklists, and rating scales. Standard questionnaires have been developed for the assessment of different emotions such as degree of anxiety (e.g., Spielberger, Gorsuch, & Lushene 1970), anger (Spielberger et al. 1983), depression (Beck 1967), and general sense of well-being (e.g., Andrews & Whitey 1976). Other questionnaires measure several mood states or mood dimensions simultaneously – for instance, the Multiple Mood Adjective Check List (Nowlis 1966), the Profile of Mood States (McNair, Lorr, & Droppleman 1971), and the Multiple Adjective Checklist (Zuckerman & Lubin 1965).

Self-observation can be combined with objective experimentation, by systematically varying the sources of information available to the subjects. Examples are the measurement of changes in felt anxiety under varying conditions, such as the gradual approach of a dangerous event (Epstein & Fenz 1965), or of differences in felt emotions with varying degrees of spinal injury (Hohmann 1966).

Elements of experience

Analysis of emotional experience has been approached with the procedure of classical introspection. In that procedure, subjects are presented with some stimulus – an odorous substance, the sound of a hammer striking metal, a word, or a picture of an accident – or are asked to call up some emotionally charged memory (Bull 1951). The subjects are instructed to describe their experience analytically, in as elementary terms as possible, and to carefully report sensations, mental images, or other mental content as well as the development of the experience in time.

It was concluded from these introspection studies that affective experience contains three kinds of constituents: elementary "feelings," body sensations (visceral, kinesthetic, and pressure sensations), and ideas associated to the stimulus. Elementary "feelings" form the core characteristic that differentiates affective from nonaffective experience. According to Wundt (1903), Titchener (1908), and others, "feelings" are a basic, irreducible kind of mental element. They cannot be analyzed in terms of the other kinds of mental elements, sensory sensations, and images (and "thoughts," imageless [*nicht-anschauliche*] mental contents that were admitted by other investigators such as Bühler 1907).

"Feelings" differ from sensory sensations, images, and thoughts in a number of properties. They presuppose the presence of sensations, images, or thoughts; that is, they presuppose some object the feeling is about. They have the property of subjectivity: They are experienced as one's own subjective response, rather than as asserting a property of the object. They are evaluative: They imply acceptance or nonacceptance of the stimulus or of the experience itself. They cannot be localized in space; they cannot be objectified, that is, referred to stimulus properties, and they are independent of the sensory modality of the sensations or images evoking them. They are evanescent when attention is directed upon them (Titchener 1908; Alechsieff 1907).

At the time, the issue was hotly debated whether "feelings" (in this technical sense of the word, as elements of experience, and in which sense we will continue to put the word in quotation marks) indeed constitute a distinct class of experience. Wundt and Titchener thought so; others did not. According to these others, "feelings" could be reduced to body sensations. Pleasantness, they argued, is nothing but "bright pressure" in the chest and unpleasantness "dull pressure" in the abdomen (Koch 1913; Nafe 1924). These sensations themselves might be the result of muscular adjustments, preparing approach and withdrawal movements (Beebe-Center 1932).

Lehmann (1914) argued that this could not be so, since reaction time of affective experience, upon presentation of smells or other stimuli, was faster than that of physiological or other bodily response. Also, the introspective descriptions carry overtones that go beyond the purely sensory; even those of the body sensations concerned carry such overtones. Terms used by the subjects – *bright* versus *dull, light, smooth, alive* versus *leaden, dead, hard, constraining* (Nafe 1924) – clearly split into positive and negative ones; they were applied to pleasant and unpleasant experiences, respectively. Arnold (1960), in a careful review of this debate, concludes that the evidence favors the hypothesis of "feeling" as a distinct, irreducible kind of experience. The experiences have clear links to acceptance or nonacceptance of the stimuli. Those links appeared in the very same introspective studies. Thus a blindfolded subject feeling cold metal said: "It became very unpleasant and repulsive, and I wished you would take it away" (Conklin & Dimmick 1925); another: "When I say, 'pleasant,' it doesn't stand for anything more than 'I would smell it more if I could'" (Young 1927; both quoted in Arnold 1960).

"Feelings," then, constitute a class of experiences sui generis. The class comprises different experiences. According to Wundt, "feelings" can vary along three dimensions: pleasantness–unpleasantness, ("hedonic quality"), excitement–calmness, and tenseness–relaxation.

Elementary "feelings," said Wundt, combine into complex ones. Emotions (*"Affekte"*) are composite consciousness structures consisting of complex feelings together with body sensations and associated ideas. Different emotions are characterized by the specific time course of change of the composing elementary "feelings," along each of their three dimensions, and by the type of composition and succession of the feeling composites.

Dimensional analysis

An entirely different approach to the structure of emotional experience consists of analyzing similarities and differences between emotional

Table 4.1. *Mood dimensions: Nowlis (1966)*

Aggression	Social affection
Anxiety	Sadness
Surgency	Skepticism
Elation	Egoism
Concentration	Vigor
Fatigue	Nonchalance

states, or between the meanings of words denoting emotional states. Such similarities and differences suggest the presence of underlying dimensions of experience.

Nowlis (1966) developed a "Multiple Mood Adjective Check List" (MACL) consisting of 33 adjectives selected from a large pool of emotion and mood terms. In a mood checklist, subjects are asked to check each item that applies to their mood state of the day; answers are given on a 5-point scale, for instance from "no" to "very." In Nowlis's study, correlations were computed between the items, on the basis of their being checked concurrently. Factor analysis of the correlation matrix produced 12 dimensions, which are listed in Table 4.1. The dimensions are unipolar. That is, no substantial negative correlations were obtained; "elation" and "sadness" did not truly exclude each other, and so for other opposites.

Several studies of the same general kind have been conducted, each having somewhat different sets of items and producing varying numbers of dimensions. Lorr, Daston, and Smith (1967), for instance, found 8 dimensions. However, considerable overlap is obtained with respect to the nature of the dimensions identified, differences in item sets and selection procedures notwithstanding. Sonneville et al. (1985), for instance, collected all mood and emotion terms from a Dutch dictionary and presented a checklist containing the 231 items found to a group of subjects. Cluster analysis of results led to a reduction to 100 items and, after presentation to a new group of subjects, to a final list of 60 items. The 10 dimensions represented in the latter list are given in Table 4.2 (in English translation, arranged to correspond with Table 4.1.). The similarities with Nowlis's set appear to be considerable.

Some additional differentiation in the mood structure can be obtained by special attention for subdomains. Thayer (1978a,b) investigated the "activation" area. Beyond confirming most of Nowlis's dimensions, he found the dimensions "sleep" and "calm" for Nowlis's "fatigue," and "vigor" and "excited" for Nowlis's "vigor," thus demonstrating the existence of several distinguishable mood dimensions in the activation

Table 4.2. *Mood dimensions: Sonneville et al. (1981)*

Angry	—
Anxious	Depressed
—	Irritable
Elated	Arrogant
Conscientious	—
Tired	Indifferent
	Timid

domain; Sjöberg et al. (1979) confirmed the distinction.

Mood scales have been validated, to some extent, by comparing different populations (for instance, anxious vs. nonanxious patients), the effects of drugs (e.g., Nowlis 1970), physical effort and time of day (Thayer 1978b), and the like. Scores on some dimensions differ in these comparisons, whereas others do not, which is as it should be.

Evidently, then, mood states can be analyzed in terms of a small number of basic components. They can be considered to consist of such components, with some moods representing instances of only one of them and others being blends. The same might hold for emotions. Bartlett and Izard (1972) asked subjects to rate each of a number of emotional experiences, as indicated by name, in terms of the presence of the eight "fundamental emotions" hypothesized. "Joy," a fundamental one, not surprisingly rates high on "joy"; "anxiety" appeared as a blend of interest, distress, and fear; "depression" as a combination of distress, fear, and hostility (Izard 1972). Plutchik's (1980) approach is rather similar. Subjects were asked to indicate, for each of a number of emotion words, which two or three of eight "primary emotions" composed the emotion concerned. "Guilt" was found to consist of sorrow plus fear, "love" of joy plus acceptance.

It is not clear what these studies by Bartlett and Izard and by Plutchik demonstrate. Evidently, subjects obediently utilize the set of basic emotions they are offered; but this does not prove that the "complex" emotions can be considered blends of simpler ones. What is offered to the subjects as simple is treated by them as simple, and what is offered as complex they cannot but treat as complex or as blends.

Whatever the merits of these studies with respect to emotion complexity, they beg an important question: The basic emotional experiences are left unanalyzed. They do not provide insight into what the experiences of joy, fear, interest, and so on consist of. Are these experiences unanalyzable "qualia," like "red" and "green"? That is indeed what they appear to be to Plutchik and Izard.

Analysis can be pushed further, though. Wundt, as will be remembered, suggested that "feelings" vary along the three dimensions pleasantness–unpleasantness, excitement–calmness, and tenseness–relaxation. It is conceivable that each emotion, even each simple one, is located at a unique point in this three-dimensional space, or in a space of different dimensionality. It is also conceivable that each emotional experience is fully defined by such a location. A number of investigators have indeed taken this position.

Block (1957) presented his subjects with 15 emotion words, which were to be rated upon the bipolar 7-point scales of Osgood's semantic differential ("good–bad," "active–passive," "weak–strong," etc.). Most of the variance of the ratings was accounted for by two factors, pleasantness–unpleasantness and activation. Plutchik (1980) and Fillenbaum and Rapoport (1971) reanalyzed Block's data and found that the emotion names could be arranged along the circumference of a circle. Opposition on this circle circumference represents polar opposition of emotions, such as fear and anger or joy and grief. The structure was rather similar to that obtained by Schlosberg (1952) with judgments of facial expressions, where the two dimensions were those of pleasantness–unpleasantness and attention–rejection.

Lorr, Daston, and Smith (1967) and Lorr and Shea (1979) found their mood dimensions to be intercorrelated and to admit of a partial circular ordering. Russell (1980) obtained similar and consistent results with a variety of procedures. Sorting emotion words into eight preestablished categories yielded a circular ordering of these categories, if categories showing highest overlap were put in adjacent positions. The ordering was the same as that obtained by having the words placed directly upon a circle's circumference and as that derived from ratings upon the two dimensions of pleasantness–unpleasantness and degree of activation. It was the same, again, when higher-order analysis was performed upon the dimensions obtained from a mood inventory of the type of Nowlis and McNair et al.

The many dimensions in the various mood studies, indeed, appear not to be independent of one another. They show relationships that could be explained the way Russell did in his study. It is true that mood dimensions obtained from checklists tend to be unipolar rather than bipolar; the phenomenon, in fact, is quite a research issue (see Lorr & Shea 1979; Russell 1979). However, unipolarity to a large extent is an artifact of checklist format and therefore does not conflict with the major dimensions being bipolar and producing circular ordering. The circular ordering may be somewhat too simple. Daly et al. (1983) found evidence in support of a conical rather than a circular model, as had Schlosberg (1954) before them for facial expressions. The vertical axis in this model is intensity or activation, again in agreement with Schlosberg.

Still, all is not well. Dimensional analysis does not truly represent emotional experience in a satisfactory manner. Intuitively quite different emotions, like anger and fear, occupy the same position in two- or three-dimensional plots. Quite different principles, namely cognitions, have to be invoked to explain these anomalies (Russell 1980), which more or less brings the analysis back to where it started.

In fact, whether analysis of emotional experience, as that of Izard and Plutchik does, remains at the level of basic categories – joy, sorrow, fear, and so on – or is pursued toward Wundtian dimensions, it leaves one dissatisfied. Both kinds of analysis do so for quite similar reasons. What, in Izard's and Plutchik's analysis, constitutes the specific experience of anger or fear? What, in Russell's analysis, is the nature of the cognitions responsible for the experiences of emotions occupying the same place in the dimensional plot? Dimensional analysis is unsatisfying for an additional reason. The dimension values do not truly explain the experience. "Distress" would appear to be more than high degree of activation plus unpleasantness, and "fear" more than unpleasantness plus moderate activation. One could not reconstruct the experience if only the dimensional values were known. Something essential appears to be lacking.

Descriptive analysis

Rather than ask the subject to introspect or to rate his feelings in terms of a set of emotion labels or dimensions, one might simply ask him what he experienced when he was angry, happy, and so on, and what he means when describing himself with such words. The answers to such questions are of the kind that novelists produce and that are obtained in autobiographical reports such as those of psychotic patients (Kaplan 1964) or in interview studies like those by Parkes (1972) with widows, Rowe (1978) with depressives, or Hite (1976) on sexual emotions.

Descriptive information can be analyzed systematically, when transformed into questionnaire format. Davitz (1969), in an original and valuable study,* obtained detailed accounts of the emotional experiences

---

*The present author at the time wrote a rather critical review of this study. He made an error of judgment.

Table 4.3. *Clusters: Davitz (1969)*

Activation	Comfort
Hypoactivation	Discomfort
Hyperactivation	Tension
Moving toward	Enhancement
Moving away	Incompetence/
	dissatisfaction
Moving against	Inadequacy

of 30 subjects: Each subject was asked to recall some experience of each of nine emotions and to describe these experiences as fully as possible. The 270 descriptions were broken down into 556 statements, which were then transformed into a checklist. Fifty new subjects checked off that checklist for each of 50 emotion words. In this way, "definitions" were obtained of each of these 50 emotions, the definitions consisting of the statements checked frequently for that word. As an example, some of the statements considered applicable to "grief" were the following (numbers in parentheses refer to percentage of subjects who checked that statement for that emotion): "I can't smile or laugh" (56); "There is an inner ache you can't locate" (48); "There is a sense of regret" (54); "There is a sense of longing" (46); "There is a sense of being incomplete, as if part of me is missing" (40); "I feel choked up" (50); "There is a sense of loss, of deprivation" (84); "There is a sense of disbelief" (68) (Davitz 1969, pp. 60–61).

The statements drawn from the original accounts fall into a number of categories, not all of them present in the previous analyses; apparently, emotional experience is richer, more diversified than suggested so far. The statements refer to expressive movements, inner feelings, attitudes toward events and toward implications concerning those events ("regret," for instance), relational notions ("incomplete," "part of me is missing"), cognitive attitudes ("disbelief"), and body sensations. As with other questionnaire studies, the frequencies with which the statements were checked together in defining the given emotions were analyzed and the correlations were submitted to a cluster analysis. Table 4.3 lists the 12 clusters as labeled by Davitz. The clusters are not independent.

Factor analysis produced two dimensions, yielding three emotion classes. The first dimension represents the opposition between pleasant and unpleasant emotions; the second splits the latter into, roughly, the fearful and the angry ones (moving away versus moving against). Inspection of content suggested to Davitz four bipolar aspects of emotion: activation, hedonic tone, relatedness (moving toward, away, or against), and competence.

As with the previous analyses, reduction to basic dimensions involves information loss: Specific emotions do not appear merely to represent combinations of basic dimension values. Descriptive analysis may provide the full array of constituents of emotional experience. It thereby allows insight into the nature of cognitive and perhaps other components that are part of emotional experience, in addition to the general facets identified by dimensional analysis.

4.3. The nature of "experience": reflexive and irreflexive consciousness

Critique of introspectionist analysis

The search for the constituents of emotional experience has produced two major conclusions. First: Experience is composed of elements of various different kinds, each irreducible and sui generis – "feeling" is one of these kinds and is characteristic of affective experience. Second: "feelings," or the mental complexes in which they participate, have the property of "subjectivity." Affective or emotional experience is a kind of awareness ascribed by the subject to himself and occurring, in some sense, "within" him.

These conclusions are colored by a premise that underlies the search. Experiences in general are considered "mental contents," kinds of entities coming and going upon the stage called consciousness. That premise and thus the search for constituents of experience have been criticized by Brentano (1874), and by Köhler (1929) and Sartre (1934) (and others) taking their cue from him. Introspection involves a specific mental attitude that creates the mental contents as described, says Köhler. Sensations are its products (see also Gibson 1966), and so are "feelings." This is the reason why, in the beginning of this section, introspection ("classical introspection," as in the investigations reviewed) was distinguished from self-observation generally. In introspection, attention is directed "inwardly"; the mode of mental operation is analytical.

The very notion of mental contents and of experience as a collection of conscious qualities or elements is the product of this mental attitude. The analytical mental attitude has important consequences. The relationships between the conscious elements are lost. More importantly: The external object of consciousness is lost. In introspection, the notion disappears that consciousness involves the act of taking cognizance of something. The notion also disappears that every consciousness includes a kind of assertion about that something. Perceptual awareness, for instance, asserts external existence of its object: It asserts that the object can be approached or handled or inspected. Imagination, by contrast, asserts the object's absence or nonexistence; and so forth. These assertions form part of consciousness, although they are not objects of it, when perceiving or imagining. They are implicit in perceived affordances (Gibson 1966) and in readiness or unreadiness to act.

The notion of "object of consciousness" is important and enlightening. Introspection is an act of consciousness that has awareness as its object, and not the object that was intended in the first place. In other words, introspection involves reflexive awareness, or "reflexive consciousness," as Sartre called it. And that is not the natural form of emotional experience.

One of the major consequences of reflexiveness is a transformation of awareness and the creation of subjectivity, as described above. The "me" who does the becoming aware becomes part of awareness, rather than merely being its condition or theoretical point of reference. "I know that I am perceiving X" takes the place of "There is X."

Another major consequence of introspective reflection, as said, is loss of the relation between subject and object. The experiencing subject is floating in the mist of his experience, and isolated from an outer world with which to interact. The loss is evident in the way experience is treated in dimensional analyses, as well as in introspectionist analysis: It is the relationship with the world that is lost when anger is described as unpleasantness plus high activation.

The distinction between reflexive and irreflexive experience has important consequences for the conception of experience generally. In reflexive experience, awareness itself is the object of attention. It is thus reduced to an object: to content, or to a mere fact of consciousness. It appears to consist of discrete "feels," qualities, perceptual images, or whatnot, rather than of phenomena – that is, experiences with sense and significance for the subject that embody assertions about the experienced object. Irreflexive consciousness should be described in terms not of contents, but of those of objects intended, and of acts of consciousness that intend.

Irreflexive experience: situational meaning structure

The distinction between reflexive and irreflexive experience clarifies the nature of emotional experience. Emotional experience, in its more direct manifestations, is not conscious of itself. It is not a "subjective state." It is, as Sartre argues, primarily a perception: a mode of appearance of the situation, whether truly perceived or merely thought. Emotional experience is perception of a certain kind, to be specified later; different kinds of emotional experience are different kinds of perception. Emotional experience is "objective," in the sense that it grasps and asserts objects with given properties. Irreflexive emotional experience also, by its very nature, is "projective": The properties are out there. These properties contain the relationship to the subject: Emotional experience is perception of horrible objects, insupportable people, oppressive events. They contain that relationship implicitly: the "to me" or "for me" dissolves into the property.

The phrase to catch the meaningfulness involved is that emotional experience consists of the perception of situations rather than of stimulus events. Situations may contain a focus, as in the examples given, or they may not: One may be confronted with barren emptiness; one is hemmed in on all sides, without ways of escape; one is confronted with a situation that does not yield, even to the most empathic appeals; and so on.

Such description of emotional experience has intrinsic phenomenological merit. More important, perhaps, is that it permits ascribing emotional experience to animals and young children and that it accounts for experience in such self-forgetting states as ecstasy. In those organisms, and in such states, experience may be considered pure perceptual awareness without a trace of reflexive awareness. Experience is glued, as it were, to its object, coinciding entirely with apprehending that object's nature and significance. In this fashion, McDougall (1923) once supposed a breeding hen to perceive an egg as a "never-too-much-to-be-sat-upon-object," and so the experience of desire in adult humans primarily is that of perceiving a never-too-much-to-be-fondled-child, or a never-too-much-to-be-kissed-girl (or boy). Calling this "having the subjective experience of desire" may come as a surprise to many, or as an afterthought.

The notion of irreflexive experience is that of awareness without awareness of itself, without some supervisor inspecting it. Such a notion is not a product of phenomenological considerations only. Similar notions have been developed from an entirely different angle, namely the study of modes, or levels, of consciousness. Hilgard (1977) introduced the concept of variable modes of cognitive control, in connection with hypnotic phenomena. During hypnosis, a subject may receive impressions that he simultaneously knows and knows not of. Upon hypnotic suggestion of deafness, he may deny hearing anything, behaviorally not showing any reaction, but in automatic writing report hearing as in the normal state.

Experience during low cognitive control is what some investigators, in noncommittal fashion, merely call "information processing" and what others call "unconscious experience." In fact, irreflexive experience in ecstasy, or in animals, might tempt one to use that latter anomalous expression. Zajonc (1980) indeed uses the term *unconscious* in connection with discrepancy between the information processing demonstrably involved in affective impressions and the lack of reflexive knowledge of the information processed; the discrepancy meant will be illustrated presently.

Reflexive experience admits of degrees, without, for the most part, becoming true subjective awareness. A subject usually is part of his own awareness; however, he then plays this part more as condition of experience and subject of action than as subject of experience. "I feel I am running up against a wall," "Nothing interests me any more," "I ran out of ways to handle this situation," "I feel in control" and "I feel proud" are, as far as reference to the self is concerned, linguistic formalities rather than descriptions of experience.

It is true that some emotions do presuppose the self as constituent of awareness: pride, shame, guilt feeling, and anxiety when understood as awareness of one's powerlessness (Sartre 1943, after Kierkegaard); but here the self is object of experience ("I admire I who has done that deed"); the experience itself still is not subjective, or not necessarily so. Note that all examples can be rephrased in perceptual terms, with the self appearing only in the last ones: "There is an impenetrable barrier," "There is nothing of interest any more," "The situation is desperate," "The situation as a whole is approachable and yielding," "There is an act that increases the value of me."

Whereas emotional experience can be described as mode of appearance of the given situation, this situation cannot be turned around. Not every mode of appearance is emotional. Delineations may vary, according to the inclusiveness of one's categorizations. Roughly speaking, emotional experience corresponds to a mode of appearance involving "demand characeristics" (Lewin 1937). Demand characteristics, again roughly speaking, refer to the "valence" (again Lewin's) of the situation as a whole: whether it is attractive or aversive or merely "demanding." Efforts toward more specificity will be presented in the next section. We will refer to such a mode of appearance of situations as *situational meaning structures*.

The situation as it appears to the subject, and toward which or away from which his behavior is directed, is called the *object* of emotional experience. It is important not to confuse the object of emotion with its cause. *Object* refers to a datum of irreflexive experience (or to one of behavioral observation). *Cause* refers to explanation, to reflexive analysis, which may or may not also be a datum of experience. It is not such a datum in morphine-induced euphoria, which still has a delightful world as its object. Even if a cause is an object of experience, object and cause (the eliciting stimulus event) need not coincide. If someone is angry because he has been ill-treated, he is angry at the other person and not at that person's acts.

Emotional experience often gives no clues as to its causes; different causes may produce an identical experienced object. A given situation may appear as threatening because of the dangers it entails, or because the subject lacks strength and competence even in relation to an innocuous event. Depression may be caused by loss or by drugs, which both may render the world empty of objects to strive for. Experienced threat or experienced barrenness of the world do not differ for their being justified or not.

The distinction between cause and object implies that the object, the perception of situational meaning structure, cannot be the cause of emotional experience, but *is* emotional experience. It may be meaningful to ask someone why he thinks someone else a horrible person; it is not meaningful to ask why he detests a horrible person. Experience of serious loss *is* grief; otherwise it is no experience of loss, or of its being serious.

Such emotional experience, however, itself appears to be the cause of something. It motivates or causes emotional behavior. One will recall the issue referred to in section 4.1, concerning the causal relation between emotional experience and emotional behavioral response. It is nonsense, said James (1884), to consider emotional experience the cause of such response. We are afraid because we run: How could running be elicited by subjective feelings of unpleasantness, tenseness, and excitement? Rather, James argues, running is elicited by the "perception of the exciting fact." That perception, of course, is what is being discussed

here. The causal issue appears to resolve itself upon recognition of irreflexive, perceptual experience. Such experience does cause response:
The terrifying bear, the serious loss, the horrible persons do precisely
that. The terrifying bear motivates flight, the serious loss causes loss of
motivation.

Reflection

Reflexive consciousness, in Sartre's study of the emotions, has two components that should be kept separate: turning awareness into subjective
experience, in the sense described, experience with conscious representation of the self as experiencer; and occurrence in experience of the self
in its relation to intended objects. "I want to smash him in the face"
may be read, or felt, as "I have the experience of wanting to . . . ," or as
"I am ready for the desired situation of him being slapped in the face,"
as a promise yet unfullfilled. The first we will call true reflexiveness, the
second self-awareness. True reflexiveness is involved in introspection;
some measure of self-awareness is present in most experiences of an
adult human being.

Even so, every reflection involves an activity of taking stock. It is an
activity distinct from the activity that is taken stock of. This holds with
respect to action or its preparation, as well as with respect to the apprehension of situational meaning structure. Experiencing an event as
horrible is different from categorizing one's response as one of horror,
and even more so from knowing what makes it horrible. Slapping someone's face (which can be called an "act of consciousness" since the action
must be prepared and the other must be hit) is different from observing
that one slaps his face, and why, and how it is done. Reflection and the
reflected result form two quite different processes.

There is no reason why the results of the two processes should correspond. Taking stock may be faulty, and it may err in its endeavor to
get hold of the features that constituted the irreflexive experience and
that actually motivated and guided behavior. It may err in assessing that
the mode of appearance is called "horrible," or that the state is called
"horror." It may also err in assessing the intentional properties of action – concluding that the action meant inflicting pain rather than punishment, for instance. Reflection usually involves acts of categorization.
Also, it usually involves inference and reconstruction: whether one did
think him horrible; why one did so; what precisely the action readiness
was aiming at. These processes may utilize other information than that

immediately at hand; justifying the assessment "horrible" requires analysis that was not involved in forming it.

There is ample evidence that such processes result in discrepancies between categorization and original inputs. Nisbett and Wilson (1977) have given an extensive review of experiments in which manipulations with stimuli, conditions, or instructions modified the subjects' affective judgments and in which these subjects did not realize what caused the modifications or attributed them to other causes than the true ones. An experiment by Zajonc (1980) further illustrates the viscissitudes of reflexive cognition. Subjects were presented with nonsense figures or syllables; different stimuli were presented with different frequency. Liking for these stimuli, as subsequently rated upon a 10-point scale, correlated with prior frequency of presentation; estimates of that prior presentation frequency correlated with actual frequency to a significantly smaller extent, and under some conditions not at all: the discrepancy between reflexive knowledge and information processing mentioned earlier in this section.

Labeling, naming one's own emotion, talking about it, and justifying it involve attribution processes, as has been argued by cognitive theorists (Schachter 1964; Mandler 1975; Weiner 1974; and Bem 1972; among others). This does not imply that these processes are involved in emotional experience, nor that such processes necessarily underlie emotional behavior. They may be of influence when situational meaning structure is indistinct, inarticulate. They may also be of influence when there are pressures toward reflexive categorization and justification. Interpretation and inference generally are effective in perception mainly when stimulation is impoverished or has to be justified (cf. Neisser 1976). They have not much influence when information is aplenty.

The results of reflexion, of course, themselves constitute experience. Categorizing one's own state has effects upon behavior. Saying "I am afraid" justifies avoidance more than mere awareness would. These points lead to discussions of the experience of the apparent reality of events and of the ambiguity of experience, which will only be briefly touched upon toward the end of this chapter.

Forms of emotional experience

Irreflexive experience, then, is not the only mode of experience, and reflexive experience is not necessarily what we called subjective experience. Awareness can take stock of one's state or one's relation to the environment without, on the one hand, losing itself in perception of situational meaning structure and, on the other hand, without losing the relationship with the self or with the environment. Neither "There is something horrible" nor "I am upset by X" nor "I want to flee from X" need dissolve into disembodied body sensations or feelings floating in consciousness, as these are generated by classical introspection.

Emotional experience can take three major forms: awareness of situational meaning structure, awareness of autonomic arousal, and awareness of action readiness. The three modes are correlated with the three sources of information: the environment, autonomic response, and both readiness for and feedback from behavioral response. Through all three modes of experience runs the attribute of hedonic quality. In addition, emotional experience in any of the three modes may, or it may not, gain depth by the emotion's "significance."

The three modes usually occur together; and they occur together with the significance they engender. Emotional experience usually is made up of all these: the three modes, hedonic quality, and significance. They can also be said to form the constituents of full emotional experience.

4.4. Emotional experience as experience of the situation

Emotional experience, first of all, is experience of the situation. Experience of the situation, of significant objects, significant goals, and significant absences, makes up a large part of spontaneous descriptions of emotions. To Parkes's (1972) widows, grief is being left behind and alone, living without a point, in a world devoid of objects of true interest, and it is having to carry out tasks heavy with pointlessness.

Situation refers to more than the event that elicits the emotion: to the loss, the threat, the achievement, or whatever. It refers to everything that event carries with it or around it. It includes the potentialities of the situation, to the extent that these affect the person; it includes what is incomplete in gain, remains in loss, or is glimpsed concerning the future. How the situation looks to a person depends as much upon that situation's inherent properties as upon those of the person himself. The overpowering nature of an event is complementary to the person's powerlessness, the painfulness of an event to the person's vulnerability, the accessibility of an object to the degree to which the person feels he can grasp opportunity. Relevance for action and response to action, actual or potential, are etched into the perceptual world, in its "barriers" and "open spaces" (Lewin again). As said, to that perceptual world the subject himself may belong as an object: His value and his competence are, in his own eyes, etched upon him, in pride and shame and loss of self-confidence.

Situational meaning structure, then, can be considered to comprise three kinds of elements: cognitions of what the situation does or offers to the subject, or withholds from him, or might do or offer or withhold; cognitions of what the situation allows him to do, prevents him from doing, or invites him to do; and evaluations of whether the various outcomes are desirable or not.

Cognition and emotion

Of course, this discussion of experience of the situation is a discussion of the importance of cognitive factors in emotion. That importance was emphasized by older writers like Spinoza and by Sartre and is emphasized again in current cognitively oriented psychology. It is emphasized on two counts: Cognition is a determinant of emotional response, through processes of "appraisal" (Arnold, Lazarus), "interpretation"(Schachter), or "meaning analysis" (Mandler); and it is a constituent of emotional experience. The appraisal process will be discussed in the next chapter, which is concerned with the causal role of stimuli and cognitions. Here, cognition is being considered from the second, phenomenological angle: as a constituent of emotional experience.

The role of the cognitive consitutent of emotional experience is drastically different from that assigned to it by Schachter and the other attributional theorists. Awareness of the situation is emotional, not by virtue of being linked to something else, such as arousal; and it is emotional not because it serves the subject to explain his arousal. It is emotional by virtue of the situation being meaningful for the subject, and by virtue of that situation's particular meaning structure. The situation is perceived as meaningful because it contains demand character and because of its other action-relevant features that make it represent obstruction, irretrievable loss, or some other event category. By virtue of these features, inherent in the cognitions themselves, are these cognitions emotional and do they form what we call situational meaning structures. The cognitions contain direct links to calls for action and to perceived control precedence.

How can that be? We will be very brief at this point. It can be because cognitions as elements of experience are not necessarily mere representations or mere images. They are references to readinesses or necessities or possibilities to act, and to pains and pleasures actual or forthcoming.

Situational meaning structures and emotions

The hypothesis in this analysis of emotional experience is that different emotions are characterized by different situational meaning structures. This applies to emotions distinguished by name: Situational meaning structure is one of the cues by which the subject distinguishes and names his emotions. It also applies to emotions distinguished by mode of action readiness, since situational meaning structure is what elicits or motivates the latter.

Each emotion corresponds to a different appraisal – a different situational meaning structure – and is characterized by it. The hypothesis has been brought forward, in particular, by Arnold (1960) and Lazarus (1966; Lazarus et al. 1980) and can be found in several cognitively oriented clinical approaches, notably that of Beck (1971, 1976). One and the same event can give rise to a variety of emotions in behavior and in experience, depending upon how it is appraised, what aspects are emphasized or focused upon or overlooked – that is, depending upon the situational meaning structure of the particular moment. If a situation of danger is seen as one of threat that one doubts can be countered, it produces fear; if as one that is a willful obstruction, it produces anger; if as a challenge that can be met, it produces enthusiasm and eagerness. The influence of subjective assessments upon the kind of emotion elicited and the influence of slight variations in the context of the events in fact form the main reason for using the notion of situational meaning structure rather than of stimulus pattern for describing what motivates emotional behavior.

Different emotions correspond to different situational meaning structures. Different situational meaning structures map onto different emotions and thus onto different modes of action readiness. This correspondence thesis, it is true, meets with a complication. The complication is due to the fact that the situational meaning structures of events that stretch out over time manifest major and stable aspects as well as variable and incidental ones. The major and stable ones determine intentional structures that, like the meaning structures that motivate them, stretch out over time. Loss of a dear one dominates the mind and robs life of its major interest for an extended period. The variable and incidental aspects participate in shaping actual action readiness. When loss is, at a given moment, perceived from the perspective of its being something irrevocable, it induces sorrow and weeping; when it is perceived from the perspective of its being a condition that ought not be so, it stirs anger and protest. It may even not be focally perceived at all, and any other emotion may be evoked, but still that emotion unfolds within a wider context of unstable interest due to nagging emptiness.

Co-occurrence of major and stable situational aspects and variable and incidental ones causes confusion in talking about one's emotions or those of someone else. Response to the major and stable aspects is called "grief," whether the precise response to full structure including variable aspects is that of sorrow, anger, or despair. The confusion – grief causes sorrow or anger – of course is precisely the same as that discussed earlier in connection with emotion definition by object or by action readiness mode.

The relationship between situational meaning structure, as labeled, and action readiness change thus is not always strict. It is, however, always intimate. A given kind of action readiness change – abandoning striving, helplessness, in the case of grief – if the "logical" response to the major and stable features; and therefore that kind of action readiness change (grief, in fact) is the most "typical" response to grief.

The present hypothesis of correspondence between situational meaning structures and emotions requires that, for every different emotion as distinguished either by name or by action readiness mode, a unique situational meaning structure can be specified. It should be possible to present, for every emotion, a corresponding description of how the world looks to the subject. The descriptions should make clear when and why a given emotion rather than another is experienced by the subject or is identified by a spectator.

The above requirement of course cannot be really met. For one thing, emotion words have shifting meanings, for a given person as well as from one person to another. For another thing, emotions have not been explored systematically from this angle, although some of the older literature, Spinoza in particular, comes close. Still, plausible descriptions can be construed. Information to be used for such descriptions is of various sorts: analyses in the philosophical literature, which contains penetrating discussions of specific emotions (Scheler 1923 on love is a good example); self-reports of literary and psychological origin, as in clinical studies of grief or depression; and experimental and observational studies of eliciting conditions (e.g., Hoppe 1931 on pride; Dembo 1931 on anger; Hebb 1946 on fear; Sroufe & Waters 1976 on amusement).

Although eliciting conditions are not situational meaning structures, they of course hang closely together.

Description of situational meaning structures for the various emotions has theoretical value in that it renders intelligible why and when a given emotion occurs. Also, those descriptions provide a basis for accounting for transitions between and similarities among emotions. Transitions occur when one aspect of situational meaning structure changes. When, for instance, the idea of personal causation of some loss arises, sorrow changes into anger. Similarities between emotions can be supposed to derive from partial identity of situational meaning structures. It can be predicted that intuitive similarity of emotions and similarity of situational meaning structures correspond.

Description of situational meaning structure also has practical implications: Under depression, anger, or anxiety, given cognitive structures must be present. Descriptions may serve as heuristics in the search of what, for this individual, corresponds to each meaning structure aspect, and why that aspect is perceived in the event. In that vein, situational meaning structure analysis is in fact applied in cognitive behavior modification (e.g., Beck 1976), as well as in the practice of psychoanalytic therapy.

Some examples will be given to show what kind of description is meant.

Description of some situational meaning structures

Fear has been called the "sense of impending evil" (Aristotle, cited in Krause 1961) and "an inconstant sorrow arising from the idea of something past or future whereof we in some respect doubt the issue" (Spinoza 1677 [1979, p.187]). The components mentioned are threat, uncertainty about the issue or about the ability to cope; the uncertainty goes both ways, since evil issue is not certain either.

There exist many fears, not just with respect to the kind of harm expected, but also with respect to further components of experience. The issue may be evil because of the sheer powers of the event, or because of the fact that escape probably will not be fast enough, or because there is no way of escape at all. The threat may be seen as going to last indefinitely, or expected to be over when the bridge has been crossed or flight has succeeded, or as something that can be ended by an act of will, by returning home or leaving the game. The threat may be coming from a specific location in space, so that it can be avoided; or there may not be a single safe place, whatever one does or wherever one goes, as in racial or political persecution and the threat of nuclear war.

Features such as those mentioned are what shape behavior: carefulness when the threat is transitory; protective effort when there is no immediate way of escape or immediate need to escape; escape when such is possible and the threat is more than protective behavior can handle. Features may combine to a point where no behavior is possible, no fearful behavior, expression included, is shown except trembling and being sleepless, and emotional experience merely consists of persistent awareness of the evils that may strike.

Anxiety. There exist experiences of apprehension, anxiety, and panic without object, without specification of possible harm, or with apprehension far exceeding the specific harm expected. Subjects make the distinction "I am afraid of dogs, that they bite; but with spiders it is the other thing" (Barendregt 1982). The situational meaning structure can be designated, not danger but as "weirdness," "eeriness," "the void."

The structure appears to consist of absence of cognitive grip, with concomitant absence of cues for coping actions (McReynolds 1976; Barendregt & Frijda 1982). The world, or some pivotal object, cannot be grasped; it is unclear what might issue forth from it and what one is required to do about it. Sartre (1943), following Kierkegaard, views anxiety in a similar vein: as experience of total incompetence, as confrontation with nothingness. Anticipatory fear and anxiety thus appear to involve entirely different meaning stuctures. Or rather, two entirely different structures exist, which can be given the names of fear and anxiety.

Anger, to Aristotle, is the passion evoked by being slighted or hurt, or perceiving to be slighted or hurt, directing behavior to punish the true or perceived attacker. According to Spinoza, anger is the desire to injure one whom we hate; and hate is sorrow accompanied by the idea of an external cause. Modern approaches (Dollard et al. 1939; Rosenzweig 1944; Buss 1961) emphasize frustration, personal loss, and insults. These interpretations have two features in common: expectation of harm and attribution of this harm to a freely acting agent. Spinoza indeed says: The more the other is free, the more we hate him if he is a cause of our pain.

However, the two features do not fully account for the structure of an angering event. On the one hand, one does not get angry at the dentist drilling, although one might if he is careless; "arbitrariness" has been mentioned as an element in what angers (Pastore 1952). On the other hand, sheer lack of attention or love may be maddening; and so may be that little screw that continues to slip from one's fingers, or someone violating social norms. These conditions all figure prominently in the survey by Hall (1899) of what made people angry.

An apt characterization of the structure of anger is given by De Rivera (1977): An angering event is one in which someone or something challenges what "ought" to happen. De Rivera, following Heider (1958), defines "ought" as "correspondence to some suprapersonal objective order." This sounds somewhat sophisticated for anger in infants or animals, supposing that one is willing to grant them experience of anger; and also for the anger upon hammering your finger or bumping into the kitchen shelf. Still, the kitchen shelf ought to have behaved differently, and fate was unjust and ought to change. What "challenge to what ought to happen" appears to imply is violation of rules, that is, violation of what the subject counts upon that will happen.

A number of implications are packed into this feature of "challenge to what ought." One is explicit reference, in the aspect of challenge, to what ought to be: to nonoccurrence of the present event and the possibility of a different outcome. Anger implies nonacceptance of the present event as necessary or inevitable; and it implies that the event is amenable to being changed. We will call this aspect *controllability*. Another implication is that some agent does the challenging. Since the event goes counter to what one counts upon, causation has all the marks of spontaneity or, as we shall say, *intentionality*. The naming is not too far off, considering that even fate can be damned, as if it listened. It is evident that the most blatantly angering events – neglect and carelessness, insults, unjustified harm, willful intrusions – have a large share of both intentionality and controllability.

Sadness and grief correspond to the situational meaning structure of emptiness or barrenness; that is, to the explicit absence of something valued. Loss, of course, is one of the most distinct forms, and "pining" a word designating orientation toward something explicitly absent. "I never stopped missing him," says one of the widows interviewed by Parkes (1972); "There is the feeling that the world is a dangerous, insecure place," says another. Absence pertains not only to loss of a person: There is grief upon the loss of an ideal once cherished. It need not even pertain to loss; there exists grief concerning absence that never was filled: a love affair that never managed to become what it could have become, or an unhappy childhood recollected. Of course, these can be construed as losses, of hopes and of opportunities.

For absence to truly constitute grief, it must possess the property of finality: the notion that absence will be forever. Without finality there is misery or distress or anger. Anger upon loss indeed appears to function as a means to ward off realization of finality: "I wish there was something I could blame," to quote again one of Parkes's subjects.

The term *absence* here means absence of some intentional object, some object of interest. Such absence may extend to the world as a whole, and in fact every grave personal loss tends to rob the entire world of its color. To the extent that absence spreads beyond a specific focus and global emptiness takes over, grief turns into depression. In depression (meaning the mood, not the clinical syndrome) there is no object serving as focus for behavior or nonbehavior. There is, however, a situation with a meaning structure; only that situation is the world as a whole, and situational meaning structure invests it in global fashion. That structure is barrenness and isolation (Rowe 1978).

Joy. The situational meaning structure can be said to be either one of accomplished striving or one in which the way to accomplishment appears open, unencumbered, or conquerable. The object of desire appears available, attainable, or in possession; or it is yielding to the actions of possessing. Openness and attainability are the irreflexive counterparts of one's own sense of competence as well as of external absence of obstacles.

Openness and attainability indeed appear to form the core of the experience of joy. In Davitz's (1969) study, the items checked most frequently for "enjoyment" were "I'm in tune with the world," "There is a sense of harmony and peace within," and "I seem to be immediately in touch with the world; a sense of being very open, receptive, with no separation between me and the world."

Joyous states differ in the extent to which closeness to or openness of the world dominates or that attainment and possession do. Often joy and enjoyment vacillate between the two: when events are eluding, asking to be grasped or caught, are obtained, and subsequently are obtained to the point of oneness.

Challenge is an aspect of situational meaning structure; so is probable success; so is success. The three aspects help characterize the more subtle as well as the more earthly joyful experiences. Further variations of joyful meaning structure regard degrees of difficulty and uncertainty involved in achieving success and, particularly, amount of difficulty and uncertainty that were overcome. Joy after anxiety is a different joy from that which came without risk: Situational meaning structure carries more than what the instant presents.

Guilt and remorse. There is no need to consider guilt feeling an irreducible mental quality, as Tomkins (1962) appears to suggest. Guilt feeling is characterized sufficiently and adequately as painful self-evaluation due to some action evaluated negatively and for which action the person holds himself responsible. That evaluation *is* guilt feeling. The cognitive structure is quite involved. First, there is the action or actions evaluated negatively in a moral sense. Second, this action is attributed to one's own intentionality; one was free to have acted otherwise, in one's own judgment. Third, negative evaluation is extended from the act to oneself as an actor: It is I who is bad, and not merely what I did. This last step appears to distinguish guilt feeling from mere sense of being guilty.

Behavior motivated by feelings of guilt reflects the situational meaning structure indicated; conversely, guilty behavior gives the clues to the meaning structure concerned. Three types of behavior follow from different aspects of the structure. Mere suffering, wringing one's hands, and beating one's head comprise one of these types: Since the pain is caused by confrontation with the self, there is little else one can do. Atonement is a second mode of behavior, which aims at undoing, or at least counterbalancing, the causes of negative self-evaluation. Suicide is, logically, a third type of action: Since the self has caused the pain, only removal of the self can end the pain.

Language is fairly subtle in distinguishing different meaning structures and the corresponding sets of possibilities for action. *Contrition* does not emphasize negative self-evaluation but refers to negative evaluation of the deed and to one's responsibility. *Remorse* adds the pain caused by having done the deed and the wish that it had not been done. *Self-hatred* is forceful negative self-evaluation only.

Componential analysis of situational meaning structure

One would wish for systematic description of situational meaning structures – even, if possible, for a principle from which all possible meaning structures, and thus emotions, could be derived.

One way to arrive at systematic description of situational meaning structures is componential analysis: viewing situational meaning structures as composed of a restricted set of components. This is a plausible way since, as already indicated, componential analysis can explain similarities between emotions and transitions between emotions. Further, componential analysis can easily be seen as reflecting the operation of a set of coding principles in terms of which subjects code events. Componential analysis can thus be seen as reflecting the process that generates emotion: the organism "computes" the pattern of components and searches the corresponding action readiness mode. A matrix of permissible combinations of components could be set up, each cell of the matrix corresponding to a different emotion (as to name), and many of them to a different mode of action readiness. The result is what is called a "structural theory" of emotion.

Analyzing emotions in terms of situational meaning components is an old and respectable undertaking. Spinoza's theory is of this sort. It starts from three basic components – joy, sorrow, and desire – each defined in terms of a contingency: enhancement of mode of activity, diminishment of mode of activity, endeavor to persist in one's given nature. It then adds components to each of the basic ones: "uncertainty," "doubting the issue," "with conception of its cause," "with respect to something past"; it adds further components to such combinations; and so forth. In the *Ethics*, the components are not systematically enumerated, but one might easily arrange them so.

Arnold (1960) did construct a system. Appraisals, she argued, vary along three dimensions. Events can be seen as (1) beneficial or harmful, (2) to relate to either presence or absence of some object, and (3) to be easy to approach or to avoid or, rather, to present difficulty in that respect. "Basic" emotions are those defined and determined by these contingencies. The major problem with Arnold's classification is that it appears too simple: Different emotions fall in the same cell, and some emotions cannot easily be accommodated.

Roseman (1984) proposed a system with five two-valued dimensions; plausible combinations produce "thirteen or so" basic emotions. The dimensions are (1) desirability: an object is desirable or undesirable; (2) outcome: an object is present or absent; (3) probability: an outcome is certain or uncertain; (4) agency: outcomes are caused by circumstances, by some actor, or by the self; (5) legitimacy: outcomes can be deserved or undeserved. "Desirability" crossed with "outcome" yields a basic fourfold division of having what you want, not having what you want, having what you don't want, and not having what you don't want – with enjoyment, grief, distress, and relief in the four cells. Agency and legitimacy are debatable as basic dimensions, and so are also some of the allocations ("hatred" as the response to deserved distress.)

De Rivera (1977) advanced a "structural theory of emotion" in which emotions are analyzed in terms of three dimensions: inherent movement tendency (toward self, toward other, away from self, away from other); object of these movements ("it" or "me"; the movement "toward other," for instance, becomes "allowing the world to come into the self" when the object is "me"); and kind of relationship involved ("belonging," "recognition," "being"). A "fluidity–fixity" distinction is added. Emotions are placed into the 48 cells resulting from crossing the three dimensions. The dimensions are intuitively appealing, and elements of them will be met below. Some of them, however, the last one in particular, offer little foothold for solid verification, although it is true that assignment of emotion labels to the cells by a group of subjects corresponded reasonably well with De Rivera's own analysis (De Rivera 1977).

More systems have been proposed over the last several years. Kemper (1978) presented an analysis restricted to emotions arising in interpersonal relationships; admittedly, that restriction leaves in the larger share of human emotions. The analysis is based upon whether interpersonal events are relevant to two general concerns: for power and for status. Different emotions arise when events are relevant to either the one concern or the other, and further according to four kinds of contingency. First, events can imply continuation of a given power or status state, or decrease, or increase. Second, such constellations can regard the self or the other in the relationship. Third, they can apply to continuous state, to an anticipated interaction outcome, or to an actual outcome. Fourth, within these constellations "agency" plays a major role: Agency can reside in the self, the other, or a third party. Relevance to the power concern implies what in other proposals is the important feature of controllability.

Solomon (1976) presents a list of 13 "categories of judgment" that together constitute the "logic" of emotions. The categories include "direction" (outer–inner), scope/focus (something–everything as the object), evaluation, responsibility, and power. A number of emotions (from anger–anxiety to vanity–worship) are analyzed in terms of these categories, illustrating the power of the approach; but assignments of categories to emotions are intuitive only.

In Scherer's (1984a,b) approach, people are viewed as constantly performing a series of "stimulus evaluation checks" upon the environment; performing these checks constitutes the appraisal phase of the emotion process. He presents a set of "facets," each comprising one of the coding categories for one of the stimulus evaluation checks. The stimulus evaluation checks with their facets are novelty (expected or unexpected); pleasantness (pleasant or unpleasant); goals/plan relationship (with the facets relevance, conduciveness, justice or equity); relevance for coping (with the facets agency, motive or cause, influence potential, and coping potential); norm consistency; and self-consistency. Each emotion corresponds to a given outcome of the series of checks and thus to a given string of facet values.

More restricted proposals concerning relevant categories have been advanced by Weiner (1982) and Clore and Ortony (1984).

Among the components, dimensions, or checks mentioned by the various authors, there intuitively appears to exist a large amount of overlap or consensus. Criteria with which to evaluate the relative merits of the proposals, or their correspondence, so far are absent.

The list of situational meaning components that follows contains yet another proposal. It intends to go some way toward accounting for the elicitation of the different action readiness modes discussed in chapter 2. The list was inspired initially by Spinoza's analyses. His definitions clearly indicated which set of features might account for differentiation between the major emotions. Components have been modified or added when experimental or clinical literature suggested their importance or when distinctions between certain emotions appeared to call for additions. The general perspective in organizing and viewing situational meaning components is the notion, stemming from Lazarus (1966; Lazarus et al. 1980) that appraisals result from the interaction between appreciation of what the event can do or offer – primary appraisal – and appraisal of one's coping potential with respect to that event – secondary appraisal.

Components of situational meaning

A general distinction will be made between "core components," "context components," and "object components." Core components are those that make (or do not make) the situation an emotional one. They pertain to emotional relevance and constitute emotional experience per se. Their assessment corresponds to primary appraisal.

Context components are those features of situational meaning structure that determine the nature of the emotion. They pertain to what the subject feels he can or cannot do with respect to the situation and are in fact action relevance components. Their assessment corresponds to Lazarus's secondary appraisal; their contents with "affordances" in the Gibsonian sense (Gibson 1966).

Context components also determine whether an emotion actually results: Core components in part depend upon context. That is, whether an event that is potentially relevant indeed is so in actual fact depends not merely upon the event's core of being potentially beneficial or harmful, but also upon its context making or not making action with respect to that event difficult.

Emotional experience and emotional behavior, as argued in section 2.8, depend not only upon event relevance and context, but also upon the nature of the emotional objects; hence "object components." Emotion shows indefinitely large variation with respect to objects and corresponding actions or intentional structures. Some distinctions in the relationship between events and their basis of relevance, however, require explicit discussion.

Components are illustrated by their participation in given emotions. A component is assumed constitutive of a given emotional experience when it appears indispensible for an experience to be called by the given name or for an action readiness mode labeled in that fashion to emerge.

Core components

1. Objectivity. An emotional situation imposes its meaning upon the subject. The situation is "spontaneous"; the subject experiences himself as affected and passive in this regard: He does not confer meaning. The sense of being overcome by the event as well as by one's own response is the reflexive counterpart of the situation's apparent objectivity.

This component is called "objectivity," from the phenomenological point of view. Although we may know better, in emotion events carry their significance as inherent features. The spider phobic's knowledge that the animal can do no harm does not assuage his fear: The animal is gruesome and remains so. Emotional significance of events is there "forever"; it is invested with qualities of absoluteness and everlastingness. Temporal absolutes play a conspicuous role in the language of emotion and translate emotional intensity more than anything else: "You never listen to me," "You always reject my proposals," "I will always love you" are all proven untrue the next day, but still reflect how things are honestly felt. Intense desire and intense pain carry the feeling that the world will crumble, that life is not worth living if the desire is not satisfied or the pain taken away *now*; and this is so even when the subject knows that in five minutes desire will have waned and pain subsided (as they may sometimes do in pangs of longing or of jealousy).

Without the feature of objectivity, experience is not emotional. Willful judgment of relevance neither constitutes nor engenders emotional experience (Arnold 1960).

2. *Relevance*. An emotional situation is one of interest and claims attention. "Relevance" is a slightly awkward term to denote what is meant, since it extends to situations lacking anything whatever worth paying attention to, as in boredom or apathetic depressiveness.

3. *Reality level*. The notion stems from Lewin (1937), if not from Freud. A situation may in principle be relevant, but be only play, or a fantasy, or an abstraction; or the subject may succeed in considering it so. Nuclear holocaust may be made to appear a remote possibility; by contrast, one may convince oneself of conspiracy when there is mere opposition. Emotional involvement varies correspondingly. Subjects repeating to themselves that a motion picture showing a bloody operation was merely staged showed decreased emotional response (Koriat et al. 1972).

4. *Difficulty*. The world of emotion is a difficult world, according to Sartre: There is no direct solution for responding to the situation's demands. The situation is relevant, but there is uncertainty about whether opportunity indeed can be grasped, threat countered or evaded, challenge met.

5. *Urgency*. Situations differ in the degree to which they require immediate response. One of the variables contributing to urgency is proximity of event effects in space or time; another is inability to cope with or counter or evade events that appear to ask for it. When a caged animal is approached, its state changes from attention over wariness to fear to panic.

Urgency is the irreflexive counterpart of felt emotional intensity. Difficulty and urgency are the situational meaning components corresponding to emotional upset, to emotion in the excited sense of the word.

6. *Seriousness*. Situations differ in the degree to which they or their implications are felt to be serious. "Seriousness" refers to expected or

felt scope of consequences, both in time and in number. Loss of a limb is more serious than severe pain, both because the first will last forever and because it has multiple consequences. Seriousness corresponds with emotional intensity in the second, nonacute sense discussed in section 2.10.

7. *Valence*. Events, objects, and situations may possess positive or negative valence; that is, they may posses intrinsic attractiveness or aversiveness. The adjective *intrinsic* serves to distinguish these features from derived attractiveness or aversiveness: Loss derives its aversiveness from the positive valence of the object lost.

8. *Demand character*. "Valence" corresponds to intrinsic value and thus to potential outcomes. "Demand character" refers to actual or signaled outcome: Threat to peace has negative demand character, whereas (and because) peace has positive valence.

Four types of demand character are distinguished: positive and negative demand character (or pleasantness and aversiveness), desirability, and interestingness. "Desirability" refers to the characteristic of certain objects not in possession that they appear to demand possession, proximity, or access; it is the perceptual component corresponding to desire. "Interestingness" refers to events, objects, or situations claiming attention. It is the situational meaning component corresponding to interest, wonder, or curiosity.

Note that "desirability" refers to positive valence of some (potentially accessible) object, not to positive demand character. That is: Desire, like interest or wonder, is considered an emotion that is neither pleasant nor unpleasant. Additional contingencies might make it so; indeed, the fact that desire can be pleasurable as well as painful is the main reason to consider it hedonically neutral by itself. A similar argument goes for interest or wonder.

9. *Clarity*. Situational meaning structures vary in distinctness and articulation; the value of one or more of the core or context components may be undefined. When one is notified that a friend is seriously ill, the true significance is still unknown, or implications have not yet crystallized; they have not penetrated yet. Situational meaning structure in these cases lacks clarity. The result is mere "emotion" – mere upset or alarm, or mere confusion, when implications just begin to sort themselves out.

This is to say that not all emotions are of the same order. Not all

Valence

		Positive	Negative
		Positive	Negative
Presence	Present	Contentment; enjoyment	Suffering
	Absent	Desire	Contentment; safety

Figure 4.1. Valence × Presence.

emotional states can be considered to occupy some region of an emotion space. The states referred to by the terms *anger*, *fear*, and *joy* do, but those meant by *excitement*, *upset*, and *confusion* do not. They correspond to dedifferentiations of that space.

10. Multiplicity. Situational meaning structure can be compound. It may comprise more than one event; or it may correspond to one event carrying different implications and perhaps even different valences. Multiplicity of meanings corresponds to mixed and compound emotions. The fact of multiplicity itself can constitute a meaning component. That component forms part of the structure of doubt or uncertainty; and a structure with clarity about multiplicity of valences corresponds to ambivalence and sense of conflict.

Context components: action-relevant components

1. Presence and absence. Positive demand character can be generated by the presence of something of positive valence or by the absence of something of negative valence; likewise for negative demand character. This combination of valence and presence–absence gives a basic fourfold division of emotional situations, which can be recognized in many discussions of emotion: in the behaviorist formulations of contingencies of reinforcement (Mowrer 1960; Gray 1971) and in the classifications of Arnold or Roseman. We give the fourfold table in Figure 4.1.

The content of the table may be somewhat suprising: "Presence" and "absence," however, are taken in a strict sense. Most emotions caused by absence are marked by more than absence. Loss, for instance, implies change over former presence. Similarly, joy is caused not by sheer presence of something agreeable, but by its appearance.

Context components are linked to action readiness modes, either alone or in conjunction with other components. Presence of positive valence by itself motivates action to effect that which the object of valence calls for: look at it, possess it, eat it, or whatever may be the case. Absence of an object of positive valence, when it is felt as such, dictates readiness to get it. Presence of negative valence moves to escape or to achieve change generally; its absence is motivationally neutral.

2. Certainty and noncertainty. This component can also be called "anticipation of effects to come." Effects are certain when they have actually materialized. Effects that have not yet fully materialized are uncertain: They may still pass by, be warded off, or be borne more or less well. Both fear and hope look at the future, and with a measure of doubt. Aristotle and Spinoza mention that aspect; anticipatory signaling is central in Mowrer's (1960) analysis of fear.

Joy, distress, grief, desire all imply absence of uncertainty. Uncertainty about how one's friend will respond takes away much of the joy of going to meet her or him. Note that what counts is not objective certainty or uncertainty, but whether or not being certain is explicitly part of the situational meaning structure. Joyful anticipation may not be sure about its issue, but it does not bother about it.

Yet in grief, joy and distress, the aspect of certainty is implicit rather than explicit. It is an explicit component only of emotions looking into the future. Despair and trust form true counterparts to fear and hope. The present component dimension can therefore best be assigned three values: certainty, noncertainty, and non-uncertainty, a default value.

Noncertainty motivates behavior to change the situation and to avert negative effects or to advance the advent of a positive one. Certainty cannot motivate behavior other than waiting, seeing, relishing, or enduring.

3. Change. Situational meaning can contain definite reference to a previous and different state. Such reference is implicitly present in the notion of "event": Events are changes. In fact, in enjoyable events it is change rather than mere presence of something positive that counts: joys that go on and on become boring or maddening. To Schopenhauer, all happiness is mere decrease of unhappiness; to Spinoza, it is change to greater perfection, and not having it, that constitutes joy (*Ethics*, Part III, Def.2). It is change over a baseline, or contrast with something else, that differentiates joy from contentment, as it differentiates distress from suffering.

In some emotions, change is realized explicitly. Comparison with a previous state then is an explicit component of experience: Some valence goes, or does not materialize, contrary to expectation. Relief and disappointment are the clearest examples, and are defined by Mowrer (1960) in this manner. "Frustration-effects" (Amsel 1962) and "elation-effects" (Karabenick 1969) spring from the constellations of reduction and increase of previously given rewards. Note that it is cognitive content that is essential here. In experience, relief and joy succeed one another, according to whether previous state or present state preoccupies the mind.

Loss, as said, is not mere absence, but absence of what was or what could have been in the subject's thought. Both grief and nostalgia contain the past as an element of experience, the first focusing upon now, the second upon then. The past shines through in more emotions. Conquered fear – threat considered supportable – feels differently from equanimity that never knew unease.

4. Openness–closedness. Openness and closedness modulate presence and absence: There is access only with what we call openness. Accessibility ranges over a continuum, from openness over presence of obstructions to being hemmed in on all sides by barriers that block goal achievement or escape.

Openness or apparent penetrability of barriers is a condition for positive emotions. Closure is the situational meaning component corresponding to frustration in the sense that this word is used in clinical psychology. It is the major determinant of the feature of difficulty.

Closure varies, during encounters with a given situation or event, as a function of whether efforts prove successful or unsuccessful. Dembo (1931) describes the development of anger as contingent upon progressive failure of efforts at solving an unsolvable task and at leaving the situation; Janis et al. (1955; Janis 1971) describe panic as resulting from escape routes gradually closing.

5. Intentionality. This has been discussed in the preceding subsection. Events can be seen as caused by some live intending agent. Intentionality can take two values: other and self; the first is important in anger, the second in self-hatred and in guilt. If neither applies, causation is by circumstances.

Intentionality is linked to three facets: spontaneity, which is its cue; freedom, which is part of its cognitive content, and controllability, an implication of causation by intentionality that, however, on occasion also may accrue to events seen as caused by circumstances. As for spontaneity: It probably is because their actions are perceived as originating in the acting entities that animals and human beings treat live creatures differently from objects (see Michotte 1950); even a decorticated cat does so when it attacks the experimenter and not the equipment. Sudden intrusions generally, like pains and noises, momentarily share this feature, as do stubborn bolts and objects hiding themselves from search. Freedom, here, means that the agent could have acted differently.

Controllability is meant to imply that controlling behaviors are in order; and since here it is connected to intentionality, the controlling behaviors are of the interactive sort: threatening, bluffing, weeping.

6. Controllability. Controllability refers to the perspective that the course of events is capable of being modified by one's own actions. Controllability is an aspect of how the world looks when having a sense of "internal control" (Rotter 1966).

Intentionally produced events are by their very nature controllable, unless unequal power relationships destroy that controllability; fear rather than anger is the response to the political police. Impersonal circumstances differ in their controllability, depending upon both their resistance and your power, or your confidence in it. Controllability is the component that turns danger from threat into challenge and thus negative into positive emotion (Lazarus 1966; Lazarus et al. 1980). Generalized controllability is the perceptual counterpart, and the source, of self-confidence and arrogance – nonangry, "tyrannical" aggression; generalized uncontrollability is that of anxiety (Averill 1973; McReynolds 1976). To repeat: Uncontrollability may be due to the environment's unpredictability as well as to weakness of the subject's coping potential (Barendregt & Frijda 1982).

The significance of openness and closedness of situations derives from controllability: Barriers may appear penetrable or impenetrable, leading to anger or to panic or despair.

Controllability, as perceived, changes with prolonged interaction and accumulation of experience. Events may turn out to be capable of yielding, and thus turn from occasions for fear or submission to occasions for anger; so in the changeover from subjection to revolt. Conversely, efforts toward control may turn out to be fruitless, and events may reveal

themselves as immutable; which is what happens in the course of prolonged uncontrollable stress (Seligman 1975).

The succession of grief phases as described by Bowlby (1969) and
Parkes (1972) can be understood in a corresponding manner. Change
from angry protest to despair and resignation can be interpreted as a
consequence of the fact that uncontrollability gradually dawns, and only
gradually, through vain attempts. The succession, in other words, may
be interpreted as consequent upon inevitable cognitive change rather
than as produced by a biologically determined response sequence, as
Bowlby suggests.

7. Modifiability. "Modifiability" refers to duration and time perspective;
it refers to judgment that a course of events is capable of changing.
Events may or may not be controllable; but even if uncontrollable, they
might still turn out differently from how they are or look, and do so
through circumstance or luck or outside help. What is uncertain is modifiable; what is certain now still may be different later. Unmodifiability,
the negative pole of this component, is to a large extent an event feature
that carries with it the past. What has been so for a long time may well
be so forever. It may also exist, however, with respect to events actually
going on – suffering experienced as if it will never end – as well as with
respect to events still to come, when it shapes feelings of confidence
and trust, for instance, or certainly that a person will never come back.

Unmodifiability was also called "finality." Loss through death is final
only when it is accepted as such. As long as grief is loud and wailing,
there still is a glimmer of hope; the possibility of restoration, of loss
proving untrue, is still envisaged. And even passive despair considers
finality against a background of what could have been: Something of
that sort separates despair from resignation.

8. Object evaluation versus event evaluation. This component is similar to
De Rivera's (1977) distinction between "fluid" versus "fixed" emotions.
Some emotions involve attaching positive or negative valence to a person
or object rather than to the outcome of an action or event. Valence
becomes a property of the person or object; the emotion involves "dispositional attribution" (Nisbett & Ross 1980). For instance, suffering
someone's despicable action turns him into a despicable character; anger
thereby turns into hatred, or is complemented by it. *Hatred* is an emotion
that contains the component of object evaluation. *Love,* of course, is of
a similar structure: One may enjoy an event or outcome, but one loves

a person. Actions differ according to whether the emotion involves event evaluation or object evaluation. In anger, action is directed against occurrence of an outcome; in hate it is directed against a person and his very existence. In enjoyment it accepts an outcome; in love it seeks to further someone's mode of being.

Object evaluation applies to objects and event types as much as to persons. *Liking*, *dislike*, and *aversion* are names for the corresponding emotions: One likes hot chocolate and enjoys drinking a cup of it. All emotions that imply valuing a person or object contain this component: admiration, awe, disgust, sympathy, guilt feeling (because, or to the extent that, this implies self-hatred), pride. They form a separate class of emotions, different from the event-provoked emotions, because of this feature of object evaluation. All these emotions can be defined as modes of love or hatred rather than of joy and sorrow; indeed, this is the approach adopted by Spinoza.

Within object evaluation, a number of subcomponents could be distinguished that might differentiate between various forms of like and dislike. "Totality" is one, differentiating love from sympathy; "closeness" is another, being specific to disgust (in the moral sense) as opposed to distaste. They will not be systematically analyzed here; they pertain to subtle, probably idiosyncratic, distinctions.

9. Focality–globality. Meaning can attach to a specific object or event; it can also attach to the environment or the life space as a whole. Globality is the component that differentiates depression from sadness, bliss from joy, and anxiety from fear. In depression, as said, the world as a whole appears barren and devoid of intentional objects. In anxiety, the environment as a whole lacks support for orientation or a focus that might make meaningful any efforts to protect oneself. In bliss or true happiness, the environment as a whole appears accessible and invested with positive valence. The component was employed by Spinoza for the distinctions mentioned. It is an interesting one: Joy and bliss, sadness and depression, fear and anxiety, in this view, do not merely differ in intensity but also structurally. Behavior differs accordingly: It possesses direction toward or away from the focus in situations with focality, and it lacks such direction in those with globality. Globality is a component that differentiates experience of moods from that of emotions.

10. Strangeness–familiarity. Strangeness means lack of support for the preparation of definite actions: It is unknown what can be expected and what, if necessary, can be done with or about the event or object. Strangeness per se motivates cognitive activity: It is one of the situational meaning components shaping the feature of interestingness. When global, the feature of strangeness turns into that of chaos, which, as said, can be considered one of the major determinants of anxiety.

Familiarity is an important component of feelings of security and of liking; Zajonc (1968) showed that familiar stimuli, by reason of their being familiar only, are more likable or attractive than unfamiliar stimuli. Familiarity must be a composite component, however, since familiarity in an objective, frequency-of-encounters sense may also determine boredom; as it also breeds contempt.

Object components

Both Spinoza (1677) and De Rivera (1977) emphasized the nature of the emotional object as a differentiating dimension. De Rivera distinguishes three types of object relation: "belonging" (love is an instance), "recognition" (e.g., esteem, humility) and "being" (e.g., acceptance, serenity). The object types to be discussed here are in part related to De Rivera's distinctions.

1. Ego as constituent. As said, "situational meaning structure" refers to the situation as perceived and as imbued with the meaning it has for the subject; the subject himself is not part of that situation, but merely the condition for its existence and appearance. As also said, however, the subject can on occasion be a constituent of his own experience and figure in the situation as perceived. This is emphatically so when, as in guilt feelings, the subject perceives himself as the actor of some act he evaluates. We will refer to the subject as constituent of his experience as the *ego.*

Most human experiences do involve the ego, if only in a marginal way. In most experiences, emotional or otherwise, there is awareness of events-out-there, and "out there" is not the ego. This aspect of experience tends to go unnoticed, except when suddenly thrown into relief by two contrasting modes of experience that have emotional impact by themselves: ego–object fusion and depersonalization. By *ego–object fusion* we mean loss of awareness of events-out-there, as distinct from the ego; perhaps the experience should be referred to as awareness of oneness. It occurs in mystic experience but also in rare but still down-to-earth experiences of ecstasy, aesthetic understanding, and close interpersonal contact. "Depersonalization" is taken to refer to awareness of loss of sense of meaningfulness of events, even when rationally their impact may be appreciated; such loss of meaningfulness tends to enhance the sense of subject–object separation. Neither ego–object fusion nor depersonalization is adequately characterized by the ego not being, or emphatically being, a marginal constituent of experience; they do illustrate however, that marginal constituency.

2. Ego as object. The ego is an explicit constituent of experience in some emotions; guilt feeling and remorse are examples. The most explicit occurrence is in shame. Lewis (1971) has given a penetrating analysis of this latter emotion. In shame, the subject perceives himself, or one of his acts; in addition he perceives others perceiving him; imputes condemnation of his acts to those others; and shares in their condemnation. Perhaps ego as object should be classed among the context components rather than among the object components, since true action tendency can be determined by it: desire to disappear from the eyes of others and sometimes from one's own as well. How real this desire can be is evident from voodoo death, dying because of a ritual curse, which can be analyzed as a shame reaction (Cannon 1942).

3. Object fate versus *subject fate.* In emotions proper, the subject's own well-being is involved in the emotion-provoking event. In other types of emotion, someone else's fate is at stake, and that fact in its complexity shapes the subject's situational meaning structure. The other person's situational meaning structure forms part of it, in some sort of recursive manner. Examples of emotions where this is the case are pity, compassion, empathic distress (Hoffman 1978), malign joy (enjoying someone's else's misfortune), some forms of jealousy ("pain caused by someone else enjoying what I want to enjoy"), sadistic pleasure. Every subject-fate emotion, it would seem, can be duplicated by some object-fate emotion in either the sympathetic or antipathetic mode.

Whether the object's fate has positive or negative valence depends upon what his or her good or bad fortune means to the subject, which is many things: "In the misfortune of our friends there is always something which does not displease us," observed La Rochefoucauld.

The object in object fate can be the ego. Self-pity, pleasure in self-abasement, and self-indulgence involve the complex cognitive structures that can be deduced from this and the preceding subsections.

4. Value relevance versus contingency. In common emotions like fear and anger the eliciting event just happens to happen and to possess positive or negative valence: Valence exists because one happens to have the concerns involved. Other events appear to possess intrinsic positive or negative valences: they are good or bad with respect to a suprapersonal value, a suprapersonal basis for judgment. We will call this the feature of *value relevance*.

Indignation, admiration, respect, and contempt belong to emotions that owe their emergence to values rather than to personal concerns. One is indignant not because some personal concern has been frustrated but because Friendship, Human Dignity, Discretion have been offended. Admiring someone does not mean that he or she perfectly serves one's needs, but that he or she is as one ought to be, or that he or she exemplifies the realization of some ideal. Clearly, emotions exist that owe their emergence to values rather than to personal concerns.

Value relevance makes a difference, in experience as well as in behavior. In experience: The category "ought" is explicitly implicated. In behavior: The ideals of self-control are not relevant when values are involved. Ideology strengthens emotions; time, forgetting and forgiving, play a role that is different, because it is not merely personal. Hence the advantages of the emotions with value relevance. Turning anger into indignation provides moral support, as does the switch from devotion to admiration.

Further object components. Object components could be added ad infinitum, since social values strongly influence whatever distinctions are made. For instance, village Eskimos are reported to distinguish fine shades of meaning in their terms for affection and hostility (Briggs 1970). Javanese vocabulary, as said, makes fine distinctions among feeling states associated with respectful behavior (Geertz 1959).

Meaning component profiles

The various situational meaning structures can be represented as vectors of component values; we call them *profiles*. Such profiles define the various emotions with respect to their situational meaning structure or cognitive content.

Situational meaning profiles indeed appear to provide plausible descriptions of the emotions concerned. Fear, for instance, is uncertain expectation (the above context component no. 3) of the presence (component no. 1) of negative valence (core), or absence of positive valence, over which there is insufficient control (no. 6), but which event is modifiable (no. 7); its degree corresponds to the measure of closure (no. 4) and urgency (core) of the situation. Anger is experience of presence (no. 1) of negative valence (core), or of barriers (no. 4) toward obtaining positive valence (core), either certain or uncertain, and attributed to an intentional agent (no. 5) that is controllable (no. 6). Intuitively constructed profiles for most emotions mentioned in this section are given in Table 4.4. This arbitrary selection of emotion names is used to explore and illustrate the plausibility of the present component set. The profiles are all different, as they should be, since among the emotion names there are no synonyms.

The present approach can to some extent be validated by comparing the similarity between profiles with some other measure of similarity between emotions. One such measure is simultaneous occurrence of the emotional state, or simultaneous applicability of the emotion names: In the responses to mood adjective checklists, mood or emotion terms frequently checked off together may be considered to be similar in meaning. Data of this sort were derived from the Sonneville et al. (1981) mood adjective checklist. Thirty-six mood names were selected, representing the four items loading highest on each of nine of the mood dimensions; items from the same dimension were considered more similar than those from different dimensions (since the dimensions are based upon high interitem correlations). Subjects were asked to check the situational meaning components described for each of those 36 mood states. Profiles were constructed by assigning a plus or minus sign to each component that was checked for that mood state by at least two-thirds of the subjects; the empirically obtained profiles thus were similar in nature to the constructed ones in Table 4.4.

Indices of profile similarity (correlations between strings of frequencies, and measures of profile match) between items from the same mood dimension were considerably higher than those between items from different dimensions. Also, all but one of the 36 profiles turned out to be different. Certain components were found to discriminate between dimensions, in the sense that all four items from one dimension obtain an identical mark for them; these components are given in Table 4.5. Other, different components discriminated between items within dimensions (Frijda & Bovenkerk 1985; "responsibility" corresponds to "intentionality" earlier in this section).

The present approach asserts that, in general, component profiles map onto emotions. This means that, by and large, different emotions as language distinguishes them should correspond to different profiles;

Table 4.4. *Profiles for selected emotions*

	Positive character	Negative character	Desire	Interest	Positive valence	Negative valence	Presence	Absence	Certainty	Uncertainty	Change	Open	Closed	Intentionality of other	Intentionality of self	Controllability	Noncontrollability	Modifiability	Finality	Object	Event	Focality	Globality	Strangeness	Familiarity	Value
Joy	x				x	x	x	x			(x)	x						x			x	x				
Distress		x			x	x	x											x			x	x				
Desire			x		x		x														x	x				
Interest				x	x		x														x	x				
Grief		x			x		x				(x)								x		x	x				
Sorrow		x			x		x				(x)										x	x				
Fear		x			x	x	x	x		x					x	x	x				x	x				
Hope	x				x	x	x	x		x		x									x	x				
Anger	x	x			x	x	x							x		x					x	x				
Challenge	x				x	x			x																	
Boredom		x	x			x												x			x	x				
Satisfaction	x		x		x					x											x		x			
Contentment	x				x		x														x	x			x	
Security	x				x		x														x	x				
Relief	x				x		x		x												x	x		x		x
Anxiety		x			x	x				x											x	x				
Despair		x			x	x		x					x					x			x		x	x		
Disappointment		x			x		x		x		x							x			x	x				
Hate		x			x	x												x			x	x				
Frustration		x			x	x	x							x	x			x		x	x					

Table 4.4. (cont.)

	Positive character	Negative character	Desire	Interest	Positive valence	Negative valence	Presence	Absence	Certainty	Uncertainty	Change	Open	Closed	Intentionality of other	Intentionality of self	Controllability	Noncontrollability	Modifiability	Finality	Object	Event	Focality	Globality	Strangeness	Familiarity	Value
Guilt		x				x	x								x					x	x					x
Contempt		x				x	x													x		x				
Resignation						x	x												x	x	x					
Love	x				x		x													x	x					
Admiration	x				x		x							x						x	x					x
Pride	x				x		x								x					x	x					
Disgust		x				x	x							x						x	x					
Self-hatred		x				x	x														x		x			
Depression		x				x		x													x		x			
Bliss	x				x		x							x						x	x					x
Indignation		x				x	x													x	x					

each emotion name that is not a synonym of another one should correspond to a unique profile (or, in case of polysemy, to several unique profiles). Support for this hypothesis has recently been obtained by Smith and Ellsworth (1985), with respect to 15 major emotions.

It also means that profiles consisting of core and context components (thus leaving out object components) should map onto action readiness modes; each different profile restricted in this manner should map onto a different action readiness mode, and vice versa. In particular, different profiles should exist for the different emotions considered basic along the lines sketched in chapter 2, since these were defined by action readiness modes. Evidence collected so far supports this prediction. Some of the mood dimensions in the study just discussed parallel emotions usually classed as basic: anxious, depressed, angry, and elated. Each of these corresponds to a distinct profile, as presented in Table 4.5. Further,

Table 4.5 *Components sufficient for distinguishing dimensions*

	Valence	Unexpectedness	Control	Social Context	Responsibility	Self-esteem
Anxious	−	+	−	+		+
Timid				+		+
Depressed	−	−	−	+		
Angry	−	+		+	+	+
Irritable	−	−		+		
Elated	+	+		+		−
Conscientious		−		−		−
Arrogant						
Indifferent		−				−

Key: +, All four words scored by 75% or more of subjects for this component; −, all four words scored by 75% or more of subjects for opposite component.
Source: Adapted from Frijda & Bovenkerk 1985.

a study in progress obtains high correlations between presence of action tendencies in given emotions, as reported by the subjects, and profiles of those same emotions (Frijda 1986).

Furthermore, certain components or component combinations can be expected to map onto physiological parameters and patterns. Scherer (1984b) has emphasized this aspect in his work and has produced a systematic prediction set, as well as evidence, with respect to voice intonation parameters. Other correspondences may be expected to exist along the lines suggested in section 3.9. It is to be noted that core components like urgency and difficulty are absent from Table 4.4 (and Table 4.5), whereas they are hypothesized to correspond to autonomic response variables.

This list of components presented above is, as said, derived in empiricist fashion. No generative principle appears available from which a nonredundant and sufficient set of components could be derived; the principles reviewed earlier are too simple for emotions generally. The redundance in the set presented above is obvious, and was evident in the results of the Frijda and Bovenkerk study mentioned: Full differentiation of 35 out of 36 items could be retained with 7 components or with 12 component values; Smith and Ellsworth obtained 6 bipolar components. No solid theoretical principle for reduction has as yet come to mind.

4.5. Emotional experience as experience of autonomic arousal

The problem

As mentioned when discussing peripheralist theories, there is near-unanimity that awareness of autonomic arousal (or, in the terms of earlier times, visceral sensations or organ sensations) is an important component of emotional experience. Nearly all theorists of emotion would subscribe to James's (1884) statement that if awareness of one's breathing, heartbeat, trembling, and muscle tenseness is discounted, the remaining experience is cold and bleak. The major theoretical issue, however, is whether autonomic awareness is essential for emotional experience.

The second theoretical issue mentioned concerns the experience of different emotions. Are different emotional experiences based upon awareness of different patterns of autonomic arousal?

A third question followed from the previous ones: If autonomic awareness turns out not to be a necessary component of emotional experience, and not to be a necessary condition for emotional behavior, how shall its role in emotional experience be characterized?

The importance of autonomic feedback

If awareness of autonomic response is essential to emotional experience, the intensity and frequency of such experience should increase when such awareness is increased and decrease when it is decreased.

Autonomic arousal (and thus its awareness) can be increased by the administration of epinephrine. Epinephrine injections usually do not produce distinct emotional experience. Subjects report feeling jittery, pent-up, sometimes agitated and aroused. They often feel nothing emotional at all, or they feel "as if" nervous or excited or anxious (Marånon 1924; Landis & Hunt 1932). Only occasionally is true anxiety felt, and in rare instances happiness.

On the whole, experience induced by epinephrine injections is not truly emotional, but neither is it emotionally neutral: It is biased toward unpleasant feeling tone and toward unpleasant response to stimuli, particularly with higher epinephrine dosage (Hawkins et al. 1969; Maslach 1979; Marshall & Zimbardo 1979). What epinephrine does distinctly do, however, is render the subject "jumpy," that is, more responsive to unexpected or unpleasant stimuli. Startle responses are enhanced (Cantril & Hunt 1932); and rats injected with epinephrine show more fear behavior than placebo-injected rats when placed in unfamiliar surroundings (Haroutunian & Riccio 1977).

Although autonomic awareness, according to the above data, does not by itself constitute emotional experience, it still might be one of its necessary components. According to Schachter (1964), it indeed is: Emotional experience consists of awareness of autonomic arousal, when such arousal is interpreted by the subject as caused by emotionally meaningful situational cues. Different emotional experiences consist of awareness of autonomic arousal attributed to different (that is, enjoyable, fearful, angering, etc.) situational cues. No emotional experience results when there is no arousal, or when arousal is attributed to nonemotional sources.

Confirmation of this hypothesis was sought in that well-known experiment (Schachter & Singer 1962) in which subjects (1) received either epinephrine or placebo injections; (2) received the epinephrine injection either under the condition of being informed or of not being informed about its autonomic effects; and (3) were placed in the presence of either "happy" or "angry" situational cues (a confederate who behaved happily or angrily). After receiving the injections and being confronted with the situational cues, subjects filled out rating scales asking how happy or how angry they had felt.

Ratings by uninformed epinephrine-injected subjects confronted with the happy cues were happier than those of informed subjects confronted with the same cues; and similarly for anger after confrontation with the "anger" cues. Behavior ratings by observers tended to corroborate the subjective feeling ratings. The authors considered these experimental results to support their hypothesis. The situational cues appeared to determine the kind of emotion felt, and to do so only when arousal could not be attributed to the injections; arousal and its attribution consequently could be considered the core of the experience.

These conclusions have been seriously questioned by various investigators (see Reisenzein 1983 for a review). Some of Schachter and Singer's own data are inconsistent with their hypothesis – for instance, the fact that feeling ratings in the unexplained arousal and placebo conditions did not significantly differ (see Plutchik & Ax 1967). Replications, with slight variations, by Maslach (1979) and by Marshall and Zimbardo (1979) failed to reproduce the findings: replications by Erdmann and Janke (1978) and by Gerdes (1979) only partly so. Further, even where Schachter and Singer's findings are replicated, they can be interpreted in plausible alternative ways – for instance, by the enhanced emotional responsiveness under epinephrine mentioned above. Lower emotion ratings in drug-informed subjects may well be due to these subjects correcting for their drug-induced jumpiness. Contrary to the hypothesis again is the fact that some subjects receiving epinephrine and knowing it may still experience strong genuine emotions, particularly if predis-positions for such emotions exist (e.g., for anxiety; Breggin 1964).

The role of autonomic arousal in emotional experience has also been investigated along somewhat different lines, namely, in studies of "arousal transfer." It has been shown that arousal elicited by given stimuli contributes to the intensity of emotions elicited by subsequent different stimuli. For instance, Cantor, Zillman, and Bryant (1975) had male subjects rate the attractiveness of female nudes after having in-duced arousal by making the subjects ride a bicycle ergometer. Attrac-tiveness ratings were highest briefly after exercise, when arousal was still objectively present but no longer felt by the subjects. Ratings were lower immediately after exercise, presumably (according to the authors) because arousal was attributed to the efforts made; and they were lowest when arousal had completely died down.

The fact that previously elicited arousal produces enhanced subjective response (and sometimes objective response) to subsequent emotional stimuli appears well established (see Reisenzein 1983): For instance, provoked aggressive response is enhanced after viewing erotically stim-ulating materials (Cantor, Zillmann, & Einsiedel, 1978) and after expo-sure to uncontrollable loud noise (Donnerstein & Wilson 1976). Interpretation of this fact is less clear. It is difficult to separate the con-tributions of "misattribution" of arousal from enhanced responsivity to the later stimuli because of the state of arousal existing then. Also, as said earlier (section 2.8), various motivations (such as sex and aggres-sion) maintain other, more intrinsic relationships than merely that of sharing autonomic arousal (if they do that). It is therefore difficult to conclude that these experiments demonstrate the importance for emo-tional experience of feedback from autonomic arousal, misattributed or not.

A number of other types of experiment have tried to show the decisive influence of appropriately attributed autonomic awareness upon experienced emotional intensity. Many of these experiments suffer from serious methodological and conceptual flaws. Schachter and Wheeler (1962), for instance, considered that influence of arousal attribution upon emotion was demonstrated by an experiment in which subjects reacted with more laughter to a comedy film after epinephrine than after chlorpromazine; chlorpromazine, a tranquillizer, acts centrally, however, and does not merely suppresses autonomic response. Valins (1966) demonstrated faked autonomic feedback (alleged heart rate changes made audible through loudspeakers) to affect attractiveness ratings of female nudes. The higher the alleged heart rate, the higher the rated attractiveness. Clearly, autonomic "awareness" cannot be playing a role in this experiment, and what in fact appears to have taken place is an entirely different process, namely, enhanced attention for attractive details when the heart rate allegedly rose (Barefoot & Straub 1974).

The experiments on arousal transfer at most demonstrate that awareness of autonomic arousal contributes to intensity of emotional experience; they do not demonstrate that such awareness is indispensable for emotional experience per se. A more direct demonstration can perhaps be found by investigating conditions of decreased autonomic feedback.

Autonomic feedback can be decreased pharmacologically by reducing autonomic response; this in turn can be achieved by the administration of beta-blocking agents. Beta-blocking agents prevent naturally occurring epinephrine from acting upon some of its receptors (the beta receptors) in their target organs.

Beta blockers are capable of reducing discomfort due to autonomic responses, particularly if those responses interfere with efficient performance; the latter is the case in stage fright of professional musicians. Performance of violinists improves and their feelings of anxiety and nervousness decrease, after administration of propanolol (Brantigan, Brantigan, & Joseph 1982). Subjective feelings of anxiety, in clinical populations, have been found to be reduced by beta blockers in some studies but not in others (see Jefferson 1974; Reisenzein 1983). The divergence of results may be due in part to the fact that some studies used beta blockers with central as well as peripheral effects. It may be due also to the fact that anxiety reduction appears to occur in some subjects and not in others. It appears to occur mainly – perhaps only – in patients whose anxiety strongly depends upon perception of peripheral symptoms (e.g., cardiac neurotics; Lader & Tyrer 1972, Tyrer & Lader 1973).

However this may be, several studies find no reduction in subjective anxiety after administration of beta blockers; in at least one study, psychiatrists' ratings of the patients' anxiety decreased after such administration, whereas those by the patients themselves did not (Tyrer & Lader 1973). Evidently, emotional experience does not necessarily presuppose autonomic awareness and can exist without the latter. The same conclusion is drawn from failures to achieve reductions in experimentally induced anxiety (e.g., Tyrer 1976) or anger (Erdmann & Van Lindern 1980; see Reisenzein, 1983).

The effects of reduction of autonomic awareness through sensory nerve damage have been studied in patients of various kinds, primarily hemiplegics. James (1884) mentioned a case of "general anaesthesia" in which the patient's emotionality appeared to have suffered greatly: The man was "tranquil and phlegmatic." Dana (1921) reported on a 40-year-old woman whose "neck was broken" between the third and fourth vertebrae. Spinal cord lesions abolish or reduce sensitivity of those parts of the body innervated below the level of the lesion. The higher the lesion, the more extensive sensitivity loss; in a "broken neck," the loss is considerable. In the year Dana's patient lived after her accident, no changes were observed in manifestations of joy, sorrow, displeasure, and affection; severance of the spinal cord may not have been complete, however.

Hohmann (1966) conducted a study of 25 men with spinal cord lesions. Ages varied from 27 to 47 years; duration of lesion varied from 2 to 17 years. The group was divided into five subgroups of five men, according to how high the lesion was located. The higher the lesion, the larger indeed was the reported loss in emotional responsitivity. Fear, anger, and sexual excitement appeared to have decreased in nearly all subjects. The emotions still existed, but had become more purely cognitive and less pressing: "Formerly I became red. I did not reason, I just hit him and beat him up or was beaten up. Now I am a lot quieter, I don't any more feel as if I would explode"; "I still feel I am afraid, as when before a difficult examination, but I do not really feel afraid, not tense and shaky all over, with that hollow feeling in my stomach, as formerly."

The comments are what could be expected: Sensations of shakiness and of a hollow stomach are necessarily abolished, and emotional vivacity is thereby reduced. Yet some subjective as well as overt emotional response remained. Fear, anger, and sexual excitement persisted to some extent. Nearly all patients mentioned an increase in "sentimentality": They wept easily and felt a lump in the throat on the occasion of farewells, moving films, or ceremonies or when expressing feelings of tenderness.

Hohmann's findings have been widely cited as evidence that aware-ness of autonomic feedback is central to emotional experience. Consid-erable caution is needed, however, before agreeing with that conclusion. For one thing, as said, some anger, fear, and the like remained, and sentimentality had increased: Autonomic awareness evidently was not indispensable. For another thing, conditions of life and the meaning of events had considerably changed because of spinal injuries: Why get sexually excited, for instance, when there is little one can do about it? (Higgins 1979). Also, other studies did not find decreases in all types of emotional response (e.g., Jasnos & Hackmiller 1975) or found no de-crease whatsoever (Nieuwenhuyse & Bermond, 1986).

It may be concluded from the above that no adequate evidence exists for the hypothesis that autonomic awareness is an indispensable com-ponent of emotional experience; nor for the hypothesis that whenever such awareness is reduced, intensity of experience is necessarily re-duced. This, indeed, is also Reisenzein's (1983) conclusion in his exten-sive review of the evidence regarding Schachter's hypothesis.

Discrepancies between arousal and emotional intensity

The above conclusions do not alter the fact that autonomic awareness forms an important part of emotional experience, particularly of expe-rienced intensity. The relationship between arousal and experienced intensity, however, is complex. The complexity is evident from the dis-crepancies found between measures of strength of autonomic response and of subjective experience. Correlations between such measures tend to be moderate or low; we recall the Morrow and Labrum (1978) study on anxiety in heart patients, in which correlations were zero (section 3.4).

Some of the discrepancy may be due to misattribution of arousal to neutral, nonemotional sources, in line with Schachter's theorizing; such attribution would decrease experienced emotional intensity. A number of studies have found something of that nature to occur. Nisbett and Schachter (1966), for instance, found increased tolerance for electric shocks, and less distress, when experimental manipulations led subjects to attribute their arousal to a drug rather than to the shocks.

The moderating effect of certain cognitive manipulations upon inten-sity of emotion is clear from this kind of study. These studies do not provide convincing demonstrations of a decisive contribution of arousal – when appropriately attributed – to emotional experience. The manipulations may have actually decreased autonomic response, or emotional response generally; they may, for instance, have directed the subject's attention away from the emotional stimuli (Weiner 1980). Also, "misattribution" is not the best conception of the process involved, even when autonomic response is unchanged but experienced emotion still is modified. Apart from attention diversion, manipulations affect the significance attached by the subject to his autonomic arousal. Leventhal (1979; Calvert-Boyanowski & Leventhal 1979) has shown the effect of reducing the subject's uncertainty regarding the meaning of his aroused responses: Relevant information distinctly reduced subjective distress.

Other, related processes are also involved. Weinstein et al. (1968) found frequent and considerable discrepancies between autonomic indices (heart rate, EDR) and subjective distress ratings, in subjects viewing gruesome films; the discrepancies were shown particularly by subjects classified as "repressors" on the basis of MMPI profiles. Similar discrepancies occur in clinical cases. Individuals may complain of and suffer from dizzy spells, palpitations, and hyperventilation that they attribute to unknown illness but that in all likelihood constitute anxiety responses (Barendregt, pers. commun.). Evidently, arousal awareness contributes to emotional exprience only when factual coding (Leventhal 1980; see section 5.2) does not divorce that awareness from its sources.

All this illustrates the plausible supposition that awareness of bodily response may contribute to experience of emotional intensity. Additional suggestive evidence on this score is provided by a study by Nieuwenhuyse and Bermond (1986). The investigators had subjects record their emotional experiences over a period of two weeks. For each occurrence of emotion the subjects rated both it intensity and the presence of body sensations in 63 body areas; sensations were marked on a chart outlining those areas. Rated emotional intensity significantly correlated with number of areas marked for most emotions; exceptions were anger and fear. It must be added that the method did not tap autonomic awareness only: Marking of areas could indicate awareness of somatic activity as well as of autonomic activity.

Autonomic awareness and quality of emotion

For James, different emotional experiences come from different patterns of body sensation. For Cannon, this could not be true, since he considered autonomic response patterns in different excited emotions to be essentially the same. This argument was taken over by Schachter and

Mandler, who drew the conclusion discussed above: Differentiation of emotional experience must be due to cognitive cues.

The discussion centers around the amount and kind of differentiation present in autonomic awareness. Research on differentiation in autonomic response patterns does not favor the Jamesian view. The evidence has been reviewed in the preceding chapter. Autonomic response does show distinctly different patterns; the patterns do not, however, appear to correspond to emotions as classified and referred to by different names. They provide a basis for distinguishing experiences of excitement or calm, tenseness or relaxation, activity or passivity; but they do not appear to provide sufficiently distinctive and invariable cues for enabling the subject to identify his state as one of anger, or fear, or joy, and so forth.

Even when information for differentiation is available, subjects might be unable to use it. According to Mandler (1975), subjects are unable to discriminate between different levels of heart rate acceleration or blood pressure, and of course EDR goes largely unnoticed. Subjective estimates of arousal show higher correlations with the sum total of all physiological parameters than with any of them separately. Mandler concludes that a global arousal awareness is all that subjects can have.

Mandler's conclusion almost certainly is false. There exists a large variety of different emotionally significant body experiences: trembling; sweating; feeling choked; having a lump in one's throat; feeling oppressed; breathing freely; blushing; feeling one's face flush; feeling one's knees shake or teeth chatter; feeling butterflies in the stomach; having a sinking feeling in the pit of one's stomach; and many more. Note the differing experiences corresponding to roughly (but only roughly) similar physiological events: Blushing in embarrassment does not feel like flushing in anger. Note also the many experiences that are related to respiration and that probably stem from respiration parameters rarely recorded in emotion research.

Systematic description of body sensation patterns in emotion has hardly begun. Mason (1961) collected introspective reports illustrating the large variety of body experiences mentioned and the wide array of body parts differentially involved; the usual psychophysiological measurement probably taps only part of these. Nieuwenhuyse (Nieuwenhuyse, Offenberg, & Frijda, in prep.) further analyzed the data collected in the Nieuwenhuyse and Bermond study referred to above. The 63 body areas were reduced to 15 larger areas and scores from areas composing each larger area combined; profiles of the frequencies with which subjects had checked each area for each emotion were constructed. Iz-ard's 10 "fundamental" emotions were studied: joy, sadness, fear, anger, interest, disgust, guilt, shame, contempt, and shyness. Differences be-tween all parts of profiles were computed. All differences but two were significant. The profiles were readily interpretable: "face" being checked frequently for shame, probably reflecting blushing, etcetera. From this study it appears that emotions do differ in body experience and that each of the "fundamental" emotions, at least, corresponds to a distinct pattern.

The significance of these results should not be overrated. There is no evidence that each occurrence of a given emotion invariably corresponds to a given body awareness pattern; there thus is no evidence that the latter serves as the cue for the former. Also, many of the sensations probably correspond to awareness of somatic rather than autonomic activity: "front" presumably was checked when subjects felt they were frowning (its highest value was for "interest"), and "hands" probably was checked because of fist clenching (its highest value was for "anger"). The conclusion appears valid that emotions cannot be distinguished by autonomic sensation patterns. Still, the results underscore the viewpoint that the contribution of body awareness to emotional quality is too easily dismissed by the Schachter–Mandler or related approaches.

Autonomic awareness and behavior

Autonomic awareness does not seem to be a prerequisite for emotional behavior; the various pieces of evidence have been presented above. On the other hand, after sympathectomy, dogs do not learn an avoidance response, although responses learned before the lesion was made remain unaffected (Solomon & Wynne 1954; Wynne & Solomon 1955). During establishment of a conditioned avoidance response, response probability correlates with increases in heart rate; again, response probability after learning shows no such correlation (Black 1959). Wenzel (1972) reports that serological sympathectomy reduces open-field emotionality (defe-cation of rats in an open field), increases variability of aggressive re-sponse, slows down active and passive avoidance learning, and produces overreaction upon stimulus presentations. Mandler (1975, p.97) quotes Wenzel as concluding that "the immunosympathectomized animal [is] somewhat less reactive to *threatened* aversive stimuli but also somewhat overreactive to certain *actual* stimuli" (italics are Wenzel's). It might be, therefore, that autonomic awareness is either particularly important in anticipatory situations, where actual aversive stimuli are absent, or that it is important when learning, rather than execution of well-learned or unlearned responses, is involved. Under these conditions it may serve as a signal that something of importance is happening and needs checking (Mandler 1975).

Mandler also argues that emotional response under sympathectomy, as in Cannon's, Hohmann's, and Wenzel's subjects, is due to residual autonomic feedback or to the occurrence of "autonomic imagery." The latter hypothesis seems far fetched and lacks evidence; both hypotheses conflict with the unstable correlations between autonomic parameters and emotional experience and with the variable results with administration of beta blockers.

The significance of autonomic awareness

We conclude: Autonomic awareness is not a prerequisite for emotional experience or emotional behavior. It contributes to intensity and quality of experience, although it probably is not the cue for distinguishing the different emotions of fear, anger, joy, and so on. It may be necessary for acquisition of learned emotional or fear responses.

Autonomic sensations give emotional experience the distinct flavor of excitement and upset, of hotness, of being affected, that marks its most characteristic occurrences. Sartre (1934) has phrased it thus: Physiological changes in emotion represent to the subject the fact that his appreciation of the events is in earnest; they represent "le sérieux de l'émotion." We called it the emotion's *urgency*. They show the subject that he is affected and overcome without his wanting to. They signal the subject that events important to him occur. This, as just said, is precisely what Mandler emphasized. According to him, autonomic arousal motivates the subject to scrutinize the situation, realize its impact, and devise appropriate action. In addition, bodily changes have motivating properties of their own. They are disturbing sensations one wants to get rid of, or pleasurable sensations one may want to get back.

These kinds of significance attach differentially to different body changes. Shaking knees impede locomotion, and trembling hinders finer movement. Gastrointestinal upset generates weakness; dry mouth and a lump in the throat hamper speech; pressures on the chest demolish feelings of freedom and block urges to action. The different changes vary in experienced closeness to the "self," and thus in the degree of feeling shattered and of being unable or able to respond.

4.6. Emotional experience as awareness of action and action tendency

Awareness of action and action tendency

To James, emotional experience did not consist of visceral feedback alone. It also consisted of awareness of one's own actions: We are afraid because we run.

Indeed, action and impulse for action, or their absence, make up a large portion of the descriptive language of emotion. One wants to hit, destroy, or retaliate, to jump and shout, to regain the lost person. One finds oneself setting a second plate although the husband has been dead for a year (from Parkes 1972, again). One feels listless, lacks interest, would like to leave or to rid oneself of something. One wants to undertake things, to possess, to be with or to care for. One feels powerless or incompetent or full of vitality; or frozen, blocked, incapable of moving. One feels as if he were running into a wall, or in control and capable of succeeding. Varieties of cognitive action, as well as overt actions and tendencies, figure in experience: feeling confused, off balance, uncertain, unable to think clearly, or lucid and thinking without effort.

The items in Davitz's study, discussed in section 4.2., are largely of this kind; subjects deemed them appropriate in describing the various emotions. To again cite sample items: "I feel outgoing,"; "I want to be tender and gentle with another person"; "My senses are alert"; "There is a sense of vitality." As was pointed out, the majority of clusters obtained in his analysis refer to action tendencies or action tendency and activation states: activation (e.g., "sense of vitality"); hypoactivation ("I feel heavy, sluggish"); hyperactivity; moving toward; moving against; tension; enhancement; inadequacy. Some emotions, particularly the more subtle ones, can hardly be described otherwise than as action tendencies, and reflexively they certainly feel that way. A "kick" can be described as sudden felt activation and increase of interest, plus perhaps increased lucidity. "Being moved" can be characterized by what it says: falling into passivity and being carried by the significance of the event. Love is characterized by Scheler (1923) as "tendency towards being increased of a value." Awareness of one's passions, as defined in section

2.10, also consists of awareness of persistent tendency to act in given ways or of persistent absence of such tendency.

The major questions for understanding this mode of emotional experience concern the information upon which it is based and the process by which it comes into existence.

Awareness of action; self-attribution theory

One can, of course, observe one's own actions: One can perceive their nature, their outcomes, or the outcomes they appear to aim at. One then can attribute these actions to internal causes named after these actions: One attributes to oneself emotions post hoc, and one does so because causal attribution is a general cognitive propensity.

This is the theory of self-attribution. A person knows his emotions, according to Bem (1972), "partly by inferring them from observations of his own overt behavior and/or the circumstances in which his behavior occurs."

There can be little doubt that people do try to explain their own behavior and that they sometimes do so along the lines described by Bem. It happens that one infers one's liking from one's lenience, or one's anger from having acted disrespectfully. However, emotional experience itself often requires explanation, and then it is explained in similar fashion. One endeavors to explain one's anger by the offensiveness of some remark, whereas the true reason might have been the other person's show of superiority. Explanation of emotion is often a problem, for the subject himself. Anxiety attacks and depressions emphatically seek their causes, often in vain, sometimes inventing them. The issue is, then, whether emotions generally result from self-attributional judgments.

It was argued (section 4.3) that reflexive labeling of emotion is not the same thing as having an emotional experience. Labeling may be based upon emotional experience; it may also be based upon inference from awareness of action. It will be based upon inference, one may assume, when experiental cues are indistinct or ambiguous. Bem (1972) himself restricts his theory to such situations.

Self-attribution theory is not a general explanation of emotional experience, for other reasons than the above phenomenological argument. There is emotional experience in the absence of overt behavior. Instructions to inhibit expression sometimes decrease rated intensity of experience, but sometimes they do not; evidence will be discussed in the next subsection. There often exist clear discrepancies between experience and overt behavior. In experimental studies such discrepancies not infrequently crop up. Valins and Ray (1967) found fearful behavior to decrease through some cognitive manipulations but fearful experience to remain unaffected. Cupchick and Leventhal (1974) found degree of laughter and rated funniness of cartoons to be uncoupled under certain conditions–namely, precisely when the subject directed his attention toward his own spontaneous laughter. Lanzetta et al. (1976), by contrast, found intentional enhancement of pain expression to increase pain experience; intent here should have constituted "sufficient justification" in Bem's terms and should have rendered the self- attribution of feeling unnecessary. Indirect evidence is further provided by negative correlations sometimes observed between autonomic indices and overt behavior (see below, this section).

The role of proprioceptive cues; facial feedback theory

One of the cues for awareness of action is proprioceptive feedback from one's movements. Instead of considering such proprioceptive feedback as a basis for self-attribution, it may be considered directly to be part of emotional experience and even to constitute the major component of such experience.

Tomkins (1962) and Izard (1971) hypothesize that different emotional experiences consist of feedback from different facial expressions. Smiling feels different from frowning, and thereby happiness feels different from seriousness. The hypothesis can account for the differentiation of emotional qualities. Whereas autonomic response is relatively unspecific, facial expressive behaviors are reasonably characteristic for the various emotions (chapter 2). Tomkins and Izard restrict their hypothesis to facial expression; there is no good reason to do so, and the hypothesis may be extended to expressive behavior generally.

The hypothesis implies that voluntarily producing facial expressions, or expressive behaviors generally, should generate the corresponding emotional experiences. Indeed, it is common belief, and cited as such by James (1884), that giving vent to anger or grief intensifies the experience. However, the contrary opinion is also common belief, and is cited by Cannon (1927): Vent your anger to more readily get rid of it.

Experimental results tend to favor James. Bull (1951), without using emotion terms, asked her subjects to contract given facial muscles; these expressions were then "frozen" by hypnotic suggestion, and the subjects, still under hypnosis, were asked to experience a given emotion.

If the suggested emotion was incompatible with the frozen expression, the subjects were unable to experience it.

Laird (1974) gave his subjects similar emotion-neutral instructions. The subjects were asked either to contract the eyebrows (thus producing a frown), or to lift the corners of the mouth (thus producing a smile), both alledgedly for measuring muscle tension during a perception task. They then were asked to look for 15 seconds at cartoons projected on a screen. Ratings of mood showed higher ratings for anger in the "frown" condition and for happiness in the "smile" condition. The same experimental manipulation produced differences in recall of either sad or happy memories (Laird et al. 1982). Laird interprets his results by means of Bem's self-attribution theory, but they may also be interpreted as support for the Tomkins–Izard hypothesis, and are indeed quoted by Izard (1977) to that effect.

Ekman et al. (1983), with again similar types of instruction, found different physiological response patterns with different expressions voluntarily adopted. Subjective ratings showed that corresponding feeling states were indeed evoked.

Lanzetta et al. (1976) found that ratings of painfulness of electric shocks were higher when subjects were encouraged to express their pain, or even to pose as if the pain were intense, than when they were asked to hide their pain and to deceive observers as to the presence of shock. Autonomic arousal (EDR) corresponded to the differential pain ratings. Kleck et al. (1976) found lower pain ratings and EDR to be caused by the mere presence of observers, which induced suppression of expression (according to behavior ratings).

These results to not prove, however, that emotional experience consists of proprioceptive feedback from expression. Control of expression does more than merely decrease feedback; it may easily lead to efforts at controlling pain by what is called disengagement (see chapter 8) or by muscular relaxation. Apart from that, findings are far from uniform. Kotsch and Izard (cited in Izard 1977, p. 63) failed to obtain emotion-induction effects. Tourangeau and Ellsworth (1979) likewise found no effect of maintaining sad or fearful facial expressions upon reported sadness and fear in subjects watching emotion-inducing films; Hager and Ekman (1981) doubted the validity of the put-on expressions, however (see also Laird 1984).

Leventhal and Mace (1970), who asked their subjects to either express or inhibit laughter while looking at a slapstick movie, found positive effects (respectively, higher and lower funniness ratings) for girls, but an opposite effect for boys. Also, inhibition of laughter did not abolish funniness. Observation of the moments of laughter led to the interpretation that truly amused laughter (which girls appeared to do more) does influence experienced funniness, but that deliberate laughter (which boys appeared to produce more) does not. The results could be explained by self-attribution theory: Intention to laugh is a sufficient justification for laughter and does not necessitate emotion attribution. This explanation does not account, however, for the finding that instructions to observe one's laughter, while increasing expressiveness, tended to decrease rated funniness (Cupchik & Leventhal 1974).

When expression does appear to influence emotional experience, as in the studies by Laird and Ekman et al., that influence is not necessarily based upon proprioceptive feedback from expression itself. More likely it is due to other changes accompanying adoption of facial expressions, notably changes in respiration and general muscle tension. The influence of both upon mood of course is known from biofeedback studies (see section 3.4). In connection with the present issue, the effect of respiration rate upon emotion rating was demonstrated by McCaul et al. (1979). Changes in EDR, found when subjects had to put on expressions, can likewise be explained by respiration, tension, and movement. McCaul et al. (1982) and Tourangeau and Ellsworth (1979) both obtained evidence supporting such an explanation.

Further reservation concerning the facial feedback hypothesis comes from the inverse relationship sometimes found between overt expression and subjective experience or autonomic response. Some of the evidence has been mentioned earlier (section 3.9). Lanzetta and Kleck (1970), Buck et al. (1974), and Notarius and Levenson (1979) all found that subjects who were the most expressive facially were least responsive physiologically (with respect to EDR); all three studies investigated response to arousing situations such as threat of shock. Feeling intensity tends to follow autonomic response rather than overt response in these conditions (Notarius et al. 1982). Inverse relationships were also observed in hyperreactive children, but not in normal controls (Jones 1935; Hare 1976).

Taken together, the findings reviewed (see also Buck 1980) indicate that expression can influence emotional experience; that it sometimes does and sometimes does not; that the magnitude of effects is not impressive; and that when expression influences experience, it does not necessarily do so directly by proprioceptive feedback. These conclusions throw considerable doubt upon the Tomkins–Izard facial feedback hypothesis. Feedback from expression is not the major determinant of emotional experience, and cannot be a sufficient condition for it.

At the same time, the data suggest an explanation for the inconsistencies found. They also suggest a more satisfactory hypothesis concerning the role of proprioceptive feedback. Feedback from expression contributes to emotional experience if, and only if, it complements an action tendency or activation state.

What is meant can be clarified by introspective considerations. Movements as such do not feel the same as expressions, and expressions do not feel like mere kinesthetic sensations. They have direction and relational aspects. These properties can be illustrated by the difference between how it feels to point and how it feels merely to stretch your arm and index finger; the difference can be sensed when you point toward something and then, once you point, concentrate upon the muscle sensations produced. Awareness of pointing gets lost, precisely as amusement tends to get lost when observing your laughter.

What distinguishes awareness of pointing from that of stretching one's index finger is that in pointing, the muscular sensations confirm the intention to point. Quite generally, awareness of action consists of proprioceptive (or other) feedback signifying and signaling fulfillment of intention, along the lines of "feedforward biasing" (Pribram 1971). This in turn means that awareness of action includes awareness of the relational aspects of the action: what it wants and how far that has been accomplished. The same applies to expression, with the only difference being that action tendency or activation mode takes the place of intention. Experience of frowning is experience of concentration intent or of withdrawal urge realized in fact. Awareness of one's own smiling is that of friendly attitude actually achieved. Awareness of apathic posture is that of absence of interest that one has abandoned oneself to. More precisely: Only to the extent that awareness of expression implies those complements does it contribute to emotional experience. This conceptualization is quite similar to the conclusion Leventhal (1979) draws from his experiments.

The feedback expression hypothesis can be modified along these lines. Emotional experience can be considered to consist, or consist in part, of proprioceptive feedback from expression, when this expression confirms some action tendency or activation state. Emotional experience, in other words, does not consist of proprioceptive feedback, but of awareness of *action* readiness in the sense defined in chapter 2, in which proprioceptive feedback plays a confirming, informative role.

The point of "confirming action tendency" and "awareness of relational aspects" can be further illustrated, and perhaps supported, by observations from an old introspective study by Flach (1928). Flach, too, asked her subjects to execute certain movements designated in objective terms – for instance, "Move your hands forcefully forward, palms up" (a gesture of begging). She carefully interviewed her subjects, however.

The movements made were experienced as "striving," as emotional attitudes "contained in the dynamics of tension and countertension," and as establishing relationships with the environment (Flach, 1928, pp. 449, 460 ff., 521). They were experienced so only, however, if the subject "identified" with her movements, made them "from the inside," and put herself "behind" her gestures. These qualifications can be understood as referring to setting the relational goals proper to the action tendencies involved. It need not surprise one that such goal setting comes naturally and involuntarily, at least to some subjects. It may be supposed to come naturally whenever subjects produce expressions with conviction. Point your finger and you feel you are pointing; look surprised and you feel you are stopping and waiting and watching. The relational goal is the common denominator of all components of the movement one tries to produce, just as the goal of hitting a target is the common denominator of all movements comprising, say, throwing darts. It is also their integrating principle. The integration is what is manifest as "activated" behavior, in which all body parts participate in some balanced manner (see section 2.4). It is manifest also in general tenseness or relaxation and, particularly, in respiration. Respiration and degree of tension set the tone for a smile, a frown, a fearful grimace not to be isolated facial events; their importance for expression feedback effects to occur has been underlined above.

All this, incidentally, implies that merely executing expressive movement does not generate true emotion. It generates the image of an emotion; it establishes from the outside the nonverbal, imaginal representation of an action tendency's aim; it does only that unless there is preexisting readiness to go with that particular tendency. The conditions under which execution of expressive movement truly generates emotion are of a quite different, and considerably more complex, nature; they form a contingency that will briefly be dealt with in section 5.5, under "Elicitation of activation."

Felt action tendency; action tendency theory

Arnold (1960) has assigned felt action tendencies the central place in emotional experience. Emotion is defined by her as felt action tendency

– that is, first of all, as felt tendency toward approach or withdrawal. Further principles yield further differentiation of emotions. As discussed in chapter 2, action tendency is too restrictive a notion to do justice to the variety in emotional response, and activation modes had to be added; together they constitute modes of action readiness. Emotion thus is felt mode of action readiness.

Felt action readiness modes contain the information needed to account for the distinction between the major emotions like anger, fear, and joy and for many distinctions within those concepts. Action readiness modes contain all the information needed for the subject to distinguish one major emotion experience from another.

There is ample evidence to consider action readiness a major mode of emotional experience in actual fact, and not merely because it contains all the necessary information. As argued above, spontaneous descriptions of experience to a very large extent consist of what one wants to do or cannot do or does not know how to do or does without wanting to do it, or to what one feels able or unable to do. Subjects assign action readiness modes to emotions without difficulty, with a high degree of intersubjective agreement and with considerable specificity regarding the assignments made; the assignments tend to be those that can be expected, and to follow the suggestions made in Table 2.1 (Frijda 1986).

One may wonder whether awareness of action readiness is in fact dependent upon feedback from muscular response – whether proprioceptive feedback is necessary for such awareness. One may wonder whether that awareness could not be entirely central. It can be questioned whether feedback from actual muscular activity is necessary for awareness of action readiness. Actual movement does not seem indispensable; the pattern of muscular readiness may well be sufficient, since the specific experiential character may be assumed to derive less from actual feedback than from intent. That pattern might even be fragmentary and still suffice: Even tensing one arm might suffice to feel anger, if it is embedded in the central readiness for offensive action.

There is no good reason why central readiness itself could not be represented in consciousness, even in a nonverbal, nonsymbolic mode. No doubt, actual feedback from the muscles gives awareness substance and urgency. Yet awareness of action tendency can exist without it. We often know what we want to do and what action programs press for control precedence. We know of our being preoccupied, restless, unable to concentrate, or of our being preoccupied by a particular event. Restlessness, preoccupation, preoccupation with revenge or escape or anticipated enjoyment need no muscle twitches to come to awareness. For much in emotional experience, it would seem, the periphery is peripheral. On the other hand, the periphery – muscle twitches or autonomic upset – probably offers the most direct signals of control precedence and urgency.

Components of action readiness awareness

As with situational meaning structure, components can be systematically described that alone or in patterns make up awareness of the action readiness modes corresponding to the different emotional states. The major of these components, of course, parallel the modes of action readiness as derived from behavior and enumerated in Table 2.1.

It is important to recall: *Action readiness modes* meant modes of readiness for entertaining or abandoning given types of relationship with the emotional object. The relational aspects form the dominant features in awareness of these modes, too. Weeping is felt not as contorted face, sobbing convulsions, and wet eyes only: It is *felt* as capitulation, giving up resistance, helpless surrender to one's helplessness. Being attentive is felt as one's focusing upon an event, following how it develops, linking to it. Mere excitement – sheer arousal – is felt as being gripped by something and not knowing what to do, or as not knowing what grips you. And so on. Awareness of action readiness is awareness of its sense (cf. section 2.1).

Awareness of action readiness is not awareness of momentary state only: It is awareness of such a state within a temporal context, as an element in a development from what precedes and toward what comes. The future is evidently present in the sense of readiness itself, and in the anticipations, uncertainties, thwartings, incompletednesses that constitute major readiness modes and their monitoring. Monitoring was discussed earlier as one of the aspects of action tendency and action readiness generally (chapter 2). Feelings of being unable, of powerlessnes, success, and probable success are as much parts of awareness as doing, not doing or wanting to do.

The past is present in awareness of action readiness in that relaxation after excitement is, and feels, different from just relaxing; having abandoned struggle is, and feels, different from mere rest. Here, too, muscle sensation, proprioceptive feedback, gains meaning from the intentional context within which it is received.

Awareness of action readiness mode hovers, one may assume, between true awareness of action readiness and awareness of the goals of such action. One can feel an urge, or intent to act, and one can anticipate an outcome. The more the latter dominates, the more there is awareness of intention; the more the former dominates, the more pronounced the awareness of "emotion," of being gripped. Note that intentional structures, passions even, do not distinctly "feel" like emotions. This holds to such an extent that love is not usually considered an elementary emotion in psychological theory; and yet to naive subjects it is the most prototypical instance of emotion (Fehr & Russell 1984).

As with situational meaning structure, here too there are core components: attributes of experience that identify that experience as an emotional one and that constitute its intentional dimension or dimensions.

Foremost among these components is what we will call *passivity*; it is the attribute underlying the designation "passion."Emotional urge and emotional apathy are felt as not chosen; no intention, no voluntary goal setting precedes them. The emotion as a whole may be chosen – one may decide to view events in a certain way – but action readiness change then follows of its own accord. Intentions do play a role in emotional action, but they follow emergence of action tendency. Passivity, of course, is to action readiness awareness what objectivity is to situation meaning structure.

Related to passivity is sense of control precedence. "Passivity" refers to awareness of involuntary origin of action readiness mode, "sense of control precedence" to that readiness's mode of operation.

Inhibition and control

Awareness of action readiness includes awareness of inhibition and voluntary self-control. One can be aware of being inhibited: of desire to act, to change the situation, or to grasp opportunity, but, at the same time, of being unable to let that desire develop into true action readiness or action. One can even be aware of absence of emotional response to stimuli one knows call for such response: the feeling of numbness or that of depersonalized detachment. All this, too, has its peripheral feedback that confirms inability: the feeling of one's own rigidity, one's inability to move properly, one's cramps, in fear, shyness, nervousness. And one can notice one's inability to think straight and clear, thoughts not coming, words not coming. All this shares in the features of passivity and control precedence just mentioned: It comes, unasked for, and there is not too much one can do about it.

One is also aware, most of the time, of one's voluntary self-control; awareness comes from peripheral feedback of the efforts made – suppression of movement, jaws set, teeth clenched (although aching muscles sometimes betray this only afterward) – or by awareness of a more cognitive nature: of not letting imagination run wild, thought pursue its train, and action tendency take shape. There often is a strong sense that cognitive self-control is exerted: the sense that, were something to slip, panic, uncontrollable anger or weeping, or laughter, might burst out. The sense of being on the brink of panic has often been described: so has the possibility of suppressing rising panic, unless it has risen too far. Janis (1971) has reproduced the account of a man in danger of drowning. Beijk (1963) reports retrospective accounts of actors experiencing blackouts: They often mention that split second in which they decide, as it were, to panic or to find a solution. Piët (1986) gives similar descriptions from mountainclimbers. Kaplan (1964) reproduces a moving account of a woman fighting her rising madness by writing with all effort she can muster. These experiences of control and capability for control mitigate or qualify the features of passivity and control precedence.

Regulatory functions of expression

The research reviewed above suggests that expressive behavior is important for emotional experience. Emotional experience consists, in part, of feedback from expressive behavior; according to the present interpretation, it does so primarily because it is experienced as confirmation or fulfillment of action tendency. We are afraid because we run, if the running feels motivated and with control precedence.

Control of expression can exert a regulatory influence upon emotional experience that extends beyond providing or withholding feedback. Several of the results suggest that expression retrogradely affects both action tendency and the control processes keeping it in check, with concomitant effects upon experience. If an action tendency has been aroused, or was in abeyance under inhibitory control, letting expressive movement go undermines further control; letting control slip has the same consequence. The issue has been touched upon in chapter 2, in discussing the "point of no return" in control of anger, weeping, and the response to pain. "Count till ten when in wrath" is a manifestation of the inverse process. This regulatory function also shows in the difficulty of retaining or regaining mental concentration without outward action such as frowning. Regaining self-possession, too, often involves tensing up and clenching teeth. The results by Lanzetta et al. (1976) and Kleck et al. (1976) are, we think, to be interpreted along these lines, rather than as mere effect of proprioceptive cues upon self-awareness.

Freely giving way to expression stimulates development of emotion both through generating the image of a given relationship with the situation and through self-generated change in situational meaning. Expression is relational action that modifies relations with the environment. Giving in to anger elicits fresh encounters with the offender or his offense; giving in to grief creates self-pity and sharpens appreciation of hopelessness. Perhaps this explains the opposing effects of expression upon experience, the Jamesian and the Cannon ones. To the extent that letting expression go undermines control, it enhances emotional intensity. To the extent that it effectively changes relationships (makes the offender draw back, or satisfies the offended) it permits emotion to die down sooner. To the extent, moreover, that control of expression is due to fear of its effect upon others, that control itself is a source of frustration that increases emotional arousal.

4.7. Hedonic quality

Implicit in the preceding is the presence of hedonic quality as a further ingredient of emotional experience. Situational meaning structure involves valence; that is, situations and outcomes are liked or disliked; so are one's own actions. Reflexively, subjective experience can be pleasant or unpleasant. Body response, arousal, too, can be pleasurable or disagreeable.

The psychology of mental content, it will be recalled, distinguished "feelings" as mental elements that could not be reduced to mere sensory sensations. In addition to this introspective point, pleasantness and unpleasantness must necessarily be irreducible, on logical grounds. There must be something in the individual's experience that makes him welcome or accept certain events and reject others; there must be signals that lead to and trigger these different sorts of behavior. These events, of course, include physical pain and autonomic or other bodily sensations: There must be something to them that makes one seek aspirin to end some of them and to seek a partner to produce others. In other words: The facts of preference require the assumption of some basis for preference. Young (e.g., 1961), in particular, has untiringly argued the vital role of hedonic quality for understanding preference behavior and thereby motivation.

Hedonic quality, pleasure, and pain are nevertheless evasive notions, and were fiercely debated in the era of introspective psychology. The quality was called "evanescent" by Titchener, when it was observed as accompaniment to sensory impressions – some pleasant taste, some harsh sound – in the introspection experiments. Others doubted its existence as nonsensory quality or denied its particular properties. However, its existence and properties are neither evasive nor evanescent in those emotional experiences that appear as nearly unalloyed instances of "hedonic tone": anguish, as in depression, and anxiety, as in anxiety states. These experiences impress as elementary, as experiential rock-bottom. Neither the presence of cognitive contents like self-deprecation, guilt, the end of the world, nor loss of interest as such, nor awareness of autonomic arousal (which may even be absent) explain the torment and the sense of white blazing hell, or the sense of absolute nothingness which may make death preferable. Autobiographic accounts of mental illness, like Sutherland's (1977) *Breakdown*, or the selections of Kaplan (1964) give evidence of what is meant. It is pure silliness to essay explanations of such experiences as mere organic sensations or cognitive assessments or some combination of both.

The introspectionist account of hedonic quality is nevertheless unsatisfactory, due to its reflexive nature. Pleasantness and unpleasantness in that account are represented as "feelings," that is, as mental elements rather than as apparent states of the world or of the subject as seen by himself. Reflexive reduction destroyed the true nature of experience, here more than anywhere else. It destroys relations between the so-called elements. In the introspectionist account "feelings," perceptions, and images just float around together in the consciousness bowl.

That account invites odd consequences. Since "feelings" of pleasantness and unpleasantness are "not localized" (see section 4.2), they should add and subtract. Eating steak while listening to a concert should increase the pleasure one takes in the latter, or the former, or both. Usually this does not happen. Usually, simultaneous experiences of pleasure or pain are kept distinct, unless combined in an overall evaluation of one's condition.

The present point is Aristotle's and is extensively discussed by Kenny (1963). Simultaneous hedonic experiences are kept distinct because the relationship between an event and its concomitant pleasure or displeasure is an intrinsic one. Both belong together. They do so not because of one's attributional or reflexive activities: uncertainty about what caused one's pleasant feeling, which motivates attributions, forms a particular constellation and not a paradigmatic case.

Hedonic quality is not a mere contingent fact – pleasure or pain happening to be around when a given event happens to be around. It is a meaningful experience. Hedonic quality is a comment upon the event or the action concerned. Hence Aristotle's formulation which is followed in substance by Spinoza and by Arnold (1960) and Kenny (1963): Pleasure is the sense of unimpeded functioning; unpleasantness is the sense of impeded functioning. In Spinoza's phrase: Joy is a passive state wherein the mind passes to a greater perfection; sorrow is a passive state wherein the mind passes to lesser perfection (*Ethics*, Part III, Prop. II). The perfection, of course, is in the eye of the beholder: it is being closer to one's own nature.

In the preceding, hedonic quality has figured under a variety of designations: "feelings," of pleasantness and unpleasantness; positive and negative valence; attractiveness and aversiveness; joy and sorrow. The different labels apply to what may be called different manifestations in experience. "Feelings" of pleasantness or unpleasantness are more or less self-contained experiences; the others are embedded in the context of actual or potential action and do not come into separate existence as "experiences."

By this description, "feelings" (in quotation marks) and emotions are different kinds of experience. There exist experiences of an evaluative nature that stand by themselves and those in which evaluation is manifest through the call for action or through elicitation of action tendency; "*feeling*" is a name for the first; *emotion* for the latter. The typical situations in which they occur are different. "Feelings" are concomitants of stimulus reception and imply mere acceptance or nonacceptance of the stimulus: A tone is disagreeable, a person pleases the eye, or mind. Emotion (or valence, or attractiveness and aversiveness, or joy and sorrow) implies that an interest is touched upon and action or activation change is called for. The distinction may be taken as a matter of definition. However, the latter kind of experience (emotion) also corresponds to outwardly visible emotional behavior (if it occurs), whereas the former does not: It at most underlies preference behavior.

The distinction between "*feeling*" as defined here and *emotion* has been forcefully argued by Arnold (1960). The distinction refers, according to her, not to a difference in intensity but to a difference in nature. "Feeling" is sense of enhanced or impeded functioning; (felt) emotion is felt action tendency. The distinction is important, as it clarifies confusions and relationships. Certain objects or situations elicit "feelings"; opportunities and risks in obtaining or avoiding those objects or situations elicit emotions (see section 6.5 for further discussion).

4.8. The significance of emotion

Emotional experience itself can become an object of experience, through reflection, as can emotional action, through awareness of action. They carry their own meaning, which then becomes part of emotional experience. That meaning will be called the *significance* of an emotion.

Significance has many sources and facets. We distinguish three: self-significance, external consequence, and social significance.

Self-significance

Emotion may reveal to the subject that the stimulus event for him, possesses a given meaning; and it may reveal his sensitivities that make that meaning come into existence. Through being upset upon hearing her name, one may discover not really to have become indifferent. One discovers, by one's timidity, that social situations are situations one cannot cope with. By again falling in love with a gentle man, one discovers that one falls for gentle men. Through emotion one gets acquainted with one's world. At the same time, one gets acquainted with oneself: as being insecure; or dependent; or desirous of care and tenderness. Awareness of emotion can modify the self-image. A given fear is "that fear again," with its implications for future vulnerability. At a higher level of abstraction, that fear shows me to be a sensitive person, or a weak person, or whatever the inference.

There are not only general assessments. Every emotional response tends to be evaluated in terms of one's self-evaluation and other norms or values. One is in grief and helpless and may hate oneself for it. One is afraid and considers oneself a coward. One is angry and considers oneself entitled to one's anger. Emotional experience, in other words, extends beyond emotion proper: It extends to how the emotion itself is felt; how it is welcomed or rejected.

This applies also to having emotions as such, and to being able or unable to experience and handle given specific kinds of them. Suffering great fear and being able to stand it, or continuing to act coolly in danger and suspense, can be a source of sense of power and adequacy and, under the circumstances, of peak experience. Quite generally, emotions enhance a sense of experiencing and functioning, of possessing and utilizing resources. This also applies to negative emotions, to sorrow and anxiety. Anxiety in particular is an experience that is not only valued negatively. The positive emotional value of anxiety stems in part from the variety it provides. It stems also, and more importantly, from the sense of functioning and of mastery, of being able to face it (Piët 1986).

Significance of this type does not come only to anxiety. It comes as much to grief, or hatred, or guilt. Any great passion can enhance the feeling of being alive and functioning to one's limits; and so, to some extent, do their poor man's alternatives in viewing sentimental or suspense films. Lack of emotion, by contrast, as it occurs in some depersonalization states, is terrible. It increases the sense of nonexistence. As for guilt, Dostoyevski describes the pride that can be derived from it.

Of course, self-significance can also go the other way. Emotions can be considered exhausting, irrational, a bother, or a waste of time. What determines either the one or the other is complex. Ability to handle strong emotions may be one factor; so may be the dreariness of what life otherwise would be; so is one's value system.

Magnitude and kind of self-significance can be assumed to color particular emotional experiences, making one joy, fear, or anger different from another. Self-significance probably accounts for the experienced "depth" of an emotion. Self-significance certainly influences emotional control, since what is accepted needs less control than what is rejected.

An important aspect of self-significance is the evaluation of one's sense of control over emotion and of one's sense of responsibility for feelings and acts involved. One can feel guilty about one's anger, even if that anger is never expressed; and one can feel free from responsibility for acts committed impulsively, under the power of emotion. One can fear emotions generally because of the threat to control over events, or specifically because of fear of being unable to resist a particular temptation. Monitoring of emotion occurs at various levels simultaneously.

External consequence

Emotions have external consequences. In part these have been discussed in connection with what were called interactive expressions: Other people react to one's signs of emotion. In part the consequences were discussed along with the topic of emotion as disturbance or energizer (section 2.12). External consequences can go far, of course: The environment can retaliate, be envious, punish, censure, take advantage of weaknesses, or it can join in the fun, respond to interest and invitation, feel sorry or guilty or taken aback. All this is obvious. The point here is that emotional experience includes or entails awareness of these consequences. This aspect of the significance of emotion determines how emotion is controlled, or enhanced and used; it will be discussed more extensively in chapter 8. The distinction between awareness of external consequence and self-significance is vague: Feeling sorry for oneself when sad merges into putting on its manifestations because of the fruit that that yields.

Social significance

External consequences are to a very large extent due to social response. By *social significance* is meant something else, however.

Emotions may be felt to isolate or to unite. They can be considered by the individual as events that throw him back upon himself, leave him to himself, are his private affairs that may not or cannot be shared; or they can be considered essentially public or social affairs that will be accepted and understood by others and that confer upon the subject a well-defined place: as a bereft one, or a successful one, or an indignant one, or a deranged one. Certain emotions, in given cultures, constitute "transitory" social roles (Averill 1982), and the subjects know this. We will briefly return to these points in chapter 8, when discussing social regulation of emotion (section 8.5). They are mentioned here to indicate that actual or anticipated isolation or social embedding, through emotional experience and response, are part of the emotion's significance – that is, they are constituents of how emotions are felt.

It is clear that the wider social context – cultural norms and beliefs – strongly determines all three sources of emotion significance. Self-significance is highly dependent upon the social environment's "feeling rules" (Hochschild 1983), external consequence upon rules of behavior (see Gordon 1981).

4.9. Intensity of emotional experience

So far, discussion has centered around emotional quality: what makes the difference between emotional and nonemotional experience and between the experience of the different emotions. Other aspects of quality were touched upon in passing – depth, for instance.

Still other aspects of quality concern intensity differences. This way of phrasing of course is wordplay, but it serves to underline that the entire notion of intensity of experience is problematic, particularly when it comes to emotional experience. Is rage merely stronger than anger? Certainly not: There is an allusion to loss of control. The phrasing also serves to underline that whatever can be meant by "intensity of emotional experience" is not unidimensional. The point was raised in connection with intensity of emotional behavioral response. We briefly come back to it here.

What constitutes intensity of emotional experience, or (what is not necessarily the same) the experience of emotional intensity? The preceding sections have mentioned a number of different constituents, that is, a number of different dimensions that allow of quantitative variation. Awareness of autonomic arousal is one of these, but it is only one among several.

Situational meaning structure contains a number of "intensity parameters": urgency of the events; relevance of the event; seriousness of the event; inescapability (closedness, unmodifiability, objectivity). Action readiness change also has several quantitative aspects. Passivity, the sense of being overcome, and impulsion, the sense of control precedence, both can vary in degree. There is also awareness of degree of activation and of response vigor and amplitude. Another variable again consists of the amount of time and effort one is inclined to spend in intentional activity, the execution of plans, and the abandonment of current goals, which underlies one's awareness of the long-range intensity discussed in section 2.10. Such inclination, incidentally, does not directly translate into awareness in the guise of strength, but of frequency. We noted the apparent absoluteness of emotional events as appraised; it was included in the situational meaning feature of "objectivity." A similar characteristic applies to awareness of action readiness. "I often think: I always want to be with him" was one of the statements by which subjects described their feeling of being in love (Rombouts 1983).

As said, it is unknown how the various subjective parameters correlate with one another and with the various behavioral and stimulus parameters. Almost certainly, there is more than one underlying intensity dimension.

4.10. Emotional experience: its structure and varieties

Emotion

Emotional experience, in its most prototypical form, is a complex of the three kinds of awareness: situational meaning structure, arousal, and action readiness, with hedonic quality involved in each. To these kinds of awareness may be joined awareness of actions, plans, and goals and of the significance of emotion. In this complex, situational meaning structure and action readiness mode specify a given kind of emotion.

The elements of the complex are not just mixed or juxtaposed; they fit together. Meaning structure motivates action readiness; action readiness is the felt answer to meaning structure. Awareness of arousal represents the urgency of the situation–action structure, and it participates in awareness of action readiness, both as an element of such readiness and as an element of disturbance of action. Hedonic quality is a felt comment upon event and upon response. Significance manifestly flows from the preceding. Actions, plans, and goals are instrumental in fulfilling that which action tendency tends toward.

Emotional experience, at its most prototypical, is not subjective experience. It is in part a perception and in part a felt interaction with the environment, or felt inclination or disinclination thereto. It is something between him and me, or between her and me, or it and me. It is, moreover, not "an" experience, in the sense of a mental content or a state of mind. Sometimes it is, when things are stable. Mostly it is not: Most emotions, being interactions, are events over time and are felt as events over time. They not only have a beginning and an end, but also an initiation and a resolution, or an explicit nonresolution. Fear not merely ends; it is overcome; or not needed any longer, or assured that nothing will happen, or left dangling, unresolved.

Of the preceding components of emotional experience, action tendency would seem to be the most criterial attribute for identifying an experience as emotional. Action tendency can exist in isolation: in dejection, in anxiety attack, and in mood. Anxiety attack may search a matching situation, and it does create one by projecting a world without hold; but it was there first as inability to act and find a hold, and this was the basis, for the subject, to identify his state as one of anxiety.

It has been argued that the above components – awareness of situational meaning structure, of arousal, and of action readiness – represent antecedents and consequents of emotion, and not emotional experience itself. Izard (1977), for one, appears to take this position. We do not think this to be an appropriate point of view. There is no need, nor any evidence, for an irreducible *quale* over and beyond the experiential structure described. The components of that structure account for the specificity of particular emotional experiences.

That structure can have the appearance of a quale, though – as something sensed at once and at one instant of time. It does so in the same way that a the meaning of a word can be sensed at one instant of time. Experience of word meaning is a pointer to what could be explicated; it is awareness that one could explicate, by telling or pointing or doing, were there time to do so. That much is evident from old-time introspection on imageless thought (e.g., Bühler 1907; see Woodworth 1938). The same applies to emotional experience.

Emotional experience at a given instant of time points beyond itself in several directions. Situational meaning structure contains the past and the future: Relief contains the past, and grief the future, in the loss being felt as irretrievable. Similar pointers are contained in awareness of action readiness mode. Sense of incompetence implies that everything has been tried and nothing will succeed; joy implies the power over moments to come.

Emotional response, moreover, hardly ever is felt as an isolated response to an isolated event. It is an element from a string, a series, a system of responses to some life event: an event that, for instance, is manifestly unique, unrepeated, unrepeatable; or, on the contrary, a recurrent one, one more of it. It is felt as response to an event located at a given time or place, or rather as response to an instantiation of what crops up everywhere. It also is felt as an element in a series of different kinds of, or instances of, responses: I am angry now, whereas I may be contemptuous later and aloof, indifferent tomorrow. Emotional response at a given instant projects toward an intentional structure of which it may be the germ, the beginning, or out of which it has emerged. It projects toward the actions that the intentional structure contains: My admiration for that flower is different from that for that piece of music because the interactions announced by the admirations are not the same, because the time perspectives for the interaction are different, because the concerns they impinge upon are different.

All this is the flesh adorning the skeleton of the three components defining emotional experience: situational meaning structure, awareness of arousal, and awareness of action readiness mode, along with hedonic quality and possibly significance. From that skeleton components may be missing or modified, thereby producing other modalities of affective experience.

Feeling

The word has many meanings. Earlier in this chapter it was used in the technical sense of an element of experience or as a self-contained evaluative experience of pleasantness or unpleasantness. The introspectionists and Arnold employed it in that sense; and when used in that sense "feeling" is being put in quotation marks.

The word has a different meaning in sentences such as "I feel angry," "I feel insecure," or "It makes me feel lonely." Sentences like these are of two sorts: those in which an emotion word occurs, as in "I feel angry," and those affairs in which this is not the case, as in "I feel lonely" or "I feel insecure." Loneliness and insecurity are states of affairs that can be described more or less objectively, as being without company and as being subject to risks, respectively.

There is a difference in emphasis between "I am angry" and "I feel angry." A feeling like that of anger has the same structure as the corresponding emotional experience, except that action tendency does not truly press for action. The action tendency – action readiness mode generally – is known as an implication of the situational meaning structure, but it is not actually competing for control precedence, at least with respect to overt action. It is virtual, so to speak. A feeling consists of awareness of situational meaning structure plus anticipation that a given mode of action readiness will develop if the situation becomes urgent. In other words: There exist experiences similar to emotions in which action readiness change is virtual and belongs to the domain of imagery or mere knowledge. Hedonic quality may be pronounced, though, in these experiences, too, and control precedence can be pronounced in cognitive activity – in preoccupation, that is. It is to such experiences that the name of *feeling* is usually given.

One may consider *feeling* to be merely a word referring to emotions of lesser intensity. However, as actually used it mostly refers to experiences with a different structure. There exist weak emotions and strong, very powerful feelings, to judge from the degree to which one can be absorbed in them and abstain from other actions. Also, emotions can be transformed into feelings, by a process which will be called "reflexive control": by reflecting upon action tendency, by contemplating it rather than having it (see section 8.5).

Feelings of loneliness, insecurity, and the like are slightly different. They refer to states of satisfaction or nonsatisfaction of concerns. They are equivalent to awareness of situational meaning structures, but transformed into subjective states, through reflection. Phrased differently: They are awareness of the kind of relevance of events and of what these events are relevant for: for the sense of security, for the desire to be with others, and so on. They are such awareness experienced as subjective states rather than as states of the world. In that, of course, they correspond more closely to the "true" state of affairs, as reflection teaches that to be: The world as a barren place, when looked at closely, turns out to be nothing but my feelings of loneliness, and that, in turn is acute awareness of the fact that my desire for being together with others is unsatisfied. Feelings are monitors in Pribram's (1970) phrase: They monitor the state of satisfaction of the organism, with respect to concerns sometimes identified in the feeling's name; and they do so in a way that is accessible to reflection.

Mood

Moods are experiences underlying completions of the sentence "Today, I feel _____," where an emotion word is to fill the blank. The term *mood* is applied to affective states, often of relatively long duration, not elicited by an external event or outlasting such an event, or disproportionate to such an event in intensity or duration.

Mood, as experience, can be characterized more precisely in terms of the components of emotional experience enumerated earlier. Moods are action tendencies or activation states not felt as motivated by situational meaning, which action tendencies or activation states are directed toward, or away from the surroundings in general rather than toward or away from a specific object or event. There is general increased or decreased interest, or easily provoked readiness for aggressive response, or whatever the nature of the mood. Alternatively, moods can be described as experiences of situational meaning structure with the characteristic of globality (section 4.4): Everything seems open and attainable, or nothing is attractive, or nearly everything is irritating.

That moods are not felt as motivated by situational meaning does not exclude their having been caused by some meaningful event; and the subject may know it. Known causation, however, is different from experienced motivation. In mood experience, the cause has become detached from felt action readiness. The cause indeed may not be an experienced meaningful event. It may be biochemical. For experience, as said before, the kind of cause makes no difference. Morphine makes things easy, accessible, and beautiful.

"Feelings"

"Feelings" (in quotation marks) are self-contained experiences referring to acceptance or nonacceptance of an object or situation – that is, to sense of unimpeded or impeded functioning. Feelings are self-contained in that they do not involve action tendency or other mode of action readiness change. For further discussion, see the section on hedonic quality (section 4.7).

Sentiments and passions

We defined (section 2.10) sentiments as dispositions to habitually appraise given objects or kinds of event in certain ways, or as awareness itself of these appraisals. Sentiments, then, are feelings in which object evaluation is the major situational meaning component.

Passions are goals springing from action tendency known to be of long standing, and in which either the actual situation or the desired situation has strong relevance; they are felt to be such as to generate action readiness change under appropriate conditions of urgency.

The varieties of emotional experience

Emotions, moods, feelings, sentiments, and passions are not sharply separate classes of experience, as may be evident from the above analysis. Feelings may turn into emotions when urgency increases or when loosening of self-control allows action tendency to change from virtual to actual. Moods and passions may form the background for emotions to emerge upon the advent of specific events; mood again may remain when the confrontation is over. Common to all varieties are action tendency and situational meaning structure, varying in urgency and in call for action or action abandonment.

Incompleteness, undeterminedness, and ambiguity

Emotional experience can vary in other ways. One or more of the four basic components may be absent. Situational meaning structure may be absent, due to reflection. The experience then becomes "subjective," an inner feeling in which the projective nature of irreflexive experience is lost. Reflection easily occurs when situational meaning structure has no focus, as in mood; moods readily are felt as subjective states, particularly if they have not been precipitated by external events.

Situational meaning structure itself also may be undifferentiated and lack context components. Fleeting impressions, associations of thoughts barely noticed, or sudden brief stimuli may lead to mere excitement before context is perceived or has crystallized in thought. One may become moved or begin trembling upon hearing the name of a person once loved, without much articulation as to why or how; and by consequence no definite action tendency can develop. Such emotions are called "being startled" or "being moved"; or they may have no name. Often further confrontation, in reality or in thought, clarifies the situation and leads to the development of a more specific emotion: of regret, of nostalgia, of anger, and so forth.

Action tendency may be lacking, except for mere arousal and its relational significance; this is the case in most of the examples just mentioned. Arousal may be absent: in feelings, in the peaceful emotions, perhaps in many of the emotions elicited by solitary thoughts rather than by external events. Some anxiety states and depressed states show no arousal change. Absence of noticeable arousal change is of course more or less definitory for calmer, more self-contained emotions.

Hedonic quality is absent in moderate, unthwarted desire and in attention or interest as such. Hedonic quality may disappear for defensive reasons: As mentioned before, autonomic arousal is sometimes felt as mere body sensation when in fact it is emotional response. In depersonalized states the same may happen with action tendency or expressive behavior: "He opened his mouth, so that excitement could escape through the mouth" (Kafka, *The Trial*). Introspection can produce the same result when pleasantness and unpleasantness evaporate, leaving mere pressure sensations. Loss of hedonic quality in emotional reaction clearly can go so far as to destroy emotional experience.

In all these variants, emotional experience is somewhat atypical. "Being moved" is not one of the emotions considered basic; it falls in fact outside the usual classifications. Attention and desire are often not considered emotions. The status of startle as an emotion has been debated; Dumas (1948a), for instance, considers it one of the "general emotional reactions" and separates it from the true emotions like joy, anger, and fear; Ekman, Friesen, and Simons (in preparation) consider it a reflex.

In many of these variants, emotional experience is incomplete and inarticulate. When no articulate situational meaning structure exists, no articulate action tendency can develop. When no articulate situational meaning structure can be found, the subject may search for one: The need for evaluation may arise that Schachter (1964) and others invoked and that leads to search for causal attributions. None may be found, or not at once. The resultant emotion is confused, unclear. A stinging remark may cause an uncomfortable, perturbed feeling only, because the remark struck home without the subject being able to pinpoint that fact.

When efforts at causal attribution are made, they may yield unstable results. The emotion vacillates; the subject is uncertain whether he feels fear, anger, distress, or sorrow; he is uncertain which action tendency and corresponding action might resolve his uncomfortable feeling. This may even happen when awareness of the situation is articulate. Interpretation may emphasize now this, now that component; the subject may wonder whether he really blames the other or primarily feels loss of love or his incompetence to cope; he hovers between anger, grief, and distress.

Situational meaning structure can thus be diffuse or open to changing, unstable interpretation; and action tendency may lack direction and consist of mere excitement that is uncertain as to what might relieve it. In such cases, emotional experience is not only inarticulate: It is also ambiguous. The subject senses the various options that he has or has had and that he has more or less arbitrarily chosen among. This also applies to core components: to choice of having an emotion, and of its strength. One may be uncertain about one's emotion and about the necessity of having one.

Causal attribution

As said, indistinct emotional experience motivates search for causes explaining that experience. The same may hold for more articulate experiences: depressed mood, anxiety, anger, joy. Causes are often evident because situational meaning structure is transparent to reflection and existed prior to the urgent confrontation that triggered the emotion. But causes also may be obscure: Why this angry mood? or what, precisely, in the other's actions made one white with anger? The causal attribution that results does not produce emotional experience, since such experience motivated the search; also, the search may fail and leave the subject in doubt. Causal attribution may modify the experience, however, and contribute to "significance."

Nisbett and Ross (1980), as discussed in section 2.12, have emphasized that causal attributions employ certain heuristics and algorithms concerning which kinds of behavior tend to follow which kinds of event. Self-attribution, in this view, is preconception that may on occasion happen to hit the mark. Experiments demonstrate this often to be an appropriate description, as does introspective awareness of those many occurrences of uncertainty, unclarity, and ambiguity.

However, introspection suggests preconception not to be the only source of causal attribution in indistinct emotional experience. In the search for causes, the true cause may make itself known when considered as a candidate. It can be recognized as the true one, simply because (and when) the thought stirs the corresponding action tendency and thereby clarifies the unclear disturbance. Self-exploration is inner experimentation as much as it is inner theory construction. It is not surprising that such inner experimentation may work. If relevant event features generated emotion in the first place, recurrence in thought of these features may be expected again to be responded to in somewhat similar fashion.

4.11. Definition of emotion and kinds of emotion

Definition of emotion

Emotional experience, as said, can take three different forms: awareness of situational meaning structure, awareness of autonomic arousal, and awareness of action readiness. Each of these can be used to define emotional experience. Emotion is awareness of situations as relevant, urgent, and meaningful with respect to ways of dealing with it. Or: emotion is awareness of action readiness – readiness with respect to changing or maintaining relationships with the environment – or other intentional objects which readiness is such as to require control precedence. The three forms of awareness define overlapping but nonidentical sets of experiences.

The three forms usually occur together, as constituents of emotional experience. *Emotion*, as experience, can then be defined as: awareness of some mode of action readiness of a passive and action-control-demanding nature, involving readiness to change or maintain relationships with the environment (or intentional objects generally); which action readiness is experienced as motivated or caused by situations appraised as relevant, urgent, and meaningful with respect to ways of dealing with it; which situations are felt to affect the subject, and affect him bodily. The definition is that of experience of "emotions proper" (see section 2.8). Leaving out the phrase about "involving readiness to change or maintain relationships" brings enjoyments and desires, within the definition. Leaving out further parts yields the several varieties just discussed.

The definition closely parallels the definition of emotion in section 2.8, which was based upon behavioral phenomena and their supposed internal antecedents – action tendency and activation state. Of course the definitions are parallel. Emotion conceived as experience is from the inside what emotion conceived as internal antecedent of behavior is when it is approached from the outside.

The definitions given above, and the one given in chapter 2, tell what the word *emotion* is supposed to mean. That, of course, is not very interesting. What the definitions actually try to do is to replace the working definition from the Introduction by a more substantial description of the kind of events for which the following chapters will try to determine the antecedents, functions, and mode of operation.

Kinds of emotion

The present chapter discussed the bases for distinguishing different emotions. Only in passing did it touch upon the questions of when two emotions are "different emotions" and how different emotions are related to one another.

In section 4.2 two viewpoints were mentioned regarding the relationship between different emotional experiences; the viewpoints extend to emotions generally. They are the dimensional and the categorial viewpoint. The first, originating in Wundt's (1903) analysis (see section 4.2), considers emotions as states varying along a few dimensions such as pleasantness–unpleasantness and intensity. The second, taking its cue from common tradition and from Darwin (1872), considers the domain of emotions to consist of a small set of "discrete emotions" (Izard 1971,

1977) and their blends. The two viewpoints are not as different as they seem. On the one hand, the number of dimensions may prove to be large, as we saw (see Nowlis 1966 for moods, Frijda 1969 for facial expressions, and Smith & Ellsworth 1985 for emotional experience); this moves the dimensional viewpoint toward the categorial. On the other hand, discrete emotions do vary along common dimensions (Izard 1977) and can be ordered in terms of similarities and as pairs of opposites (Plutchik 1980); this pushes the categorial viewpoint in the opposite direction. For Izard, the common dimensions are pleasantness, activity, deliberateness, tension, impulsiveness, control, self-assurance, and extraversion.

The two viewpoints are not alternative, competing interpretations. They are complementary because they apply to different phenomena belonging to different parts of the emotion process.

There do exist discrete, qualitatively different response systems. They were described in chapter 2, as action readiness modes. They correspond to more or less well-defined behavior systems; they also correspond to different facial expressions; they produce qualitatively different kinds of awareness, through awareness of action readiness and of feedback from expressive behavior.

However, these well-defined response modes cover only part of the emotion domain. They do not include the desires and enjoyments. Nor do they include all emotions proper. They do not include those modes of action readiness that manifest the fact that well-defined response cannot develop: states of excitement, being disturbed, being moved, states of inhibition. Most of these states, as said earlier, cannot be considered to form a class of emotions on a plane with other classes like anger or fear; they are less articulate; they correspond to a dedifferentiation of the emotion space. Nonetheless, they make up a large share of human emotional responses.

Still, the better-defined modes of action readiness are discrete, qualitatively different events. Moreover, they have something in common. They are responses to context components of situational meaning structure – to cues concerning which coping actions are or are not possible. Other aspects of emotional response, by contrast, follow the core components.

Core components of situational meaning structure vary continuously over several dimensions. So do the response variables that respond to them. The core component dimensions are demand character that varies from positive to negative, urgency, and seriousness. The response variables are tendency for continuation or for change, control precedence, autonomic arousal, and time spent and efforts made. On both sides the variables define dimensions, not categories.

It would be incorrect to view the mentioned response variables merely as parameters of the state of action readiness. Since the mode of action readiness – the specific emotion – that exists at a particular moment is elicited by context components, different modes of action readiness may replace one another within a given confrontation as defined by core components. Faced with an event of some duration – a given threat of given urgency, for instance – fear, anger, despair, mere excitement may alternate within an unchanging general readiness to do something about it and to interrupt ongoing activity. The various emotions alternate, depending upon the aspect of the situation that comes to the fore or that is focused upon, and upon variations in sense of competence.

That is to say, emotions are discrete states when considered at the level of actual response readiness – at the level of particular action tendencies. They are states varying along a set of continuous dimensions, however, when considered at the level of response to the event's valence and urgency. They are, in other words, states defined by a restricted set of dimensions when considered at a higher level in the hierarchy of action instigation and action control processes as discussed in section 2.8. The dimensional and the categorial view are both valid because they apply to different levels of the emotion process, corresponding to different sets of phenomena.

In addition to the levels of core and context components, there is the level of object components. That is: In addition to the levels of global readiness and specific readiness mode there is the level of intentional structures (section 2.10). It is difficult to say whether intentional structures form a dimensional or categorial space. Probably, neither model is meaningful in view of the considerable overlaps. Jealousy, envy, remorse, nostalgia in all likelihood do not cut out neat coordinate portions of an emotion space; whereas at the same time any dimensional approach must fail in view of the large number of specifics involved, as manifest in definition of emotions by object and the cultural differences in emotion taxonomies.

In fine, we must conclude that the discrete-emotions view, the dimensional view, and the third, cognitive view, which is neither discrete nor dimensional, are all valid, since all three focus on different phases of the emotion process. No one view is any more fundamental than the others with respect to what emotions are.

PART II

Antecedents

5. Emotional stimuli, or situational antecedents

In Part I, *emotion* was defined as action readiness change elicited by certain external events and thoughts. We can now ask what these kinds of events and thoughts are: What are the stimuli eliciting emotions?

5.1. Theoretical viewpoints

Specific-stimulus theories

The different emotions, it can be said, are elicited by specific stimuli or groups of stimuli. Pain, hunger, and cold cause distress; threat of pain, hunger, or cold causes fear; insults and frustrations cause anger; personal loss causes grief; satisfactions cause joy. Watson's (1929) theory was of this nature: Three basic emotions are each innately elicited by a specific kind of event. What is called fear is, in Watson's view, the innate response to loud noises and loss of support; what is called anger is the response to movement restraint; what is called love is the response to caresses. Other stimuli become emotional stimuli through conditioning, through having been paired with one of the unconditioned stimuli.

The specific-stimulus viewpoint occurs in a variety of guises. It is the dominant viewpoint in ethology, particularly that of lower animals. Emotional behavior systems are triggered by specific, sometimes quite specific, stimuli. In the male ruff, a red patch a little below eye level elicits attack; in the duck, the silhouette of a bird of prey in flight elicits fear; in animals, and perhaps in humans (Murray 1979), distress calls from the young elicit care-giving behavior. The viewpoint underlies a search for the precise stimuli that elicit the various emotions. As we shall see, there do exist specific stimuli that tend to elicit emotions in a given kind of animal or in humans. Yet the specific-stimulus viewpoint does not appear the most plausible one for understanding human, or primate, emotion. A rather large number of different stimuli appear capable of

263

innately evoking given emotions; fear, for instance, is innately elicited by painful stimuli, intense lights and sounds, darkness, unfamiliar objects, certain social stimuli (Gray 1971). Conversely a given stimulus can give rise to a number of different emotions. Hebb (1949) observed that confrontation of a chimpanzee with an unfamiliar object (a snake, a skull, the animal's keeper with a new cap) can provoke either fear, anger, lively curiosity, or mere excitement. Personal loss, in humans, can induce anger, panic, restlessness, or numbness in addition to sorrow and despair (Bowlby 1969; Parkes 1972). Rough-and-tumble play induces fear in small infants and merriment in those same infants a few weeks later (Sroufe & Waters 1976). Of course, the stimuli may be said to possess different meanings in the different circumstances; this, however, robs the specific-stimulus viewpoint of its point.

Intensity theories

It can be argued that stimuli of weak or moderate intensity induce pleasant emotions, and intense stimuli unpleasant emotions. Support for this viewpoint is drawn primarily from sensory experience. Mild sweetness, saltiness, and bitterness, soft touches, weak sounds tend to be agreeable; strong salt solutions, strong lights, loud sounds, and the like tend to be unpleasant (Wundt 1903; Young 1961; Dumas 1948a). Also, weak and moderate stimuli tend to elicit approach behavior in young animals, whereas strong stimuli elicit withdrawal (Schneirla 1959). Strong anxiety, it has been argued in this connection, is aversive, whereas mild anxiety is often sought, as in merry-go-rounds or suspense movies. This issue, however, is considerably more complex; the attractiveness of mild anxiety results from the sense of challenge and mastery it entails, and has little to do with its intensity per se.

The intensity viewpoint also occurs in many forms and places. Freud (1900) initially gave it a central role when he explained anxiety by intense excitations threatening to penetrate the "stimulus protection barrier." According to Tomkins (1962), different emotions are elicited by different "densities of neural firing" and their patterns of rise and fall in time. Presumably, density of neural firing is determined by stimulus intensity. Since time course pattern as well as density per se contribute to emotion differentiation, this theory is a cross-breed of the intensity and specific-stimulus viewpoints. It is doubtful, however, that "density of neural firing" can be defined independently of intensity of emotional response, which makes this explanation largely post hoc; the same holds for

Freud's "intensity of excitation." Also, "stimulus intensity" is but a figure of speech when applied to other than sensory stimuli; it thus requires further explanatory principles. With regard to Schneirla's theory, it is doubtful that innate approach and withdrawal responses are determined primarily by stimulus intensity differences; there is nothing inherently intense in unfamiliar stimuli, which stimuli tend to be approached hesitantly or avoided.

Related to the stimulus intensity viewpoint are theories relating emotion to the presumed hedonic qualities of arousal levels or changes therein. According to Hebb (1955), moderate degrees of (cortical) arousal are pleasant and supportive for behavior, and strong degrees are unpleasant and disruptive: the famous inverted U-curve. In Leuba's (1955) view, shifts away from some optimal arousal level are unpleasant, and those toward that level are pleasant. In Berlyne's (1971) later view, both very low and very intense levels are unpleasant, whereas decrease from intense levels as well as increase toward moderate levels evoke pleasant affect. Arousal, in most of these theories, is in part a function of stimulus intensity. In part, however, the theories view it as a function of degree of match or mismatch of stimuli with expectations and other cognitive schemata (Hebb 1949; Berlyne 1971); this, in fact, transforms these theories into instances of the third approach.

Match–mismatch theories

Emotion may be viewed as the result of stimuli interacting with dispositional entities like response tendencies, motives, goals, expectations; or, equivalently, as the result of stimuli being relevant to obtaining incentives or reinforcements or to maintaining well-being. Positive emotions can be seen as produced by stimuli representing match with expected or desired situations: with achievement of goals, satisfaction of motives, realization of response tendencies, acquisition of incentives. Negative emotions can be seen as the result of stimuli representing mismatch with any of the above. The different emotions, in such a view, are determined by variants of the constellations of actual or predicted match and mismatch.

Spinoza's (1677) theory is of this nature, and worth mentioning since it demonstrates that so little but the words is new. Pleasure exists when the mind passes from a state of lesser to one of higher perfection; a state of perfection exists when the mind is true to its nature; the manifestation of the mind's persistence in its nature is desire. Hence, pleasure exists upon fulfillment of desire, and pain upon fulfillment being impeded.

Modern variants differ in the supposed nature of the dispositions with which stimuli match or do not match; they differ in the name given to what invests those stimuli with their emotional impact. Behaviorist theory referred to them as "response tendencies," or anticipations of reinforcement. According to Brown and Farber (1951), frustration or emotional upset generally is produced when execution of an activated response tendency is obstructed; obstruction can be caused by physical blocking, by reduction in expected reward, or by elicitation of incompatible or conflicting response tendencies. Emotional stimuli are thus stimuli that produce or signal obstruction. Mowrer (1960), Hammond (1970), and Millenson (1967) saw emotion as produced by stimuli producing or predicting reward or punishment, or by changes in reward or punishment. Pattern of signaling and kind of change determine what kind of emotion results; stimuli thus owe their emotional impact to what happens to constitute reward or punishment for the individual. A current version of this approach is that of Gray (1971, 1982).

Hebb (1949) emphasized cognitive structures: Negative emotion is produced when stimulus events do not match available cognitive structures; one of the major forms of lack of match is when events do not fit expectations. Mandler (1984) views emotion as caused by interruptions, where "interruption" includes impossibility of executing plans as well as thwarting of expectations; the nature of the interrupted plan or thwarted expectation determines which emotion results. Another cognitive match–mismatch theory is that of Pribram (Pribram 1981; Miller, Galanter, & Pribram 1960). Emotions, according to Pribram, are "nogo" plans: plans put into operation when normal plans are blocked; or (Pribram 1970) they are "monitors" signaling the state of achievement or nonachievement of plan completion. In another of his formulations again, they result from the generation or resolution of uncertainty.

In psychoanalytically oriented thought, emotional stimuli are those that signal drive satisfaction or threats to such satisfaction; or those that elicit unacceptable wishes and thus generate conflict (Freud 1926). Lazarus (1966; Lazarus, Kanner, & Folkman 1980; Lazarus & Folkman 1984) views emotion as dependent upon the evaluation of events with respect to their significance for the individual's well-being. Events are appraised as benign–positive, stressful, or irrelevant; if stressful, they may constitute harm or loss, threat, or challenge. These appraisals depend upon the individual's goals, values, and commitments, and their importance to the subject: Goals, values, and commitments "affect the personal stakes with respect to which well-being is defined" (Lazarus et al. 1980, p. 192).

Simonov (1970, 1975) has given a formal representation of the view that motivation is what underlies emotion and invests emotional stimuli with their significance. Emotion results when the information contained in stimulus events differs from the information needed for the satisfaction of motives. If stimulus information is less than the desired information, negative emotion is produced; if it is more, the product is positive emotion.

Clearly, the language in the above approaches differs. Dispositional entities are called response tendencies, reinforcements, expectations, motives, goals, values, or commitments; and stimuli are said to elicit emotion because they obstruct or provide, predict or contradict, thwart or confirm, frustrate or satisfy. Nevertheless, the approaches all share several essential features. First, eliciting conditions are described for emotion in general – or, if for positive and for negative emotions in general, both still are derived from a single principle. Focus is not upon the different emotions. Second, elicitation of the different emotions is in some way secondary to elicitation of emotion as such. Third, the notion of "emotional stimulus" somewhat recedes into the background: Mismatch – interference, interruption, discrepancy – or match – attainment of incentives, correspondence with expectations – is what counts, rather than the precise stimulus that causes that mismatch or match. Finally, the distinguishing feature for grouping these approaches together is that they all imply a distinction between eliciting events and the dispositional entity to which those events owe their eliciting power. This viewpoint appears to be the most fruitful of the three sketched, as will be argued further down.

5.2. "Stimuli," events, and cognitive processes

The word *stimulus* is used in a shorthand way, and by convention. The subject matter of the present chapter is more adequately indicated as "situational antecedents of emotion" and these antecedents are "events" rather than "stimuli." Emotions are rarely, if ever, elicited by an isolated stimulus. Rather, the emotional effectiveness of sensory stimuli depends upon the spatial, temporal, and meaning context in which they occur, the adaptation level upon which they impinge, and the expectations with which they clash or correspond. Being alone is not the same as being alone after one's partner died; no food is different from no food when food was expected; threat when there is a way of escape is different from that when there isn't. Hence, in what follows, there will be free alternation of *stimuli, events* and *situations*. The latter two designations are to be preferred: *Events* because so often it is change that counts, or the perspective that that change entails, *situations* because so often the context is decisive for emotion: the possibilities for coping or avoidance, the whole history of interaction with the object or event concerned. In fact, the best designation is *transaction* (Lazarus & Folkman 1984), which, as mentioned in section 2.8, is defined both by what the event can do to the subject and what the subject can do and wants to do with the event, in their development in time.

Stimulus is a shorthand term for further reasons. Emotions can be elicited by imagination and fantasies – things that could occur or could have occurred may make you start up in cold sweat – by recollections, by thoughts revealing the significance of events encountered and remarks received. Also, emotions are elicited by one's own actions, quite apart even from the products these actions produce or the satisfactions to self-esteem they may engender; as in the joys of walking, and of smooth performance of skilled action generally.

Furthermore, on the whole it is impossible to define effective emotional stimuli independently of the subject: of his goals and desires, his expectations, and his abilities for coping with the events involved. Abilities and inabilities for coping are important in determining whether events become emotional stimuli, and in determining which emotion will arise: Coping abilities determine secondary appraisal, and thus the context components of situational meaning structure. What is a threat to one person is a challenge to another one and a passing encumbrance, or even a diversion, to a third. As Lazarus phrased it: "The consequent emotional state at any moment . . . is a product of the balance of forces between the capacity of the event to harm him and the potency of his resources to prevent, tolerate, profit from, postpone, or overcome that harm" (Lazarus 1975, p. 48). The same holds for the capacity of events to favor the person.

Goals, desires, and expectations interact with thoughts and associations emanating from actual events in forming the effective emotional stimulus. What is enjoyable in having climbed a difficult mountain peak is not the scenery as much as the fact of having been better than someone else, or having conquered one's fears, or having mastered difficulties by one's own forces; what makes someone else's forgetfulness a cause for grief or anger is its significance as sign of loss of attention or love. That is to say: The emotional "stimulus" is in part self-generated, the thought attached to the event; and a thought that is but loosely connected with the event, dependent as it is upon one's goals.

Effective emotional stimuli thus are products of a subject's cognitive activity, except perhaps in the case of hunger, cold, and pain; and even there cognitive factors are potent, considering hunger in hunger strikers and pain in martyrs. They cannot be defined, generally speaking, independently of that cognitive activity. Let it be clear what is meant here by *cognitive activity*. It does not refer, or not necessarily, to conscious thought, conscious deliberation, or even mental imagery. What it does refer to is the demonstrable interposition, between objective stimulus input and emotional response, of cognitive variables: selection of stimulus aspects, effects of previous experiences and preceding interactions with the stimulus, effects of implications of stimuli rather than of stimuli themselves only, effects of event features simply not physically present when the response is elicited. *Cognitive* refers to intervening processes between stimulus and response, assumed to occur because the relation between the latter two is variable, dependent upon previous history, the state and activity of the organism, and stimulus context – a common, traditional definition of *cognitive* (cf. Hebb 1970). To what extent these processes are conscious or modifiable by the subject will concern us later.

The cognitive processes to which the effective emotional stimuli are due have been variously named. *Appraisal* (Arnold 1960; Lazarus 1966; Lazarus & Folkman 1984) and *stimulus coding* (Leventhal 1979, 1980) are the most current terms. Experiments and observations are numerous that show the effects of cognitive processes upon emotional response.

Mention has already be made of the series of studies by Lazarus and coworkers in which gruesome films were shown under various conditions influencing the viewer's appraisals; the films depicted either a painful circumcision rite or a woodshop accident. In one experiment, subjects were told either that the film was a real one or an arranged, enacted one (Lazarus & Opton 1966). In another experiment, subjects were told either to empathize with the persons shown or to intellectualize what they saw (Koriat et al. 1972). Subjective and physiological distress responses varied with the experimental conditions.

Leventhal et al. (1979) nicely demonstrated how distress can be affected by the way a stimulus is coded. Subjects were submitted to the "cold-pressor test": immersing one hand in ice-cold water. Prior to the test, subjects were told either about the sensory sensations to expect or about the coming autonomic arousal and tenseness; there also was a control group that did not get information on sensations to come. Half the subjects in each of the three conditions were told that the experience would be painful. "Arousal" forewarning resulted in significantly more intense pain experience and subjective distress ratings than mere sensation information; pain forewarning augmented the response difference. Similar effects of advance information were demonstrated in real-life settings – for instance, in endoscopy (Johnson & Leventhal 1974) and dental treatment (Johnson 1975).

What these studies demonstrate is that emotional stimuli are the stimuli that the subject sees, or as the subject sees them. Other relevant studies come under the heading of studies in causal attribution. Storms and Nisbett (1970), for instance, gave subjects suffering from insomnia a placebo pill; half the subjects were told the pill would cause arousal symptoms, the other half that its effect was relaxing. The former subjects fell asleep more readily than the latter (according to self-report), presumably because they now could interpret their restlessness in bed as physiological rather than due to worries. Zimbardo et al. (1969) asked subjects to accept electrical shocks while active at some task; half the subjects were told this was highly important to the experiment, the others were not. Task performance of the first-mentioned subjects was better, and electrodermal response lower; pain, presumably, was less, presumably because suffering the shocks was perceived as useful, a contribution, a nonarbitrary event.

Pain response generally varies according to meanings attached. Tursky (1974) studied pain thresholds for electrical shock, pain intensity estimates, and pain tolerance limits in women from varying cultural background: American Protestant, Irish, Italian, and Jewish. Pain thresholds did not differ among groups; intensity estimates and tolerance limits did. The differences appeared to be caused by the significance of pain: to the Jewish women, pain seemed to signify possible irreversible damage or illness, to the Italians an indignity, to the Protestants something you should stand without flinching. Beecher (1959) reported observations on wounded soldiers in World War II who hardly seemed to suffer from very serious wounds, relatively seldom complained of pain so much as to require morphine, and often said they did not need pain-alleviating medication. Civilians with similarly severe wounds tended to suffer and complain bitterly. The wounds, argued Beecher, meant having escaped alive from the battlefield for the soldiers and a calamity for the civilians (although other explanations might be advanced for the difference). Dependence of pain response upon meaning is not confined to humans: Pavlov reported that, in dogs, violent defense reactions upon strong electric shocks disappeared when shock became the signal for the presentation of food (after Melzack 1973).

As a final example we mention the studies on attribution of causes for success and failure. Extensive studies by Weiner (1974) show that feelings of pride and shame, or performance-related joy and distress, depend upon attribution to personal effort and ability as opposed to external factors such as good or bad luck and easiness or difficulty of the task – and upon such attributions rather than upon success or failure per se. Obviously, succeeding by effort and ability is a different stimulus from merely arriving at some favorable outcome.

Several of the above outcomes have been explained by variations in stimulus coding (Leventhal 1980); others by shifts in attention (Weiner 1980): Diversion of attention tends to diminish pain or distress (Bloom et al. 1977). Both evidently alter the effective stimulus, the effective stimulus aspects, or the effective stimulus compound. The same holds for thoughts about the significance attached to events: They add to the stimuli. As said, a certain forgetfulness – sugar in your coffee which she knows you always take without – is seen as lack of love, and thus elicits violent anger or grief. A certain failure – not knowing how to counter a joke or strike up a conversation – may, to you, exemplify your general social inability, and thus precipitate anguish or dejection. Situations that elicit social anxiety are imbued with "irrational beliefs," as Ellis (1970) argued, or with "dysfunctional thoughts" (Beck 1976). Such a failure constitutes a different failure, a different emotional stimulus, from one that does not have these attributions attached.

5.3. Unlearned emotional stimuli

The present section discusses stimuli that, according to some evidence or other, are candidates for being considered unlearned stimuli. Unlearned emotional stimuli we define as stimuli capable of evoking emotional response without previously having occurred together with other stimuli capable of evoking similar emotional response, and without the subject having seen others respond emotionally to it or having had occasion to infer its emotional consequences. This does not imply that no learning was involved: A stimulus can be considered unlearned when its effect depends upon other learning than about that particular effect.

To cite Hebb's (1970) example of such a contingency: Strangeness may be an innate stimulus for fear even if identifying an object as strange presupposes learning that has rendered other objects familiar. Evidence for stimuli to be considered unlearned elicitors of emotion consists of occurrence of response to these stimuli in animals that could not have learned about their effects, or of universality of effectiveness in the species. Innateness of stimulus effectiveness does not necessarily imply that the stimuli always evoke response: Context, inhibition, and habituation may neutralize it. Nor does it imply that response is shown from birth onward: Sexual stimuli present the obvious contrary example. Furthermore, innateness admits of degrees. Seligman (1971) introduced the notion of "preparedness." Fear for some kinds of stimuli is much more readily learned than for others. The organism is apparently "prepared" for them. Human beings very readily learn to be afraid of spiders and snakes (Öhman, Erixon, & Löfberg 1975; see Öhman 1979). Preparedness can be specific to certain kinds of stimuli for certain kinds of response. Pigeons easily learn an avoidance response to a sound signal and a food-getting response to a light signal, but not vice versa (Forge & LeLordo 1973). The notion of preparedness has not gone unchallenged (e.g., Bitterman 1975), and different interpretations of relevant findings have been advanced (e.g., Testa 1974); the facts of differential ease of learning of emotional response to certain stimuli remain, however.

The list of unlearned emotional stimuli to follow is no doubt incomplete. It serves to indicate the range of likely or possibly innate stimuli. Animal data are included to support the possibility of similar propensities in humans.

Several elementary response patterns are innately elicited by more or less well-defined stimuli. The startle response (section 2.1) is evoked by sudden, intense stimuli: loud noises, light flashes, unexpected tactile stimuli. "Suddenness" refers to rise time: In rats, maximal startle is obtained upon a 90-dB sound when peak intensity is reached within 12 msec (see Hoffman & Ison 1980). Animal species differ with respect to effective stimulus modalities: Rats show startle to sounds, pigeons to light flashes, but not the other way around.

The orienting response is elicited by what Berlyne (1960) called "collative" stimulus variables: novelty, unexpectedness, complexity. Any stimulus change elicits the orienting response; this includes omission of an expected stimulus (Sokolov 1963; Grings 1960; Badia & Defran 1970). The orienting reaction, according to Sokolov (1963), is evoked by discrepancies between what the organism is used to or geared to (his "neuronal model") and stimulus input; the discrepancy, then, is the effective stimulus.

Unusual, unfamiliar stimuli generally tend to evoke curiosity, approach, and exploratory behavior; they also tend to evoke apprehension or fear. They may do both together, as when children keep looking from the safety of their mother's lap. Attention for and approach toward novel objects is present quite early in infants, human as well as primate; it is manifest in rhesus monkeys as soon as attachment to a mother figure is established and her presence supersedes apprehension (Suomi & Harlow 1976). The more unusual a stimulus, the more curiosity tends to be evoked (Berlyne 1960), up to some upper limit of unusualness or complexity (Boselie 1984). As said, the same kinds of stimuli that evoke orienting and curiosity tend to evoke fear, apprehension, or other distress; they do so when they are more intense, closer, or in a generally unfamiliar or unsafe context. Loud sounds, intense lights, unusual tactile stimuli, being moved in unusual ways, and environmental instability (e.g., earthquakes) all lead to fear in many animal species, including monkeys (Suomi & Harlow 1976) and humans. Strangeness as a stimulus is exemplified in the fear of dogs and apes for people dressed or behaving in unfamiliar ways (Hebb 1946) and of horses for flapping plastic bags. Rhesus monkey infants become terrified by moving mechanical monsters (Novak, quoted in Suomi & Harlow 1976). New, unfamiliar situations are mentioned in several studies as a major source of fear in children up to the age of six (Jersild & Holmes 1935; Shephard, Oppenheim, & Mitchell 1971). Fear of the unfamiliar decreases or disappears through general increased competence or self-confidence (Sroufe, Waters, & Matas 1974); presence of the mother tones it down and allows fear to be replaced by curiosity (Suomi & Harlow 1976) or merriment (Sroufe & Waters 1976). Fear of strangers in human infants at around 8 months ("8-month anxiety") probably is innate, in the sense that propensity for fear of the novel appears to peak around that age; it also does so in rhesus monkeys of equivalent age (Suomi & Harlow 1976).

Loss of orientation can be considered an innate source of distress. Hebb (1946) found fear of the dark in chimpanzees, and it is widespread in children (Jersild & Holmes 1935). Loss of support is an obvious fear stimulus, at least in humans. Mild panic is frequent in humans when losing back–front orientation in unfamiliar buildings (Katz 1944); the terror of depersonalization can perhaps be understood along the same lines (Barendregt & Frijda 1982). Similarly, distress or anxiety evoked by internal or external conflict, by lack of congruence between expectations and events, and by lack of control can all be understood as unlearned, unconditional response to unassimilable, unmanageable situations (McReynolds 1976; Gray 1982).

Other unlearned sources of distress include perception of dead or mutilated members of one's species or, generally, immobile unresponsive ones (Köhler 1917; Hebb 1946; Van Lawick-Goodall 1972). Of particular importance is the evidence for innate fear evoked by threat gestures of conspecifics. Rhesus monkeys reared in social and visual isolation when shown slides of other rhesus monkeys reacted with strong fear response to those showing facial threat expressions; but not to other slides (Sackett 1966). In humans, conditioned autonomic response with angry facial expression as the conditioned stimulus shows slower extinction than when the conditioned stimulus is a happy or neutral face, which distinctly suggests "preparedness' for angry expressions (Öhman & Dimberg 1978). Perhaps being looked at fixedly itself constitutes an innate negative stimulus. "Staring down" seems to be an effective intimidation technique among chimpanzees (mentioned by Marks 1969; Kendon 1972); it often is among humans, to the extent that some cultures forbid looking straight at superiors or entertain notions of the "evil eye."

Being rejected from the group and other forms of social isolation are potent sources of distress; they may lead to suicide or voodoo death; Gray (1971) counts them among innate distress stimuli. However, they are perhaps to be understood as exemplars of loss of satisfying, or merely of familiar, conditions. Separation from the attachment figure, in animal and human infants, innately evokes distress, independently of the loss of the food provider (Bowlby 1969; Harlow 1958; Suomi & Harlow 1976); it probably functions in human adults in similar ways and, on occasion, with similar intensity (Klein 1981).

For innate fear of strangers there is no clear evidence, at least as regards rhesus monkeys (Suomi & Harlow 1976). Fear, hostility, or excitement upon confrontation with strangers may be innate in other species, though, as argued by Scott and Fredericsson (1951). It is a general occurrence in animals, and conspicuous and easily evoked in humans (Tajfel 1982), who appear quite "prepared" for it. It is of wide cross-cultural generality; hospitality rituals may well be restraint measures to keep it in check; but of course, there also is ample occasion to learn to fear strangers. Fear expressions in others of the same species generate excitement (e.g., Miller, Murphy, & Mirsky 1959); in humans, conditioned responses (with shock as the unconditioned stimulus) are more easily established to fearful than to neutral facial photographs as the conditioned stimulus (Lanzetta & Orr 1981; Orr & Lanzetta 1984).

Infant distress calls induce prompt response in most higher animal species, from birds to humans, at least women. Infant crying can probably be considered an innate releaser of care-giving behavior, perhaps through evoking "empathic distress" (Murray 1979). One of the main arguments for this view is the brief latency, of about 6 seconds, of mothers picking up a child after it starts crying, under favorable cultural conditions (DeVore & Konner 1974; Konner 1972).

Fear of snakes apparently is not innate, at least in the rhesus monkey: It was not found in laboratory-raised animals (Joslin et al. 1964). The point is of importance since fear of snakes is common in humans, which fact has been suggestive of the notion of preparedness and of its explanatory value for phobias (Seligman 1971). As said, pictures of snakes and spiders show slower habituation of orienting response than neutral stimuli in nonphobic human subjects (Öhman et al. 1978) and more rapid acquisition of conditioned fear response (Öhman et al. 1975).

Note that, according to the evidence reviewed, few if any of the stimuli discussed induce one specific emotional response. They tend to evoke fear or anger or distress, depending upon circumstance. Hebb (1949) noted the variability of emotions evoked by strangeness, Bowlby (1969) that evoked by personal loss. The various stimuli discussed are stimuli for negative emotion generally. Specific unlearned elicitors for fear, anger, or distress separately are hard to find.

The lack of specificity in the kind of emotion aroused by the above stimuli suggests that they be considered not stimuli for emotion proper but as inherently aversive stimuli: stimuli to be avoided. This certainly holds for the traditional negative reinforcers: cold, hunger, and other bodily discomforts, pain, certain smells and tastes. Except for some smells and tastes, which perhaps can be viewed as elicitors of loathing and disgust, these aversive stimuli all underlie a variety of different emotions and may give rise to unpleasant "feeling" only.

Unlearned stimuli for positive emotions include the inherently pleasant stimuli: certain tastes and smells, bright colors, bodily comfort, caresses. Most of these stimuli, too, are not so much elicitors of emotions proper as elicitors of positive "feeling" and, in the event, of desire. For caresses this may be different. Caresses can probably be considered innate stimuli for peacefulness and quietness. Stroking tends to quiet excited animals (dogs, horses) as well as humans. Gellhorn (1964) cites a study by Edinger and Fisher (1913), who observed the quieting effects of stroking on an idiotic child lacking both cerebral hemispheres, and one by Euler and Söderberg (1957), who found that stroking increased parasympathetic dominance of hypothalamic action. Caressing of erogenous skin zones, of course, is an innate stimulus for sexual emotions.

Innate stimuli for sexual excitement other than skin contact exist in all animal species, smell being foremost; visual displays and complex action sequences are particularly important in lower animals like birds and fish, and visual stimuli again become important in apes. Innate stimuli for sexual excitement other than stroking and kissing are plausible in humans, but have not been unambiguously determined. Plausible candidates include provocative gestures and movements, winking, and flirtatious eye contact sought by women; they appear to occur nearly everywhere, in almost every culture. Morphological female characteristics (breasts, full red lips, prominent buttocks) are suggested by Morris (1967) as possible releasers for sexual excitement in men; "provocative movements" are movements bringing these and other characteristics into visual prominence. "Macho" behavior may well represent their counterpart as an arousing stimulus for women, considering the cross-cultural generality of its manifestations in, for instance, folk and other dancing.

There are many more unlearned positive stimuli; the list of "primary reinforcers" is relatively large. In addition to the sensory stimuli mentioned, it includes stimulus variety, at least to some optimal amount (Harlow 1950; Berlyne 1960), smooth performance of skilled actions, exertion of power and control, and achievement of mastery over the immediate environment; these sources of satisfaction will be discussed further in the next chapter. The classes of stimuli are wide and ill specified. There probably exist more specific unlearned stimuli with motivational significance. Lorenz (1963) and Eibl-Eibesfeldt (1974) have suggested the roundness of a baby's head to be a releaser of care-giving behavior and concomitant feelings of tenderness; Brooks and Hochberg (1960), in a psychophysical study, found this feature, together with relative size of the eyes, to be a stimulus determinant of the "cuteness" of teddy bears. Proximity of the mother figure appears to be a "stimulus" for security and well-being (Bowlby 1969); the mother figure role can be fulfilled by anything soft that one can cling to (Harlow 1958). Characterization of proximity of the mother as a stimulus for security and well-being derives from the fact that such proximity is sought before fear responses develop; it thus is not derived from protection from the latter

(Suomi & Harlow 1976). Contact with peers likewise appears to be an innately positive stimulus (Harlow 1969).

"Friendliness" (nonaggressive contact signs) can be viewed as eliciting quietness, or perhaps specifically social positive emotions; or perhaps it merely alleviates social fear. The smile is universal as a contact and appeasement sign; its probable chimpanzee precursor so functions in chimpanzee encounters (Van Hooff 1972); the infant smile has been interpreted as a trigger or as a reinforcement for maternal (or perhaps parental) care-giving behavior (Vine 1973). There is some evidence for the smile as an innate releaser of positive affect in infants (Spitz 1957). Crying has already been mentioned as a stimulus for care giving.

Most of the above, again, concern positive motivational stimuli, stimuli for desires, rather than elicitors of positive emotions proper. Stimuli that qualify as unlearned elicitors of joy or amusement as such are few; tickling might be one. Laughter generally is elicited by a complex course of events, which cannot properly be called a "stimulus."

5.4. The elicitation of emotion

Stimuli and constellations

The preceding covers only a fraction of the emotional stimuli. Of course, most stimuli that elicit emotion, particularly in humans, do not innately do so. Many stimuli do so as a result of previous experience or through cognitive activities such as foresight.

More importantly, the majority of events eliciting emotion cannot be properly designated emotional "stimuli." No sugar in your coffee does not constitute an emotional stimulus. What elicits emotion is a constellation of an event and some desired or undesired condition for which that event is relevant. That is to say: Emotions are elicited by constellations consisting of an event and of some satisfying or aversive state of affairs that the event appears to advance or harm. Or, as we will phrase it: Emotions are elicited by constellations in which a stimulus event is relevant for one (or more) of the individual's concerns. *Concern* is the general name adopted here for the dispositions (see section 5.1), the inner conditions, to which stimuli owe their emotional significance.

Elicitation of emotion thus does not involve one entity, the stimulus, but two: the stimulus event and a concern that exists prior to the stimulus event and that the subject carries with him when the event confronts him. In the constellations formed by events and concerns, event and concern stand in a particular relationship. Different kinds of emotion are evoked by different constellations. That is, different emotions are evoked by different constellations, and not by different sorts of stimulus, nor even by different sorts of concern. Loss of a partner causes grief, and so do loss of hope concerning the future, not being promoted to the position one desired, and change of place of residence (Marris 1974). What triggers grief is loss of a thing of importance, whatever the thing and whatever the reason for importance. Partner, hope, desired position, and place of residence are among the things; attachments, life perspectives, self-esteem, and preference for a familiar environment are among the reasons for importance – that is, concerns.

That which triggers emotions can be compared to functions in the mathematical sense. Constellations define types of relationship that each have a particular outcome, regardless of what the variables in the relationship represent; that is, regardless of the particular nature of the events and concerns. Outcomes of constellations are invariant when events and concerns vary. They are also invariant over other aspects of events and concerns. Emotions are elicited by change brought about by events rather than by absolute amounts of satisfaction or harm that these events carry. There is joy in heaven over a sinner who repented as well as over just persons who need no repentance. Similarly on earth: Loss of expected reward is roughly equivalent to obtaining unexpected punishment, and joy results from escape from threat as much as from receiving satisfactions. Don't take this lightly: There is despair when thrown from rich into modest circumstances; there is true elation when emerging from inhuman circumstances into just bearable ones, as any political prisoner can tell you.

What elicits emotions, then, are constellations of events relevant to concerns. Emotions result from match or mismatch between events and concerns. Positive emotions can be said to result from events that represent match: actual or signaled concern satisfaction. Negative emotions result from events that represent mismatch: actual or signaled interference with concern satisfaction. Neutral, cognitive emotions result from events that appear as possibly relevant to some concern, and from events that merely deviate from what was expected. Desires result from the absence of concern satisfaction and from recognition of fit objects for concerns.

The various different positive, negative, and neutral emotions are produced by variants of the above constellations. In these variants, the

	Event	Event
Presentation	Joy	Distress
Withdrawal	Frustration	Joy

Figure 5.1. Constellations of primary reinforcement. (After Millenson 1967)

nature of match or mismatch is further specified. The major constellations figure prominently in common speech and in the psychological literature on the elicitors of emotion: loss, threat, challenge, frustration in its various overlapping meanings of blocking of goal directed activity or of desire fulfillment, or decrease in expected reward (Yates 1962; Lawson 1965). Even some of the "stimuli" discussed in the preceding section, when looked at closely, turn out to represent constellations: novelty, for instance, which obviously refers to a relationship between events and expectations or cognitive schemata rather than to a class of stimuli.

A systematization of basic constellations has been provided in the behaviorist literature. Millenson (1967) gave a fourfold division of constellations of primary, actual reinforcement. What constitutes reinforcement – what is aversive or rewarding – of course depends upon the individual's concerns. The fourfold division is equivalent to that of situational meaning structures presented in chapter 4; the scheme of reinforcement constellations is given in Figure 5.1. The emotion words in the figure are illustrative only.

Mowrer (1960) has discussed the constellations of secondary reinforcement, that is, of signaling and anticipation of the above contingencies; these are shown with Hammond's (1970) phrasing in Figure 5.2; the emotion words are those used by Mowrer, and again are illustrative only. Gray (1971, 1982) has recently revitalized this conceptualization of conditions for emotions. He pointed out that the emotional effects of the constellations indicated are also determined by the extent to which occurrence of rewarding and aversive events depend upon the individual's responses. This aspect provides further differentiation of constellations; the subject's assessment is what was described in section 4.4 as secondary appraisal and the corresponding situational meaning aspects as action-relevant components or context components. Despair results

	Event	Event
Signaled increase	Hope	Fear
Signaled decrease	Disappointment	Relief

Figure 5.2. Constellations of signaled reinforcement. (After Mowrer 1960 and Hammond 1970)

when signaled aversive events are inevitable; grief when termination of reward will be forever; anger when aversive events, signaled or not, appear controllable, and so forth.

There is one class of constellations that does not fit smoothly into the above schema and that was mentioned by Gray to that effect: novelty or unfamiliarity. The class of constellations in fact underlies a separate class of emotions – the cognitive ones: attention, surprise, interest, curiosity.

Analysis of elicitation of emotion in terms of constellations throws into relief the fact that it is not presence or absence of concern-relevant rewarding or aversive events per se that elicits emotion: It is these events in their action-relevant context and in the context of prevailing expectations. Joy is not elicited by the mere presence of the beloved, but by her appearance after absence or by the realization that her presence is not to be taken for granted. Joy generally is elicited by a particular constellation that is variously called the "arousal jag" (Berlyne 1960), the "arousal–safety sequence" (Sroufe & Waters 1976), or the "challenge–mastery sequence" (Rothbart 1973). It was touched upon when discussing laughter: Laughter in infants is elicited by stimuli that also elicit wariness or apprehension, or did so a few weeks earlier, but which stimuli have just become familiar, or which are experienced from the safe position of being held by a trusted person.

There are constellations that pertain not so much to the occurrence of events as to the monitoring of ongoing events or of one's own activity in progress: suspense – uncertainty whether an outcome will be achieved; uncertainty proper – uncertainty which of several outcomes will be achieved; disappointment – nonachievement of an expected outcome; discouragement – lack of prospect for positive outcome achievement; contentment – expected or obtained outcome achievement (Simon 1967; Abelson 1983). The constellations have been given the names of the emotions that they elicit when the outcomes are of importance to the individual's concerns.

The various constellations not only describe the eliciting conditions for those full-fledged emotions of grief, fear, joy, or anger that make a person weep, flee, laugh, or strike. They also describe the conditions for that multitude of "small" emotions that continuously accompany daily events and that merely make a person pause, or fall into reverie, make one restless, briefly disturb concentration, or influence mood, to crop up later, perhaps when work is over, when they may crystallize into larger ones. These small emotions may reflect relevance of events to the goal at hand, or to concerns such a self-esteem or social acceptance that may be secondary at that moment to what one is engaged in or focusing on. Current goal achievement or nonachievement may, as an aside, imply that some disagreeable outcome cannot be modified, and thus cause a fleeting depressed feeling or that it may come to someone's notice and thus induce a moment of nervous apprehension.

The notion that the different emotions are elicited by different constellations in which objects and concerns are not specified applies to emotions like anger, fear, and joy that are defined by mode of action readiness. It obviously does not apply to emotions that are defined by objects (see "Definitions of emotion" in section 2.8). Within emotions defined this way – within, say, grief, or jealousy, or revengefulness – constellations as meant do decide which the precise response will be. Within grief, for instance, different constellations, at different moments in time, determine whether passive despair, or excited distress, or angry protest occurs. Of course, emotions defined this way still are elicited by the general constellation of an event impinging upon a concern.

Considering emotions to be responses to constellations has consequences for the issue of the innateness of emotional stimuli. Constellations can be considered the original, and by and large unlearned, elicitors of emotion. That is to say: The constellations, the assessments of concern relevance, the kind and context of concern relevance, are the unlearned "stimuli" for the behavioral systems and activation modes, activation of which composes action readiness change. Fear – protective and escape readiness and response – is the unlearned response to danger signals, even if it has to be learned what constitutes a danger signal. Loss of some object or person of value that is considered as final is the unlearned elicitor of grief – of activation loss, helplessness, and apathy – even if it has to be learned which stimuli signify loss with finality, and even if the value of the object was acquired. Similarly for mastery after suspense as a stimulus for joy, for free activation increase: What constitutes mastery is acquired, but once the situation has been so defined, laughter and shouting are unconditioned responses. This, it would seem, is the only consistent interpretation of what elicits the unlearned response modes. It is meaningful to ask why a fire, or a spider, spells danger to a person; it is not meaningful to ask why danger induces fear. Generally, wherever emotions are said to have been learned, what is meant is that learning has produced a definition of the situation such that the constellation corresponding to the given emotion prevails and the unlearned response to that constellation can follow.

Central to the above analysis is the hypothesis that emotions by and large arise through events conducive or obstructive to concern satisfaction, to the advent of positive or negative reinforcers; and through events that do not fit expectations or cognitive schemata. This analysis agrees with that of other match–mismatch theories mentioned earlier. It is distinct from those among them (Hebb's or Mandler's, for instance) that focus upon mismatch with expectations or schemata, but do not include concerns (hedonic outcomes, reinforcers, and motives) in their analysis. It differs from behaviorist accounts primarily in the cognitive approach to the eliciting constellations.

The present analysis of emotion elicitation harbors the hypothesis that all emotions, all occurrences of emotional response, flow from relevance of the eliciting event to some concern. This hypothesis has to face the objection that some emotions appear to be disinterested – the aesthetic emotions in particular, but also sympathy, pity, and the like. The issue will be discussed in chapter 6.

Desires and enjoyments

Fear can be understood as response to something that spells threat to some concern, joy as response to something that provides or promises some concern's satisfaction. What is spelled by the objects and elicitors of admiration, tenderness, and love? And which is the constellation through which these emotions arise?

The answer has been given earlier: These emotion arise when objects are recognized as fit objects for concerns. In tenderness, the concern is caring-for; in admiration, the concerns can be several but tend to involve values; in love, the desire is for proximity, among other things. The constellation within which this recognition occurs and within which the emotions arise is that of mere presence of the object, not its unexpected appearance, not promise of its presence, not call for its possession: It is there, available for consummation or enjoyment, by whatever action is appropriate: care giving in tenderness, cognitive appropriation in admiration, staying close, et cetera, in love. Many emotions answer to this constellation description: delights and pleasures of all sorts, fascination, peacefulness, pride in the sense of enjoyment of one's achievement. In fact, these emotions can all be grouped under the term *enjoyments*.

The various classes of emotions distinguished here arise from conditions that each has a different place in the course of events leading to concern satisfaction. Desire is engendered by the thought of, or encounter with, a fit object not in possession, and when such possession seems called for. Emotions proper arise from events that are encountered on the way to possession or that interfere or undo interference when in possession. Enjoyments arise when being there; they respond to unobstructed possession.

As there are emotions contingent upon recognition of fitness as objects of concern, so there are emotions that arise through recognition of unfitness as objects for concerns: hatred, dislike, aversion – in fact, all emotions with the feature of negative "object evaluation" (section 4.4). These, too, are elicited by mere confrontation with the objects. Here, however, the distinction with emotions proper rapidly becomes less fruitful, since presence of unfit objects rapidly becomes interference with concerns.

Inhibitors and facilitators

Occurrence of emotion depends not only upon the presence or absence of eliciting events; it depends also upon the presence or absence of stimuli that cause inhibition. Inhibitors will be discussed in chapter 8. As there exist inhibitors, there exist facilitators: stimulus conditions that facilitate elicitation of emotion without themselves being stimuli for such an emotion. Warm, accepting, and understanding people function as facilitators for grief and distress, for instance, perhaps by counterbalancing inhibitory elements. So do conditions promising secondary gains of having and expressing the emotions. Facilitators of these sorts will also be discussed in chapter 8.

We want briefly to discuss the point that facilitation of response by subsidiary stimuli can be often understood as due either to decrease of inhibitory control or to the contributions of these stimuli to the situational meaning structure: The stimuli may enhance the salience of seriousness in the case of distress, for instance, or the controllability in the case of anger. Berkowitz (1974) favors this latter interpretation to explain the facilitating effect of stimuli associated with aggression (weapons, prior exposure to images of violence, stimuli associated with previous aggression success) upon aggressive behavior. Berkowitz and Le Page (1967), for instance, had a confederate play the role of experimenter and deliver shocks to subjects upon alleged failure in a so-called learning experiment. When the subjects' turn came to play experimenter they delivered more forceful shocks when a pistol happened to be lying around than under control conditions without such an object. Bandura (1973) favors the decrease-of-inhibition interpretation to explain these phenomena.

In general, it is not easy to decide between the two kinds of interpretation, elicitations or facilitation versus decrease of inhibition. For instance, presence of the mother and comforting actions like stroking or rocking decrease fearfulness and distress in infants. Such presence and such actions can be considered either stimuli for security or inhibitors of distress. Mandler (1975) proposes the latter: The stimuli supposedly tone down a "fundamental distress" thought to be caused merely by autonomic arousal of purely physiological origin.

Objectless emotions and internal causes

Not every emotion is elicited by some stimulus. There exist depressions (meant as mood or emotion, not as clinical syndrome), anxiety attacks, and states of joy or distress that appear to come spontaneously. There are several possible explanations. The emotion or mood can have been induced by the prevailing general situation rather than by some specific event; or it can be thought to have broken through brusquely after slow accumulation of stresses or satisfactions, or because of fluctuations in coping effort, or because of the lifting of control. In all these examples, stimuli were in fact present.

A second possibility is that emotion or mood is of internal origin. Mandler's (1975) just-mentioned notion of "fundamental distress" is an example: It supposedly consists of nothing but bodily discomfort and unexplained (to the infant) arousal. The notion is hazy, since bodily discomfort and unexplained arousal are uncomfortable stimuli. Nevertheless, the hypothesis is plausible that some internal states are inherently emotional. This may apply in particular to activation modes. Activity is activating, and loss of drive, interest, or intentionality may well be inherently depressing. Such variations in activation state could themselves be due to purely biochemical causes, as they probably are in some manic and depressive mood swings.

Anxiety can occur for similar nonpsychological reasons: Coping potential may be low, or felt to be low, owing to exhaustion, brain damage, or hormonal deficiency. However, these internal conditions can still be considered to determine emotion through psychological factors. Coping potential *is* low, and the world thus unsafe; otherwise, it might be assumed, there would not be anxiety but mere slowness and cognitive, or energic, deficiency; similarly for biochemically induced euphoria and depression, and for the pleasurableness of activation.

As a third possibility, emotions could occur for reasons of emotional metabolism or internal regulatory processes. R. L. Solomon (1980; Solomon & Corbit 1974) presented an "opponent process theory" of motivation and emotion. Affective processes, elicited by some stimulus or activity, and supposed to induce complementary, "opponent," compensating ones. Pleasure is supposed to generate a compensatory depressive process, and vice versa. In the presence of the stimulus the direct process is the stronger of the two: but the indirect, opponent one outlasts the former. The result is a rebound, a mood switch, when the direct effects of the stimulus have worn off: elation after anxiety, dejection after drug-induced euphoria, hangovers after enjoyment. The evidence adduced by Solomon and Corbit admits of several alternative interpretations; support for the theory is therefore weak. Nevertheless, the hypothesis of processes restabilizing the affective system after disturbance is a plausible and attractive one. If true, the mood swings involved have no external or truly psychological reason.

5.5. The description of emotional stimuli

The various emotions, it was argued in the preceding, are elicited by constellations rather than by specific stimuli; different emotions correspond to different constellations rather than to specific kinds of stimuli. Even so, it is important to describe the specific stimuli that make people angry, or amused, or jealous and so forth. Apart from being interesting by itself, such description must form the basis for the proper definition of the constellations concerned. If, for instance, it is held that anger is elicited by frustrations (Dollard et al. 1939) or by attributing distressing events to the intent of someone having control over the events (Weiner 1981), description of the conditions that actually elicit anger will have to show whether frustration – or attribution of intent – is present in all of them; which was in fact shown not to be the case for both inter-pretations.

Another goal for the description of emotional stimuli is analysis of the concerns involved in the various emotions. Is anger (or irritable anger) contingent upon frustration of the desire for control, or upon that of any concern? What are the concerns offended in erotic jealousy; is it safeguarding the relationship or is it self-esteem? According to the ex-isting studies (e.g., Buunk 1980; White 1981), it is both. What causes depressive mood: loss of reinforcers, loss of reinforcer effectiveness, or loss of social reinforcers (Eastman 1976; Costello 1972)? What are the sources of amusement? Can they always be subsumed under the arousal–safety constellation or its equivalents? Much, in fact, is unclear.

Description of the major stimuli for the various emotions exceeds the scope of this volume; each emotion (or what is, or can be considered, a particular emotion) deserves a monograph, and many are the subjects of one. To mention a few: Averill (1982) and Tavris (1983) on anger; Berlyne (1960) on curiosity; Marks (1969) and Gray (1971) on fear; Selig-man (1975) on helplessness and despair; Stotland (1969) on hope; Schoeck (1966) on envy; Clanton and Smith (1977) on jealousy; Zimbardo et al. (1974) on embarrassment; Lynch (1976) on loneliness; Lewis (1971) and Lynd (1961) on shame and guilt; Marris (1974), Parkes (1972), and Freud (1915) on grief; Freud (1905), Gregory (1924), and McGhee (1979) on amusement; Stoller (1979) on sexual excitement; Stendhal (1820) on falling in love.

The eliciting conditions for some major aspects of emotion will be briefly discussed here, because of their general theoretical relevance.

Stimuli for autonomic arousal

It was argued in chapter 3 that not all emotions are necessarily accom-panied by autonomic arousal. "Emotion" and "arousal" do not cover the same domain. The question thus arises: What kind of conditions specifically lead to autonomic arousal or excitement?

According to Mandler (1984), these conditions are "interruptions": interruptions in ongoing activity, expectations, goals, or execution of plans. The notion of interruption is stretched beyond useful, however, since it is unclear how expectations can be interrupted. Yet the conno-tation of the notion of interruption might be quite appropriate for the specific eliciting conditions for autonomic arousal that is not due to actual physical effort. That connotation is need for readjustment. Any sudden event, painful stimuli and sudden pleasurable events included, requires, or might require, some immediate readjustment, even if it does not truly interrupt anything; it must, at the very least, be located and identified. So, of course, does any true interruption of ongoing activity or attentional deployment, unless continuation of that activity is of no concern. Even if the change is expected or anticipated, readjustment often is called for: assimilation of the event when it arrives and preparation for subsequent action, or new attentional deployment: From now on, for instance, that soccer match I view has to be viewed from the 1–0 score angle. *Interruption* in this sense, refers to the same domain of conditions as that characterized by the situational meaning component *difficulty*. The explanation of autonomous excitement in joy then becomes similar to that given by Sartre (1934) for joyful behavior generally: It is difficult to rapidly process a new acquisition or achievement, and in any event it has to be acted upon and adjusted to. Emphasis upon readjustment requirements agrees with the considerable influence of unpredictability and uncontrollability in the elicitation of arousal (section 5.6).

Positive emotional stimuli

The conditions that elicit positive emotion have been characterized in general terms as achievement of concern satisfaction, or as promises of such achievement. *Promise* means encounter with an event conducive to achievement of satisfaction, or with signals announcing increase in the likelihood of achievement.

Signals of likely achievement include evaluations of the likely success of one's actions; that is, they include obstacles to some valued goal that look like they can be mastered: the constellation of challenge. Meeting a challenge is pleasurable, provided it remains challenge and does not turn into threat – and provided it does not remain challenge rather than mastery for too long: Promises generally turn into disappointments when not fulfilled.

As said earlier, it is achievement of positive outcomes rather than having them that generates positive emotion. Continued enjoyments are taken for granted or get stale; adaptation level shifts. Generally, one can say that the more unexpected the positive outcome, or the greater the effort spent in achieving it, or the greater the uncertainty that preceded, the more intense and long-lasting is the positive emotion that follows. The arousal–safety or challenge–mastery sequence exemplifies this general rule in the constellations leading to laughter, but it can be recognized also in the joy upon receiving an unexpected gift or in the peak experience of a mountainclimber or stuntman feeling that he has surpassed his limits (Piët, 1986). In these events, degree of challenge differs, as does the relative amount of mastery or safety thereafter; but the constellations are essentially the same. As discussed in connection with laughter, theories of humor generally invoke a sequence of a similar kind.

As also discussed in that connection, it is unclear to what extent these positive emotions result from relief and release of bound activation built up previously or from sense of mastery and competence gained or regained. At any rate, these latter belong to the major specific determinants of positive emotions. Triumph, it has been said, is a regular component of joy (Bull 1951), and most achievements of satisfaction entail some gain in self-esteem in having achieved it. The joys of thrill and adventure probably derive in part, and perhaps primarily, from these sorts of gain; at any rate, they are prominent in the accounts that experienced mountainclimbers and stuntmen give of their experiences. Anticipation of mastery, challenge appraisal, is a source of positive emotion that stands in relation to achieved mastery as promise generally does to achievement generally; the significance of challenge has been elaborately discussed by Lazarus (1966; Lazarus, Kanner, & Folkman 1980).

There are two classes of stimuli that cause activation increase and positive emotion but that do not smoothly fit the above specifications: activity performed for its own sake and not in response to external demands; and exciting stimuli such as lively music and perhaps also vivid stimulus variety generally. As to the first, there is, as remarked earlier, pleasure in walking and other forms of exercise, and in waking up healthily in the morning with the sun shining and the air brisk; such pleasures can reach all the way to exhilaration. Thayer (1978a,b), as mentioned, observed increased feelings of vigor and vitality after physical exercise. Perhaps such enhanced vitality and mood result from enhanced sense of competence and well-functioning. Intuitively, however, the effects of exercise upon mood would seem to be more direct; exercise would seem to stimulate activation directly, and physiological hypotheses may be the most adequate. The same holds for the second class. Lively music, as well as dancing, are not stimuli that elicit pleasure but rather stimuli that are invigorating by themselves, and therefore releasers of available activation resources. Why some music is constituted so as to have these effects is unclear. It may well be that it answers the principle of assimilation-with-some-effort, which appears to underlie attractive stimuli generally (Kreitler & Kreitler 1972; see chapter 6) and which is related to the challenge–mastery sequence; this still does not specify or explain their activating properties. For the moment, they have to be taken for granted.

Activating stimuli

That which was discussed in the last paragraph has wider relevance. There exist stimuli that alter the emotional state of the organism because of their temporal (and perhaps other) characteristics; they do so not primarily because of their meaning. Among these stimuli are certain movements: repetitive movements, and perhaps expressive movements executed repeatedly and with conviction. What we mean are those external stimuli and movements that may induce trance states and those willfully adopted expression-like movements that truly manage to lead to emotional arousal. Precise conditions for the effects of both types are unknown to the present author, and so, by consequence, are the possible mechanisms involved; some reflections on some aspects of the latter are given in section 8.5. Repetitive stimulation, of course, tends to desynchronize the EEG; whether it does so under the conditions indicated is unknown, and anyway this would not really explain what happens. Generation of emotional awareness through proprioceptive feedback from the movements made is an unlikely or at least incomplete hypothesis: There is true elicitation of emotion, and not merely awareness of the emotion that corresponds to the movements. So far, a process of major significance for understanding the mechanisms of emotion remains not understood.

The elicitation of moods

No elaborate discussion will be devoted to the elicitation of mood, since no systematic treatments exist in the literature. One may guess that the elicitation of mood falls into the following three categories: (a) aftereffects of emotions; (b) organismic conditions such as illness, fatigue, previous exercise, and good health, or pharmacological agents; (c) general environmental conditions and side-effects of activities: heat, noise, environmental variety, stressful conditions. Why and when emotions result in longer-lasting mood changes is, so far, a largely unexplored question.

Stressors

Stressor is the term used for a stimulus or event or, rather, a relationship between the person and the environment "that is appraised by the person as taxing or exceeding his or her resources and endangering his or her well-being" (Lazarus & Folkman 1984, p. 21). The word thus does not refer to a specific class of stimuli, since whether a given stimulus constitutes a stressor depends upon both the individual's appraisal of it and his resources. Also, although stimuli for negative emotions tend to be stressors, particularly when intense or enduring, stimuli for positive emotion may equally be so: Mastering challenge requires efforts, and so does relishing many an inherenly pleasurable situation. The notion of stressor, as defined, extends to events – tasks, stimuli – requiring sustained attention, although it is likely that their taxing properties to a large extent reside in the emotional effects that failures of attention would entail, that is, in the burdens of responsibility.

5.6. Factors affecting emotional intensity

Emotional intensity, as has been stressed repeatedly, is not a unitary concept. What affects one index of intensity need not affect another one: Events that cause no acute upset may keep nagging the subject for days.

Obviously, factors that affect emotional intensity also determine whether or not emotion is elicited, according to one or more of the criteria: No response is the lower bound of response intensity.

The following discusses some major stimulus or stimulus-dependent factors affecting occurrence and intensity of emotion upon the advent of potentially emotion-eliciting events.

Stimulus intensity and seriousness

Emotional intensity may be assumed to be a function of stimulus intensity or of the gravity of the eliciting events. The physiological response to aversive stimuli (shock, noise) tends to increase with intensity of those stimuli; so does rated aversiveness (e.g., Tursky 1974). Seriousness of air raid victimization (having or not having been pulled out of ruins, having or not having had friends or relatives killed, etc.) was observed to be related to probability of later emotional disturbances (Janis 1951); soldiers' amount of exposure to combat has been shown to be related to later anxiety symptoms (Star, cited in Janis 1971). Aggressiveness increases, on the whole, with amount of frustration (Dollard et al. 1939; Berkowitz 1962). Graham et al. (1951) asked subjects for their most likely response to various hostile behaviors, ranging from unfriendliness to physical violence; intensity of presumed response was directly related to seriousness of the offense.

Rarely, however, can gravity of events be expressed in stimulus terms. It often resides in relative rather than absolute amounts: getting less than expected, more than deserved, or less or more than others with whom one compares (Festinger 1954). It also depends upon proximity of meaningful events in space or time: upon the event's urgency (section 4.4), which will be discussed below. More importantly, seriousness depends upon the concerns to which the event is relevant. A given event is more serious to one person than to another because it relates to more of his concerns or to more focal concerns; it has more or farther-reaching meaning. This, in turn, is mediated by cognitive processes, by what a person thinks the implications are, as much as by actual event effects. Tursky's experiment on pain in women of different cultural groups may again be cited as an example: Pain was merely something disagreeable to some subjects, an affront to others, a threat to health or a challenge to bravery to others again. Pain estimates and tolerance limits differed accordingly. Anecdotal illustrations of differences between objective intensity and subjective seriousness are easy to find. Mild reproach hurts more than physical violence when the first means loss of love or loss of "face." Loss of life is sometimes preferred over loss of limb, sexual prowess, or financial position when any of the latter means life as a dependent cripple or a life of shame.

Events often are serious because not one but several concerns are involved; events can have multiple significance. An injection may be frightening because lack of control over the aversive situation, in addition to the pain; and because that lack of control means detested passivity. Loss of a friend or spouse, of course, is serious not merely because the attachment was strong, but also because the number of losses it implies – of exchanges, of support, of going shopping together; and because it brings home the fact of one's own mortality.

Expectation strength

Expectation strength is a subject variable rather than a stimulus variable; as meant here, it is strongly tied, however, to stimulus variables like temporal or spatial proximity of the satisfiers and annoyers; and it is tied to actions that are under way. We may say that expectation strength regarding the likelihood that an aversive event will materialize, a satisfaction be obtained, or a consummatory act performed increases with these two factors.

The proximity variables determine the situation's urgency; emotional intensity may be assumed to be highly dependent upon them. Anticipatory fear may be held to increase as the feared event draws nearer, desire when fulfillment seems around the corner, frustration when fulfillment is blocked at the very last moment. There is ample evidence to support this assumption. Epstein and Fenz (1965) found fear ratings by novice parachutists to rise from the evening before the jump until just before jumping; Ursin et al. (1978) confirmed this by physiological measurements. Rats' speed of running for food tends to increase as they approach the goal box; it tends to slow down when the goal box emits shocks in a passive avoidance set up: The "goal-gradient" hypothesis (Miller 1959), of course, is a theoretical statement of the above assumption, as is Sheffield's (1965) generalization that thwarting of strong actual expectations engenders more intense emotion than mere absence of satisfaction. Indeed, ratings of the attractiveness of incentives tend to be higher after frustration than before (Brehm 1972; Mischel & Masters 1966), a quite general phenomenon well known, for instance, by whoever was in danger of being left by his or her partner. Proust has illustrated it in *Albertine Disparue*, and it is what we will later (section 5.8) refer to as the Law of Regret. There is some evidence for increases in appetitive response intensity after frustration, although the evidence has been debated (see Klinger 1975 for comment). Frustration response is the more intense the closer to the goal the frustration occurs. Haner and Brown (1955) interrupted children's play, consisting of putting marbles into holes in certain patterns. The closer the interruption to task completion, the more vehement the force with which the children slammed the button switching off the interruption signal. Hotton (1961) presents similar results. The same again has been found in rats: Interrupting approach close to the goal box produced more excitement than did interruption at the beginning of the runway (Lambert & Solomon 1952).

Anticipation and uncertainty

Anticipation, of course, intensifies emotional experience in that it considerably extends the time period over which a given event exerts emotional influence; the event casts its shadow or shine forward. In addition, anticipation affects the response to the emotional event when it comes. It determines surprise and disappointment; it permits preparatory actions like relaxing or bracing or writing one's will; and it gives opportunity for advance coding or recoding of the events, with corresponding change in situational meaning structure.

Evidence concerning the effects of anticipation is provided by experiments in which aversive stimuli (shocks, sound bursts) are or are not preceded by a warning signal. Autonomic response tends to be lower when a warning signal is given than when not (see Averill 1973). Responses are more intense when time of occurrence of aversive stimulation is uncertain than when it is precisely known (Monat, Averill, & Lazarus 1972; Glass & Singer 1972). Unsignaled shock produces stronger response than signaled shock in both dogs (Seligman 1968) and rats (Weiss 1970) as well as in humans; which indicates the generality of the effect. Signaled shocks are generally preferred over unsignaled shocks by rats and by humans. However, subjects differ in this regard; also, preference does not necessarily imply smaller response magnitude, and autonomic response magnitude does not always correspond with subjective distress (Lykken et al. 1972; Averill 1973): the former may represent coping effort rather than distress.

Decrease of distress through predictability has been explained by preparatory responses (e.g., emotional control – Epstein & Fenz 1965; Lykken et al. 1972), or the sense of control that comes from knowing what will happen (e.g., Glass & Singer 1972). However, advance warning is by no means always beneficial. Signaled shock, for instance, does not always lead to lower autonomic response, nor does it not lead to lower aversiveness ratings of pain stimuli (Furedy & Klajner 1974; Furedy & Doob 1972). Advance warning leads to anticipatory fear and is stressful due to maintaining vigilance and preparatory coping efforts. Hence preferences for immediate over delayed forewarned shock (D'Amato & Gumenick 1960; Maltzman & Wolff 1970; Averill & Rosenn 1972). Sometimes signaled shock has been observed to cause more upset than unsignaled shock (Lidell 1950; Brady, Thornton, & Fisher 1962). In most experiments on humans, 10–20% of subjects prefer unsignaled over signaled shocks (Averill & Rosenn 1972). Evidently, net effects of anticipation result from the opposing factors of stress produced by anticipatory fear and reduction of surprise with its possibilities for anticipatory coping.

These net effects particularly depend upon the nature of the advance information, the way the subject handles that information, and his own anticipatory cognitions. Staub and Kellet (1972) gave some subjects full information on the effects of the electric shocks to come, on the apparatus, absence of risk, the nature of subsequent sensations, and the like. Other subjects received only part of that information, or none at all; these latter presumably were free to fear what they imagined could happen. The fully informed subjects accepted stronger shocks as non-painful than did the others. Epstein (1973) found that announcing "severe shock" (rather than just "shock") enhanced autonomic reactivity upon a shock of given intensity. He also explains habituation to successive shocks by disappearance of unnecessary apprehensions.

Janis (1958) studied surgical patients before and after operation. Both those who did not worry in advance and those who worried very much showed slower recovery than patients worrying in realistic measure and fashion. Janis introduces the notion of "work of worry": establishing adequate anticipations of coming hardships so as not to be taken unprepared and developing adequate preparatory sets, such as trust in the medical treatment. Patients who did not show anticipatory fear failed to develop such anticipations; those who worried too much did not develop adequate ones. Egbert, Battit, Welch, and Bartlett (1964) verified the favorable effects of adequate anticipations: Patients given information both about postoperative pain and about the way it should be handled needed significantly less pain-reducing medication than patients in the uninformed control group.

Whether information is favorable or harmful depends upon how the subject uses it, however. Cohen and Lazarus (1973) conducted preoperative interviews with 61 surgical patients and assessed their coping styles as vigilant, avoidant, or a mixture of both. Five variables of recovery after operation were recorded. Vigilant patients scored less favorably than the others on two of these variables (days in hospital and minor complications), and their recovery was more complicated. The authors conclude that advance information is useful only to the extent that the patient can do something positive with it.

Leventhal et al. (1979), in the studies reviewed before (section 5.2) demonstrated that advance information exerts its influence through coding of the coming stimuli. If that coding is an emotionally loaded one, distress is enhanced; if it is more matter-of-fact (or more adequate to what is really happening), distress may be diminished. The same, incidentally, holds for positive stimuli – for instance, sexual ones. If these are coded as mere bodily sensation, delight may be less than when coded as aspects of action and feedback from accomplished tender or enjoying intent; this would seem to be what accounts for the beneficial effects of "sensate focus" and "pleasuring" exercises employed in therapy of sexual dysfunctions (Masters & Johnson 1970).

Peculiar manifestations of anticipation are contrast effects. Estimates of pleasurableness or aversiveness depend upon reference levels. As a somewhat trivial example, an explosion sound was rated as less loud when a very loud one was made to be expected than when a moderate one was expected (Epstein & Clarke 1970). Present satisfaction in life was rated higher after studying the miserable aspects of life of previous generations than after studying its more pleasant aspects (Dermer et al. 1979). Related to contrast effects are increases in emotional response shortly before an aversive situation is expected to terminate. Phobic anxiety has been observed to increase, in claustrophobic subjects, just before the train or streetcar journey ends; prisoners are said to try to escape more often toward the end of their terms. The same goes for combat soldiers and fighter pilots: "Four years ago I didn't mind. I remember distinctly not minding about it four years ago. I didn't mind three years ago either. . . . It is always fine to fight when you are going to lose anyway, and that was how it was four years ago, but now we are going to win" (Dahl 1945 [1976, p. 14]). Perhaps under such conditions the apparent modifiability of the situation is increased, or the sense is intensified of being in a situation that need not be so (the goal-gradient hypothesis of behaviorism); or control efforts may slacken upon expectations of misery's end.

Controllability

Controllability means dependence of the outcome of events upon the subject's actions. It has been shown to be an important factor in determining emotional intensity as well as quality. Uncontrollability makes worse what is already bad and detracts from the joy of what could be good. Having to wait passively for the development and onslaught of distressing events may be intolerable. Janis (1971) cites Grinker and Spiegel (1945), who studied bomber pilots, and Schmideberg (1942), who studied bombardment victims, to demonstrate that experience of having been powerless is the major factor responsible for enduring aftereffects of traumatic events. General uncontrollability, or feeling of incompetence in dealing with daily events, has been proposed as the primary source of anxiety (it is one of the major tenets of existential philosophy; see also McReynolds 1976; Mandler 1975; Barendregt & Frijda 1982).

When control is interfered with by willful agents (agents that look like they are, in principle, controllable), however, anger is evoked or, more generally, "reactance": increased motivation to reassert control (Brehm 1972). Being, or just feeling, reduced to impotence probably is the most important cause of violent anger.

Uncontrollability of a more drastic or unresolvable nature leads to depressed affect and loss of motivation, as in the learned helplessness paradigm. A large number of experiments have demonstrated these effects in human subjects faced with persistent unavoidable shock or noise, with unsolvable problems, or with tasks in which success or failure appears unrelated to expended effort (e.g., Glass & Singer 1972; Miller & Seligman 1975; Abramson et al. 1978; Wortman & Brehm 1975). Often depression is determined not by events that are actually uncontrollable, but by the conviction that outcomes are uncontrollable, whatever one does. Such convictions are held to be major determinants of clinical depression, since they are conspicuous in depressive patients' self-reports (Beck 1967; Abramson et al. 1978); the convictions may equally have been consequences of depressive mood, however.

Stress effects are enhanced when uncontrollability is added to aversive stimulation as such (Glass & Singer 1972; see Cohen 1980 for a review). When subjects can control the administration of shock or noise bursts, their distress ratings, autonomic response, and aftereffects are less extreme than when they receive the same amount of shock or noise independently of their actions (Pervin 1963; Staub et al. 1971; Sherrod et al. 1977); the same holds for subjects who can choose time off from such experiences, as compared to yoked controls who have the same time off imposed upon them (Hokanson et al. 1971). Subjects working under noise stress, when angered, become more angry if they have no control over noise termination (Donnerstein & Wilson 1976). Frankenhauser (1975) reports studies showing that epinephrine excretion correlates inversely with amount of control over shock administration. In many of these experiments, controllability and predictability are linked: Self-administration implies knowing when aversive stimulation will come; and subjects may choose shock or time off to come when they feel most ready for it (Averill 1973). In fact, controllability and predictability are closely related: Predictability involves a kind of cognitive control and permits more adequate preparation (Averill 1973; Rothbaum et al. 1982).

Controllability need not involve actual control in order to reduce distress, depressiveness, or anger; the mere possibility of exerting control, of not having to passively submit, can be sufficient. Subjects who are allowed to terminate aversive stimulation manifest less distress than those who are not, even if they do not actually make use of the opportunity (Sherrod et al. 1977). Sense of control, the conviction of not merely being the victim of events, appears to be one of the factors determining "hardiness" when confronted with stressful life events (Kobasa 1979). Rats that can be active and, for instance, fight other rats when subjected to uncontrollable shock suffer fewer stress effects than shocked rats not having that opportunity (Laborit 1979). Goal-directed activity in humans likewise tends to decrease stress effects, whether the activity aims at the source of stress or elsewhere. This subject has been reviewed by Gal and Lazarus (1975). During aircraft carrier landings, pilots experience less anxiety and fewer autonomic arousal symptoms than do their radar intercept officers. The difference presumably is caused by the fact that there was nothing the latter could do once landing operations had set in; they also had more opportunity for anxious anticipatory thoughts. Similar interpretation is offered for differences in physiological recovery time between soldiers from an attacking and an attacked platoon: Recovery time was twice as long for the attacked (Davis, cited in Gal and Lazarus 1975). Similar interpretation, again, appears appropriate for the surprisingly low plasma cortisol levels of ambulance helicopter crews operating in a combat area.

The influence of uncontrollability is dependent upon the degree of uncontrollability. Moderate degrees of uncontrollability tend to induce reactance (anger, hostility, increased vigor); more extreme degrees tend to lead to depressed mood and passivity (Wortman & Brehm 1975). The relationship is modified by the subject's generalized expectations concerning locus of control, that is, whether the subject feels his behavior predominantly to be controlled internally, by himself, or externally, by others or by circumstance (Rotter 1966; Lefcourt 1976). "Internals" can be expected to suffer more from loss of control than "externals"; externals should not show response increment. Indeed, internals show reactance after mild "helplessness training" (mild exposure to uncontrollable outcomes in, for instance, a problem-solving task), but performance decrement and depressed mood after more severe training, as compared with no-training controls; externals show performance decrement under both forms of uncontrollability experience, but less so than internals under more severe training (Pittman & Pittman 1979).

Controllability is not an invariably favorable feature of events. It imposes loads of sustained vigilance and control effort upon the subject, may bring disappointments when control fails, and puts the burdens of responsibility upon him. These costs of coping may outweigh the advantages of controllability, particularly when control is only moderately effective (Weiss 1971a,b); of course, these disadvantages also are part of situations of uncontrollability that are recognized as such and yielded to, in what Rothbaum et al. (1982) called "secondary control": gaining control through changing the self, its desires, efforts, and attitudes, rather than the world. In fact, ability to abandon efforts at control, and thus concomitant frustrations and damage to self-esteem, appears to be vital for survival under prolonged stressful conditions. Such ability may be involved in the presumed greater endurance of women for prolonged stress. For such greater endurance there is some evidence, for instance in their lower epinephrine secretions under stress (see Frankenhauser 1975); as will be recalled, epinephrine appears to respond particularly to (perceived) requirements for active coping (see section 3.8). Anecdotal evidence for women's greater endurance comes from observation of concentration camp reactions (e.g., Wilbaut-Guillonard, pers. commun.).

Controllability is determined not merely by event properties that permit control, but also by availability to the subject of means with which to exert control. This goes two ways. On the one hand, what counts in the development of depressive response, as said, is not controllability of events per se, "universal controllability," but "personal helplessness" of the individual with respect to those events (Abramson et al. 1978; Garber & Hollon 1980). On the other hand, the major factors that permit mountainclimbers and stuntmen to face the hazards they seek are their extensive training, skill, and equipment (Piët, 1986). The personal side of controllability is usually referred to as "competence" (White 1959; Mischel 1973) or "self-efficacy" (Bandura 1977b). In line with the above examples, competence or self-efficacy is generally considered to moderate stressfulness of aversive events; it also is the factor that differentiates a situation of challenge from one of threat (Lazarus 1966). Acquisition of coping modes is, according to Bandura (1979a,b), the operative factor in behavior therapy of phobias, weight control problems, and the like; this applies to modes of coping with the environment as well as with one's desires and emotions. In all this, appraisal of controllability of events and of one's efficacy counts as much as the actual facts.

Imagination

As has been repeatedly stressed, emotion is elicited by situations as the subject sees them; this mode of seeing includes his thoughts, associations, and fantasies. Thoughts, associations, and fantasies belong to the stimuli; they can be proper elicitors of emotions; they also contribute to the impact of actual events. One can considerably enhance one's jealous sufferings by visualizing what might be going on. Jealous suffering can even be created entirely in this fashion: Iago, as said, is part of Othello himself. As mentioned, Beck (1976), Meichenbaum (1977), and others have emphasized the role of self-defeating thoughts in depression and anxiety. Spielberger (1975) adduced evidence to show that performance decrement due to test anxiety is mainly caused by the activities of worrying; predominance of such thoughts correlates with decrement, which can be explained by the attention the thoughts deflect from the task. Deleterious, distress-amplifying effects of worrying have been discussed in the preceding subsection on anticipation; "sensitizers," who think of what may happen, suffer more from information about surgical operations (Andrew 1970) or about their children's illnesses (Wolff et al. 1964) than do "avoiders." The upsurge of fear after a sudden emergency has been adequately responded to and is over is due to the emergence of thoughts of what could have happened. Increase in fear with prolonged combat duty has been explained in a similar way (Grinker & Spiegel 1945): One has seen and realized what can happen, and of course imagination was entirely realistic there. Courage often can be said to be due to lack of imagination.

Dependence of sexual arousal upon imagination is commonplace. It also adds to nonimaginary pleasures, not only by sheer fantasy, but also by awareness of the interpersonal aspects of the situation and the emotional intent involved; imagination blends over into nonsensory stimulus coding, as discussed before in connection with Leventhal's studies (section 5.2). Generally, the pleasure of positive events is amplified by imagination: by the new possible prospects that a given achievement opens, the imagined acclaim of valued possible spectators, the potential love obtained even from deceased people, and so forth. Imagination widens the scope of concerns for which a given event can be relevant and forms the substance of what was earlier termed the "significance" of an emotional experience.

Thresholds

Wherever there are stimuli, there is question of thresholds; so also in the elicitation of emotion. Not every sudden stimulus produces startle, and not every loss of a cherished object causes sorrow; some are just too unimportant, or attention is invested elsewhere.

The existence of thresholds with respect to elicitation of emotional response does not follow from the above facts only. It also follows from variations in responsivity to emotional stimuli as a function of the individual's state: Exhaustion and adrenaline tend to enhance startle; alcohol may enhance both aggressive and affectionate responses; exhaustion would seem to first potentiate irritability and then to induce indifference. Also, responsivity changes as a function of previous events: Violent anger leaves the subject irritable for a while, and grief may make him susceptible to self-neglect. Further, there exist individual differences with respect to responsivity – for instance, as regards nervousness, upset, or fear, usually referred to as "emotionality" or "neuroticism" (Cattell 1957; Eysenck 1967). Threshold changes or differences may be specific to a given type of emotional response or generalized and apply to a range of responses, as in the exhaustion syndrome.

"Threshold" refers, first of all, to nothing but the above facts: to unresponsivity to stimuli considered weak and to intra- and interindividual differences in responsivity. There are three ways to conceive of the mechanism behind these facts: variable degrees of readiness of emotional response systems per se with trigger-happiness as an example of high degree of readiness; as variable degrees of weakness of inhibitions with respect to a given response system or with respect to emotional response generally; and as variable degrees of readiness of given ways of event coding. Some people may have a stronger tendency to perceive events as threatening, or as infringements, or as damaging generally than have other people or than they themselves have at other moments. It will not be easy to generate differential predictions to test the three hypotheses against one another, but in some conditions such predictions can perhaps be made.

Summation and sensitization

Intensity of response to a given stimulus depends not only upon the properties of that stimulus as such, but also upon the place of that stimulus in a time series. Successive, more or less similar stimulus events may produce summation, increase in response intensity, or sensitization, decrease in stimulus thresholds. Repetitions may also cause response decrement – habituation, which will be discussed in the section on loss of emotions (section 5.7).

Repeated frustrations accumulate. The frustration–aggression theory supposes them to do so (Dollard et al. 1939), and there is some experimental evidence that they do in fact. Berkowitz (1962) reviewed that evidence. For instance, Otis and McCandless (1955) repeatedly obstructed the play of children, who became increasingly angry. Berkowitz (1960) frustrated his subject's activities and in addition had them receive unfriendly messages; hostility increased with increasing number of messages. Common experience provides numerous examples of minor aggravations and contretemps that add up during the day, so that a final minor event elicits explosion of anger.

Accumulation of aversive effects is observed in a wide range of situations: from learned helplessness and apathy upon prolonged exposure to inescapable shock to battle fatigue. Fear responses to phobic stimuli may increase in strength with successive presentations, and in fact generally tend to do so during the development of a phobia. Repetitive infant–infant separations, in motherless rhesus infants, produces cumulative effects upon distress and behavior disturbance (Suomi et al. 1970).

Several variables are responsible for seeing to it that summation or sensitization, rather than habituation, occurs. Stimulus intensity probably is a major one. Strong simple sensory stimuli (loud sounds, intense light flashes) produce little or no habituation (Thompson & Spencer 1966); neither do traumatic events such as inescapable shock and combat experience. Klorman (1974) repeatedly showed snake-phobic subjects films of snakes of three different degrees of fearfulness; summation occurred in response to the most fearful series and habituation in response to the other two. Eysenck (1968, 1979) discusses the phenomenon of what he called "incubation": response increase to a brief conditioned stimulus, after this stimulus had once been paired to a traumatically intense shock (e.g., Napalkov 1967); the relevant evidence has, however, been seriously questioned (Evans 1976; Bersh 1980).

Frequency, or duration of interstimulus intervals, appears to be a second important variable, although the evidence is conflicting. Epstein (1971), for instance, found habituation of response to electric shock with repetitions on any one day, but sensitization with repetition on successive days; Lazarus and Opton (1966) found the reverse with responses to stressful films. The lack of consistent findings is not surprising, since frequency by itself facilitates habituation (Thompson & Spencer 1966); also, with truly emotional events various things may happen in the interstimulus intervals. Longer intervals permit recovery from excitement and fatigue but can also lead to dissipation of preparatory readiness and inhibitory control; they favor worrying as well as reassuring recoding.

The three types of interpretation of threshold changes mentioned in the previous subsection have all been advanced to explain summation or sensitization; they may all be valid in different instances of response increment. Increased response readiness forms part of the original frustration–aggression hypothesis: Drive strength from successive frustrations (and from other sources) adds up unless longer interstimulus intervals allow it to dissipate. In more modern variants, arousal or activation is supposed to accumulate (e.g., Groves & Thompson 1970). Arousal may accumulate even when it originated in different sorts of events; evidence for this was discussed in section 4.5. Presumably, such effects are effective over relatively brief interstimulus intervals, since autonomous arousal usually dissipates rather rapidly and hormonal effects in an hour or so. Very intense stimuli may well considerably extend these periods, though, as was discussed in chapter 3.

Decreased effectiveness of inhibitory control has been held responsible for the effects of prolonged stress: Control presumably requires effort, of which there may be a limited supply (the "adaptive cost hypothesis" of Glass & Singer 1972). Continued stress may also exhaust attentional capacity, thereby diminishing sensitivity to others and its controlling influence (Cohen 1978; 1980). Such effects are presumably of much longer duration: "Nervous exhaustion" may take months to recover from.

Finally, repetition and continuation of given events progressively changes situational meaning structure; the situation becomes increasingly serious or closed. A new aggravation is one aggravation more; a series of insults cannot be ignored or explained away, whereas a single one could; the store of possible ways of coping gets exhausted et cetera. Also, more concerns gradually come into play; fatigue, for instance, mobilizes desires for help or rest that in their turn are frustrated. These, indeed, are the kinds of explanation advanced by Dollard et al. (1939) and Berkowitz (1962) with respect to summation of frustration, and by Seligman (1975; Abramson et al. 1978) with respect to prolonged uncontrollable events. Cognitive explanations such as these make the assumption of accumulation of drivelike states unnecessary; they would seem to apply particularly to decrease of anger thresholds with indefinitely widely spaced frustrations. Repetitions giving rise to progressive change in the situation as perceived probably operate over long time periods. They may in fact lead to persistent dominance of given modes of coding situations: to persistent readiness to see events as frustrating or threatening or challenging. That is to say: Threshold differences may originate in differing cognitive dispositions, built up in the manner indicated.

5.7. Acquisition of emotion

Direct experience: conditioning and expectancy learning

Stimuli in the appropriate constellations elicit emotion either because they are originally pleasurable or aversive stimuli or because they are signals for the advent or nonadvent of aversive and pleasurable stimuli. *Signals* is to be understood broadly: It includes appearance of objects from which pleasant or unpleasant consequences can be expected to issue forth (dogs that bite, people who caress), of objects that are instrumental to such consequences, and of objects that make the subject think of such consequences.

There are several ways in which originally neutral stimuli can turn into signals and thus into emotional stimuli. The simplest of these corresponds to the classical conditioning paradigm: A neutral stimulus that accompanies an emotional stimulus and thus the latter's emotional effect thereby tends to become a conditioned stimulus that may elicit an emotional reaction by itself. The classic demonstration of "conditioned fear" is Watson and Rayner's (1920) experiment with little Albert. Showing the child a white rat while simultaneously producing a sudden loud sound led to subsequent fear when seeing the rat only; the fear generalized to other white furry objects. The conditioning paradigm not only fits acquisition of emotional response to external stimuli. It also fits acquisition of emotional response to one's own actions, and to one's impulses to perform certain actions: Acquisition can be supposed to occur when execution of these actions, or when thought thereof, is followed by reward or punishment.

"Conditioning" primarily refers to the arrangements of events as described: Coincidence of some neutral stimulus with emotional consequences produced by another stimulus results in the former becoming an emotional stimulus. It is best understood as signal learning or expectancy learning, because what is learned is a correlation between advent of the stimulus and that of the emotional consequences (Rescorla 1969).

Establishment of conditioning, or expectancy, usually requires several encounters with coincidence of neutral and emotion-arousing events. However, one-trial learning can occur under traumatic circumstances. Smells of burning may cause panic in subjects who have been fire victims; cancer patients who receive cytostatic drug therapy may become nauseated by the sight of the injection syringe, or even of the nurse, after the first injection that caused nausea. Experimentally, one-trial learning of fear has been produced, for instance in dogs, by very severe electric shock (Napalkov 1963; Wynne & Solomon 1955), and in humans by the injection of a drug that produces paralysis and blocking of respiration for about a minute (Campbell et al. 1964).

Strength of conditioning, that is, response intensity and persistence in time, generally is dependent upon number of reinforced encounters. The effects of successive encounters summate, perhaps even when they are of somewhat different kinds (Levis 1966; Levis & Hare 1977). It has been hypothesized that phobic anxieties may have been caused by trains of "subtraumatic" aversive events: parental rejections and punishments, minor frustrations, and so on (Eysenck 1979). Direct evidence for this hypothesis is lacking, however.

Rate of conditioning, that is, ease of acquisition, appears to depend upon the "congeniality" of the conditioned stimulus, with respect to the kind of unconditioned consequences involved (Bolles 1975; Seligman & Hager 1972; Seligman 1971). Watson and Rayner (1920), as mentioned, obtained one-trial acquisition of fear for a white rat. Bregman (1934) failed to obtain such acquisition when using a wooden block or a curtain as the stimulus to be conditioned. Valentine (1930), on reviewing his children's fears, concludes that some stimuli are more conducive to learned fear than others; English (1929) came to similar conclusions. Seligman (1971) notes that the bulk of phobias comprise only a limited number of phobic objects: certain animals (snakes, spiders, mice), heights, open spaces, narrow enclosures; the notion of preparedness (section 5.3) was suggested by observations such as these. Garcia and Koelling (1966) could rapidly establish food aversion in rats by adding taste to food that had made the animals ill (or rather after consumption of which they had been made ill by X-rays); they did not succeed when combining food presentation with noise or light flashes, which stimuli easily become effective warning signals for shock but that taste, in turn, does not.

Variations in ease of acquisition may reflect innate propensities, as assumed in the preparedness hypothesis, or more general principles of perception. Testa (1974), as said, has argued that coincidence of stimuli in space and time may facilitate recognition of their covariation as cause and effect or as signals and events to the signaled. Other principles may concern ease of recognition, orientation, and perceptual surveyance. It is likely that stimuli that are more difficult to survey and movements that are difficult to predict generally evoke alertness and wariness; they thus readily may evoke fear or become signals of danger. Animal movement may be considered to belong to this class of stimuli, that of snakes and spiders in particular, as well as that of mice and rats. Rats are "potentially fearsome," as Thorndike (1935) remarked in connection with the conflicting findings of Watson and Rayner and of Bregman.

Acquisition of emotional response to a given stimulus is not an inescapable consequence of the conditioning contingency. If the to-be-conditioned stimulus is not perceived or attended to, no acquisition is to be expected. Also, there is some evidence that current arousal level (or apprehensiveness, or jumpiness) influences ease of acquisition. Spence (1964) found rate of eyelid conditioning to be correlated with the subject's degree of "manifest anxiety"; Bandura and Rosenthal (1966) found observational learning to be facilitated by medium but not by low or high epinephrine-induced arousal level; Marks and Herst (1970) found that the phobias of a large proportion of agoraphobic women had started during periods of emotional stress, such as illness or divorce (however, it is unlikely that agoraphobia is due to conditioning in the first place).

Rate of acquisition may also be dependent upon subject characteristics. There might exist individual differences in "conditionability" (Eysenck 1975, 1979), or more specifically in sensitivity for fear conditioning (Gray 1971), or in conditionability of autonomic arousal (Hare 1976). This last has been invoked to explain the relative indifference to aversive consequences in psychopathic individuals. There are several ways in which such individual differences can be understood; we will briefly return to them in section 6.6.

The importance of conditioning in the development of naturally occurring anxieties, or of negative emotions generally, is not easy to assess. Phobias have been explained in conditioning terms (e.g., Eysenck & Rachman 1965); however, in a very large proportion of phobics, no precipitating event involving the phobic object could be traced (Rachman 1968; 1974). Lautch (1971) did find at least one possible relevant traumatic incident in the childhood of each of 34 subjects with strong fear for the dentist. Goorney and O'Connor (1971) identified an accident or some other anxiety-provoking incident in the history of one-fourth of a group of 79 air force personnel with excessive fear of flying; but in at least one-third no such incident could be found (in the remainder, precipitating incidents were of nontraumatic kinds, such as returns to flying after long absence). Also, conceptually as well as empirically, with respect to various features, phobias generally cannot be considered conditioned avoidance responses (Costello 1970).

Studies on expectancy learning of positive emotions are few, except for the (presumably joyful) learned anticipation of food. Several studies have investigated conditioning of sexual responses to more or less neutral stimuli. Rachman (1966) paired presentation of photographs of ladies' boots with those of female nudes; thereafter presenting the photographs of boots only produced some erection, that is, some penile tumescence. It is doubtful that mere conditioning was involved; intervention of imagination is likely, and at any rate it appears unwarranted to call the experimental result "an experimental analogue of fetishism" (Rachman 1966) or the prototype of how sexual deviations originate (Eysenck 1975). Findings have been inconsistent. Langevin and Martin (1975) failed to obtain conditioning when using meaningless drawings as conditioned stimuli; they doubt that sexual responses can be classically conditioned.

Indirect experience

Learning of emotions can be established through observing others react emotionally with respect to given stimuli and by being told what to fear or enjoy or be angry about or what consequences of a given event to expect. Bandura (1977a) has called these two forms of learning "vicarious learning" (or learning through vicarious reinforcement) "and symbolic learning," respectively.

Direct evidence of acquisition of emotions through observational learning comes from several experiments. Miller, Murphy, and Mirsky (1959) established, and then extinguished, an avoidance response to a given object in rhesus monkeys; the response reappeared when the subjects observed the frightened facial expressions and cries of other monkeys that approached the same object. Berger (1962) had human subjects watch a performer feign pain reactions upon a buzzer and light signal, as if receiving shock; the subjects came to manifest, in response to the signals, EDRs that were larger in magnitude than those of control subjects not seeing a performer. Craig and Weinstein (1965) obtained similar results in an experiment in which a performer ostensibly received shock upon failing at some task. However, in these experiments subjects may well have reacted sympathetically to another's suffering rather than have learned to fear some stimulus.

Indirect evidence for observational or symbolic learning of emotions comes from the correspondence between children's fears and those of their close relatives. Hagman (1932) reports a correlation of .32 between the number of fears of children and their mothers. May (1950) finds correlations of .65 to .74 between the number of fears of siblings and high correspondence in what things are feared. Bandura and Menlove (1968) report that parents of children who are afraid of dogs are more often afraid of dogs than other parents from the same population. Of course, these findings can also be interpreted in different ways (similar environments, neurotic constitution, etc.). Nevertheless, observational and symbolic learning can be, and have been, held responsible for the origin of animal phobias since evidence of relevant direct traumatic experiences is absent in a majority of cases (Rachman 1974).

Emotion learning through being told is demonstrated in simple conditioning experiments. Telling a subject that shock will follow a light signal is sufficient for that signal light to evoke a GSR and thus tenseness or apprehension (Cook & Harris 1937). Instruction that shock will follow a high tone, but not a low tone is sufficient for differential GSR responding to these tones (Bridger & Mandel 1964). Telling the subject that no further shock will follow immediately diminishes subsequent response to the signal (Silverman 1960). Telling someone that handling an object is unsafe produces aprehensiveness when he touches it or fright when he is forced to do so.

Yet reservations are in order. Direct experience of some sort strongly supports observational and symbolic learning and may well be a necessary condition for such learning. Simple warnings are usually of little consequence; so, in general, are the mistakes of others (or one's own, for that matter). The monkey subjects in Miller, Murphy, and Mirsky's experiment first had had their own aversive experience. Church (1959) reports observational learning in rats, but only when they themselves first had had painful experiences, and more so if they had suffered pain together with the animals they observed. In the experiment by Bandura and Rosenthal (1966), strongest vicarious conditioning (acquisition of GSR to a signal when this signal had been seen to be followed by pain response in a performer) was obtained when the subjects themselves had earlier been threatened with shock. Observational learning of fears in children might well occur only upon real fright: seeing one's parents be frightened is itself an unsettling experience. Instilling fears through verbal exhortation usually is accompanied by vivid description of dire consequences, among them loss of love or of social acceptance or being seen by the all-seeing eye of God. Differences in the amount of direct experience involved may account for the variable effects of observation and of verbal information upon acquisition and relinquishing of fears and other emotional responses.

Imprinting

Ducklings and jackdaws become attached to the first animate object they meet after hatching. They follow a human being if that object happens to be a human being. The phenomenon is called "imprinting," which thus constitutes a mode of learning different from expectancy learning (Lorenz 1952).

Imprinting is a learning mode not usually ascribed to humans. However, something at least similar is occurring in human acquisition of attachment objects. The propensities for forming attachments, whatever they are, become focused upon one single individual; such focusing blocks the formation of other, simultaneous attachments of the same nature. Focusing upon specific objects as satisfiers and consequent restriction in the range of acceptable satisfiers probably is typical in the acquisition of satisfiers generally. It is found in food preferences and other preference for what is familiar: housing, culture, the fatherland. It is notably found in falling in love, where infatuation with one usually bars all other similar ones from attention.

Cognitive processes

Emphasis upon previous direct and indirect experience unduly simplifies the way emotional stimuli actually come into existence. Direct experience with pleasant and aversive consequences probably always forms the ultimate source of emotional impact of learned stimuli; this appears to be so even with objects of observational and symbolic learning. However, that direct experience may have had nothing to do with occurrence of the stimulus under concern.

Simplest examples come from generalization. Stimuli may elicit emotion because they resemble either unconditional or acquired stimuli. Generalization is of course a basic property of conditioning. Fear conditioned to a white rat generalized to other white furry objects. It is as basically a property of innate response. Ducklings fear silhouettes resembling those of birds of prey (Tinbergen 1951).

Generalization occurs at different cognitive levels. Emotional reactions may spread to stimuli perceptually similar to the original stimuli, as in the above examples; to stimuli that are semantically similar, as a word is to its denoted object, or one word to another with similar meaning or connotation ("semantic generalization," see Razran 1961); to stimuli that are conceptually related, belonging to a class the original stimulus also belongs to; to real events from imagined events and vice versa (Lang 1977). Sexual arousal, alertness, and nervousness can be elicited by words denoting parts of the female body; such words may make an adolescent fall into reverie. Physiological response occurs to words denoting feared objects; spider phobics may shudder upon mention of the word *spider*. Generalization can occur on the basis of accidental similarities unrelated to the stimulus properties essential for the original emotional response: from object to word to different word with similar sound, for instance. Such generalization underlies responses to sexual and aggressive symbols as these occur in dreams, jokes, and coarse or oblique speech (Freud 1917).

Emotions evoked by words and images usually are not the same as those elicited by the real thing. As said, warnings are often not heeded, declarations not believed, or not truly so; fear of an imagined spider is not usually the same as fear of a real spider. Of course, verbal signals and images differ from true events in their reality and in possibilities for coping actions. On occasion, however, emotions evoked by words and images can be as violent as any other. We will explore the conditions later.

Stimuli may become emotional stimuli through their resemblance or association with original emotional stimuli, even when response to those original stimuli is lost through inhibition or by being overrun by other, incompatible emotions: the phenomenon of displacement. Displacement of aggression is frequently discussed in the aggression literature (see Berkowitz 1962 for experimental evidence). It has been invoked by Freud (1900, 1917, 1926), who invented the term, to explain sexual variations and phobias: Emergence of fear of a powerful horse was explained as displacement of fear of the powerful father, the displacement being due, presumably, to suppression of the latter fear and of the anger that was thought to have generated it. Displacement can be explained by differences in gradients of generalization and of inhibition, respectively, of response to the original object (Dollard & Miller 1950); it can also be explained in terms of cognitive procedures.

Generalization is not a learning mechanism. True acquisition is involved when stimuli become emotional stimuli on the basis of general knowledge and of cognitive rules of inference. Such general knowledge, or these rules of inference, may have been acquired from experience that has nothing to do with emotional situations. When the ship's engine stalls during a storm at sea it precipitates fear even though one has no such experience in fearful situations; stalling engines make one powerless, whatever the condition. When husbands start to whistle in the bathroom after 10 years of marriage, or wives resume making up, there is occasion for worrying; and so forth. These are logical rather than merely empirical relationships between cue and possible consequence, and if the consequence happens to be aversive under the circumstances, the cue becomes an emotional stimulus.

The above examples again illustrate that emotions result from meanings, and meanings, to a large extent, from inferred consequences or causes. The aversiveness of being given coffee without sugar, understood as a sign of neglect, derives not from prior experience but from causal attribution based on general rules. These rules may involve supposed empirical connections; they may also involve norms and values: Certain events, given certain other events, ought to happen, or ought not to happen, even if they constantly do. Indignation gives examples of eliciting conditions that have nothing empirical about them, although their impact is acquired: violations of norms, of standards of behavior.

A majority of emotional stimuli derive their emotional impact along these lines: those of generalization or, rather, abstract thought, of application of rules and general knowledge schemata, of generalized and normative expectations. That impact thus has little to do with conditioning, whether direct or vicarious. It has little to do with having experienced aversive or pleasurable consequences accompanying a particular kind of stimulus. Losing one's job, receiving criticism, perceiving signs of being neglected or slighted, being praised, and seeing norm violations are all quite indirectly or remotely connected to the actual aversive or pleasurable conditions that they somehow signal and that give them emotional life.

On the other hand, immediacy and strength of emotional response would seem to depend upon intensity of direct experience with the aversive or pleasurable conditions involved, whether in connection with the learned stimuli or otherwise. Where there is smoke, there is fire, and apprehension generally follows; but panic seizes when one once was in a conflagration, even if smokeless. A whistling partner causes worry; but cold sweat breaks out if one has ever been left before.

The above mechanisms of emotion acquisition leave out what is perhaps the major source of acquired emotional stimuli: acquisition of concerns. Some goals, objects, and values become important for a variety of reasons; events relating to achievement of these goals, welfare of these objects, and maintaining these values thus generate emotions. Emotional stimuli thus differ when concerns differ, from one individual to another. When honor is considered important, loss of honor becomes an offense to self-esteem and an elicitor of grief or anger. When social power is considered of high value, loss of social power forms such an offense. When material possessions are valued, emotions attach particularly to their acquisition and loss. And of course, one's particular attachments generate particular emotional stimuli: the fate of that mother, that child, that partner.

Social sources of emotions

As said, many objects and events become emotional stimuli because of the operation of rules, norms, and values. Many of these rules, norms, and values are of social origin; they are rules, norms, and values of the individual's society. Also, many concerns that underlie emotion derive from society's norms and values.

The influence of society upon emotion has been discussed extensively by Gordon (1981). Rules, norms, and values contribute in at least two ways to the emotions of the individual. First, they provide him with positively or negatively evaluated goals, concerns, and objects. Honor was already cited as a concern or goal that is highly valued in some cultures, and the concept of which may be nonexistent in others. Virginity, deference to superiors, the Fatherland, control of emotional expression may be mentioned as various other examples. Among the products of rules, norms, and values are socially defined positively or negatively valued objects: taboo objects and objects of veneration.

The second contribution of rules, norms, and values to the individual's emotions consists of the emotions contingent upon adherence to these norms, or upon norm violation: comfort in one's sense of propriety, pride in one's outstanding achievements, admiration for those of others; shame and guilt upon one's own infringements and distrust, anger, and indignation upon those of others. Norm violation, in fact, is one of the major anger stimuli, both in the old study by Hall (1899) and in the current one by Scherer et al. (1986).

Society can contribute to emotion in still other ways: by providing the individual with particular emotions and with definition of particular emotionally relevant situation aspects. Certain things may be emotional objects in some culture, even form a separate class of objects at that, and not be so in others. Sexual jealousy is a case in point: It is sometimes said not to exist in certain cultures. If true, this might be because society defines or sanctions unique sexual rights over given other persons, or because its conceptual system focuses upon the third party in sexual infidelity rather than upon one's pain of loss. Gratitude provides an other example: Gratitude, beyond doubt, is more important in Javanese and Japanese culture than in ours. Those cultures presumably have "feeling rules" (Hochschild 1983) in this regard; but they have them because they have embedded services rendered in systems of interpersonal relationships and obligations. As a final example: The culture may or may not stress individual identity and responsibility. If it does not, emotions like guilt feeling and remorse must be different or even absent.

How does society do all this? The mechanisms, no doubt, are primarily observational learning and being told; together with the actual rewards of social approval and the actual punishments of social disapproval and parental discipline. With, no doubt, the added impact of imagination: stories about the terrible fate of those who trespassed.

Discussion of social origins of emotions cannot be concluded without a caveat. Firm conclusions about social origins of given emotions are not easy to draw; and the tendency exists to rashly declare culture to be the origin of whatever shows intercultural difference. The caveat is twofold. First, whenever there is cultural difference, culture may have been of positive influence in either of the differing cultures or in both. Presence of sexual jealousy in one culture and not in another may mean cultural definition (of sexual rights, of possession) in the first *or* cultural denial, prohibition, and repression in the second. Second, whenever there is difference, it may be nothing but a veneer around a common core. What is "honor" in one culture might be "self-esteem" in another. We do not stab rivals in love, but fail to appear at work in the morning.

5.8. Loss and persistence of emotions

Emotions come, and they often go. Stimuli that elicit emotion at one moment may fail to do so at some later time. Objects lose their appeal, grief fades, anxieties and apprehensions vanish without change in external circumstances. The relevant questions are: When do they do so? and Why?

Emotions also may persist indefinitely in the absence of circumstances that seem to warrant persistence. Phobias are enduring anxieties evoked by harmless objects or situations. Traumatic events carry their aftereffects for years. Archibald and Tuddenham (1965) report that 7 out of 10 men who had suffered from battle fatigue during World War II showed depression, jumpiness, restlessness, and irritability 20 years later. Dobbs and Wilson (1960) exposed war veterans to tape recordings of battle noises; several of those who had suffered from war neurosis reacted with acute anxiety attacks. Similar persistence of sensitivities and disturbance exist among concentration camp survivors (Chodoff 1963; Matussek 1971): depression, nightmares, anxiety attacks, violent anger or panic reactions to stimuli resembling stimuli from camp situations – tiled walls, chimneys, crudeness of behavior. Sometimes these symptoms emerge only after an interval of 20 years or more, probably because of slackening of emotional control consequent upon the remoteness of the events of time or the subject's advancing age; the latency of the syndrome has given rise to the designation "late injury" (German *Spätschädigung*).

Grief upon loss of a spouse or child may continue unabated for long periods. There can be extended apathy, depression, or restlessness (Parkes 1972). Chance encounters, years after, with objects once belonging to the lost person, or stumbling upon a memory, may elicit unexpected outburst of sorrow, as if the loss was fresh. The dictum that time heals all wounds is empirically incorrect.

Several different constellations can be distinguished that may account for loss of emotional impact, and several conditions can be outlined that may account for its persistence.

Change in concerns

Emotions are elicited when some event favors or interferes with satisfaction of some concern. It follows that the event should cease eliciting emotion when the concern has disappeared. Joy upon meeting one's friend is gone when love for him has gone; and jealousy, too, evoked by behavior that provokes suspicion. Swann decides that, when their affair will be over, he will ask Odette who it was that visited her that one night; he then realizes that by that time he will no longer care (Proust, "Swann in Love" in *Swann's Way*).

Emotions may vanish because concerns have changed at a more general level. Old age is said to bring rest because lovely shapes no longer stir youthful agitations. The nature of children's fears changes with age, presumably because security and competence grow and because social interactions and self-esteem become relevant. Small children primarily fear sounds, objects, certain people, and being left alone; older children come to fear failure in social situations and performance (Jersild & Holmes 1935).

To the extent that concerns remain in force, relevant events tend to retain their emotional power. Presumably, distress by being abandoned by one's partner does not last so long when a new relationship can be established and is found satisfying. Conversely, continued pining is taken to indicate that the attachment is still alive. Waning and persistence of the concerns themselves may be understood by the other mechanisms adduced to explain loss of emotions.

Extinction

"Extinction" refers to decrease in response when this response is no longer reinforced: when a signal stimulus is no longer followed by the aversive or profitable consequent (in classical conditioning constellations) or when a response is no longer followed by its aversive or profitable outcomes (in operant or instrumental learning). The classical illustration of the first is given by the experiment of Jones (1924): A child who was afraid of a white rabbit lost its fear when the rabbit was repeatedly presented together with sweets, first in a cage and at a safe distance, and gradually moved closer. Extinction of the operant type may be illustrated by decrease of anger or fear when secondary gains (others giving in to bullying, providing attention and support, etc.) are taken away (see Bandura 1977a).

Extinction, like conditioning, can be understood as change in expectancy: expectancy, in this case, that signals and actions will no longer be followed by emotionally relevant consequents. Extinction, in fact, is accelerated when reinforcement and extinction conditions are made clearly distinct, for instance with the help of discriminative stimuli (e.g., Bolles & Grossen 1969), and is slowed down when they cannot easily be told apart, as after partial reinforcement. A love object is more easily relinquished after a distinct than after a provisional no.

However, not every change in circumstances produces prompts extinction; not all information regarding absence of reward or punishment generates effective change in expectancies. Bridger and Mandel (1974) told subjects that shock would follow a light signal; "Conditioned" EDR promptly appeared at the first signal presentation. Half the subjects then actually received an occasional but intense shock; the others received none. Telling that no (or no more) shock would follow and disconnecting the electrodes produced immediate extinction in the unshocked subjects, but only gradual extinction in the others. For one thing, this proves that actual, direct experience has different consequences from only being told; for another, it proves information not to be the same as expectancy change.

Emotional response to very intense aversive stimuli often does not appear to extinguish at all. Mention has been made of traumatic aversive conditioning (Solomon & Wynne 1954 with dogs; Campbell et al. 1964 with humans) that persists, unreinforced, for hundreds of trials and of the fact that inescapable, uncontrollable shock led dogs to remain passive and apathetic indefinitely after shock termination (Seligman 1975). Non-extinction has been explained by the principle of "anxiety conservation." Rapid avoidance behavior in response to the danger signal, as in Solomon and Wynne's experiments, reduces fear before the subject has had the opportunity to find out that the situation had become harmless (Dollard & Miller 1950); alternatively, such rapid avoidance behavior forestalls the emergence of fear, which then has no opportunity to extinguish (Solomon & Wynne 1954). Persistent learned helplessness is explained in a similar way. Eysenck's (1968, 1979) incubation hypothesis is of a related nature: Persistence of anxiety occurs if the conditioned stimulus is so brief as to preclude extinction.

Persistence of unreinforced anxiety thus is explained either by absence of "reality check" through avoidance or by relative absence of to-be-extinguished anxiety. Both may be effected by psychological rather than overt actions. Defensive avoidance of thinking of the traumatic event, avoiding confrontation with anxiety-provoking situations, and suppression of anxiety (see chapter 8) all lead to conditions equivalent to those sketched, actual confrontations with fear-provoking stimuli notwithstanding; Marks (1975) blames failures of "flooding" procedures (see below) on such cognitive manipulations. In addition, restriction of awareness and disturbance of thought processes during strong emotion may make the subject fail to attend fully to the actual harmlessness of the stimuli. Persistence of grief can in a similar way be understood as due to avoidance of realizing that the loss is final, of thinking of the loss, of confronting the situation that might bring the loss truly home. Inclination to avoid confrontation with the loss is strengthened by avoidance of inadmissible feelings of anger, guilt, and relief, which bereavement may also bring about and which appear to be the strongest obstacles against full realization (Ramsay 1979).

Persistence of anxiety and grief or of the attachment underlying grief may in many cases be due to the fact that emotions are connected with a number of different stimuli rather than a single one. Not all these stimuli are encountered for extinction until stumbled upon much later.

Grief may persist because the myriad of habits and expectations comprising attachment have to be extinguished one by one; when, years later, the dead child's wet nurse is met, the lost endearment still appears in force. Anxieties, according to Stampfl and Levis (1973), persist until all contributing subtraumatic events have come to the fore.

The above mechanisms and contingencies form the foundations upon which the various procedures are built that are employed in the behavior therapy of phobic anxiety, social fears, sexual dysfunction, and protracted reactions to bereavement. "Systematic desensitization" confronts the patient with graduated series of (real, imagined, or verbal) fear stimuli or images of loss. In treatment of anxiety, the series is called an "anxiety hierarchy" (Paul 1969; Bandura 1969; Wilson & Davison 1971); the gradually moving closer of Jones's rabbit is an in vivo example. Graduation is supposed to prevent too strong anxiety and subsequent avoidant behavior (or to favor incompatible "reciprocal and inhibitory responses" – Wolpe 1969); its actual contribution to anxiety is doubtful (Wilson & Davison 1971). "Flooding" (Baum 1970; Marks 1975) and "implosion" (Stampfl & Levis 1973) involve confronting the patient with maximally anxiety-provoking but harmless stimuli, again either in reality ("in vivo treatments") or in imagination ("imaginal treatments"), and for extended periods – for 100 minutes or more; intensity and duration are aimed at maintaining opportunity for anxiety extinction, keeping attention focused upon the situation, and counteracting avoidant efforts. "Response prevention" (of avoidance responses) indeed appears to cause considerably faster extinction in animals than the usual avoidance paradigm (Baum 1970), and duration of flooding or desensitization sessions indeed appears to be an important variable, in animals (Wilson & Davison 1971) as well as in humans (Stern & Marks 1973; Levis & Hare 1977). Muscular relaxation training, which is often added to desensitization procedures (Wolpe 1969; Paul 1969), appears to contribute to extinction when (and only when) it functions to facilitate nondefensive exposure to the anxiety-provoking stimuli (Wilson & Davison 1971).

Confrontations with anxiety-provoking situations may be arranged indirectly, vicariously, rather than directly. "Modeling" involves having the patient observe a model behaving fearlessly toward the phobic object (Bandura 1977a). Geer and Turtletaub (1967), for instance, found less avoidance of snakes in 10 out of 20 snake phobics after they watched a calm model approach the snakes (4 out of 20 behaved less fearfully after watching a fearful model, which is less, but still nonnegligible).

In general, in vivo treatments appear superior to verbal or imaginal treatments (Bandura 1977a), except when anxiety would rise too much in actual confrontation (Wolpe 1969). Modeling accompanied by "guided participation" tends to be superior to mere observational learning; in guided participation or "participant modeling," the patient participates in the model's actions (Bandura, Blanchard, & Ritter 1969). Behavioral methods in the therapy of sexual dysfunction are said to be more effective in overcoming anxieties than discussion and interview techniques. If this superiority of treatments involving direct experience turns out to be consistently present, this would support the hypothesis that expectancy change is effected more readily, or more effectively, through direct experience than by way of merely cognitive mediation.

Persistence of emotion is not only due to avoidance of confrontations or thoughts. It may be due to the emotion's secondary gains; emotion may produce gains that interfere with extinction of the operant type. Many emotions, even painful ones, provide the subject with some sort of gain. Grief implies a tie with the lost person; as long as grief persists, the lost person is not entirely gone. Jealousy often implies a claim upon the partner; admitting to the unreasonableness of one's jealousy threatens to give license to one's partner. Letting go of a grudge recognizes the other person's power or right to do what he did; letting go of resentment toward a lover who left abandons the lover as well as the fantasy of still extracting satisfaction. "Secondary gains" is an awkward expression when it comes to understanding the same mechanisms in connection with truly serious harm. By accepting past horrors as well as by facing one's helpless terror, the enemy may be felt to gain more of a late victory (Epstein 1979).

The various procedures mentioned, generally speaking, appear reasonably effective, although the accumulated evidence is not so solid as to permit firm statements (Kazdin & Wilson 1978). Effectiveness does not necessarily demonstrate that extinction is the process involved. Decrease of response may result from habituation, to be discussed below. Moreover, expectancy change may be produced through increase in competence, to be discussed later in this section. Extinction interpretation of decay of anxiety, phobic or otherwise, hinges upon the assumption that the anxieties are of the conditioned variety, which is not necessarily so (see Costello 1970). They may result from actual weakness of control, competence, or cognitive grip; and posttraumatic anxieties rather seem to be unconditioned responses to remembered horrible experience. Bereavement also can hardly be seen as a conditioned stimulus.

More important, perhaps, with respect to the explanation of persistence of emotions is the assumption that the consequences of intense emotional experience should extinguish unless counteracted by avoidance or secondary gain. For this assumption there in fact is no evidence; it is theoretical dogma. One may hold that Solomon and Wynne's dogs simply did not forget. It may be in the very nature of severe trauma and personal loss to produce effects that persist. In fact, this is not contradictory to the notion of extinction. Extinguished responses generally do not really disappear; they may show spontaneous recovery. Extinction, according to Pavlov, is a process of suppression rather than of decay. Put differently, expectancies are only overwritten by new experience; the older ones are not erasable. Significant expectancies may never be fully overwritten. Late injury, the resurgence of concentration camp or war effects after years of apparent adjustment, attests to this; as said, resurgence appears to depend upon slackening suppression or decreased coping potential. Time, it may be ventured, does not heal wounds at all; it only provides plasters.

Habituation

Habituation, in a technical sense, means decrease of response to unconditioned stimuli due to repeated occurrence of those stimuli. Magnitude of the orienting response to neutral stimuli (clicks, light flashes) or to weak electric shock decreases upon successive presentations, for instance.

Habituation of the orienting response is explained by Sokolov (1963) in terms of the gradual establishment of a "neuronal model" of the stimulus. Orienting is the outcome of a mismatch between stimulus input and neuronal model; as the neuronal model develops, mismatch disappears. Other theories explain habituation somewhat differently. According to Groves and Thompson (1970) habituation is the outcome of two competing processes: habituation proper of a given type of response to a given type of stimulus; and sensitization, a change in the organism's general state of activation that, upon stimulus repetition, first grows and then decays. Manifest habituation occurs when habituation proper outscores sensitization, which it does when stimuli are frequent and not too intense.

There are a number of properties that define *habituation* in a technical sense. The following generalizations are derived from Thompson and Spencer (1966):
1.　Habituation is faster with weak than with intense stimuli. With

intense stimuli and stimuli that have to be responded to, response increase rather than habituation may occur. Stimuli requiring response do not habituate, or less so.

2. Habituation rate is faster, the smaller the interstimulus interval.
3. Habituated responses show spontaneous recovery with longer interstimulus intervals.
4. Dishabituation occurs upon different, and mostly upon more intense, stimuli.
5. Habituation manifests stimulus generalization: Upon habituation to certain stimuli, similar stimuli also elicit decreased response.
6. Rehabituation after dishabituation is faster than the original habituation.
7. Repeated dishabituations decrease in magnitude.

Further, habituation of arousal occurs more slowly under high arousal, as under the influence of stimulant drugs (see Groves & Thompson 1970); it also is slowed down by very low arousal state, as in somnolence or sleep (Johnson & Lubin 1967; Sokolov 1963).

Many of these features seem to apply to some of the more complex situations of emotional response. They apply to orienting reactions, from which they are to a large extent derived; and to the related reactions of curiosity and interest. Emotions contingent upon novelty generally show loss upon repetition and recovery after long intervals. The same occurs with the boredom upon hearing the same piece of music over and over and the regain of appeal after a period of nonexposure; or the excitement and wariness of novel environments giving way to the security of familiar surroundings.

Fear and distress also tend to show habituation, at least with weak or moderately intense stimuli – so with successive electric shocks of moderate intensity (Epstein 1973), repeated presentations of a gruesome film (Averill, Malmstrom, Koriat, & Lazarus 1972; Maguire et al. 1973), and progression of parachutist training (Epstein & Fenz 1967; Ursin et al. 1978). Habituation in these studies concerns physiological response as well as subjective distress ratings. The relation between habituation and stimulus intensity holds for fear. Even experienced parachutists show strong physiological and subjective apprehension response, albeit in a different temporal pattern from novices (Epstein & Fenz 1965).

Flooding and desensitization are perhaps better explained by habituation than by extinction. The effectiveness of flooding, since it involves massed stimulation, supports a habituation interpretation, but stimulus intensities would make one predict that no habituation should occur;

on the other hand, sensitization in flooding sessions appear not to be a rare occurrence (e.g., Wolpe 1969; Barret 1969).

People get used to continuous aversive events like lack of attentiveness, repetitious aggravations, minor harassments, material deprivations, and not too extreme hardships; to continuous pleasures, too, and more so, for that matter. To what extent this is due to habituation or to the development of adaptive forms of coping, the aftereffects of which may show up sooner or later, is unknown. The two, moreover, are not clearly separable if a cognitive theory of habituation is espoused; Sokolov's theory, after all, is an expectancy theory. Cognitive adjustments clearly seem important in the conditions indicated, as they do in the simpler habituation constellations. Epstein (1973), as already stated, explains habituation to repeated mild shock by worries proving unnecessary; Lazarus and Opton (1966) give a similar explanation for diminishing effects of repeated stress-film exposures. Bandura, Adams, and Beyer (1977) find reduction in ruminations instrumental in the reduction of snake phobia. Cognitive adjustments to continuous frustrations, hardships, and the like can be effected by change in attributions (from "bad intent" to "that is the way he is") and various other coping strategies.

Predictions concerning where and when habituation will occur, and where and when not, are hard to make. This is particularly so because signal stimuli – stimuli that have to be responded to – habituate slowly, if at all (Thompson & Spencer 1966); and whether a stimulus has to be responded to is, within limits, a matter of the subject's discretion. When the need is felt to counter harassments, slightings, and reproaches, anger or distress may well persist more strongly for that reason than when the subject is forced to remain passive or has decided to let those events pass by, as a mode of "secondary control."

Competence gain

As indicated above, habituation to recurrent or continuous aversive or challenging events does not consist of mere decrease in sensitivity. To a large extent, it consists of the development of new ways of coping with those events. Diminishment of emotional response reflects, at least in part, growth of competence.

There are many circumstances in which acquisition of coping skills causes reduction of emotional impact in obvious fashion. Learning how to drive a car, finding ways of obtaining food under shortage, and learning social skills are examples, as are the acquisition of skill in dangerous sports and professions. Learning to suppress unnecessary worry, to discard "irrational beliefs," and to focus upon tasks at hand are slightly less obvious examples. Acquisition of these modes of coping may enhance actual control, thereby changing situational meaning structure. In addition, they enhance trust in one's coping ability and sense of control, one's sense of not being at the mercy of events. Whereas such skill acquisition is part of the natural process of getting used to or training for new conditions, it is sought explicitly in some of the behavior therapies. Social skills training (e.g., Salter 1961; Wolpe & Lazarus 1966) presumably works to combat social anxiety, to the extent that it does, in these two ways. The cognitive therapies of Ellis (1970) and Beck (1976) endeavor to change competence by combating irrational beliefs and self-defeating worries.

Acquisition of coping actions blends in with a second mode of competence gain: acquisition of confidence in one's ability to stand suspense or distress. Approaching a live snake, even when one is sweating, in desensitization or flooding, not only may change outcome expectancies of a snake's actions. It also changes expectancies concerning one's response; it proves, or may prove, that the anxiety does not block action or incapacitates, and that it passes. The same holds for people successfully facing real dangers, such as combat, mountain cliffs, or fires. In life's ordinary hardships, too, habituation – or, rather, adaptation – occurs through learning to endure and stand fear, pain, helplessness, or jealousy, or pleasurable suspenses. Meichenbaum's (1977) "self-inoculation training" is specifically geared to anxiety manipulations of this kind.

The importance of subjective competence in decrease of distress is attested to by the influence of social, relational factors and expectations of improvement upon therapeutic success in behavior (or other) therapy. Wilkins (1971) reviewed the evidence on the contributions made by the patient–therapist relationship, feedback concerning therapeutic gains, encouragement, and patients' confidence in therapy effectiveness. These factors probably do not explain all the therapeutic success (Davison & Wilson 1971), but their contribution appears to be considerable. For instance, procedures that prove superior to others also tend to be more credible to the patients (Kazdin & Wilcoxon 1976); such credibility may account for a sizable proportion of demonstrated emotion change.

Bandura (1977a,b) has subsumed all effects of behavior therapies under the heading of increase in "self-efficacy expectations," that is, in convictions that one can successfully execute the behavior required to produce the desired outcomes. Self-efficacy ratings correlate more closely with actual behavior improvement in phobics than does, for instance, nonavoidance of phobic imagery during desensitization (Bandura 1977b). There is something circular in the argument, since self-efficacy ratings would seem to reflect (assumed) ability to cope rather than to cause it. It appears more appropriate to juxtapose outcome expectancy and competence expectancy as two major determinants of resistance to potentially distressing situations. Even so, competence (or self-efficacy) can be viewed, as it is by Bandura, as the common final pathway of at least many of the procedures that prove effective in achieving emotional change.

Emotional processing

Achieving the conditions for extinction, habituation, and competence change in part occurs naturally. In part these conditions must be brought about actively, by effort and the deployment of attention, thought, and imagination. This holds for the natural course of events as much as for behavior therapy. Freud (1915) describes the "work of grief": Active evocation of painful memories, voluntarily looking at the deceased's photograph, thinking of one's loneliness and abandonment that serve as self-generated extinction conditions. Some time later (Freud 1920) he considered recurrent nightmares of traumatic events not as wish fulfillment but, similarly, as endeavors to process these events. Janis (1958) writes about the *work of worry*: anticipatory creation of conditions for expectancy change, so as to forestall future surprise and future need for habituation.

Rachman (1980) introduced the concept of "emotional processing" to cover the entire gamut of activities described; in fact, Dutch and German possess accepted and current words for referring to what one should do with intense painful experiences that are precise equivalents of the verb *to process* (the Dutch word is *verwerken*; the German words are *verarbeiten* and *durcharbeiten*). The concept of processing aptly denotes the work involved, and how remote the processes of overcoming suffered anxiety, trauma, or loss are from the automaticity suggested by *extinction* and *habituation* in their original theoretical meanings.

Emotional processing, as may be inferred from the preceding, involves more than active confrontation with the events or thoughts one wishes to avoid. It also involves or should involve active exploration of antecedents of anxiety and loss, and the risks of confrontation. The roles of imagery and of surrendering to one's imagination, of identifying and acknowledging implicit assumptions and beliefs, and devising new modes of coping have been discussed in preceding subsections. We add the importance of exploring the secondary gains one covertly hopes to achieve and, according to psychoanalytic views, the historical background and precise content of these hopes.

Emotional processing comprises activities at quite different levels: from attention to chance encounters with events and thoughts through actively opposing tendencies to shrink from such events and thoughts and coming to accept anxiety and distress and on to reinterpretation of events with a view toward obtaining secondary control and relinquishing obsolete concerns and secondary gains. "Integrating" experience probably refers to the entire range concurrently, with the extensive cognitive change that implies.

The laws of hedonic asymmetry

Habituation, as discussed in this section, plays an important role in the disappearance of emotional response. However, habituation does not work in equal measure for all stimuli. There often is a limit to habituation. Responses may decrease but not disappear altogether. This is the case particularly with signal stimuli that have to be acted upon. Pain and sorrow, for instance, never really subside, even (and perhaps especially) when its causes continue for a long time.

Habituation is strong when stimuli do not require response. Continuous, safe presence of the attachment figure, enough food in the morning, regular satisfactions of self-esteem, when they are there, can be taken for granted; emotions regarding having and getting all these recede. As argued earlier in this and the preceding chapters, positive emotions are responses to change. Even explicit contentment is; it only emerges as an emotion when contrasting possibilities are envisaged.

This state of affairs can be generalized. We may phrase it as the *First Law of Hedonic Asymmetry*, specifically the *Law of Asymmetrical Adaptation to Pleasure and Pain*: Pleasure results from change toward achieving satisfaction and disappears under persistent satisfaction, whereas Pain persists under persistent dissatisfaction. The law is important in evaluating the net quantity of pleasure in a person's life and is a source of ever-recurring surprises and disappointments. That other law, the terrible *Law of Regret*, is derived from it: In Dory Previn's version, "One never stops to wonder until a person's gone." One knows what one had more than what one has. This law was illustrated earlier by reference to Proust's *Albertine Disparue*: After he had wished Albertine away, her actual disappearance shattered him; many a marriage can tell the same story. Discontentments swap places after achievement; what one has counts less than what one has not; the grass is always greener on the other side of the fence.

This is not generally true, however. Many things give pleasure that were never missed. Even losses can live a silent life, calling out only upon confrontation with that which reminds of what could have been. We may thus propose a Second Law, the *Law of Preponderance of Pleasure*: Pain upon not having satisfaction tends to be less than pleasure upon having it. The two regularities, fortunately, tend to counterbalance. The conditions under which either the first or the second is operative can be distinguished. The second applies when there is nothing to call attention to absence of satisfaction; the first when absence is obtrusive or when the situation consists of presence of aversive events rather than absence of satisfying ones. Also, the first is a law of adaptation and thus of recurrence or persistence of events; the second one of actual conditions.

5.9. The stimulus reception process

Stimuli for emotion, as we argued and tried to show in the preceding, largely consist of cognitions, as defined in section 5.2. They consist of expectancies, interpretations, comparisons, and attributions; actual stimuli depend upon such cognitive elements for their effectiveness. They – the effective stimuli – result from appraisal processes in which actual stimulus events interact with previously acquired knowledge, with available coding categories, and with available rules of inference. Coding categories such as "modifiability" and "controllability" and "change" (chapter 4) and coding in terms of these categories are responsible for emergence of the different emotions. Scherer (1984a,b), as said, views the appraisal process as the sequential application of a number of "stimulus evaluation checks," each (roughly) corresponding to one of our components. All that takes time and, on occasion, effort, particularly with regard to making inferences from the concrete stimulus events. Consequential events take time to sink in; people quite often have to think out what the implications are; realization of impact may come only after a while, when significance has dawned.

In these cognitive processes, people have a large measure of latitude of operation. Stimulus aspects may or may not be considered; implications may or may not be drawn out; aspects may or may not be coded in a given way. Leventhal (1980), as said, emphasized stimulus coding: stimuli are apprehended in terms of given coding categories, and which category to apply at a given moment is to some extent at the individual's discretion. Physiological arousal can be coded by the subject as itches and twitches or as excitement and apprehension, with concomitant difference in emotional impact (Leventhal et al. 1979).

Yet at the same time, emotional impact is often immediate. It is unpremeditated. Events impose their meaning upon the subject; he does not feel that he attributes that meaning to the event. Processing emotional input sometimes must be so simple as hardly to deserve the name *appraisal*, or not to deserve that name at all – as when a dozing cat, upon being touched unexpectedly, angrily strikes out. Appraisal of an event's significance is neither deliberate nor a conscious process. One can influence that process's conditions, but not the process itself. How can the contradiction, which forms the substance of a recent polemic (Zajonc 1980, 1984; Lazarus 1982, 1984) be reconciled?

First of all, cognitive processes can be complex and at the same time automatic and immediate. Object recognition offers the clearest example: Its complexity is obvious from the influence of expectancy and context, and yet one can recognize a very large number of objects or faces with apparent immediacy. Recognition of concern relevance is in principle no different from that of objects: A steep cliff is as dangerous as it is steep. That is, you can see that you can fall off it with awkward results; and you can see that it comes into the category "close to the perpendicular"; and you can see both with equal ease. You can perceive affordances (Gibson 1966).

There are, in fact, no true "stimulus evaluation checks" in event appraisals; or at least there by no means always or necessarily are. In the more elementary emotional conditions, there are no special or explicit tests applied by the subject to perceived events. It is not that the subject perceives an event and then asks: Is it novel? Can it harm? Is it relevant and concern-satisfying? Is it controllable? Rather, the more elementary coding categories are implicit in the very processes by means of which input is assimilated and perceived in the first place. The code "novelty" is nothing but the signal emitted by mismatch between input and existing knowledge dispositions, and it is that signal that triggers orienting or alerting. Appraisals of "change" and "loss," too, are nothing but outcomes of discrepancies with expectations that differ in what they are discrepancies from. Other codes – the action-relevant ones – are the direct outcomes of monitoring the actions executed, availability of further actions, anticipation of given actions' effectiveness. The coding "controllability" is what is noticed and felt when events conform to one's actions or look like they will: assessment of controllability is an aspect of every planning of action, and is simply the result of the same process that makes a ditch to be seen as within, or not within, one's jumping capacity. "Uncontrollability" is the outcome of having noticed that everything miscarries or looks like it will; and "finality" is the result when everything has been tried unsuccessfully and the coping repertoire is exhausted; or when anticipation shows endeavors to be futile.

In short, the coding categories of appraisal come from input procedures and from the organism's action monitoring (see section 2.8). This also applies to the core appraisal category, relevance. When events or their implications happen to match or mismatch desired situations or expectations and do so with some urgency, pleasure and pain result as direct outcomes of the relevant comparison process; the next chapter will discuss this further.

Obviously, cognitive operation at some more explicit and reflexive level can equally be involved – in assessments of novelty, of favorableness of outcome, and of the other components. There are levels of processing (Leventhal 1979). The point is that explicit and reflexive cognitive operations do not have to be involved in order that the "tests" may operate; and further along we will discuss the fact that for their emotional effectiveness they rather appear to depend upon the more elementary perception-bound and action-bound processes.

It should be realized, furthermore, that few emotional events fall upon an unprepared mind. The general situation is that events correspond with or deviate from prior expectations. It can be argued that truly unexpected events – sudden events that do not give time to see how they develop – never produce an emotion of a structured kind; that is, that they do not generate action tendency, but merely "shock" or "emotion," or mere excitement: interruption, behavioral inhibition, autonomic arousal, and, in experience, a blank. In other words, when there is no time for nor previous preparation of cognitive processes, none will ensue, and appraisal remains rudimentary. Expectations, by contrast, form a cognitive background that holds relevant coding categories in readiness and upon which the events impinge: I wait for an aversive event to end, and it does not end – it is unmodifiable; I wait hopefully for a friendly comment to be given and am bitterly disappointed that a comment is both given and not friendly, one that I thereby perceive as both frustrating and "intentional." Minimal stimuli and minimal stimulus processing are therefore often all that is needed. As for the dozing cat and similar instances: It may be that simple startle-like stimuli elicit reflex-like responses that perhaps should not be called emotions (Ekman, Friesen, & Simons, in preparation, so argue for ordinary startle). But even these may perhaps still be understood, and better understood, along the lines sketched. After all, being touched against the background of being at rest is an infringement; its very unexpectedness makes it appear "spontaneously"; its moderation and specific location make it manifestly not uncontrollable: All the cues for anger, as mentioned in chapter 4, are there.

There remains another problem, however, a problem that touches upon vital aspects of the emotional stimulus reception process and upon the major question of what constitutes an emotional stimulus. Emotional stimuli are, we said, cognitions about personal harm or opportunity, or about novelty. But that description cannot be complete. Not all cognitions of personal harm or opportunity or of novelty elicit emotion; nor do all cognitions of harmlessness, lack of opportunity, or familiarity take emotion away. Several instances of this were mentioned along the way. Verbal assurance of the innocuousness of spiders, and even one's conviction of innocuousness, does not abolish the spider phobic's fear. In the Bridger and Mandel study, knowing that no more shock will follow, or even can follow, does not erase conditioned apprehension. Irrational beliefs and social fears, if they do abate in cognitive behavior therapy, do so only after extensive and intensive training.

Cognitions, then, are often impotent, and they are often more impotent than they seem. A distinct no from a rejecting love object may be honestly believed and still not abolish hope; and it will certainly not abolish striving and longing as long as he or she remains kind or beautiful or both. Attributions that are meant to produce indifference upon frustration, such as "He is not really to blame" or "It is my fault, not hers," or "He could not have acted otherwise," do not prevent anger and blaming to emerge spontaneously half an hour later. Intellectualizing the content of gruesome films, as in the experiment by Koriat et al. (1972), does decrease distress, but it can be expected that disturbing unbidden images will start cropping up in the course of the day, or night. In fact, they actually do (Horowitz 1976).

The opposite also occurs: Stimuli of potential emotional significance leave the subject cold, even if he wants it to be otherwise. Intellectualizing often comes unwanted, and not only in the face of distressing events. "Spectatoring" demolishes sexual excitement in sexual interactions (Masters & Johnson 1970). There exist pervading and chilling feelings of unreality in depersonalization, and affective remoteness of events. These instances are of defensive kinds, but there are others. Emotions cannot be called up willy-nilly by calling up relevant thoughts or images; and even a visit to a cemetery or any other place that carries old memories, rereading old letters in search of old affect, or listening to one's favorite music in the hope of delight may leave one emotionally empty. The emotions rather come unasked for and surprisingly, at moments when one is least prepared for them, when tying one's shoelaces or tasting a certain type of biscuit, or hearing a shred of the music over the radio. So much so that we may propose the *Law of Intermittences*, enunciated earlier by Proust (*Sodom et Gomorrhe*): Emotional susceptibility for given events is present only intermittently, and at irregular intervals, and its awakening is outside the individual's will.

Evidently, then, some qualities of stimuli and cognitions are more emotionally effective than others. The problem is to determine the relevant difference. That difference, it may be proposed, resides in what has been called the "reality" of situational meaning structure. Reality is determined by one of two factors: previous direct experience with affective consequences of the stimuli involved, together with access to that previous experience, and actual interaction between the stimulus event and one's action tendencies.

As to the first, we cite as evidence the Bridger and Mandel experiment and the evidence of the effects of trauma. Note that previous direct experience can be operative even when not present in conscious awareness. It may merely act as an expectancy and not as an expectation; it may make itself known only in panic or the fast-beating heart. That is the case when panic comes first and realization that it was the smell of burning that did it comes later; or when a Bridger and Mandel subject is startled and then realizes how silly he is. Access to previous experience may be cut off by appropriate stimulus coding if advance warning and time for preparation exist.

As to the second: Some stimulus events actually block ongoing activity or interfere with the successful completion of actions for which readiness exists. This is a different situation from one in which it is merely known that a stimulus event would block or interfere if action readiness were to be present – that is, in which the stimulus event does not actually sensibly block or interfere. Merely knowing that a goal cannot be reached is not what generates the sense of frustration. What does is that action that is under way is halted, is blocked, cannot go on to completion; the action involved may exist merely in imagination, but then imagination halts before it can imagine consummation. Similarly with respect to opportunities. Opportunities may be known; but that is different from opportunity being in fact accessible to actual desire and to readiness for grasping, or being relished in fantasy.

Interaction between action readiness and stimuli is emotionally relevant not only in frustration or satisfaction. The interaction pervades even neutral perception, and may be held to constitute sense of perceptual reality. It may be recalled (section 4.2) that perceptual awareness, according to phenomenological analysis, implies implicit expectancy that the object can be approached and touched, and inspected at will; such an expectancy may well depend upon one's actual potential to approach, touch, and inspect, as is indeed argued in some theories of perception (e.g., sensory–tonic field theory; Werner & Wapner 1953). Derealization may be supposed to result when the interlocking of stimulus and potential action is disturbed, as it does, for instance, upon disturbance of the body image (e.g., Schilder 1950).

In this vein, loss can be considered to be affectively real not by virtue of the mere absence of a valued person or object, but by the running idle of actual bodily or mental tendencies toward interaction – arms reaching out in vain. In fact, grief often does not emerge when one is notified of death or departure; such notification consists only of words. Grief strikes when one comes home to the empty house.

This discussion is in line with the evidence on the role of imagery in behavior therapy. Lang (1977) has emphasized that, in desensitization and flooding procedures, vivid imagery appears essential: no imagery, no desensitization. Effectiveness of desensitization appears to correlate with heart rate increase during fear imagery (Lang, Melamed, & Hart 1970). Lang also emphasized that vivid imagery instructions refer to imagining emotional response and stimulus content. The present argument is further supported by the claims by Bandura (1977a) and others concerning the superiority of in vivo treatments over imaginal and verbal ones.

The importance of links to direct experience and reality, as defined, is not surprising. The unconditioned stimuli for emotional response are direct experiences: perceptual stimuli and sensory signals for actual harm or satisfaction, and response tendency interferences or affordances. Direct experience in this sense may be said to be the proper "input format" for the emotion system: for the behavior systems and activation modes, arousal included. Symbolic input, words and thoughts, has first to be translated into that format before emotional response can be evoked. This can be phrased in a different way: Stimuli are emotional stimuli only when contact is actually made with the individual's concerns, with the positive or aversive outcomes to be expected.

The notions of "proper input" and "translation of improper inputs" is not precise enough really to explain the phenomena discussed. In particular, it does not explain nonoccurrence of emotions in the presence of proper input: music that you like but that leaves you cold today, without any possibility of doing anything about it, or absence of sexual excitement in the presence of appropriate and desired stimuli, as a consequence of whatever "spectatoring" refers to. But the hypothesis might help. Intellectualizing can be understood as an activity that replaces "proper input." Even the phenomena just referred to might perhaps be understood by such replacement, be it an involuntary one: replacement by abstract input codings, caused by inability to let the stimuli come as they are.

There is a twofold implication in the preceding. First, conscious cognitions are emotionally effective only if the translation into the proper input format is made, internally; where "translation" means the emergence of associations with direct experience. Such translation does not seem to be accessible to intent. It can only be helped by voluntary imagery. There is no reason why voluntary imagery would guarantee success; associations can never be forced to emerge. Even actual physical stimulation does not guarantee access to the proper emotion elicitors, as is evidenced by the effects of stimulus coding discussed. Second, conscious cognitions are largely irrelevant to the elicitation of emotion. As said, interpretation is to a large extent an automatic process, and recognition usually consists of assimilating input to existing schemata without the intervention of a conscious or intentional comparison process.

There is a further point. Emotion, it is argued here, is elicited when the system recognizes stimuli as blocking or permitting the completion of action tendencies or as related to actual pain or satisfaction. There is no reason to assume that they should at the same time be recognized in terms of the categories upon which conscious awareness is based. In other words: There is no reason to assume that conscious categorization must correspond to what in fact is emotionally effective. The content of conscious categorization may be different, and it may contain less than what is in fact effective. Recall the distinction made earlier between irreflexive and reflexive experience. The latter is a response system of its own, which is largely governed by the abstract and symbol-supported categories that underlie verbal expression. True enough, the conscious awareness response system is presumably fed by the same information that leads to concern relevance recognition; still, as a response system, it is a distinct one. The internal schema in terms of which the conscious judgment "threat" is made is distinct from that in terms of which adverse concern relevance is recognized. The latter uses, for instance, the direct, sensed, clash with action or desire; the first may not do so. The decision rules for what are acceptable inputs also may be different for both systems. That this is in fact the case is evidenced by a study by Abelson et al. (1982) in which subjects' statements of affective responses to politicians better predict their overall evaluations of these politicians than did descriptions of the properties of these politicians upon which the evaluations were presumably based.

The notion of two separate output systems, one consisting of conscious awareness and categorization, the other of emotional response, has been advanced by Zajonc (1980) on the basis of his experiments described before (section 4.3). Explicit conscious recognition of a stimulus as familiar is distinct from the implicit recognition as manifest in affective experience of like or dislike; the threshold for the latter is lower than that for the former. The view is supported by the evidence reviewed above. Zajonc, in the debate referred to above, has argued that his view and findings conflict with emphasis upon the importance of cognition in the elicitation of emotion. Obviously, this argument comes from equating the two different meanings of *cognition* – the one referring to complex stimulus processing and the other to conscious awareness, as a specific form of input (thoughts, images) as well as of outputs (again, thoughts, images) (Lazarus 1982, 1984).

The proper input format for emotional response corresponds to the format of unconditioned emotional stimuli and constellations, apprehended as real. Emotion is elicited by a few true innate stimuli or by stimuli sufficiently similar to those in appearance and particularly in reality characteristics; far more importantly, emotion is elicited by constellations in which the elements are apprehended as real – real signs of real promise of satisfaction or frustration of real, behavior-governing concerns.

Specific emotions are elicited by specific situational meaning structures, again apprehended as real. The notion of "reality" applies to meaning components generally, and not merely to threat and opportunity. Intentionality (the situational meaning component), for instance, is real to the extent that its cues are perceptually present; the cues are initiation of the event and persistence in producing it. One may ever so much know that harm was not truly intended: Anger still lurks behind those rational considerations and flares up upon pretext, because the act concerned had the characteristics of intention. In love, friendly acts and beauty are more potent than declarations of not being wanted. It was suggested above that conscious categorization may well employ different acceptance rules for emotional categorization; the latter's acceptance rules may well be more lenient, involve a quite different payoff matrix, and use a decision criterion that takes fewer risks of false negatives. Rational, reflexive attribution thus can be at variance with attribution based upon the evidence of the eyes and body: The latter may be expected to dominate in emotion, and the more so the more the payoff distribution in the matrix is skewed.

6. Concerns and other dispositional antecedents

6.1. Dispositional sources of emotion

The major tenet of the preceding chapter is that emotions result from the encounter between an event and a concern to which that event is relevant and to which it owes its emotional impact. That is to say that emotions result from the encounter of an event occurring at some given moment of time with a disposition that the subject carried with him prior to that moment of time.

Assuming dispositions that the subject carries with him or her prior to the event that elicits emotion is a logical necessity: The subject must harbor sensitivity to certain events since not all events elicit emotion. What characterizes the notion of "concerns" as a particular conception of such dispositions, however, is that it refers to dispositions that manifest themselves in other ways than only by emotions proper; and that it refers to dispositions that can underlie the entire gamut of emotions proper, according to the constellation in which the object of concern figures. The term refers to dispositions that can account for the facts of intraindividual and interindividual differences. These facts are that some events elicit emotion whereas other, closely similar ones do not. The departure of Ms. R saddens, whereas that of Ms. S does not. Also, given events affect some people and leave others indifferent. The departure of Ms. R does not touch those who do not love her. And events that affect one at some time fail to do so at other times: when love is over, for instance, and interest is lost.

The present conception is a variant of what were called match–mismatch theories in chapter 5. That class of theories was contrasted with two other classes, which view the dispositions in other ways. According to specific stimulus theories, specific sensitivities, on occasion even "templates," must be supposed to mediate between specific stimuli and the various kinds of emotional response. As we saw, however (section

5.3), the sensitivities that mediate response to unlearned emotional stimuli – to the silhouette of a bird of prey, for a duck, or to novelty or to pain – serve to class these stimuli as aversive generally, or rewarding generally, rather than as stimuli for fear or anger or distress or joy; they thus function like concerns. According to intensity theories, special sensitivities must exist for intense stimuli, or for stimuli with given intensity gradients. To the extent that stimulus intensity results from discrepancies, however, rather than from stimulus intensity per se, again these sensitivities function like concerns.

"Concern" is a motivational construct: It refers to the dispositions that motivate the subject, that prompt him to go in search of given satisfactions or to avoid given confrontations. Equivalently, it refers to the dispositions that allow certain classes of stimuli to act as reinforcers or serve as incentives. The concept fulfills the same function that in other theories of emotion is fulfilled by "needs" (Dollard et al. 1939; Berkowitz 1962), "motives" (Simonov 1970, 1975; Tomkins 1962), or major "plans" or "goals" (Mandler 1984; Abelson 1983). These concepts all are motivational constructs invoked both as reasons to act, search, or avoid and as leading to emotions when frustrated, satisfied, or confirmed. All theories that invoke one of these concepts see emotion as based upon motivation and dependent upon it. The same is true for the present conception. No concern, no emotion. Conversely, when it is known what an individual desires or abhors, the conditions under which emotion will arise are known: when something happens that is relevant to fulfillment of desire or mobilization of aversion, and when that happens in one of the emotion-eliciting constellations.

The viewpoint is plausible. Yet, it is not without its problems, because desire and aversion, positive and negative reinforcement, and thus also concern may themselves be taken as emotional concepts. The viewpoint begs the question regarding the emotional status of *concern* (or any of its functional equivalents), and therefore might involve circular reasoning, since the concepts are to explain emotion. We will return to the issue after discussing the nature of concerns. Apart from these problems (and assuming that they can be satisfactorily solved), the statement appears to hold that emotion depends upon motivation and that emotions proper derive from the fate, the "life history" (Shand 1896), of the individual's concerns.

The present chapter investigates the nature of these and other dispositional antecedents of emotion and examines how far the statement just presented might be valid.

6.2. Concerns

Properties of concerns

The word *concern* is preferred over the more usual alternatives like *motive* or *goal* because these latter terms all carry connotations of activity, actual striving, or awareness of future state to be reached, which are inappropriate with respect to many of the conditions under which emotions arise. The motivational background of emotion often is silent until an emotional event makes it cry out. Also, *motive* and *goal* tend to emphasize control of behavior and of emotion by behavior propensities (tendencies to do something) rather than by cognitive, informational dispositions from which those behavior propensities arise. Again, *concern* appears to suit interest in, say, stamp collecting, or in the well-being of Ms. R, as well as that in not being alone generally or competence generally; the word *motive* tends to be reserved for the latter kind of interests. The term *concern* is borrowed from Klinger (1975), who favored it for similar reasons.

Concern is defined as a disposition to desire occurrence or nonoccurrence of a given kind of situation. Such dispositions are assumed to exist when an individual initiates activity to achieve given kinds of situations and spends time, effort, or money in doing so; or when he explicitly expresses desire to achieve such a kind of situation; or when there is emotional response upon events implying achievement or nonachievement of such a kind of situation. An infant tries to follow his mother when she leaves the room; he expresses desire that she stay; or he is upset when he cannot follow her: Evidently the mother's presence represents a concern, and each of the three elements – expressed desire, action, and emotion – indicates this.

Obviously, occurrence of emotion cannot here be used to define the presence of concerns, since the latter are invoked to explain the former; in actual practice, however, occurrence of emotion is one of the clues.

Concerns equivalently can be defined as the dispositions that turn given kinds of events into satisfiers or annoyers, into positive or negative reinforcers, for the subject or for the species as a whole. The dispositions can be conceived as internal representations serving as standards against which actual situations are tested. When actual situations do not correspond to these standards, and if circumstances permit, action to achieve correspondence ensues: action to achieve a situation that does correspond, or to abolish one that does not. The kind of situation corresponding to the standard will be called the concerns' *satisfaction condition*.

Concerns, in this way of phrasing, are largely dormant demons: They are dispositions that remain silent as long as conditions conform to the standards, within reasonable bounds. Concerns for bodily welfare are unnoticed and unobtrusive until something happens that makes bodily welfare a matter for concern; desire for the mother's presence cannot be observed or inferred as long as she is there and stays there. Concerns make themselves known only when actual conditions deviate from their satisfaction conditions in some appreciable measure, or when they signal a satisfaction condition that could obtain, as in acute desire or lust.

Interpreting the occurrence of emotional response in terms of concerns to some extent merely describes what the subject is disposed to like or dislike, and thus what things may cause emotion. Positing a disposition would not seem to add to the explanation of emotion. However, it does add. Identifying a concern predicts that the various emotions will occur when events involve achievement or nonachievement of the concern's satisfaction condition, under the various constellations described in the previous chapters. Positive and negative emotions and their various subspecies are thus derived from one single disposition: the concern, the disposition to like or dislike a given thing. In addition, concerns do not merely describe what kinds of event cause emotion. For many concerns there exists independent evidence in the subject's, or the species', recurrent and persistent goal-searching activities. Moreover, making the supposition of a concern means what supposing any other kind of disposition means: issuing a "promissory note" (Feigl 1958; Van Heerden 1982). There must be something to be found and identified, some process or sensitivity, that accounts for the like and dislike observed and to which, waiting such identification, the name "concern for . . ." or "concern of . . ." is given. Some discussion of these "somethings" will be presented later (section 6.4).

A concern, of course, need not be dormant. It can be "awake" when a stimulus or thought has given rise to true desire, an actual motive or an actual goal that governs behavior. Stimuli, we may suppose, give rise to actual desires, motives, or goals when these stimuli evoke expectations of possible satisfaction or dissatisfaction, or when they make some dissatisfaction to be actually felt. Achievement of the goals of these desires and motives, fulfillment of these expectations, and the completion of actions undertaken then become awake concerns. It will be clear that *desire* here refers to an emotion, a state of readiness as defined in chapter 2. We will also use *motive* and *actual expectation* to refer to awake concerns.

Emotions proper arise both when events correspond or interfere with awake concerns and when they correspond or clash with latent concerns. Distress caused by unexpected pain illustrates the second of these two contingencies: No prior desire for no pain was manifest in consciousness or action, and no such prior desire has to be, for pain to arise. Other examples of emotions contingent upon latent concerns are those of a dozing male animal becoming sexually aroused when a female passes by, or of a man working when an equivalent thought crosses his mind; the distress caused by hearing about the serious illness of a friend; or being hurt by a rude remark when no action toward maintaining self-esteem was, at that moment, in operation.

Emotions, as said earlier, can come as thieves in the night, the night being the dormant demon. Latent concerns are responsive, are constantly alert, and can be awakened; they can be awakened also in minor but no less important ways in the multitude of fleeting emotional reactions merely felt when reading or during conversations. Such reactions faithfully reflect the significance of what is said and unsaid, and particularly the overtones and undercurrents of what is said, making one wonder what one was reacting to, and why, until the fleeting reactions burst out in well-defined and overt emotional response.

With respect to the elicitation of emotion, the distinction between latent and awake concerns is inessential, except for the fact that awake concerns carry higher expectation strength (see section 5.6), with its consequences for emotional intensity. Beyond that, the differences between latent and awake concerns is important in that the subject has more chances of not knowing about the former than about the latter. Hence, the surprisingness of many emotions, as mentioned, or the tears elicited by sentimental stories or films; and hence that discoveries are made when the emotion shows that, for instance, a forgotten attachment is still alive.

Concerns vary in aspects other than their being dormant or awake. One aspect is their temporal stability, the time period over which they exist (Klinger 1975). Intention for a given act or expectation of a given important outcome may endure only a minute or a day; an attachment can last a lifetime, and so, of course, do basic concerns like those for food and shelter. These aspects are mentioned merely to indicate the variety of dispositions underlying the occurrence of emotions. The notion of concern is applicable to all, in that they all involve representations of desired kinds of situations serving as standards and existing prior to events that elicit emotion; and all underlie emotions in similar fashion. Anger may result from a momentary goal being interfered with, from one's friend being annoyed by someone else, from interference with a lasting attachment, or from the unattainability of a life goal. Although all the various concern parameters probably influence the nature and intensity of emotions, in terms of conceptual structure all concerns are equivalent.

Source and surface concerns

One distinction between two kinds of concern deserves somewhat more extensive discussion, since it is needed to clarify what we mean by the term *concern* itself and thus how the dispositional antecedents of emotion should be viewed. It is the distinction between source and surface concerns.

Source concerns are defined in terms of satisfaction conditions pertaining to states of the individual: security, sexual satisfaction, competence, being well oriented, and the like. Some source concerns are basic in the sense that they cannot be seen as subspecies of other source concerns or as derived from any of them; others are not. Concern for self-esteem, for instance, might derive from concern for parental or societal rejection (Bandura 1977a); concern for such rejection might itself be basic or derived: and similar options apply to other concerns.

Surface concerns are defined in terms of specific objects and goals: love for that person, attachment to that toy, indignation concerning human rights violations, jealousy with respect to that person, getting the car started now (all but the last of these examples were also called "passions"; see section 2.10). Surface concerns, it can be held, derive from source concerns. Achievement of their satisfaction states is a subgoal in the achievement of the satisfaction states of source concerns or of other surface concerns. The former achievements are instrumental to the latter; or they are instantiations of source concerns, in the way indicated in the discussion of imprinting in the previous chapter. Love for a given person because he or she offers security or care or sexual satisfaction illustrates instrumentality; love for a given individual, and exclusive love at that, because she represents proximity, illustrates instantiation. A third form of surface concern involves objects that spell offense to source concern satisfactions: dogs that bite, spiders that upset. Surface concerns generally are "sentiments": They correspond to the existence of loved or hated objects or to cherished goals.

Objects of surface concerns thus by and large evoke expectancies of source concern satisfaction or offense and by and large have become objects of concern for that reason. However, surface and source concerns can give rise to different goals, and emotion elicited by events relevant to surface concerns has often to do with source concerns only by proxy. What elicits joy when the beloved recovers from illness is not, or not in the first place, his or her recovering availability for sex or succorance; it is approximation to the satisfaction condition of love that was characterized as "optimal existence of the love object." This is not a play on words. There usually is a time lapse, sometimes considerable, between his or her inability to satisfy source concerns and the disappearance of love. Also, action to further the goals of love (that optimal existence) may conflict with, or at least be independent of, action to further the satisfaction of relevant source concerns. Surface concerns, in other words, often have a measure of what Allport (1937) called "functional autonomy." For that reason, even when source concerns (or deeper surface concerns) explain the development and perpetuation of surface concerns (or shallower surface concerns), they do not as such explain emotions elicited by events relevant to the latter. Availability for sex and succorance may explain a given love; it does not (does not necessarily) explain the joy upon recovery from illness.

Yet source concerns, too, can directly explain emotions elicited by what befalls the object of surface concerns. Frustrations do in fact occur when he or she is ill because sexual and other satisfactions are withheld; they do occur even when bravely and loyally denied. Sometimes no independent surface concern is involved in the same general situation as the one sketched: If he or she falls ill, someone else can serve as well. Direct recourse to source concerns also appears called for as an explanation of emotion when emotional response is unduly strong: Why is he upset to that extent by the loss of his favorite teddy bear, and why does she still cling to that unhappy marriage – what do the bear and the man mean to them?

One of the main roots of functional autonomy, of the relative self-sufficiency of surface concerns, is probably the multiplicity of source concerns that the object is expected to satisfy and perhaps does; surface concerns usually represent subgoals for many supergoals simultaneously. As said, a partner in love is expected to satisfy many needs; a job represents income, social contacts, social prestige, and so on. Response to emotional events such as loss, as remarked earlier, is correspondingly complex, each source concern seeking and recognizing its own constellation in the event.

Emotions and the strength of concerns

It is plausible to assume that intensity of emotion is related to strength of the underlying concern, or to the added strength of concerns when more than one are involved. In fact, the assumption follows from the general hypothesis concerning the source of emotions. The assumption indeed has been stated, in some form or other, by various theorists sharing the hypothesis. Thus, for instance, Dollard et al. (1939): Interference with a strongly instigated striving toward some goal produces a more intense hostile reaction than does the thwarting of a weaker drive. In formula, $E = f(D, I)$, where E is hostile reaction or emotion generally, D is drive strength, and I the degree of interference (or event importance generally, since the latter also affects emotional intensity; section 5.6). Brown and Farber (1951) proposed a more complex relationship, which extends to emotions generated by conflict or competing motives: Emotional intensity is a monotonic function of the relation between the strengths of opposing response tendencies. In its mathematical form:

$$E = R(w)^n / R(s)^{n-1}$$

where E is emotional intensity, $R(w)$ the strength of the weaker response tendency, and $R(s)$ that of the stronger. In case of external interference, $R(s)$ could be set to unity, in which case the expression reduced to the Dollard et al. relationship.

A different expression, again, is produced by Simonov (1975, p. 89):

$$E = f(N, I_n - I_a)$$

where E is emotional intensity, N motive strength, I_n information needed for satisfaction and I_a information available to the subject. $I_n - I_a$ represents the conditions for either positive or negative emotion: positive when information available (that is, likelihood of satisfaction) exceeds information needed, and negative when it is less (see section 5.1).

"Strength of motives" in the above formulas has a double meaning. It can be taken to refer to concern strength proper – to intensity of need, amount of deprivation, attractivity or inherent incentive value of the object – and it can be taken to refer to what we will call "desire strength": intensity of actual action instigation in the face of the given stimuli. Desire strength can be assumed to depend both upon concern strength proper and upon "expectation strength" as defined earlier (section 5.6) – upon degree of being set for obtaining the object. Both desire strength and concern strength proper can be held to provide independent contributions to the intensity of emotion when satisfaction of the concern is thwarted (see Bolles 1975 and Atkinson & Birch 1978 for all these issues).

Determination of concern strength, necessary for testing the above relationships, is a tricky matter since concern strength itself is not a very clear concept. Conceptually, it probably can best be viewed as defined by intensity of response or threshold for response: how fast or vigorous is the response, how weak a stimulus evokes action, how large a range of stimuli evokes action, how strong an obstacle the subject will try to overcome, how frequently he will engage in concern-relevant action. Methods for determining motive strength attach to these response intensity and threshold measures. The "obstruction box technique" (Warden 1931) measures the severity of discomfort a subject is willing to accept to attain his object; analysis of fantasy – dreams, play themes, daydreams – logically measures frequency of action or response to weak stimuli. Response latency and vigor are often used in animal research. The measures readily and plausibly translate into what are considered signs of concern strength in daily situations: how fast the telephone is picked up, how much money is spent in taking her or him to dinner, how persistent is the wooing, how long one stands in the rain under her or his window, how much reverie one indulges in. But it is unclear to what extent the various measures covary. Sometimes, in fact, they interfere with one another. Fear, of obstructions and pneumonia, inhibits hunger and sexual or other desire; extreme food deprivation weakens hunger; and so on.

The evidence that exists tends to support the hypothesis of a monotonic relationship between concern strength and emotion intensity. Some of this evidence was collected in connection with the frustration–aggression hypothesis; it is not always clear whether desire strength or concern strength should be considered to be involved. Doob and Sears (1939) asked subjects to indicate frustrating experiences they had had, how badly they had wanted their objectives, and whether they had become angry or had shifted to some nonangry substitute activity. Intensity of desires correlated with frequency of angry or aggressive reaction and inversely with nonaggressive substitute activity. Miller (quoted by Berkowitz 1962, p. 52, from Dollard et al. 1939) "had his subjects rate the degree of annoyance they would feel if various people whom they liked to different degrees had snubbed them." Annoyance was greater when the people were liked more than when they were liked less. Sears and Sears (same source) interrupted feeding of a 5-month-old baby by taking away the bottle after he had taken varying amounts of milk; crying after removal of the bottle started later when the child had become less hungry.

Correlations were shown to exist between some personality traits as measured by questionnaires and emotions in response to specific events. General apprehensiveness concerning social and intellectual performance ("trait anxiety") correlated with actual anxiety ("state anxiety") just prior to academic or medical examinations (Spielberger et al. 1970). "Sensation seeking," as measured by the Sensation Seeking Scale, correlated with positive, playful, enthusiastic mood when subjects were about to participate in an experiment on hypnotic induction or drug experience; correlations ranged from .26 to .57, and were higher than those with mood measured under ordinary classroom conditions (Neary, cited in Zuckerman 1979).

In addition to "absolute strength," there is relative strength of concerns; relative strength, too, has implications for emotional response. People devote their time to different pursuits, and they react differently when the pursuits conflict. For some, wealth dominates at the cost, if need may be, of some loss of honor; for others it is the other way around. Obtaining wealth thus is what produces emotion in the first instance, and maintaining honor is what produces emotion in the other, under similar circumstances. At least, regret of loss of possible wealth will probably be weaker for the latter, or held more in check.

The issue of priority ordering of concerns is an interesting but complex one, particularly because of the various forms of interactions that exist. Stress, as said, inhibits hunger and sexual desire. Satisfactions of concerns that are satisfied appear less important than satisfaction of concerns that are unsatisfied – the hedonic asymmetry underlying the Law of Regret (section 5.8). Investigation of the determinants of concern priorities and concern interactions, although of obvious emotional significance, is outside the scope of this study (but see Atkinson & Birch 1978).

Commitment to and disengagement from concerns

For the sake of completeness, brief mention must be made of commitment to and disengagement from concerns. Surface concerns mostly develop because objects or goals are expected to lead to satisfaction, or to relief from dissatisfaction, with respect to source concerns. The ways in which these expectations can emerge have been touched upon in section 5.7. However, the acquisition mechanisms such as conditioning, inference, instantiation describe development of surface concerns only in principle. How attachments and interests are established, and how expectations come to be sufficiently strong to lead to more or less persistent goals, is a complex process to which Klinger (1975) gave the name of *commitment to concerns*; in connection with attachments it is extensively discussed by Bowlby (1973, 1980). Cognitive processes other than those resulting from mere past frequency of satisfaction play an important role. Surface concerns can develop and even survive in the face of low likelihood of actual satisfaction, because of the mere apparent aptness of the object. Imagination can take over even when the subject is aware of discrepancies between what imagination promises and actual fact presents. An example is given by infatuations. Falling in love, probably, is triggered by signals of acceptance from an interesting object. An object can become interesting, it would seem, merely because of those signals. In falling in love, a single glance from the other, a small sign that can be interpreted as a sign of interest, can be a sufficient (and probably necessary) condition and give rise to infatuations that persist in the face of unpromising further evidence (Stendhal 1820; Rombouts 1983).

Disengagement from concerns (again, Klinger 1975) is an equally involved topic, as grief processes demonstrate. This also has been briefly touched upon in the previous chapter. The point to be emphasized here is that cognitive processes exert their influence, and that these, in part at least, are motivated by emotions resulting from concern dissatisfaction. We want and try to disengage from unsatisfactory attachments or unrealistic desires; sometimes we do. Unattainability evokes anger, distress or depression (Klinger 1975), depending upon further aspects of meaning structure, and these motivate efforts toward goal abandonment. Successful goal abandonment when the underlying concern is still alive, is what we call resignation; this state has a somewhat different structure from that of most or all other emotions arising on the basis of actual desires. Others have as their background persistence of desire. Grief and even despair presuppose some measure of hope. They presuppose that truly the situation could have been otherwise; not so with resignation. When, under what circumstances, abandonment of surface concerns themselves occurs, according to Klinger, is unclear. Perhaps it only occurs when they can be replaced by other ones pertaining to the same source concerns. Perhaps they never can, as old griefs suggest, and can merely be overwritten. At any rate, disengagement from concerns requires some sort of work. Depressive response upon loss has been interpreted by Klinger as a mechanism of disengagement, operative perhaps through introjection of the lost object (Freud 1920); perhaps through inoculation against painful impressions (Price 1972), and perhaps through inhibition, voluntary or not, of futile tendencies toward the lost or foresworn object. To consider depressive response a disengagement process is, in fact, in line with the concept of secondary control, abandonment of futile efforts as a means of dealing with unconquerable aversive events (Rothbaum et al. 1982).

6.3. Discussion of some source concerns

In the preceding, source concerns were named loosely. They were named on the basis of what appear to be the preferred or disliked implications of given events and the sought-for aspects of given goals. To what extent these concerns all are distinct basic ones is a matter for debate and falls outside the scope of the present review. However, they do point to the fact, apparent already from the discussion of unlearned emotional stimuli in chapter 5, that the variety of sources of emotion is much larger than that of receiving or not receiving the more tangible rewards and punishments of food, drink, sex, bodily comfort, and pain, even in animals.

   At least as important as concerns for food, drink, and sex, are the concerns for self-esteem and the regard of others; for personal warmth and attention; for smooth, not too effortful functioning; for achieving what one had set out to do; for the welfare of others, and particularly of close relatives. The warp and woof of emotional life in times of peace and plenty are based upon concerns like those; and perhaps even those in war and dearth. These concerns coalesce, as indicated, in the surface concerns that motivate daily activities: work, attachments, social encounters, interest in things seen along the way. One continually is admitted and rejected, attracted and repulsed, belongs and is left or clings, achieves and falls short of achieving. Also, one continually is faced with, challenged by, recoils and hesitates and despairs before the expenditure of effort. In sheer number of emotion occurrences, these concerns are probably more important than the concerns linked to the tangible rewards and punishments. Also, what makes them so important is the fact that they in a sense are insatiable. Of personal warmth one can hardly have enough; or, if one can, it is a different sort of satiation than that with sex or steak.

We will discuss a few of these concerns in a little more detail, for several reasons. First, the general thesis of this chapter holds that every emotional event harbors relevance for some concern, and this thesis should at least be made plausible by indicating some of the variety of what is meant by *concern*. Second, what will be discussed are those concerns that play a central role in current theory of emotion and motivation. They do so because, bringing no tangible rewards, it is not obvious that the behaviors and experiences concerned can profitably be said to be instigated by a concern; we will try to show that this is nevertheless the case, that the behaviors and emotions can be seen to flow from match or mismatch with an internal representation corresponding with a given kind of situation and serving as a standard against which actual situations are tested (see section 6.4).

Curiosity

Mention was made in chapter 5 of the arousing effects of novel, unexpected, and complex stimuli. Such stimuli not only elicit arousal, they also tend to evoke exploratory, investigative activity; moreover, they are often actively sought out. Curiosity motivation has long been recognized because of such exploratory behavior, and because of the reinforcement value of exposure to novel and varied stimuli (see Toates 1980). The concern is evident, with the usual concern properties of interindividual differences in propensity and intraindividual variations dependent upon the individual's wakefulness, fatigue, or freedom from worry. As evident as the concern are the emotions depending upon it: curiosity proper, interest, and fascination as emotions of the desire and enjoyment types, and the excitements, joys, and discouragements upon being confronted with relevant stimuli or failing to apprehend them, as emotions proper occurring in connection with exploration in the same way as in connection with any other concern. A distinct "need" for novel, complex, or varied stimuli appears from "stimulus hunger" and concentration loss after prolonged sensory deprivation (Bexton et al. 1954), from boredom and listlessness under more modest deprivation conditions, and from increase in activation when being and having been exposed to varied stimulation.

Curiosity, as the impulse behind investigation of novel or complex stimuli, has been explained by the same mechanism as the orienting response: by occurrence of mismatch between stimulus input and preexisting cognitive dispositions (knowledge, expectations). Orienting and investigation tend to continue until matching cognitive dispositions have been found or construed; "match," evidently, is the concern's satisfaction condition. Although this describes the conditions for initiating and terminating exploration when collative stimuli are met, it does not explain active seeking of such stimuli nor their reinforcement value for humans and monkeys in uninteresting environments. Hebb (1955), Berlyne (1960), and others advanced the "optimal level of arousal" hypothesis mentioned in section 5.1: Absence of informative stimulus input decreases cortical arousal, through decrease in activation of the brain stem reticular formation; stimuli with informational content restore it. Such restoration is presumably rewarding. Since high levels of arousal tend to be disliked as much as very low levels, a "drive" exists to restore optimal level when input pushes it too high or lack of input lets it sink too low. Furthermore, since return from high levels toward optimal level is pleasurable, people may be hypothesized to seek such high levels in order to have them drop afterward; excitement and complex, conflictual information are sought because of the "arousal jag" (Berlyne 1960).

Berlyne (1971) later revised his theory, to account for the fact that excitement and cognitive effort are often sought without subsequent drop. Arousal is supposed to be simultaneously pleasant and unpleasant. Which of the two dominates depends upon arousal intensity: Pleasantness and unpleasantness both rise with intensity, but unpleasantness starts doing so later and reaches its maximum later; at that maximum unpleasantness outweighs pleasantness. The result is the curvilinear relationship between stimulus intensity and hedonic value (the "Wundt curve") referred to in section 5.1, and the aversive effect of stimuli with extreme "arousal potential."

The theories, in both versions, are not really satisfactory, at least for explaining curiosity, for one thing because there is no evidence that degrees of interestingness are related to absolute and not relative degrees of arousal (cortical or autonomic), as the theory requires; and for another thing because there is no reason why the pleasures and displeasures of collative stimuli should be linked to arousal rather than directly to that arousal's cause, mismatch. Mismatch that can be overcome, one might say, is pleasurable; mismatch that cannot, unpleasant. That is to say, these pleasures and displeasures can be linked to the end result that the stimuli met or sought incite the subject to achieve: cognitive assimilation. As regards stimuli met, cognitive assimilation is rewarding when it succeeds; it is aversive when it fails. As regards stimuli sought, letting capacity for cognitive assimilation run idle is aversive, as in boredom; exercising capacity for cognitive assimilation is rewarding, as is responding to any challenge of what one is well able to do. Curiosity, then, can be understood to be the concern of cognitive assimilation, with input being assimilated as its satisfaction condition, *and* as the concern for successfully exercising the cognitive assimilation apparatus. The organism, evidently, is constructed so as to have spare capacity for cognitive assimilation as long as it is healthy and free from worry.

This rephrasing justifies considering curiosity a concern. It is, moreover, plausible because it describes the activities of attending to and seeking out collative stimuli from a functional psychological perspective and not merely as results of a physiological contingency. Such a description appears to be appropriate particularly because it fits that physiological contingency itself. Cortical arousal through reticular activity, according to Pribram and McGuinness (1975), is not a mere stimulus-dependent brain event: It represents, or serves, the process of cognitive assimilation, the construction of a neuronal model (chapter 7). The rephrasing further implies that unpleasantness in cognitive situations corresponds not to high arousal per se but to assimilation failure or absence, which may or may not be reflected in cortical or autonomic arousal. It asserts that when collative variables are aversive, this is not because they generate high arousal; rather, they generate high arousal when aversive for the reason stated.

Sensation seeking

The above rephrasing does not account for the pleasures of suspense and of bright colors, good sex, good food and drink, nor for the fact that these are often sought actively. Cognitive assimilation does not seem to be the primary element in them. In fact, a sensation-seeking motive is distinguished from curiosity; it has been extensively investigated by Zuckerman (1979). It has to be distinguished from curiosity because the mechanism must be different: Although both involve exploratory activity, individual differences in sensation seeking and in cognitive curiosity do not correlate (Zuckerman 1979).

Sensation seeking refers to the motivation to undertake risky activities like dangerous sports or gambling and to obtain strong sensory or sensual experiences; risky activities are sought, presumably, for the strong sensations they provide. The concern has been investigated mainly through individual differences in responses to the Sensation Seeking Scale. Analysis of these differences reveals existence of four distinguishable submotives, which tend to go together (although weakly), and together are taken to form the sensation-seeking motive: "thrill and adventure seeking" (liking mountain climbing, surfboard riding, etc.); experience seeking (liking earthy body smells, new foods, unknown places, new drugs); disinhibition (liking wild parties, drinking, sexual excitement); and boredom susceptibility (dislike for predictable or boring situations). As with curiosity, the range of consequent emotions is vast. Note, however, that the emotions primarily derive from other concerns: They are contingent upon the dangers of the risky undertakings, the sense of competence when having overcome them, the satisfaction of drinking and sex, and so on. The sensation-seeking motive generates the occasions for these experiences for its own proper pleasure of having them. In addition, the motive underlies, as said, the usual emotions proper: frustration upon failure in its undertakings, anger at obstruction of its concomitant surface concerns, and so on.

Sensation seeking might be considered a negative thing, the result of some deficit such as habitually falling below one's optimal arousal level or incapability of obtaining more usual satisfactions. The evidence, however, contradicts this. Individuals high on sensation seeking tend to show a number of "positive" features: stronger orienting responses to novel stimuli than subjects low on it (Neary & Zuckerman 1976); "augmenting" of the cortical average evoked response (increase of the AER with increased stimulus intensity), as opposed to "reducing" (no increase, or decrease in AER amplitude with increased stimulus intensity) (Zuckerman, Murtaugh, & Siegel 1974); lower concentration of monoamine oxidase (MAO) in the blood cells (Zuckerman, Buchsbaum, & Murphy, 1980). Low MAO concentrations appear to be related to activity, playfulness, and sociability in animals (Murphy 1977). Cats with augmenting AER patterns are described as exploratory, active, aggressive, and responsive to novel stimuli; reducer cats, as shrinking from novel environments and as socially avoidant (Hall, Rappaport, Hopkins, & Griffin 1970). These characteristics tally with those of the "impulsiveness" personality trait discussed by Gray (1971; see section 6.8) and suggest that the above physiological variables are unique not to sensation seeking but to impulsivity generally (or extraversion; see section 6.8). What they do underscore, however, is that the concern of sensation seeking reflects a capacity, a potential, and not the making up for a deficit.

Zuckerman interprets sensation seeking as the outcome of an inherent rewarding effect of sensation generally: Experience, like arousal in Berlyne's later theory, is by its very nature both rewarding and punishing, for no other reason than that it stimulates both the reward and the punishment centers of the brain. It is more rewarding than punishing when reward sensitivity is higher than punishment sensitivity and when approach behaviors are readily evoked; this, supposedly, is the case in some individuals more than in others. The theory is unconvincing: Logically, preference for strong sensations would suggest lower rather than higher sensitivity. More plausible appears the hypothesis that strong sensations are liked by subjects who can manage them, and because they can manage them: They are able to process them and cope with them and are bored with stimuli that are too easy to handle. This is in line with the fact that the behavioral and neural properties described are considered suggestive of a "strong nervous system" (Nebylitsyn & Gray 1972); it also accords with the behavioral features of vitality and activation in the descriptions of Murphy and of Hall et al. just quoted. If such an interpretation is correct, it would transform sensation seeking, more so still than curiosity, into a concern toward doing and experiencing what one can do and experience well; being able to do and experience well then would be the concern's satisfaction state – which indeed is what mountainclimbers appear to climb mountains for (Piët, 1986).

Familiarity and orientation

Novelty, and experience generally, can be aversive as well as interesting or attractive. This is evident from the upsetting effects of "strangeness," uncertainty or unfamiliarity (section 5.3), for which, indeed, the theories of both Berlyne and Zuckerman try to account. There is, one may conclude, a desire for familiarity or orientation. The concern is not, in terms of mechanisms, the inverse of the two just described. The desire is not just the opposite of the desires for novelty and sensation. Fearfulness, or "emotionality," as it is usually called, is not negatively correlated with impulsiveness, extraversion, or sensation seeking (see Zuckerman 1979, ch. 6 for the evidence); curiosity and fear of the novel may exist side by side, or alternate, in rats (Whimbey & Denenberg 1967), infant monkeys (Suomi & Harlow 1976), and human infants (Bowlby 1969) – or in human adults, for that matter.

The upsetting effects of strangeness do not depend upon expectancy of physical harm, as appears (chapter 5) from the observations of Hebb, of Suomi and Harlow, and of Bowlby; strangeness by itself can be a sufficient condition for fear. Also, familiar stimuli, as mentioned, are liked better than unfamiliar ones, for that sole reason (Zajonc 1968). More importantly, people generally dislike drastic changes. All drastic changes, and not merely personal loss, can lead to depressive reactions and grief (Marris 1974).

When is unfamiliarity upsetting, and when is it interesting? As described, Berlyne assumes magnitude of unfamiliarity, of mismatch, to determine whether unfamiliarity is pleasant or unpleasant. Magnitude of mismatch is not easy to formalize, except in simple stimuli; and it is doubtful that it can be formalized in simple ways, since mismatch with expectations, rather than sheer unfamiliarity, often appears to be the most upsetting. Hebb's (1946) chimpanzees became upset not by a complete stranger but by the attendant with another than his usual cap.

We may suggest that what makes unfamiliarity upsetting and familiarity comforting is unavailability or availability of coping actions: of ways to deal with the environment in case the events call for it. Familiar surroundings afford habitual actions, unfamiliar ones require effortful readjustments or leave helpless; and these affordances are there even when no action is actually called for. This would explain the potent emotional effects of the partly unfamiliar: An attendant with an unusual cap is a small mismatch stimuluswise but a large mismatch copingwise. Also, negative attitudes toward strangers, like those toward ethnic minorities, may in part feed upon the strangers' very strangeness: It is expected that they will behave in ways one cannot deal with in one's habitual manner, which forms a fertile ground for malignant ideology. Failure in cognitive assimilation, in other words, is truly aversive when it has consequences for potential inability to act. This interpretation accords with current notions with respect to the cognitive structures to which perceived information is assimilated: not merely schemata, but "frames" (Minsky 1975), which are structures of cues giving access to actions. The interpretation makes familiarity–preference a concern, with availability of potential coping action as its satisfaction condition.

Proximity and coherence

Proximity to the mother figure is desired by infants. They try to follow her, cling to her if possible, and get upset when she is not near, particularly in unfamiliar environments (Bowlby 1969). Concern for proximity to a mother figure is present in all higher animal species; at least, it has been described in a large variety of them (Hinde 1974). Concern for proximity is an essential ingredient of affectional bonds throughout life (Bowlby 1980), as is evident from actual proximity seeking as well as from fantasy and symbolic behavior such as carrying photographs in one's wallet. In fact, *proximity seeking* is but another, albeit better, name for dependency needs (Bowlby 1969); it is considered the source of separation anxiety (Bowlby 1973) and of grief upon completed separation (Bowlby 1980; Parkes 1972). The rewarding effect of proximity to a mother figure, as said, is not derived from other satisfactions she might offer, as was evident from Harlow's (1958) studies of rhesus monkeys: The infant clings to a mother surrogate as long as that surrogate provides occasion for comfortable clinging, even when the infant is fed from another source; and punishing behavior by the surrogate only tends to make it cling more. Proximity desire in later life can equally be assumed to exist for its own satisfaction, with loneliness as state of absence of its satisfaction condition; and, of course, in later life, proximity comes to mean more or other things than merely physical proximity and physical clinging.

There exist other concerns for closeness and coherence than that with respect to an attachment figure, which may or may not be dependent upon it. Harlow (1969) presents evidence for strivings after peer group participation in rhesus monkeys, independent of the mother-proximity concern. Concerns for social closeness and coherence, at any rate, are powerful. They may not be as evident in our culture as they are in certain others, where social isolation can cause severe distress, where a separate ego identity can hardly be said to exist (Parin & Morgenthaler 1963), and where even being alone for some extended time tends to induce fear or despair (ibid.). Yet in Western cultures, too, social rejection constitutes severe punishment, and most likely not merely because of its more remote adverse consequences. Social affiliation is sought with increased intensity under threat (Schachter 1959), and there exists intense hankerings after group participation in religious groups and sects (Aberle 1965) and social movements generally (see Zurcher & Snow 1981).

Motivation toward identity loss, or coherence, exists also with respect to the nonsocial environment. Mysticism appears to offer that reward, as does "empathy" with spaces and movements. Awe inspired by vast spaces (cathedrals, nature) seems related to it. On a more commonplace, and again social, level, concern for closeness may well be that which accounts for the "sentimental" emotions. By *sentimentality* here is understood the occurrence of strong emotions, mostly conducive to tearfulness, in response to relatively weak stimuli. These stimuli usually have to do with love, affection, devotion, or solitude and often have no direct personal significance for the subject: seeing brides in white wedding gowns, hearing stories about poor small boys being lost and lonely but finally finding a loving home. Tearjerkers and three-penny novels usually have such themes and readily elicit tears, secret or open, even in critical, sophisticated adults (Efran & Spangler 1979).

The origin of these latter concerns is unclear. They all may reach back to the elementary proximity concern and connected childhood experience (Freud 1930 argues so for "oceanic feelings"); they may derive from the abandonment of efforts toward coping and retaining separate identity (sentimentality appears to increase in old age, severe illness, some forms of brain damage, hemiplegia and, generally, in conditions of helplessness; although these may equally promote proximity desires), or they may be related to sensitivity for shelter, comfort, and being cared for. The three possibilities are not mutually exclusive.

Concern for control over one's movement and action

Animals tend to struggle when their movements are restrained. Even pets do when held by their owners, or when held longer than they desire. Movement restraint was the first major stressor employed by Selye in his early stress research on rats, and was considered by Watson to be the unconditioned stimulus for anger. Frustration, in the sense of blocking of ongoing activity, of course has played a considerable role in theory and research on emotion. The ongoing activity does not need to be very important for irritation or anger to arise: bumping into someone when walking, having to brake for a slow-moving car. Nor is true activity necessarily involved: Being bumped into merely upsets the habitual endeavor to keep upright. Nor again does blocking have to be done by someone else. Irritation follows even when no one else is to blame, but only circumstance or one's maladroitness: when unsuccessfully threading a needle, when stumbling, and the like.

The concern can equally be called concern for freedom of movement and action. Brehm (1972) developed a "theory of psychological reactance": People manifest "reactance" upon elimination of any of those of their behaviors that they consider to be "free behaviors." This phrasing includes the constellations of frustration and of challenge. Reactance consists of protest, anger, increased effort, or increased desire. Increased desire is illustrated by an experiment in which subjects had been promised a valued outcome (a phonograph record as reward for some activity) and the outcome did not materialize: Attractivity of the outcome was rated higher than before, but only on the condition that the promised outcome had been chosen by the subject himself from among several alternatives, which underlines the relevance of free behavior.

The importance of this concern, in the sense of frequency of events relevant to it and strivings coming from it, is obvious. The independent contribution of sense of control to stress effects has been discussed in the preceding chapter (section 5.6); locus-of-control attributions intervene in many emotional responses (Weiner 1974; Lefcourt 1976). The concern may be more important still than appears at first glance, since it may well be behind the fears and distresses of passivity, where self-initiated action is not blocked but impossible, as it may be behind the stress-reducing effect of control discussed earlier. Fears and distresses of passivity include those contingent upon having to submit to aversive events or wait for them to occur; but they also include more common instances of emotion such as impatience while and distaste for standing in line or waiting in a waiting room, fear of flying and of trains; and many of the complexities of sexual interaction. Also, concern for control may be a contributing factor in the power motive, through anticipation of infringements upon control or operantly reinforced reactance (Bandura 1973).

Whether infringement upon control or freedom incites reactance or depression depends upon one's expectancies with respect to control: Reactance should occur more readily in subjects whose dominant locus of control is internal, as indeed has been found (Wortman & Brehm 1975; see section 5.6).

Values

All concerns discussed so far are of a personal kind. They pertain to preferences with respect to the subject's own state of activity. Values, by contrast, involve preferences with respect to what "ought" to be or not to be. They concern conditions in which the subject himself is not, or not necessarily, involved. Values can become concerns: values such as justice, or freedom or respect for human dignity; or belief in a certain god, or political doctrine; or conformation to social norms or to certain modes of conduct such as politeness, sincerity, or optimal deployment of one's abilities. People may get enraged upon offenses against any of these values to an extent that would in all likelihood be exceptional for them in personal matters; they will denounce you to the police, or burn you at the stake; or risk their lives for them. They may become afraid to see adherence to these values slacken, depressed when it has disappeared altogether, joyous when it is restored or offenses to the values righted, and they feel guilty when they themselves offend – all according to the usual constellations.

Why values can become concerns is a matter for speculation. Hypotheses about this mostly involve references to concerns such as social conformity or coherence or to the vicissitudes of attachments to and expectations of punishment from parents. The violence of value-dependent emotions probably is caused by awareness of social support or suprapersonal justification, which latter again may amount to the imagined support of some powerful reference figure looking over one's shoulder. An important role is perhaps also played by the fact that, since values guide an individual's judgments and, in some measure, his actions, offense against values becomes an offense against concerns for familiarity and competence.

Emotions and concerns

The main point in the present section is to investigate to what extent emotions arise as responses to events relevant to concerns. It is guided by the hypothesis that behind every occurrence of emotion there is relevance for a concern. The hypothesis is considered valid to the extent that satisfaction conditions can be plausibly construed or assumed to exist behind each such occurrence and that these appear to serve also as goals for striving.

This general hypothesis does not appear to be the appropriate one for emotions elicited by very specific unlearned stimuli: startle stimuli; some innate fear and aggression stimuli perhaps, such as the red patch of a rival ruff; hedonically toned sensual and sensory stimuli. Even those, however, are perhaps more compatible with the hypothesis than they seem. In part, the above stimuli (tastes and smells) are not stimuli for emotion as much as for "feelings" (see section 5.3); they are just pleasant or disagreeable, unless they fit into some constellation. In part they belong to various behavior systems and correspond to those systems' "go" condition; the point will be elaborated in section 6.5. Startle, as said, should perhaps be considered a reflex rather than an emotion (Ekman, Friesen, & Simons, in preparation).

A different problem is presented by the unselfish emotions: compassion, pity, suffering when seeing others suffer, joy upon their success or escape from danger. Why do we care? Where is the concern? Obviously, we do care, on occasion; and the welfare of others, or certain others, can be a goal toward which to strive. The question is, Why does seeing others suffer elicit pity (when it does)? Is it because there is an elementary stimulus for feelings of pity or helping behavior, or because it conflicts with some desired state of affairs?

The answer is complex and involves both. Hoffman (1978) distinguishes as sources of "emphatic distress" or pleasure: (a) the distress evoked, probably innately, by distress calls; (b) the distress or pleasure that results from the adverse of beneficial consequences of the other's mood; (c) associations between the situation evoking emotional expression in others and one's own experiences under such conditions; (d) direct expressive contagion ("motor mimicry"); and (e) imagining oneself in the place of the other. All of these probably contribute to the formation of unselfish emotions. Some of them – c, d, and e – involve the subject's own concerns by proxy. Others do not: Distress calls are specific stimuli touching upon specific sensitivity. On the other hand, they, and perhaps distressed facial expression (Miller, Murphy, & Mirsky 1959; Miller, Caul, & Mirsky 1967), serve as releasers of care-giving behavior (Murray 1979) and so can be considered relevant to a true prosocial concern: to that care giving. Distressed facial expression of others generally tends to induce worry; it facilitates establishment of conditioned responses to shock (Lanzetta & Orr 1981). The unselfish emotions can thus, at least in part, be considered expressions of such care-giving tendency. Cognitive transformations, according to Hoffman, then may turn that tendency into true sympathy or, in the event, pity.

We conclude: The unselfish emotions rest, in part, upon specific sensitivity for distress expressions in others, which sensitivity is itself part of a behavior system or concern; in part they derive from the individual's own concerns, either directly through what the other means to him or by proxy, through empathy or identification.

Aesthetic emotions

More serious questions are presented by the aesthetic emotions. By *aesthetic emotions* are usually meant two distinct classes of events. First, the emotions such as sadness, joy, excitement, suspense that may be generated by the specific nature of a given work of art or nature (let us call it a stimulus) and that are related to its particular content or form. We will call these *complementing emotions*. Second, the emotions evoked by the quality of the stimulus: "emotion," fascination, pleasure, admiration, being moved. We will call these *responding emotions*. Emotions more or less similar can be evoked by other kinds of stimuli, which then also are called "beautiful": a masterly chess move, elegant technical solution, clever turn of phrase. All emotions indicated, and particularly those in the second group, are intriguing not only from the present point of view. Beauty evokes disinterested pleasure. Why and how?

The subject, obviously, is far beyond the scope of the present study and its writer's ability; yet some remarks have to be made to consider the position of aesthetic emotions in the present interpretation of emotion. As far as I can see, two broad classes of theory can be distinguished. The first consists of those theories that seek connections between the impact of the aesthetic stimuli and the individual's personal concerns. Psychoanalytically oriented theories are primarily of this kind. Art, according to these theories, associatively evokes latent, mostly problematical, desires. It thereby allows some imaginary, substitute satisfaction and permits some processing of these desires (Freud 1930; Kris 1952). A condition for such processing and substitute satisfaction is that the subject not be directly, personally involved in the perceived events, in order to permit slackening of resistance. There should, in other words, be "aesthetic distance" (Kreitler & Kreitler 1972). The desires are not necessarily repressed ones; they can just be unsatisfied desires being kept under control: Consider the impacts of songs of loss upon people who have lost. Personal concerns, in these views, are thus involved in aesthetic emotion, albeit in indirect fashion. The type of theory explains emotions contingent upon thematic contents – so, for instance, the appeal of fairy tales (Bettelheim 1976). Formal aspects of art are considered means of controlling too strong arousal of the latent wishes or attenuation of their frustration. About formal beauty the theory has little to say. For Freud, formal beauty derives from sexual attraction, although he admits the process of derivation to be obscure (Freud 1930).

The second theoretical approach seeks the source of aesthetic emotion in the processing of the stimuli as such, and in particular in the resulting dynamics of tension increase or of successions of tension and relief (Kreitler & Kreitler 1972); the approach is not incompatible with the first, and can be made to encompass it. In Berlyne's (1971) variant, pleasantness, as discussed earlier, results either from moderate arousal increase or from its decrease from high levels. Arousal increase can come from touched-upon concerns as well as from collative stimulus variables such as complexity. Arousal increase is moderated by order in the arrangement of the stimuli. In this way the theory accounts for the coupling of order and complexity, or the "unitary connection of the manifold" (Fechner 1876), which is a recurrent theme in aesthetic theory. For the importance of this coupling there exists good experimental evidence. Orderly but complex drawings tend to be preferred over just orderly or just complex ones; the relationship has been quantified (Birkhoff 1932), and precise definition of both order and complexity, with a revised formula, has been shown to possess good predictive power with respect to preference judgments (Boselie 1984).

The difficulties with Berlyne's theories have been noted earlier: There is no evidence that absolute levels of arousal, or of arousal jag, correspond with given degrees of pleasantness or unpleasantness – certainly not when it comes to degree of aesthetic appreciation. Also, one would say that arousal is caused by appreciation, and not vice versa. The difficulties resolve themselves when tension and tension relief, arousal and the arousal jag, are recognized as representing challenge and the challenge–mastery sequence – constellations discussed in chapter 5. Challenge and mastery can be assumed to play a role in aesthetic appreciation; they may be held to apply either to one's powers of cognitive assimilation or to one's efforts, under the safe conditions of aesthetic distance, at coping with reality and with one's own emotions. In both these cases, one's concerns are involved. And in such a view, it makes sense that certain increases and decreases – of activation, of readiness and coping, rather than of mere arousal – are pleasurable; it makes sense that they are when they are: when assimilation, cognitively or emotionally, is offered a task successfully accomplished.

Yet this cannot be the whole story. Aesthetic emotion is not mere pleasure, like that produced by sexual climax. It implies a relationship with the aesthetic object; it is based, as said, upon appreciation, like that produced by a beautiful body. This is particularly clear from the responding emotions. Why should a work of art be moving, or staggering, or bring excitement, as even formal art can be or do? The nature of the emotion of "being moved" may give a clue. Being moved, to the point of tears, has been interpreted in an earlier section as surrender to something greater than oneself. It is, we argue, not mere tension release. The moving object of art is recognized as something that is greater than oneself and that one can surrender to; and, of course, excitement (other than that resulting from "exciting" colors and rhythms) results from confrontation with unusual quality or meaning. That is to say: Aesthetic emotions result from the confrontation with objects that are recognized as challenging and guiding one's powers of assimilation, cognitive or emotional. Objects are admirable to the extent that they invite and permit such assimilation; and the concern from which the responding emotions spring is that for commerce with such objects. Note that, as before, *assimilation* not only means fitting input into existing cognitive dispositions, but also means "accommodation" in the Piagetian sense: the construction of new cognitive dispositions and new action potentialities – of new modes of seeing or responding. Such construction increases both the inherent pleasures of experience and one's sense of mastery and competence, even if only for the moment of aesthetic appreciation. More importantly, perhaps, in recognition of an object that permits and invites all this, the object offers proof that certain modes of being exist toward which one can unambiguously orient, as perfect examples of challenge that can be resolved, of unitary connections of the manifold, whether – again – formally and merely cognitively or also emotionally.

This feature of existence of perfect examples toward which one can orient brings us to another aspect of aesthetic emotion, one that is distinctly of less cognitive nature: relevance to desire to join and to possess, that is, relevance to concern for proximity and coherence. Empathy, identification even with spaces and forms, has often been named as an aspect of the aesthetic process (e.g., Lipps 1903); so has "losing oneself" in the work of art or in natural scenery. Music tends to induce paralleling movement and in part takes its forms from such movements. Vigorous, exciting music tends to excite, and soothing music tends to soothe. This can be interpreted as instances of "direct effect upon the nervous system"; but perhaps it should be seen as consequences of willingness to "go with" the stimuli, since such activation change may well only occur when the subject abandons himself to those stimuli. Music may well derive some of its impact from a game of losing and catching, with respect to mental grasp as well as with respect to awareness of closeness and distance. At least, music "activates tendencies, inhibits them, provides meaningful and relevant resolutions," and "affect or emotion-felt is aroused when an expectation – a tendency to respond – activated by the musical stimulus situation, is temporarily inhibited or permanently blocked" (Meyer 1956, pp. 23, 31).

All this is not to deny that suspense and arousal can be pleasurable by themselves and can contribute to aesthetic pleasure. This is implicit in the above and evident in the earlier discussion of sensation seeking. Also, there is pleasure in variety as such, as when seeing a flowering meadow; this is evident from the discussion of curiosity. Probably there does exist an optimal level of stimulation or arousal or excitement, for a given individual at a given moment of time, depending upon his resources for processing. But it would seem erroneous to see those factors as the sole, or even major, root of aesthetic emotions. Even these last-named factors probably are not as simple as they seem. The appeal of variety may well come from the fact that, quite generally, satisfactions fade when not regularly obtained or affirmed anew (see section 5.8).

6.4. The structure of concerns, pleasure and pain, and the problem of circularity

Emotions arise when events are relevant to the individual's concerns; they arise, in particular, when events represent match or mismatch with those concerns' satisfaction conditions. This view, as said earlier, is not new. It is that of Mowrer (1960) and Simonov (1975) and of Gray (1971, 1982) and Pribram (1971), whose formulations resemble the present one. For this view to be truly meaningful, there must be independent evidence for concerns, and it must be there whenever emotions occur.

To some extent these conditions are met. There exists evidence for many concerns apart from the occurrence of emotion, in goal-directed and persistent strivings and from the subjects' expression of their wishes; such evidence can often be found in conjunction with emotional phenomena. Even in the absence of this sort of evidence, the viewpoint represents gain. Is is parsimonious. It explains the occurrence of different, both positive and negative, emotions by reference to a single underlying event: the concern with which events match or mismatch. It is not that, each time, two separate facts exist: that, for instance, familiar stimuli evoke pleasant affect and that unfamiliar ones are aversive. There is one preference for familiarity, upon which emotional response builds according to Mowrer's four contingencies and further contextual detail. Further, no matter which the concern, which the specific reinforcements implicated, the same emotions proper emerge in response to the same constellational contingencies.

Still, there are problems. Many concerns are inferred from the occurrence of emotions only. "Concern for familiarity" is known mainly by the upset caused by unfamiliar stimuli. Also, the independent evidence from goal-directed strivings may not be as independent as it seems. There is danger of circularity in the reasoning that emotions arise in response to events relevant to concerns. *Concerns* were defined as dispositions to prefer, and people may be said to prefer what they do because they like the preferred outcome. They try to achieve certain ends because these ends make them happy or remove distress.

Surely it can be countered to this objection that achievement of situations that make happy or removal of those that cause distress are to the subjects' benefit. There is an external criterion. It advances their interests. But benefit and interests cannot, in general, be defined in objective terms, independently from subjective evaluations. As Spinoza said: We do not like what is good and dislike what is bad, but we consider good what we like and consider bad what causes us sorrow. *Concerns* cannot, in general, be defined in terms of benefits or harms beyond hedonic ones. Craving for heroin is no different, in terms of motivational mechanism, from craving for food. In other words, when emotions are said to arise in response to events relevant to concerns, are we not saying that emotions arise in response to events that can cause emotions?

There is no true circularity, however. The last statement is not generally correct, nor are several of the arguments leading up to it.

First, emotions are not "feelings," as these were defined in section 4.7. By "feelings" were meant subjective responses of acceptability and nonacceptability; emotions are defined as changes in action readiness. Like and dislike are not emotions, although they can give rise to them. Concerns can be said to be dispositions to like or dislike given kinds of situation, but are not thereby necessarily dispositions to have emotions.

Second, it appears incorrect to say that people, or animals, desire what they do because they like the desired outcome – because they anticipate pleasure. This is not generally true. People like the outcomes of what they desire. As Tolman phrased it: "The organism does not, according to us, do things in order to feel pleasant, and not to feel unpleasant. . . . Pleasantness and unpleasantness are, as we see it, results not causes. They are indicators of cognitive expectations already made" (Tolman 1932, p. 263). These expectations, in turn, are not necessarily anticipations. Desire is not always the product of anticipation of outcomes. The latter cannot be supposed to be present in naive subjects whose desires can be evoked by appropriate objects, their naiveté notwithstanding. It or he or she smells good or looks good, and that is in many instances what evokes desire. Moreover, the assertion that people, or animals, desire what they like, if not tautological, still requires explanation why they like what they like, and one is again forced to assume dispositions that themselves are not of hedonic character, since liking is a response. These dispositions are what is meant by *concerns*. Concerns are the final point in tracing back occurrence of emotion to its sources.

This leaves the question of why we desire what we desire, and how pleasantness and unpleasantness are related to it. An answer to this question amounts to clarification of the nature of concerns; that is, it amounts to going from the intentional to the functional level of description (Dennett 1978) and analyzing the organism's mechanisms of motivation.

The structure of concerns

Motivation, to a large extent, can be considered the elicitation of behavior systems by appropriate external stimuli. A behavior system is defined as a potential action (a program), or a sequence of potential actions, equipped with some "sensitivity," a disposition to recognize occasions for activation of the system; and a "set-point," a disposition that recognizes conditions for terminations of action. Sensitivities are "go" provisions; set-points are "stop" provisions. Stimuli are "appropriate" when they match the specific sensitivity for that system: for a smell or appearance that, by virtue of that match, appears attractive to the subject. Sensitivities can be set. Motivational variables such as deprivation time (in the case of the food consumption system) or hormone levels (in the case of sexual desire) increase the sensitivity and thus prime the behavior system; they increase the readiness to act.

The model of motivation, as sketched, is found in Gallistel (1975), Toates (1980), and others; the present formulations are in debt, in addition, to Pribram (1971, 1980; Miller, Galanter, & Pribram 1960). A concern can thus, first, be identified with a stimulus sensitivity plus the consequent behavior potential. This means that, as far as this specification of concerns applies, we desire what we desire because we are made to become enflamed by desire for given things. We are made so, either by Nature, which provided us with sensitivity for a specific stimuli (it did so more in lower animals than in us), or by Experience, which made stimuli become signals for correspondence with a set-point (it does so more in us than in lower animals).

A concern, second, can be identified with a set-point. Match the actual conditions and set-points, as said, signals termination of the behavioral sequence: achievement of adequate glucose balance or a distended stomach or whatever the cue, in the case of hunger; relaxation upon sexual discharge, or whatever the cue, in the case of sexual desire; proximity of the attachment figure; and so on. Correspondence between set-points and actual conditions thus is a desired condition, in the sense that action continues until it is achieved, that no action from the behavior system or subsystem concerned follows after it has been achieved, and that its achievement engenders pleasure and obstruction of its achievement, unpleasantness.

Insofar as this applies, we desire what we desire because we are made to get satisfied by certain conditions corresponding to whatever set-points there are. We are made so, either by Nature, which provided us with certain set-points, or by Experience, which made some situations instrumental to achieving others provided by Nature.

Set-points can equally be set (Stellar 1954). In fact, sensitivities and set-points, go provisions and stop provisions, are usually interdepedent. What primes search for food is, at least in part, hunger, which, at least in part, depends upon mismatch between set-points and actual conditions. Set-point mismatch thus can directly or indirectly provide the stimulus for the go provision.

According to this account of motivation, behavior is not instigated by a low threshold setting of the sensitivity for need-relevant stimuli as such (as this may be due to deprivation, for instance), nor by mismatch between set-point and prevailing conditions as such; nor does either of them trigger the emotion of desire. Low threshold setting and mismatch can be considered to constitute a "central motive state" (Morgan & Stellar 1950): a state of readiness in terms of both enhanced sensitivity to relevant stimuli, and priming of relevant actions. By itself, a central motive state does not lead to actual motivation or desire, or rarely so. It does so only, or mainly, in response to stimuli impinging upon this readiness. Central motive states, at most, produce internal stimuli, such as result from stomach contractions, dry mouth, genital swellings and the like; and discomfort and restlessness, probably caused by these internal stimuli; but both, again, are as much a function of external stimuli and actual expectations as of the internal conditions of deprivation or hormone level (see Bolles 1975, ch. 7).

The most important conditions, then, for true motivation to arise – for the emotion of desire, for actual behavioral activation, actual goal-seeking activity – are external stimuli and thoughts of them. Actual motivation – impetus to act – is to be considered almost fully dependent upon stimuli (thoughts included) that notify the subject of mismatch or of potential match, the availability of goal objects. Motivation is a cognitive matter, even at the biological level, and much more so, of course, at the level of social propensities and concerns for self-esteem. True enough, it emphatically is a cognitive matter upon the noncognitive background of sensitivities and set-points, and with the noncognitive consequence of control precedence of action instigation. Still, mismatch of actual conditions with set-points and absence of satisfaction objects induce desire or emotions proper only when stimuli set off a signal.

Absence of social partners or attachment figures – the objective fact of loneliness – can be supported and go more or less unnoticed until one sees others playing together or is made to think of what could have been. The monk is quite contented, at most feeling a little empty or restless, unless plagued by images or a glimpse of something. Unfulfilled concerns exist without one being aware of them until events or thoughts make them become known as desires. We only miss things when we miss them; the same holds for having things, for that matter. All this pertains to what was called the second law of hedonic asymmetry (section 5.8) and to what was discussed in connection with "latent" concerns. Evidence for latent concerns – the male dog dozing until a bitch in heat passes by – and the heavy dependence of desire upon incentive value and expectations have been the stronger arguments, in the motivation literature, for stimulus–sensitivity match and stimulus–set-point mismatch conceptions of motivation, as opposed to drive-reduction (Hull) or energy-reduction (Freud) ones. In the present context, unprepared emotions provide similar arguments and force us toward the same conception.

"Stimuli," in all this, does not refer to actually rewarding and punishing stimuli only. The concept includes signals that evoke expectancies of reward and punishment, stimuli that signal "frustrative nonreward" or loss, and the self-generated stimuli of longings and fantasies.

Variants in concern structure

The above account of motivation applies not merely to biological drives, although most illustrations have been taken from those, but also to, for instance, curiosity, for which no priming conditions (other than, on occasion, suboptimal arousal level) are known: "interesting" or novel objects correspond to the go condition, exploration to the action program, and successful assimilation to the set-point. The account also applies to surface concerns: Perception or thought of an attachment figure is the go condition; following, looking, looking at his or her portrait the action program; and actual or symbolic proximity the satisfaction conditon that corresponds with the set-point. Availability of preprogrammed action sequences is not part of the definition of behavior systems: The action programs can have been acquired.

When ability and experience make it possible to anticipate situations corresponding to the set-point match, through conditioned signals or thought, those situations can be sought; or one can seek for the go conditions linked to achieving them. Motivation does not always need to wait for occasions to arise. The structure of concerns then becomes slightly different: Achievement of those situations becomes a goal, and a representation of that goal mediates on the road toward source concern satisfaction. This is of course the structure of most surface concerns. Concerns can thus consist of internal representations corresponding to desired external events; these representations serve as the set-point that regulates behavior. Perhaps there exist innate structured representations; the template with which the hawk silhouette must correspond in ducks could be one, and perhaps that which corresponds with "proximity of the mother figure" in babies. However, most such set-points must be products of experience, particularly in humans.

Not all concerns can be fitted into the above model. That is, it is not as easy for all concerns to imagine a distinct set-point as it is for hunger, thirst, sex, or proximity striving. Two concerns were discussed where this is distinctly the case: curiosity and control over one's movements and actions. In fact, these are two concerns that are problems for drive-reduction kinds of theory. Curiosity, as a true motive, hardly can be said to possess a set-point; on occasion, one wants to get more and more. Concern for control manifests the peculiarity of not giving rise to strivings at all except when frustrated by external events. Yet the two can be plausibly subsumed under the general conception discussed – or so we will argue.

The notion of set-point regulation of behavior has, of course, wide application outside the realm of motivation. It is the essential element of models of organized behavior generally, from goal-directed behavior over voluntary movement down to movements at the reflex level. As such it found its expression in the TOTE concept of Miller, Galanter, and Pribram (1960), the notion of a Test–Operate–Test–Exit cycle as the unit of analysis in psychological processes. Given the fundamental nature of feedback regulation, one can plausibly assume a tendency to complete any set-point-regulated action cycle once initiated, at least when anchored in a solidly integrated behavior system. This, in fact, is the central assumption made by Mandler (1984), when giving "interruption" the place of honor in the elicitation of emotional response. Further, pleasantness or unpleasantness can plausibly be assumed to be consequent upon achievement, or nonachievement of any intention–outcome agreement. *Intention*, at this point, is meant as the goal setting, and thus, set-point setting, of any organized behavioral sequence, whether a simple voluntary movement, a sexual response cycle, or a desire put into action. In curiosity, that is, in cognitive assimilation activity, the set-point corresponds to successful assimilation, to achieved match between input and internal representation. Exploration can be held to be rewarded when the action cycle "mismatch–explore–match?" succeeds, and to be a rewarding enterprise because it usually succeeds. In the behavior suggestive of a concern for control or freedom, the set-point corresponds to completion of initiated voluntary action. Movement restraint is then resented because self-initiated movement does not arrive where it aimed to go, even when that was nowhere in particular – just its set end point. Entertaining self-chosen expectations (Brehm 1972) and just standing there or choosing to do nothing plausibly belong to initiated voluntary actions: Both, as discussed, generate reactance when disturbed.

What this means is that cognitive assimilation and control over one's movements and action may be held to be valued because the organized behavior systems for cognitive assimilation and for self-initiated action are there, because they exist as capabilities. More precisely: Their unrestrained execution is valued because the capabilities, the systems, exist. This can be generalized. Unrestrained performance of any mental function is valued. Unrestrained execution engenders pleasure when not taken for granted; restraint of execution engenders unpleasant feeling. Effort, performing against resistance, is to be included among the restraints, but overcoming restraints is successful execution. In other words, we do things, and we like to do them, because we can do them, and we hate to see them go awry.

"Function pleasure," which is what we are discussing, has been a stand-by notion in the psychology of motivation since C. Bühler (1931) introduced the term; it returned in White's (1959) "effeciance motive." I suggest that no general function pleasure exists, nor a global effectance motive. Rather, each function generates its own pleasure upon functioning well, because well-functioning is monitored. Pleasantness and unpleasantness are the outcomes of such monitoring. A general, continuous monitoring, with pleasure and unpleasantness as signals, would explain both occurrence of these feelings and actual motives to seek them. Potential well-functioning can be foreseen, and conditions for it can be sought or created. This view applies to any other behavior system: walking, playing tennis, keeping balance on a tightrope. It thereby does away with a problem that recurs in motivation theory: the proliferation of hypothesized motives or reinforcers caused by the fact that such a large variety of events are reinforcing. Everything, we may assert, gives pleasure that is done well when it can be done and – because it is in the nature of pleasure – when such doing well is not taken for granted. "Function pleasure," in this sense, can perhaps be considered *the* pleasure, since that of sexual activity, eating, and drinking can be subsumed under it: We have our sexual, feeding, and drinking behavior systems.

One result of viewing pleasure as contingent upon well-functioning of behavior systems is the explanation of desires and pleasures under abundance. There is delight upon receiving a toy never coveted before, and there is desire for compact disc equipment that never before was missed. More money and more power usually are quite welcome, whatever the baseline. This can be explained by the shifting of set-points, the moving upward of adaptation levels, or by changing evaluation of what might constitute potential deprivation, threat, or impediment. Still, that more of money, power, toys, or equipment was not missed before. They all, however, provide renewed possibilities for deployment of functions, new stimuli for action, and new occasions for playing with objects and testing success of self-initiated action. Obviously, toys, money, and power yield more than that; but there are occasions when they appear to be enjoyed for their own sake, which is what is endeavored to be understood here.

Pleasure and pain

So far, pleasure and pain (in the general sense of unpleasant feeling) have been explained as results not causes. They come from match and mismatch with concerns or, generally, from well-functioning and interference with it.

Of course, pleasure and pain can be causes as well, in a variant of concern structure that often is taken as its prototype: hedonic concerns, the pursuit of pleasure and the avoidance of pain. The hedonic principle of course is important, and Tolman was wrong in formulating his above-quoted statement in the general way he did. Pleasures and pains can be anticipated, and so become objects of desire and goals for striving; and all the emotions proper will arise in connection with the fate of these pursuits when the various constellations present themselves.

The pleasures pursued and the pains avoided by and large derive from other concerns. As discussed in connection with sensation seeking, hedonic concerns are largely parasitic on what these other concerns produce in terms of hedonic outcomes.

However, this is not so for all pleasure and pain. It is not so for pain proper – physical pain – for aversive taste and smells, and for pleasure proper – for pleasant tastes, smells, and touches. The organism is made, evidently, so as to like and dislike those stimuli as such. The reinforcing power of nonnutrient but sweet saccharose (Sheffield et al. 1954) has been widely discussed in the literature as demonstrating the point. These pleasures and pains cannot be reduced, it would seem, to fate-of-concern outcomes, to outcomes of matches and mismatches. Or can they?

For physical pain one would say they can. Pain has true motivating power. It is the go condition for action programs having no pain as their set-point or termination condition – recuperative action programs in particular, leading to taking rest and licking one's wounds (Bolles & Fanselow 1980). Archer (1976) described pain as "the simplest disparity stimulus." The only distinctive aspect of pain is that, perhaps, the set-point is not represented by a representation of no pain; the set-point is implicit in the mechanism. Pain may be said to represent a "frozen concern."

For pleasure, the situation appears to be different. Pleasure, it seems, has no motivating power once it has been obtained, and pleasant sensory stimuli do not seem to be pleasant by reason of correspondence with some behavior system's set-point; nor do unpleasant sensory stimuli, for that matter, seem to owe their unpleasantness to some mismatch. On closer scrutiny, however, neither of these statements appears to be correct.

Hedonic tone of sensations, in fact, does have some set-point-like background, as the Wundt curve shows: Very weak stimuli tend to be neutral, and stronger ones distasteful, with often a positive optimum in between. Also, hedonic tone is not altogether independent from the satisfaction state of needs. Food does not smell as good after dinner as before; the smell may even become sickening, and generally, "the level of acceptability of test-foods declines as the terminal state of satiation is approached" (Young 1959, p. 105). The concentration at which liking for a salt solution changes over into aversion, in rats, is close to the point at which the concentration is isosmotic with body fluids (Pfaffman 1960). The salinity of gastric contents affects the salt preference (Stellar, Hyman, & Samet 1954). Evidently, there exists a stop mechanism that translates into negative hedonic tone that is set by physiological state (Pfaffman 1960). As for the sexual domain, sensitivity for sex pheromones has been shown to be related to hormone levels.

Nevertheless, hedonic tone of tastes and smells is only partly dependent upon the organism's physiological state. Mild sucrose solutions are positive to rats even when the animals are completely satiated (Young 1959), and bitter is never truly positive (Pfaffman 1960). Many substances never taste well, to humans. One must assume that specific unlearned provisions exist that make certain tastes and smell sensations pleasant and others unpleasant; and this also applies to sexual sensations, caresses included. That, of course, is not surprising and it is biologically plausible; evolution may well have made it so, just as with pain. The sensations that the organism is prepared to like or dislike are clearly related to basic biological interests. Not all good tastes, odors, and touches come from biologically favorable substances or useful objects, and not all bad ones from noxious ones; but by and large one may assume a correlation to exist, or to have existed in the species' original ecology. However this may be, it appears that the formulation of what underlies the occurrence of emotions will have to be completed and has to run: Emotions are elicited by events relevant to concerns – or to sensitivities.

Although the existence of specific hedonic sensitivities for tastes, smells, touches, and the like is evident, this still may not be the whole story; the hedonic qualities may not be irreducible facts. Positive "feeling" is not really without motivational significance; it is not, in fact, correlated with behavioral end points. Quite the contrary: It is, as we argued earlier, the signal that starts and guides behavior in enjoyment. It tells you to go and to go on with consummatory activity; just imagine orgasm stopping being pleasurable in mid-course. That is to say that the pleasant tastes, smells, and other positively toned sensations are releasers and monitors of prewired behavioral systems. The provisions upon which they impinge, and by virtue of which they are experienced as pleasant, form the go condition of these systems. It can be maintained that the pleasant smells and tastes and other sensations are pleasant *because* they are recognized, by the organism, as fit to trigger and steer the behavior systems. This does not hold for sexual stimuli only. Pleasantness of sweet substances can be argued to derive from the fact that they elicit eating or drinking – that is to say, that the organism recognizes them as matching the go conditions for such behavior – and evil smells are evil because they are nauseating, and not vice versa. Goodness and badness thus can be considered outcomes of acceptability matching. The hypothesis is not implausible, because a match between stimulus and disposition to "recognize" that stimulus must exist anyway – whether it is to recognize the stimulus as pleasant or unpleasant, or whether it is to recognize it as belonging to the class of fit or unfit objects for consummatory behavior.

The problem of circularity

What do we need all this for, in the present context? It cannot be to survey theories of motivation or to advance an alternative one. It is to argue that like and dislike, pleasantness and unpleasantness, are results, not causes, except in the derived case of hedonic concerns. They are expressions of match and mismatch with sensitivities and set-points relevant for behavior, that is, sensitivities and set-points embedded in behavioral systems. They are, in principle, useful signals for learning what situations to seek or to avoid in the future and, more directly, for beginning or pursuing a given course of action, for terminating action or changing tack. This interpretation implies that a solidly obtained match needs no signal, which in fact it does not appear to produce. It explains what we have called the Law of Asymmetrical Adaptation of Pleasure and Pain: It is change that makes for pleasure, but pain can remain indefinitely.

Concerns thus are not generally defined by like or dislike, pleasure or pain. They are defined by sensitivities and set-points that happen to be there. It is of course true that the empirical determination of concerns implies reference to like and dislike, taken either in the sense of seeking and seeking to avoid, or in that of feeling of pleasantness and unpleasantness. But conceptually, concerns imply no such reference. The set-point for body temperature, when not in fever, is 98.6°F (36.7°C), whether we like it or not.

Viewed in this way, motivation, emotion, and feeling, all three, have one common source: match or mismatch between actual conditions and concerns. Which of the three occurs at a given moment (to the extent that they do not overlap) depends upon features of situational structure, as discussed earlier. Motivation, that is desire and actual striving, occurs under perceived mismatch with some perspective of success, or when confronted with potential match – a go stimulus; emotion (emotion proper) under perceived possible or actual match or mismatch; and mere "feeling" when urgency is insufficient to entail activation change.

If the above analysis is correct, pleasantness and unpleasantness are the outcomes of central monitoring of the proper functioning of the organism's behavior systems (see Pribram 1970). Proper functioning means receiving the adequate inputs and producing the adequate outputs. Note that this description is identical to that of the "feelings" of pleasantness and unpleasantness themselves, as discussed in section 4.7 and stemming from Aristotle: Pleasure is the sense of unimpeded functioning, and unpleasantness that of impeded functioning.

Also, if the above analysis is correct, motivation is the product of behavior systems pressing toward their proper functioning, given conditions for their functioning at all. That is, in fine, there is only one kind of motivation: that of establishing or maintaining proper functioning of whatever systems there happen to be, happen to be sensitized, or happen to be in mismatch with respect to their sensitivities or set points. Such general motivation is better not called motivation at all, but rather considered a basic property of animate organisms, or of the matter of which they are composed – the hardware of neurons and neuron circuits and neuroendocrine information transmission. Desire is the expression of this general property, as manifest in the activation of any given behavior system not, or not yet, having completed its proper functioning cycle.

As for the various desires: They result from the fact that given behavior systems, and thus concerns, are there. What is there just happens to be there, from the individual's perspective, that is, when leaving out consideration of how it came to be there through evolution and experience. That is to say: What one desires is what one is made to be, at a given moment of time. What one likes is what enhances that which one is made to be. This sounds like self-actualization theory, and in some sense it is; but it is a mere rephrasing of the preceding. It brings us, if the reader permits, back to Spinoza. Spinoza, it will be recalled (section 5.1), said that the nature of mind is to persist in its own nature. To quote: "The mind ... endeavours to persist in its existence for an indefinite duration. ... This endeavour, ... when referred to both mind and body in conjunction is called striving. ... Desire is striving connected with consciousness thereof" (Spinoza 1677, III, Prop. 9); and "Striving is the very essence of man, in so far as it is determined to do what promotes its own persistence" (ibid., Definitions, 1).

6.5. The function of emotions and "feelings"

Emotions are action readiness changes in response to events relevant to the individual's concerns. Emotions proper are responses to actual or potential match and mismatch of events with those concerns' satisfaction conditions.

Emotions, as actual readiness changes, are based upon relevance evaluations of these events; these are expressed in "feelings"* or in the experienced relevance of events. Emotions and "feelings" therefore can be said to serve the function of signaling concern relevance or, equivalently, the well-functioning of the individual's behavior systems. Since emotions and "feelings" have motivating properties or signal actual match, the function of emotions and "feelings" can be said to be to monitor and steer concern satisfaction – to be instrumental in obtaining or maintaining such satisfaction.

Action readiness change in part consists of action tendencies toward actions for dealing, mostly in relational change fashion, with the concern-relevant events. Insofar as emotions are overtly expressed action tendencies, emotions can be said to serve the function of ensuring concern satisfaction. Expression of desire endeavors to do so directly. Expression of emotions proper does so by trying to restore disturbed mismatch, or by aligning activity with opportunities for match.

Insofar as emotions are mere tendencies – having desire, feeling angry, being aroused – they express readiness for ensuring concern satisfaction. They are "plans."

Emotions and "feelings" thus can be said to constitute the organism's concern satisfaction system. They serve the useful functions of watching, guarding, and satisfying the individual's concerns and realigning action toward satisfaction when disturbed.

When considering the individual as such, from the point of view of his mode of operation, concerns are to be taken for granted. Whether the concerns themselves serve a useful function is outside that point of view. However, an individual's concerns are, to some extent, a reflection

---

* Recall that "feeling" – i.e., in quotation marks – is used in a special technical sense, as feeling of pleasantness or positive value, or of unpleasantness or negative value (see section 4.7).

of his biological interests, or of those of his species: survival and reproduction. Of course, the unreflecting individual who is sexually excited
does not need to know about propagation, and still less so that this is
to be valued for letting the species survive. Yet the correlation between
concerns and what may be distinguished as interests is there. This holds,
in particular, for the basic source concerns of which the sensitivities and
set points are laid down in the organism's hardware. Since this is the
case, the emotion system can be said to serve the furthering and defense
of the organism's biological interests. The point is obvious, but the distinction between concerns, which are individual "goals," and interests,
which are biological, evolutionary "purposes," needs to be emphasized,
since what is desirable or functional from the individual's point of view
is not necessarily so from an "objective," or even reflexive, point of
view.

The emotion system can be said to be *the* concern satisfaction provision. Motivation – that is, desire – serves direct satisfaction; the emotions
proper serve signaling, prudence, restoration, and alignment. How else
could concerns be satisfied than by signaling states of satisfactions and
changes in action readiness in response to events? Of course, they could
be, by rational consideration of interests and the rational planning of
action; in fact, it is often done so. But this obviously is an added complexity, a later addition in a phylogenetic and ontogenetic sense. Moreover, what we rationally desire can only have been derived from what
we feel as desirable, even if what we feel as desirable pertains only to
being rational or to conforming to what is held to be desirable by others.

Emotions are thus seen as heavily dependent upon motivation in the
dispositional sense that we distinguished under the term *concerns*. They
not only are dependent upon concerns, they also are at the service of
concerns. This view accords with the views of theorists who see emotions
as dependent upon expectations of reinforcement such as Gray (1982)
and with those of other theorists who emphasize the close relationships
with motivation, notably Simonov (1975) and Tomkins (1962; 1980).
Tomkins has for long advocated the notion that emotions "amplify" the
power of motivation. Excitement and desire make something different
out of mere sexual urge, for instance. We would say that excitement
and desire are the primary manifestations of sexual urge: They signal
recognition of a fit object, make impatiently ready for action, and steer
toward encounter and fulfillment.

Emotions and feelings thus have a useful function. There are, however, important restrictions to this functionality. Whereas the emotion

system as a whole can be said to fulfill a useful and even necessary function, individual emotions and emotional phenomena not always do; certainly not. We will discuss dysfunctionality later (section 9.4), and conclude that it does not necessarily invalidate the conception of emotion as the product of functional, useful provisions. A more essential restriction with respect to the functionality view comes from certain afunctional, rather than dysfunctional, response aspects – afunctional from the point of view of ensuring concern satisfaction. What are meant here are the activation modes and the emotions characterized by them.

Deactivation and free activation were discussed in chapter 2. Prolonged deprivation, or loss and aversive conditions considered to be final, produce deactivation, apathy; absence of intentional objects does likewise, producing spleen and listlessness, states readily bordering upon depressed mood. Achievement of satisfaction after challenge produces free activation, joy, enhanced vigor, which tend to outlast that achievement. There is no immediate functional reason, with regard to ensuring concern satisfaction, why this should be so; little or nothing can be gained by apathy or exuberance in dealing with the eliciting events. Two interpretations for the behavior changes have been advanced, which are not necessarily mutually exclusive. The first is that absence of goals, satisfaction objects, or satisfactions lets general activation level sink below the set-point of well-functioning; achievement of satisfactions keep current level at a higher point, or pushes it there. That is the way it is, the mode of functioning of the system, due to properties of the neural and neurohumoral hardware. This, of course, is not psychological explanation but mechanism; but it may be that this is all there is to be said about it.

The second interpretation is that activation changes, apart from being a function of presence or absence of interesting goals, are a function of the general well-functioning of behavior systems; that is, of confidence. In other words, free activation upon achievement of concern activation, and deactivation upon loss or discouragement result from their impact upon a different concern from that which was implicated in the achievement or failure in the first place. Nothing succeeds like success: Success reflects back, in a positive feedback cycle, upon general evaluation of competence. The inverse applies to failure, when confidence with respect to the current concern is lost. This leaves deactivation as afunctional, because what may be gained by sinking into apathy, even in loss of sense of competence?

Even if afunctional as behavior modes, activation changes "express" the concern implicated in eliciting them, in the sense that they are implementations of the current state of concern satisfaction endeavor (see section 2.8). They just *are* the modes of striving, or of abandoning striving, with respect to the current concern.

6.6. Other dispositional antecedents

Emotions arise when events and their implications – situational antecedents – interact with concerns – dispositional antecedents. For this to happen, events usually must be interpreted in terms of concern relevance; and for such interpretation the organism needs coding categories and other knowledge. Coding categories and knowledge mediate between the events and the concerns; emotions thus result from three, rather than two, entities: events, concerns, and cognitive dispositions.

To the dispositional antecedents further belong the various response modes. Obviously, whosoever has no antagonistic actions in his repertoire cannot become angry; whosoever has no inhibitory or protective potential cannot know fear.

The points would not need mention, except for the sake of completeness, were it not that both coding categories and response modes involve further dispositional antecedents: the readiness with which either of them, or any of either of them, is used. In section 5.6 we mentioned the matter of thresholds. Emotional response thresholds – and response intensity – depend either upon the readiness with which an event is seen as relevant, as harmful, as unmodifiable, and so on; or upon the readiness with which a given response system is mobilized or a given activation change triggered. These readinesses vary from moment to moment and from person to person; they, too, intervene between event and concern in the development of emotional response. For the sake of completeness, indeed, we will briefly touch upon them, under the headings "Cognitive dispositions," "Resources" and "Constitutional factors."

Cognitive dispositions

Obviously, emotions are pervaded by one's cognitive potential. In order to feel someone else's promotion as diminishing one's chances for improvement, or attention of one's beloved for a third party as negligence, coding principles of "chances for improvement" and "negligence," the rule that his chances diminish those of oneself and so forth, must be available to the subject.

The readiness with which to use these categories varies, and makes people vary in spite or reproachfulness, in envy or feelings of being abandoned. Similarly, people differ in the tendency to see either themselves or external circumstances as primarily responsible for what befalls them: They differ in expectations concerning locus of control (see section 5.6). By consequence, they differ in proneness to all emotions contingent upon those expectations. Recall that feeling slighted, abandoned, treated unjustly all imply external locus of control, whereas feeling hurt in self-esteem, feeling that one has fallen short of one's duties, and feeling humiliated, even when by actually humiliating events, are highly dependent upon internal locus control.

Personality differences are among the dispositional antecedents of differences in emotional response. Personality traits such as anxiousness and aggressiveness are best viewed as low thresholds for anxiety or anger response or as dispositions to respond frequently in such manners, rather than as continuously being a little anxious or angry. Trait anxiety, says Spielberger (1975), is the tendency to react with anxiety to a wide variety of situations; aggressiveness, says Berkowitz (1962), is the tendency to react with anger and aggression to a large variety of situations. One of the ways of conceiving these tendencies is as cognitive sets, as predominant readiness of the corresponding coding categories of threat, challenge, obstruction, and the like.

Cognitive sets of given kinds can be general over all sorts of situations, or specific to certain classes among them. Anxiousness may pertain to all sorts of events, or be restricted to possibilities of physical harm or to social situations. Endler (1975), for instance, found anxiety-proneness with respect to self-esteem, with respect to pain, and with respect to novel situations to be only moderately correlated, and in some population groups not at all. A monosymptomatic phobia, of course, illustrates the lower bound of generality.

Differential availability of coding categories explains various sorts of individual differences in emotional response – for instance, sex differences. Women cry about three times as often as men, according to one of our own studies; this applies to crying in anger and jealousy, and not merely in sorrow and physical pain. The explanation might be that they more readily see themselves as helpless than men, or are more ready to admit that they are when they are. Conversely, it is likely that men see

themselves more readily as in control, and that they more persistently try
to be, with all consequences of internal locus of control alluded to.

Cognitive sets and readiness to use given coding categories probably
have multiple origins, and schools of psychology differ in the emphasis
they place upon one or the other: the individual's history of reinforcement, social acquisition of dominant modes of interpretation of the environment, and actual conditions such as the strength or weakness of
the individual's coping resources.

Resources

Strength and weakness of response resources may color the way events
are perceived – as challenges or as threats, and so on; they may also
influence readiness for given modes of response as such, or for response
inhibition. Animals reared under prolonged social or perceptual isolation
are considerably more fearful than animals reared normally (e.g., Melzack & Scott 1957; Harlow 1949; Konrad & Bagshaw 1970), presumably
because they did not develop a coping repertoire with respect to the
social or perceptual environment. The "hyperesthetic–emotional" or
"neurasthenic" syndrome (irritability, emotional lability, concentration
loss, sentimentality) after prolonged stress or illness likewise illustrates
changed propensity for certain emotional responses due to some kind
of resource depletion. There is, of course, gradual transition from specific
weakness or strength of coping resources due to lack of skill or power
in a specific situation (say, a marriage) to generalized weakness due to
disturbed development or organismic condition.

Organismic condition is an important background variable for emotions. Individuals differ from moment to moment and among each other
in what one might call *activation resources*: They differ in vitality and
spontaneous interest, and thereby in capacity for emotional responses
of various sorts. Interests in events met, aggressive response other than
irritation, that is to say, true anger, and positive emotion, particularly
vivid joy, all would seem to covary with degree of vitality or with exhaustion. At least, one has the impression that this is so; no systematic
investigation is known to the author, except for observations on enhanced apathy, anxiousness, and irritability after sleep deprivation
(Murray 1965). To the extent that the relationship between activation
resources and emotion indeed obtains, the three interpretations given
above could all apply: Stimuli may appear demanding and unmanage-

able, powerful responses may not be available, and (for the neurasthenic syndrome) inhibition may be weakened.

Response potential is also influenced by mood, as determined by hormonal changes and life events. Propensity for angry response, in the irritability of the premenstrual syndrome, illustrates the first; propensity for happy and eager response after success and for depressed or listless response after failure or loss illustrate the second. Sense of competence and self-confidence, of whatever origin, mediate in important ways between events and emotions. Many examples were encountered in the preceding chapters. The mice that grew more aggressive by a history of success in fighting with other mice (Lagerspetz 1961) have their human counterparts. At the other extreme, mention was made of anxiety in combat pilots after having been wounded or having seen comrades die, which had shattered the subjects' implicit sense of invulnerability, and of the fact that phobias often emerge during periods of personal stress.

Constitutional factors

By *constitutional factors* are meant here general response propensities rooted, at least in part, in the individual's physical constitution.

What is often called "emotionality" or "emotion instability," or, more properly, anxiousness is the major of these factors. Individuals differ in the readiness with which autonomic emotional responses, behavioral disturbances (sleeplessness, difficulties in concentration) and worries are elicited. The notion goes back to the ancient theory of temperaments, found new formulations in the typology of Heymans (1932), which investigator was the first to obtain evidence that a hereditary trait was involved (Heyman & Wiersma 1906), and became prominent as "anxiety" in the work of Spence and Spence (1966) and Cattell (1975), and in somewhat different conceptualization as "neuroticism" in Eysenck's (e.g., 1967) studies. In Eysenck's work, factor analysis of questionnaire responses repeatedly led to the identification of a reliable neuroticism or emotional stability–instability dimension, characterized by response features as just mentioned.

In Eysenck's studies, neuroticism is one of two orthogonal dimensions found in factor analysis of his questionnaires; the other is "introversion–extraversion," to be discussed below. The dimensions identified result from appropriate rotation of the orthogonal factor axes and are labeled after items obtaining the highest loadings. Gray (1971) argued that these axes could better be shifted by 45 degrees; the two axes then become "anxiety" and "impulsivity," respectively.

In animal studies, a similar trait of "emotionality," or rather anxiousness, has been found; it is defined, in rats, by emotional disturbance in the open-field test, as indexed by amount of defecation. On that index, "emotional" and "nonemotional" rat strains could be bred, remaining reliably distinct over five or more generations (Hall 1941; Scott 1958; Broadhurst 1960). Emotional rats show less exploratory activity in the open field, flee faster when receiving electric shock, and show more pronounced conditioned response suppression (CER) (Gray 1971).

The other important dimension mentioned above, adopting Gray's conceptualizing, is "impulsivity": sensitivity, presumably, for rewards and for relief from punishment, which entails readiness for relevant approach and consummatory behaviors (Gray 1971). Impulsiveness, as defined by the questionnaires from which the dimension is derived, manifests itself in impulsiveness proper, the occurrence of unrestrained strong desires, and in aggressiveness and irritability (Gray 1971).

Sensation seeking is related to impulsivity as measured by specific rating scales, with correlations between .20 and .57 (see Zuckerman 1979), and has been interpreted as one of its variants (Eysenck & Eysenck 1979). Its physiological concomitants, AER augmenting and low platelet MAO concentrations, appear to apply to impulsivity generally, as was discussed above, and this is also suggested by the fact that correlations with impulsivity are highest for the Sensation Seeking Scale's Disinhibition subscale (Zuckerman, Murtaugh, & Siegel 1974). Extraversion, whether conceived as a basic dimension or as the mixture of low anxiety and high impulsivity, is, among other things, tendency toward being sociable and responsive to pleasurable social stimuli; the questionnaire items involved define it so.

There probably are other personality dispositions, with independent constitutional backgrounds, underlying differences in propensity for given emotional responses. Aggressiveness is one. Rat strains high and low on aggressiveness can be bred.

Interpretation of these dimensions offers the same options as before: differences in cognitive or response propensities. Probably, they are not true alternatives here: Response propensities, for aggression, inhibition, or social response, shape how events are seen and thereby determine actual response.

7. Neurophysiological conditions

The present chapter presents a brief review of major neurophysiological mechanisms involved in emotional phenomena. They are reviewed under the heading of "conditions" for emotion and discussed from that angle. In chapter 3 we touched upon neural and physiological aspects of emotional response. Here we discuss neural structures and humoral supplies, the intactness and activity of which appear to be conditions for normal emotional response.

The review will be brief and superficial, partly because the literature is vast, complex, and often confusing, partly because it is selective to suit the present purpose: to round off discussion of antecedent variables of emotion, to emphasize the biological basis of emotion, the importance of cognition notwithstanding, and to investigate what psychological theory of emotion can learn from neurophysiological analyses.

Extensive reviews of relevant literature can be found in Ruch (1979), Isaacson (1974), and Gray (1982), from which much of the present chapter has been drawn.

7.1. Brain structures involved in emotion

Major brain structures involved in emotion are indicated in Figure 7.1. Neurophysiological control of emotional behavior and experience, motivated behavior included, has been conceptualized in terms of three sets of structures: brain stem, including parts of the diencephalon; limbic system; and neocortex. The division roughly corresponds to MacLean's (1970) description of the "triune brain": protoreptilian brain, protomammalian or "visceral" brain, and neomammalian brain.

The protoreptilian brain, according to MacLean, subserves the elementary needs of food, shelter, defense, and reproduction, in the sense of containing and organizing programs for species-specific behavior. Electrical stimulation of the lower brain stem elicits unlearned behaviors,

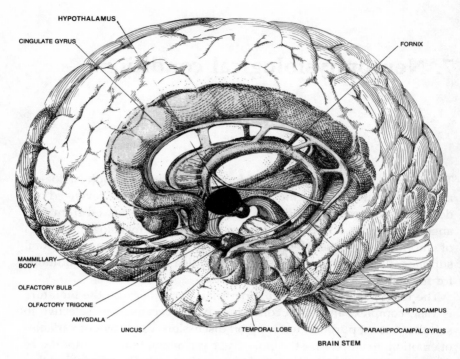

HYPOTHALAMUS

CINGULATE GYRUS

FORNIX

MAMMILLARY
BODY

OLFACTORY BULB

OLFACTORY TRIGONE

AMYGDALA

UNCUS

TEMPORAL LOBE

BRAIN STEM

HIPPOCAMPUS

PARAHIPPOCAMPAL GYRUS

Figure 7.1. Major brain areas involved in emotion. (Adapted from F. Snyder, Opiate receptors in the brain, *Scientific American* March, 1977)

although mostly only fragments of them. The midbrain, among other things, contains mechanisms that govern wakefulness and that influence arousal of higher brain structures. In the diencephalon, the hypothalamus is considered the "head ganglion" of autonomic responses and also ensures activation and integration of species-specific behaviors like those of defense, feeding, and sex. It is the major control structure for emotional arousal and need-related behaviors. Its importance appears from the fact that removal of the entire cerebral cortex in dogs or cats leaves an animal capable of "sham rage": Minor stimuli evoke violent responses such as hissing, spitting, struggling, clawing, and the full gamut of autonomic accompaniments (Goltz 1892). Transsection of the brain stem behind the hypothalamus abolishes this response, thus identifying the hypothalamus as the primary affective integration center (Bard 1928). Brain stem, midbrain, and diencephalon also contain the origins and major course of neural pathways – the monoamine pathways, excreting norepinephrine, dopamine or serotonin – which extend into the limbic system and far into the neocortex and are considered important in attentional control, in reinforcement, and in mood (Ungerstedt 1971; Clavier & Routtenberg 1980; McGeer & McGeer 1980).

Considered by MacLean to form part of the protoreptilian brain are the basal ganglia: caudate nucleus, putamen, globus pallidus. The basal ganglia are involved in the organization and regulation of need-related and goal-directed action.

Limbic system is the name for a number of interrelated structures, for the most part belonging to the phylogenetically old parts of the brain. Its major structures are the amygdala, hippocampal formation, and septal area; some authors include the cingulate cortex and anterior thalamus (Isaacson 1974). This set of structures is considered to regulate responses organized, in principle, by hypothalamus and basal ganglia and to provide them with much of the necessary information; it integrates cognitive aspects with commands for action.

The neomammalian brain, the neocortex, contributes extensive cognitive analysis to emotions: It is responsible for foresight, finer discriminations, and analysis of linguistically mediated information. In addition, it contributes construction of plans and spontaneous interests, which are vital in engendering occasions for emotions proper, as well as in generating the emotions of interest and of desire for future accomplishments.

The discussion of neurophysiological conditions will be organized around a number of psychologically relevant topics.

7.2. Elicited behavior

Electrical stimulation of specific brain sites is capable of eliciting emotional and motivational behavior of various sorts. Evidently, such behaviors are organized at, or below, the locations stimulated. Stimulation elicits such behaviors on condition that appropriate stimulus objects are also present and generally fails to do so in their absence. Also, external stimuli may elicit emotional and motivational behaviors in animals in which parts of the brain have been removed or connections severed. Evidently, again, the behaviors are organized by the remaining or still-connected structures.

Stimulation of the lower brain stem in intact animals elicits fragments of emotional behavior: clawing, facial expressions, or vocalizations (e.g., Delgado & Mir 1969, with monkeys). In humans, irritative lesions in the pons may elicit compulsive laughter or crying, without emotional content (see Loeb & Meyer 1969). Evidently, at low brain levels programs of elementary behaviors are laid down, but with a low degree of organization. These facts are indicated also by responses to painful exteroceptive stimuli in animals in which the brainstem is severed just below the hypothalamus. The animals show defensive responses – clawing, spitting – which, however, are poorly coordinated and do not show signs of general excitement; responses terminate as soon as stimulation ends (Woodworth & Sherrington 1904). The responses were termed "pseudoaffective" responses because of the absence of general excitement.

Stimulation of hypothalamic and limbic sites, by contrast, produces full-fledged emotional response patterns consisting of both autonomic and somatic components. Hess (1957) gives the following description of "affective defense" in a cat, elicited by medial hypothalamic stimulation. A few seconds after stimulus onset, the animal shows signs of attentional arousal and excitement. It looks around, hairs stand up, pupils dilate, it starts to breathe heavily. It focuses on a person standing nearby, strikes out when approached, and prepares to jump from the experimental platform. The cat's behavior, according to Hess, can hardly be understood otherwise than as the expression of a feeling of being seriously threatened. Also, it can hardly be understood otherwise than as activation of an "action tendency": thresholds for signs of threat and for corresponding behaviors are lowered, and after termination of stimulation the animal for a while remains irritable and growls when approached. During stimulation, behavior develops in coherence with the situation: It is directed toward people and toward escape routes. Such adaptive flexibility is the rule in behavior elicited by hypothalamic, limbic, and some midbrain stimulation. Chickens aim their elicited attack at the experimenter's face (Von Holst 1957); stimulation of midbrain central grey elicits aggression in monkeys when the animal is surrounded by monkeys lower in the social hierarchy, and submission when faced with higher placed ones (Delgado 1967); defensive attack in cats is directed toward live rats rather than towards stuffed ones if both are available (Wasman & Flynn 1962).

Many different modes of emotional and motivational behavior can be elicited from more or less discrete hypothalamic and midbrain locations. It appears that various behavior systems are neuroanatomically more or less distinct and that even various components of given systems might be. It can be argued, however, that stimulation that elicits affective defense merely does so because it is aversive to the animal. It is true that such stimulations indeed appear to be aversive (see section 7.6);

still, when small electrodes are used, different points can be shown to yield either defensive attack or escape, and different points may yield different patterns of escape or of attack (Romaniuk 1967; Brown, Hunsperger, & Rosvold 1969; Wasman & Flynn 1962). Predatory attack (Flynn 1973; Panksepp 1971), intermale aggression (Koolhaàs 1978; Adams 1971; Kruk et al. 1979), and defensive aggression (Brown et al. 1969) are elicited from distinctly different lateral and medial hypothalamic sites (see Moyer, 1971). The response systems are physiologically differentiated also by the fact that intermale aggression responds to testosterone manipulations, whereas other systems do not (Bermond 1978).

Stimulation at other lateral hypothalamic placements elicits appetitive behaviors: eating, drinking, gnawing wood (in rodents). Sexual response to appropriate objects has been evoked, in male rats, by stimulation of posterior hypothalamus (Caggiula & Hoebel 1966) and area preoptica (Van Dis & Larsson 1971).

As said, the various stimulations result in the various behaviors only when suitable objects are present. Predatory aggressive behavior is elicited only in the presence of potential prey (Flynn 1973), intermale aggression only in the presence of conspecifics behaving submissively (Koolhaas 1978). The effect of hypothalamic stimulation is to lower thresholds for response to given cues or to mobilize attention for given cues rather than, or as much as, to elicit a given response. A cat that disregards a rat begins to get interested upon the onset of stimulation in the "predatory attack area." Changes in threshold are particularly evident in this case. Increasing intensity of stimulation increases the sensory fields in face and forepaws from which tactual stimuli elicit the relevant predatory response components – opening the mouth and clawing, respectively (Flynn 1973). Hypothalamic damage, by contrast, causes "sensory neglect": absence of orienting toward given stimuli, at least during a certain period postoperatively (Marshall & Teitelbaum, 1974). All this suggests that stimulation activates an entire behavior system – elicits action tendency – rather than a given response as such. That this is the case is suggested also by the fact that subthreshold stimulation of predatory attack sites facilitates response to potential prey for a certain period of time after termination of that stimulation and by the fact that the stimulated animal appears to search for appropriate prey or opponent if none is present (Flynn 1973).

Generally, behavioral systems rather than behaviors are activated by brain stimulation. In the case of stimulation at affective defense locations, weak stimuli produce attentional arousal and exploration. Stronger stimuli do the same when no potentially threatening stimuli are present; attack or escape occurs when there are. In the case of appetitive behaviors – eating, drinking, gnawing, sexual activity – the same regularity holds: Appropriate behaviors are shown when suitable objects are present, and attentional arousal, exploration (in rats, sniffing in particular), and locomotion when there are not (Panksepp 1982). Which type of behavior is elicited at a given stimulus location is not strictly determined by that location. Stimulation at an electrode placement that elicited feeding may elicit carrying pups or gnawing wood when one of the latter stimuli is substituted for food (Valenstein, Cox, & Kakolewski 1970). Further, which behavior is elicited depends as much upon the nature and history of the individual as upon external stimuli and electrode placement (Panksepp 1982; Ploog 1970). Mouse killing is evoked electrically only in rats which are natural mouse killers (Panksepp 1971), just as violent mood in humans is elicited by brain stimulation only in subjects who were susceptible to attacks of violence prior to such stimulation. These observations suggested to Valenstein (1969) that hypothalamic stimulation in rewarding areas activates motivational systems that are "prepotent" at the time of stimulation. As Panksepp (1982) phrases it: stimulation can be said to activate desire, or expectancy, or satisfaction, or whatever goal is at the time suggested to the individual by external stimuli and his own propensities.

There are limits to the validity of the prepotent response or "expectancy" hypothesis. Not all behavior can be elicited from all sites, or with equal ease; predatory behavior, to name an example, is elicited from quite specific locations. Still, the assertion that brain stimulation elicits action tendencies or behavior systems, with the states of readiness and behavioral flexibility implied, appears to hold for all structures above the brain stem.

As said, behaviors can be elicited from various limbic and other locations, too. These behaviors tend to have the features indicated; in humans, stimulation often leads to articulate emotional experiences. Orienting and fearful and angry responses can be evoked by stimulation of the amygdala, for instance, in which both behavioral and autonomic components are present (Ursin & Kaada 1960; Fonberg 1979); elicited attack behavior builds up gradually, more gradually than hypothalamically induced attack, and subsides still more slowly after stimulus termination (King, after Isaacson 1974). In man, rage attacks occur in patients with temporal lobe tumors, temporal epileptic foci, and temporal lesions; the attacks usually are triggered by insignificant events and are often accompanied by aura experiences (Poeck 1969). Amygdaloid stimulation in temporal lobe patients leads to buildup of anger and aggressive urge, felt as uncontrollable, and similar to what the patients say they experience in spontaneous attacks (Mark & Ervin 1970; King 1961).

Stimulation at other locations (head of caudate nucleus, Heath 1976; Hassler & Riechert 1961; anterior thalamus, see Poeck 1969) can produce smiling and hearty laughter that the patient is unable to suppress, often with feelings of intense pleasure or amusement: "Everything appears quite funny to the patient" (Hassler & Riechert, 1961). However, elicited behavior is not always accompanied by distinct and appropriate emotional content. As said, irritative pontine lesions sometimes cause nonemotional laughter and crying. Lesions higher up along the pathway from the thalamus to pons (in "pseudobulbar palsy") give rise to uncontrollable fits of crying or laughter in about half the patients. The fits are provoked by insignificant stimuli, or no stimuli at all, and are usually devoid of feelings of grief, joy, or amusement; they may even be accompanied by entirely incompatible emotions (Bekhterev 1894; see Poeck 1969; Rinn 1984). Crying and laughing fits sometimes occur in the same patients; other patients show only one of them (Poeck 1969).

By contrast, disturbances in certain regions – neurotransmitter disorders in the basal ganglia in Parkinson's disease – disrupt some emotional behaviors, facial expression in particular. Patients with such disturbance show "mimetic facial paralysis": absence of spontaneous facial expression while retaining the capacity voluntarily to move their facial muscles (see Rinn 1984).

The phenomena of elicited behavior – and their counterparts in lesion effects – indicate various points of interest for the study of emotion.

First, many elementary behaviors, facial expression included, are evidently laid down at subcortical levels; some even in the lower brain stem. They thus must be considered unlearned behaviors. Also, regulation of these behaviors is different from that of voluntary behavior. That latter fact is evident in particular from the mimetic facial paralysis just mentioned and from its converse, "volitional facial paralysis": retention of spontaneous expression with paralysis of voluntary movement. Volitional facial paralysis occurs with lesions of the cortical portion of the motor pathway from cortex to brainstem (e.g., Monrad-Krohn 1924; see Rinn 1984).

Second, the phenomena discussed show that there exist different levels of organization of the emotional and motivational behaviors concerned. At more central levels they are organized into systems showing adaptive flexibility and involving sensory receptive arrangements; also, subjectively their activation is accompanied by feelings and sense of urge.

Third, evidence was encountered that various behavioral systems are neuroanatomically distinct. Some appear distinct that behaviorally might not be unambiguously separated, as for instance defensive, predatory, and intermale aggression (Moyer 1971); others are more closely related than emotion theory might have supposed, such as escape and defensive attack (variants of fear and anger), which together constitute "affective defense" (Hess 1957; Gray 1982), and those behavior aspects subsumed under "desire" or "expectancy" in Panksepp's (1982) view.

7.3. Activating mechanisms

One of the recurrent issues in the psychology of emotion is the relationship between emotional phenomena and those of behavioral intensity. In preceding chapters we discussed the notions of arousal and activation, and the question of whether the phenomena warrant a unidimensional concept. We thought fit, from a descriptive perspective, to make a number of distinctions (section 3.9). Neurophysiological investigation likewise necessitates the distinction of several different activating systems related to different behavioral or physiological phenomena.

The classical system held responsible for the phenomena of activation is the midbrain reticular formation. Stimulation of that structure causes awakening in a sleeping animal, behavioral and autonomic orienting responses, and desynchronization of the EEG (Magoun 1958; Lindsley 1951). Destruction of the reticular formation tends to render the animal comatose, or to cause EEG synchronization, or both. The reticular formation is activated, under normal circumstances, by stimulus change or informative input generally, that is, by novel stimuli, by interruptions of behavior, or by stimuli conflicting with expectations. In turn, it is held to facilitate processing of sensory information in the cerebral cortex and to activate autonomic arousal response and behavioral alertness by way of mechanisms in the anterior hypothalamus. Routtenburg (1968) interprets the function of the system of which the reticular formation forms a part to be regulation of general response readiness or "drive." Pribram and McGuinness (1975) reserve the term *arousal* for this system; they consider its function to be that of interrupting ongoing behavior, ensuring registration of events in awareness, and instigating cognitive assimilation – the formation of "neuronal models."

Wakefulness and EEG desynchronization, and behavioral responding generally, do not uniquely depend upon an intact reticular formation, however. Reticular lesions do not always render an animal comatose; lesioned animals may still show low-voltage fast activity in the EEG, and they may still be capable of performing complex behavioral tasks. Also, animals may be rendered unresponsive by other lesions, with reticular formation untouched. Lesions in the posterior hypothalamus, for instance, may produce lethargic animals that when aroused by stimuli, settle down to sleep again as soon as they can (see Routtenberg 1968 for references on all these points). Damage to the major midbrain catecholamine pathways – the dopaminergic nigrostriatal system and the dorsal noradrenergic system – likewise tends to cause lethargy or hypersomnia (Jouvet 1972).

Evidence of the kind mentioned points to a second activating system, called "arousal two" by Routtenberg and "activation" by Pribram and McGuinness. Its function, according to the latter authors, is the preparation of response mechanisms, in terms of both maintaining expectations and establishing somatomotor readiness; it is activation of intentional directedness, of tonic, vigilant readiness, as well as of specific intentional actions. The system comprises the dopaminergic nigrostriatal pathway just mentioned and the basal ganglia that are known to be involved in the organization of voluntary movement, in active postural readiness, and in the organization of need-related behaviors such as feeding and drinking. The system includes all or part of the lateral hypothalamic locations whence appetitive behaviors can be elicited (see section 7.2). As will be recalled, there is evidence that such elicitation involves activation of response systems prepotent because of stimuli or the subject's history. Pribram and McGuinness also call this system the "go" system.

The dopaminergic nigrostriatal pathway, as the name implies, leads into the striatum and the basal ganglia generally. As said, its destruction causes lethargy. Its mode of proper functioning appears to be the non-specific activation of the basal ganglia, that is, generation of that tonic level of readiness mentioned above. Specific inputs by other routes prepare specific actions upon that tonic background. The dopaminergic pathway, it appears, can produce such unspecific activation because the mode of action of dopamine in the basal ganglia is neuromodulatory rather than neurotransmitting; that is, it modulates the operation of neural systems subserved by neurotransmitters proper (acetylcholine in this case) (Fuxe, qouted in Pribram 1977).

The distinction made by Pribram and McGuinness between arousal and activation is important in the present context not merely because it has helped clear the air concerning these concepts, but also because separate systems are suggested underlying emergence of emotions proper and motivational behavior or desires: "Arousal," in the sense used by Pribram and McGuinness, activation of a stop-and-see system, is identified with the former, and "activation" with the latter – with action tendencies as we described them, tendencies toward flight and fighting, included among the "activation" states.

Pribram and McGuinness (1975) distinguish a third system involved in the regulation of activity: the "effort" system, centered around the hippocampus. The system is responsible for willful concentration and for the organization of response modes other than those habitual or natural as responses to the stimuli present. These other response modes include behavioral inhibition, and we will further mention the system in that connection. We will also discuss later (section 7.6) the neuro-modulatory hormones, ACTH and corticosteroids, which enhance alertness, probably by sustaining hippocampal functioning.

The activating systems are embedded in complex relationships with other systems from which they receive inputs and which they influence with their outputs. An example is provided by the influences to and from the posterior hypothalamus, which probably can be considered to form part of both the "arousal" and "effort" systems above. As said, lesions in the posterior hypothalamus cause somnolence and lethargy. Its stimulation, by contrast, results not only in sympathetic arousal and EEG desynchronization but also in potentiation of muscle movements, which later effect appears to be independent of the former (Gellhorn 1968). This appears to be the way by which active emotions produce activated behavior. Activity of the posterior hypothalamus is itself a function of feedback from muscles and joints: Curare diminishes that activity and thereby, indirectly, cortical arousal. Muscular activity thus enhances that arousal and sustains itself (Gellhorn 1968). This appears to be the way in which physical exercise exerts its activating, arousing influence.

Other structures than those mentioned are involved in behavioral activation phenomena and in the emergence of emotional response, notably the amygdala and frontal lobes. These structures, in fact, are considered by Pribram and McGuinness to form part of the arousal system. The amygdala is seen as embodying that system's major regulatory mechanisms. We will, however, discuss it under a slightly different heading.

7.4. Evaluation functions

Bilateral destruction of the temporal lobes in monkeys leads to dramatic changes in emotional responsiveness. The monkeys become tame and placid, indifferent to ordinary fear-evoking stimuli such as snakes or strangers, and lose their habitual aggressiveness. At the same time, they may become "hypersexual" – at least animals in captivity do. They lose discrimination of what are and are not appropriate sexual objects; they may try to copulate with, for instance, a cat or a rabbit. Also, they tend to manifest profound orality, compulsively putting every object into their mouth. This "Klüver–Bucy syndrome" (Klüver & Bucy 1937), or major aspects of it, is found also in humans with bilateral temporal lobe damage. Mood in such patients tends to be indifferent, orality can be pronounced, and they may show compulsive, greedy eating; indiscriminate sexual manifestations, without concern for the presence of others, have also been observed (Poeck 1969).

Major features of the syndrome are shown when lesions are restricted to the amygdala and surrounding tissue (Schreiner & Kling 1953). Aggressiveness is lost, in dogs and cats and even in aggressive animals like the lynx. In monkeys and, to judge from the clinical observations, in humans, amygdalectomy seriously impairs sensitivity to social signals. In zoo colonies, amygdalectomized rhesus monkeys lose status in the social hierarchy, particularly because they do not modulate their behavior in accordance with the specific situation (Rosvold et al. 1954). In the wild they become social outcasts, get into unusual social conflicts, and withdraw from the group (Dicks et al. 1969). Amygdalectomized dogs lose their affectionate behavior toward their keepers and thereby deteriorate in all performances reinforced by those keepers' affectionate approval (Fonberg 1981).

As Isaacson (1974) puts it: Amygdalectomized animals, at least in protected surroundings, "seem content with their particular lot." They generally appear unconcerned with unexpected events and hardly react to them (Bagshaw et al. 1972). Fonberg (1981) describes her dogs with dorsomedial amygdala lesions as indifferent and emotionless. Yet such animals are not entirely emotionally blunted. Orienting does occur when stimuli are sufficiently rewarding (Pribram, Douglas, & Pribram 1969), and fear or aggressive response is evoked when events are manifestly important, such as under attack by conspecifics (Rosvold et al. 1954). Amygdalectomized animals continue to react to those unfamiliar events they do react to as if these stimuli remain novel, regardless of repeated presentations (Schwartzbaum et al. 1961).

What seems particularly deficient in animals and humans with temporal lesions is their capacity to regulate motivated behavior in accordance with potentially modifying circumstances. The phenomena called hypersexuality and compulsive eating in particular illustrate this: Animals and patients do not stop where normals would and are blindly subjected to attractive stimuli. Mark and Ervin (1970) present cases of violent aggressive behaviors in response to quite minor provocations, presumably due to temporal damage.

The above data suggest the existence, in intact organisms, of evaluating functions that test events for their hedonic or regulatory relevance and feed activating or inhibiting information to the hypothalamic systems controlling emotional response proper. Pribram and McGuinness (1975), as said, consider the amygdala the major control center of the arousal system that is responsive to changes in stimulus contingencies; and thus it is considered the major control center for emotions proper.

The above description of observations on temporally lesioned subjects emphasized their bluntness and, by inference, the activating effects of the evaluative functions. These activating affects, however, appear to be counterbalanced by opposite, moderating effects, since temporal lesions may result in hypersexuality and orality, as well as emotional bluntness. The amygdala, in fact, contains divisions that in many respects act antagonistically (Kaada 1967; Fonberg 1979). Lesions in some regions produce extremely aggressive, rather than placid, animals (Wood 1958; Fonberg 1979); and whereas electrical stimulation in some amygdala areas elicits arousal and aggressive responses, in others it causes dearousal, fear, or sexual arousal (Ursin & Kaada 1960). In humans, stimulation of amygdaloid nucleus has been observed to produce anxiety (Heath, Monroe, & Mickle 1955; Chapman 1958). Observations on reciprocal effects such as mentioned led Pribram and McGuinness (1975) to postulate the presence of reciprocal controls that, by that reciprocal control, can exert a finely graded regulatory tuning of hypothalamic arousal; this tuning is presumably based upon evaluations of information generated elsewhere.

As said, certain regions of the frontal lobes are considered by Pribram and McGuinness to form part of the "arousal" system, in their sense of the word. Frontal lobe ablation, in monkeys and apes, considerably reduces initiative, persistent goal-directed activities, and aggressive responses to frustration (Jacobsen 1936). Animals with frontal lobe lesions indiscriminately devote attention to all environmental change but are unable to maintain orientation toward future events, as in delayed response tasks (see Rosenkilde 1979 for a review). In humans, frontal lobe lesions result in "drive deficit" (Kleist's term): apathy and loss of interest, initiative, and purposeful control of action when meeting with difficulties (Powell 1979). Mood is indifferent or blandly euphoric. As in animal studies, orienting by irrelevant stimuli is readily evoked and habituates badly. Severe deficits are noted in the actual regulation of activity by plans that the subjects can still state verbally. From these observations, Luria (1973) concludes that "the frontal lobes in man participate directly in the state of increased activation which accompanies all forms of conscious activity." That "increased activation" appears essential for entertaining interests and the more subtle emotions. Luria (1969) in fact describes the frontal lobe syndrome as marked by narrowing of interests and disintegration of higher forms of emotional life. The functions involved appear essential even for more elementary emotions. Prefrontal lobotomy is capable of relieving intractible pain – the subject notices the pain but it does not bother him – as well as severe anxiety and obsessions (Powell 1979), be it at the mentioned costs of apathy, loss of interest, and loss of planning ability.

The frontal lobes, like the amygdala, show functional differentiation. Orbitofrontal lesions in monkeys may lead to increased fear and anger responses (Butter & Snyder 1972) and in humans to severe affective disinhibition, violent outbursts, and gross changes in character. Planning disturbances and apathy mostly occur in lateral lesions (Luria 1969, 1973). Like the amygdala, the frontal lobes can be considered to contain antagonistic, reciprocally acting divisions located in the orbitofrontal and frontolateral regions, respectively (Pribram & McGuinness 1975).

7.5. Inhibitory and regulatory functions

Inhibitions of various kinds are involved in antagonistic, reciprocal controls upon a number of functional systems. One set of these, dual controls of emotional arousal by the reciprocal amygdala and frontal circuits, has been discussed in the preceding section. Other such dual controls are involved in hypothalamic functioning. On the whole, stimulation of the posterior and medial hypothalamus produces predominantly sympathetic response, and that of anterior and lateral hypothalamus predominantly parasympathetic response. For this reason, Hess (1957) and Gellhorn (Gellhorn & Loofburrow 1963) make the distinction between "ergotropic" and "trophotropic" hypothalamic zones, which together determine a shifting balance of control of autonomic functioning. There also appears to exist some reciprocal control of go and stop functions with respect to the appetitive behaviors of feeding and drinking, in part also at the hypothalamic level. Initiation of feeding and drinking is regulated by lateral hypothalamic or adjacent subthalamic mechanisms, and termination of eating and drinking by mechanisms influenced by ventromedial hypothalamic processes; the latter might have to do with inhibition of the pleasures of eating (see Grossman 1979 for a review). There is some evidence that the two stand in mutually inhibiting relationships (see Pribram 1980).

Different from the regulatory tuning of impulse by the reciprocal action of inhibitory and facilitatory mechanisms is the more direct inhibitory control of emotional behavior or impulse as such. Removal of entire cerebral cortex in dogs and cats, as said, produced violent sham rage in response to slight provocations (Bard & Mountcastle 1948). Evidently, the cortex exerts inhibitory influence over underlying structures. Inhibitory control is also manifest in voluntary self-control and in the modifying influence of display rules upon spontaneous facial expressions (Rinn 1984). Weakening of cortical inhibitory control accounts for disinhibitions – for instance, under the influence of alcohol.

Mechanisms of behavioral inhibition are found in brain stem and limbic structures, as well as in higher cortical structures. Hess (1957) found that stimulation of basal ganglia – caudate nucleus and striatum – interrupted spontaneous activity and caused immobility. Delgado (1975, 1979) observed such stimulation to block ongoing feeding and aggressive behavior, whether such behaviors were spontaneous or elicited by stimulation of other brain structures. According to Delgado, stimulation of specific sites can selectively inhibit given behavior systems. For instance, an animal that is stimulated by a certain electrode placement while eating stops chewing and loses interest in his food or actively rejects it with grimaces of distaste; it does not, however, become immobile. Similarly, a charging bull stimulated at a presumed aggression-inhibiting point will stop charging and start making other movements (Delgado, 1964). Interpretation of these observations in terms of specific inhibitory circuits has been contested, however: Stimulations might, for instance, elicit incompatible behaviors (Valenstein 1973).

Lesions in the septal area lead to hyperactivity in response to elementary startle stimuli like light flashes, sudden sounds, and electrical shocks; startle responses are greatly enhanced in magnitude (Lubar et al. 1970), suggesting normal startle to be under inhibitory control. Hyperactivity is evident also in "septal rage" shown after septal lesions by rats and perhaps by other animal species (Brady & Nauta 1955); septal hyperactivity appears to be only temporary, however.

Stimulation of the hippocampus, like that of certain basal ganglia locations, produces arrest reactions: interruption of ongoing activity and immobility (MacLean 1957; Kaada, Jansen, & Anderson 1953). Hippocampal lesions, by contrast, lead to unstable activity increases. More acts are initiated, more novel events are responded to, responses to unexpected and aversive events are strongly enhanced, but responses lack duration or persistence (Isaacson 1974). Hippocampectomized animals tend to perseverate in trained activities, or in approaches once adopted, when circumstances change. Spontaneous alternation, the tendency to explore regions different from those just visited, is severely impaired (Kimble 1968).

All this suggests some behavioral inhibition function to be impaired under hippocampal and septal damage and thus such a function to be operative under normal circumstances. Such a function would indeed seem to be implicated in other activities affected by hippocampal or septal lesions. These activities include passive avoidance, that is, refraining from approaching an attractive stimulus because of resultant punishment; postponement of responding in "delayed reinforcement learning," where reward is given only if the animal has refrained from responding during a certain interval; and extinction, where the animal must stop responding since reward is no longer coming. All three are impaired (see Gray 1982 for a review). In all three kinds of impairment one might detect a weakness of operation of a "behavior inhibition system" responsive to conditioned punishment or to frustrative nonreward, which is Gray's (1982) hypothesis. The hypothesis equates the operation of this system with the mechanism of anxiety: anxiety as inhibitory response to signals of punishment and frustrative nonreward.

Weakness of inhibition, in the above observations, need not have been caused by damage to inhibitory mechanisms as such; it may have been caused by damage to structures that provide information for inhibitory mechanisms. Such, indeed, is the interesting kind of interpretation advanced by various theories.

The hippocampus appears to be involved in certain cognitive functions, such as memory or the construction of cognitive maps. Behavioral deficits upon hippocampal lesions often have distinct cognitive aspects. For instance, in addition to the deficits mentioned above, hippocampectomized animals appear to fail to make adequate use of information encountered or are slow to do so; they tend to behave as if situations met repeatedly remain novel to them (see O'Keefe & Nadel 1978 and Gray 1982 for reviews). Also, deficiencies are most apparent when the animals are faced with conditions of uncertainty that necessitate shifts in behavior (Isaacson 1974; Pribram and Isaacson 1975). Further, electrical activity in the intact hippocampus suggests that the structure is involved in the detection of novelty and of match and mismatch with expectations (see Pribram & Isaacson 1975 and Gray 1982 for reviews) – types of information of obvious relevance for emotional control.

In Gray's view, as said, a major function of the above system is to command behavioral inhibition and attentional arousal in response to the system's detection of novelty or mismatch. In the view of Pribram (Pribram & McGuinness 1975; Pribram & Isaacson 1975), it is to control immediate response to stimulation to see whether such response is appropriate or whether to instigate other, less dominant response modes. These response modes include inhibition, non-specific defensive readiness – anxiety – and concentration, the organization of voluntary, reasoning-controlled activity. As said, they call the system the *effort* system.

The behavioral inhibition or effort system can exert its functions only if given access to relevant information. Such information, it appears, might well come by way of anatomically connected areas, particularly the cingulate cortex, which is included in the system both by Gray and by Pribram and McGuinness; in fact the hippocampus and cingulate cortex are the major structures composing the "Papez circuit," which Papez (1937) proposed as responsible for emotion. At any rate, stimulation of the cingulate cortex produces signs of emotional excitement: heart rate changes, pupillary dilation and hair erection (Smith 1944). Lesions, by contrast, result in "tameness" and loss of emotional responsivity; aggressive responses after frustration disappear (Brutkowski & Mempel 1961). Lesioned monkeys display no grooming activity and no affectionate behavior toward their companions. They treat humans and other monkeys as inanimate objects, sit upon them, and bump into them. They do not fight and do not try to escape when given the opportunity; they generally act as if unable to forecast the emotional consequences of their own actions (Smith 1944; Ward 1948).

Lesions of the cingulate cortex appear to cause loss of impetus to do anything about aversive events and to reduce response to signals of forthcoming stressors (Gollender 1967). In humans, cingulectomy is performed in cases of severe intractable pain, severe anxiety states, obsessional behavior, and rage attacks (Le Beau 1952; Powell 1979). Pain is still felt but does not appear unduly to bother the patient. The effects of cingulectomy have been interpreted as due to interference with generation of predictions concerning external events and the intended consequences of the subject's own actions, possibly on the basis of information provided by other cortical centers (Gray 1982).

7.6. "Feeling" and mood

As said, electrical stimulation of hypothalamic sites can elicit appetitive behaviors such as feeding, drinking, copulation. Such stimulation is probably pleasant to the animals since usually the locations from which these behaviors are elicited also support intracranial self-stimulation (ICSS): The animal, given the opportunity, will learn to press a lever that turns the current on, and will then do so avidly, often at high rates and for extended lengths of time (Olds 1962). "Rewarding" sites are found all through the midbrain and limbic system; highest self-stimulation rates are obtained in the lateral hypothalamus, in or near the medial forebrain bundle. The nature of the stimulation effects can differ: In the hypothalamus, self-stimulation induces increased heart rate; in the septum, it appears rather to quiet the animal, since heart rate and blood pressure decrease (Routtenberg 1968). Whether all self-stimulation results from the pleasure it evokes is a matter of debate; at some sites, tendency to self-stimulate and aversion to stimulation appear to alternate. In humans, brain stimulation at certain hypothalamic and other sites can produce intensely pleasurable feelings, sometimes of an orgastic nature (Sem-Jacobsen & Styri 1975; Bekhtereva 1969; Heath 1976). Stimulation can sometimes attenuate severe pain (Heath 1976). The reservation must be made that, in humans, observations of rewarding brain stimulation come only from disturbed patients or from patients in which, as said, it produces relief from pain (Valenstein 1973). Still, the observations support the conclusion that "feeling" can be of entirely central origin, without peripheral or cognitive sources.

Stimulation at hypothalamic or other points that elicit defensive behavior in the presence of suitable objects clearly is unpleasant to the animal. Animals readily learn to "switch off"; that is, they readily learn a response that switches the current off (Nakao 1958). Also, they readily learn to escape and to show passive avoidance (Nakao 1967; Cox 1967). Some stimulations in humans (e.g., amygdaloid nucleus; Heath, Monroe, & Mickle 1955; Chapman 1958) produce anxiety attacks. Anxiety states as well as states of bliss are known to occur in patients with temporal epileptic foci and temporal irritative lesions (Williams 1969).

Mood and "feeling" are probably dependent upon activity of the brain monoamines: norepinephrine, dopamine, and/or serotonin. There appears to exist a relationship between the subcortical catecholamine pathways and self-stimulation sites: As said, these sites are concentrated along the medial forebrain bundle (see Rolls 1975). The locus coeruleus, the place of origin of the dorsal noradrenergic bundle, supports high rates of self-stimulation (Crow, Spear, & Arbuthnot 1972). The correlations are points of debate, however (Rolls 1975). Manipulations of norepinephrine and dopamine neurons, and of these neurotransmitters' metabolism affect self-stimulation rates; the relationships are complex and confused (Routtenberg 1978).

Opinions about the precise function of the monoamines in reward effects differ. Stein (1968) considered the dorsal noradrenergic bundle responsible for "mediating the behavioral effects of reward" – for pleasure signals, that is. This probably is incorrect, since the bundle's destruction does not abolish learning with food, drink, or sex as rewards (see Rolls 1975). More likely is involvement in aversive experience: Stressors lead to increased brain norepinephrine (and other monoamine) turnover (Stone 1983; Stein, Wise, & Belluzi 1975). Gray (1982), upon extensive review of the evidence, considers the function of the dorsal noradrenergic bundle to be conveyance of relevance signals generally; it signals importance, be it because of reward, punishment, or novelty.

Dopamine is clearly relevant for reward experience. Administration of dopamine antagonists removes the effects of elementary rewards upon learning and self-stimulation (Fourezios & Wise 1976). However, dopamine blocking may well affect attention for the stimuli rather than hedonic experience: For instance, destruction of dopamine pathways causes "sensory neglect" with respect to several different sense modalities (Ljundberg & Ungerstedt 1976).

Serotonin may be involved in the transmission of signals related to aversive experience. Stimulation of serotonin pathways or of serotonin turnover elicits signs of fear (Stein, Wise, & Belluzi 1975). Pathway destruction and administration of antagonists diminish response suppression caused by punishment signals; benzodiazepines reverse the effects of pathway stimulation (see Gray 1982, ch. 11, for a review). For these reasons, Gray hypothesizes that serotonin pathways mediate signals of aversive events. Pribram and McGuinness (1975) hold these pathways to convey relevance signals and to serve behavioral interruption and attentional arousal generally.

The brain monoamines, in all likelihood, are involved in depressive mood and perhaps also in depressive illness. Stress, as said, increases their turnover. It has been argued that prolonged stress leads to depletion of either brain norepinephrine in particular (Weiss, Glazer, & Poherécky 1976) or of all three monoamines (Anisman & Zacharko 1982). It can be argued that such depletion occurs particularly, or only, when stress is uncontrollable and coping actions are ineffective, as in the learned helplessness paradigm (Weiss et al. 1976; Anisman & Zacharko 1982; Laborit 1979). Depression thus might be a consequence of monoamine depletion: of norepinephrine, as in Schildkraut's hypothesis (Schildkraut & Kety 1967), of serotonin (Van Praag 1983), or of several monoamines together, including brain epinephrine (Roth 1983). Alternatively, or complementarily, depressive mood could be due to neural overstimulation caused by the enhanced neurotransmitter turnover (Stone, 1983). The relationship between depressive mood and illness and monoamine depletion or turnover is largely conjectural and a subject of controversy. Yet a relationship between them – and mood generally – and the monoamines is quite likely, considering the effects of mood-altering drugs upon monoamine metabolism or transmission. Amphetamine, with its activating and euphoric effects, is a catecholamine agonist; tricyclic antidepressants such as imipramine inhibit monoamine reuptake; monoamine oxidase (MAO) inhibitors, which facilitate monoamine neurotransmission, have antidepressant effects; both amphetamine and MAO inhibitors facilitate self-stimulation; drugs such as reserpine that disturb monoamine metabolism can cause serious depressed states.

Of probably considerable importance in the processes underlying "feeling" and mood are the endorphins. Endorphins are opiate-like substances present in the brain and elsewhere; they are excreted particularly during stress. They have potent affective properties. Certain endorphins produce pleasurable experience or euphoria, as does morphine; rats learn to self-stimulate for met- and leu-enkephalin (Belluzi & Stein 1977), and these substances appear to be addictive, again like morphine. Administration of beta-endorphin blocks pain sensitivity or, at least, pain experience (Snyder & Childers 1979), and decreases pain-related reflexes (Belluzi et al. 1976); the beta-endorphin antagonist naloxone enhances these reflexes (Fanselow & Bolles 1979). Other endorphins have narcoleptic, calming effects: Gamma–endorphin and derivatives speed up extinction of conditioned avoidance (De Wied et al. 1978); the derivative DT-gamma-G induces grid clasping, like haloperidol does. These effects might be due to attenuation of aversive experience. In fact, Wise (1982) advanced an "anhedonia hypothesis" to account for the effects of narcoleptics: These substances might moderate negative hedonic tone as mediated by dopamine pathways; by inference, the hypothesis might hold for gamma–endorphin.

Investigation of the emotional implications of naturally occurring endorphins has scarcely begun. These implications, as said, may be expected to be considerable, particularly in view of their neuromodulatory rather than neurotransmitter mode of functioning.

Neurohumoral substances other than neurotransmitters and endorphins also influence emotional behavior and experience, notably adrenocorticotropic hormone, ACTH. ACTH has been called "the neurohormone which mediates fear" (Jacquet 1980). It influences fear responding: Acquisition and extinction of both active and passive avoidance decrease after removal of the anterior hypophysis, which abolishes ACTH secretion; subsequent administration of ACTH restores avoidance learning (De Wied 1964; Levine & Jones 1965). Mesencephalic and diencephalic implantations of ACTH 4–10 enhance avoidance learning (De Wied et al. 1978; see De Wied 1980). Extinction of appetitive behaviors (performance for food or sex as reward) similarly diminishes when ACTH secretion is blocked and becomes normal again when ACTH levels are restored. ACTH appears to produce the above-mentioned effects centrally: Its administration affects hippocampal electrical activity (Urban & De Wied 1976).

Other hormones that are centrally active are the corticosteroids and testosterone, and in fact all hormones involved in the hypothalamic–hypophyseal–gonadal system. Activation of this system, by direct hormonal manipulation such as testosterone administration (Bermond 1978) or otherwise, facilitates both sexual and aggressive behavior and, presumably, the corresponding emotions of excitement and anger, or irritation (Beach & Holtz 1946; Bermond 1982; Poshilavov 1982); lowered thresholds for irritation, anger, and depressed moods due to hormonal influences are distinctly suggested by the premenstrual syndrome (Parlee 1973; Smith 1975).

Corticosteroids and ACTH have varied effects upon avoidance, fear, and aggression. The behavioral effects of these two are variable and complex (see Leshner 1978, 1983 for reviews). They can perhaps best be accounted for by the hypothesis that they increase attention and intentional readiness and thereby intensify whatever emotional impact the situation carries (Bohus 1975; Leshner 1983). They thus do influence mood, but may not do so directly and specifically: They may well influence mood by increasing sensitivity for the environmental stimuli, and readiness to respond to them. This underscores the complexity of dispositional antecedents of emotion.

The interpretative problems apparent from the above also underscore that the mode of operation of most neurohumoral factors upon mood and "feeling" is unclear and open to various interpretations. That is to say, it is unclear which is the precise process that they affect and that is responsible for the effects upon experience. Do monoamines directly produce "feeling" as one of their effects, or do they affect activation generally, or specific response propensities, and thereby sense of competence? Or do they affect alertness, and thereby stimulus sensitivity? One of the few analyses that goes some way in explaining experience is that of anxiety by Gray, since the activity of the neurophysiological system under concern, the behavioral inhibition system, is assumed to have those cognitive and hedonic antecedents and behavioral consequences that in fact account for the experience; but the hedonic nature of the antecedent remains unexplained and may, indeed, be irreducible.

7.7. Hemispheric differences

It is currently being argued that the two cerebral hemispheres are not equivalent with respect to emotion: The right hemisphere presumably is more emotional than the left at least in right-handed individuals.

There is some evidence to support this notion; Flor-Henry (1979), Campbell (1982), and Kinsbourne and Bemporad (1984) have recently reviewed it. For instance, depressed patients show larger electrodermal responses at the left hand than at the right; epileptic foci in the right temporal lobe produce more mood disturbance than left-sided foci; pain after amputations tends to be felt more intensely left than right (remember that both sensory and motor nerves are crossed). The evidence is decidedly weak. Somewhat stronger is that concerning hemispheric difference in normal subjects with respect to sensitivity for emotional stimuli such as the affective value of voice intonation (e.g., Safer & Leventhal 1977) or of other people's facial expressions; right-hemisphere superiority with respect to the latter was found in 11 studies (Campbell 1982).

It is true that the right hemisphere is superior in many nonverbal tasks; specific superiority in the processing of emotional information is suggested by at least one of these studies (McKeever & Dixon 1981). Experiments with patients with either right- or left-hemisphere lesions have produced conflicting results, although on the whole right-hemisphere damage tends to affect nonverbal emotion recognition tasks more severely than left side damage.

Facial expressions tend to be more pronounced on the left side of the face than on the right side, suggesting more intense involvement of the right hemisphere (Sackheim, Gur, & Saney 1978), but the finding applies more generally to facial gestures than to true facial expressions (Ekman, Hager, & Friesen 1981). To the extent that it applies to facial expression proper – and does not reflect general dominance of left-side facial mobility (Campbell 1982) – it might indicate more pronounced left hemisphere inhibition rather than right-hemisphere emotionality: Facial expressions proper are of subcortical origin (Rinn 1984).

Another suggestion is that of qualitative emotional difference between the hemispheres; there are various pieces of evidence on this score, also reviewed by Flor-Henry (1979), Campbell (1982), and Kinsbourne and Bemporad (1984). The right hemisphere appears more inclined to sad or depressed mood, the left to euphoric mood. For instance, right-sided electroconvulsive shock appears to be more effective in lifting depression than left-sided shock (Galin 1974); and left-sided brain damage tends to produce sad mood, whereas right-sided lesions rather tend to lead to emotional flatness or jollity (Gainotti 1972). Interpretation of the findings is quite complex, though, and findings have not always been replicated (Campbell 1982). Still, the evidence is suggestive and converging (see also Fox & Davidson 1984). An interesting hypothesis has been advanced by Kinsbourne and Bemporad (1984). According to this hypothesis, the left frontal area subserves action control, or "activation" in Pribram and McGuinness's sense; lesions therefore lead to apathy and incompetence with respect to action planning, with depression as a secondary result. The right frontal area is considered to serve emotion control, or "arousal," and the evaluation of emotionally relevant information (see also Tucker 1981); lesions therefore lead to either inappropriate and undercontrolled affect or indifference.

8. Regulation

8.1. Regulation phenomena

The notion of regulation

Emotions have been described in the preceding chapters as changes in action readiness elicited by meaningful events. The individual, we said, is confronted with events; these events are appraised with respect both to their concern relevance (primary appraisal) and to the coping actions they do or do not allow (context evaluation, secondary appraisal); action readiness change – impulse – follows from the event as appraised; response is then selected from the available response repertoire; response, if one is possible, aims at affecting or maintaining the relation between individual and event and at maintaining, changing, advancing, or forestalling the event's effects.

However, this description is incomplete. People not only have emotions, they also handle them. They take a stance toward their emotions and the consequences of their emotional actions. They like them or they do not like them. They take action accordingly. They may do so while the emotion is in progress; or anticipatorily, before it occurs. These actions interact with their emotions: They shape the emotions and are part of them.

Emotions are subject to regulatory action throughout all phases of the emotion process as just sketched. There is regulation of confrontation with events: Emotional events are sought and avoided. There is appraisal regulation: Appraisals can be modified within a considerable range by selective attention and self-serving congnitive activities. There is impulse control: Emotional urges can be suppressed so as to disappear from consciousness as well as from behavior, and they can be amplified. Overt response can be checked, or attenuated, shaped, or replaced by some other response.

401

Thus, emotions are handled. *Handling* has overtones of involving voluntary action and planning. That is not what is meant. Regulation of emotion is not always voluntary; it mostly is not. The stance taken toward one's emotional experience or response is mostly involuntary, and so are the reactions instigated by that stance. *Regulation* therefore refers to all processes that have the function of modifying other processes – actions, experiences – instigated by a given stimulus situation.

Regulation implies a duality of activity that regulates and activity that is being regulated. There is a problem here. The notion assumes readiness for a response that is not forthcoming, or not fully so, or more vigorously than corresponds with that readiness; and it assumes some process to which that incomplete or exaggerated manifestation is due. Two unobservable processes are invoked to explain one single manifestation. In the event, two unobservables are even invoked to explain no manifestation at all: An animal merely sits motionlessly, or a person continues with his work as usual after receiving some important news.

The duality implied by the notion of "regulation" sometimes is readily apparent in subjective experience or in behavior. In self-control, an upsurge of impulse is felt, followed by intent to suppress; or a violent movement unexpectedly stops. More generally, however, regulatory processes are invoked not to explain obvious duality, but inconsistencies. Discrepancies can be observed between different behavior signs: The animal, while motionless, is yet highly tense and alert. Or discrepancies exist between feelings reported and behavioral signs: A trembling subject denies feeling anxious. Or discrepancies occur between behaviors or feelings at different times: Anger is absent or moderate at one moment but shows up when sources of possible punishment are removed or when the subject is under the influence of alcohol. Notable with respect to inconsistencies among feeling is what has been termed "middle knowledge" (Weisman 1972). In fatally ill patients, for instance, doubt and depression, or just realistic assessments, may break through their optimistic mood and denial of the gravity of the condition.

Inconsistencies can also be found between the content of thoughts or feelings and that of fantasy or dreams. Anxiety or anger themes may appear in fantasy and dreams when such themes are absent in the subject's direct preoccupations with given events (e.g., Fenz 1964, Fenz & Epstein 1968, who studied such discrepancies in novice parachutists).

If regulation is assumed to be involved in inconsistencies as described, it is only logical to assume that such regulation may also have occurred when there is no trace of inconsistency. Inconsistency may be considered to result from regulation that slips, which is only partly successful in its endeavors to control. Indeed, completely successful regulation is often assumed when a subject shows unbroken cheerfulness in the face of misfortune, balanced mood, or denial of appreciable impact. There exists what Lazarus and Alfert (1964) called "short-circuiting of threat" or of harm. The reasons for assuming regulation under those conditions still are good, or can be. They consist of inconsistency between the individual's response and the response that "should" have occurred, given the stimuli known to be present or the information known to be available to the subject.

Generally speaking, assumption of regulation – successful regulation in particular – is based either upon knowledge of the "history of the process" (Lazarus 1966, whence this discussion is borrowed) or upon a theory, a model of animal or of human functioning. Unfamiliar stimuli elicit attention, important news elicits upset, threat evokes fear, humiliation evokes anger: If any of these does not appear, something must have made it so. Such models are fallible, of course, but they serve as good heuristics, theoretically as well as in practice. If someone does not show anger after humiliation, do not take that at face value. Ask where the anger has gone. Quite often it can be shown to have gone somewhere; that is, some behavioral inconsistency still shows up.

The duality between processes that regulate and processes that are being regulated is of general psychological significance. It does not merely represent the fact that two processes are often involved in shaping one response. It reflects a general and basic duality in the principles governing behavior and in the way the system that produces that behavior is built. On the one hand, there are primary instigators of response; on the other hand, there is some provision for controlling that response and for keeping it in check. This general duality is expressed in the very notion of "self-control" and in the traditional opposition between Emotion and Reason; or in that between the Pleasure and Reality Principles. The problem for psychology is, of course, to determine what Self, Reason, and Reality are, and how they operate.

It can be argued that the duality reflects a duality, not in the system, but in the external contingencies of reinforcement with which the system is faced. Actions can have both rewarding and aversive consequences. Skinner (1953) has emphasized this duality for explaining self-control. The opposition between Emotion and Reason, he argues, or between Pleasure and Reality, is nothing but that between short-term reward and long-term punishment – or later larger reward, for that matter.

However, these contingencies by themselves do not explain the facts of regulation. These facts are that processes – actions, thoughts – are often suppressed, attenuated, or modified before they arise or during their execution. This means that evidently the human and animal system is so designed that it can intervene in the execution of its own processes. It is capable of inhibition and of replacing a given process by another one when this appears to be more appropriate. The facts of caution, emotion handling, self-control, and following Reason are thus outgrowths of this general capability: intervention in the execution of one's own processes.

To intervene effectively in the execution of its own processes, the system must be capable of process monitoring. We encountered the notion before when discussing action tendency (section 2.8). With respect to regulation, it means two things. First, it means outcome monitoring: The system must know and heed the outcomes of its planned or executed actions, because that is the function of regulation. Regulation serves to regulate outcomes of the regulated processes. Inhibition serves to avoid adverse consequences of action; defensive denial serves to reduce discomfort brought about by cognitions. Second, regulation means action monitoring: The system must know what it does or plans to do before it can infer the outcomes of what it does or plans to do, and before it can take appropriate regulatory action. In the phrasing given by Gray (1982): Inhibition involves predictions about the outcomes of motor programs and assessment of failures of these programs to produce expected reward, or of the fact that they have produced punishment.

Of course, action and outcome monitoring are in no way peculiar to emotion. However, puzzles emerge because sometimes outcomes are avoided before they are known: In defensive denial and repression the subject is not supposed to know what he denies or represses, because that is what defensive denial and repression are meant for. We will return to it.

Regulation does not proceed in an inhibitory or attenuating direction only. It also proceeds in augmenting fashion. As said, responses can be enhanced over and beyond what actual emotional stimuli instigate. They are enhanced in view of favorable consequences. While crying from pain or misery, the subject may look out of the corner of his eye to watch the effect. One can prolong or seek pleasurable stimulation; one can dwell upon grievances and get madder and madder. There is full symmetry here between attenuation and enhancement.

The symmetry extends to all phases of the emotion process. Stimulation can be sought as well as avoided. Appraisals can be made better, to shield oneself, and they can be made worse, to steel oneself, or to be prepared for the worst. Emotional impulses can be checked, and they can be "psyched up." "Feeling management" (Hochschild 1983) has the power to do both. Behavior can be inhibited and willfully controlled, and it can be put on. "Display rules" (Ekman 1973) and impression management in the presentation of self (Goffman 1959), too, have the power to do both.

This possibility of two-way regulation, of getting more as well as getting less, poses the problem of how to distinguish between what is the primary response being regulated and what is due to regulation that attenuates or augments. Theoretically, the distinction is relatively clear: Regulatory processes are outcome-controlled, whereas processes to be regulated are not, or not to the same degree. In practice, and for the subject himself, however, the problem can be serious. The subject is faced with obscure questions: How necessary, how sincere and how true was my response, how inescapable, uncontrollable my emotion? To what extent was it outside my responsibility?

In fact, it is for these reasons that phenomenologically oriented theorists like Solomon (1976, 1980) regard emotions as outcomes of choices. To some extent they are right. They are not right to the extent that regulation has limited power in the face of direct impact of events, although these limits are yet to be determined.

Ubiquity of regulation

Regulation is an essential component of the emotion process. Emotion – outwardly manifest emotion, but equally emotion as experienced – is to be considered the product of excitation of action tendency on the one hand and of inhibition of that same action tendency on the other. What is observed or felt depends upon the balance between these two.

The emotion system should be viewed as a system governed by dual, reciprocal control. Dual control is rather usual in biological systems. It is found in movement control by the simultaneous action of antagonistic muscles, in autonomic response in the interplay of sympathetic and parasympathetic activity, in hormonal response, to name a few instances. Evidently, dual control permits finer tuning than does single-graded excitation.

Evidence for dual control of emotional response, and thus for the ubiquity of regulation, can be found at various levels and in various domains of phenomena. Neurophysiological evidence was discussed in the previous chapter: the general control exerted by neocortical mechanisms and the attunement of emotional arousal by the reciprocal circuits in the amygdala and frontal lobes. Note that neocortical control, too, is dual. Removal of cortex may both disinhibit and enhance indifference. Duality is present in many arrangements. For instance, cortical arousal upon arrival of unfamiliar stimuli does not arise from those stimuli exciting the reticular formation; rather, it comes from the hippocampus temporarily loosening its inhibitory hold upon reticular activity (Lindsley & Wilson 1975).

As for behavior, emotional behavior shows a continually shifting balance between letting go and restraint (section 2.4). Restraint is almost never entirely absent; and there is continuous vigilance as to whether is might be needed. Degree of restraint is a function of a variety of situational factors such as risks of retaliation in anger or of inflicting undue damage. This is so even in animals. Anger in an irritable dominant male chimpanzee fails to appear when the irritation comes from an infant tugging the male's fur (Van Lawick-Goodall 1972). Also, attack, both angry and predatory, is usually graded in form, scope, and timing in relation to the nature, location, and actions of opponent or prey.

The fact that all normal emotional response is dampened, graded, and monitored is highlighted by what happens when all that is absent – in panic, frenzy, or blind rage. As argued in chapter 2, panicky flight and normal fearful escape differ not merely in intensity; they differ also in feedback regulation of behavior, which in these blind responses is lost. Ubiquitous emotion control under normal circumstances is further evident from the increase in intensity of some emotional responses as a function of exhaustion, prolonged stress, or illness; presumably, these general conditions affect inhibitory potential. We refer here to the complex of enhanced irritability, anxiousness, and sentimentality, of enhanced startle responses and diminished concentration and pain tolerance. Alcohol intoxication produces similar changes, together with loss of restraint with respect to gaiety, violent anger, and expression of sexual desire. In all this, not only manifest, overt behavior is affected: Anxiousness, irritation, gaiety, anger, and sexual desire as experiences and impulses are more readily evoked or more intense. Presumably these same impulses are potentially there, but controlled, under normal conditions.

The ever-presence of inhibitory control is suggested also by the strong impact of sudden, unexpected events. Evidently, suddenness prevents the preparatory instigation of control measures. The particular impact of suddenness appears from some evidence of stronger response to unsignaled than to signaled electric shock (see section 5.6); this evidence gave rise to the "preception hypothesis" implying inhibitory preparation (Lykken et al. 1972). The evidence for weaker response has been contested (Furedy & Klajner 1974), but tendency to prefer signaled aversive events over unsignaled ones is unmistakable, as is that to prefer certainty regarding the time at which they may strike and to be given appropriate warning intervals (Monat, Averill, & Lazarus 1972). All this is presumably because watchfulness can take controlling measures. The generality of preparatory control measures is also evident from the fact that startle responses are considerably stronger after unsignaled than after signaled intense stimuli. Anecdotal evidence and intuition of course are in line with this: One tends to lead up slowly to delivering shattering news.

Furthermore, situational tolerance, intolerance, appropriateness, and the like produce distinct variations in emotional intensity; the variations do not appear to concern manifest behavior only. Sexual excitement, one can observe, is conspicuously weak under public conditions such as nudist beaches or pornographic stage shows, unless the general mood invites participation. Sorrow tends to mount, or to return, when one is among sympathetic listeners. Anger, of course, is highly sensitive to anger tolerance in the social environment. Acts of communal violence, as in lynch mobs, are explained in part by disinhibition through such tolerance and in part by decreased self-monitoring, decreased awareness of what one plans and does and what the outcomes will be (Diener 1980; see section 8.6).

Finally, we venture to adduce a Freudian argument for the conclusion that inhibitory regulation is ever-present in emotional response. Emotional language and fantasy often are considerably more violent than the emotions felt when using the language or indulging in the fantasy. "I could have killed him" can be spoken or thought, laughingly and without any impulse to kill, then or at any other time; people often have fantasies of cruel revenge, or of sexual assault, or of endless disputes with people who have slighted them, often without much accompanying affect. We venture to hold that language and fantasy recognize the impulse behind the inhibition and speak truly for it. Note that inhibition in these examples has nothing of the neurotic or conflict-ridden about it. It is merely normal not to kill, and not even to wish to kill, a person who has merely slighted one; still, the thoughts were in one's words or fantasies, and could be taken seriously. Freud may well be right in emphasizing the murderous, violent, lascivious nature of the "unconscious," that is, of impulses before they are subjected to immediate, regulatory, realistic inhibition.

One may hypothesize, then, that regulatory processes are constantly present, constantly modulating, permitting emotional impulse to come through in various degrees rather than suppressing impulses after the fact, in the manner of hippocampal control over reticular arousal. It may also be that emotional impulse as evoked by relevant stimuli potentially always is of maximal intensity, regardless of realistic or moralistic considerations; this impulse is toned down by inhibition, as a permanent stabilizing counterforce governed by reality and morality. Sham rage, Mark and Ervin's observations on unrestrained anger (section 7.4), enhancement of startle response after septal damage and hippocampectomy (section 7.5) and when a stimulus is unexpected, the Freudian reflections, irritability after stress and under alcohol – all suggest that such maximal impulse propensity lurks behind inhibitory control.

8.2. Instigation of regulation

Regulation has been defined above as occurrence of processes the function of which is to modify other processes – actions, experiences – elicited by the given situation. Such modifications consist of attenuation, enhancement or, in the event, transformation.

The outcomes of regulatory processes are of two general kinds. We may assume achievement of these outcomes to be the function of these processes, and we may assume that signals that such outcomes might be desirable or can be achieved form their instigation. The first kind of outcome regards the consequences of behavior: reduction of adverse consequences or increase in favorable ones. The second concerns the nature of emotional experience as such: reduction of discomfort and disturbance or increase of comfort and pleasure. The first of these kinds of outcome, by and large, is the domain of inhibition and self-control, the second that of intrapsychic coping, of appraisal change.

Regulation of behavior and impulse

Behavior, emotional behavior included, can bring about adverse consequences of various sorts – in the first place, nonreward and punishment. Nonreward results when unrestrained emotional action and uncontrolled execution of motivational behavior produce suboptimal action. One runs the risks of stumbling when fleeing too hastily and of seeing the alerted object of desire escape before being caught; keeping a poker face likewise serves to avoid alerting others who might take advantage. There also is nonreward consequent upon approach–approach conflict: Gaining one thing may mean losing another. Punishment results when the environment retaliates, envies, disapproves, or despises because of emotions shown.

These external outcomes have their internal counterparts in the calls of conscience and the sense of propriety. Norms of behavior and rules of conduct underlying calls of conscience and propriety can be more or be less internalized; their regulating powers can be more or be less dependent upon the actual presence of others. As a consequence of internalization, regulation may come to affect mere feeling and impulse, even in the absence of action of any kind. Mere feeling and impulse can evoke shame, guilt feeling, and fear of the opinion of others.

The positive consequences of emotional action include those of impression management (Goffman 1959): acceptance, respect, approval, submission, help. Crying can elicit help, and anger conformity to one's desires. The benefits can be subtle. Anger may elicit counteranger, which then serves as an excuse for one's various further sentiments and actions.

As said, regulatory processes are instigated by signals that any of these outcomes is likely to occur. These signals are in part stimuli actually present – either external ones or ones coming from one's own action or impulse. To the extent that this applies, regulation is under stimulus control; this in turn implies that to that extent regulatory response is emotional response just like the response it regulates. There exist situational meaning components that correspond to the call for inhibition, restraint, or reticence and components that correspond to the call for letting go of or shedding prudence or civility. These situational meaning components correspond to the instigations, response-dependent threats, when those appear invested with "urgency" (see section 4.4).

Emotions resulting from those aspects and features of situational meaning structure are anxiety or caution or considerateness; but any of these may just dissolve into attenuation or disappearance of the emotion that is controlled. Such attenuation or disappearance is itself emotional, in the sense that it has control precedence to the same degree that an anxiety response such as freezing has. One cannot lose civility at will, nor shed modesty when stimuli in the environment do not cooperate; and when one is forced to, control precedence immediately manifests itself in strong discomfort. In the same vein, there exists emotion-enhancement emotion: mass-behavior-instigated enthusiasm that amplifies devotion, cheering, fleeing, or killing.

When actual stimuli and urgency are absent, mere thoughts and anticipations can signal desirability of regulation; they may instigate voluntary self-control. Voluntary self-control and restraint stand to inhibition as well-considered avoidance stands to fear.

Regulation of experience and arousal

There are, as said, endeavors to reduce the discomfort and disturbance caused by emotional response itself. In coping with stress, one must deal with those aspects of emotion as well as with the stressor itself. Lazarus and Folkman (1984) make the distinction between "emotion-focused coping" and "problem-focused coping"; emotion-focused coping is often the only resource remaining.

The discomforts and disturbances of emotion are several. Lazarus and Launier (1978) list three main categories. The first includes the painfulness of emotions such as anxiety, guilt, or grief per se. The second includes interference with task performance, both with respect to problem-focused coping – efforts toward escape, attack, control, observation – and with respect to other tasks the subject may, or must, be engaging in; emotions can affect thought efficiency, concentration, and motor performance (section 2.12). The third category includes the discomforts and disturbances caused by physiological responses – sweating, trembling, shortness of breath. The discomforts and disturbances of the second and third kinds occur under positive as well as negative emotions. Careless driving can result from exuberance and the driver's thoughts being elsewhere. Attempts at reduction of discomfort and disturbance thus are undertaken not merely for hedonic reasons. They may be vital: One has to pilot one's ship on fire, or one has to take care of the children.

Lazarus and Launier (1978) refer to activities to reduce discomfort and disturbance as "palliative endeavors." They distinguish four modes: information seeking, intrapsychic coping, inhibition of action, and direct action. "Information seeking" refers to selectively seeking information that supports a favorable appraisal of events. "Intrapsychic coping" is defined as "cognitive processes designed to regulate the emotion by making the person feel better, in short, things a person says to himself or herself and forms of attention deployment such as avoidance" (Lazarus and Launier 1978, p. 317). "Inhibition of action" refers to response suppression and self-control; "direct action" refers primarily to seeking distraction and help or taking actions like consuming alcohol or taking tranquilizers.

"Intrapsychic coping," as said, refers to cognitive processes designed to obtain a more supportable appraisal of stressful events. These processes are not necessarily "palliative" in a strict sense. There exists cognitive activity designed to cope with unalterable loss, harm, or threat, and to continue functioning without bogging down, while still fully experiencing their impact. Such activity will be called *constructive reappraisal*.

As to the advantages of emotion enhancement, those of comfort and pleasure are obvious. Enhancement of discomfort and disturbance, too, can have advantages: Discomfort and disturbance offer excuses. They can serve in moral blackmail: Who wants to make you suffer so? They disinculpate, since you already suffer; they satisfy self-pity. All these are daily occurrences that account for stronger grief, more intensely being hurt, more shame, more feeling of loneliness than are absolutely necessary. The mechanisms of feeling enhancement are roughly the same as those of palliation, as will be clear in later sections.

Social sources of regulation

Much of regulation is of social origin; that is, it is instigated by social repercussions, disapprovals, and approvals, or by social norms acting through the sense of propriety and feelings of shame and guilt.

It bears emphasizing that not all regulation is of social origin. That which comes from desire for optimal performance is not; nor that which comes from the desire to know what one is doing and where one is going – general caution and wish to be the master of one's actions; nor those regulatory processes that aim at reduction of discomfort and disturbance or at enhancement of feelings and that are primarily motivated by direct hedonic and pragmatic considerations. Nor is all social restraint of social origin in the sense defined above: Considerateness, restraint instigated by unselfish emotions generally, are to a large extent independent of social disapproval or approval and of social custom (see section 6.3).

To a very great extent, however, regulation of emotion does flow from social sources. These sources consist in part of the interests of others and the norms of social interaction: Others often do not want to be bothered; revenge usually is supposed not to take on bloody forms; and so on. In part these sources consist of the expression display rules (Ek-man 1973) and feeling rules (Hochschild 1979; 1983) of the society: Boys don't cry; grief should not be too loud; upon loss of a parent one should mourn and one is expected to feel grief. Display rules and feeling rules are of all sorts of specificity: They can be particular to a given culture, a given social class or role, a given interaction context or response mode, a given individual relationship. Englishmen show expressive reticence; civilized people behave in civil fashion; pastors behave with dignity; superiors are to be treated respectfully, and their reproaches to be taken with humility and gratitude; boys, as said, don't cry.

Many of these rules are merely implicit, for the individuals concerned, and only manifest in sense of propriety or shame. Often they are overtly expressed, though, and explicitly acknowledged: "You don't have a right to feel jealous, given our agreement" and "You shouldn't feel so guilty, it wasn't your fault" are two quotations from Hochschild's (1979, p. 564) interviews. Rules apply, as said, to feelings as well as to expression or behavior. In certain social groups, one should not feel jealous; in certain others, one should. In certain cultures one should deeply feel offense to honor, and is a coward when one does not; in others the concept of honor is almost nonexistent. The various rules are often explicit to the degree of being codified in books of etiquette (Granet 1922; Elias 1939). And of ethics. The fifth commandment, the injunction to honor your father and your mother, is a feeling rule as much as a rule for behavior; and a feeling rule that enjoins one to feel respect as well as not to feel disrespectfully.

Feeling rules are so deeply embedded in social relationships that they are part of social exchange, as Hochschild shows. Certain other people are entitled to be the object of certain feelings on your part: love, grat-itude, or respect – even anger, if they are to obtain proof of being taken seriously. Of course, being entitled does not imply that one is in fact given what one is entitled to; but as Hochschild's interviews make clear, people do try hard to oblige and, presumably, often succeed.

Some rules are quite general in a given culture. In Western culture, an ethic of control of emotion and impulse prevails – probably still does, sexual revolutions notwithstanding – that may well be so pervasive that it obscures the proper extent of that control: It may give the illusion of a "natural" state of affairs where there is not. In fact, the entire phe-nomenon of "civilization" can be considered to consist of control of emotion and of natural impulse. Elias (1939) extensively argues this thesis with respect to Western civilization, from the Middle Ages onward; the argument is based upon analysis of historical accounts and etiquette books. Such accounts and books suggest that once such anger was normal as would be considered psychopathic now. Lust in destruction avowed openly then would only be admitted shamefacedly now, on the therapist's couch or among mercenaries. Elias convincingly shows how acts and experiences close to the emotional or belonging to it – spitting, eating with the fingers, bodily contact – were progressively "civilized," suppressed, and channelized. Ample information probably exists concerning emotion and impulse control in other than Western cultures that could substantiate Elias's argument with respect to these points. Emotion theory, based as it is upon studies with contemporary Western subjects, might well underestimate the extent to which emotion is shaped by inhibitory control as determined by social ideology.

Of course, it is difficult to decide to what extent freer modes of feeling and expression resulted from less inhibition or from greater enhancement. When it is proper to enjoy watching torture or to smash the skulls of enemies, there will be more occasion for such enjoyment: Occasions are created, and people will endeavor to see the jolly sides of it, along the general lines of feeling management. And ideology helps appraisal. It is good to see a heretic burn; one does not need to live in the Middle Ages for that. On a more modest scale: just as there existed etiquette books that said not to be loud and exuberant, there were such books that said, "Young men should certainly be gay and lead a joyful life. It does not suit a young man that he be sad and pensive" (quoted by Elias 1939).

Something else, too, characterizes "civilization" according to Elias: increased self-awareness with respect both to emotional response and its reasons and to the reasons for restraint. One questions the justification of one's emotions as well as one's taboos; there is plenty of reason to doubt that the same held for as many people in other times or that it holds for as many people now in other places. As an African subject of Parin and Morgenthaler (1963) phrased it: White man thinks too much. Obviously, such self-awareness and this self-questioning provide continuous readiness, as well as continuous material, for regulations of various sorts. If what Elias and others assert in this respect is true, emotion regulation in different social contexts not only attaches to different impulses or objects or relationships, and not only can be deployed in different social contexts to different degrees. Emotion regulation, it appears, can take on qualitatively different forms: less emphasis upon outright response control, and more upon the conscience that makes cowards – that is, upon intrapsychic coping modes.

In Elias's view, civilization and emphasis upon restraint are consequences of the progressive centralization of economic and political power; progressive centralization vastly increases the kind and number of interactions that individuals are exposed to and the kind and number of strivings for maintaining power and status within the contexts that remain one's own.

Elias may be right, or he may not be. Whether his or a different hypothesis holds, social dynamics and ideologies do not influence emotion or emotion control directly. They do so by way of the feeling and expression rules that the practice of these social dynamics and ideologies generates. These rules, in turn, operate by way of the instigations sketched earlier; these instigations, in their turn, operate largely through what subjects have learned regarding the valuation and other consequences of emotional experience and overt response. That is, they operate through what constitutes the "significance" of emotion, as that term is defined in section 4.8. Significance, as part of experience, arises during and after the fact of responding. Shame, sense of propriety, and inhibition do the work before the fact.

8.3. Major regulatory mechanisms

Several rather different processes are involved in attenuation of emotional response; the same, to some extent, applies to response enhancement. Regulatory processes can be divided into inhibitory mechanisms, outcome controlled processes, and voluntary actions. It will not be easy to assign each regulatory process to one or another of these three kinds; their distinction nevertheless appears to be called for, as they belong to different levels of psychological functioning.

Inhibitory mechanisms

By *inhibitory mechanisms* are meant true prewired automatic mechanisms, like those involved in the startle and freeze reactions. In startle, current activity is interrupted and respiration is briefly blocked; freezing consists of total or near-total immobility. The same mechanism as in freezing is presumably operative in rigidity of movement and deterioration of thought processes in many human anxiety responses. Arrest of information processing can be striking: In a serious blackout, in which an actor onstage has forgotten his lines, he may not hear or understand the prompter's words even when the last row in the theatre does (Beijk, 1968).

According to Gray (1982), anxiety generally is a response of behavioral inhibition coupled to attentional arousal. Behavioral inhibition, as we argued in chapter 2, can be seen as response of prudence, of caution, in view of the possibility of undesirable consequences of unrestrained behavior. Cautious control of behavior generally might result from activity of the behavioral inhibition system, with full-blown anxiety as its more or less unamalgamated manifestation.

Stimuli for behavioral inhibition – therefore for anxiety – according to Gray are novelty, unlearned fear stimuli, nonreward, and conditioned stimuli that signal aversive events. Unconditioned aversive stimuli, by contrast, trigger fear (escape) or anger. This distinction of anxiety and fear stimuli (or of stimuli for inhibition and for defense) is not satisfactory: Too many conditioned stimuli actually elicit defense. Rather, inhibitory stimuli appear to be stimuli, conditioned or not, that signal aversive consequences that may come from unknown locations, or from everywhere, or otherwise permit no coping action.

Inhibition such as described mostly affects the response end of the emotion process. Other inhibitions attack stimulus processing, the front end of the emotion process.

Traumatic events have as one of their major immediate consequences what Horowitz (1976, 1982) calls "denial states." These have been described in quite diverse contexts: after personal loss, disaster, and war events. After disasters, victims are seen wandering aimlessly among the ruins, without tears or overt signs of despair (Tyhurst 1951, cited by Hebb 1970). Parkes (1972), in his study of bereavement, observed in at least half the widows studied that the first reaction to their husband's death had been one of being stunned, a feeling of being dazed, of unreality, extending sometimes to depersonalization, sometimes to unmoved stupor slowly merging into depression.

When told of the death of her husband, Mrs. K. remarked: "Ok, would you give me a cigarette?" She went about her household tasks automatically and her sister thought, "It hasn't penetrated; how awful when she realizes." Mrs. K. said, "I just couldn't believe it. I didn't realize he was not coming back."(Parkes, 1972, p. 134)

Horowitz (1976, 1982) lists among the major properties of denial states: being dazed, selective inattention, inability to appreciate the significance of stimuli, amnesia, nonexperience, loss of realistic sense of appropriateness, constriction of associational width, numbness. The experiential syndrome tends to be accompanied by autonomic upset, particularly bowel symptoms and fatigue, and by frantic overactivity.

Denial states of the kind described resemble states of detachment and depersonalization-like states occurring during severe stress such as very strenuous or dangerous performance or prolonged severe pain, as under torture. People under torture may experience their body as being far away, burning with pain, subjected to maltreatment, and observe or even smile at its antics and those of its torturers: "During this half-hour I only kept thinking: 'So this is how it is, – so that is how it is' I no longer felt any fear. It was as if I was someone else watching himself lying on the floor." "They strike my bare bottom with their truncheons. I almost ceased feeling. I felt no more pain. As if drugged. As under anaesthesia. Only my brain was awake. Curiously awake. I could watch everything in detail. Each stroke I registered quite objectively. Each time the heavy truncheon came down upon my flesh, my body flew to and fro. As if I were made of rubber. In thought I began to accompany the beatings: 'Now this one! That one came home! – And now that one! And one more.' " (Langhoff 1935 [1978, pp. 83, 86]; present author's translation). Experiences like these lead to needle-sharp memories, even 40 years after, in which the ego is seen from the outside, from above, with the observing self as a spider clinging to the ceiling. The depersonalization helps to withstand torture and allows the cool planning of whatever coping action is possible: "When I thought I could stand the beating no longer, I hit upon a good idea. I broke away with my last forces, threw my arms in the air and let myself fall at full length. I ceased moving. They should believe I was dead." (Langhoff, 1935 [1978, p. 86]). Langhoff was a professional actor; note the detached, almost amused ring of "I hit upon a good idea."

About the physiological mechanisms of the above, nothing is known to the present author. Whether they are the same or different from those involved in behavioral inhibition is unclear, but this is unlikely, mind blanking in anxiety notwithstanding: Attention in anxiety would seem to differ from that in numbness, and even more so from that in the detachment response. The latter response would appear to be related to what can happen under sensory deprivation and hypnosis. Sensory deprivation may induce experiences of splitoff of the soul from the body (Hebb 1955); and the hidden observer in hypnosis has the same sort of slightly amused objectivity as the overt observer under pain (see Hilgard

1977). As to denial states, suggestions concerning the psychological process will be given in the next section.

Other inhibitory mechanisms than those described may be operative in emotion regulation. In the preceding chapter mention was made of Bolles and Fanselow's (1980) theory concerning the inhibitory action of fear upon pain and its associated recuperative-action behavior system. That inhibition was hypothesized to operate by way of endorphin release. The hypothesis may be extended to the effects of concentration, or urgent coping requirements generally, upon pain and other emotional experience (Eysenck 1980). Something of the sort may be involved in the well-known phenomenon of rapid efficient action under emergency, with emotional response emerging with violence after the facts, as your car skids or when your child runs across the highway.

Outcome-controlled and voluntary processes

Behavioral inhibition and numbness must be considered stimulus-controlled: They are triggered by relevant stimuli without regard for their regulatory outcomes. These outcomes are gifts of nature; they happen to be brought about by unlearned or classically conditioned responses. Other regulatory processes are outcome-controlled, in the same sense that instrumentally reinforced responses are. They are executed because they were profitable in the past or because they turn out to be profitable now, because favorable events and experiences are perceived to be response-dependent.

Passive avoidance provides a clear example, insofar as it consists of refusal to approach a desirable goal that also caused punishment. Another example is intellectualization of unpleasant events, because intellectualization can be felt to diminish those events' aversive impact.

Outcome-controlled regulation activities are initiated because previous experience has strengthened the tendency to perform them or because actual feedback shows them the way to go. This holds for emotion-enhancing as well as for emotion-reducing operations. Weeping may increase and decrease with the wax and wane of other people's attention.

Outcome-controlled processes such as these merge into voluntary regulation: self-control, and self-regulation generally. In voluntary self-control the desired outcome is clearly anticipated and taken as a goal for action. One may decide to abstain from drinking, or not to get angry during a quarrel, or to put that person or event out of one's mind; and one may decide to enjoy oneself, or to try to love someone, or to psych oneself up.

The distinctions made between various regulations are of some consequence. They try to account for some other differences among regulation phenomena. There are controls that one can lift at will, and others that one cannot. *Inhibition* is the word usually employed for the latter, and *self-control* for the former, with merely outcome-controlled activities somewhere in between. One cannot retrieve sexual excitement at will when unsafe conditions have blocked it, or let come the grief that is choked up in a disturbed process of mourning. Also, there is the difference between regulations in which one is aware of regulation and controlled impulse and others in which one is not: In the latter, there is mere emptiness, or neutrality; one just does not become angry, or happy, or excited.

Admittedly, the dividing lines between the various modes are thin. What appears to the subject as restraint that he might let go may turn out to be inhibition that he cannot shed. And regarding many instances of apparent involuntary denial, one wonders whether the subject did not, in fact, consciously settle upon a convenient mode of seeing that he might easily change if he wished.

Regulatory processes of each of the various modes can affect emotion in each of the phases of the emotion process. Each of those phases can be regulated reflexly by inhibitory mechanisms, by involuntary outcome-controlled processes, and by voluntary action. For the next two sections we will work through the phases of the emotion process, in order to describe the various kinds of regulatory activity. We will first consider stimulus processing, with the phases of stimulus intake and appraisal; these phases correspond to input regulation and intrapsychic coping, respectively. Second, we will consider output generation with its phases of action readiness generation and behavior programming, which phases correspond to impulse control and response control.

8.4. Input regulation and intrapsychic coping

Input regulation

Behaviorists (e.g., Skinner 1953; Kanfer 1980) view regulation as produced by influencing behavior's stimulus control or response control; input regulation is influencing stimulus control. Input regulation is effected by approach and avoidance, by looking and not looking, listening and not listening, and by producing changes in the environment. Fear of spiders can be controlled by meticulously cleaning the house; "family secrets," as in families of ex-concentration camp inmates (H. Epstein 1979) serve to shield against stimuli for traumatic memories.

Many emotions can be avoided or attenuated by avoidant behavior. Jealousy can be fought by breaking contact with the unfaithful or suspected partner; disappointment can be prevented by not running risks. Phobics can forestall their fear by avoiding contact with the phobic object or situation: Agoraphobics can live a reasonably comfortable life when they decide to stay home. Freud (1926) calls such restrictions of free movement space "ego-restriction"; it is one of the "defense mechanisms."

Selective exposure to information, as a means of reducing discomfort, is illustrated by smokers who read less about the dangers of lung cancer caused by smoking than do (or did) nonsmokers (Festinger 1957). Information gathering often serves to reduce the stresses of uncertainty, as was discussed in connection with work of worrying (Janis 1958); it may exaggerate into hypervigilance that compulsively tries to put itself at rest by incessant preoccupation (Janis & Mann 1977).

Complementary to avoidance is seeking distractions, both to relieve distress and to bar the way to distressful ruminations. Joking under stress in part serves this purpose of diversion.

Active regulation of external input and thought is manifest also in selective attention and, particularly, in concentration: focusing upon the tasks at hand and not allowing thoughts of loss or danger to intrude. Concentration is of course part of problem-focused coping, with warding off of disturbing thoughts as a useful spinoff. It often is actively employed for the latter purpose, however, as in burrowing in work to forget one's troubles, or as in fanatic concentration upon what the task demands. Extreme concentration on the days before and day of performance is the major means by which stuntmen manage to emotionally cope with the enormous hazards of their undertakings; of the double function of their concentration they are well aware (Piët, 1986). Of course, for them anxiety not only is discomfort, but is disastrous for performance, and defensive coping an absolute necessity. Anxiety is avoided not by avoiding thinking about relevant aspects of the situation. On the contrary. Concentration meticulously focuses on all dangers and risks involved. It merely cuts off dwelling upon the personal consequences of what might go wrong.

Input regulation was defined above as the set of processes that influence stimulus control. This includes more than approaching and avoiding external stimuli and modifying the environment. Input for emotional response includes self-generated stimuli: thoughts, fantasies, memories. It includes the thoughts that attach to external stimuli. No sharp dividing line can therefore be drawn between input regulation and intrapsychic coping: Regulation of external stimulus input and of thoughts and images are fully equivalent.

Input regulation and intrapsychic coping are emphatically continuous when it comes to stimulus processing. What elicits emotion is the relevance of stimuli, whether external stimuli or thoughts. Assessing stimulus relevance involves internal processes by which the subject links the stimulus to his cognitive dispositions and which from there lead to meaning awareness.

These processes can be interrupted. They are so interrupted automatically and involuntarily in anxiety inhibition and in numbness. In anxiety inhibition, words are heard but not understood. In numbness, the facts of threat or trauma are known but their significance is not realized. After personal loss, it may take weeks before being stunned or dazed, and unmoved pursuance of daily duties, give way to grief. Numbness, as said, may be assumed to be a protective mechanism; it is still more clearly so when it merges into a consciously outcome-controlled process. Often after loss, says Parkes, there are "strong attempts to avoid grieving." There often is a "willing suspension of disbelief," which enables the person to retain the feeling that the partner has not truly gone. "Numbness comes as a blessing," again to quote one of Parkes's subjects. Numbness and slow, gradual dawning of significance have also been observed in children after loss of a parent:

> That evening the children seemed relatively unaffected and for a time were busy playing "London Bridge is falling down." ... During the days that followed Wendy invented two games to play with her father, in both of which she would twirl around and then lie down on the floor. In one she would then quickly stand up with the remark "You thought I was dead, didn't you?" (Bowlby 1980, p. 279)

Intrapsychic coping and defensive appraisal

Lazarus's definition of *intrapsychic coping* was given above (section 2.2). Intrapsychic coping corresponds to constructing situational meaning structure in such a fashion that the situation is appraised more favorably, less harmfully, or more tolerably than the actual state of affairs warrants or imposes in the first place. Such construction is achieved in various ways. Some of these ways involve distortions of reality; others attenuate one's affective relationship with reality; others again modify appraisal without distorting or attenuating anything.

Intrapsychic coping, insofar as it involves distortion of reality or attenuation of affective relationships, was previously referred to by Lazarus (1966) as "defensive reappraisal." The term was not entirely fortunate in that it suggested (though was not intended to mean) that a first nondefensive appraisal is subsequently defensively modified. Such true reappraisals do occur. Grapes are often sour only after unsuccessful attempts to pick them. But it is not what necessarily happens when appraisals differ from what they "should" have been, given the nature of the events and the information accessible to the subject. Often, the more favorable appraisal is there, right from the start. *Defensive appraisal* thus appears to be a more neutral term, which we will retain for this subset of intrapsychic coping strategies and their results.

Denial

Denial is a blanket term used to denote defensive distortions of reality. Extensive discussions of the term and the processes it covers are presented in Breznitz (1983a) and Lazarus and Folkman (1984). The term covers a variety of processes. For instance, in avoidant thinking, aspects of situational meaning structure are simply omitted. The stunted assessment of reality that such omission results in may or may not be truly believed in; it may or may not form the basis for action or inaction, as it does when, for instance, a person with heart complaints does not attend to them and fails to get medical assistance. In other modes, the truth of information is actually denied; or denial affects the information's relevance, its urgency, or one's own vulnerability (Breznitz 1983b).

A general denial strategy consists of assigning low likelihood to certain implications of the events. It cannot happen here, or to me. Credibility and likelihood estimates are easy prey for defensive operations. Friedman, Mason, and Hamburg (1963), for instance, describe how some parents of leukemic children underrate the seriousness of their child's condition, voice false hopes, and believe in the effectiveness of new, untested cures in a way that staggers hospital staff and other parents. Hamburg et al. (1953) described thoughts and behavior of severely burned disaster victims: One of these patients gave a cheerful account of his plans and projects for after release from the hospital. Weisman (1972) extensively reports on the way cancer patients deny or disbelieve their diagnosis or its prognostic implications.

Omissions, denials, and disregard for likelihoods – they lie quite close together – are not restricted to serious life events. Disbelief is frequent when a girl says no upon being propositioned – so much so that propaganda slogans were deemed necessary to bring the issue home. Love affairs may drag on indefinitely because one of the parties simply disregards or reinterprets messages of disinterest or disinclination: "She just wants to hide her true feelings," et cetera.

Denial-like processes can be implicit in behavior and feelings. Conscious thought may accept what implicit presuppositions, feelings, and behavior deny. We gave the illustration of a widow who acts as if her husband is still alive and might come home at any time, always keeps his chair unoccupied, once a month brushes his clothes, and continues to set the table for two (Parkes 1972). Grinker and Spiegel (1945) describe how combat soldiers entertain a feeling of "It can't happen to me," even when seeing others around them die. The same feeling occurs during accidents and disasters, or upon loss, or when the partner announces intent to divorce. The feeling that it can't happen to me, observe Grinker and Spiegel, is most noticeable and sincere in earlier phases of combat duty; it is maintained, but with more cynicism, less conviction, less consistency as time goes on. It dwindles as exhaustion sets in, or as defensiveness becomes dysfunctional: when hope comes back, toward the end of combat duty or of war itself (see the quotation from Dahl, section 5.6). More or less deliberately enacted denial is illustrated by the attitude of indifference and bravado among soldiers, which Grinker and Spiegel interpret as masked depression: As a mask, it is still more or less effective in warding that depression off.

Denial-like process, as said, may be implicit in feelings. Pining is an example: It maintains sense of presence of a lost person, just as do behaviors such as brushing his clothes. Pining, argues Parkes, represents search for the lost object, and abandoning pining means abandoning illusionary hope or sense of presence.

Other defensive appraisal modes

A variety of defensive appraisal modes have been distinguished in the literature: A. Freud (1946), Menninger (1954), Haan (1977), and Vaillant (1977) are major sources; Lazarus and Folkman (1984) offer a critical discussion. We describe a few of these modes since they provide both problems and insights with regard to the psychological processes of emotion regulation.

We mentioned, above, defensive appraisals that attenuate the affective relationship of the subject with the event. The term *detachment* is used to refer to them: There is awareness of the facts of harm, danger, or loss – or even promise – but the sense of personal involvement in them has gone or is weakened. Numbness and depersonalization-like responses are automatic forms of such change; both were described as inhibitory mechanisms and as parts of the denial state response to stress described by Horowitz (1976). *Intellectualization* is a name for detachment when it is achieved more cognitively by coding the event in an impersonal, factual, or harmless manner. Detachment can be achieved voluntarily, as in the experiments by Lazarus and his group briefly referred to in section 5.2.

In the study by Speisman et al. (1964) intellectualizing appraisal of a stressful film (showing a crude circumcision ritual) was promoted by a soundtrack describing the events in a detached, scientific manner. In the study by Koriat et al. (1972), instruction encouraged defensive procedures; intellectualizing was one of those spontaneously adopted by the subjects. Lief and Fox (1963) extensively describe procedures adopted institutionally to achieve "detached concern" in the medical dissecting room. The room itself is furnished in a dry, matter-of-fact, clear, and spotless manner. Behavior of the staff is efficient, professional, and businesslike. The face and genitals of the cadaver are covered. The general mood is impersonal. Students hardly talk about the autopsy, and when they do, the tone again is detached. No jokes are made in the dissecting room, and manifestations of emotion or sympathy are avoided. Note that the intrapsychic regulatory processes are aided by external measures. The same occurs when dehumanization is sought in abhorrent settings such as slave camps: Behavior of victims must be unassertive, dress deindividuated.

States similar to numbness can be adopted more or less voluntarily, but distinctions get blurred. What is voluntarily, and what outcome-controlled, and what true numbness, under certain circumstances? Margaret Bourke-White, photographer, in the Buchenwald concentration camp, 1945, writes "I have to work with a veil over my mind. In photographing the murder camps, the protective veil was so tightly drawn that I hardly knew what I had taken until I saw the prints of my own photographs. I was seeing these horrors for the first time. I believe many correspondents worked in the same self-imposed stupor. One has to, or it is impossible to stand it" (Bourke-White 1963, pp. 259–260).

More or less involuntary detachments occur outside numbness or traumatic conditions, notably in conditions of conflict. Bleakly noting one's absurd actions, such as opening letters when sick with suspicion, or compulsively washing one's hands; or bleakly harboring obsessional images of killing an enemy or murdering one's child, or bleakly, detachedly remembering severe sufferings – all may come about without conscious intent, or contrary to intent. Freud refers to these processes as "isolation": "The experience is not forgotten [as in repression], but divested from its affect, and its associative connections are suppressed or interrupted" (Freud 1926, [1959, p. 120]).

When isolation affects not just a specific event or memory but experience generally, detachment fades into depersonalization; this, too, may occur outside acute traumatic conditions. In depersonalization, the subject, without wanting to, observes himself acting and experiencing, as from a distance. Detachment can go as far as consisting of loss of the feelings of familiarity normally accompanying perception of familiar objects and execution of familiar acts. When detachment becomes an enduring state, it is experienced as extremely painful, where even the painfulness is felt as remote, a mere isolated mental occurrence. It can be so painful as to drive the subject to suicide in a shockingly detached manner.

Denial and detachment work by and large by taking away elements from the situational meaning structure: They remove facts, or sense of reality, or sense of personal involvement. Defense can also operate by adding elements. Continued sense of presence after loss, in fact, is achieved by adding through action and fantasy. Additions may pertain not only to facts but also to sense of control and of coping ability; this helps since, as we have seen earlier, emotion is determined both by appraisal of danger or harm and by appraisal of coping potential. Anything that strengthens sense of coping potential detracts from the appraisal of threat. Self-instructions such as "I am not afraid" or "I can handle this" and correction of self-critical beliefs may succeed in modifying situational meaning structure. Self-instructions are used, to that end, in cognitive behavior therapies (Beck 1976; Kanfer, Karoly, & Newman 1975) and, at any rate, are employed spontaneously when facing danger or challenge (e.g., Prins 1985, with children afraid of the dentist). Illusionary feelings of invulnerability can be viewed from this same angle. They can be bolstered by vows, magical beliefs ("I am Sunday's child"), the wearing of charms, the performance of rituals. Such practices are not restricted to former ages or outlandish tribes. Grinker and Spiegel (1945) describe them as occurring among combat soldiers. And who has never made a secret promise to be kept when the examination is passed, the child has recovered from illness, or the adored one is responding favorably?

Then, of course, there is addition by wishful thinking: that discovery of a cure is certainly imminent; that bombs never hit twice at the same site; that there is an afterlife; that suffering makes sense and your son died for a good valuable cause.

At this point, the boundary between defensive appraisal and non-defensive appraisal becomes blurred. The same sort of thoughts that arise to soften impact of painful events can arise because the subject honestly thinks that that is how things are. It will often be impossible to distinguish between what are, psychologically, optimistic evaluations or irrational hopes. Also, it is sometimes difficult to distinguish between endeavoring to distort reality by seeing hopes where there are none and endeavoring to grasp or extend reality by seeing hopes that might be. The latter endeavors, while still intrapsychic coping, cannot be called defensive; they are not even merely palliative, and they contribute to problem-focused coping, as we will argue later.

Another mode of activity that straddles the boundary between problem-focused coping and palliative coping is joking. Jokes are sometimes made to relieve tension, and they do this by the dual functions of distracting and of attenuating the stressor's importance. In his detailed study of medical students' modes of coping with examinations for the doctorate, Mechanic (1962) describes these two functions. Joking increased as examinations drew nearer. Well before the examinations it was primarily directed at poking fun at the study materials, thereby making them look less important or threatening. Later on it took a more avoidant character, mainly serving to divert attention away from the situation at hand.

All this is defensive. However, in order to fulfill these defensive functions, joking presupposes an ability to make and appreciate jokes under the given circumstances. That is to say, joking is a defensive maneuver that presupposes some measure of aloofness from the source of stress or some willingness not to take it seriously all the time. Adoption of the aloofness and the willingness represent a constructive and not merely defensive coping effort. As a matter of fact, Mechanic found joking primarily among the moderately anxious students, and less frequent among the highly anxious ones, in whom presumably aloofness was less easily attained. We will return to the more constructive aspects of joking in a later subsection.

Deployment of overt activity likewise has this double, defensive and constructive or problem-focusing, aspect. As discussed in section 5.6 it helps, when under stress, to do something and not sit there passively waiting for things to happen. The sense of possessing a measure of control obtained by action and the readiness sustained by that action, again not only are palliative but also contribute to maintaining a problem-focused stance.

Pertinent information regarding this point comes particularly from the disastrous effects of giving in to apathy under severe stress. In German concentration camps, such apathy was called the "mussulman syndrome": the man sitting hunched up, not stirring or eating or acting otherwise, rapidly wasting away. The response pattern and its fatal course are known from other similar camps and in general from conditions of extreme and extended hardship. In all these conditions, getting the apathetic subject on his feet, and keeping him active, however trivial the activity, could mean saving him from death (e.g., Strassman, Thaler, & Schein 1956 reporting on prisoners of war in North Korea). The syndrome, and its issue, resemble that leading to voodoo death (Cannon 1942). By inference, activity would serve to counteract what causes "voodoo death," which according to Cannon is despair, the sense of total helplessness together with loss of interest in maintaining bodily functioning.

Effectiveness of defensive appraisal

Studies of the relationship between indications of defensive appraisal and subjective, autonomic, and endocrine responses show that defensive appraisal can indeed reduce discomfort and disturbance. Most of the evidence has been mentioned already in earlier chapters. Fenz and Epstein (1967) compared parachutists who did and who did not deny their anxiety prior to jumping: Nondeniers were subjects whose stories to jumping-relevant pictures mentioned anxiety, deniers those whose stories mentioned only joy and excitement. Electrodermal response was measured upon exposure to words either relevant or irrelevant to parachute jumping. Difference in response to relevant and irrelevant words was smaller for deniers than for nondeniers. Friedman, Mason, & Hamburg (1963) determined the defensiveness of parents of leukemic children on the basis of denials like those mentioned earlier and found significantly lower cortisol (17-OHCS) levels in well-defended than in poorly defended parents. Wolff et al. (1964) scaled the well-defendedness of these parents from the presence or absence of overt distress and disturbance as assesses during interviews. Again, 17-OHCS response was lower in well-defended than in poorly defended parents. Assessment of defendedness in these three studies is somewhat problematic since it is based upon rather indirect indices. Harder evidence is obtained from the experiments by Lazarus's group, which were mentioned above. The intellectualizing soundtracks or instructions were shown to reduce distress ratings and autonomous response (EDR, heart rate) during the viewing of the stressful films.

Denial or intellectualization is seldom complete or stable; defensive appraisal usually is not entirely successful. Mention was made of Weisman's (1972) observations of "middle knowledge" in severely ill patients. Middle knowledge probably is the rule rather than an exception whenever denial is effected. Intellectualization, too, probably is unstable, with affect breaking through. It can hardly be otherwise, since events are there and remain there, even if only in thought. Also, thought is continuously mobile, tending to scan now this, now that facet or implication of an event. And cognition is not a one-level process. Thought goes on at the irreflexive as well as the reflexive level. That is to say: Defensive appraisals to a large extent are verbal injunctions and thoughts that the subject himself generates; by consequence, they have limited power in comparison to actual events and ingrained expectancies (see section 5.9).

The effectiveness of these injunctions and thoughts, moreover, tends to be of limited duration. Words and thoughts fade when facts remain. Intellectualizing detachment may work to keep distress down when viewing a stressful film; but the stressful images may spontaneously crop up later, at unguarded moments; and they crop up in the night, at even more unguarded ones. Horowitz (1976, 1982) describes how intrusion states alternate with denial states after traumatic events. In intrusion states unbidden thoughts and images keep coming, sometimes as hallucinations or illusions, and they do so particularly when the person is relaxing his or her control, as when lying down to sleep.

The effectiveness of defense indeed appears to depend highly upon opportunity for preparing such defense. As said in section 8.1, events that take one by surprise hit harder than those for which one could mentally brace oneself. Emotion-laden stimuli that leave one cold when sought out or turned to in thought may move strongly when stumbled upon – Proust's "Law of Intermittences" (section 5.8). True enough, Nature has not left the organism entirely unprepared for being unprepared; it has given it the gift of numbness.

All this implies that defensive appraisal is not performed once and for all in a given connection. It has to be constantly renewed and maintained. The fact has been emphasized by Freud in relation to repression: "An important element in the theory of repression is the view that repression is not an event that occurs once but that it requires permanent expenditure of effort" (Freud 1926, [1959, p. 157]).

Effectiveness of defensive appraisal in warding off discomfort and disturbance has to be sharply distinguished from its adaptation value in actual dealings with the environment. As Lazarus (1966) argues, the two are quite distinct matters. With respect to adaptive value there exists an ideology that frowns upon defensiveness and considers full awareness of harm and threat commendable. That ideology is clearly in error. Whether defensive appraisal is maladaptive or not depends upon whether such defensiveness does or does not interfere with taking adaptive action and to what extent full awareness of threat or loss does or does not do so, given the emotions that such awareness brings about. It also depends upon whether the defensiveness enables one to carry on, aversive conditions notwithstanding, and to what extent full awareness of those conditions, with all the emotions that entails, enables one to do so.

On the one hand, palliation often gains short-term comfort at the cost of long-term loss. It gains mere comfort at the possible cost of not seeing or not grasping opportunities for action. Many Jews in Germany, 1933 and after, were unwilling to view the situation as it was and as it quite clearly was; they were not unique in that, but paid more dearly than others. Less dramatic examples of the losses of short-term gain abound. Neglect of bothersome blinking warning lights has resulted in many an explosion. Nagging unhappiness breaks out in despair when, in a marriage, too late, after years, realization is allowed that it was an unsatisfactory relationship. Defensive appraisals are distinctly maladaptive when they become a cognitive set and generalize over other contexts than merely those that palliation was meant for: when they blunt the subject for many other things than the emotions of loss or abandonment or trauma that they were to protect him from.

On the other hand, just as numbness after loss comes as a blessing, so do detachment under torture, the hopeful peace of mind of the terminally ill patient, the avoidant thinking when dangerous tasks have to be accomplished in war or peace or when the children have to be cared for after loss, when despair has to be warded off under extreme hardship, or when the will to live has to be retained when one's child has died.

The "costs and benefits of denial" (Lazarus's expression) and of other forms of defensive appraisal vary from one situation to another. Probably the most adequate generalizations as to their relative value are given by Lazarus and Folkman (1984): Benefits outweigh costs when there is nothing constructive that people can do to overcome harm and threat; benefits outweigh costs when defensive appraisal is restricted to certain facets of the situation and does not extend to the whole; and particularly when it is not applied to facts that can and should be dealt with at that moment.

Emotion transformations

Palliative endeavors consist not merely of strategies to tone down emotional response but also of endeavors to transform one emotion into a different, more supportable, more favorable, more advantageous one.

Every emotion has its advantages and disadvantages. These advantages and disadvantages can be inferred from the various situational meaning structures. Grief is the emotion of finality, of definitive, irreparable loss. Finality has its specific painfulness in the helplessness that it implies. It also has its advantages: No efforts make sense, nothing has to be endeavored, no effort has to be spent.

Similar considerations apply to anger. Its situational meaning structure involves an obstacle that in principle might not have been there. The antagonist could have acted otherwise; something or someone else is to blame. This implies that behind the obstacle the blocked goal still exists, still is available; and the nature of the obstacle is such that, in principle it can be controlled and modified. Anger implies hope. Further, anger implies that fighting is meaningful; one is not reduced to mere passivity. These are the advantages. The disadvantage resides in the effort and alertness required and the burden of responsibility for effecting or not effecting the change that is possible. Efforts toward that change, moreover, may fail and thus produce humiliation and disappointment.

Fear is the emotion of uncertainty and lack of control. In uncertainty and lack of control, it is of no use to stick your neck out in efforts at control. That is an advantage. Also, at the same time, the situation is seen as one that could be other than it is; it is a "modifiable" one, in contrast to the situation of grief. But in contrast to that of anger, it is not one that looks controllable; it tends to leave you passive and apprehensively waiting for what is to come.

Changes in appraisal can be effected in order to obtain what looks the most profitable for the given subject and under the given circumstances. There is leeway for appraisal to stress now this, now that feature of the situation in direct perception, in causal attributions made, in thinking about probable consequences and about possibly effective coping actions. Preference for one or the other mode of appraisal is particularly sensitive to the different "significance" of different emotions for the particular subject. One does not want to be a coward, which pleads against fear; or a tyrant, which pleads against anger; or one detests passivity, which pleads against grief and anxiety. Particular emotions have their particular values: anger as an aspect of manliness, guilt feeling as conferring a glow of moral standing that shields one from moral attacks because one was there first in moral reprobation.

These advantages of certain emotions over others explain emotional persistence; they also explain occurrence of one particular emotion rather than another that could also have occurred. Consider again anger. As mentioned earlier, anger is one of the regular responses to loss: Anger can be directed against the lost person as well as against others, such as well-meaning friends (Lindemann 1944). Bowlby interprets such anger as search for the lost object. It might also have a defensive function, particularly when protracted. Anger helps to maintain the illusion that the lost object is still to be found, that the situation of misery can still be modified. As one of the widows interviewed by Parkes (1972) said, after a period in which she had been angry with all and everything, including her dead husband: "Only after I could abandon protest did grief really break through." In marital quarrels and other misfortunes, too, anger often serves to avoid perceiving an unlucky situation as one that cannot be modified, and thus to avoid being helplessly unhappy, or resigned. Grief, being faced with a sad situation that cannot be undone, appears to be one of the most difficult conditions to support – one that is to be avoided at high costs and that prompts various maneuvers at escape.

Guilt feeling, we suggest, also can fulfill an avoidant function with respect to grief. Guilt feeling shares with anger that someone – the ego in this case – is to blame as a causal agent. One could have acted otherwise; the situation could have been other than it is. It thus could as yet be different: It is of a controllable and modifiable nature; action is possible, even if only in the mind. Guilt feelings, we suggest, are clung to, and often even called up, to ward off finality. In fact, guilt feelings do give rise to endless ruminations as to what could have happened had one acted otherwise.

Guilt feelings are conspicuous after personal loss (Ramsey 1979). They may well be so because they make events appear as less definitive. Perhaps the same mechanism is operative in the guilt feelings that are prominent in depression. There, they may provide an explanation for one's misery, an explanation that provides an aspect of controllability, some shred of it, in the morass of helplessness; it permits acts of contrition and efforts at paying penance. The guilt feelings may be defenses against depression as such. This explanation of guilt feelings may also hold for the guilt feelings of ill-treated children: If there is guilt, ill-treatment at least has a reason.

Similar processes can explain clinging to jealousy, and occurrence of jealousy instead of mere sorrow or unhappiness over the partner's unfaithfulness, emotions that are equally possible under the circumstances. To the extent that jealousy is anger, the controllability component of anger applies. To the extent that it is acute, anxious suffering, the modifiability component of fear is present: The situation is kept alive as one that should not be so. Abandoning outer or inner protest means abandoning desire to keep a hold and gives free license to the other, which is precisely what is abhorred. There seems to be a paradox here: One retains suffering because abandoning that suffering would make one suffer. The paradox is merely apparent. What is preferred is anger or suffering over loneliness or being left behind.

Then there is clinging to grief and sorrow and preference for sorrow over indifference. As long as grief is there, the object is in some way there; one's readiness to interact is there; some actual, albeit merely mental, interaction with the lost one is there. Abandoning grief throws one into emptiness, or sometimes into disloyalty. People often resist letting grieving go, as Parkes's report extensively illustrates. In addition, there are the secondary gains of grief: avoidance of some of the pains of having to face the world alone. One is entitled to not going to the office; one is entitled to assistance and considerateness and care by others, and to regressive, low-energy behaviors of various sorts.

In this view, even depression – acute depressed mood – can be defensive. It can avoid grief, or effort. Depression, however much a torture, shields from having to cope actively, from having to confront the loss as well as the task, from full awareness of both. This applies not merely to personal loss; it also applies to marital disharmony, to professional failure, to any kind of misery. Note that it may not be unwise to behave in this fashion and to go under the covers. If nothing else can be done, coping efforts are wasteful; and apathy gives time for readjustments and for realization to seep through. These interpretations of depressive response to loss and stress have been advanced by Klinger (1975), who views depressive response as disengagement strategy, and by Rothbaum et al. (1982), who view it as "secondary coping."

We mention briefly a somewhat different mode of transformation: reflexive analysis. I can replace my anger by awareness of my own vulnerability or of my own strong concerns at stake -- my desires for control, my fear of loss, my being dependent, or whatever the deeper reason for taking things so heavily. By this reflexive action, interaction with the object of concern tends to be broken; ties to the object are cut. Anger toward the other is replaced by something subjective within myself. Sometimes, again, this is as it should be; it can be fully realistic. Why reproach someone else when more justifiably, or as justifiably, I can view the situation as a result of my long toes being stepped upon? But often it should be considered defensive, as a method of escaping from the emotion or from the object.

Explanation of defensive appraisal

Defensive appraisal is outcome-controlled; the same holds for emotion transformation. The process seems puzzling, for how can someone prefer a more comfortable appraisal over a more uncomfortable one without first having experienced the latter; how can someone deny without first knowing what he wants to deny? The paradox is present already in numbness: How can someone close himself off from shattering news without first realizing that it is shattering?

The paradox is known from discussions of repression: How can a desire or memory be repressed without knowing what the desire or memory is? One knows the solution proposed by traditional psychoanalytic theory. The desire or memory evokes unconscious anxiety, which triggers the repression process. Of course, this is mere metaphor. Anxiety is an overt and experiential response, and, as Lazarus (1966) argues, nothing is gained by doubling it with a nonovert, nonexperiential equivalent.

The issue, actually, is relatively simple, with respect both to defensive appraisal and to repression; in fact, the two can be considered to be roughly the same. The key phrase is *defensive exclusion* (Bowlby 1980), and the context is the perceptual cycle as described by Neisser (1976). The present account is taken from Bowlby (1980), modified on the basis of Neisser's model.

Perception, in Neisser's analysis, is the outcome of informational input being assimilated in terms of cognitive dispositions that comprise the individual's store of knowledge; these dispositions are called schemata. Partial information – the first glimpse plus, generally, current expectations – calls up a schema. The schema directs further information intake and selection; that further information either confirms appropriateness of that schema or leads to change in the schema applied. The process is cyclical: input–schema–exploration–input–schema, and so on. It is a process that extends over time. It comes to rest, and "perception" is achieved, when information and schema fit and, presumably, when internal criteria as to what constitutes fit are satisfied; at some times we are more readily satisfied than at others.

The process is called "analysis by synthesis" because information pickup is controlled by its contributing to successful synthesis into some schema. The model applies to cognition generally: to judgmental thought as well as to perception proper. "Thinking about" an event – the emergence of expectations, inferences, and estimates of the likelihood of their being appropriate – is part of calling up the schema, insofar as it serves to put questions to the knowledge store of the environment. It is part of exploration and information pickup, however, insofar as the expectations and so on are considered, by the subject, as answers. The process can be cut off at any stage in the cycle, and after any given cycle. It can be cut off whenever the system – the subject – is satisfied, or loses interest, or when his attention is drawn elsewhere. This is where "defensive exclusion" can come in.

Defensive exclusion, in fact, is nothing more than refusal further to explore the content or implications of given information, whatever the stage of the process of information pickup one has arrived at. Such refusal, of course, is often evident at the conscious level. Its signal is discomfort, uneasiness, disinclination – not "unconscious anxiety," as anomalous psychoanalytic parlance has it (see Lazarus 1966). The signal can also be mere anticipation of danger – that is, perception of threat. One knows of course what can lead to what, and thus avoid it. Right now, while writing, I am not looking at *The Boys from Brazil*, that movie suggesting that Nazism is still alive, showing on television elsewhere in this room and being watched by someone who thinks she can stand it. The signal may even be nothing but a glimpse of potential threat, as indeed it is in this actual example. That is to say: Refusal to go on, cognitively, may be triggered merely by an event that *would* be true threat were the urgency of the event to be increased – when the event would move closer, become more vivid, more compelling, as it will do when thoughts start to run off about it, consequences come to mind, and images emerge.

One does not have to assume that such appraisal of actual or potential threat must necessarily be conscious in the sense of reflexive awareness. It may operate preattentively, and may preattentively block attending. The notion of preattentive assessment of meaning is a familiar one. Unattended messages – a conversation during a party going on behind one's back, while one is listening to someone else – are not consciously heard and understood; still, they are heard and understood in some sense since they draw attention when touching upon important concerns – when mentioning one's name for instance, or sex (see Norman 1976). Unattended messages are thus evidently processed, but they are processed only up to a point. They do not come into conscious awareness unless subjected to that further processing that is called "attending to." Also, they are rapidly forgotten and leave the processing system without a trace, or nearly so, unless attended to within a few seconds (Norman 1976).

Defensive exclusion, as said, can occur at any stage of information processing. That is to say: Processing may be interrupted at any moment from the first evocation of some schema by some input onward. It may be interrupted before or during sampling of further information or before the process of attending to or before or during the mobilization of associations, expectations, inferences and the like. Exclusion can thus be effected before the information reaches reflexive awareness: before the process of attending to. Such blocking occurs during hypnotic analgesia or deafness. The "hidden observer" phenomenon shows that indeed some sort of blocking is involved: Awareness does not come through in the hypnotic's "ordinary" consciousness, although it does in his hidden observer part (Hilgard 1977). Somewhat similar blocking occurs under more commonplace conditions, when attention drifts away from problematic, potentially painful material: One cannot focus upon it, the mind keeps wandering, the words, while heard, do not penetrate and are forgotten as rapidly as those from unattended messages.

Stimulus processing may thus be interrupted, for instance, during that stage of processing that ensures realization of what the stimuli – things seen, words heard – mean; the stage corresponds to exploration of the information contained in the schema. And it can be interrupted at that stage of processing when the links are followed that connect the identified stimuli with expectations, associations, actions, and concern relevance. Most emotional stimuli, in fact, are signals or symbols – stimuli that arouse emotion only by virtue of such links with expectations et cetera. Thought can refuse to follow the links and to go further than merely register and classify. It can see blood as just a red liquid; unwilling thought can make it remain so. It can hear "He is dead" just as a string of words; processing can be interrupted before it goes on to realizing that he will never come back; or before realizing what that in turn implies.

Numbness corresponds to interruption early in the process, which may extend to interrupting active input scanning. Detachment corresponds to interruption before thought goes on to personal relevance, or to associations accessing that. Denial corresponds to nongeneration of implications, nonconsideration of facts, and to selective pursuance of favorable implications. Repression easily fits this analysis. Freud, as the quotation earlier in this section showed, viewed repression as a continuous process. In his phrasing, impulses have to be kept down continuously. In the present way of phrasing (and more in line with present-day conceptualizations of motivation; see section 6.4), concern-relevant events have to be continuously appraised defensively, by defensive exclusion.

The processes that ensure defensive exclusion at various points in the process do not all consist of simple interruptions or refusals to go on. Numbness involves general cognitive and attentional inhibition. Involuntary detachment, as said, looks similar to the "dissociations" under hypnosis and sensory deprivation. Hilgard (1977) hypothesized that under both conditions higher-order control processes that involve reflexive awareness become dissociated from the more automatized and autonomous action and information-processing routines.

"Noting" of events, in some forms of detachment, appears to sidetrack information processing that otherwise would have led to meaning awareness, to imagination and emotion. Noting can be effected voluntarily: One can shield oneself from experiencing the aversiveness of an event, just as one can shield onself from sexual arousal, while still noticing the object and even its attractiveness. Noting, it appears, is achieved by abstract or factual stimulus coding, as described by Leventhal et al. (1979), and by controlling further processing by stubbornly keeping that coding in awareness – the technique of defense-by-concentration. Verbal

recoding, naming the event, assists in this, and is one of the intellectualizing techniques. Naming and noting, as well as factual stimulus
coding, appear to operate by substituting mere words and thoughts for
the proper input of the emotion system, which, as said, consists of
images, sensory stimuli, and sensed interaction with the event (see section 5.9).

Involuntary processes and voluntary strategies are continuous with
one another. One may yield to involuntary numbness, abandon to it,
permit it to continue. Conversely, voluntarily fixing attention may fade
over into "blanking," into arrest of purposive mental activity not unlike
that in meditation. Noting may become a habit.

Finally, many defensive exclusions are results of quite general modes
of behavior control, which extend to cognitive behavior. Thought often
actively, and sometimes even deliberately, recoils before drawing disagreeable inferences, or cuts off undesirable images, because they are
undesirable or because present assessments are well enough as they
stand. Or it pursues attractive lines of thought, thus producing comforting additions.

It may be emphasized again that appraisals are not usually made at
one shot, or once and for all. Appraising is mobile: It tries to make sense
as much as it tries to make hopeful sense, and sense is the outcome of
a net balance of positive and negative features considered. Balance shifts
with degree of elaboration of both, and why continue considering negative ones? Which is to say that in defensive appraisal the motivational
and nonmotivational explanations of reality distortions (Nisbett & Ross
1980) meet rather than that they form alternatives.

The main point of the analysis in the present section is this: Defensive
appraisal is outcome-controlled. Appraisals are selected that entail reduced discomfort or, in the event, enhanced comfort. Yet they do not
result from bad faith or self-deception. They do not really involve the
paradox that something must be known or felt in order to be kept out
of awareness. Defensive appraisals are instigated by present discomforts
or comforts or by present signals of threat and escape from threat, and
not (not necessarily) by foreknowledge of discomfort that might be.

Nondefensive intrapsychic coping

Hardship and suffering have to be dealt with, even if only because
defensiveness has limited power. Also, one may desire to face the hardships as they are, or one may have to for the sake of coping. Coping

often requires that one not bog down and not let the emotional response have its way. How is this accomplished, when it is?

Self-control may be used as a designation for what is required and done. However, self-control in the sense of not giving in to emotional impulse would not seem adequately to describe the modes of coping with prolonged uncontrollable stress: with personal loss, physical misery, or continuous humiliation and threat. And if the term is chosen, the question is how self-control is achieved and maintained under the conditions mentioned.

There exist, it is argued here, constructive, nondefensive modes of intrapsychic coping in which events are perceived as they are, but still made more or less tolerable and withstood mentally. They are called upon in the sadnesses of daily life as well as under extreme and enduring adverse circumstances. We venture some guesses as to what some of these modes of coping might be and how they might operate.

Joking was mentioned above as not merely serving defending, but also withstanding. It was argued that joking implies a measure of aloofness from a stressor the impact of which is recognized, and particularly that it implies a willingness or ability to adopt that aloofness. By virtue of these properties, joking is, or rather can be, a powerful coping mode; the same applies to the use of irony.

More precisely, the coping mode consists of the readiness to adopt the stance, and a way of looking, from which the joking and irony as meant derive. That way of looking is one that both fully recognizes the threat or harm and puts it between brackets, so attenuating its scope or importance. Serious events are divested of part of their seriousness by discerning features that include them in a different context. Joking and irony, as meant here, imply distancing, but differently from detachment as described earlier. They do not deny, avoid, or diminish personal involvement but give it a double implication, by discerning both implications in the events. As in that joke of the two political prisoners when they hear of the razzia going on outside: "We are lucky; we cannot be arrested." Events are made to appear more relative, by embedding them in alternative viewpoints – one of the core elements of humor generally.

To be able to perceive these alternatives, as said, presupposes a willingness to step back. For the moment, one adopts the perspective of a nonparticipant who takes time to view things from different angles. The cognitive process involved may be called one of *constructive reappraisal*: "constructive" because it adds realistically. The distancing involved is an instance of acting in a different way from what seems to be required by the situation. It is an act orthogonal, so to speak, to the emotional response that appears to be called for by the situation. In performing this act, one gains, or regains, a measure of independence. One gains or regains a measure of "inner control": control not over the event but over its appraisal and over one's own response. *I* determine how the event shall be seen, and *I* determine how I shall act.

Constructive reappraisal, distancing, and inner control seem to be the essential elements of nondefensive intrapsychic coping generally; joking is used merely to introduce them. They can be recognized, at least in part, in the dimensions that make for "hardiness" in dealing with life stress, according to Kobasa's studies (Kobasa 1979; Kobasa, Maddi, & Kahn 1982): commitment, challenge, and control. Tendency to perceive difficult events as challenges rather than burdens or threats obviously is readiness for some kind of constructive reappraisal. "Control," here, refers to the sense of not being the victim of events, which is quite close to what we mean by inner control.

Exerting inner control, as said, means executing some action that is independent of what the situational meaning structure appears to dictate. Self-willed action is substituted for abandoning struggle in a hopeless situation, or for aggression or protest in one of humiliation, or for cowering or flight in one of threat. The self-willed action can be overt action: a smile, or remaining silent. First and foremost, it is mental action: precisely the distancing and reappraisal described. Because it is mental action, it is action that is always possible, whatever the event, given sufficient inner resources. One always can retain some measure of initiative, one never has to be entirely victim, as long as the resources last. By resources is meant some remnant of physical energy and mental alertness and not being overwhelmed by pain.

Constructive reappraisal can take several forms; perhaps it can take many. One is perceiving events as challenges, as events to be coped with or mastered. As discussed earlier (section 5.6), perceiving an event as challenge rather than as threat depends upon one's sense of competence or trust in one's coping potential. However, trust in one's coping potential is not something given and unalterable. It is itself amenable to reappraisal, as will be further discussed in the section on self-control (section 8.5). The reappraisal can be variously motivated: by indignation; by anger or disgust; by sense of moral obligation and ideological commitments. Anger and disgust can be directed against oneself as much as against the offender – for instance, because one sees oneself on the verge of bogging down. Sense of moral obligations can concern obligations toward oneself as much as toward others or toward values per se. Coping under adversity, indeed, often appears to be inspired by such emotions and commitments, as evident from accounts of those who did put up resistance against oppression (e.g., P. London, pers. comm.) or manage to survive in concentration or prisoner-of-war camps (e.g., Dimsdale 1974).

Another mode of constructive reappraisal is perceiving the stressful event within a context of "necessity." The notion is taken from Spinoza: Nature follows its course, and present events can be seen as mere instantiations of that fact; seeing them so can help in controlling emotion. "The mind has greater power over the emotions, or suffers less from them, in so far as it understands all things as necessary" (Spinoza 1677, part V, prop. 6). It probably is true. Appraisal of necessity can appease suffering and help to conquer desire because it removes closeness of the goal for striving or change. It weakens expectations of possible achievement or relief that contribute to intensity of desire and of frustration upon its thwarting (section 5.6). It does so, in part, by removing attributions of personal causation, by self or others. It more particularly does so because it relieves from the burdens of controllability (section 5.6). Necessity cannot be changed; nor can it humiliate, nor does one fail when submitting to it.

What is called "necessity" has, in actual experience, different names: the human condition, embodying both the course of events and the nature of response to them; contribution of events to some higher purpose; for some, it is God's will. Making sense of distressing events is in fact but a variant of it, and has often been mentioned as a coping device or attenuator of distress (e.g., Rothbaum et al. 1982); the same goes for the support provided by suprapersonal beliefs and values. But there is also sheer appreciation of necessity, in the sense meant, which, when one is capable of such appreciation, permits one to carry burdens otherwise unbearable. One sometimes gets the impression that women are better at it than men.

Again: A thin line divides defensive and constructive reappraisal. Whether reappraisal is to be considered either the one or the other depends upon whether meaningful direct coping actions are or are not excluded for the benefit of fatalism; and upon how realistic the assessment of necessity is – that is, how much one remains alert for event features that are relevant for coping and how real are one's aloofness and the degree to which the reappraisal is chosen voluntarily.

8.5. Regulation of emotional impulse and response

A distinction was made earlier between action readiness – action tendency and activation – and overt response (section 2.7). The distinction was made, among other reasons, because both can be controlled separately. One can be angry and rein it in; one can truly suppress one's anger. "Controlling emotion" and "impulse control" refer to both together, and rightly so since the two subprocesses interact, but to some extent they can be discussed separately. They also should be discussed separately because, for the subject, focus can be either upon the one or upon the other.

Insofar as impulse control involves inhibition, it has been discussed in an earlier section of this chapter. It is stimulus-controlled rather than outcome-controlled. Outcome-controlled and voluntary processes are instigated by actual or anticipated adverse response consequences. In addition, impulse control may be motivated by desire to reduce the discomforts and disturbances of pent-up, unsatisfied desires such as impotent anger and sexual excitement without outlet and the discomforts and disturbances of efforts for voluntary response suppression.

Impulse control: regulation of action readiness

Emotion, once it has arisen, can be made to die down, or kept within bounds, by many of the procedures discussed in the preceding section: by directing attention elsewhere, by affecting the stimulus, by modifying its appraisal, by reappraising one's coping potential. The event can be denigrated or made to look attractive; one can say to oneself that one can cope with it. Cognitive behavior modification approaches concerned with weight control, control of impulsiveness, or control of anxiety stress these procedures (e.g., Meichenbaum 1977; Kanfer 1979). Kanfer, Karoly, and Newman (1975), for instance, instructed children who were afraid of the dark to repeat either that the dark is a nice place to sleep and dream (situation reappraisal) or that they could manage well in the dark (competence reappraisal). During testing, these children remained in the dark longer than equally anxious controls. Similar procedures were used to learn to control dentist anxiety, although here effects did not differ from anxiety reduction in control subjects (Prins 1986). Weight control programs stress the control of stimulus conditions by regulating time and place of eating and buying food and by programming substitute activities when one is tempted (Stuart & Davis 1972; O'Leary & Wilson

1975). Whether these programs do indeed modify emotion or desire and not merely suppress response is unclear; overt behavior and subjective anxiety ratings, for instance, tend to diverge (Prins 1986). Subjects do spontaneously use the cognitive maneuvers that the various programs try to instill; in spontaneous use these maneuvers may, however, reflect anxiety rather than procedures that actually control it.

Control of emotional impulse can also be effected by response suppression. Clenching one's teeth, relaxing, breathing deeply, and counting to 10 may help in letting that impulse die down. There are several explanations. Each of these formulates a separate kind of condition under which response suppression sometimes may affect emotional impulse; clearly, it by no means always does or can.

Response suppression may prevent cycles of self-reinforcement in which emotional response generates further stimuli for emotional response: Anger may incite insults in the antagonist, which incites anger, and so on – the escalation cycle. Or crying makes one only more miserable because no one comes to help. Response suppression also assists in keeping impulse below the threshold beyond which control is lost; loss of control again may instate a self-reinforcement cycle. Furthermore, response suppression may provide a time interval during which immediate stimulus impact – of the insult, the grievous thought – can fade and one's attention turned elsewhere. All these effects can also be achieved by initiating incompatible behaviors such as engaging in work, or smiling when in fact angry, rather than by outright response suppression.

Response suppression, particularly willfully adopting a different, incompatible, posture or expression, may also affect emotional impulse directly. In the first place, there is some interaction between impulse and its overt expression, as discussed earlier (section 4.6). Adopting some behavior may interfere with readiness for a different behavior, which is what impulse consists of (section 2.8). In the second place, willfully adopting a given overt attitude may lead to "discovery" that such an attitude, as inner attitude, is in fact a possibility, under the given conditions. Bodily relaxing when faced with threat may lead to the discovery that that attitude's relational content – not cringing, not offering resistance, letting things come – is within one's capacities, or that such an inner attitude is feasible at all. Similarly, feigned indifference may give one self-confidence in being able to perform it, and also make one hit upon the idea of being indifferent in fact. That is to say: Willfully adopting some attitude may lead to seeking situational support for that attitude, as a Stanislavsky actor in real life; it may lead to seek support for a different appraisal. When smiling in anger, support for that posture of superiority can be found in the other's lesser worth or the stupidity of his reproaches; when relaxing in anger, one can tell oneself that it can safely be done. This brings us back to the cognitive procedures, which, of course, could have been instigated to begin with.

Impulse control, like appraisal regulation, has its reflexive variant; we will call it *reflexive control*. Action tendency is transformed into mere "plan," mere intention without activation or direct instigation to act. Action tendencies are made purely conceptual; emotions are turned into feelings (see section 4.10); they thereby can be made objects for reflexion.

A prerequisite for the transformation appears to be abandonment of the desire to actually change the situation; the same prerequisite was found in constructive reappraisal. Attentional focus is shifted from dealing with the event to one's own subjective response.

Suspension of actively dealing with the situation can serve as preparation for dealing better: for fleeing or striking out in a more optimal way. It also can, however, be an act of reflexion per se. Reflexive control is reflexive not merely in the sense of self-observation and of making affective experience a "subjective" phenomenon (section 4.3), but also in that it permits reflexive investigation of the nature of one's action tendency: what it wants, what it seeks to obtain.

Response control

Response control, if not produced by way of impulse control or true inhibition, is effected by direct response suppression or by initiating responses incompatible with those to be controlled. One tenses, or busies oneself with something else, or grasps the table edge, or kicks the cat. Acts like grasping the table edge or kicking the cat rather than the partner are compromise forms of control. In such "displacement of aggression" behavior is allowed to come forth but deflected from its purpose. Deflection itself is usually controlled, as is evident when the less costly possessions are selected for enraged destruction.

As said in section 8.1, response control presupposes two activities that are necessary before the above actions can be applied: action monitoring and outcome monitoring. In learning theory these together are called "self-monitoring" (Kanfer 1979; Bandura 1977). Both are continuously involved in ordinary, daily control of behavior, that of emotion included.

This assumption follows from theoretical analysis, but is supported by some of the evidence demonstrating the ubiquity of inhibition and the impact of sudden, unprepared-for events. Note that enhanced impulsiveness under distraction or after prolonged stress may result from weakened monitoring as well as from decreased readiness of inhibiting responses.

Self-monitoring presumably proceeds at a covert level in most daily regulation. It comes to the fore when restraining stimuli have little urgency, that is, under the conditions of voluntary self-control. Under temptation, or under threat that has to be withstood, children can be observed to tell themselves what will happen when they do what they should not do, or what the rewards are when they abstain (Kanfer 1979; Mischel et al. 1972).

As said, response control serves to attenuate discomfort and disturbance accompanying emotional response itself, in addition to forestalling aversive external consequences. The discomforts and disturbances come primarily from the autonomic response components. Autonomic responses, to some extent, can be regulated by the techniques of biofeedback (see section 3.4), and indirectly by everything that can regulate emotional impulse. Autonomic response can also be regulated by physiological means, and it is of theoretical as well as practical importance to include that regulation mode in a survey of regulation procedures. Tranquilizers, sedatives, and alcohol affect autonomic response centrally, by affecting emotion or alertness; some beta-blocking agents affect such response peripherally, as discussed in section 4.5.

Effectuating response control depends not only upon stimuli. As with everything connected with emotion, stimuli interact with dispositional factors. There are relevant dispositions with respect to stimulus effectiveness, with respect to effort needed for self-monitoring and maintaining control, and with respect to availability of regulatory behaviors and strategies. We will very briefly touch upon each of these.

Variability in either monitoring or control potential, or stimulus effectiveness, is implied in intrapersonal variations of regulation due to, for instance, alcohol, and in interindividual variations in the personality trait of impulsiveness (Eysenck & Eysenck 1979). As we saw, Gray (1971) hypothesized that trait to be due to variation in sensitivity for conditioned punishment. Both his later theory (Gray 1982) and the work of Pribram and McGuinness (1975) would rather implicate control potential. Others voice other hypotheses. Mischel (1973), for instance, stresses intolerance for delay of gratification as an encumbrance to self-control, Bandura (1973, 1977) learning experiences and modeling with respect to both aversive behavior consequences and self-regulation.

Weakness of available control strategies is emphasized in investigations of impulsive children, for instance by Meichenbaum (Meichenbaum & Goodman 1969). Behavior modification programs focus upon remedying impulsiveness by teaching control strategies (e.g., Hartig & Kanfer 1973; Patterson & Mischel 1976).

Catharsis

Response suppression by itself, as said, does not abolish or weaken action tendency. It does so only when the conditions mentioned in the above subsection are fulfilled. When they are not, response suppression engenders tenseness and discomfort. Letting go of control, by contrast, is felt as relief and release. Relief and release give rise to the notion of "catharsis": purifying oneself of pent-up or blocked emotion (Breuer & Freud 1895).

The issue as to whether cathartic effects in fact exist has been much debated. Experiments have investigated whether overt aggression after frustration produces faster autonomic recovery than when aggression is inhibited (Hokanson 1961; cf. 3.3), or whether engaging in aggressive play or action reduces aggression on subsequent occasions (see Geen & Quanty 1977 for a review of both kinds of studies), or whether watching violence on TV does so (e.g., Stener, Applefield, & Smith 1971). Results have mostly, though not always, been contrary to the catharsis hypothesis. On the other hand, as said, giving in to bottled-up anger does relieve, and being able to let oneself go in weeping can produce relaxation of previous tenseness and excitement.

A distinction, we think, must be made between short-term effects of release of control – getting rid of actual excitement and preoccupation – and those long-term effects that concerned Breuer and Freud: getting rid of a persistent inhibition or a persistent behavior tendency. As to short-term effects, giving free rein to anger or grief can instate the self-reinforcing cycle described above. Abandoning control of anger can lead to escalation, or to reinforcement of desire to hurt when anger was successful. Whether or not the self-reinforcement cycle develops would seem to depend upon presence or absence of the conditions for that cycle, such as actual maintaining stimuli, provocation of response, and occurrence of rewards for behavior. On the other hand, anger in quarrels may clear the air; the other may understand, modify his behavior, or restore one's own self-esteem. The example of anger indicates that letting go of control can provide all the things that control seeks to avoid. For grief, for instance, that can mean confrontation with memories or images or acceptance of others; or acceptance of oneself when self-control was dictated by self-esteem; or acceptance of situations as they are. We suggested earlier (section 2.5) that giving way to weeping, after loss, amounts to truly acknowledging the finality of that loss.

These elements, rather than release of pent-up impulse, can be supposed to play a role also in long-term cathartic effects. The analysis suggests the conditions under which such effects can be expected to occur. Catharsis, in reliving trauma, grief, or anger, is not letting off steam from an overheated boiler. This is an outdated energy metaphor, and the getting-rid-of-impulse notion is almost certainly inappropriate. Catharsis is renewed confrontation, and to the full, with a given kind of event, as fully as is necessary to perceive the situation as it really is, or in terms of what it really means to the subject, and acceptance of one's own mode of response. It is, in other words, much more like extinction than like tension release (section 5.8). It may be supposed to occur, and to occur only, when such confrontation and acceptance have been warded off in the past and can be effected now: when, in other words, letting go of control can produce, or is accompanied by, cognitive change.

8.6. External regulation

External and social regulation

The preceding description of regulation as produced by processes from within the subject may have obscured the fact that regulation, to quite an extent, is a function of actually prevailing external conditions: the existence of task demands that must be met, and of current social norms regarding acceptable modes of expression and acceptable emotions; and the presence of sympathetic, judging, or unsympathetic others. Control is a function of the environment's demands and permissiveness, both materially and socially. Observation suggests that this holds for inhibition almost as much as for voluntary self-control. Breakdown occurs more readily when one can afford it, with respect to stance and face, and when it is greeted with warmth and sympathy. Sexual inhibition, too, appears to some extent to respond to warmth, acceptance, and absence of demands (Masters & Johnson 1970). Anger occurs more readily when others yield to it.

"External regulation" has an obvious "internal" side. Permissive and supportive, avoidant and controlling environments are sought as well as met or offered. People tend to arrange or select their environment, manipulating "stimulus control" as discussed in connection with input regulation. Seeking encounter groups or friends helps to undo control. Seeking or keeping a phobic companion helps to keep anxiety within bounds. Seeking the AA helps to uphold drinking control. Discouraging others to talk about painful events prevents recurrence of painful memories and thoughts. Response suppression and enhancement, as said before, in part serve to control the environment in its production of emotional stimuli.

External regulation, social regulation in particular, operates because its agents form part of the stimulus environment. Other people provide and withhold emotional stimuli and take part in what the subject can or cannot do. They are punishing and rewarding agents, or reminders of punishing and rewarding consequences.

The social environment has some particular features over and above these matters. Other people guide attention toward relevant event features. By their actions, they provide and uphold social definition of the significance of objects and events (Gordon 1981). They create and support given appraisals. Hostility of others toward a given object creates or underscores that object's offensiveness; others acting with sympathy define a given situation as one in which letting go is appropriate and dependent behavior commendable; and so on. Attitudes and behavior of others signal what are rewards and punishments; they indicate possibilities for concern satisfaction and reasons for discontent. All this operates with force because one wishes to belong to, or be like, those others. It also operates because those others provide or take away signals for inhibition, and because they may stress or lift the individual's responsibility for what he feels and does.

Deindividuation

These latter factors are emphasized in the deindividuation hypothesis advanced to explain crowd behavior: communal enthusiasm and communal acts of violence. The hypothesis was proposed originally by Festinger, Pepitone, and Newcomb (1952) and has been elaborated by Zimbardo (1970) and Diener (1980). Deindividuation involves reduced self-monitoring, which was just described as essential for self-control. Antecedents for deindividuation, according to Diener, are the excitement, the focus upon external events, and the anonymity, all caused by being in a crowd and in the midst of its activities. Consequents are decreased concern about evaluation of oneself by others, enhanced sensitivity to immediate cues, and decreased effort toward self-awareness and self-control.

The theory has found some experimental support. Anonymity produced by dressing subjects in hoods and capes and by keeping them nameless for one another was shown to increase aggressiveness of action when instigations for such action exist (Zimbardo 1970); anonymity produced by darkness increases intimate behavior, given appropriate stimuli (Gergen, Gergen & Barton 1973); in both kinds of study, enhanced sensitivity to stimuli rather than anonymity might have produced the results, however (Johnson & Downing 1979).

Deindividuation may provide the explanation of the disinhibitions of sentimentality, dependency feelings, sexual arousal, and grief manifest in ultrapermissive surroundings like encounter groups. Identification with leaders, so important in crowd behavior, can be fitted into the deindividuation conception: Attentional and behavioral control are transferred to that leader.

Social support

Regulation by social factors extends to palliation. People in acute distress, anxiety, or grief tend to seek company (Schachter 1959); and when they do not, they still might need it. It is a common adage never to leave someone in acute distress alone; one should be there, talk or just hover in the background. The literature on social support identifies such support as an important moderator of stress effects (Cobb 1976; Antonovsky 1979); experience with self-help groups of mourners, rape victims, alcoholics, and the like suggests a strong need for sharing and exchange as well as their providing true relief.

The palliative effects of social support are of various sorts. Schaefer et al. (1982) distinguish three types of function. The first is emotional support. Warmth, sympathy, and understanding, which are never wasted, are particularly timely when succorance needs run high. Also, receiving warmth and an attentive ear, apart from providing satisfactions and consolations, change the situational meaning structure of the aversive event: They make that meaning less all-encompassing and provide a place and time of rest. The second function is that of tangible support. Other people may take some of the burdens and cares away; they also, in this way, may relieve the feelings of guilt or sorrow about not being able to perform one's duties. The third function is informational support. Talking to others may help in the work of grief or worry, relieve uncertainties, clarify the nature of events. Note that in all three respects, other people can be pests and burdens as well as supports. Suls (1982) extensively discusses the "benefits and liabilities" of social support.

Something more than the benefits mentioned probably is involved in social palliation. As said, people in distress tend to seek company. Affiliation needs rise in anxiety, and many people prefer companions in distress to suffering alone (Schachter 1959); the benefits mentioned do not seem to provide the major motivation. Schachter argues that other people – by their responses to the events as much as by what they say – influence self-evaluation of one's own response. That is, response by others modifies both one's appraisal of the event and of one's coping ability; one does better or worse than they do, or one does as well. Evidently, this may go both ways; it may aggravate as well as palliate.

More important would seem that others, both by their presence as companions in distress and by sharing one's experiences, influence appraisal qualitatively, in a general way. Their presence and sharing render the impact of events more objective. They make that impact more a feature of the world outside and less a subjective experience in the sense discussed in section 4.3. Loss that is deplored by others as much as by oneself turns it into deplorable rather than deplored loss; shared fear makes fear into danger; shared indignation supports awareness of indignity instead of being faced with one's indignation. In the absence of sharing, sympathy, or participation, strong emotions tend to isolate, particularly emotions that are caused by events one can do little about: grief, severe worry, humiliation, impotent indignation. They force the subject into the "subjectivity" of emotion: It is his response, his fate. Sharing, argues Cassel (1976), helps to maintain social identity and a sense of social integration.

Social embedding

A reason to stress this more subtle aspect of affiliation, of sharing and of experiencing emotion in the presence of others, is to get to the important function of society at large with respect to the regulation of the individual's emotions. Perhaps the aspect is not so subtle, since it is tied up with the fact that so many emotions and their causes are public events, with consequences for others and even for society as such. This subject is beyond the scope and intent of the present review. Here we may just emphasize the social functionality of many emotions in given cultures that contributes to the reduction of isolation and subjectivity.

Many emotions are embedded in a social, public context, both because the eliciting event is publicly acknowledged and because the emotion is. Grief upon loss of spouse, child, or face may be given its public place. It is not inevitable to lose contact with society, in such grieving; being thrown back upon oneself is not a necessary part of grief. The same applies to the joys of marriage and birth, and of sanctioned social benefits. Clearly, huge cultural differences exist in these regards. Other peoples' grief, in our culture, often repels and is a bother, and there are strict rules as to its appropriate amount and duration; the rules are shared by the mourner. "No flowers, no visits" is, however, unthinkable in other cultures (Aries 1974). Loss of honor is another example of an emotion that is considered quite differently in different places and times.

Society provides powerful supports for social embedding. By its display rules and feeling rules (Ekman 1973; Hochschild 1983), it ensures recognition and possibility for communication, as well as decrease of frictions. As a still stronger support, it provides models of appropriate behavior. Such models not only guide in adopting behavior that is socially acceptable, they also provide the individual with ready-made modes of expression that give shape and substance to his emotions. Wailing, beating one's breast, heaping ashes upon one's head, tearing one's clothes are presents of the culture. So are the more elaborate emotional patterns such as that of being a "wild man," discussed by Averill (1982). Among several peoples in New Guinea, individuals may go into a state of frenzy, roam about, and shout for days or weeks as release for pent-up tensions of hypercontrol. This syndrome, and others like it occurring elsewhere (e.g., running amok in Southeast Asia, *tunu* among the Kaingaug Indians of Brazil; Averill 1982) probably are instances of a generally occurring psychological mechanism of tension release and consciousness change. Still, in the cultures indicated, culture offers the form, the pattern is recognized by the culture, and is accepted as a temporary, classifiable aberration – or so, at least, anthropologists report.

Society also provides rituals that give time and place for emotional expression and that detail its form. Ritual, of course, is explicit in embedding individual emotion in a social context. It explicitly shields the individual from his exposure and isolation – for instance, by drowning his or her grief in the true or ritualized sorrow of others. It powerfully assists in objectifying emotion (Scheff 1977, 1979). In fact, it is a pitiful sight, in present-day lack of ritual, to see a widow or widower at a funeral swallowing her or his tears, lonely in front of respectful but watching relatives, friends, and strangers. Other cultures, less cruel, provide wailing women, or encourage more general participation in overt despair, to permit the individual her or his full portion of grieving without conspicuously standing alone. Present society is generally poor in rituals, and those that exist are poor in requiring or permitting emotional involvement, thus robbing the individual of a powerful regulatory mode (Klapp 1969; Gordon 1981).

But, of course, society also compels, forcing to show and feel what is not there, and forbidding to show and feel many things that are there, in accordance with its feeling and expression rules.

PART III

Synthesis

9. Theory of emotion

9.1. The emotion process

Chapter 1 started out by outlining a set of phenomena calling for the designation "emotional": behaviors, including behavioral disruptions; physiological changes; and experiences. Chapters 2, 3, and 4 endeavored to determine the nature of these phenomena; they are the phenomena asking for explanation.

The phenomena are evoked by certain stimuli; the stimuli were discussed in Chapter 5. One of the main questions with which chapter 1 started was: *Why* do certain stimuli elicit the emotional phenomena? The answer given was that they do so because of the individual's concerns: The stimuli are relevant to these concerns' satisfaction. A second question was: *How* do the stimuli elicit the phenomena? The answer suggested in the preceding chapters is that a sequence of steps leads from the stimuli to the phenomena to be explained, that sequence being under the influence of a number of side conditions. We will call the sequence of steps and the operation of side conditions the *emotion process*.

The emotion process can be described in terms of information processing. The description is given in the form of a diagram in Figure 9.1. Other information-processing models of emotion have been suggested in the literature (Abelson 1983; Toda 1982; Sloman & Croucher 1981; Pfeifer & Nicolas 1981; Wegman 1985; Bower & Cohen 1981). All these models share essential features with each other and with the present one. The present description, modified from Frijda (1984), embodies the considerations of the preceding chapters.

In describing the process, three lines will be distinguished: the core process or emotion process proper, leading from stimulus event to response; the regulation line, containing processes that intervene in the core process; and the line of inputs other than the stimulus event proper.

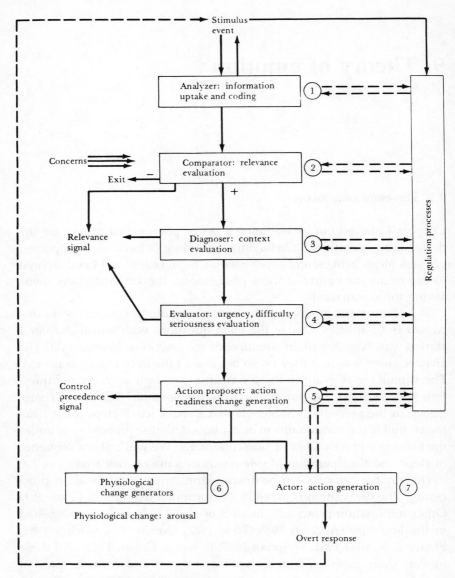

Figure 9.1. The emotion process.

In addition, there are the outputs: the responses, overt, physiological, and experiential.

Core of the emotion process

1. *Analyzer:* The subject is confronted with a stimulus event, or has sought one, or has generated one in thought; the event, or aspects of it, are received as input or actively scanned. The Analyzer codes the event, if it can, in terms of known event types and what they might imply with respect to cause or consequence.

2. *Comparator:* The stimulus event is appraised as to its relevance for one or more of the subject's concerns: relevance evaluation, or primary appraisal. Relevance evaluation results from comparing the event as understood with the satisfaction conditions or sensitivities (section 6.5) of the various concerns, for many, or all, concerns in parallel. Outputs of the Comparator are, in principle, the four relevance signals: pleasure, pain, wonder, or desire; or, by default, irrelevance, whereupon the process exits.

3. *Diagnoser:* The stimulus situation as a whole is appraised in terms of what the subject can or cannot do about it. Context evaluation or secondary appraisal diagnoses possibilities or impossibility for coping. For doing so, it employs a set of coding categories relevant for selection among its fund of action possibilities; their utilization can be regarded as a series of diagnostic tests. Output is a patterned diagnosis: situational meaning structure. In addition, the Diagnoser, together with relevance evaluation, provides the next process with information as to how difficult, urgent, or serious events really are.

4. *Evaluator:* Urgency, difficulty, and seriousness are computed on the basis of previous information. They combine in a signal of control precedence for dealing with the current event. They thus cause action interruption if need may be, or else they cause distraction when previous action happens to continue.

5. *Action Proposer:* On the basis of the information generated hitherto, action readiness change is generated: a plan for action – action tendency – and/or for mode of activation. Readiness mode presses for, or occupies, control precedence.

6. *Physiological change generator:* Physiological change is effected, in accordance with the action readiness mode generated before.

7.   *Actor:* Action – overt or cognitive – is selected, as determined by action readiness mode and by further aspects of the situation insofar as regulation permits.

Phases 1–5 compose stimulus processing as described in section 4.4 and chapter 5. Phases 6 and 7 compose generation of responses as described in chapters 2 and 3.

Regulation

As discussed in section 8.1, every phase in the core process is subject to regulatory intervention by mechanisms, outcome-controlled processes, or voluntary self-control. Inputs to these processes are partly external stimuli: directly inhibitory stimuli and stimuli announcing adverse response consequences. Simultaneous inputs come from core processes themselves: signals that a response to be regulated is planned or actually under way.

Inputs and side conditions

The major inputs to the emotion process are stimulus events (including thoughts) and concerns. "Stimulus events" refers both to things that happen and to situations that prevail. Concerns are dispositions that the subject brings to the transaction: They were defined as dispositions to prefer occurrence of given states of affairs (chapter 6). Stimulus events and concerns meet at the Comparator. There, as said, stimulus events are compared to the satisfaction conditions of concerns; or with "sensitivities" – dispositions to recognize fit objects for achieving satisfaction; or with dispositions to recognize objects as aversive (section 6.4).

Stimulus events also constitute inputs to regulatory processes; and they are inputs to the Diagnoser, which uses their "contextual" properties to decide what actions are and are not possible. To that purpose the entire history of the transaction – the outcome of the previous attempts to cope and other previous experiences – is combined with actual stimuli.

External stimuli, finally, influence selection and guidance of specific actions motivated by action tendency: Whether jumping, running, or freezing occurs in response to conditioned signals for shock, in rats, depends upon spatial context; whether insult or brute force toward an annoyer, upon his apparent strength or age.

For all this to work, the process needs additional inputs: dispositional inputs, referred to here as "side conditions." Input coding needs coding categories; context evaluation needs the context coding categories or tests; both they and the Evaluator need knowledge and the system's inferential capabilities in order to deduce event implications. Regulation operates by means of feeling rules and expression display rules (section 8.2). Note that not all these cognitive dispositions are necessarily implemented as true tests or coding principles: Some are implicit in information processing as such; we will come back to that.

Coding categories, inference rules, and concerns can be assumed to differ in availability, preference, or sensitivity. With respect to concerns, this means priority parameters; with respect to other dispositions, this means tolerance or preference parameters: for "novelty," for "control failure," and so on. These parameters characterize and bias the system at any given moment; they underlie interindividual differences and intraindividual state differences. Some of these dispositional attributes were mentioned in section 6.6.

Action tendency is generated from a repertoire of possible action tendencies: behavioral systems and specific action modes. Physiological response patterns and activation modes, too, form a repertoire that is laid down in the organism's constitution. Similarly, there is a repertoire of specific action programs, including those for facial expressions.

The system must know what action readiness change to instate upon what situational meaning structure. There must be something equivalent to a "table of correspondences" between situational meaning structures, on the one hand, and action readiness modes, physiological changes included, on the other: a system of stimulus-to-response connections, or of "production rules" linking acceptance conditions recognizing given situational meaning profiles to given action readiness change and action programs.

The system, finally, must possess a set of threshold rules: thresholds defining which degree of mismatch or match constitutes "relevance" as opposed to irrelevance; which degree of urgency, difficulty, or seriousness triggers action readiness change, or a given kind of action readiness change; and which degree of possible response consequences trigger regulation, or a given kind of regulation. The issue of thresholds was touched upon in section 5.6. Thresholds have logically to be postulated; differences in thresholds also underlie interindividual differences and intraindividual state differences.

There are a number of further inputs to the emotion process: prevailing mood, prevailing state of arousal, previous experience with a given type of event, examples set by other people, social definitions of events. All these belong to the side conditions and thereby to the dispositional antecedents of emotion (6.6). They need not be considered separately in a description of the emotion process since they all operate by way of situational meaning structure, by way of preference orderings and availability parameters of coding categories and response modes, and by way of the thresholds mentioned.

Outputs

The major outputs of the process are overt behavior and physiological manifestations of action readiness change. Overt behavior feeds back into the process: It affects the eliciting stimulus event either in the sense for which that behavior is functionally meant (as flight increases the distance of danger) or in other ways (as flight draws attention from others, or angry outbursts provoke retaliation). Physiological response affects behavior (as trembling disturbs writing) and behavior potential (as exhaustion diminishes coping potential); chapter 8 discusses a number of these feedback effects, which are among the instigators of regulation.

Two other major output modes are the process's influence upon the flow of action control, control precedence, which will be discussed in the next subsection, and experience, which we will discuss separately.

Embeddedness of the emotion process

In the diagram of Figure 9.1, the emotion process is presented in isolation, and as a nearly linear chain starting from a neatly isolated event. This misses part of the process's point.

First, emotion processes are not discrete events; not in all of their phases. Information uptake and accompanying relevance evaluation go on continuously. The environment is scanned continuously as long as the individual is awake; at least, all impinging information is subjected to some analysis and some relevance testing (sections 5.9 and 8.4). Relevance signals are emitted whenever the outcome of that testing surpasses the relevance threshold. Action tendency also varies continuously and leads to physiological arousal, to activation change, and to actual action whenever intensity is sufficient, considering prevailing conditions of regulation.

Second, emotion processes are events over time; and each of the sub-processes is, or can be. This holds emphatically for uptake and processing of stimulus events. "Emotional stimulus," as said in section 5.2, is merely a shorthand for what more properly is referred to as a transaction. That which actually elicits a given emotion may have been sought as well as encountered; it is elicited by the subject himself as well as imposed upon him by others or by the course of events; and it develops through this transaction in such a manner that it becomes relevant and loses its relevance, varies in urgency and in quality, and so on: "flux" (Lazarus & Folkman 1984). This whole history of the process coalesces into the situational meaning structure as it exists at a particular moment. Situational meaning structure is continuously updated, complete with the changing perspectives regarding the future that each assessment entails and the changing perspectives regarding impact upon one's estimated coping potential, upon controllability of the events, or upon helplessness. In terms of the processing model, this implies feedback loops between information uptake and coding, as in the analysis-by-synthesis model of perception (section 8.4), but also between actions envisaged and information scanned or evaluated; and of course it implies the feedback over the environment mentioned above, that of response affecting the stimulus situation in coping with it, appeasing it, or provoking it.

All this requires a general, overall monitoring of the process, of its elicitation, its course, and its results, as well as of the relation of the emotional process to other processes of the system. Assumption of monitoring has been found essential in order to understand regulation (section 8.1) and action readiness changes such as in helplessness (section 2.8). Monitoring needs central integration of all relevant information coming from different sources and moments, as mentioned. Such monitoring by centrally integrated information has been called a "blackboard control structure" (Bower & Cohen 1982). The blackboard contains the situational meaning structure. In fact, accounting for information integration is what the concept of "situational meaning structure" is for.

The third aspect that is missed when regarding the emotion process in isolation is the relation of that process to other processes and its place in the overall action control structure. A central place in the notion of emotion has to be assigned to what we called "action control precedence." Emotion, as action readiness state or as emotional action, has action control precedence in two senses. It can interrupt other processes and block access to action control for other stimuli and other goals; it invigorates action for which it reserves control and invests that control with the property of indistractibility or persistence (section 2.8).

This is the proper place to return to a distinction made earlier in this book and perhaps not sufficiently emphasized: that between emotions proper and desires or enjoyments (sections 2.8, 4.4).

Emotion and motivation

The distinction between emotions proper and desires plus enjoyments reflects the distinction often made between emotion and motivation. However, as argued in section 6.4, these latter two cannot be put in opposition, or even juxtaposition. For one thing, *motivation* means several different things. For another, *hunger, craving,* and *sexual excitement* refer to emotions, both by denoting feeling states and by denoting modes of action readiness. What is meaningful in the distinction is that some emotions, some modes of action readiness – emotions proper – involve relational states or tendencies toward relational change, and others, the desires and enjoyments, tendencies toward obtaining given satisfactions (section 2.8).

Emotions proper and desires plus enjoyments have different roles with respect to action and action goals in the system. Emotions proper result from monitoring whether events promise, or threaten to interfere with, concern satisfaction. That is to say: Emotions proper result from monitoring whether events permit or interfere with action toward getting, keeping, or enjoying that satisfaction. What emotion proper does – what the action readiness change does – is to align (invigorate, focus on course, prepare for enjoyment) these actions upon promise; or to realign (remove obstacles in the path of, remove oneself from obstacles in the path of, etc.) those actions upon interference; or to regulate endeavor (continue action, change goals, marshal resources, abandon action) in correspondence with observed chances for goal completion, in emotions such as hope, disappointment, discouragement. In short, emotion proper serves to facilitate or regulate action belonging to other goals and other programs than its own.

Desires, by contrast, initiate and maintain new courses of action; they establish goals and activate programs for achieving them. They result from recognizing existence – potential availability or just existence – of fit objects for satisfaction (section 5.4). Such recognition occurs because those objects fit "sensitivities," internal representations, memory images, biological dispositions which enable perception or thought of these objects to evoke behavior programs for obtaining them (section 6.4). The action readiness of desire serves its own program only. Enjoyments result from recognizing that those objects are within reach of consummatory activity; they consist of the impulse for executing that action itself. They do not monitor arrival or achievement of concern satisfaction, as joy does, or pride, or contentment; lust, tenderness, and admiration monitor and motivate the accomplishment of concern satisfaction (of sex, or caring for, or sharing in the value of someone) as such.

Variants of the emotion process

The emotion process sometimes is a linear process, as suggested in Figure 9.1. More often it is not: Figure 9.1 should contain bidirectional links. Most of the time, information flow is not from the top down only. Information uptake is guided by information already processed, from all stages of processing, as detailed in section 8.3: Initial appraisals ask for confirmation, evaluation of what actions might or did achieve influences appraisal, overt response psyches up action tendency, and so forth. Regulation responds to processes planned as well as executed, and this is so essential to regulation that the bidirectional links have been drawn.

The process not always runs in the sequence as depicted. Context evaluation may precede relevance evaluation, as when, coming to an unfamiliar hotel, one looks for the emergency exit and fire escape, and thus already knows the layout when a fire breaks out.

Emotion in its typical form embodies the process in its entirety, from information uptake to overt response, with the part from appraisal to action readiness change as the trunk – that which is properly emotion. But subprocesses can be skipped, and the process can be interrupted at any point, thus producing the variants of emotional phenomena (section 4.10).

Input processing is skipped when emotion is aroused by internal processes such as pharmacological agents, as in pharmacologically induced anxiety or depression. Context evaluation is skipped in the response to unexpected sudden events or when otherwise there is no time for information gathering or processing: in emotional shock, or startle and the mind going blank; or in instances of mere excitement. Everything that comes between context appraisal and overt response is skipped when the individual is fitted out with highly automatized acquired behaviors or with stereotyped unlearned ones: as the driver who brings the car out of a skid, the trained jiu-jitsu fighter who hits in reflex fashion, or again the startle response. In many instances of the above, processes are not truly skipped or omitted by interruption, but temporarily bypassed by other, faster or overlaying ones; fear still comes after having regained control of the car, upset still comes with unbidden images after denial (sections 5.9, 8.3).

The emotion process may halt after the Action Proposer has done its work: after action tendency is generated. Action tendency may be too weak to really translate into action or physiological arousal; or it might be, on occasion, in its nature not to translate into action. Both occur, and the result is what we termed feeling, without quotation marks (see section 4.10).

Then there is the path through the process diagram that finds no urgency in the Evaluator, but does find seriousness, and that also does not go on to action. That path, like that of feeling, does not lead to control precedence. Its action sequel consists of true plan construction and plan execution: Intentional structures and passions (section 2.10) result.

Finally, both urgency and seriousness may be nil, control precedence does not ensue, and the label "emotional" loses its sense: It is the process of cool, goal-directed action with respect to matters of personal interest. Many goal-directed actions result from the interaction of events or of thought about them and concerns, or they can be traced back to such interaction. This structure of action generation can be seen as a complication of the more "original," more elementary structure of behavior as outlined in the diagram. It is a complication, in an evolutionary sense, that goals emerge in the absence of actual stimulus events and urgent context. Goals can emerge because foresight can foresee the eventual advent of relevant events; or because rationality generates the idea that their advent is possible; or because habit ensures that they never occur. What foresight, rationality, and habit do is to forestall occurrence of urgent, that is emotional, events. Cool, ordinary, instrumental, or goal-directed action – a dog smoothly and coolly jumping the shuttle box fence upon the warning signal, we humans going shopping or going to work in the morning – is nonemotional only because desire and fear, and thereby joy, are forestalled by habit and anticipation, through previous experience and reasoning.

As said, goal-directed action to a large extent flows from goals for obtaining concern satisfaction or dealing with anticipated interference.

Emotion and goal-directed action thus have much in common. They both serve concern satisfaction; they both flow from signaling actual or potential concern relevance of actual or thought-of events. The difference resides in the appraisals that start the processes – urgent or not, difficult or not – and in the control precedence signals and processes that result.

9.2. Emotional experience

Emotional experience is an output from various phases of the emotion process sketched. In chapter 4 we argued that emotional experience consists of awareness of situational meaning structure, awareness of autonomic arousal or dearousal, and awareness of state of action readiness, both as impulse and as feedback from behavior. In addition, it consists of pleasure or pain, either truly in the form of subjective experience or as the "relevance" aspect of situational meaning structure – as perception of the horrible, or the delightful, or the enjoyable. In addition, it further contains awareness of control precedence or its complement, the sense of being overwhelmed. In addition, it may contain the response's "significance," not matched to a specific phase in the diagram of Figure 9.1.

These various experiential components together constitute emotional experience. From them, emotional experience can be reconstituted, in the sense that they can be used to produce descriptions that are unique and recognizable as descriptions of any given emotional experience. This, at least, is the theoretical claim. The claim is not exaggerated because it says that emotional experience consists of what novelists put into their descriptions.

The claim may appear unwarranted, since many emotional experiences are ill understood. What, for instance, distinguishes panic from anxiety, as some authors assert something does (Klein 1981; Van Dis 1985)? But the fact that some emotional experiences are ill understood underscores the point that emotional experiences can be analyzed, if understood – and then, presumably, along the lines given.

As said earlier, it is sometimes asserted that emotional experience is an irreducible quale – if not all emotional experience, then at least that experience that gives each basic emotion its specific flavor. This position cannot be proven incorrect: One can always hypothesize an irreducible quale. However, there is no need to do so. The components mentioned contain all the information needed for reconstitution of unique experience.

We make an exception for one of the components themselves: hedonic experience. The basic hedonic experiences of pleasure and pain appear indeed to be basics (section 4.7). They are to be considered signals provided by nature for alerting the organism to its well-functioning and malfunctioning (section 6.4).

Experience is not merely a result, an output, of the emotion process. It also is one of its essential ingredients. The output of the appraisal processes is situational meaning structure – the event as perceived. Situational meaning structure is the input to response generation: It triggers control precedence and motivates action tendency and activation change (sections 4.3 and 4.4). Furthermore, situational meaning structure itself is determined in part by feedback from action or action tendency, from previous coping success or anticipated present potentials: an event is overpowering by virtue of one's own lack of power (sections 4.4 and 5.6). And, of course, action itself can be regulated by, and because of, its actual and expected effects (section 8.2).

The experience as sketched is not necessarily reflexive awareness; usually it is not. As will be recalled, it was deemed necessary to distinguish irreflexive and reflexive awareness – one's knowing something, as evident from behavior, and one's knowing that one knows it, one's awareness of awareness (section 4.3). Experience as referred to in the previous paragraph is, first of all, irreflexive experience – experience that, presumably, an animal is also capable of. One may object to the word *experience* in this connection, and prefer the word *unconscious*.

What is quite distinctly unconscious, usually, is the appraisal process, the series of processes that generate situational meaning structure. One usually knows not which stimulus event feature interacts with which concern; and one does not have to know that in order for situational meaning structure – perception of something horrible or delightful or attractive – to emerge. When one does know, it often is after the fact. It is also after the fact of situational meaning structure having elicited action readiness change. Because of this limited effect of reflexive awareness, emotion can be said to be an essentially unconscious process. One knows, generally, that one has an emotion; one does not always know why, and what exactly makes one have it; and if one does know, it is a construction, a hypothesis, like those one makes about the emotions of someone else (sections 4.3 and 5.9).

Nonetheless, emotional experience in the sense of reflexive awareness plays an important role in the development of emotional response, and it is an important aspect of that response. That role of experience is highlighted by the phenomena of feeling, in the sense in which this word is being used here.

Feelings, we said (section 4.10), consist of awareness of situational meaning structure and of action readiness change at the level of mere potentiality, mere inclination, mere plan. Feelings, in the phrase of Pribram (1970), are monitors. They register relevances: relevant concern–event interactions. They register the context of these relevances: that there are events that are angering, saddening, et cetera. They may register urgency and seriousness. But they do so without the need for actual action readiness change with concomitant control precedence, or without the subject allowing the process to go that way.

Such monitoring is not for the record only. It serves analysis of the concerns and event features involved: What is it that angers me, and why? It serves evaluation, not only of the event but also of the object concerned: He may not be worth getting angry at. It serves planning: in intentional structures and passions (section 2.10). And it serves regulation: Better get overtly angry, or better keep out of his way. In other words, it serves all these responses that are not under direct stimulus control or stimulus-elicited expectancy control.

Experience also plays all these roles in true emotion. Awareness of what one feels, does, or is inclined to do, and why, adds to the situational meaning structure. It is input like any other input and is added to the blackboard; it modifies subsequent evaluations. Experience of what one does or is inclined to do also belongs to the input to regulation, for which self-monitoring is one of the important aspects (sections 8.1, 8.5).

9.3. Psychological theory of emotion

The preceding sections discussed emotion in information-processing terms and from a functionalist perspective. Emotion is seen as the output of a provision, a system, for ensuring concern satisfaction and for monitoring ongoing events for that purpose (section 6.5).

Description of function and information flow does not suffice as a psychological theory. To become a psychological theory, mechanisms must be specified – that is, constraints posed by the organism upon information processed and upon the modes of processing, modes of action the organism has at its disposition, and the major goals that determine those modes of action. A psychological theory of emotion must thus specify whether there are constraints upon the concerns that emotion endeavors to safeguard and satisfy; upon the stimuli considered when doing so, and the processing these stimuli are subjected to; whether the human or animal organism brings specific action modes to the process; how it coordinates stimuli with those actions, and under what conditions or restrictions it does so.

Emotions

Emotions, in this perspective, are defined as changes in action readiness. That is: Emotions are changes in readiness for action as such (we called these changes in activation), or changes in cognitive readiness (they have come under investigation as attentional arousal), or changes in readiness for modifying or establishing relationships with the environment (we called these action tendencies), or changes in readiness for specific concern-satisfying activities (we called these desires and enjoyments).

Concerns

Concerns underlie emotions. They underlie the meaningfulness of action readiness change; their satisfaction or safeguarding is what action coming out of action readiness is for.

The concerns of higher animals and humans largely develop through experience; and in humans more so than in animals. They are in large measure tied up with the presence of specific other individuals (partners, parents, other familiar individuals), specific environments (familiar places, one's own territory, house, or nest), and specific life goals; in humans they are also tied up with values and objects proposed by the society one lives in. We called all those concerns "surface concerns." They depend upon the particular environments in which the individual has grown up and moves about.

But surface concerns must be considered to derive from elementary forms of satisfaction and aversion rooted in the species' constitution. Emotions thus are tied up, in large measure, with the particular behavior systems with which the species happens to be endowed: those involved in sex, in attachment to particular individuals, in social propensities with their two major motives of power and prestige (Kemper 1978), in preference for the familiar, in care for one's young, and so on (section 6.3).

Emotions are not tied up only with the particular environments of the individual and the particular behavior systems of the species. They also are tied up with every major function that the individual or the species is equipped to perform and that he or it can perform well. As argued in sections 6.3 and 6.4, performance of every such function constitutes a concern: Challenge to such performance produces positive emotions, and its frustration, all negative emotions imaginable. Such concerns include cognitive assimilation, freedom for self-initiated action, and having experiences one is able to handle.

Some concerns, and thus emotions, are intimately linked to the general mode of functioning of the organism, and even to the hardware: to the general monitoring of success of planned action, for instance, which constitutes sense of competence, or to the fact that optimal cognitive functioning just happens to depend upon an optimal cortical arousal level, which may account for need for variety.

Of particularly pervasive consequence is the fact that human and animal response propensity happens to be highly dependent upon prevailing level of activation: the level of alertness and "interestedness" and eagerness for interaction. That level is variable and itself dependent upon a number of conditions: physical well-being or exhaustion, recent successes and failures; direct central nervous system factors (neurotransmitters) perhaps. Prevailing level of activation forms a side condition for emotional responses generally: It is manifest as positive or negative mood. In addition, as general propensity for interactions, it is itself a source of emotions, of the free activation or joy variety, in playful activities – and of other emotions upon its frustration or running idle.

Stimuli

Stimuli elicit emotions when they are relevant to concerns: when they constitute or signal match or mismatch with conditions of concern satisfaction.

However, not all stimuli constituting or signaling match or mismatch do in fact elicit emotion. Match and mismatch only occur when stimulus inputs have the proper formats so that comparisons with conditions of concern satisfaction can be made. Emotion is elicited only when inputs have the proper format. That proper format appears to be sensory stimulation associated with pleasure and pain, with actual match or mismatch, or else the hampered or unhampered execution of consummatory action (see section 5.9). One fears pain, not warnings of pain that were never followed by pain. One does not suffer from mere absence of the beloved who left or died, one suffers when one's arm reaches out in vain. In humans, imagery supplements sensory stimulation and action's outcomes (see section 5.9).

The inverse of the preceding also applies. Stimuli are indifferent, emotionally, when they do not imply concern relevance: when they do not promise or threaten satisfaction. This again only applies when they have the proper format; it does not when stimuli have not that proper format, and particularly not when other available stimuli do. We know that that other person is not to blame, but still we saw what he did. Here, too, imagination may take over and fill the gaps.

This is to say that, even if emotion elicitation is to a very large extent cognitive (chapters 4, 5, and 8), it has not, as it is called, "cognitive penetrability" (Pylyshyn 1984). One cannot really elicit emotion at will; one can only work oneself into it, to some extent. Also, one cannot really abolish emotion at will; one can only work oneself out of it, to some extent, for some duration (see chapter 8). This has two sides. Emotion elicitation is not cognitively penetrable from the stimulus angle: One cannot choose to have or not to have emotions, given certain stimuli; there is a margin, but no license. The same from the concern angle: One cannot get into touch with what counts, one cannot "get into touch with one's feelings," unless the stimuli, as processed, cooperate. The mode of operation of the organism imposes constraints.

Appraisal mechanisms

Appraisal mechanisms, with the help of coding principles proper to the subject, turn stimulus events into events-as-appraised or "situational meaning structure." It is the latter which in fact elicits emotion.

The coding principles, as we argued in section 5.9, in large measure are not special tests applied by the subject to perceived events. The more elementary ones, at least, are not truly knowledge categories. They are implicit in the very processes of information uptake and recognition, built into the system, and in the processes of action monitoring. Novelty, as said, is an outcome of the stimulus-reception process. Pleasure is the direct outcome of match of events as perceived with sensitivities or expectancies of rewarding outcome, and pain that of mismatch – both due to prewired arrangements with respect to matches and mismatches. The elementary coding principles do not come from the outside but from the way the system is built and operates.

The processes of appraisal – considering and evaluating aspects and implications of the stimulus event, and comparing these to the satisfaction conditions of concerns – are in part consciously controlled. Current goals play a role in focusing attention, and so do individual preferences for particular points of view, for particular coding principles (sections

5.2, 5.9, 6.6). However, important aspects of the process again are closed for cognitive penetration. Concern relevance is generated by a process akin to recognition: The stimulus is seen first as bad, and then as harmful, or unfavorable, or whatever reason badness may have. The fact that mechanisms, and not only cognitive strategies, are involved in appraisal is apparent from disturbances in the process: numbness (section 8.3), depersonalization states (section 8.3), and intrusion states (section 2.12) – inhibitory blockings on one side, unbidden images on the other. The fact that numbness, depersonalization, and perhaps intrusions can be given functional interpretations does not alter the fact that all three cannot, or cannot easily, be modified by efforts of will; and that all three are subject to stimulus parameters or stimulus effect parameters, and perhaps individual state parameters (exhaustion?), which, so far, are largely unexplored and thus unknown.

Action readiness change

Action readiness change is the major feature of emotion; it is, in the present perspective, the defining feature. The notion of "action readiness" includes action tendencies and activation modes; it also includes their absence, in relational null states and deactivations (sections 2.2, 2.4). The notion refers to the inner disposition (and its absence) for performing actions and achieving relational change, as it exists at a particular moment. Emotional experience largely consists of experienced action readiness or unreadiness: impulse to flee or strike or embrace; lack of impulse, apathy, listlessness.

Which various emotions humans or animals can have – the various action readiness modes they may experience or show – depends upon what action programs, behavior systems, and activation or deactivation mechanisms the organism has at its disposal. Biological constitution brings along a number of these programs and mechanisms: for defense and attack, for protection, for attentional readiness, for inhibition. Were there to be other behavior systems and mechanisms, there would be other emotions: Chameleons (if they have emotions) must have emotions other than those of humans, and so must geese, which evidently like to fly just behind and askew from other geese. The programs and mechanisms brought along by constitution comprise the "basic" emotions, distinguished along the lines of Darwin, Tomkins, and Plutchik (chapter 2). The programs can accommodate learned behaviors; they also command a number of specific, prewired, innate action modes, some more flexible and themselves program-like, others more rigid. Facial expressions belong to those modes; so do the activation patterns like invigoration, apathy, tenseness, and the various autonomic response modes and vocal intonation patterns. They all represent particular instantiations, by the human and animal organism, of the relational and concern-satisfying aims; as said, they form the means and logistic support for achieving the latter.

Not all action readiness modes spring from specific prewired behavior systems with their specific action patterns. Action tendencies also originate in the general modes of relational change that are available to the individual and that are not particular to emotional response. Part of the action tendency repertoire is both given and constrained by the general action capabilities of the organism: approach, withdrawal, turning toward, turning away from, opening or closing of sensory receptivity. An organism that could not locomote or conceive of locomotion, or otherwise conceive of promoting the occurrence of events, would not be capable of desire; it would merely be capable of want, or distress.

Stimulus–response connections

The vital link in the emotion process is that between situational meaning structures and modes of action readiness change. It is the pivot of the emotion process. Where does the link come from?

As argued in section 5.4, action readiness change is not elicited, properly speaking, by "stimuli" but by "constellations": stimuli-as-signals of given modes of promise of concern satisfaction, or of threat thereto. The emotional impact of stimuli, we also argued, on the whole is learned; that of constellations is not. The links between given constellations and given modes of action readiness must be considered largely preestablished by the structure of the organism. Uncontrollable threat is originally linked to fear – to tendency to protect oneself, to flee or to avoid, or to freeze. Loss that is final, which will never change, is originally linked to depression or grief: to abandonment of interests and helplessness and what more goes with these. In similar fashion, there are innately prepared links between given event features and inhibition and between given event features and physiological response modes: controllability and sympathetic arousal, uncontrollability and heart rate decrease; and what other linkages there are (sections 3.8 and 3.9).

These links, as said, have to be considered preestablished by the structure of the organism. That may mean, and in many instances does mean, that the links are prewired, innate stimulus–response connections; or rather, constellation–response program connections. There can be little doubt that controllable frustration (or a constellation like it) is an innate elicitor of anger, of reactance; that promised and actual goal achievement are innate elicitors of joy, of activation increases; and that interruptions, unexpected events, are innate elicitors of attentional arousal and behavioral arrest. All this, and more, must be assumed. Yet at the same time, what is innately elicited are programs, not responses. Being programs, there must be a measure of goal awareness, that is, of sensitivity to regulating feedback, in them (section 2.8).

Prewired links to prewired programs are not the only means by which the structure of the organism determines what response is made under particular circumstances. In section 2.11, we discussed the "intuitive" type of link: the type of link where action tendency is felt or discovered to be the proper one, by following the "field forces" – the lines of manifestly decreasing punishment and manifestly increasing reward. This type of link, it would seem, connects the general response modes referred to earlier – approach, retreat, sensory exposure and shutting off – to their eliciting conditions.

Regulation

Regulation extends over all phases of the process; dual control, we said, is characteristic of emotional response in various respects and at various levels (chapter 8).

Regulation is exerted at various levels of control. There are inhibitory mechanisms that respond to external stimuli; and there are inhibitory mechanisms that respond to actions elicited, planned or under execution. There are outcome-controlled restraining and enhanced processes, which are better described in cognitive and strategic terms; and there is cognitively penetrable, voluntary self-control; that is, regulation under the control of the topgoals of the organism. Levels correspond to adaptability to details of the situation at hand. True inhibitions cannot be lifted when reason says they are not needed; they are dependent upon inputs in the proper format. Self-control responds to abstract considerations – to the extent that it does respond.

Pleasure and pain, and control precedence

Control precedence is probably the most specific distinguishing mark for the emotional. It is not to the nature of particular behavior modes

per se that emotional action tendencies owe the character of urges or
impulses; it is to their place in the action control structure, once they
are activated. It is control precedence that makes emotional impulse
different from other forms of action instigation (section 2.8).

Control precedence has some particular features that are connected
with the nature of human and animal organisms.

First, control precedence for a given action mode does not merely
mean that that action mode is placed at the top of a priority list, a goal
stack. It means that action readiness, if not actually taking control of
action, impatiently waits to do so. Effort is needed to keep it from taking
control; and readiness insinuates itself into the gaps of current action
planning and information processing; which is what "preoccupation"
is. All this implies some form of parallel processing, the simultaneous
operation of two action control processes, of which dual control as discussed with "regulation" is an instantiation.

Second, control precedence is forced upon the organism primarily by
those peculiar relevance signals, pleasure and pain. These signals are
persistent and insistent: They continue, and are noticed, as long as an
eliciting event continues or a desire is evoked and unsatisfied. They
force themselves upon attention when ongoing activity is not interrupted
for their benefit. As argued earlier (section 2.8), emotional impulse,
desire included, overwhelms and is uncontrollable largely because the
subject allows himself to be overwhelmed and does not truly want to
control, because of the pain that then has to be sustained or the pleasure
foregone.

We found it necessary (section 4.4) to distinguish four relevance signals: pleasure, pain, desire, and "interestingness." Control precedence,
it would seem, falls to the first two only. The uncontrollability of desire
and of curiosity derives, one may argue, from the fact that it is almost
unthinkable to keep them in check – that is, it flows from the violence
of the emotions proper engendered by their frustration.

"Control precedence" has been used to refer to the effects of emotional
impulse and desire upon the general control of action in the organism:
interruption of other activities, preoccupation, and persistence of activity
in the face of obstacles and other distracting events.

Persistence would appear to depend also upon additional properties
of the organism. Action readiness of certain kinds – action tendencies,
presumably, states of activation with specific aims – appeared to have
dynamics of their own. Action programs once triggered have a tendency
to run off until spent, particularly if activation is so strong as to surpass

inhibition thresholds or "points of no return" (sections 2.4 and 2.8). Anger, panic, laughter and weeping were mentioned in this regard; evidence for tension release in connection with laughter and weeping pointed in a similar direction. The concepts of "activation," "dynamics of their own," and "tension release" are vague and largely metaphorical; parameters of intensity, time course, thresholds, and so on are unknown. Also, in desire and in fits of anger, it is difficult to distinguish between "dynamics of its own" and the tempting forces of reward. Still, the phenomena point to what might be a major feature of the emotion process and its mechanisms.

9.4. The concept of "emotion"

The concept

It has been debated whether "emotion" is a substantive category in psychology or rather merely a chapter heading. Duffy (1941, 1962), for one, advocated this latter view: "Emotion," according to her, sloppily refers to the extreme ranges of the activation continuum or to the more pronounced occurrences of ever-present hedonic experience.

The present analysis leads to the conclusion that "emotion" is, in fact, a substantive psychological category. There is a mechanism, or set of mechanisms, ensuring concern satisfaction. That is, there is a mechanism or set of mechanisms that compare stimuli to preference states of the organism and thus turn stimuli into rewards and punishments; it generates pleasure and pain. There is a mechanism that generates expectancies concerning rewards and punishments. There is a mechanism that dictates actions accordingly. There is furthermore a mechanism capable of assuming control precedence for these actions, which interrupts ongoing activity and marshals resources for these actions' purposes. That mechanism, or set of mechanisms, is "emotion" in a wide sense. It is the mechanism that produces readiness change with control precedence, both for motivation (desire, enjoyment) and in emotions proper.

There is a subset of these mechanisms, or part of the overall mechanism, that serves ensuring concern satisfaction by monitoring whether events are conducive or obstructive to concerns already being satisfied or to expectancies and actions toward such satisfaction. These mechanisms command their own specific action programs and provisions for physiological activation and suppression. That mechanism or set of mechanisms is emotion proper. It is the set of mechanisms that produces relational action tendency and activation change.

The mechanisms operate by way of dual control. The mechanisms mentioned contain duplicates, as it were, that attenuate their own functioning, attune it to the situation, and in the event enhance it.

There are thus two definitions of emotion, one encompassing the other. *Emotion* is action readiness change. *Emotion proper* is relational action tendency and change in relational action tendency generally (activation).

One might add still a third definition, one still more restrictive. *Emotion* might be defined as action readiness change in response to emergencies or interruptions; and this action readiness change itself might be restricted to activations and deactivations of actual, overt response: activated behavior and physiological arousal or upset. That definition, of course, yields the "excited" emotions, the typical, or paradigmatic, emotional responses.

The concept of emotion, as defined, might seem to extend to phenomena that one would call "emotional": an ant scurrying forward when touched or upon smelling food; a worm cringing when grasped. Such extension, however, is excluded by the notions of "readiness" and "tendency." These notions point to the central features of emotional behavior: Responses can be held in abeyance, by control, inhibition, or obstruction; and certain responses appear to be manifestations of flexible programs, which programs persist in execution until some termination point; these programs command a variety of responses, each flexibly adapting to circumstances (section 2.8). Flexibility, when it is present, resides not only in the action programs proper, but also in the mechanisms of general activation and attentional arousal. Both are preparatory and facilitatory for a number of action programs. Flexibility also resides in cognitive capacity. Cognitive capacity serves discrimination of differences between emotion-eliciting events; it thus serves both adaptive flexibility of response and flexible regulation.

Abeyance and flexibility are essential features of emotion. That is to say: The concept of "emotion" is meaningful to the extent that fixed action patterns turn into multifaceted, flexible programs that can be inhibited and held in abeyance. The concept of "emotion" is meaningful to the extent that aim and tendency become loosened from the actions performed. Flexibility and inhibitory control, of course, are not all-or-none attributes. There is no sharp dividing line between "reflexive" or "instinctive" behavior and emotion; behavior organizations can be ordered on a continuum in this regard. Hence the possibility of differing in opinion as to whether, say, disgust is or is not an emotion; and hence the possibility of differing in opinion as to where, in evolution, emotion begins: with the worm, or the lizard, or the mouse, the chimpanzee, or the human animal.

Functionality of emotion

The present account of emotion is, quite evidently, a functionalist account. Emotions serve something, and presumably they serve it well. They serve concern satisfaction; they do so by monitoring the relevance of events and by modulating or instigating action accordingly.

Equally evidently, this account collides with the many obvious non-functionalities of emotion: behavior disturbances (section 2.12); exhaustion and the illnesses of adaptation (section 3.10); irrational emotions and emotional actions (section 2.12); useless or damaging emotions such as panic, depressions, nostalgia, emotions contingent upon obsolete attachments; many occurrences of every kind of emotion, such as jealousies, fears, and joys that were better not there, as they turn out to be detrimental to the subject or his relationships.

Some of these emotions, or occurrences of emotions, can be given functional interpretations, and many have been given them in the preceding. It must be emphasized, however, that the functional perspective is a point of view, an a priori. Functionalism assumes that both psychological and biological phenomena make sense and do not represent mere contingencies, merely the way things happen to be. The point of view is not really open to test: Some function, some usefulness, can almost always be found.

Still, the functionalist perspective is a powerful heuristic. It generates useful questions, hypotheses, and evaluations. We will try to evaluate the nonfunctionalities of emotions from this angle.

The major points that are relevant in this connection have been mentioned throughout the preceding chapters. The first: Much of the nonfunctionality of emotion, its harmful effects, derives from the nonfunctionality not of emotions as such, but of the concerns underlying them. When a junkie manifests asocial behavior, blame not his desperation, nor even his desire for heroin, but his need for it; when someone abandons house, spouse, and children, blame not his new infatuation or his old anger, but his concerns for tenderness, or self-importance, or novelty, or whatever moved him or her. In particular, blame not emotion's control precedence: precedence follows preference; it is preference that does the trick (section 2.8).

Why are there nonfunctional concerns? Why do people have the concerns they do? Why are certain goals clung to regardless of their having proven unattainable, attachments clung to despite constant disappointment and contrary to all reason? The motivating powers of distress do not always steer toward disengagement from concerns when this would mean the larger gain; heroin addiction again is the prime illustration. Why? These questions are not for this book to answer. The only aspect within reach of the present review is a mechanical aspect of emotion, which indeed is central in this connection and which forms the following point.

The second major point is that many dysfunctionalities, apparent or real, come from suboptimal evaluations of what weighs most heavily in conflict between concerns (pleasure or health?), in conflicts with regard to any one concern (she or no she?), and most of all in conflicts between short-term gain and long-term gain.

The preponderance of short-term over long-term gain is in the nature of emotion. This is because the short-term gains that are under consideration now are embodied by actual stimuli: escape from the actual distress of no she or no heroin; obtaining the tempting satisfaction dangling before one's eyes. Such stimuli, as said, form the proper input of the emotion system (section 5.9); the system is made to respond to them. Long-term gains, by contrast, are remote, symbolic, have to be thought out, inferred, are told to one by others.

Even so, it might be unfair to blame suboptimal evaluations entirely upon the organism and its equipment for responding to input. They can equally be blamed upon the contingencies of life, which are not always clear in their implications, and which often are in the habit of occurring together and of not admitting of synthesis. In other words: Many irrationalities do not stem from suboptimal design of the human or animal system, but from the fact that we do not live in the best of all possible worlds.

The third major point: A human being cannot have been made to stand and withstand all contingencies life presents. What can you expect from a system that only takes nine months to produce and merely weighs about 70 kilograms? Also, there exist contingencies, both natural and fellow-man-made, that no system can be constructed to cope with and still function adequately in other regards.

That is to say: Many nonfunctional aspects of emotion – dysregulations, disturbances – simply manifest the limits of capacity of the system, the limits of what it can deal with, and the limits of its resources. The role of capacity limitations of course has to be evaluated against the weight of the contingencies such as these are for the subject. A panic attack may be sheer dysregulation, a flaw in the system; but it may also be that concern for being separated (Klein 1981) is so focal for that particular individual.

The fourth, and final point: One may assume that humans have been fitted out with provisions to deal effectively with a number of important contingencies. There is necessarily a cost to this. Several emotion provisions, for instance, are emergency provisions. They produce response fast, and upon a minimum of information processing. If the system can do that, one should not complain that its information processing on these occasions is truncated, or that response is being made when finer meaning analysis might have shown it to have been unnecessary. What counts, of course, is whether overall, and considering the size of risks, there is gain. That is to say: Emotion may be considered an overall functionally adequate, useful provision even if it is not adequate or useful in all of its manifestations.

Nonfunctionality due to overall functionality not merely applies to response to emergencies, but to emotional response generally. Emotion, feeling included, results from ever-ready monitoring of event relevance and concomitant adjustment of action readiness. Such monitoring and adjustment also occur when adjustment is meaningless and of no further consequence. It is a small price to pay for ever-readiness and, moreover, usually evident as meaningless only after the event. This principle may explain many entirely "nonfunctional" emotions. Nostalgia provides an example. Of what use is nostalgia? None, one may assume. But nostalgia is response to thought about an object or event known to be lost or gone. The response is a brief hankering, a reaching out known to be in vain. However, it is an appropriate response for things lost, and which can be seen as vain only after it has occurred; and which response is aimed at an object known to be so valuable only after the response has been made, and because of it. Many other emotions and occurrences of emotions follow the same pattern: old griefs, old grievances, impotent angers. Note that these emotions are not really as useless as they might seem. The action tendencies – reaching out in nostalgia, withdrawal in bitterness over old wrongs, and the like – as such are useless, but awareness of them participates in the functions of emotional experience mentioned in section 9.2: recognition and registration of the events as relevant.

The four points discussed imply extension of the functional viewpoint of emotion over several seemingly nonfunctional manifestations. To repeat: The system may be functionally adequate even if not all its manifestations are; these manifestations do not necessarily evidence flaws in the system or useless additions. As formulated in section 6.5, many emotions "express" rather than ensure concern satisfaction endeavor. In that, they reflect the system's mode of functioning.

To some extent that mode of functioning is just as it is; that is, it cannot meaningfully be considered useful or functionally geared to the events under which it is deployed. In section 6.5 activation modes were discussed from that angle. Activation increase after success and activation decrease after failure or loss – some forms of joy and grief, that is – cannot be interpreted as useful in dealing with successes that are accomplished and losses that are final. They just reflect (or can be seen to reflect) the fact that the system happens to modulate its activity resources in accordance with its current accomplishments.

Many other emotions – desires in particular – should be seen in a similar way. Desires are not generally useful; they just *are*. The same for that multitude of emotions that remain action tendencies without turning into action or even into activation change. They cannot be said to ensure concern satisfaction: They are plans and readiness for ensuring satisfaction. What they all do, though, is reflect and "express" what the individual is concerned with.

The most general statements regarding emotions therefore are: Emotions are the manifestations of the individual's concern satisfaction system; and: Emotions express the individual's concerns and the satisfaction state of these concerns.

Emotion and emotions

This last discussion underscores what has recurred at several points in this chapter: Overt emotional action, activated behavior, and marked arousal emerge from action readiness changes that are largely tentative, subdued, internal – true changes in readiness only. Moreover, they emerge from mere readiness only under particular conditions, which we identified as those of interruption, urgency, and difficulty.

That is to say that excited emotions – emotions under the third definition – emerge as discrete events from action readiness that itself is continuous.

Excited emotions are paradigmatic for the phenomena investigated in this book. They manifest apparently useless behaviors, physiological upset. The phenomena have a distinct beginning and end in time. However, these discrete events only represent the rocks sticking out of the deep continuous streams of emotional responding. In emotional responding generally there is no succession of discrete events so much as flow of varying attitudes, acceptances, rejections, abandonments, and reserves; and that flow may be manifest in experience only. Only sometimes – when events are sudden or urgent and dealing with them is difficult, when control fails or is let go of – does the subject settle upon actually achieving, maintaining, or changing a given transaction, or is forced so to settle, or abandons it. Then full-blown, paradigmatic emotional response bursts loose, overtly or inwardly, and the subject has "an" emotion.

Emotions in this paradigmatic sense, however, are but crystallizations in a stream of emotional response, of readiness and tendency, that faithfully follows the continuous bed of concern-relevant events and overflows that bed in intentional activities and passions; but which stream of relevance appraisals goes on incessantly, mostly only felt by the person herself or himself; which is what we wanted to try to understand.

References

Abelson, R. B. 1983. Whatever became of consistency theory? *Person. Soc. Psychol. Bull.* 9, 37–54.

Abelson, R. B., Kinder, D. R., Peters, M. D., & Fiske, S. T. 1982. Affective and semantic components in political person perception. *J. Pers. Soc.Psychol.* 42, 619–30.

Abelson, R. B., & Sermat, V. 1962. Multidimensional scaling of facial expressions. *J. Exp. Psychol.* 63, 546–664.

Aberle, D. 1965. A note on relative deprivation theory as applied to millenarian and other cult movements. In W. A. Lester & E. Z. Vogt (eds.), *Reader in comparative religion: an anthropological approach.* New York: Harper & Row, 537–41.

Abramson, L., Seligman, M., & Teasdale, J. 1978. Learned helplessness in humans: critique and reformulation. *J. Abnorm. Psychol.* 87, 49–74.

Adams, D. B. 1971. Defence and territorial behavior dissociated by hypothalamic regions in the rat. *Nature* 232, 573–4.

1979. Brain mechanisms for offense, defense, and submission. *Behav. Brain Sci.* 2, 201–41.

Ahrens, R. 1954. Beiträge zur Entwicklung des Physignomie und Mimikerkennens. *Z. Exp. Angew. Psychol.* 2, 414–54.

Ainsworth, M. D. S. 1967. *Infancy in Uganda.* Baltimore: Johns Hopkins University Press.

Alechsieff, N. 1907. Die Grundformen der Gefühle. *Psychol. Stud.* 3, 156–271.

Allport, G. W. 1937. *Personality: a psychological interpretation.* New York: Holt.

Allport, G. W., & Vernon, P. 1935. *Studies in expressive movement.* New York: Macmillan.

Ambrose, A. 1963. The age of onset of ambivalence in early infancy: Indications from the study of laughing. *J. Child Psychol. Psychiat.* 4, 167–81.

Amsel, A. 1958. The role of frustrative nonreward in non-continuous reward situations. *Psychol. Bull.* 55, 102–19.

1962. Frustrative nonreward in partial reinforcement and discrimination: some recent history and theoretical extension. *Psychol. Rev.* 69, 306–28.

Anand, B. B., Chhina, G. S., & Singh, B. 1961. Some aspects of electroencephalographic studies in Yogis. *Electroencephalogr. Clin. Neurophysiol.* 13, 452–6.

Ancoli, S., Kamiya, J., & Ekman, P. 1980. Psychophysiological differentiation of positive and negative affects. *Biofeedback and Self-regulation* 5, 356–7.

Andrew, J. N. 1970. Recovery from surgery, with and without preparatory instruction, for three coping styles. *J. Pers. Soc. Psychol.* 15, 223–6.

Andrew, R. J. 1963. The origin and evolution of the calls and facial expressions of the primates. *Behavior* 20, 1–109.

1972. The information potentially available in mammal displays. In R. A. Hinde (ed.), *Non-verbal communication*. Cambridge, England: Cambridge Univ. Press, 179–203.

Andrews, B. K., & Whitey, S. B. 1976. *Social indications of well-being: Americans' perceptions of life quality*. New York: Plenum.

Anisman, H., & Zacharko, A. M. 1982. Depression: the predisposing influence of stress. *Behav. Brain Sciences* 5, 89–138.

Antonovsky, A. 1979. *Health, stress and coping*. San Francisco: Jossey-Bass.

Archer, J. 1976. The organisation of aggression and fear in vertebrates. In P. P. G. Bateson & P. Klopfer (eds.), *Perspectives in ethology* (Vol. 2). New York: Plenum, 231–98.

Archibald, H. C., & Tuddenham, R. D. 1965. Persistent stress reactions after combat. *Arch. Gen. Psychiat.* 12, 475–81.

Argyle, M., & Cook, M. 1976. *Gaze and mutual gaze*. Cambridge, England: Cambridge Univ. Press.

Argyle, M., & Dean, J. 1965. Eye-contact, distance and affiliation. *Sociometry* 28, 289–304.

Argyle, M., & Kendon, A. 1967. The experimental analysis of social performance. In L. Berkowitz (ed.), *Advances in experimental social psychology* (Vol. 3), New York: Academic Press, 55–98.

Aries, P. 1974. *Western attitudes towards death*. Baltimore: Johns Hopkins Univ. Press.

Arnold, M. B. 1960. *Emotion and personality* (Vols. I and II). New York: Columbia Univ. Press.

1970. Perennial problems in the field of emotion. In M. B. Arnold (ed.), *Feelings and emotions*. New York: Academic Press, 169–86.

Atkinson, J., & Birch, D. 1978. *An introduction to motivation*. New York: Van Nostrand.

Averill, J. R. 1968. Grief: its nature and significance. *Psychol. Bull.* 70, 721–48.

1969. Autonomic response patterns during sadness and mirth. *Psychophysiology* 5, 399–414.

1973. Personal control over aversive stimuli and its relationship to stress. *Psychol. Bull.* 80, 286–303.

1982. *Anger and aggression: an essay on emotion*. New York: Springer

Averill, J. R., Malmstrom, E. J., Koriat, A., & Lazarus, R. S. 1972. Habituation to complex emotional stimuli. *J. Abnorm. Psychol.* 80, 20–8.

Averill, J. R., & Rosenn, M. 1972. Vigilant and non-vigilant coping strategies and psychophysical stress reactions during anticipation of electric shock. *J. Pers. Soc. Psychol.* 23, 128–41.

Ax, A. F. 1953. The psychological differentiation between fear and anger in humans. *Psychosom. Med.* 15, 433–42.

Azrin, N. H., & Hutchinson, R. R. 1967. Conditioning of the aggressive behavior of pigeons by a fixed-interval schedule of reinforcement. *J. Exper. Anal. Behav.* 10, 395–402.

Bacon, S. J. 1974. Arousal and the range of cue utilization. *J. Exp. Psychol.* 102, 81–7.

Badia, P., Culbertson, S., & Harsh, J. 1973. Choice of longer or stronger signalled shock over shorter or weaker unsignalled shock. *J. Exper. Anal. Behav.* 19, 25–32.

Badia, P., & Defran, R. H. 1970. Orienting responses and GSR-conditioning: a dilemma. *Psychol. Rev.* 77, 171–81.

Bagchi, B. K., & Wenger, M. A. 1957. Electrophysiological correlates of some yogi exercises. *Electroencephalogr. Clin. Neurophysiol. Suppl.* 7, 132–49.

Bagshaw, M. H., Mackworth, N. H., & Pribram, K. H. 1972. The effect of resections of the inferotemporal cortex or the amygdala on visual orienting and habituation. *Neuropsychologia* 10, 153–62.

Bandura, A. 1969. *Principles of behavior modification.* New York: Holt, Rinehart & Winston.

1973. *Aggression: a social learning analysis.* Englewood Cliffs, N.J.: Prentice-Hall.

1977a. *Social learning theory.* Englewood Cliffs, N.J.: Prentice-Hall.

1977b. Self-efficacy: towards a unifying theory of behavior change. *Psychol. Rev.* 84, 191–215.

Bandura, A., Adams, N., & Beyer, J. 1977. Cognitive processes mediating behavioral change. *J. Pers. Soc. Psychol.* 35, 125–39.

Bandura, A., Blanchard, E. G., & Ritter, B. 1969. The relative efficacy of desensitization and modelling approaches for inducing behavioral, effective and attitudinal changes. *J. Pers. Soc. Psychol.* 13, 173–99.

Bandura, A., & Menlove, F. L. 1968. Factors determining vicarious extinction of avoidance behavior through symbolic modeling. *J. Pers. Soc. Psychol.* 8, 99–108.

Bandura, A., & Rosenthal, T. L. 1966. Vicarious classical conditioning as a function of arousal level. *J. Pers. Soc. Psychol.* 3, 54–62.

Bard, P. 1928. A diencephalic mechanism for the expression of rage with special reference to the sympathetic nervous system. *Am. J. Physiol.* 84, 490–515.

1934. On emotional expression after decortication with some remarks on certain theoretical views (parts I and II). *Psychol. Rev.* 41, 309–29; 424–49.

Bard, P., & Mountcastle, V. B. 1948. Some forebrain mechanisms involved in the expression of rage with special reference to suppression of angry behavior. *Res. Publ. Assoc. Res. Nerv. Ment. Dis.* 27, 362–404.

Barefoot, J. C., & Straub, R. B. 1974. Opportunity for information search and the effect of false heart rate feedback. In H. London & R. E. Nisbett (eds.), *Thought and feeling: cognitive alteration of feeling states.* Chicago: Aldine, 107–15.

Barendregt, J. T. 1982. *De zielenmarkt.* Meppel, Netherlands: Boom-Pers.

Barendregt, J. T., & Frijda, N. H. 1982. Cognitive aspects of anxiety. *J. Drug Res.* 4, 17–24.

Barrett, C. L. 1969. Systematic desensitization versus implosive therapy. *J. Abnorm. Psychol.* 74, 587–92.

Bartlett, E. S., & Izard, C. E. 1972. A dimensional and discrete emotions investigation of the subjective experience of emotion. In C. E. Izard (ed.), *Patterns of emotions.* New York: Academic Press, 129–75.

Bartoshuk, A. K. 1971. Motivation. In J. W. Kling & L. A. Riggs (eds.), *Woodworth and Schlosberg's experimental psychology.* New York: Holt, Rinehart & Winston.

Basowitz, H., Persky, H., Korchin, S. J., & Grinker, R. R. 1955. *Anxiety and stress.* New York: McGraw-Hill.

Baum, M. 1970. Extinction of avoidance responding through response prevention (flooding). *Psychol. Bull.* 74, 276–84.

Beach, F. A., & Holtz, M. 1946. Mating behavior in male rats castrated at various ages and injected with androgens. *J. Exp. Zool.* 101, 91–142.

Beck, A. T. 1967. *Depression: clinical, experimental and theoretical aspects.* New York: Harper & Row.

1971. Cognitions, affect and psychopathology. *Arch. Gen. Psychiat.* 24, 495–500.

1976. *Cognitive therapy and the emotional disorders.* New York: International Univ. Press.

Becker, J. 1974. *Depression: theory and research.* Washington, D.C.: Winston.

Beebe-Center, J. G. 1932. *The psychology of pleasantness and unpleasantness.* New York: Van Nostrand.

Beecher, H. K. 1959. *Measurement of subjective responses.* London: Oxford University Press.

Bekhterew, A. 1894. Zwangshaftes Lachen und Weinen in zerebralen Affektionen. *Arch. Psychiat. Neurol.* 26, 791–802.

Bekhterewa, N. P. (ed.). 1969. *Physiologie und Pathophysiologie der tiefen Hirnstrukturen des Menschen.* Berlin: Verlag Volk und Gesundheit.

Bell, C. 1844. *The anatomy and philosophy of expression* (3rd ed.). London: Bohn.

Beluzzi, J. D., Grant, N. Garsky, V., Sarantakis., D., Wise, C. D., & Stein, L. 1976. Analgesia induced in vivo by central administration of enkephalin in rats. *Nature* 260, 625–6.

Belluzi, J. D., & Stein, L. 1977. Enkephalin may mediate euphoria and drive-reduction reward. *Nature* 266, 556–8.

Bem, D. J. 1972. Self-perception theory. In L. Berkowitz (ed.), *Advances in experimental social psychology* (Vol. 6). New York: Academic Press, 2–62.

Benesch, H. 1960. *Der Ausdruck im Momente des Versagens.* Bericht 22 Kongr. Deutschen Ges. Psychol.

Berger, S. M. 1962. Conditioning through vicarious instigation. *Psychol. Rev.* 69, 450–68.

Berkowitz, L. 1960. Repeated frustrations and expectations in hostility arousal. *J. Abnorm. Soc. Psychol.* 60, 422–9.

1962. *Aggression: a social psychological analysis.* New York: McGraw-Hill.

1974. Some determinants of impulsive aggression: role of mediated associations with reinforcements for aggression. *Psychol. Rev.* 81, 165–76.

Berkowitz, L., & LePage, A. 1967. Weapons as aggression-eliciting stimuli. *J. Pers. Soc. Psychol.* 7, 202–7.

Berlyne, D. E. 1960. *Conflict, arousal and curiosity.* New York: McGraw-Hill.

1969. Laughter, humor and play. In G. Lindzey & E. Aronson (eds.). *Handbook of social psychology* (Vol. 3). Reading: Addison-Wesley, 795–852.

1971. *Aesthetics and psychobiology.* New York: Appleton-Century-Crofts.

Bermond, B. 1978. *Neuro-humoral regulation of aggressive and sexual behavior in the rat.* Amsterdam: Univ. Amsterdam.

1982. Effects of androgen treatment of full-grown puberally castrated rats upon sexual behavior, intermale aggressive behavior and the sequential patterning of aggressive interactions. *Behavior* 80, 144–73.

Bernick, N., Kling, A., & Borowitz, G. 1971. Physiologic differentiation of sexual arousal and anxiety. *Psychosom. Med.* 32, 341–51.

Bersh, P. J. 1980. Eysenck's theory of incubation: a critical analysis. *Behav. Res. Ther.* 18, 11–17.

Bettelheim, B. 1943. Individual and mass behavior in extreme situations. *J. Abnorm. Soc. Psychol.* 38, 417–52.

1976. *The uses of enchantment.* London: Thames & Hudson.

Bexton, W. H., Heron, W., & Scott, T. H. 1954. Effects of decreased variation in the sensory environment. *Can. J. Psychol.* 8, 70–6.

Beyk, M. 1968. *A study of black-outs in actors.* Amsterdam: Report, Univ. Amsterdam.

Bezooyen, R. A. M. C. van, 1984. *Characteristics and recognizability of vocal expressions of emotion*. Dordrecht: Foris Publ.

Bills, A. G. 1927. The influence of muscular tension on the efficiency of mental work. *Am. J. Psychol.* 38, 227–51.

1937. Blocking in mental fatigue and anoxemia compared. *Am. J. Psychol.* 43, 230–45.

Birkhoff, G. D. 1932. *Aesthetic measure*. Cambridge, Mass.: Harvard Univ. Press.

Bitterman, M. E. 1975. Issues in the comparative psychology of learning. In R. B. Masterton, M. E. Bitterman, C. B. G. Campbell, & N. Hotten (eds.), *The evolution of brain and behavior in vertebrates*. New York: Erlbaum.

Black, A. H. 1959. Heart rate changes during avoidance learning in dogs. *Can. J. Psychol.* 13, 229–42.

Black, A. H., & Young, G. A. 1972. Electrical activity of the hippocampus and cortex in dogs operantly trained to move and to hold still. *J. Comp. Physiol. Psychol.* 79, 128–41.

Black, A. H., & deToledo, L. 1972. The relationship among classically conditioned responses: heart rate and skeletal behavior. In A. H. Black & W. Prokasy (eds.), *Classical conditioning: current research and theory*. New York: Appleton-Century-Crofts, 290–313.

Blanchard, E. B., & Young, L. B. 1973. Self-control of cardiac functioning: a promise as yet unfulfilled. *Psychol. Bull.* 79, 145–63.

Blatz, W. E. 1925. The cardiac, respiratory and electrical phenomena involved in the emotion of fear. *J. Exp. Psychol.* 8, 109–32.

Block, J. 1957. Studies in the phenomenology of emotions. *J. Abnorm. Soc. Psychol.* 54, 358–63.

Bloom, L. J., Houston, B. K., Holmes, D. S., & Burish, T. G. 1977. The effectiveness of attentional diversion and situational redifinition for reducing stress due to a nonambiguous threat. *J. Res. Pers.* 11, 83–94.

Blurton-Jones, N. G. 1972a. Comparative aspects of mother–child contact. In N. Blurton-Jones (ed.), *Ethological studies of child behavior*. Cambridge, England: Cambridge Univ. Press, 305–28.

1972b. Non-verbal communication in children. In R. A. Hinde (ed.). *Non-verbal communication*. Cambridge, England: Cambridge Univ. Press, 271–96.

Board, F., Persky, H., & Hamburg, D. A. 1956. Psychological stress and endocrine functions. *Psychosom. Med.* 18, 324–34.

Boas, E. P., & Goldschmidt, E. F. 1932. *The heart rate*. Springfield, Ill.: Thomas.

Bogdanoff, M. D., Combs, J. J., Bryant, G. D., & Warren, J. V. 1959. Cardiovascular responses in experimentally induced alterations of affect. *Circulation* 20, 353–9.

Bohus, B. 1975. The hippocampus and the pituitary–adrenal system hormones. In R. L. Isaacson & K. H. Pribram (eds.). *The Hippocampus* (Vol. 1). New York: Plenum.

Bolles, R. C. 1970. Species-specific defense reactions. *Psychol. Rev.* 77, 32–48.

1972. The avoidance learning problem. In G. Bower, *The psychology of learning & motivation* (Vol. 6). New York: Academic Press.

1975. *Theory of motivation* (2nd ed.). New York: Harper & Row.

Bolles, R. C., & Fanselow, M. S. 1980. A perceptual-defensive model of fear and pain. *Behav. Brain Sci.* 3, 291–323.

Bolles, R. C., & Grossen, N. E. 1969. Effects of an informational stimulus on the acquisition of avoidance behavior in rats. *J. Comp. Physiol. Psychol.* 68, 90–9.

Boselie, F. 1984. Complex and simple proportions and the aesthetic attractivity of visual patterns. *Perception* 13, 91–6.

Bourke-White, M. 1963. *Portrait of myself.* New York: Simon & Schuster.

Bourne, P. G., Rose, R. M., & Mason, J. W. 1967. Urinary 17-OHCS levels: data on seven helicopter ambulance medics in combat. *Arch. Gen Psychiat.* 17, 104–111.

Bower, G. H., & Cohen, P. R. 1982. Emotional influences in memory and thinking: data and theory. In M. S. Clark & S. T. Fiske (eds.), *Affect and cognition.* Hillsdale: Erlbaum.

Bower, G. H., Monteiro, K. P., & Gilligan, S. G. 1978. Emotional mood as a context for learning and recall. *J. Verb. Learn. Behav.* 17, 573, 585.

Bowlby, J. 1969. *Attachment (Attachment and loss,* Vol. 1). London: Hogarth Press.
  1973. *Separation: anxiety and grief (Attachment and loss,* Vol. 2). London: Hogarth Press.
  1980, *Loss: sadness and depression (Attachment and loss,* Vol. 3). London: Hogarth Press.

Brady, J. V. 1970. Endocrine and autonomic correlates of emotional behaviour. In P. Black (ed.), *Physiological correlates of emotion.* New York: Academic Press.

Brady, J. V., & Hunt, H. F. 1955. An experimental approach to the analysis of emotional behavior. *J. Psychol.* 40, 313–24.

Brady, J. V., & Nauta, W. J. 1955. Subcortical mechanisms in control of behavior. *J. Comp. Physiol. Psychol.* 48, 412–20.

Brady, J. V., Porter, R. W., Conrad, D. G., & Mason, J. W. 1958. Avoidance behavior and the development of gastroduodenal ulcers. *J. Exp. Anal. Behav.* 1, 69–72.

Brady, J. V., Thornton, D. R., & Fisher, D. 1962. Deleterious effects of anxiety elicited by conditioned pre-aversive stimuli in the rat. *Psychosom. Med.* 24, 590–5.

Brantigan, C. O., Brantigan, T. A., & Joseph, N. 1982. Effect of beta blockade and beta stimulation on stage fright. *Am. J. Med.* 72, 88–94.

Breggin, P. R. 1964. The psychophysiology of anxiety. *J. Nerv. Ment. Dis.* 139, 558–68.

Bregman, E. 1934. An attempt to modify the emotional attitude of infants by the conditioned response technique. *J. Genet. Psychol.* 45, 169–98.

Brehm, J. W. 1966. *A theory of psychological reactance.* New York: Academic Press.
  1972. *Responses to loss of freedom: a theory of psychological reactance.* Morristown: General Learning Press.

Brentano, F. 1874. *Psychologie vom empirischen Standpunkt.* Leipzig: Duncker & Humboldt.

Breuer, J., & Freud, S. 1895. *Studien über Hysterie.* Vienna: Deuticke (Ges. Werk Bd I. Frankfurt, Fischer).

Breznitz, S. 1976. False alarms: their effects on fear and adjustment. In I. G. Sarason & C. D. Spielberger (eds.), *Stress & anxiety* (Vol. 3), New York: Halstead.
  (ed.) 1983a. *The denial of stress.* New York: International Univ. Press.
  1983b. The seven kinds of denial. In S. Breznitz (ed.), *The denial of stress.* New York: International Univ. Press.

Bridger, W. H., & Mandel, J. J. 1964. A comparison of GSR fear responses produced by threat and electrical shock. *J. Psychiatr. Res.* 2, 31–40.

Briggs, J. L. 1970. *Never in anger: portrait of an Eskimo family.* Cambridge, Mass.: Harvard Univ. Press.

Broadbent, D. E. 1971. *Decision and stress.* New York: Academic Press.

Broadhurst, P. 1957. Emotionality and the Yerkes–Dodson Law. *J. Exp. Psychol.* 54, 345–52.

1958. Determinants of emotionality in the rat, III: strain differences. *J. Comp. Physiol. Psychol.* 51, 55–9.

1959. The interaction of task difficulty and motivation: the Yerkes–Dodson Law revisited. *Acta Psychol.* 16, 321–38.

1960. Studies in psychogenetics: applications of biometrical genetics to the inheritance of behavior. In H. J. Eysenck (ed.), *Experiments in personality* (Vol. 1). London: Routledge & Kegan Paul, 3–102.

Brooks, V., & Hochberg, J. 1960. A psychophysical study of "cuteness." *Percept. Mot. Skills* 11, 205.

Brown, B. B. 1971. Awareness of EEG-subjective activity relationships detected within a closed feedback system. *Psychophysiology* 7, 451–64.

Brown, C. H., & Van Gelder, D. 1938. Emotional reactions before examinations, I: Physiological changes. *J. Psychol.* 5, 1–9.

Brown, J. L., Hunsperger, R. W., & Rosvold, H. E. 1969. Defense, attack and flight elicited by electrical stimulation of the hypothalmus of the cat. *Exp. Brain Res.* 8, 113–29.

Brown, J. S. 1961. *The motivation of behavior.* New York: McGraw-Hill.

Brown, J. S., & Farber, I. E. 1951. Emotions conceptualized as intervening variables – with suggestions towards a theory of frustration. *Psychol. Bull.* 48, 465–95.

Brutkowski, S., & Mempel, E. 1961. Disinhibition of inhibitory conditioned responses following selective brain lesions in dogs. *Science* 134, 2040–1.

Buck, R. 1980. Nonverbal behavior and the theory of emotion: the facial feedback hypothesis. *J. Pers. Soc. Psychol.* 38, 811–21.

Buck, R., Miller, R. E., & Caul, W. F. 1974. Sex, personality and physiological variables in the communication of affect via facial expression. *J. Pers. Soc. Psychol.* 30, 587–96.

Bühler, Ch. 1931. *Kindheit und Jugend.* Leipzig: Hirzel.

Bühler, K. 1907. Tatsachen und Problemen zu einer Psychologie der Denkvorgänge. I. Über Gedanken. *Archiv. Ges. Psychol.* 9, 297–365.

1934. *Ausdruckstheorie.* Jena, East Germany: Fischer.

Bull, N. 1951. The attitude theory of emotion. *Nerv. Ment. Dis. Monogr.* no. 81.

Bumke, D. 1911. *Die Pupillenstörungen bei Geistes- und Nervenkrankheiten.* Jena, East Germany: Fischer.

Bunney, W. E., Jr., Mason, J. W., & Hamburg, D. A. 1965. Correlations between behavioral variables and urinary 17-hydrocorticosteriods in depressed patients. *Psychosom. Med.* 27, 299–308.

Buss, A. H. 1961. *The psychology of aggression.* New York: Wiley.

Butter, C. M., & Snyder, D. R. 1972. Alterations in aversive and aggressive behaviors following orbital frontal lesions in Rhesus monkeys. *Acta Neurobiol. Exp.* 32, 525–65.

Buunk, B. 1980. *Intieme relaties met derden.* Alphen, Netherlands: Samsom.

Cacioppo, J. T. 1979. Effects of exogeneous changes in heart rate on facilitation of thought and resistance to persuasion. *J. Pers. Soc. Psychol.* 37, 489–98.

Caggiula, A. B., & Hoebel, G. 1966. "Copulatory-reward site" in the posterior hypothalamus. *Science* 153, 1284–5.

Calvert-Boyanowski, J., & Leventhal, H. 1979. The role of information in attenuating behavioral responses to stress: a reinterpretation of the misattribution phenomenon. *J. Pers. Soc. Psychol.* 32, 214–21.

Campbell, D., Sanderson, R. E., & Laverty, S. G. 1964. Characteristics of a conditioned response in human subjects during extinction trials following a single traumatic conditioning trial. *J. Abnorm. Soc. Psychol.* 68, 627–39.

Campbell, R. 1982. The lateralisation of emotion: a critical review. *Int. J. Psychol.* 39, 106–24.

Cannon, W. B. 1927. The James–Lange theory of emotion: a critical examination and an alternative theory. *Am. J. Psychol.* 39, 106–24.

  1929. *Bodily changes in pain, hunger, fear and rage* (2nd ed.). New York: Appleton.

  1942. "Voodoo" death. *Am. Anthropol.* 44, 169–181.

Cantor, J. R., Zillmann, D., & Bryant, J. 1975. Enhancment of experienced sexual arousal in response to erotic stimuli through misattribution of unrelated residual excitation. *J. Pers. Soc. Psychol.* 32, 69–75.

Cantor, J. R., Zillmann, D., & Einsiedel, E. 1978. Female response to provocation after exposure to aggressive and erotic films. *Commun. Res.* 5, 395–412.

Cantril, H., & Hunt, W. A. 1932. Emotional effects produced by the injection of adrenalin. *Am. J. Psychol.* 44, 300–7.

Carroll, D., & Anastasiades, P. 1978. The behavioral significance of heart-rate: the Lacey's hypothesis. *Biol. Psychol.* 7, 249–73.

Cassel, J. 1976. The contribution of the social environment to host resistance. *Am. J. Epidemiol.* 104, 107–23.

Cattell, R. B. 1957. *Personality and motivation: structure and measurement.* New York: Harcourt, Brace & World.

Chance, M.R.A. 1962. The interpretation of some agonistic postures: the role of "cut-off" acts and postures. *Symp. Zool. Soc. Lond.* 8, 71–89.

Chapman, W. P. 1958. Studies of periamygdaloid area in relation to human behavior. *Res. Publ. Assoc. Res. Nerv. Ment. Dis.* 36, 258–77.

Charlesworth, W. R., & Kreutzer, M. A. 1973. Facial expressions of infants and children. In P. Ekman (ed.), *Darwin and facial expression.* New York: Academic Press, 91–168.

Chevalier-Skolnikoff, S. 1973. Facial expression of nonhuman primates. In P. Ekman (ed.), *Darwin and facial expression.* New York: Academic Press, 11–89.

Chiva, M. 1985. *Le doux et l'amer.* Paris: Presses Universitaires de France.

Chodoff, P. 1963. Late effects of concentration camp syndrome. *Arch. Gen. Psychiat.* 8, 323–33.

Church, R. M. 1959. Emotional reactions of rats to the pain in others. *J. Comp. Psychol.* 52, 132–4.

Clanton, G., & Smith, L. G. (eds.). 1977. *Jealousy.* Englewood Cliffs, N.J.: Prentice-Hall.

Clark, M. S., & Isen, A. M. 1982. Toward understanding the relationship between feeling states and social behavior. In A. Hastorf & A. M. Isen (eds.), *Cognitive social psychology.* Amsterdam: Elsevier.

Clavier, R. M., & Routtenberg, A. 1980. In search of reinforcement pathways: a neuroanatomical odyssey. In *Biology of reinforcement: a tribute to James Olds.* New York: Academic Press.

Clore, G. L, & Ortony, A. 1984. Some issues for a cognitive theory of emotion. *Cahiers de Psychol. Cogn.* 4, 53–7.

Clynes, M. 1977. *Sentics: the touch of the emotions.* New York: Anchor/Doubleday.

  1980. The communication of emotion: theory of sentics. In R. Plutchik & H. Kellerman (eds.), *Emotion: theory, research and experience.* New York: Academic Press, 271–304.

Cobb, S. 1976. Social support as a moderator of life stress. *Psychosom. Med.* 38, 300–14.

Cohen, F., & Lazarus, R. S. 1973. Active coping processes, coping dispositions and recovery from surgery. *Psychosom. Med.* 35, 375–89.

Cohen, H. D., Goodenough, D. R., Witkin, H. A., Oltman, P., Gould, H., & Shulman, E. 1975. Effects of stress on components of the respiratory cycle. *Psychophysiology* 12, 372–80.

Cohen, M. E., & White, P. D. 1951. Life situations, emotions and neurocirculatory asthenia (anxiety neurosis, neurasthenia, effort syndrome). *Psychosom. Med.* 13, 335–7.

Cohen, S. 1978. Environmental load and the allocation of attention. In A. Baum, J. E. Singer, & S. Valins (eds.), *Advances in environmental psychology* (Vol. 1). Hillsdale: Erlbaum.

1980. Aftereffects of stress on human performance and social behavior: a review of research and theory. *Psychol. Bull.* 88, 82–108.

Cohen, S., & Spacapan, S. 1978. The aftereffects of stress: an attentional interpretation. *Environ. Psychol. Nonverbal Behav.* 3, 43–57.

Conklin, V., & Dimmick, F. L. 1925. An experimental study of fear. *Am. J. Psychol.* 36, 96–101.

Cook, S. W., & Harris, R. E. 1937. The verbal conditioning of the galvanic skin reflex. *J. Exp. Psychol.* 21, 202–10.

Costello, C. G. 1970. Dissimilarities between conditioned avoidance responses and phobias. *Psychol. Rev.* 77, 250–4.

1972. Depression: loss of reinforcers or loss of reinforcer effectiveness? *Behav. Ther.* 3, 240–7.

Cowan, P. A., & Walters, R. H. 1963. Studies of reinforcement of aggression, I: effects of scheduling. *Child Dev.* 34, 543–51.

Cox, V. C. 1967. Avoidance conditioning with central and peripheral aversive stimulation. *Can. J. Psychol.* 21, 425–35.

Craig, K. O., & Weinstein M. S. 1965. Conditioning vicarious affective arousal. *Psychol. Rep.* 17, 955–63.

Crow, T. J., Spear, P. J., & Arbuthnot, G. W. 1972. Intracranial selfstimulation with electrodes in the region of the locus coeruleus. *Brain Res.* 36, 265–73.

Cupchik, G. C., & Leventhal, H. 1974. Consistency between expressive behavior and the evaluation of humorous stimuli: the role of sex and self-observation. *J. Pers. Soc. Psychol.* 30, 429–42.

Dahl, R. 1945. *Over to you* (1976. Harmondsworth, England: Penguin Books).

Daly, E. M., Lancee, W. J., & Polivy, J. 1983. A conical model for the taxonomy of emotional experience. *J. Pers. Soc. Psychol.* 45, 443–57.

D'Amato, M. E., & Gumenick, W. E. 1960. Some effects of immediate versus randomly delayed shock on an instrumental response and cognitive processes. *J. Abnorm. Soc. Psychol.* 60, 64–7.

Dana, C. L. 1921. The anatomic seat of emotions: a discussion of the James–Lange theory. *Arch. Neurol. Psychiat.* 6, 634–9.

Darrow, C. W. 1939. Emotion as relative functional decoration. *Psychol. Rev.* 42, 566–78.

1950. A new frontier: neurophysiological effects of emotion on the brain. In M. L. Reymert (ed.), *Feelings and emotions*. New York: McGraw-Hill, 247–60.

Darrow, C. W., & Freeman, G. L. 1934. Palmar skin-resistance changes contrasted with non-palmar changes and rate of insensible weight-loss. *J. Exp. Psychol.* 17, 739–48.

Darwin, Ch. 1872. *The expression of emotions in man and animals*. London: John Murray (1965. Chicago: Univ. of Chicago Press).

Davis, R. C. 1934. The specificity of facial expressions. *J. Gen. Psychol.* 10, 42–58.

1938. Relation of muscle action potentials to difficulty and frustration. *J. exp. Psychol.* 23, 141–58.

1953. Response and adaptation to brief noises of high intensity. USAF Sch. Aviat. Med. Rep. no. 55.

1957. Response patterns. *Trans. N.Y. Acad. Sci.* 19, 731–9.

Davis, R. C., & Buchwald, A. M. 1957. An exploration of somatic response patterns: stimulus and sex differences. *J. Comp. Psychol.* 50, 44–52.

Davis, R. C., Buchwald, A. M., & Frankmann, R. W. 1955. Autonomic and muscular responses and their relation to simple stimuli. *Psychol. Monogr. Gen. Appl.* 69, 20 (whole no. 405).

Davison, G. C., & Wilson, G. T. 1972. Critique of "Desensitization: Social and cognitive factors underlying the effectiveness of Wolpe's procedure." *Psychol. Rev.* 78, 28–31.

Davitz, J. R. 1969. *The language of emotion*. New York: Academic Press.

(ed.) 1964. *The communication of emotional meaning*. New York: McGraw-Hill.

Day, M. E. 1964. An eye-movement phenomenon relating to attention, thought and anxiety. *Perc. Mot. Skills* 19, 443–6.

De Jong, M. A. 1981. *Emotie en respons*. Lisse, Netherlands: Swets & Zeitlinger.

De Rivera, J. 1977. A structural theory of the emotions. In *Psychological issues* (Vol. 10). New York: International Univ. Press.

De Wied, D. 1964. Influence of anterior pituitary on avoidance learning and escape behavior. *Am. J. Physiol.* 207, 255–9.

1980. Hormonal influences on motivation, learning memory and psychosis. In D. T. Krieger & J. C. Hughes (eds.), *Neuro-endocrinology*. Sunderland, England: Sinauer Assoc.

De Wied, D., Bohus, B., Van Ree, J.M., & Urban, I. 1978. Behavioral and electrophysiological effects of peptides related to lipotropin (beta-LPH). *J. Pharmacol. Exp. Therapeutics* 204, 570-80.

Delgado, J. M. R. 1964. Free behavior and brain stimulation. In C. C. Pfeiffer & J. R. Smythies (eds.), *International review of neurobiology* (Vol. IV). New York: Academic Press, 349–449.

1967. Social rank and radio-stimulated aggressiveness in monkeys. *J. Nerv. Ment. Dis.* 144, 383–90.

1969. *Physical control of the mind*. New York: Harper & Row.

1975. Inhibitory systems and emotions. In L. Levi (ed.), *Emotions: their parameters and measurement*. New York: Raven Press, 183–204.

1979. Inhibitory functions in the neostriatum. In J. Divac & R. G. Öberg (eds.), *The neostriatum*. Oxford: Pergamon, 241–62.

Delgado, J. M. R., & Mir, D. 1969. Fragmental organization of emotional behavior in the monkey brain. *Ann. N.Y. Acad. Sci.* 159, 731–51.

Dembo, T. 1931. Der Ärger als dynamisches Problem. *Psychol. Forsch.* 15, 1–144.

Den Uyl, M. J., & Frijda, N. H. 1984. Mood, emotion and action: a concern-realization model. *Proceedings sixth annual conference cognitive science society*. New York: Boulder, 137–141.

Dennett, D. C. 1969. *Content and consciousness*. London: Routledge & Kegan Paul.

1978. *Brainstorms: philosophical essays on mind and psychology*. Montgomery, Ala.: Bradford Books.

Dermer, M., Cohen, S. J., Jacobsen, E., & Anderson, E. A. 1979. Evaluative judgements of aspects of life as a function of vicarious exposure to hedonic extremes. *J. Pers. Soc. Psychol.* 37, 247–60.

Descartes, R. 1647. *Les passions de l'âme.* Amsterdam: Elsevier 1970. (Paris: Vrin).

DeVore, I., & Konner, M. 1974. Infancy in a hunter-gatherer life: an ethological perspective. In N. White (ed.), *Ethology and psychiatry.* Toronto: Univ. of Toronto Press, 285–99.

Diamond, E. L. 1982. The role of anger and hostility in essential hypertension and coronary heart disease. *Psychol. Bull.* 92, 410–33.

Dicks, D., Myers, R. E., & Kling, A. 1969. Uncus and amygdaloid lesions: effects on social behavior in the free-ranging rhesus monkey. *Science* 165, 69–71.

Diener, E. 1980. Deindividuation: the absence of self-awareness and self-regulation in group members. In P. B. Paulus (ed.), *The psychology of group influence.* Hillsdale, N.J.: Erlbaum.

DiMascio, A., Boyd, R. W., & Greenblatt, M. 1957. Physiological correlates of tension and antagonism during psychotherapy: a study of "interpersonal psychophysiology." *Psychosom. Med.* 19, 99–104.

Dimsdale, J. E. 1974. The coping behavior of Nazi concentration camp survivors. *Am. J. Psychiat.* 131, 792–7.

Dittman, A. T. 1962. The relationship between body movements and moods in interviews. *J. Consult. Psychol.* 26, 480.

Dobbs, D., & Wilson, W. P. 1960. Observations on persistence of war neurosis. *Dis. Nerv. Syst.* 21, 686–91.

Dollard, J., Doob, L. W., Miller, N. E., Mowrer, O. H., & Sears, R. R. 1939. *Frustration and aggression.* New Haven, Conn.: Yale Univ. Press.

Dollard, J., & Miller, N. E. 1950. *Personality & psychotherapy: an analysis in terms of learning, thinking and culture.* New York: McGraw-Hill.

Donnerstein, E., & Wilson, D. W. 1976. Effects of noise and perceived control on ongoing and subsequent aggressive behavior. *J. Pers. Soc. Psychol.* 34, 774–81.

Doob, L. W., & Sears, R. R. 1939. Factors determining substitute behavior and the overt expression of aggression. *J. Abnorm. Soc. Psychol.* 34, 293–313.

Drozýnski, L. 1911. Atmungs- und Pulssymptome rytmischer Gefühle. *Psychol. Stud.* 7, 83–140.

Duchenne, G. B. 1876. *Mécanisme de la physionomie humaine.* Paris: Baillère.

Duffy, E. 1941. An explanation of "emotional" phenomena without the use of the concept "emotion." *J. Gen. Psychol.* 25, 283–93.

   1962. *Activation and behavior.* New York: Wiley.

   1972. Activation. In N. S. Greenfield & R. A. Sternbach (eds.), *Handbook of psychophysiology.* New York: Holt, 577–623.

Duke, J. D. 1968. Lateral eye movement behavior. *J. Gen. Psychol.* 78, 189–95.

Dumas, G. 1932. La mimique des aveugles. *Bull. Acad. Med. Paris* 107, 607–10.

   1933. L'expression des émotions; Les mimiques. In G. Dumas (ed.), *Nouveau traité de psychologie* (Tome 3). Paris: Alcan, 39–249, 293–360.

   1948a. *La vie affective.* Paris: Presses Univ. France.

   1948b. *Le sourire.* Paris: Alcan.

Eason, R. G. 1963. Relation between effort, tension level, skill and performance efficiency in a perceptual motor task. *Percept. Mot. Skills* 16, 297–317.

Eason, R. G., & Branks, J. 1963. Effects of level of activation on the quality and efficiency of performance of verbal and motor tasks. *Percept. Mot. Skills* 16, 525–43.

Eason, R. G., Harter, M. R., & Storm, W. F. 1964. Activation and behavior, I: relationship between physiological "indicants" of activation and perfor-

mance during memorization of nonsense syllables using differenting induced tension conditions. *Percept. Mot. Skills* 19, 95–110.

Easterbrook, J. A. 1959. The effects of emotion on cue utilization and the organization of behavior. *Psychol. Rev.* 66, 183–201.

Eastman, C. 1976. Behavioral formulations of depression. *Psychol. Rev.* 83, 277–
91.

Edelberg, R. 1972. Electrical activity of the skin. In N. S. Greenfield & R. A.
Sternbach (eds.), *Handbook of psychophysiology*. New York: Holt, Rinehart
& Winston, 367–418.

Edinger, L., & Fischer, B. 1913. Ein Mensch ohne Grosshirn. *Arch. Ges. Physiol.*
152, 535–61.

Efran, J. S., & Spangler, T. J. 1979. Why grown-ups cry. *Motiv. Emot.* 3, 63–72.

Egbert, L. D., Battit, G. E., Welch, C. E., & Bartlett, M. K. 1964. Reduction of
postoperative pain by encouragement and instructions of patients. *N. Eng.
J. Med.* 270, 825–7.

Eibl-Eibesfeldt, I. 1973. The expressive behavior of the deaf-and-blind-born. In
M. von Cranach & I. Vine (eds.), *Social communication and movement*. New
York: Academic Press, 163–94.

   1974. Similarities and differences between cultures in expressive movements.
In R. A. Hinde, (ed.), *Nonverbal communication*. Cambridge, England: Cambridge Univ. Press, 20–33.

Ekman, P. 1972. Universals and cultural differences in facial expressions of
emotions. *Curr. Theory Res. Motiv. Nebr. Symp. Motiv.* Vol. 19 207–83.

   1973. Cross cultural studies of facial expressions. In P. Ekman (ed.), *Darwin
and facial expression*. New York: Academic Press.

   (ed.) 1982a. *Emotion in the human face*, 2nd ed. Cambridge, England: Cambridge Univ. Press.

   1982b. Methods for measuring facial action. In K.R. Scherer & P. Ekman,
(eds.), *Handbook of methods in nonverbal behavior research*. Cambridge, England: Cambridge Univ. Press, 45–90.

Ekman, P., & Friesen, W. V. 1969a. Non-verbal leakage and clues to deception.
Psychiatry 32, 88–105.

   1969b. The repertoire of nonverbal behavior: categories, origins, usage and
coding. *Semiotica* 1, 49–98.

   1975. *Unmasking the face*. Englewood Cliffs, N.J.: Prentice-Hall.

   1978. *The facial action coding system*. Palo Alto: Consulting Psychologist Press.

   1982. Felt, false and miserable smiles. *J. Nonverb. Behav.* 6, 238–52.

Ekman, P., Friesen, W. V., & Ancoli, S. 1980. Facial signs of emotional experience. *J. Pers. Soc. Psychol.* 39, 1125–34.

Ekman, P., Friesen, W. V., & Ellsworth, P. 1972. *Emotion in the human face:
guidelines for research and a review of findings*. New York: Pergamon.

Ekman, P., Friesen, W. V., O'Sullivan, M., & Scherer, K. 1980. Relative importance of face, body and speech in judgments of personality and affect.
J. Pers. Soc. Psychol. 38, 270–7.

Ekman, P., Friesen, W. V., & Simons, R. C. (in preparation). Is the startle reaction
an emotion?

Ekman, P., Hager, J. C., & Friesen, W. V. 1981. The symmetry of emotional
and deliberate facial actions. *Psychophysiology* 18, 101–6.

Ekman, P., Levenson, R. W., & Friesen, W. V. 1983. Autonomic nervous system
activity distinguishing among emotions. *Science* 221, 1208–10.

Ekman, P., & Oster, H. 1979. Facial expression of emotion. *Ann. Rev. Psychol.*
30, 527–54.

Elias, N. 1939. *Der Prozess der Zivilization (The civilizing process.* New York: Urizen Books, 1969).

Elliot, R. 1974. The motivational significance of heart rate. In P. O. Obrist, A. H. Black, J. Brener, & L. V. DiCara (eds.), *Cardiovascular psychophysiology.* Chicago: Aldine.

Ellis, A. 1970. *The essence of rational psychotherapy: a comprehensive approach to treatment.* New York: Institute for Rational Living.

Ellson, C. D., Henri, P., & Cunis, D. 1977. Physiological changes in yoga meditation. *Psychophysiology* 14, 52–7.

Elmadjian, F. J., Hope, J., & Lamson, E. T. 1957. Excretion of epinephrine and norepinephrine in various emotional states. *J. Clin. Endocrin.* 17, 608–20.

Endler, N. S. 1975. A person–situation interaction model for anxiety. In C. D. Spielberger & I. Sarason (eds.), *Stress and anxiety* (Vol. 1). New York: Wiley, 145–64.

Engel, B. T. 1960. Stimulus-response and individual-response specificity. *Arch. Gen. Psychiatr.* 2, 305–313.

Engel, J. J. 1785. *Ideeen zu einer Mimik.* Berlin: Mylin.

English, H. 1929. Three cases of "conditioned fear response." *J. Abnorm. Soc. Psychol.* 34, 221–5.

Epstein, H. 1979. *Children of the holocaust.* New York: Putnam.

Epstein, S. 1971. Heart rate, skin-conductance and intensity ratings during experimentally induced anxiety: habituation within and among days. *Psychophysiology* 8, 319–25.

  1973. Expectancy and magnitude of reaction to a noxious UCS. *Psychophysiology* 10, 100–7.

Epstein, S., & Clarke, S. 1970. Heart rate and skin conductance during experimentally induced anxiety: effects of anticipated intensity of noxious stimulation and experience. *J. Exp. Psychol.* 84, 105–12.

Epstein, S., & Fenz, W. D. 1965. Steepness of approach and avoidance gradients in humans as a function of experience: theory and experiment. *J. Exp. Psychol.* 70, 1–12.

Erdmann, G., & Janke, W. 1978. Interaction between physiological and cognitive determinants of emotions: experimental studies on Schachter's theory of emotions. *Biol. Psychol.* 7, 61–74.

Erdmann, G., & van Lindern, B. 1980. The effects of beta-adrenergic stimulatioin and beta-adrenergic blockade on emotional reactions. *Psychophysiology* 17, 332–8.

Euler, C. von, & Söderbert, U. 1957. The influence of hypothalamic thermoceptive structures on the electroencephalogram and gamma motor activity. *Electroencephalogr. Clin. Neurophysiol.* 9, 391–408.

Evans, I. M. 1976. Classical conditioning. In M. P. Feldman & A. Broadhurst (eds.), *Theoretical and experimental bases of the behaviour therapies.* New York: Wiley.

Exline, R. V., & Fehr, B. J. 1982. The assessment of gaze and mutual gaze. In K. R. Scherer & P. Ekman (eds.), *Handbook of methods in nonverbal behavior research.* Cambridge, England: Cambridge Univ. Press, 91–135.

Exline, R. V., Gray, P., & Schuette, D. 1965. Visual behavior in a dyad as affected by interview content and sex of respondent. *J. Pers. Soc. Psychol.* 1, 201–9.

Exline, R. V., & Winters, L. C. 1965. Affective relations and mutual glances in dyads. In S. S. Tomkins & C. Izard (eds.), *Affect, cognition & personality.* New York: Springer.

Exline, R. V., & Yellin, A. 1969. Eye contact as a sign between man and monkey. Unpublished (quoted in Argyle & Cook, 1976).

Eysenck, H. J. 1967. *The biological basis of personality*. Springfield, Ill.: Thomas.
  1968. A theory of the incubation of anxiety/fear responses. *Behav. Res. Ther.* 6, 309–21.
  1975. Anxiety and the natural history of neurosis. In C. D. Spielberger & I. G. Sarason (eds.), *Stress and anxiety* (Vol. 1). New York: Wiley, 51–94.
  1979. The conditioning model of neurosis. *Behav. Brain Sci.* 2, 155–65.
  1980. Commentary to Bolles' & Fanselow's "A perceptual model of fear and pain." *Behav. Brain Sci.* 3, 307–8.

Eysenck, H. J., & Rachman, S. 1965. *The causes and cures of neurosis*. London: Routledge & Kegan Paul.

Eysenck, S. B. G., & Eysenck, H. J. 1979. The place of impulsiveness in a dimensional system of personality description. *Br. J. Soc. Clin. Psychol.* 16, 57–68.

Fanselow, M. S., & Bolles, R. C. 1979. Naloxone and shock-elicited freezing in the rat. *J. Comp. Physiol. Psychol.* 93, 736–44.

Farber, I. E., & Spence, K. W. 1953. Complex learning and conditioning as a function of anxiety. *J. Exp. Psychol.* 45, 120–5.

Farr, C. B., & Lueders, C. W. 1923. Gastric secretory functions in the psychoses. *Arch. Neurol. Psychiatry* 10, 548–61.

Fechner, G. T. 1876. *Vorschule der Aesthetik*. Leipzig: Breitkopf & Hartel.

Fehr, B., & Russell, J. A. 1984. Concept of emotion viewed from a prototype perspective. *J. Exp. Psychol. Gen.* 113, 464–86.

Fehr, F. S., & Stern, J. A. 1970. Peripheral physiological variables and emotion: the James–Lange theory revisited. *Psychol. Bull.* 74, 411–24.

Feigl, H. 1958. The "mental" and the "physical." In H. Feigl, M. Scriven, & G. Maxwell (eds.), *Minnesota studies in the philosophy of science* (Vol. 2). Minneapolis: Univ. Minnesota Press, 370–498.

Féléky, A. 1916. The influence of emotions on respiration. *J. Exp. Psychol.* 1, 218–41.

Fenz, W. D. 1964. Conflict and stress as related to physiological activation and sensory, perceptual, and cognitive functioning. *Psychol. Mon.* 78, 8; whole No. 585.

Fenz, W. D. & Epstein, S. 1968. Specific and general inhibitory reactions associated with mastery of stress. *J. Exp. Psychol.* 77, 52–6.

Festinger, L. 1954. A theory of social comparison processes. *Hum. Relat.* 7, 117–40.
  1957. *A theory of cognitive dissonance*. Evanston: Row, Peterson & Co.

Festinger, L., Pepitone, A., & Newcomb, T. M. 1952. Some consequences of deindividuation in a group. *J. Abnorm. Soc. Psychol.* 47, 383–9.

Fillenbaum, S., & Rapoport, A. 1971. *Structures in the subjective lexicon*. New York: Academic Press.

Flach, A. 1928. Die Psychologie der Ausdrucksbewegung. *Arch. Ges. Psychol.* 65.

Flor-Henry, P. 1979. On certain aspects of the localisation of the cerebral systems regulating and determining emotion. *Biol. Psychiat.* 14, 677–98.

Flynn, J. P. 1973. Patterning mechanisms, patterned reflexes and attack behavior in cats. In J. K. Cole & D. D. Jensen (eds.), *Curr. Theory Res. Motiv. Nebr. Symp. Motiv.* 20, 125–154.

Folkins, C. H. 1970. Temporal factors and the cognitive mediators of stress reactions. *J. Pers. Soc. Psychol.* 12, 211–28.

Folkow, N., & Neil, E. 1971. *Circulation*. New York: Oxford Univ. Press.

Fonberg, E. 1979. Physiological mechanisms of emotional and instrumental aggression. In S. Feshbach & A. Fraczek (eds.), *Aggression and behavioral change.* New York: Praeger, 6–52.

1981. Amygdala and emotions. In L. Cioffi, W. P. T. James, & T. B. van Itallie (eds.), *The body weight regulatory system: normal and disturbed mechanisms.* New York: Raven Press, 25–32.

Ford, A. 1929. Attention-automatization: an investigation of the transitional nature of mind. *Am. J. Psychol.* 41, 1–32.

Forge, D. D., & LeLordo, V. M. 1973. Attention in the pigeon: differential effects of food-getting versus shock-avoidance procedures. *J. Comp. Physiol. Psychol.* 85, 551–8.

Forsyth, R. P. 1969. Blood pressure responses to long-term avoidance schedules in the restrained rhesus monkey. *Psychosomat. Med.* 31, 300–9.

Fouriezos, G., & Wise, A. 1976. Pimozide-induced extinction of intracranial self-stimulation: response patterns rule out motor or performance deficits. *Brain Res.* 103, 377–80.

Fox, N. A., & Davidson, R. J. 1984. Hemispheric substrates of affect: a developmental model. In N. A. Fox & R. J. Davidson (eds.), *The psychobiology of affective development.* Hillsdale, N.J.: Erlbaum, 353–82.

Fraiberg, S. 1971. Intervention in infancy: a program for blind infants. *J. Am. Acad. Child Psychiatry* 10, 381–405.

Frankenhauser, M. 1975. Experimental approaches to the study of catecholamines and emotion. In L. Levi (ed.), *Emotions: their parameters and measurement.* New York: Raven Press, 209–34.

Frankenhauser, M., & Rissler, A. 1970. Effects of punishments on catecholamine release and efficiency of performance. *Psychopharmacologica* 17, 378–90.

Freeman, G. L. 1948. *Physiological psychology.* New York: Van Nostrand.

Freeman, G. L., & Katzoff, E. T. 1942. Methodological evaluation of the galvanic skin response, with special reference to the formula for RQ. *J. Psychol.* 31, 239–48.

Freud, A. 1946. *The ego and the mechanisms of defense.* New York: International Univ. Press.

Freud, S. 1895. *Entwurf einer Wissenschaftlicher Psychologie (Project for a scientific psychology.* London: Hogarth Press).

1900. *Die Traumdeutung.* Leipzig und Wien: Deuticke (*The interpretation of dreams,* standard ed., Vols. 4, 5. London: Hogarth Press, 1953).

1905. *Der Witz und seine Beziehung zum Unbewussten (Jokes . . .* , standard ed., Vol. 8. London: Hogarth Press, 1962).

1909. *Analyse der Phobie eines fünfjährigen Knaben (Analysis of a phobia . . .* , standard ed., Vol. 10. London: Hogarth Press, 1960, 3–151).

1915. *Trauer und Melancholie (Mourning and melancholia,* standard ed., Vol. 14, 237–58. London: Hogarth Press, 1957).

1917. *Vorlesungen zur Einführung in die Psychoanalyse (Introductory lectures,* standard ed., Vols. 15, 16. London: Hogarth Press, 1961).

1920. *Jenseits des Lustprinzips (Beyond the pleasure principle,* standard ed. London: Hogarth Press, 1955, 3–66).

1922. *Einige neurotische Mechanismen in Eifersucht, Paranoia und Homosexualität (Some neurotic mechanisms . . . ,* standard ed., Vol. 18. London: Hogarth Press, 1955, 221–33).

1926. *Hemmung, Symptom und Angst (Inhibition, symptom and anxiety,* standard ed., Vol. 20. London: Hogarth Press, 1959, 77–178).

1927. *Die Zukunft einer Illusion (The future of an illusion,* standard ed., Vol. 21. London: Hogarth Press, 1953).

1930. *Das Unbehagen in der Kultur (Civilization and its discontent,* standard ed., Vol. 21. London: Hogarth Press, 1961, 59–148).

Friedman, S. B., Mason, J. W., & Hamburg, D. A. 1963. Urinary 17-hydroxy-corticosteroid levels in parents of children with neoplastic disease: a study of chronic psychological stress. *Psychosom. Med.* 25, 364–76.

Frijda, N. H. 1953. The understanding of facial expression of emotion. *Acta Psychol.* 9, 294–362.

1969. Recognition of emotion. *Adv. Exp. Soc. Psychol.* 4, 167–223.

1982. The meanings of facial expression. In M. Ritchie-Kye (ed.), *Nonverbal communication today: current research*. The Hague: Mouton, 103–20.

1984. Toward a model of emotion. In C. D. Spielberger, I. G. Sarason, & P. Defares (eds.), *Stress and anxiety* (Vol. 9). Washington, D.C.: Hemisphere, 3–16.

1986. Action tendencies in emotions. Report Psy.5.2.86.98. Dept. of Psychology, Amsterdam Univ.

Frijda, N. H., & Bovenkerk, G. 1985. Cognitive structures and emotions. Report Psy.6.12.84.11, Dept. of Psychology, Amsterdam Univ.

Fulcher, J. S. 1942. "Voluntary" facial expression in blind and seeing children. *Arch. Psychol.* 38, 5–49.

Funkenstein, D. H. 1956. Nor-epinephrine-like and epinephrine-like substances in relation to human behavior. *J. Ment. Dis.* 124, 58–68.

Funkenstein, D. H., King, S. H., & Drolette, M. E. 1957. *Mastery of stress.* Cambridge, Mass.: Harvard University Press.

Furedy, J. J. 1968. Novelty and the measurement of the GSR. *J. Exp. Psychol.* 76, 501–3.

Furedy, J. J., & Doob, A. N. 1972. Signalling unmodifiable shocks: limits on human informational cognitive control. *J. Pers. Soc. Psychol.* 21, 111–15.

Furedy, J. J., & Klajner, F. 1974. On evaluating autonomic and verbal indices of negative preception. *Psychophysiology* 11, 121–4.

Gainotti, G. 1972. Emotional behavior and hemispheric side of the lesion. *Cortex* 8, 41–55.

Gal, R., & Lazarus, R. S. 1975. The role of activity in anticipating and confronting stressful situations. *J. Hum. Stress* 1, 4–20.

Galin, D. 1974. Implications for psychiatry of right and left cerebral specialisations. *Arch. Gen. Psychiat.* 31, 572–83.

Gallistel, C. R. 1975. Motivation as central organizing process: the psychophysical approach to its functional and neurophysiological analysis. In J. K. Cole & T. B. Sonderegger (eds.) 1974. *Curr. Theory Res. Motiv. Nebr. Symp. Motiv.* 22, 183–250.

Garber, J., & Hollon, S. D. 1980. Universal versus personal helplessness in depression: belief in uncontrollability or incompetence? *J. Abnorm. Psychol.* 89, 56–66.

Garcia, J., & Koelling, R. A. 1966. Relation of cue to consequence in avoidance learning. *Psychon. Sci., Sect. Anim. Physiol.* 5, 121–122.

Gatchel, R. J., & Proctor, J. D. 1976. Psychological correlates of learned helplessness in man. *J. Abnorm. Psychol.* 85, 27–34.

Geen, R. G., & Quanty, M. B. 1977. The catharsis of aggression. In L. Berkowitz (ed.), *Advances in experimental social psychology* (Vol. 10). New York: Academic Press, 2–39.

Geer, J., & Turtletaub, G. 1967. Fear reduction following observation of the model. *J. Pers. Soc. Psychol.* 6, 327–35.

Geertz, H. 1959. The vocabulary of emotion. *Psychiatry* 22, 225–37.

Gellhorn, E. 1964. Motion and emotions: the role of proprioception in the physiology and pathology of the emotions. *Psychol. Rev.* 71, 457–72.

1968. *Biological foundations of emotion.* Glenview, Ill.: Scott & Foresman.

Gellhorn, E., Cortell, R., & Feldman, J. 1941. The effect of emotion, sham rage and hypothalamic stimulation on the vago-insulin system. *Am. J. Physiol.* 132, 532–41.

Gellhorn, E., & Loofburrow, G. N. 1963. *Emotion and emotional disorders.* New York: Haber Medical Division.

Gerdes, E.P. 1979. Automatic arousal as a cognitive cue in stressful situations. *J. Pers.* 47, 677–711.

Gergen, K. J., Gergen, M. M., & Barton, W. H. 1973. Deviance in the dark. *Psychol. Today* 7, 129–33.

Gibson, J. J. 1966. *The senses considered as perceptual systems.* Boston: Houghton Mifflin.

Glass, D. C., & Singer, J. E. 1972. *Urban stress: experiments on noise and social stressors.* New York: Academic Press.

Goffman, E. 1959. *The presentation of self in everyday life.* Garden City, N.Y.: Doubleday/Anchor.

Goldstein, J. B. 1972. Electromyography: a measure of skeletal muscle response. In N. S. Greenfield & R. A. Sternbach (eds.), *Handbook of psychophysiology.* New York: Holt, Rinehart & Winston, 329–65.

Goldstein, K. 1939. *Der Aufbau des Organismus.* Den Haag: Nijhoff.

Goldwater, B. C. 1972. Psychological significance of pupillary movements. *Psychol. Bull.* 77, 340–55.

Gollender, M. 1967. Eosinophil and avoidance correlates of stress in anterior cingulate cortex lesioned rats. *J. Comp. Physiol. Psychol.* 51, 520–23.

Goltz, F. 1892. Der Hund ohne Grosshirn. *Pflügers Arch. Ges. Physiol.* 51, 570–614.

Goodenough, F. 1932. The expression of emotion in a blind-deaf child. *J. Abnorm. Soc. Psychol.* 27, 328–33.

Goorney, A. B., & O'Connor, P. J. 1971. Anxiety associated with flying. *Br. J. Psychiatry,* 119, 159–66.

Gordon, S. L. 1981. The sociology of sentiments and emotions. In M. Rosenberg & R. H. Turner (eds.), *Social psychology: sociological perspectives.* New York: Basic Books, 261–78.

Graham, F. K. 1979. Distinguishing among orienting, defense and startle reflexes. In H. D. Kimmel, E. H. van Olst, & J. F. Orlebeke (eds.), *The orienting reflex in humans.* Hillsdale: Erlbaum.

Graham, F.K., Charwat, W. A., Honig, A. S., & Weltz, P. C. 1951. Aggression as a function of the attack and the attacker. *J. Abnorm. Soc. Psychol.* 46, 512–20.

Graham, F. K., & Clifton, R. K. 1966. Heart rate as a component of the orienting response. *Psychol. Bull.* 65, 305–20.

Graham, J. D. P. 1945. High blood pressure after battle. *Lancet* 1, 239–40.

Granet, M. 1922. Le langage de la douleur en Chine. J. Psychologie 19 (repr. M. Granet, *Etudes sociologiques sur la Chine.* Paris: Presses Univ. de France, 1953).

Gratiolet, P. 1865. *De la physionomie et des mouvements d'expression.* Paris: Hetzel.

Gray, J. A. 1971. *The psychology of fear and stress.* London: Weidenfeld & Nicholson.

1982. *The neuropsychology of anxiety: an enquiry into the functions of the septohippocampal system.* Oxford: Oxford Univ. Press.

Greenfield, N. S., & Sternbach, R. A. (eds.) 1972. *Handbook of psychophysiology.* New York: Holt, Rinehart & Winston.

Gregory, J. C. 1924. *The nature of laughter*. London: Kegan Paul.

Grings, W. W. 1960. Preparatory set variables related to classical conditioning of automatic responses. *Psychol. Rev.* 67, 243–52.

Grings, W. W., & Dawson, M. E. 1978. *Emotions and bodily responses: a psychophysical approach*. New York: Academic Press.

Grinker, R. R., & Spiegel, J. P. 1945. *Men under stress*. Philadelphia: Blakiston.

Grossman, S. P. 1966. The VMH: a centre for affective reactions, satiety, or both? *Physiol. Behav.* 1, 1–10.

    1979. The biology of motivation. *Ann. Rev. Psychol.* 30, 209–42.

Groves, P. M., & Thompson, R. F. 1970. Habituation: a dual-process theory. *Psychol. Rev.* 77, 419–50.

Guernsey, M. 1928., Eine genetische Studie über Nachahmung. *Z. Psychol.* 107, 105–78.

Gunn, C. G., Wolf, S., Block, R. T., & Person, R. J. 1972. Psychophysiology of the cardiovascular system. In N. S. Greenfield & R. A. Sternbach (eds.), *Handbook of psychophysiology*. New York: Holt, Rinehart & Winston, 457–89.

Haan, N. 1977. *Coping and defending: processes of self-environment organization*. New York: Academic Press.

Hager, J. C., & Ekman, P. 1981. Methodological problems in Tourangeau and Ellsworth's study of facial expression and experience of emotion. *J. Pers. Soc. Psychol.* 40, 358–62.

Hagman, E. 1932. A study of fears of children of pre-school age. *J. Exp. Educ.* 1, 110–30.

Hall, C. S. 1941. Temperament: a survey of animal studies. *Psychol. Bull.* 38, 909–43.

Hall, G. S. 1899. A study of anger. *Am. J. Psychol.* 10, 516–91.

Hall, K. R. L., & DeVore, I. 1965. Baboon social behavior. In I. DeVore (ed.), *Primate behavior*. New York: Holt.

Hall, R. A., Rappaport, M., Hopkins, H. K., & Griffin, R. B. 1970. Evoked responses and behavior in cats. *Science* 170, 998–1000.

Hamburg, D. A., Hamburg, B. A., & Barchas, J. D. 1975. Anger and depression in perspective of behavioral biology. In L. Levi (ed.), *Emotion: their parameters and measurement*. New York: Raven Press. 235–78.

Hamburg, D. A., Hamburg, B. A., & De Goza, S. 1953. Adaptive problems and mechanisms in severely burned patients. *Psychiatry*. 16, 1–20.

Hammond, D. A. 1883. *Sleep and its derangements*. New York: Lippincott.

Hammond, L. J. 1970. Conditioned emotional states. In P. Black (ed.), *Physiological correlates of emotion*. New York: Academic Press, 245–59.

Haner, C. F., & Brown, P. A. 1955. Clarification of the instigation to action concept in the frustration–aggression hypothesis. *J. Abnorm. Soc. Psychol.* 51, 204–6.

Harburg, E., Erfurt, J. C., Hauenstein, L. S., Chape, C., Schull, W. J., & Schork, M. A. 1973. Socio-ecological stress, suppressed hostility, skin-color and black–white male blood pressure: Detroit. *Psychosom. Med.* 35, 276–96.

Hare, R. D. 1976. Psychopathy. In P. H. Venables & N. J. Christie (eds.), *Research in psychophysiology*. London: Wiley, 325–48.

Harlow, H. F. 1949. The formation of learning sets. *Psychol. Rev.* 56, 51–65.

    1950. Learning and satiation of response in intrinsically motivated complex puzzle performance in monkeys. *J. Comp. Physiol. Psychol.* 43, 289–94.

    1958. The nature of love. *Am. Psychol.* 13, 673–85.

    1969. Age-mate or peer affectional systems. *Adv. Study Behav.* 334–84.

Haroutunian, V., & Riccio, D. C. 1977. Effect of arousal conditions during reinstatement treatment upon learned fear in young rats. *Dev. Psychobio.* 10, 25–32.

Harrell, J. P. 1980. Psychological factors and hypertension: a status report. *Psychol. Bull.* 87, 482–501.

Harris, F. R., Wolfe, M. M., & Baer, D. M. 1964. Effects of adult social reinforcement on child behavior. *Young Children* 20, 8–17.

Hartig, M., & Kanfer, F. H. 1973. The role of verbal self-instructions in children's resistance to temptations. *J. Pers. Soc. Psychol.* 25, 259–67.

Hassler, R., & Riechert, F. 1961. Wirkungen der Reizungen und Koagualtionen in den Stammganglien bei stereotaktischen Hirnoperationen. *Nervenartzt* 32, 97–103.

Hawkins, D. R., Monroe, J. T., Sandifer, M. G., & Verum, C. R. 1960. Psychological and physiological response to continuous epinephrine infusions—an approach to the affect anxiety. *Psychiat. Res. Rep. Am. Psychiat. Assoc.* 12, 40–52.

Heath, R. G. 1976. Correlation of brain function with emotional behavior. *Biol. Psychiatry* 11, 463–80.

Heath, R. G., Monroe, R. R., & Mickle, W. A. 1955. Stimulation of the amygdaloid nucleus in a schizophrenic patient. *Am. J. Psychiatry* 3, 862–3.

Hebb, D. O. 1946. On the nature of fear. *Psychol. Rev.* 53, 259–76.

1949. *The organization of behavior.* New York: Wiley.

1955. Drives and the CNS (Conceptual Nervous System). *Psychol. Rev.* 62, 243–54.

1970. *Textbook of psychology* (3rd ed.). Philadelphia: Saunders.

Helder, F. 1958. *The psychology of interpersonal relationships.* New York: Wiley.

Herd, J. A., Morse, W., Kelleher, R. J., & Jones, L. R. 1969. Arterial hypertension in the squirrel monkey during behavioral experiments. *Am. J. Physiol.* 217, 24–9.

Hess, E. H. 1965. Attitudes and pupil size. *Sci. Am.* 212, 46–54.

1972. Pupillometrics: a method of studying mental, emotional and sensory processes. In N. S. Greenfield & R. A. Sternbach (eds.), *Handbook of psychophysiology.* New York: Holt, Rinehart & Winston, 491–531.

Hess, E. H., & Polt, J. M. 1960. Pupil size as related to interest value of visual stimuli. *Science* 132, 349–50.

Hess, W. R. 1957. *The functional organization of the diencephalon.* New York: Grune & Stratton.

Heymans, G. 1932. *Inleiding tot de speciale psychologie.* Haarlem, Netherlands: Bohn.

Heymans, G., & Wiersma, E. 1906. Beiträge zur speziellen Psychologie auf Grund einer Massenuntersuchung. *Z. Psychol.* 42.

Higgins, G. E. 1979. Sexual response in spinal cord injured adults: a review of the literature. *Arch. Sexual Behav.* 8, 173–96.

Hilgard, E. R. 1977. *Divided consciousness: multiple controls in human thought and action.* New York: Wiley.

Hinde, R. A. 1974. *Biological bases of human behavior.* New York: McGraw-Hill.

Hite, S. 1976. *The Hite report.* New York: Dell.

Hochschild, A. R. 1979. Emotion, work, feeling rules and social structure. *Amer. J. Sociol.* 85, 551–75.

1983. *The managed heart.* Berkeley: Univ. California Press.

Hoffman, H. S. & Ison, J. R. 1980. Reflex modification in the domain of startle, I. Some empirical findings and their implications for how the nervous system processes sensory input. *Psychol. Rev.* 87, 175–89.

Hoffman, M. L. 1978. Empathy, its development and prosocial implications. In C. B. Keasy (ed.) 1977. *Curr. Theory Res. Motiv. Nebr. Symp. Motiv.* 25, 169–218.

Hohmann, G. W. 1966. Some effects of spinal cord lesions on experienced emotional feelings. *Psychophysiology* 3, 143–56.

Hokanson, J. E. 1961. The effects of frustration and anxiety on overt aggression. *J. Abnorm. Soc. Psychol.* 62, 346–51.

Hokanson, J. E., & Burgess, M. 1962. The effects of status, type of frustration and aggression on vascular processes. *J. Abnorm. Soc. Psychol.* 65, 232–7.

Hokanson, J. E., De Good, D. E., Forrest, M. S., & Brittain, T. M. 1971. Availability of avoidance behaviors in modulating vascular-stress responses. *J. Pers. Soc. Psychol.* 19, 60–8.

Holmes, T. H., & Wolff, H. G. 1950. Life situations, emotions and back aches. *Res. Publ. Assoc. Nev. Ment. Dis.* 29, 750–2.

Holst, E. von 1957. Die Auslösung von Stimmungen bei Wirbeltieren durch "punktformige" elektrische Erregung des Stammhirns. *Naturwissenschaften* 44, 549.

Hoppe, F. 1931. Erfolg und Misserfolg. *Psychol. Forsch.* 14, 1–62.

Horowitz, M. J. 1976. *Stress response syndromes.* New York: Jason Aronson.
     1982. Psychological processes induced by illness, injury and loss. In T. Millon, C. Green, & R. Meagher (eds.), *Handbook of clinical health psychology.* New York: Plenum, 53–68.

Hotton, R. B. 1961. Amplitude of an instrumental response following the cessation of reward. *Child Dev.* 32, 107–16.

Hunsperger, R. W. 1956. Affektreaktionen auf elektrische Reizung im Hirnstamm der Katze. *Helvet. Physiol. Pharmakol. Acta* 14, 70.

Ira, G. H., Whalen, R. E., & Bogdanoff, M. D. 1963. Heart rate changes in physicians during daily "stressful" tasks. *J. Psychosom. Res.* 7, 147–50.

Irwin, F. W. 1971. *Intentional behavior and motivation: a cognitive theory.* Philadelphia: Lippincott.

Isaacson. R. L. 1974. *The limbic system.* New York: Plenum Press.

Izard, C. E. 1969. The emotions and emotion constructs in personality and culture research. In R. B. Cattell & R. M. Dreger (eds.), *Handbook of modern personality theory.* New York: Wiley, 496–510.
     1971. *The face of emotion.* New York: Appleton-Century-Crofts.
     1972. *Patterns of emotions.* New York: Academic Press.
     1977. *Human emotions.* New York: Plenum Press.

Jacobsen, C. F. 1936. Studies of cerebral function in primates. *Comp. Psychol. Monogr.* 13, 1–60.

Jacquet, Y. F. 1980. B-endorphin and ACTH: inhibitory and excitatory neurohormones of pain and fear? *Behav. Brain Sci.* 3, 312.

James, W. 1884. What is an emotion? *Mind*, 9, 188–205.

Janis. I. L. 1951. *Air war and emotional stress.* New York: McGraw-Hill.
     1958. *Psychological stress.* New York: Wiley.
     1971. *Stress and frustration.* New York: Harcourt Brace Jovanovitch.

Janis, I. L., & Mann, L. 1977. *Decision making.* New York: The Free Press.

Janis, J. L., Chapman, D. W., Gillen, J. P., & Spiegel, J. P. 1955. The problem of panic. Washington, D.C.: Fed. Civil Defense Admin. Bull. TB–19–2.

Janisse, M. P. 1977. *Pupillometry: the psychology of the pupillary response.* New York: Wiley.

Jasnos, T. M., & Hackmiller, K. L. 1975. Some effects of lesion level, and emotional cues on affective expression in spinal cord patients. *Psychol. Rep.* 37, 859–70.

Jefferson, J.W. 1974. Beta-adrenergic receptor blocking drugs in psychiatry. *Arch. Gen. Psychiat.* 31, 681–91.

Jensen, A. 1962. Extraversion, neuroticism and serial learning. *Acta Psychologica* 20, 69–77.

Jersild, A., & Holmes, F. 1935. Children's fears. *Child Dev. Monogr.* 20.

Johnson, E. & Tversky, A. 1983. Affect, generalization and the perception of risk. *J. Per. Soc. Psychol.* 45, 20–31.

Johnson, J. E. 1975. Stress reduction through sensation information. In I. G. Sarason & C. D. Spielberger (eds.), *Stress and anxiety* (Vol. 2). Washington, D.C.: Hemisphere, 361–78.

Johnson, J. E., & Leventhal, H. 1974. Effects of accurate expectations and behavioral instructions on reactions during a noxious medical examination. *J. Pers. Soc. Psychol.* 29, 710–18.

Johnson, L. C., & Lubin, A. 1967. The orienting reflex during waking and sleeping. *Electroencephalogr. Clin. Neurophysiol.* 22, 11–21.

Johnson, R. D., & Downing, L. L. 1979. Deindividuation and valence of cues: effects of prosocial and antisocial behavior. *J. Pers. Soc. Psychol.* 37, 1532–8.

Jones, H. E. 1935. The galvanic skin reflex as related to overt emotional expression. *Am. J. Psychol.* 47, 241–51.

Jones, M. C. 1924. A laboratory study of fear: the case of Peter. *Pedag. Sem.* 31, 308–15.

Joslin, J., Fletcher, H., & Emlen, J. 1964. A comparison of the responses to snakes of lab- and wild-reared monkeys. *Animal Behav.* 12, 348–52.

Jost, H. 1941. Some physiological changes during frustration. *Child Dev.* 12, 9–15.

Jouvet, M. 1972. Recherches sur les structures nerveuses et les mécanismes responsables des différentes phases du sommeil physiologique. *Arch. Ital. Biol.* 100, 125–206.

Kaada, B. R. 1967. Brain mechanisms related to aggressive behavior. In C. D. Clemente & D. B. Lindsley (eds.), *Aggression and defense.* UCLA Forum Med. Sci. no. 7. Los Angeles: Univ. of California Press.

Kaada, B. R., Jansen, J., & Andersen, P. 1953. Stimulation of the hippocampus and medial cortical areas in unanesthetized cats. *Neurology* (Minneapolis) 3, 844–57.

Kahn, M. 1966. The physiology of catharsis. *J. Pers. Soc. Psychol.* 3, 178–86.

Kahneman, D. 1973. *Attention and effort.* Englewood Cliffs: Prentice-Hall.

Kahneman, D., & Beatty, J. 1966. Pupil diameter and load on memory. *Science.* 154, 1583–5.

Kahneman, D., & Tversky, A. 1973. On the psychology of prediction. *Psychol. Rev.* 80, 237–51.

Kanfer, F. H. 1979. The many faces of self-control, or behavior and modification changes its focus. In R. B. Stuart (ed.), *Behavioral managements: strategies, techniques and outcomes.* New York: Brunner.

1980. Self-management methods. In F. H. Kanfer & A. P. Goldstein (eds.), *Helping people change.* New York: Pergamon, 334–89.

Kanfer, F. H., Karoly, P., & Newman, A. 1975. Reduction of children's fear of the dark by competence-related and situational threat-related verbal cues. *J. Consult. Clin. Psychol.* 43, 251–8.

Kaplan, B. 1964. *The inner world of mental illness.* New York: Harper & Row.

Karabenick, S. A. 1969. Effects of reward increase and reduction in the double runway. *J. Exp. Psychol.* 82, 79–87.

Katz, D. 1944. *Gestaltpsychologie.* Basel: Schwabe.

Kazdin, A. E., & Wilcoxon, L. A. 1976. Systematic desensitization and nonspecific treatment effects: a methodological evaluation. *Psychol. Bull.* 83, 729–58.

Kazdin, A. E., & Wilson, G. T. 1978. *Evaluation of behavior therapy: issues, evidence and research strategies.* Cambridge, Mass.: Ballinger.

Kemper, T. D. 1978. *A social interactional theory of emotions.* New York: Wiley.

Kendon, A. 1972. The role of visual behavior in the organization of social interaction. In M. von Cranach & I. Vine (eds.), *Social communication and movement.* London: Academic Press, 29–74.

Kenny, A. 1963. *Action, emotion and will.* London: Routledge & Kegan Paul.

Kiener, F. 1962. *Hand, Gebärde und Charakter.* Munich: Reinhardt.

Kietz, G. 1956. *Der Ausdrucksgehalt des menschlichen Ganges.* Leipzig: Barth.

Kimble, D. P. 1968. Hippocampus and internal inhibition. *Psychol. Bull.* 70, 285–95.

King, H. E. 1961. Psychological effects of excitation in the limbic system. In D. E. Sheer (ed.), *Electrical stimulation of the brain.* Austin: Univ. Texas 479–86.

Kinsbourne, M., & Bemporad, B. 1984. Lateralization of emotions: a model and the evidence. In N. A. Fox & R. J. Davidson (eds.), *The psychobiology of affective development.* Hillsdale, N.J.: Erlbaum, 259–91.

Kinsey, A. C., Pomeroy, W. B., & Martin, C. E. 1948. *Sexual behavior in the human male.* Philadelphia: Saunders.

1953. *Sexual behavior in the human female.* Philadelphia: Saunders.

Klapp, O. 1969. *The search for identity.* New York: Holt, Rinehart & Winston.

Kleck, R., Vaughan, R.C., Cartwright-Smith, J., Vaughan, K., Colby, C.Z., & Lanzetta, J. T. 1976. Effects of being observed on expressive, subjective and physiological responses to painful stimuli. *J. Pers. Soc. Psychol.* 34, 1211–18.

Klein, D. F. 1981. Anxiety reconceptualized. In D. F. Klein & J. Rabkin (eds.), *Anxiety: new research and changing concepts.* New York: Raven Press, 253–63.

Kline, L. W., & Johannsen, O. E. 1935. The comparative role of face and face-body-hands as aids in identifying emotions. *J. Abnorm. Soc. Psychol.* 29, 915–426.

Klinger, E. 1975. The consequences of commitment and disengagement from incentives. *Psychol. Rev.* 82, 1–25.

Klorman, R. 1974. Habituation of fear: effects of intensity and stimulus order. *Psychophysiology* 11, 15–26.

Klüver, H., & Bucy, P. C. 1937. "Psychic blindness" and other symptoms following temporal lobectomy in rhesus monkeys. *Am. J. Physiol.* 119, 252–353.

Kobasa, S. C. 1979. Stressful life events, personality and health: an inquiry into hardiness. *J. Pers. Soc. Psychol.* 37, 1–11.

Kobasa, S. C., Maddi, S. R., & Kahn, S. 1982. Hardiness and health: a prospective study. *J. Pers. Soc. Psychol.* 42, 168–77.

Koch, B. 1913. *Experimentelle Untersuchungen über die elementare "Gefühlsqualitäten."* Heidelberg: Quelle & Mayer.

Köhler, W. 1917. *Intelligenzprüfungen an Anthropoiden. Abh. Kön. Preuss. Akad. Wiss. Berl.*

1929. *Gestaltpsychology.* New York: Liveright.

Konner, M. 1972. Aspects of a developmental ethology of a foraging people. In N. Blurton-Jones (ed.), *Ethological studies of child behavior.* Cambridge, England: Cambridge University Press, 285–304.

Konrad, K. W., & Bagshaw, M. H. 1970. Effect of novel stimuli on cats reared in a restricted environment. *J. Comp. Physiol. Psychol.* 70, 157–64.

Koolhaas, J. M. 1978. Hypothalamically induced intraspecific aggressive behavior in the rat. *Exp. Brain Res.* 32, 365–75.

Koriat, A., Melkman, R., Averill, J. R., & Lazarus, R. S. 1972. The self-control of emotional reactions to a stressful film. *J. Pers.* 40, 601–19.

Krause, M. S. 1961. The measurement of "transitory" anxiety. *Psychol. Rev.* 68, 178–89.

Krauss, R. 1930. Ueber graphischen Ausdruck. *Z. Angew. Psychol.* 14, Beiheft 48.

Kreitler, H., & Kreitler, S. 1972. *Psychology of the arts.* Durham, N.C.: Duke Univ. Press.

Kris, E. 1952. *Psychoanalytic explorations in art.* New York: International Univ. Press.

Krout, M. 1935. Autistic gestures. *Psychol. Monog. Gen. Appl.* 46.

Kruk, M. R., Van der Poel, A. M., & De Vos-Frericks, T. P. 1979. The induction of aggressive behavior by electrical stimulation of the hypothalamus of male rats. *Behavior* 70, 292–322.

LaBarre, W. 1947. The cultural basis of emotions and gestures. *J. Person.* 16, 49–68.

Laborit, H. 1979. *L'inhibition de l'action: biologie, physiologie, psychologie, sociologie* (Vol. 1). Paris: Masson.

Lacey, B. C., & Lacey, J. I. 1978. Two-way communication between the heart and the brain. *Am. Psychol.* 33, 99–113.

Lacey, J. I., & Lacey, B. C. 1958. Verification and extension of the principle of autonomic response-stereotype. *Am. J. Psychol.* 71, 50–78.

   1970. Some autonomic-central nervous system relationships. In P. Black (ed.), *Physiological correlates of emotion.* New York: Academic Press, 205–28.

Lader, M. 1975. Psychophysiological parameters and methods. In L. Levi (ed.), *Emotions: their parameters and measurement.* New York: Raven Press, 341–68.

Lader, M. H., & Tyrer, P. J. 1972. Central and peripheral effects of propanolol and sotalol in normal human subjects. *Br. J. Pharmacol.* 45, 557–60.

Lader, M. H., & Wing, L. 1966. *Physiological measures, sedative drugs and morbid anxiety.* London: Oxford Univ. Press.

Laferla, J. J., Anderson, D. L., & Scholch, D. S. 1978. Psychoendocrine response to sexual arousal in human males. *Psychosom. Med.* 40, 166–72.

Lagerspetz, K. 1961. Genetic and social causes of aggressive behavior in mice. *Scand. J. Psychol.* 2, 167–73.

Laird, J. D. 1974. Self-attribution of emotion: the effects of expressive behavior on the quality of emotional experience. *J. Pers. Soc. Psychol.* 29, 475–86.

   1984. The real role of facial response in the experience of emotion: a reply to Tourangeau and Ellsworth, and others. *J. Pers. Soc. Psychol.* 47, 909–917.

Laird, J. D., Wagener, J. J., Halal, M., & Szegda, M. 1982. Remembering what you feel: effects of emotion on memory. *J. Pers. Soc. Psychol.* 42, 646–75.

Lambert, W. W., & Solomon, R. L. 1952. Extinction of a running response as a function of distance of block point from the goal. *J. Comp. Physiol. Psychol.* 45, 269–79.

Landis, C. 1924. Studies of emotional reactions, II: general behavior and facial expression. *J. Comp. Psychol.* 4, 447–509.

Landis, C., & Hunt, W. A. 1932. Adrenalin and emotion. *Psychol. Rev.* 39, 467–85.

1939. *The startle pattern.* New York: Farrar and Rinehart.

Lang, P. J. 1977. Imagery and therapy: an information processing analysis of fear. *Behav. Res. Ther.* 8, 862–86.

Lang, P. J., Melamed, B. G., & Hart, J. 1970. A psychophysiological analysis of fear modification using an automatized desensitization procedure. *J. Abnorm. Psychol.* 76, 220–34.

Lange, C. G. 1885. *Om Sindsbevoegelser: Et psyko-fysiologiske Studie.* (*The emotions.* Baltimore: Williams & Wilkins, 1922.)

Langevin, R., & Martin, M. 1975. Can erotic response be classically conditioned? *Behav. Ther.* 6, 350–5.

Langhoff, W. 1935. *Die Moorsoldaten* (Stuttgart: Verlag Neuerweg, 1958).

Lanzetta, J. T., Cartwright-Smith, J., & Kleck, R. 1976. Effects of nonverbal dissimulation on emotional experience and autonomic arousal. *J. Pers. Soc. Psychol.* 33, 354–70.

Lanzetta, J. T., & Kleck, R. E. 1970. Encoding and decoding nonverbal affects in humans. *J. Pers. Soc. Psychol.* 16, 12–19.

Lanzetta, J. T., & Orr, S. P. 1981. Stimulus properties of facial expressions and their influence on the classical conditioning of fear. *Motiv. Emot.* 5, 225–34.

Lautch, H. 1971. Dental phobia. *Br. J. Psychiat.* 119, 151–8.

Laville, A., & Wisner, A. 1965. An EMG study of the neck muscles during a precision task. *J. Physiol.* 57, 260–9.

Lawson, R. 1965. *Frustration.* New York: Macmillan.

Lazarus, R. S. 1966. *Psychological stress and the coping process.* New York: McGraw-Hill.

1975. The self-regulation of emotion. In L. Levi (ed.), *Emotion: its parameters and measurement.* New York: Raven Press, 47–68.

1982. Thoughts on the relations between emotion and cognition. *Am. Psychol.* 37, 1019–24.

1984. On the primacy of cognition. *Am. Phychol.* 39, 124–9.

Lazarus, R. S., & Alfert, E. 1965. The short-circuiting of threat. *J. Abnorm. Soc. Psychol.* 69, 195–205.

Lazarus, R. S., Averill, J. R., & Opton, E. M., Jr. 1970. Towards a cognitive theory of emotion. In M.B. Arnold (ed.), *Feeling and emotion: the Loyola symposium.* New York: Academic Press, 207–32.

Lazarus, R. S., & Folkman, S. 1984. *Stress, appraisal and coping.* New York: Springer.

Lazarus, R. S., Kanner, A. D., & Folkman, S. 1980. Emotions: a cognitive-phenomenological analysis. In R. Plutchik & H. Kellerman (eds.), *Emotion: theory, research and experience.* New York: Academic Press, 189–217.

Lazarus, R. S., & Launier, R. 1978. Stress-related transactions between person and environment. In L. A. Pervin & M. Lewis (eds.), *Perspectives in interactional psychology.* New York: Plenum Press.

Lazarus, R. S., & Opton, E. M., Jr. 1966. A study of psychological stress. In C. D. Spielberger (ed.), *Anxiety and behavior.* New York: Academic Press, 225–62.

Lazarus, R. S., Speisman, J. C., & Mordkoff, A. M. 1963. The relationship between autonomic indicators of psychological stress: heart rate and skin conductance. *Psychosom. Med.* 25, 19–30.

Lazarus, R. S., Speisman, J. C., Mordkoff, A. M., & Davison, L. A. 1962. A laboratory study of psychological stress produced by a motion picture film. *Psychol. Monogr. Gen. Appl.* 76 (whole no. 553).

Lazarus, R. S., Tomita, M., Opton, E. M., Jr., & Kodama, M. 1966. A cross-cultural study of stress reaction patterns in Japan. *J. Pers. Soc. Psychol.* 4, 622–33.

LeBeau, J. 1952. The cingular and precingular areas of psychosurgery. *Acta Psychiat. neurol. Scand.* 27, 305–16.

Leeper, R. W. 1948. A motivational theory of emotion to replace "emotion as disorganised response." *Psychol. Rev.* 55, 5–21.

1970. The motivational and perceptual properties of emotion as indicating their fundamental character and role. In M. B. Arnold (ed.), *Feelings and emotions: the Loyola symposium.* New York: Academic Press, 151–68.

Lefcourt, H. M. 1976. *Locus of control: current theory and research.* New York: Halstedt.

Lehmann, A. 1914. *Die Hauptgesetze des menschlichen Gefühlslebens.* Leipzig: Reisland.

Leshner, A. 1978. *An introduction to behavioral endocrinology.* New York: Oxford Univ. Press.

1983. Pituitary-adrenocortical effects on intermale agonistic behavior. In B. S. Svare (ed.), *Hormones and aggressive behavior.* New York: Plenum Press, 27–38.

Leuba, J. C. 1955. Towards some integration of learning theories: the concept of optimal stimulation. *Psychol. Rep.* 1, 27–33.

Leventhal, H. 1979. A perceptual-motor processing model of emotion. In P. Pliner, K. R. Blankstein, & J. M. Spigel (eds.), *Perception of emotion in self and others.* New York: Plenum Press, 1–46.

1980. Toward a comprehensive theory of emotion. In L. Berkowtiz (ed.), *Advances in experimental social psychology* (Vol. 13). New York: Academic Press, 140–208.

Leventhal, H., Brown, D., Shacham, S., & Enquist, G. 1979. Effects of preparatory information about sensations, threat of pain and attention in cold pressor distress. *J. Pers. Soc. Psychol.* 37, 688–714.

Leventhal, H., & Cupchik, G. C. 1975. The informational and facilitative effects of an audience upon expression and evaluation of humorous stimuli. *J. Exp. Soc. Psychol.* 11, 363–80.

Leventhal, H., & Mace, W. 1970. The effect of laughter on evaluation of a slapstick movie. *J. Person.* 38, 16–30.

Levi, L. 1972. Stress and distress in response to psychosocial stimuli. Laboratory and real life studies on sympathoadrenomedullary and related reactions. *Acta Med. Scand. Suppl.* 528.

Levine, S., & Jones, L. E. 1965. Adrenocorticotrope hormone (ACTH) and passive avoidance learning. *J. Comp. Physiol. Psychol.* 59, 357–60.

Levis, D. J. 1966. Effects of serial CS presentation and other characteristics of the CS on the conditioned avoidance response. *Psychol. Rep.* 18, 755–66.

Levis, D. J., & Hare, N. 1977. A review of the theoretical rational and empirical support for the extinction approach of implosive (flooding) therapy. In M. Hersen, R. M. Eisler & P. M. Miller (eds.), *Progress in behavior modification* (Vol. 4). New York: Academic Press, 300–374.

Lewin, K. 1927. Kindlicher Ausdruck. *Z. Paed. Psychol.* 28, 510–26.

1937. *Towards a dynamic theory of personality*. New York: McGraw-Hill.

Lewinsohn, P. M., 1956. Some individual differences in physiological reactivity to stress. *J. Comp. Physiol. Psychol.* 49, 271–7.

Lewinsohn, P. M., Weinstein, M. S., & Shaw, D. A. 1969. Depression: a clinical-research approach. In R. D. Rubin & C. M. Franks (eds.), *Advances in behavior therapy*. 1968. New York: Academic Press, 231–40.

Lewis, H. B. 1971. *Shame and guilt in neurosis*. New York: International Univ. Press.

Liddell, H. 1950. The role of vigilance in the development of animal neurosis. In P. H. Hoch & J. Zubin (eds.), *Anxiety*. New York: Grune & Stratton.

Lief, H. J., & Fox, R. S. 1963. Training for "detached concern" in medical students. In H. J. Lief, V. H. Lief, & R. N. Lief (eds.), *The psychological basis of medical practice*. New York: Harper & Row, 12–35.

Lindemann, E. 1944. The symptomatology and management of acute grief. *Am. J. Psychiat.* 101, 141.

Lindsley, D. B. 1951. Emotion. In S. S. Stevens (ed.), *Handbook of experimental psychology*. New York: Wiley, 473–516.

Lindsley, D. B., & Wilson, C. L. 1975. Brainstem–hypothalamic systems influencing hippocampal activity and behavior. In R. L. Isaacson & K. H. Pribram (eds.), *The Hippocampus* (Vol. 2). New York: Plenum Press, 247–78.

Lipps, Th. 1903. *Aesthetik: Psychologie des Schönen und der Kunst*. Leipzig: Vogt.

Ljungberg, T., & Ungerstedt, U. 1976. Sensory inattention produced by 6-hydroxydopamine-induced degeneration of ascending dopamine neurons in the brain. *Exp. Neurol.* 53, 558–60.

Lloyd, E. L. 1938. The respiratory mechanism of laughter. *J. Gen. Psychol.* 19, 179–89.

Loeb, C., & Meyer, J. S. 1969. Pontine syndromes. In P. G. Vinken & G. W. Bruyn (eds.), *Handbook of clinical neurology* (vol. 2). Amsterdam: North-Holland, 238–71.

London, H., Schubert, D. S. P., & Washburn, D. 1972. Increase of autonomic arousal in boredom. *J. Abnorm. Soc. Psychol.* 80, 29–36.

Lorenz, K. 1952. *King Solomon's ring*. New York: Cromwell.

1963. *Das sogenannte Böse*. Vienna: G. Borotha-Schoeler (*On Aggression*. New York: Harcourt Brace, 1966).

Lorr, M., Daston, P., & Smith, I. R. 1967. An analysis of mood states. *Educ. Psychol. Meas.* 27, 89–96.

Lorr, M., & Shea, T. M. 1979. Are mood states bipolar? *J. Pers. Assess.* 43, 468–72.

Lowenstein, O., & Loewenfeld, I. E. 1951. Types of central autonomic innervation and fatigue. *Arch. Neurol. Psychiat.* 66, 581–99.

Lubar, J. F., Breure, J. M., Deagle, J. H., Numan, R., & Clemens, W. J. 1970. Effect of septal lesions on detection threshold and unconditioned response to shock. *Physiol. Behav.* 5, 459–63.

Lubar, J. F., & Numan, R. 1973. Behavioral and physiological studies of septal function and related medial cortical structures. *Behav. Biol.* 8, 1–25.

Luria, A. R. 1932. *The nature of human conflicts*. New York: Liveright.

1969. Frontal lobe syndromes. In P. J. Vinken & G. W. Bruyn (eds.), *Handbook of clinical neurology* (Vol. 2). Amsterdam: North-Holland, 725–57.

1973. *The working brain*. Harmondsworth, England: Penguin Books.

Lykken, D. T., Macindoe, I., & Tellegen, A. 1972. Perception: autonomic responses to shock as a function of predictability in time and locus. *Psychophysiology* 9, 318–33.

Lykken, D. T., & Tellegen, A. 1974. On the validity of the preception hypothesis. *Psychophysiology* 11, 125–32.

Lynch, J. J. 1976. *The broken heart: the medical consequences of loneliness.* New York: Basic Books.

Lynd, H. M. 1961. *Shame and the search for identity.* New York: Science Editors.

McCaul, K. D., Holmes, D. S., & Solomon, S. 1982. Voluntary expressive changes and emotion. *J. Pers. Soc. Psychol.* 42, 145–52.

McCaul, K. D., Solomon, S., & Holmes, D. S. 1979. Effects of paced respiration and expectations on physiological and psychological responses to threat. *J. Pers. Soc. Psychol.* 37, 546–71.

Maccoby, E. E., & Jacklin, C. S. 1974. *The psychology of sex-differences.* Stanford: Stanford Univ. Press.

McDougall, W. 1923. *Outline of psychology.* New York: Scribner.

McGeer, P. L., & McGeer, E. G. 1980. Chemistry of mood and emotion. *Ann. Rev. Psychol.* 31, 273–307.

McGhee, Ph. E. 1979. *Humor: its origin and development.* San Francisco: Freeman.

McGinn, N. F., Harburg, E., Julius, S., & McLeod, J. M. 1964. Psychological correlates of blood pressure. *Psychol. Bull.* 61, 209–19.

McKeever, W., & Dixon, M. S. 1981. Right hemisphere superiority for discriminating memorised from non-memorised faces. *Brain Lang.* 12, 246–60.

MacLean, P. D. 1957. Chemical and electrical stimulation of hippocampus in unrestrained animals, II: behavioral findings. *Arch. Neurol. Psychiatry Chicago* 78, 128–42.

  1970. The triune brain, emotion and scientific bias. In F. O. Schmidt (ed.), *The neurosciences: second study program.* New York: Rockefeller Univ. Press, 336–49.

McNair, D. M., & Lorr, M. 1964. An analysis of mood in neurotics. *J. Abnorm. Soc. Psychol.* 69, 620–7.

McNair, D. M., Lorr, M., & Droppleman, L. 1971. *EITS manual: the profile of mood states.* San Diego: Educational Industrial Testing Service.

McReynolds, P. 1976. Assimilation and anxiety. In M. Zuckerman & C. D. Spielberger (eds.), *Emotions and anxiety.* Hillsdale, N.J.: Erlbaum, 35–86.

Magoun, H. W. 1958. *The waking brain.* Springfield, Ill.: Thomas.

Maguire, G. A., MacLean, A. W., & Aitken, R. C. B. 1973. Adaptation on repeated exposure to film-induced stress. *Biol. Psychol.* 1, 43–51.

Mahl, G. F. 1959. Measuring the patient's anxiety during interviews from "expressive" aspects of speech. *Transact. N.Y. Acad. Sci.* 21, 249–57.

Maier, N. R. F. 1949. *Frustration, the study of behavior without a goal.* New York: McGraw-Hill.

Mailer, N. 1979. *The executioner's song.* New York: Little, Brown.

Makela, S., Näätänen, E., & Rinne, U. K. 1959. The response of the adrenal cortex to psychic stress after mepromate treatment. *Acta Endocrinol.* (Kopenhagen).

Malatesta, C. Z. 1981. Infant emotion and the vocal affect lexicon. *Motiv. Emot.* 5, 1–24.

Malmo. R. B. 1959. Activation: a neurophysiological dimension. *Psychol. Rev.* 66, 367–86.

Malmo, R. B., & Shagass, C. 1949. Physiologic study of symptom mechanisms in psychiatric patients under stress. *Psychosom. Med.* 11, 25–9.

Malrieu, H. P. 1960. Evolution et fonction des émotions dans la première année de l'enfant. *Schweiz. Z. Psychol.* 19, 132–51.

508 *References*

Maltzman, I., & Wolff, C. 1970. Preference for immediate versus delayed noxious stimulation and the concomitant GSR. *J. Exp. Psychol.* 83, 76–9.

Mandler, G. 1975. *Mind and emotion.* New York: Wiley.

1984. *Mind and body: the psychology of emotion and stress.* New York: Norton.

Marañon, G. 1924. Contribution à l'étude de l'action émotive de l'adrenaline. *Rev. Franc. Endocrinol.* 2, 301–25.

Mark, V. H., & Ervin, F. R. 1970. *Violence and the brain.* New York: Harper & Row.

Marks, I. M. 1969. *Fears and phobias.* London: Heinemann.

1975. Modern trends in the management of morbid anxiety: coping, stress immunization and extinction. In C. E. Spielberger & I. G. Sarason (eds.), *Stress and anxiety* (Vol. 1). New York: Wiley, 213–36.

Marks, I. M., & Herst, E. R. 1970. A survey of 1200 agoraphobics in Britain. *Soc. Psychiatry* 5, 16–24.

Marris, P. 1974. *Loss and Change.* New York: Pantheon.

Marshall, G. D., & Zimbardo, P. G. 1979. Affective consequences of inadequately explained physiological arousal. *J. Pers. Soc. Psychol.* 37, 970–88.

Marshall, J. F., & Teitelbaum, P. 1974. Further analysis of sensory inattention following lateral hypothalamic damage in rats. *J. Comp. Physiol. Psychol.* 86, 375–95.

Marshall, S. L. A. 1947. *Men against fire.* New York: Morrow.

Marston, W. M. 1917. Systolic blood pressure symptoms of deception. *J. Exp. Psychol.* 117–63.

1923. Sex characteristics of systolic blood pressure behavior. *J. Exp. Psychol.* 6, 387–419.

Martin, I., & Venables, P. H. 1980. *Techniques of psychophysiology.* Chichester, England: Wiley.

Maslach, C. 1979. Negative emotional biasing of unexplained arousal. *J. Pers. Soc. Psychol.* 37, 953–69.

Mason, J. W. 1972. Organization of psychoendocrine mechanisms: a review and reconsideration of research. In R. S. Greenfield & R. A. Sternbach (eds.), *Handbook of psychophysiology.* New York: Holt, Rinehart & Winston, 3–123.

1975. Emotion as reflected in patterns of endocrine integration. In L. Levi (ed.), *Emotions: their parameters and measurement.* New York: Raven Press, 143–82.

Mason, J. W., & Brady, J. V. 1956. Plasma 17-hydroxy-corticosteroid changes related to reserpine effects on emotional behavior. *Science* 124, 983–4.

Mason, J. W., Brady, J. V., & Tolson, W. W. 1966. Behavioral adaptations and endocrine activity. In R. Levine (ed.), *Endocrines and the central nervous system* (Vol. 43). Baltimore: Williams & Wilkins, 227–50.

Mason, J. W., Hartley, L. H., Mongey, E. H., Ricketts, P., & Jones, L. G. 1973. Plasma cortisol and norepinephrine responses in anticipation of muscular exercise. *Psychosomat. Med.* 35, 406–14.

Mason, R. F. 1961. *Internal perception and bodily functioning: relationships between psychological states and physiological processes.* New York: International Univ. Press.

Masters, W. M., & Johnson, V. E. 1966. *Human sexual response.* Boston: Little Brown.

1970. *Human sexual inadequacy.* Boston: Little, Brown.

Matussek, P. 1971. *Die Konzentrationslagerhaft und ihre Folgen.* Berlin: Springer.

May, R. 1950. *The meaning of anxiety.* New York: Ronald Press.

Mechanic, D. 1962. *Students under stress.* New York: The Free Press of Glencoe.

Mehrabian, A. 1972. *Nonverbal communication*. New York: Aldine-Atherton.

Meichenbaum, D. 1977. *Cognitive behavior modifications: an integrative approach*. New York: Plenum Press.

Meichenbaum, D., & Goodman, S. 1969. The developmental control of operant motor responding by verbal operants. *J. Exper. Child Psychol.* 7, 553–65.

Meltzoff, A. N., & Moore, M. K. 1979. Interpreting "initiative" responses in early infancy. *Science* 205, 217–19.

Melzack, R. 1973. *The puzzle of pain*. Harmondsworth, England: Penguin Books.

Melzack, R., & Scott, T. H. 1957. The effects of early experience on the response to pain. *J. Comp. Physiol. Psychol.* 50, 155–61.

Menninger, K. A. 1954. Regulatory devices of the ego under major stress. *Int. J. Psychoanal.* 35, 412–20.

Meyer, H. D. 1949. Reaction time as related to tensions in muscles not essential in the reaction. *J. Exp. Psychol.* 39, 96–113.

Meyer, L. B. 1956. *Emotion and meaning in music*. Chicago: Chicago Univ. Press.

Michotte, A. E. 1950. The emotions as functional connections. In M. Reymert (ed.), *Feelings and emotions*. New York: McGraw-Hill, 114–26.

Millenson, J. R. 1967. *Principles of behavioral analysis*. New York: Macmillan.

Miller, G. A., Galanter, E., & Pribram, K. H. 1960. *Plans and the structure of behavior*. New York: Holt, Rinehart & Winston.

Miller, N. E. 1941. The frustration–aggression hypothesis. *Psychol. Rev.* 48, 337–42.

　　1959. Liberalization of basic S-R concepts: extension to conflict behavior, motivation and social learning. In S. Koch (ed.), *Psychology: a study of a science* (Vol. 2). New York: McGraw-Hill, 196–292.

　　1969. Learning of visceral and glandular responses. *Science*, 163, 434–45.

Miller, N. E., & DiCara, L. V. 1967. Instrumental learning of heart rate changes in curarized rats: shaping and specificity to discriminative stimulus. *J. Comp. Physiol. Psychol.* 63, 12–19.

Miller, R. E., Caul, W. F., & Mirsky, I. A. 1967. The communication of affects between feral and socially isolated monkeys. *J. Pers. Soc. Psychol.* 7, 231–9.

Miller, R. E., Murphy, J. V., & Mirsky, I. A. 1959. Non-verbal communication of affect. *J. Clin. Psychol.* 15, 155–8.

Miller, W. R., & Seligman, M. E. P. 1973. Depression and the perception of reinforcement. *J. Abnorm. Psychol.* 82, 62–73.

　　1975. Depression and learned helplessness in man. *J. Abnorm. Psychol.* 84, 62–73.

Minsky, M. 1975. A framework for representing knowledge. In P. H. Winston (ed.), *The psychology of computer vision*. New York: McGraw-Hill, 211–77.

Mischel, W. 1973. Toward a cognitive social learning reconceptualization of personality. *Psychol. Rev.* 80, 252–83.

Mischel, W., Ebbesen, E. B., & Zeiss, A. R. 1972. Cognitive and attentional mechanisms in delay of gratification. *J. Pers. Soc. Psychol.* 21, 204–18.

Mischel, W., & Masters, J. C. 1966. Effects of probability of reward attainment on responses to frustration. *J. Pers. Soc. Psychol.* 3, 390–6.

Modigliani, A. 1971. Embarrassment, facework and eye-contact: testing a theory of embarrassment. *J. Pers. Soc. Psychol.* 17, 15–24.

Monat, A., Averill, J. R., & Lazarus, R. S. 1972. Anticipatory stress and coping reactions under various conditions of uncertainty. *J. Pers. Soc. Psychol.* 24, 237–53.

Monrad-Krohn, G. H. 1924. On the dissociation of voluntary and emotional innervation of facial paralysis of central origin. *Brain*, 47, 22–35.

Montague, E. K. 1953. The role of anxiety in serial rote learning. *J. Exp. Psychol.* 45, 91–6.

Mora, J. D., Davies, L., Taylor, W., & Jenner, F. A. 1980. Menstrual respiratory changes and symptoms. *Br. J. Psychiatry* 136, 492–7.

Morgan, C. T., & Stellar, E. 1950. *Psychological psychology* (Rev'd. ed). New York: McGraw-Hill.

Morgan, E. 1972. *The descent of woman*. London: Souvenir Press.

Morgan, J. J. B. 1916. The overcoming of distraction and other resistances. *Arch. Psychol.* no. 35.

Morris, D. 1967. *The naked ape*. London: Jonathan Cape.

    1971. *Intimate behavior*. London: Jonathan Cape.

Morrow, G. R., & Labrum, A. H. 1978. The relationship between psychological and physiological measures of anxiety. *Psychosom. Med.* 8, 85–101.

Mowrer, O. H. 1960. *Learning theory and behavior*. New York: Wiley.

Moyer, K. H. 1971. *The physiology of hostility*. Chicago: Markham.

Mulder, G. 1980. The heart of mental effort. Ph.D. dissertation, Univ. of Groningen.

Munn, N. L. 1946. *Psychology: the fundamentals of human adjustment*. Boston: Houghton Mifflin.

Murphy, D. L. 1977. Animal models for mania. In I. Hanin & E. Usdin (eds.), *Animal models in psychiatry & neurology*. New York: Pergamon Press.

Murray, A. D. 1979. Infant crying as an elicitor of parental behavior: an examination of two models. *Psychol. Bull.* 86, 191–215.

Murray, E. 1965. *Sleep, dreams and arousal*. New York: Appleton-Century-Crofts.

Näätänen, R. 1973. The inverted-U relationship between activation and performance: a critical review. In S. Kornblum (ed.), *Attention and Performance* (Vol. 4). New York: Academic Press.

Nafe, J. P. 1924. An experimental study of the affective qualities. *Am. J. Psychol.* 35, 507–44.

Nakao, H. 1958. Emotional behavior produced by hypothalamic stimulation. *Am. J. Physiol.* 194, 411–18.

    1967. Facilitation and inhibition in centrally induced switch-off behavior in cats. *Prog. Brain Res.* 27, 128–43.

Napalkov, S. V. 1967. Information process of the brain. In N. Weiner & J. Schadé (eds.), *Progress in brain research* (Vol. 2). Amsterdam: Elsevier, 59–69.

Neary, R. S., & Zuckerman, M. 1976. Sensation seeking trait and state anxiety and the electrodermal orienting reflex. *Psychophysiology* 13, 205–11.

Nebylitsyn, V. D., & Gray, J. A. 1972. *Biological bases of individual behavior*. New York: Academic Press.

Neisser, U. 1976. *Cognition and reality*. San Francisco: Freeman.

Neumann, C., Lhamon, W. I., & Cohn, A. 1944. Study of emotional factors responsible for changes in the pattern of rhythmic volume fluctuations of the finger tip. *J. Clin. Invest.* 23, 1–9.

Newell, A., & Simon, H. A. 1972. *Human Problem Solving*. Englewood Cliffs, N.J.: Prentice-Hall.

Nieuwenhuyse, B., & Bermond, B. 1986. Relations between bodily sensations and quantitative aspects of emotions. Report Dep. of Psychology, Amsterdam Univ.

Nieuwenhuyse, B., Offenberg, L., & Frijda, N. N. In prep. Subjective emotion and reported body experience. To be published in *Motiv. Emot.*

Nisbett, R. E., & Ross, L. 1980. *Human inference: strategies and shortcomings of social judgment.* Englewood Cliffs, N.J.: Prentice- Hall.

Nisbett, R. E., & Schachter, S. 1966. The cognitive manipulation of pain. *J. Exp. Soc. Psychol.* 2, 227–36.

Nisbett, R. E., & Wilson, T. D. 1977. Telling more than we can know: verbal reports on mental processes. *Psychol. Rev.* 84, 231–59.

Norman, D. A. 1976. *Memory and attention: an introduction to human information processing* (2nd ed.). New York: Wiley.

Notarius, C. I. & Levenson, R. W. 1979. Expressive tendencies and physiological responses to stress. *J. Pers. Soc. Psychol.* 37, 1204–10.

Notarius, C. I., Wemple, C., Ingraham, L. J., Burns, T. J., & Kollar, E. 1982. Multichannel responses to an interpersonal stressor. *J. Pers. Soc. Psychol.* 43, 400–8.

Novaco, R. W. 1979. The cognitive regulation of anger and stress. In P. C. Kendall & S. D. Hollon (eds.), *Cognition-behavioral interventions: theory, research and procedures.* New York: Academic Press, 241–85.

Nowlis, D. P., & Kamiya, J. 1970. The control of electro-encephalographic alpha rhythms through auditory feedback and the associated mental activity. *Psychophysiology* 6, 476–84.

Nowlis, V. 1966. Research with the mood adjective check list. In S. S. Tomkin & C. E. Izard (eds.). *Affect, cognition and personality.* New York: Springer, 352–89.

  1970. Mood, behavior and experience. In M. B. Arnold (ed.). *Feelings and emotions.* New York: Academic Press, 261–78.

Obrist, P. A. 1981. *Cardiovascular psychophysiology: a perspective.* New York: Plenum Press.

Öhman, A. 1979. Fear relevance, autonomic conditioning and phobias: a laboratory model. In P. O. Sjöden, S. Bates, & W. Dockens (eds.), *Trends in behavior therapy.* New York: Academic Press, 107–29.

Öhman, A., & Dimberg, U. 1978. Facial expressions as conditioned stimuli for electrodermal responses: a case of "preparedness"? *J. Pers. Soc. Psychol.* 36, 1251–8.

Öhman, A., Erixon, G., & Löfberg, I. 1975. Phobias and preparedness: phobic versus neutral pictures as conditioned stimuli for human autonomic responses. *J. Abnorm. Psychol.* 84, 41–5.

Öhman, A., Fredrikson, M., & Hugdahl, K. 1978. Orienting and defensive responding in the electrodermal system: palmar–dorsal differences and recovery rate during conditioning to potentially phobic stimuli. *Psychophysiology* 15, 93–101.

O'Keefe, J., & Nadel, L. 1978. *The hippocampus as a cognitive map.* Oxford: Clarendon Press.

Oken, D., Grinker, R. R., & Heath, H. A. 1962. Relation of physiological response to affect expression. *Arch. Gen. Psychiat.* 6, 336–51.

Olds, J. 1962. Hypothalamic substrates of reward. *Psychol. Rev.* 42, 554–604.

O'Leary, K. D., & Wilson, G. T. 1975. *Behavior therapy: application and outcome.* Englewood Cliffs, N.J.: Prentice-Hall.

Orr, S. P., & Lanzetta, J. T. 1984. Extinction of an emotional response in the presence of facial expressions of emotion. *Motivation and Emotion* 8, 55–66.

Osgood, C. E. 1955. Fidelity and reliability. In H. Quastler (ed.), *Information theory in psychology.* Glencoe: Free Press, 374–90.

Oster, H., & Ekman, P. 1978. Facial behavior in child development. *Minn. Symp. Child Psychol.* 11, 231–76.

Otis, N. B., & McCandless, B. 1955. Responses to repeated frustrations of young children differentiated according to need area. *J. Abnorm. Soc. Psychol.* 50, 349–53.

Panksepp, J. 1971. Aggression elicited by electrical stimulation of hypothalamus in albino rats. *Physiol. Behav.* 6, 321–9.

1982. Toward a general psychobiological theory of emotions. *Behav. Brain Sci.* 5, 407–67.

Papez, J. W. 1937. A proposed mechanism of emotion. *Arch. Neurol. Psychiat.* 38, 725–44.

Parin, P., & Morgenthaler, W. 1963. *Die Weissen denken zuviel.* Munich: Kindler.

Parkes, C. M. 1972. *Bereavement: studies of grief in adult life.* New York: International Univ. Press.

Parlee, M. B. 1973. The premenstrual syndrome. *Psychol. Bull.* 80, 454–65.

Pastore, N. 1952. The role of arbitrariness in the frustration-aggression hypothesis. *J. Abnorm. Soc. Psychol.* 47, 728–31.

Pátkai, P. 1971. Catecholamine excretion in pleasant and unpleasant situations. *Acta Psychol.* 35, 352–63.

Patterson, C. J., & Mischel, W. 1976. Effects of temptation-inhibiting and task-facilitating plans on self-control. *J. Pers. Psychol.* 33, 209–17.

Paul, G. L. 1969. Outcome of systematic desensitization I and II. In C. M. Franks (ed.). *Behavior therapy: appraisal and status.* New York: McGraw-Hill.

Peiper, A. 1963. *Cerebral function in infancy and childhood.* New York: Consultants Bureau.

Pervin, L. A. 1963. The need to predict and control under conditions of threat. *J. Pers.* 31, 570–87.

Pfaffman, C. 1960. The pleasures of sensation. *Psychol. Rev.* 67, 253–68.

Pfeifer, R. 1982. *Cognition and emotion.* Carnegie-Mellon Univ., CIP-working paper no. 436.

Pfeifer, R., & Nicholas, D. W. 1981. Towards computational models of emotion. *Proc. 7th Int. Conf. Artif. Intell.* 2369–71.

Piderit, Th. 1867. *Mimik und Physiognomik.* Detmold, Germany: Meyer.

Piët, S. 1986. Het loon van de angst. Ph.D. dissertation. Amsterdam Univ.

Pines, L. N. 1963. Laughter as an equivalent of epilepsy. *Sov. Psychol. Psychiatry* 2, 33–8 (1964, quoted from Berlyne 1969).

Pittman, N. L., & Pittman, T. S. 1979. Effects of amount of helplessness training and internal-external locus of control on mood and performance. *J. Pers. Soc. Psychol.* 37, 39–47.

Plessner, H. 1941. *Lachen und weinen.* Bern: Francke.

Ploog, D. 1970. Social communication among animals. In F. O. Schmidt (ed.), *The neurosciences: second study program.* New York: Rockefeller Univ. Press, 349–60.

Plutchik, R. 1980. *Emotion: a psychoevolutionary synthesis.* New York: Harper & Row.

1982. Only four command systems for all emotions? *Behav. Brain. Sci.* 5, 442–3.

Plutchik, R., & Ax, A. F. 1967. A critique of determinants of emotional state by Schachter & Singer (1962), *Psychophysiology* 74, 9–82.

Poeck, K. 1969. Pathophysiology of emotional disorders associated with brain damage. In P. J. Vinken & G. W. Bruyn (eds.), *Handbook of clinical neurology* (Vol. 3). Amsterdam: North-Holland, 343–67.

Poffenberger, A. T., & Barrows, B. E. 1924. The feeling value of lines. *J. Appl. Psychol.* 8, 192.

Poshivalov, V. P. 1982. Ethological analysis of neuropeptides and psychotropic drugs: effects of intraspecies aggression and sociability of isolated mice. *Aggressive Behav.* 8, 355–69.

Powell, G. E. 1979. *Brain and personality.* London: Saxon House.

Pribram, K. H. 1970. Feelings as monitors. In M. B. Arnold (ed.), *Feelings and emotions: the Loyola symposium.* New York: Academic Press, 39–54.

1971. *Languages of the brain: experimental paradoxes and principles of neuropsychology.* Englewood Cliffs, N.J.: Prentice-Hall.

1980. Cognition and performances. The relation to neural mechanisms of consequence, confidence, and competence. In A. Routtenberg (ed.), *Biology and reinforcements: facets of brain-stimulation reward.* New York: Academic Press, 11–38.

1981. Emotions. In S. B. Filskov & T. J. Boll (eds.), *Handbook of clinical neuropsychology.* New York: Wiley, 102–34.

Pribram, K. H., Douglas, R. J., & Pribram, D. K. 1969. The nature of nonlimbic learning. *J. Comp. Physiol. Psychol.* 69, 765–72.

Pribram, K. H., & Isaacson, R. L. 1975. Summary. In R. L. Isaacson & K. H. Pribram (eds.), *The Hippocampus* (Vol. 2). New York: Plenum Press, 429–40.

Pribram, K. H., & McGuiness, D. 1975. Arousal, activation, and effort in the control of attention. *Psychol. Rev.* 82, 116–49.

Price, J. S. 1972. Genetic and phylogenetic aspects of mood variation. *Int. J. Ment. Health* 1, 124–44.

Prins, P. 1985. Self-speech and self-regulation of high and low anxious children in the dental situation: an interview study. *Beh. Res. Thes.* 23, 641–50.

1986. Efficacy of self-instructional training for reducing children's dental fear (submitted).

Pylyshyn, Z. 1984. *Computation and cognition.* Cambridge, Mass.: MIT Press.

Rachman, S. 1966. Sexual fetishism: an experimental analogue. *Psychol. Rec.* 16, 293–6.

1968. *Phobias: their nature and control.* Springfield, Il.: Thomas.

1974. *The meanings of fear.* Harmondsworth, England: Penguin.

1978. *Fear and courage.* San Francisco: W. H. Freeman.

1980. Emotional processing. *Behav. Res. Ther.* 18, 51–60.

Rachman, S., & Teasdale, J. 1969. *Aversion therapy and the behavior disorders.* London: Routledge & Kegan Paul.

Ramsey, R. 1979. Bereavement: a behavioral treatment of pathological grief. In P. O. Söden, S. Bates, & W. S. Dockens (eds.), *Trends in behavior therapy.* New York: Academic Press, 217–48.

Rapaport, D. 1950. *Emotions and memory.* New York: International Univ. Press.

Razran, G. 1961. The observable unconscious and the inferable conscious in current Soviet psychophysiology: interoceptive conditioning, semantic conditioning, and the orienting reflex. *Psychol. Rev.* 68, 81–147.

Rehwoldt, F. 1911. Über respiratorische Affektsymptome. *Psychol. Stud.* 7, 141–95.

Reisenzein, R. 1983. The Schachter theory of emotion: two decades later. *Psychol. Bull.* 94, 239–64.

Rescorla, R. A. 1969. Pavlovian conditioned inhibition. *Psychol. Bull.* 72, 77–94.

Rinn, W. E. 1984. The neurophysiology of facial expression: a review of the neurological and psychological mechanisms for producing facial expressions. *Psychol. Bull.* 95, 52–77.

Risberg, J., & Ingvar, D. H. 1968. Regional changes in cerebral blood volume during mental activity. *Exp. Brain Res.* 5, 72–8.

Roberts, L. E. 1977. The role of exteroceptive feedback in learned electro-dermal and cardiac control: Some problems with discrimination theory. In J. Beatty (ed.), *Biofeedback and behavior*. New York: Plenum Press.

1978. Operant conditioning of autonomic responses: one perspective on the curare experiments. In G. E. Schwartz & D. Shapiro (eds.), *Consciousness and self-regulation*. (Vol. 2). New York: Plenum Press, 241–320.

Roessler, R., & Engel, B. 1977. The current status of the concept of physiological response specificity and activation. In Z. L. Lipowski (ed.), *Pyschosomatic medicine*. New York: Oxford University Press.

Rolls, E. T. 1975. *The brain and reward*. New York: Plenum Press.

Roman, J., Older, H., & Jones, W. L. 1967. Flight research program, VII: medical monitoring of navy carrier pilots in combat. *Aerospace Med.* 38, 133–9.

Romaniuk, A. 1967. The role of the hypothalamus in defensive behavior. *Acta Biol. Exp.* (Warsaw) 27, 339–43.

Rombouts, H. 1983. Wat is verliefdheid? *Psychologie* 2, 10–15.

Rosch, E. 1978. Principles of categorization. In E. Rosch & B. L. Lloyd (eds.), *Cognition and categorization*. Hillsdale, N.J.: Erlbaum.

Rose, R. M., Poe, R. O., & Mason, J. W. 1968. Psychological state and body size as determinants of 17-OHCS-excretion. *Arch. Intern. Med.* 121, 406–13.

Roseman, I. 1984. Cognitive determinants of emotion: a structural theory. In P. Shaver (ed.), *Review of personality and social psychology* (Vol. 5: *Emotions, relationships, and health*). Beverley-Hills: Sage, 11–36.

Rosenkilde, C. E. 1979. Functional heterogeneity of the prefrontal cortex in the monkey: a review. *Behav. Neurol. Biol.* 25, 301–45.

Rosenzweig, S. 1944. An outline of frustration theory. In J. McV. Hunt (ed.). *Personality and the behavior disorders* (Vol. 1). New York: Ronald Press, 379–88.

Rosvold, H. E., Mirsky, A. F., & Pribram, K. H. 1954. Influence of amygdalectomy on social interaction in a monkey group. *J. Comp. Physiol. Psychol.* 47, 173–8.

Roth, K. A. 1983. Epinephrine, the neglected catecholamine. *Behav. Brain Sci.* 6, 557–8.

Rothbart, M. K. 1973. Laughter in young children. *Psychol. Bull.* 80, 247–56.

Rothbaum, F., Weisz, J. R., & Snyder, S. S. 1982. Changing the world and changing the self: a two-process model of perceived control. *J. Pers. Soc. Psychol.* 42, 5–37.

Rotter, J. B. 1966. Generalized expectancies for internal versus external control of reinforcement. *Psychol. Monog. Gen. Appl.* 80, 1–28 (whole no. 609).

Routtenberg, A. 1968. The two-arousal hypothesis: reticular formation and limbic system. *Psychol. Rev.* 75, 51–80.

1978. The reward system of the brain. *Sci. Am.* 239, 154–64.

Rowe, D. 1978. *The experience of depression*. New York: Wiley.

Ruch, T. C. 1979. Neurophysiology of emotion, affect and species-specific behavior. In W. H. Howell & J. F. Fulton (eds.), *Physiology and biophysics: the brain and neural function*. Philadelphia: Saunders, 671–722.

Ruskin, A., Beard, O. W., & Schaffer, R. L. 1948. Blast hypertension: elevated arterial pressure and victims of the Texas City disaster. *Am. J. Med.* 4, 228–36.

Russell, J. A. 1979. Affective space is bipolar. *J. Pers. Soc. Psychol.* 37, 345–56.

1980. A circumplex model of affect. *J. Pers. Soc. Psychol.* 39, 1161–78.

Sachar, E. J., Mason, J. W., Kolmer, H. S., & Artiss, K. L. 1963. Psychoendocrine aspects of acute schizophrenic reactions. *Psychosom. Med.* 25, 510–38.

Sackett, G. P. 1966. Monkeys reared in visual isolation with pictures as visual input: evidence for an innate releasing mechanism. *Science* 154, 1468–72.

Sackheim, H. A., Greenberg, M. S., Wesman, A. L., Gur, R. C. J., Hungerbucks, J. P., & Geschwind, N. 1982. Hemispheric asymmetry in the expression of positive and negative emotions. *Arch. Neurol.* 39, 210–18.

Sackheim, H. A., Gur, R. C. J., & Saney, M. C. 1978. Emotions are expressed more intensely on the left side of the face. *Science* 202, 434–6.

Safer, M. A., & Leventhal, H. 1977. Ear differences in emotional tones of voice and verbal content. *J. Exp. Psuchol., Hum. Percep. Perform.* 3, 75–82.

Salter, A. 1961. *Conditioned reflex therapy: the direct approach to the reconstruction of personality.* New York: Putnam.

Sartre, J. P. 1934. *Esquisse d'une théorie phénomenologique des émotions.* Paris: Hermann (*The Emotions*, New York: Philosophical Library, 1948).

1943. *L'Etre et le néant.* Paris, Gallimard.

Schachter, J. 1957. Pain, fear and anger in hypertensives: a psychophysiologic study. *Psychosom. Med.* 19, 17–29.

Schachter, S. 1959. *The psychology of affiliation.* Stanford: Stanford Univ. Press.

1964. The interactions of cognitive and physiological determinants of emotional state. In L. Berkowitz (ed.), *Advances in experimental social psychology* (Vol. 1). New York: Academic Press, 49–80.

Schachter, S., & Singer, J. 1962. Cognitive, social and physiological determinants of emotional state. *Psychol. Rev.* 63, 379–99.

Schachter, S., & Wheeler, L. 1962. Epinephrine, chlorpromazine, and amusement. *J. Abnorm. Soc. Psychol.* 65, 121–8.

Schaefer, C., Coyne, J. C., & Lazarus, R. C. 1982. The health-related functions of social support. *J. Behav. Med.* 4, 381–406.

Schank, R. C., & Abelson, R. B. 1977. *Scripts, plans, goals and understanding.* Hillsdale, N.J.: Erlbaum.

Schänzle, J. 1939. *Der mimischen Ausdruck des Denkens.* Berlin: Graefe.

Scheff, T. 1977. The distancing of emotion in ritual. *Curr. Anthropol.* 18, 483–505.

1979. *Catharsis in healing, ritual and drama.* Berkeley: Univ. of California Press.

Scheler, M. 1923. *Wesen und Formen der Sympathie* (5th ed.). Frankfurt: Schulte-Buhmke.

Scherer, K. R. 1979. Nonlinguistic vocal indicators of emotion and psychopathology. In C. Izard (ed.), *Emotions in personality and psychopathology.* New York: Plenum Press, 495–529.

1981. Speech and emotional states. In J. K. Darby (ed.). *Speech evaluation in psychiatry.* New York: Grune & Stratton, 189–220.

1984a. On the nature and function of emotions: a component process approach. In K. R. Scherer & P. Ekman (eds.), *Approaches to emotion.* Hillsdale, N.J.: Erlbaum, 293–317.

1984b. Emotion as a multicomponent process: a model and some cross-cultural data. In P. Shaver (ed.), *Review of personality and social psychology* (Vol. 5). Beverley-Hills: Sage, 37–63.

Scherer, K. R., Koivumaki, J., & Rosenthal, R. 1972. Minimal cues in the vocal communication of affect: judging emotions from content-masked speech. *J. Psycholinguistic Res.* 1, 269–85.

Scherer, K. R., Walbott, H. G., & Summerfield, A. B. (eds.). 1986. *Experiencing emotions: a cross-cultural study*. Cambridge, England: Cambridge Univ. Press.

Schilder, P. 1950. *Image and appearance of the human body*. New York: International Univ. Press.

Schildkraut, J. J. 1978. Current state of the catecholamine hypothesis of affective disorders. In M. A. Lipton, A. DiMascio, & K. E. Killam (eds.). *Psychopharmacology: a generation of progress*. New York: Raven Press, 1233–34.

Schildkraut, J. J., & Kety, S. S. 1967. Biogenic amines and emotion. *Science* 156, 21–9.

Schlosberg, H. 1954. Three dimensions of emotion. *Psychol. Rev.* 61, 81–8.

Schmideberg, M. 1942. Some observations on individual reactions to air raids. *Int. J. Psychoanal.* 23, 146–76.

Schneider, R. A. 1968. A fully automatic portable blood pressure recorder. *J. Appl. Psychol.* 24, 115–18.

Schneirla, T. C. 1959. An evolutionary and developmental theory of biphasic processes underlying approach and withdrawal. *Curr. Theory Res. Motiv.* 8, 1–42.

Schoeck, M. 1966. *Envy*. New York: Harcourt, Brace & World.

Schreiner, L. & Kling, A. 1953. Behavioral changes following rhinecephalic injury in cats. *J. Neurophysiol.* 16, 643–59.

Schulze, R., & Barefoot, J. 1974. Non-verbal responses and affiliative conflict theory. *Br. J. Soc. Clin. Psychol.* 13, 237–43.

Schwartz, G. E., & Beatty, J. (eds.) 1977. *Biofeedback: theory and research*. New York: Academic Press.

Schwartz, G. E., Weinberger, D. A., & Singer, J. A. 1981. Cardiovascular differentiation of happiness, sadness, anger and fear following imagery and exercise. *Psychosom. Med.* 43, 343–64.

Schwartzbaum, J. S., Wilson, W. A., & Morisette, J. R. 1961. The effect of amygdalectomy on locomotor activity in monkeys. *J. Comp. Physiol. Psychol.* 54, 334–6.

Scott, J. C. 1930. Systolic blood-pressure fluctuations with sex, anger, and fear. *J. Comp. Psychol.* 10, 97–114.

Scott, J. P. 1958. *Animal behavior*. Chicago: Chicago Univ. Press.

   1980. The functions of emotions in behavioral systems: a systems theory analysis. In R. Plutchik & H. Kellerman (eds.). *Emotions: theory, research and experience*. New York: Academic Press, 35–56.

Scott, J. P., & Fredericcson, E. 1951. The causes of fighting in mice and rats. *Physiol. Zool.* 24 273–309.

Scott, J. P., & Marston, M. V. 1953. Nonadaptive behavior resulting from a series of defeats in fighting mice. *J. Abnorm. Soc. Psychol.* 48, 417–28.

Seligman, M. R. E. P. 1968. Chronic fear produced by unpredictable electric shock. *J. Comp. Physiol. Psychol.* 16, 402–411.

   1970. On the generality of the laws of learning. *Psychol. Rev.* 77, 406–18.

   1971. Phobias and preparedness. *Behav. Ther.* 2, 307–20.

   1975. *Helplessness: on depression, development and death*. San Francisco: Freeman.

Seligman, M. E. P., & Hager, J. L. 1972. *Biological boundaries of learning*. New York: Appleton-Century-Crofts.

Selye, H. 1956. *The stress of life*. New York: McGraw-Hill.

Sem-Jacobsen, C. W., & Styri, O. B. 1975. Manipulation of emotions: electrophysiological and surgical methods. In L. Levi (ed.), *Emotions: their parameters and measurement*. New York: Raven Press, 645–76.

Shand, A. F. 1896. Character and the emotions. *Mind* 5, 203–26.

Shaw, W. A., & Kline, L. H. 1947. A study of muscle action potentials during the attempted solution by children of problems of increasing difficulty. *J. Exp. Psychol.* 37, 146–58.

Sheffield, F. D. 1965. Relation between classical conditioning and instrumental learning. In W. F. Prokasy (ed.), *Classical conditioning: a symposium*. New York: Appleton, 302–22.

Sheffield, F. D., Roby, T. D., & Campbell, B. A. 1954. Drive reduction versus consummatory behavior as determinants of reinforcement. *J. Comp. Physiol. Psychol.* 47, 349–54.

Shephard J. F. 1906. Organic changes and feeling. *Am. J. Psychol.* 17, 522–84.

Shephard, M., Oppenheim, B., & Mitchell, S. 1971. *Childhood behavior and mental health*. London: Univ. of London Press.

Sherrod, D. R., Hage, J. N., Halpern, P. L., & Moore, B. S. 1977. Effects of personal causation and perceived control on responses to an aversive environment: the more control the better. *J. Exp. Soc. Psychol.* 13, 14–27.

Silverman, A. J., & Cohen, S. I. 1960. Affect and vascular correlates to catecholamines. *Psychiat. Res. Rep.* 12, 16–30.

Silverman, R. E. 1960. Eliminating a conditioned GSR by the reduction of experimental anxiety. *J. Exp. Psychol.* 59, 122–5.

Simon, H. A. 1967. Motivational and emotional controls of cognition. *Psychol. Rev.* 74, 29–39.

Simonov, P. V. 1970. The information theory of emotion. In M. B. Arnold (ed.), *Feeling and emotions: the Loyola symposium*. New York: Academic Press, 145–9.

1975. *Visjaja nervaja tsjeloveka. Motivationno-emotionalie aspekti* (German: Höhere Nerverntätigkeit des Menschen. Motivationelle und emotionale Aspekte. Berlin: Verlag Volk und Gesundheit, 1982).

Simpson, D. D., Dansereau, D., & Giles, G. 1971. A preliminary evaluation of physiological and behavioral effects of self-directed relaxation. Texas Univ. Inst. Behav. Res. 40, 71–2.

Sjöberg, L., Svensson, E., & Persson, L. -O. 1979. The measurement of mood. *Scand. J. Psychol.* 20, 1–18.

Skaggs, E. B. 1930. Studies in attention and emotion. *J. Comp. Psychol.* 10, 375–419.

Skinner, B. F. 1953. *Science and human behavior*. New York: Free Press.

Sloman, A., & Croucher, M. 1981. Why robots will have emotions. *Proc. 7th Int. Joint Conf. Artif. Intell.* 197–202.

Smith, A. A., Malmo, R. C., & Shagass, C. 1954. An electromyographic study of listening and talking. *Can. J. Psychol.* 8, 219–27.

Smith, C. A., & Ellsworth, P. C. 1985. Patterns of cognitive appraisal in emotion. *J. Person. Soc. Psychol.* 48, 813–38.

Smith, R. 1967. Heart rate of pilots flying aircraft on scheduled airline routes. *Aerospace Med.* 38, 1117–19.

Smith, S. L. 1975. Mood and menstrual cycle. In E. J. Sachar (ed.), *Topics in psychoendocrinology*. New York: Grune & Stratton, 19–58.

Smith, W. 1922. *The measurement of emotion*. London: Paul.

Smith, W. K. 1944. The results of ablation of the cingular region of the cerebral cortex. *Fed. Proc.* 3, 42–3.

Snyder, F., & Childers, S. R. 1979. Opiate receptors and opoid peptides. *Ann. Rev. Neurosci.* 2, 35–64.

Snyder, M., & White, Ph. 1982. Mood and memories: elation, depression and the remembering of events of one's life. *J. Pers.* 50, 147–67.

Sokolov, J. N. 1963. *Perception and the conditioned reflex.* Oxford: Pergamon Press.

Solomon, R. C. 1976. *The passions.* New York: Doubleday-Anchor.

   1980. Emotions and choice. In A. O. Rorty (ed.). *Explaining emotions.* Berkeley: Univ. California Press, 251–82.

Solomon, R. L. 1980. The opponent-process theory of acquired motivation. *Am. Psychol.* 35, 691–712.

Solomon, R. L., & Corbit, J. D. 1974. An opponent process theory of motivation, I: Temporal dynamics of affect. *Psychol. Rev.* 81, 19–145.

Solomon, R. L., Kamin, L. J., & Wynne, L. C. 1953. Traumatic avoidance learning: the outcomes of several extinction procedures with dogs. *J. Abnorm. Soc. Psychol.* 48, 291–-302.

Solomon, R. L., & Wynne, L. C. 1954. Traumatic conditioning: the principles of anxiety conservation and partial irreversibility. *Psychol. Rev.* 61, 353–85.

Sonneville, L. de, Schaap, T., & Elshout, J. J. 1981. *De amsterdamse stemmings vragenlijst.* Lisse, Netherlands: Swets & Zeitlinger.

   1985. Ontwikkeling en validatie van de amsterdamse stemmings vragenlijst. *Gedrag* 13, 13–29.

Speisman, J. C., Lazarus, R. S., Mordkoff, A. M., & Davison, L. A. 1964. The experimental reduction of stress based on ego-defense theory. *J. Abnorm. Soc. Psychol.* 64, 163–74.

Spence, J. F., & Spence, K. W. 1966. The motivational components of manifest anxiety: drive and drive stimuli. In C. D. Spielberger (ed.), *Anxiety and behavior.* London: Academic Press.

Spence, K. W. 1956. *Behavior theory and conditioning.* New Haven: Yale Univ. Press.

   1958. A theory of emotionally based drive (*D*) and its relation to performance in simple learning situations. *Am. Psychol.* 13, 131–41.

   1964. Anxiety (drive) level and performance in eyelid conditioning. *Psychol. Bull.* 61, 129–39.

Spencer, H. 1870. *Principles of psychology.* London: Longmans.

Spielberger, C. D. 1966. Theory and research on anxiety. In C. D. Spielberger (ed.). *Anxiety: current trends in theory and research.* New York: Academic Press.

   1975. Anxiety: state-trait-process. In C. D. Spielberger & I. Sarason (eds.), *Stress and anxiety* (Vol. 1). New York: Wiley, 115–43.

Spielberger, C. D., Gorsuch, R. L., & Lushene, R. E. 1970. *STAI Manual for the state-trait inventory.* Palo Alto, Calif.: Consulting Psychologists Press.

Spielberger, C. D., Jacobs, G., Russell, S., & Crane, R. S. 1983. Assessment of anger: the state trait anger scale. In J. N. Butcher & C. D. Spielberger (eds.), *Advances in personality assessment* (Vol. 2). Hillsdale, N.J.: Erlbaum, 159–187.

Spinoza, B. 1677. *Ethics.* Amsterdam: Riemvest (1979, Dutch transl. N. van Suchtelen, Amsterdam: Wereldbibliotheek; English trans. present author).

Spiro, R. J. 1981. Subjectivité et mémoire. *Bull. Psychol.* 35, 553–6.

Spiro, R. J., Crismore, A., & Turner, T. J. 1982. On the role of pervasive experiential coloration in memory. *Text*, 2, 253–62.

Spitz, R. A. 1957. *No and yes: on the genesis of human communication.* New York: International Univ. Press.

   1965. *The first year of life.* New York: International Univ. Press.

Sroufe, L. A., & Waters, E. 1976. The ontogenesis of smiling and laughter: a perspective on the organization of development in infancy. *Psychol. Rev.* 83, 173–89.

Sroufe, L. A., Waters, E., & Matas, L. 1974. Contextual determinants of infant affective response. In M. Lewis & L. A. Rosemblum (eds.), *The origins of fear*. New York: Wiley, 47–72.

Stampfl, T. G., & Lewis, D. J. 1973. *Implosive theory: theory and technique*. Morristown, N.J.: General Learning Press.

Staub, E., & Kellett, D. S. 1972. Increasing pain tolerance by information about aversive stimuli. *J. Pers. Soc. Psychol.* 21, 198–203.

Staub, E., Tursky, B., & Schwartz, G. E. 1971. Self-control and predictability: their effects on reactions to aversive stimulation. *J. Pers. Soc. Psychol.* 28, 157–62.

Stein, L. 1968. Chemistry of reward and punishment. In D. H. Efron (ed.), *Pharmacology: a review of progress*. Washington, D.C.: GPO.

Stein, L., Wise, C. D., & Belluzi, J. D. 1975. Effects of benzodiazepines on central serotonergic mechanisms. *Adv. Biochem. Pharmac.* 14, 29–44.

Steiner, J. E. 1974. Innate, discriminative human facial response expressions to taste and smell stimulations. *Ann. N.Y. Acad. Sci.* 237, 229–33.

Steinman, B., Jaggi, U., & Widner, J. 1955. Ueber den Einfluss von Geräuschen und Lärm auf den Blutdrück des Menschen. *Cardiologia* 27, 233–9.

Stellar, E. 1954. The physiology of motivation. *Psychol. Rev.* 61, 5–22.

1977. Homeostasis, discrepancy, dissonance: a theory of motives and motivation. *Motiv. Emot.* 1, 103–38.

Stellar, E., Hyman, R., & Samet, S. 1954. Gastric factors controlling water and salt solution drinking. *J. Comp. Physiol. Psychol.* 47, 220–6.

Stendhal, H. 1820. *De l'amour*. Paris: Verda.

Stener, F. B., Applefield, J. M., & Smith, R. 1971. Televised aggression and the interpersonal aggression of preschool children. *J. Exp. Child Psychol.* 11, 422–47.

Stennett, R. G. 1957. The relationship of performance level to level of arousal. *J. Exp. Psychol.* 54, 54–61.

Stern, R., & Marks, I. M. 1973. A comparison of brief and prolonged flooding in agroaphobics. *Arch. Gen. Psychiatry* 28, 210.

Stern, R. M., Farr, J. H., & Ray, W. J. 1975. Pleasure. In P. H. Venables & N. J. Christie (eds.), *Research in psychophysiology*. London: Wiley, 208–33.

Sternbach, R. A. 1960a. Some relationships among various "dimensions" of autonomic activity. *J. Psychosomat. Res.* 5, 215–23.

1960b. Two independent indices of activation. *Electroencephalogr. Clin. Neurophysiol.* 12, 609–11.

1960c. A comparative analysis of autonomic responses in startle. *Psychosom. Med.* 22, 204–10.

1966. *Principles of psychophysiology*. New York: Academic Press.

1968. *Pain: a psychophysiological analysis*. New York: Academic Press.

Sternbach, R. A., & Tursky, B. 1965. Ethnic differences among housewives in psychophysical and skin potential responses to electric shock. *Psychophysiology* 1, 241–6.

Stoller, R. J. 1979. *Sexual excitement: dynamics of erotic life*. New York: Pantheon.

Stone, E. A. 1975. Stress and catecholamines. In A. J. Friedhoff (ed.), *Catecholamines and behavior* (Vol. 2). New York: Plenum Press, 31–72.

1983. Problems with current catecholamine hypotheses of antidepressant agents: speculations leading to a new hypothesis. *Behav. Brain Sci.* 6, 535–77.

Storms, M., & Nisbett, R. E. 1970. Insomnia and the attribution process. *J. Pers. Soc. Psychol.* 16, 319–28.

Stotland, E. 1969. *The psychology of hope.* San Francisco: Jossey-Bass.

Strassman, H. D., Thaler, M. B., & Schein, E. H. 1956. A prisoner of war syndrome: apathy as a reaction to severe stress. *Am. J. Psychiatry* 112, 998–1003.

Strauss, H. 1929. Das Zusammenschrecken: Experimentell-Kinematographische Studie zur Physiologie und Pathophysiologie der Reaktivbewegungen. *Z. Psychol. Neurol.* 39, 111–231.

Strehle, H. 1954. *Mienen, Gesten und Gebärden.* Munich: Reinhardt.

Stuart, R. B., & Davis, B. 1972. *Slim chance in a fat world.* Champaign, Il.: Research Press.

Suess, W. M., Alexander, A. B., Smith, D. D. 1980. The effects of psychological stress on respiration: a preliminary study of anxiety and hyperventilation. *Psychophysiology* 17, 535–40.

Suls, J. 1982. Social support, interpersonal relations and health: benefits and liabilities. In G. Sanders & J. Suls (eds.), *Social psychology of health and illness.* Hillsdale: Erlbaum.

Suomi, S. J., & Harlow, H. F. 1976. The facts and functions of fear. In M. Zuckermann & C. D. Spielberger (eds.). *Emotions and anxiety.* Hillsdale, N.J.: Erlbaum, 3–34.

Suomi, S. J., Harlow, H. F., & Domek, C. J. 1970. Effect of repetitive infant–infant separation of young monkeys. *J. Abnorm. Psychol.* 76, 161–72.

Suter, J. 1912. Die Beziehungen zwischen Aufmerksamkeit und Atmung. *Arch. Ges. Psychol.* 25, 78–150.

Sutherland, M. S. 1977. *Breakdown.* London: Granada Publishing.

Tajfel, H. 1982. *Social identity and intergroup relations.* Cambridge, England: Cambridge Univ. Press.

Tavris, C. 1983. *Anger: the misunderstood emotion.* New York: Simon & Schuster.

Testa, T. J. 1974. Causal relationships and the acquisition of avoidance responses. *Psychol. Rev.* 81, 491–505.

Thayer, R. E. 1967. Measurement of activation through self-report. *Psychol. Rep.* 20, 663–78.

   1978a. Factor analytic and reliability studies on the Activation–Deactivation Adjective Check List. *Psychol. Rep.* 42, 747–56.

   1978b. Toward a psychological theory of multidimensional activation (arousal). *Motiv. Emot.* 2, 1–34.

Thompson, J. 1941. Development of facial expression of emotion in blind and seeing children. *Arch. Psychol.* 37, 5–47.

Thompson, R. F., & Spencer, W. A. 1966. Habituation: a model phenomenon for the study of neuronal substrates of behavior. *Psychol. Rev.* 73, 16–43.

Thorndike, R. 1935. *The psychology of wants, interests and attitudes.* New York: Appleton-Century-Crofts.

Tigerstedt, C. 1926. Der Blutdruck des Menschen bei psychischer Exzitation. *Arch. Phys. Skand.* 48, 138–46.

Tinbergen, N. 1951. *The study of instinct.* London: Oxford Univ. Press.

Titchener, E. B. 1908. *Lectures on the elementary psychology of feeling and attention.* New York: Macmillan.

Toates, F. M. 1980. *Animal behavior: a systems approach.* Chichester, England: Wiley.

Toda, M. 1982. *Man, robot and society.* The Hague: Nijhoff.

Tolman, E. C. 1932. *Purposive behavior in man and animals.* New York: Century.

Tomkins, S. S. 1962. *Affect, imagery and consciousness* (Vol. 1, *The positive affects*). New York: Springer.

1980. Affect as amplification: some modifications in theory. In R. Plutchik & H. Kellerman (eds.), *Emotion: theory, research and experience.* New York: Academic Press, 141–64.

Tourangeau, R., & Ellsworth, P. 1979. The role of facial response in the experience of emotion. *J. Pers. Soc. Psychol.* 37, 1519–31.

Trap-Jensen, J., Carlsen, J. E., Hartung, O. J., Svendsen, T. L., Tang, M., & Christensen, N. J. 1982. Beta-adrenoceptor blockade and psychic stress in man. *Br. J. Clin. Pharmacol.* 13, 371–95.

Tucker, D. M. 1981. Lateral brain function, emotion and conceptualization. *Psychol. Bull.* 89, 19–46.

Tursky, B. 1974. Physical, physiological and psychological factors that affect pain reaction to electric shock. *Psychophysiology* 11, 95–112.

Tversky, A., & Kahnemann, D. 1974. Judgment under uncertainty: heuristics and biases. *Science*, 185, 1124–31.

Tyhurst, J. S. 1951. Individual reactions to community disaster. *Am. J. Psychiatry* 107, 764–9.

Tyrer, P. 1976. The role of bodily feelings in anxiety. *Inst. Psychiat. Maudsley Monogr.* no. 23. Oxford: Oxford Univ. Press.

Tyrer, P. J., & Lader, M. H. 1973. Clinical and physiological effects of beta-adrenergic blockage with Sotalol in chronic anxiety. *Clin. Pharmacol. Therapeut.* 14, 418–26.

1976. Central and peripheral correlates of anxiety: a comparative study. *J. Nerv. Ment. Dis.* 162, 99–104.

Ungerstedt, U. 1971. Stereotaxic mapping of the monoamine pathways in the rat. *Acta Physiol. Scand.* 367, 1–48.

Urban, I., & De Wied, D. 1976. Changes in excitability of the theta-activity generating substrate by ACTH(4–10) in the rat. *Exp. Brain Res.* 24, 325–44.

Ursin, H., Baade, E., & Levine, S. 1978, *Psychobiology of stress: a study of coping men.* New York: Academic Press.

Ursin, H., & Kaada, B. R. 1960. Functional localization within the amygdaloid complex in the cat. *Electroencephalogr. Clin. Neurophysiol.* 12, 1–20.

Vaillant, G. E. 1977. *Adaptation to life.* Boston: Little, Brown.

Valenstein, E. S. 1969. Behavior elicited by hypothalamic stimulation: a prepotency hypothesis. *Brain Behav. Evol.* 2, 296–316.

1973. *Brain control.* New York: Wiley-Interscience.

Valenstein, E. S., Cox, V. C., & Kakolewski, J. W. 1970. Reexamination of the role of the hypothalamus in behavior. *Psychol. Rev.* 77, 16–31.

Valentine, C. 1930. The innate causes of fear. *J. Genet. Psychol.* 37, 394–419.

Valins, S. 1966. Cognitive effects of false heart-rate feedback. *J. Pers. Soc. Psychol.* 4, 400–8.

Valins, S., & Ray, A. A. 1967. Effects of cognitive desensitization on avoidance behavior. *J. Pers. Soc. Psychol.* 7, 345–50.

Van der Molen, M. W., Somsen, R. J. M., & Orlebeke, J. F. 1985. The rhythm of the heart beat in information processing. In P. K. Ackles, J. R. Jennings, & M. G. H. Coles (eds.), *Advances in psychophysiology* Greenwich, Conn.: JAI Press, 1–88.

Van Dis, H. 1986. Paniekaanvallen: Psychobiologische aspecten en differentiaal-diagnostische betekenis bij phobische patienten. Dissertation, Univ. of Amsterdam.

Van Dis, H., & Larsson, K. 1971. Induction of sexual arousal in the castrated male rat by intracranial stimulation. *Physiol. Behav.* 6, 85–6.

Van Heerden, J. 1982. *De zorgelijke staat van het onbewuste.* Meppel: Boom.

Van Hooff, J. A. R. A. M. 1972. A comparative approach to the phylogeny of laughter and smiling. In R. A. Hinde (ed.), *Non-verbal communication.* Cambridge, England: Cambridge Univ. Press, 209–37.

1973. A structural analysis of the social behavior of a semi-captive group of chimpanzees. In M. van Cranach & J. Vine (eds.), *Social communication and movement.* New York: Academic Press, 75–162.

1982. Categories and sequences of behavior: methods of description and analysis. In K. R. Scherer & P. Ekman (eds.), *Handbook of methods in nonverbal behavior research.* Cambridge, England: Cambridge Univ. Press, 362–439.

Van Lawick-Goodall, J. 1968. The behavior of free-ranging chimpanzees in the Gombe Stream reserve. *Animal Behav. Monogr.* 1, 161–311.

1972. *In the shadow of man.* New York: Dell Books.

Van Montfrans, G. A. 1984. *Continuous ambulatory blood pressure registration in uncomplicated hypertension.* Amsterdam: Rodopi.

Van Olst, E. H. 1971. *The orientation reflex.* The Hague: Mouton.

Van Praag, H. M. 1983. In search of the mode of action of antidepressants. *Neuropharmacology* 22, 433–40.

Venables, P. H. 1976. Psychophysiological variables. In M. P. Feldman & A. Broadhurst (eds.), *Theoretical and experimental bases of the behavior therapies.* London: Wiley, 43–70.

Venables, P. H., & Martin, I. 1967. Skin resistance and skin potential. In P. H. Venables & I. Martin (eds.), *Manual of psychophysical methods.* Amsterdam: North-Holland, 53–102.

Vine, J. 1973. The role of facial–visual signalling in early social development. In M. von Cranach & I. Vine (eds.), *Social communication and movement.* New York: Academic Press, 195–298.

Von Cranach, M., & Kalbermatter, U. 1982. Ordinary interactive action: theory, methods and some empirical figures. In M. von Cranach & R. Harré (eds.), *The analysis of action.* Cambridge, England: Cambridge Univ. Press.

Wachtel, P. L. 1968. Anxiety, attention and coping with threat. *J. Abnorm. Psychol.* 73, 137–43.

Wallace, R. 1970. Physiological affects of transcendental meditation. *Science* 167, 1751–4.

Ward, A. A., Jr. 1948. The anterior cingular gyrus and personality. *Res. Publ. Assoc. Nerv. Ment. Dis.* 27, 438–45.

Warden, C. J. 1931. *Animal motivation: experimental studies on the albino rat.* New York: Columbia Univ. Press.

Wasman, M., & Flynn, J. P. 1962. Directed attack elicited from hypothalamus. *Arch. Neurol. (Chicago)* 6, 220–7.

Watson, J. B. 1929. *Psychology from the standpoint of a behaviorist* (3rd ed.). Philadelphia: Lippincott.

Watson, J. B., & Rayner, R. 1920. Conditioned emotional reactions. *J. Exp. Psychol.* 3, 1–14.

Weber, H. 1929. Untersuchung über die Ablenkung der Aufmerksamkeit. *Arch. Ges. Psychol.* 71, 185–260.

Wegman, C. 1985. *Psychoanalysis and cognitive psychology.* London: Academic Press.

Weiner, B. 1974. *Achievement motivation and attribution theory.* Morristown, N.J.: General Learning Press.

1980. A cognitive (attributional)-emotion-action model of motivated behavior: an analysis of judgments of help-giving. *J. Pers. Soc. Psychol.* 39, 186–200.

1982. The emotional consequences of causal ascriptions. In M. S. Clark & S. T. Fiske (eds.), *Affect and cognition.* Hillsdale, N.J.: Erlbaum, 185–210.

Weingartner, H., Miller, H.. & Murphy, D. L. 1977. Mood-state-dependent retrieval of verbal associations. *J. Abnorm. Psychol.* 86, 276–84.

Weinstein, J., Averill, J. R., Opton, E. M., & Lazarus, R. S. 1968. Defensive style and discrepancy between self-report and physiological indexes of stress. *J. Pers. Soc. Psychol.* 10, 406–13.

Weisman, A. D. 1972. *On dying and denying.* New York: Behavioral Publications.

Weiss, J. M. 1970. Somatic effects of predictable and unpredictable shock. *Psychosom. Med.* 32, 397–408.

1971a. Effects of coping behavior with and without a feedback signal on stress pathology in rats. *J. Comp. Physiol. Psychol.* 77, 22–30.

1971b. Effects of punishing the coping response (conflict) on stress pathology in rats. *J. Comp. Physiol. Psychol.* 77, 14–21.

Weiss, J. M., Glazer, H. I., & Poherecky, L. A. 1976. Coping behavior and neurochemical changes: an alternative explanation for the original "learned helplessness" experiments. In A. Serban & A. Kling (eds.), *Animal models in human psychobiology.* New York: Plenum Press, 141–73.

Wenger, M. A. 1950. Emotion as visceral action: an extension of Lange's theory. In M. L. Reymert (ed.), *Feelings and emotions: the Mooseheart symposium.* New York: McGraw-Hill.

Wenger, M. A., Averill, J. R., & Smith, D. B. D. 1968. Autonomic activity during sexual arousal. *Psychophysiology* 4, 468–78.

Wenger, M. A., Clemens, T. L., Darsu, M. L., Engel, R. T., Estess, F. M., & Sonnenschein, R. R. 1960. Autonomic response patterns during intravenous infusion of epinephrine and norepinephrine. *Psychosom. Med.* 22, 294–307.

Wenger, M. A., & Cullen, T. D. 1958. ANS response patterns to fourteen stimuli. *Am. Psychol.* 13, 423–4.

1972. Studies of autonomic balance in children and adults. In N. S. Greenfield & R. A. Sternbach (eds.), *Handbook of psychophysiology.* New York: Holt, Rinehart & Winston, 535–70.

Wenzel, B. M. 1972. Immunosympathectomy and behavior. In G. Steiner & E. Schönbaum (eds.), *Immunosympathectomy.* Amsterdam: Elsevier.

Werner, H., & Wapner, S. 1953. Sensory-tonic field theory of perception. In J. S. Bruner & D. Krech (eds.), *Perception and personality.* Durham, N.C.: Duke Univ. Press, 83–107.

Whimbey, A. E., & Denenberg, V. H. 1967. Two independent behavioral dimensions in open field performance. *J. Comp. Physiol. Psychol.* 63, 500–4.

White, G. L. 1981. A model of romantic jealousy. *Motiv. Emot.* 5, 295–310.

White, R. W. 1959. Motivation reconsidered: the concept of competence. *Psychol. Rev.* 66, 297–333.

Wilensky, R. 1983. *Plans and understanding: a computational approach to human reasoning.* Reading: Addison-Wesley.

Wilkins, W. 1971. Desensitization: social and cognitive factors underlying the effectiveness of Wolpe's procedure. *Psychol. Bull.* 76, 311–7.

Williams, A. C. 1939. Some psychological correlates of the electroencephalogram. *Arch. Psychol. N.Y.* 240.

Williams, A. C., MacMillan, J. W., & Jenkins, J. G. 1947. Preliminary experimental investigations of "tension" as a determinant of performance in flight training. CAA Div. Res. Rep. no. 54.

Williams, D. 1969. Temporal lobe syndromes. In P. G. Vinken & G. W. Bruyn (eds.), *Handbook of clinical neurology* (Vol. 2). Amsterdam: North-Holland, 700–24.

Wilson, G. D. 1967. GSR responses to fear-related stimuli. *Percept. Mot. Skills* 24, 401–2.

Wilson, G. T., & Davison, G. C. 1971. Processes of fear reduction in systematic desensitization: animal studies. *Psychol. Bull.* 76, 1–14.

Wise, R. A. 1982. Neuroleptics and operant behavior: the anhedonia hypothesis. *Behav. Brain Sci.* 5, 39–53.

Wolf, S., & Welsh, J. D. 1972. The gastro-intestinal tract as a responsive system. In N. S. Greenfield & R. A. Sternbach (eds.), *Handbook of psychophysiology*. New York: Holt, Rinehart & Winston, 419–56.

Wolf, S., & Wolff, H. G. 1943. *Human gastric function*. New York: Oxford Univ. Press.

Wolff, C. T., Friedman, S. B., Hofer, M. A. & Mason, J. W. 1964. Relationship between psychological defenses and mean urinary 17-hydroxycorticosteroid excretion rates, I: a predictive study of parents of fatally ill children. Psychosom. Med. 26, 591–609.

Wolff, H. G. 1950. Life situations, emotions and bodily disease. In M. L. Reymert (eds.), *Feelings and emotions*. New York: McGraw-Hill.

Wolff, P. H. 1963. Observations on the early development of smiling. In B. M. Foss (ed.), *Determinants of infant behavior* (Vol. 2). New York: Wiley, 113–34.

Wolpe, J. 1969. *The practice of behavior therapy*. London: Pergamon.

Wolpe, J., & Lazarus, A. A. 1966. *Behavioral therapy techniques*. New York: Pergamon.

Wood, C. D. 1958. Behavioral changes following discrete lesions of temporal lobe structures. *Neurology* 8 (suppl. 1), 215–20.

Woodman, D. P., Hurton, J. W., & O'Neill, H. T. 1978. Plasma catecholamines, stress and aggression in maximum security patients. *Biol. Psychol.* 6, 147–54.

Woodworth, R. S. 1938. *Experimental psychology*. New York: Holt.

Woodworth, R. S., & Schlosberg, H. 1954. *Experimental psychology* (rev'd. ed.). New York: Holt.

Woodworth, R. S., & Sherrington, C. S. 1904. A pseudoaffective reflex and its spinal path. *J. Physiol. (London)* 31, 234–43.

Wortman, C. B., & Brehm, J. W. 1975. Responses to uncontrollable outcomes: an integration of reactance theory and the learned helplessness model. *Adv. Exp. Soc. Psychol.* 8, 277–336.

Wundt, W. 1903. *Grundriss der Psychologie*. Stuttgart: Engelmann.

Wynne, L., & Solomon, R. L. 1955. Traumatic avoidance learning: acquisition and extinction in dogs deprived of normal peripheral autonomic function. Genet. Psychol. Monogr. 52, 241–84.

Yates, A. J. 1962. *Frustration and conflict*. New York: Wiley.

Young, G., & Decarie, T. G. 1977. An ethology-based catalogue of facial/vocal behavior in infancy. *Anim. Behav.* 25, 95–107.

Young, P. T. 1918. The localization of feeling. *Am. J. Psychol.* 29, 420–30.

1927. Studies in affective psychology. *Am. J. Psychol.* 38, 157–93.

1943. *Emotion in man and animal*. New York: Wiley.

1959. The role of affective processes in learning and motivation. *Psychol. Rev.* 66, 104–25.

1961. *Motivation and emotion.* New York: Wiley.

Zajonc, R. B. 1968. The attitudinal effects of mere exposure. *J. Pers. Soc. Psychol. Monogr.* 9, (2, part 2).

1980. Thinking and feeling: preferences need no inferences. *Am. Psychol.* 35, 151–75.

1984. On the primacy of emotion. *Am. Psychol.* 39, 117–23.

Zanchetti, A., & Bartorelli, C. 1977. Central nervous mechanisms of arterial hypertension: experimental and clinical evidence. In J. Genest, E. Koiw, & O. Kuchel (eds.). *Hypertension: psychopathology and treatment.* New York: McGraw-Hill, 59–76.

Zimbardo, P. G. 1970. The human choice: Individuation, reason and order versus deindividuation, impulse and chaos. *Curr. Theory Ref. Motiv. Nebr. Symp. Motiv.* 16, 237–307.

Zimbardo, P. G., Cohen, A., Weissenberg, M., Dworkin, L., & Firestone, I. 1969. The control of experimental pain. In P. G. Zimbardo (ed.), *The cognitive control of motivation.* Glenview, Ill.: Scott & Foresman.

Zimbardo, P. G., Pilkonis, P., & Norwood, R. 1974. *Shyness.* Glenview, Ill.: Scott & Foresman.

Zuckerman, M. 1971. Physiological measures of sexual arousal in the human. *Psychol. Bull.* 75, 297–329.

1976. General and situation-specific traits and states: new approaches to assessment of anxiety and other constructs. In M. Zuckerman & C. E. Spielberger (eds.). *Emotions and anxiety.* Hillsdale, N.J.: Erlbaum, 133–74.

1979. *Sensation seeking.* Hillsdale, N.J.: Erlbaum.

Zuckerman, M., Buchsbaum, M., & Murphy, D. 1980. Sensation-seeking and its biological correlates. *Psychol. Bull.* 88, 187–214.

Zuckerman, M., & Lubin, B. 1965. *Manual for the multiple affect adjective check list.* San Diego: Educational and Industrial Testing Service.

Zuckerman, M., Murtaugh, T. T., & Siegel, J. 1974. Sensation-seeking and augmenting-reducing. *Psychophysiology* 535–42.

Zurcher, L. A., & Snow, D. A. 1981. Collective behavior: social movements. In M. Rosenberg & R. H. Turner (eds.), *Social psychology: sociological perspectives.* New York: Basic Books, 447–82.

Author index

Abelson, R. B., 32, 83, 280, 331, 334, 453
Aberle, D., 351
Abramson, L., 296, 298, 302
Adams, D. B., 383
Adams, N., 320
Ahrens, R., 48
Ainsworth, M. D. S., 23
Aitken, R. C. B., 319
Alechsieff, N., 159, 164, 179
Alfert, E., 403
Allport, G. W., 339
Ambrose, A., 50
Amsel, A., 114, 210
Anand, B. B., 152
Anastasiades, P., 166
Ancoli, S., 49, 65, 66, 133
Andersen, P., 393
Andrew, J. N., 299
Andrew, R. J., 16, 18, 19, 26, 36, 50, 69
Andrews, B. K., 178
Anisman, H., 397
Antonovsky, A., 447
Applefield, J. M., 444
Arbuthnot, G. W., 396
Archer, J., 367
Archibald, H. C., 312
Argyle, M., 24, 26
Aries, P., 449
Aristotle, 197, 198, 243
Arnold, M. B., 70, 71, 72, 85, 101, 102,
    109, 116, 155, 159, 178, 180, 195, 202,
    206, 237, 244, 269
Atkinson, J., 341, 342
Averill, J. R., 20, 107, 157, 163, 164, 211,
    247, 286, 293, 296, 319, 407, 449
Ax, A. F., 128, 129, 130, 134, 143, 148,
    156, 162
Azrin, N. H., 108

Bacon, S. J., 116
Badia, P., 272
Baer, D. M., 108

Bagchi, B. K., 159
Bagshaw, M. H., 376, 389
Bandura, A., 106, 108, 284, 298, 305, 306,
    307, 314, 316, 317, 320, 321, 322, 329,
    338, 353, 442, 444
Barchas, J. D., 69
Bard, P., 139, 380, 392
Barefoot, J. C., 24, 224
Barendregt, J. T., 197, 211, 227, 273, 295
Barrett, C. L., 320
Barrows, B. E., 42
Bartlett, E. S., 182
Bartlett, M. K., 294
Barton, W. H., 447
Bartorelli, C., 128
Bartoshuk, A. K., 114
Basowitz, H., 149
Battit, G. E., 294
Baum, M., 316
Beach, F. A., 93, 398
Beatty, J., 139
Beck, A. T., 178, 195, 197, 271, 296, 299,
    321, 424
Beebe-Center, J. G., 7, 9, 180
Beecher, H. K., 270
Bekhterev, W. von, 116, 385
Bekhterewa, N. P., 395
Bell, C., 10, 15
Belluzi, J. D., 396, 397
Bem, D. J., 178, 192, 232
Bemporad, B., 399, 400
Benesch, H., 15
Berger, S. M., 306
Berkowitz, L., 284, 291, 300, 302, 309, 334,
    342, 375
Berlyne, D. E., 51, 52, 134, 152, 265, 272,
    273, 276, 280, 286, 346, 349, 350, 356
Bermond, B., 93, 226, 227, 383, 398
Bernick, N., 127
Bersh, P. J., 301
Bettelheim, B., 97, 356
Bexton, W. H., 345

527

Beyer, J., 320
Beyk, M., 241
Bezooyen, R. A. M. C. van, 36, 64, 65, 68
Bills, A. G., 41
Birch, D., 341, 342
Birkhoff, G. D., 357
Bitterman, M. E., 272
Black, A. H., 126, 229
Blanchard, E. B., 146, 317
Blatz, W. E., 126, 133
Block, J., 4, 183
Bloom, L. J., 271
Blurton-Jones, N. G., 15, 47, 69
Board, F., 149
Boas, E. P., 127
Bogdanoff, M. D., 126, 129
Bonus, B., 399
Bolles, R. C., 31, 93, 106, 304, 314, 341,
    362, 367, 398, 417
Borowitz, G., 127
Boselie, F., 273, 357
Bourke-White, M., 423, 424
Bourne, P. G., 150
Bovenkerk, G., 217, 220
Bower, G. H., 122, 453, 459
Bowlby, J., 23, 212, 264, 274, 275, 276,
    343, 349, 350, 351, 420, 433
Boyd, R. W., 127
Brady, J. V., 112, 130, 147, 149, 160, 175,
    293, 393
Branks, J., 153
Brantigan, C. O., 224
Brantigan, T. A., 224
Breggin, P. R., 223
Bregman, E., 304, 305
Brehm, J. W., 292, 296, 297, 352, 353, 365
Brentano, F., 38, 186
Breuer, J. M., 444
Breznitz, S., 421
Bridger, W. H., 307, 314, 327, 328
Briggs, J. L., 74, 216
Broadbent, D. E., 171
Broadhurst, P., 113, 378
Brooks, V., 276
Brown, B. B., 164
Brown, C. H., 128
Brown, J. L., 383
Brown, J. S., 114, 266, 340
Brown, P. A., 292
Brutkowski, S., 394
Bryant, G. D., 93, 223
Buchsbaum, M., 384
Buchwald, A. M., 129, 157
Buck, R., 235
Bucy, P. C., 389
Bühler, Ch., 362
Bühler, K., 11, 13, 56, 179, 250

Bull, N., 179, 233, 288
Bumke, D., 139
Bunney, W. E., Jr., 149
Burgess, M., 130
Buss, A. H., 198
Butter, C. M., 391
Buunk, B., 99, 286

Cacioppo, J. T., 166
Caggiula, A. B., 383
Calvert-Boyanowski, J., 227
Campbell, D., 304, 315
Campbell, R., 399, 400
Cannon, W. B., 125, 126, 128, 130, 131,
    132, 136, 137, 139, 142, 143, 144, 146,
    155, 157, 159, 163, 176, 215, 233, 426
Cantor, J. R., 93, 223
Cantril, H., 222
Carroll, D., 166
Cassel, J., 448
Cattell, R. B., 300, 377
Caul, W. F., 355
Chance, M. R. A., 27
Chapman, W. P., 390, 396
Charlesworth, W. R., 68, 69
Chevalier-Skolnikoff, S., 69
Chhina, G. S., 152
Childers, S. R., 397
Chiva, M., 11, 30, 68, 69
Chodoff, P., 313
Church, R. M., 307
Clanton, G., 286
Clark, M. S., 122
Clarke, S., 295
Clavier, R. M., 381
Clifton, R. K., 143
Clore, G. L., 204
Clynes, M., 35, 42, 43
Cobb, S., 447
Cohen, F., 294
Cohen, H. D., 132
Cohen, M. E., 117
Cohen, P. R., 122, 453, 459
Cohen, S., 116, 296, 302
Cohen, S. I., 148
Cohn, A., 131, 141
Conklin, V., 180
Cook, M., 26
Cook, S. W., 307
Corbit, J. D., 285
Cortell, R., 158
Costello, C. G., 286, 305, 317
Cowan, P. A., 108
Cox, V. C., 384, 396
Craig, K. D., 306
Croucher, M., 453
Crow, T. J., 396

Cullen, T. D., 157, 158, 159, 161
Cunis, D., 159
Cupchik, G. C., 233, 235

Dahl, R., 295, 422
Daly, E. M., 183
D'Amato, M. E., 293
Dana, C. L., 225
Dansereau, D., 159
Darrow, C. W., 117
Darwin, Ch., 9, 10, 11, 15, 18, 19, 20, 21,
    27, 29, 30, 34, 35, 36, 47, 49, 50, 54,
    55, 56, 60, 67, 69, 97, 135, 140, 167,
    257, 469
Daston, P., 181, 183
Davidson, R. J., 400
Davis, B., 440
Davis, R. C., 40, 41, 65, 129, 157, 161
Davison, G. C., 316, 321
Davitz, J. R., 184, 185, 200
Dawson, M. E., 126
Day, M. E., 22
De Jong, M. A., 164
De Rivera, J., 85, 199, 203, 212, 214
De Wied, D., 398
Dean, J., 24
Decarie, T. G., 49
Defran, R. H., 272
Delgado, J. M. R., 381, 382, 392
Dembo, T., 196, 210
Den Uyl, M. J., 123
Denenberg, V. H., 349
Dennett, D. C., 38, 361
Dermer, M., 295
Descartes, R., 178
deToledo, L., 126
DeVore, I., 27, 275
Diamond, E. L., 130
DiCara, L. V., 146
Dicks, D., 389
Diener, E., 407, 446, 447
DiMascio, A., 127
Dimberg, U., 134, 274
Dimmick, F. L., 180
Dimsdale, J. E., 439
Dittman, A. T., 111
Dixon, M. S., 400
Dobbs, D., 313
Dollard, J., 198, 285, 291, 300, 302, 309,
    315, 334, 340, 342
Donnerstein, E., 223, 296
Doob, A. N., 293
Doob, L. W., 341
Douglas, R. J., 389
Downing, L. L., 447
Drolette, M. E., 129
Droppleman, L., 178

Drozýnski, L., 133
Duchenne, G. B., 15, 49
Duffy, E., 90, 93, 153, 156, 157, 158, 169,
    473
Duke, J. D., 22
Dumas, G., 15, 18, 20, 22, 23, 30, 44, 49,
    50, 51, 54, 56, 61, 69, 135, 137, 140,
    167, 255, 264

Eason, R. G., 153, 154, 156
Easterbrook, J. A., 116
Eastman, C., 286
Edelberg, R., 133, 135
Edinger, L., 275
Efran, J. S., 352
Egbert,L. D., 294
Eibl-Eibesfeldt, I., 20, 26, 48, 68, 69, 104,
    276
Einsiedel, E., 223
Ekman, P., 14, 15, 16, 18, 19, 20, 33, 49,
    61, 62, 63, 64, 65, 66, 68, 69, 72, 73,
    85, 86, 130, 132, 133, 163, 164, 234,
    255, 327, 400, 405, 412, 449
Elias, N., 412, 413, 414
Elliott, R., 166
Ellis, A., 271, 321
Ellson, C. D., 159
Ellsworth, P., 20, 63, 64, 65, 68, 219, 234,
    235, 258
Elmadjian, F. J., 147
Endler, N. S., 375
Engel, B., 157
Engel, J. J., 10, 13
English, H, 304
Epstein, H., 317, 419
Epstein, S., 126, 127, 128, 134, 142, 179,
    292, 293, 294, 295, 301, 319, 320, 402,
    426
Erdmann, G., 223, 225
Erixon, G., 271
Ervin, F. R., 385, 390, 408
Euler, C. von, 276
Evans, I. M., 301
Exline, R. V., 23, 24, 26
Eysenck, H. J., 300, 301, 304, 305, 306,
    315, 377, 378, 417, 443
Eysenck, S. B. G., 378, 443

Fanselow, M. S., 367, 398, 417
Farber, I. E., 111, 226, 340
Farr, C. B., 136
Fechner, G. T., 357
Fehr, B. J., 23, 240
Fehr, F. S., 177
Feigl, H., 335
Feldman, J., 158
Féléky, A., 133

Fenz, W. D., 127, 128, 142, 179, 292, 293, 319, 402, 426
Festinger, L., 291, 419, 446
Fillenbaum, S., 183
Fischer, B., 275
Fisher, D., 293
Flach, A., 46, 237
Flor-Henry, P., 399, 400
Flynn, J. P., 382
Folkman, S., 5, 47, 266, 268, 288, 290, 410, 421, 429, 459
Folkow, N., 167
Fonberg, E., 384, 389, 390
Ford, A., 21
Forge, D. D., 272
Forsyth, R. P., 130
Fouriezos, G., 396
Fox, N. A., 400
Fox, R. S., 423
Fraiberg, S., 61
Frankenhauser, M., 146, 147, 148, 296, 298
Frankmann, R. W., 157
Fredericsson, E., 274
Freeman, G. L., 142, 169
Freud, A., 422
Freud, S., 5, 51, 96, 99, 119, 264, 265, 266, 286, 309, 322, 344, 352, 356, 363, 419, 424, 428, 435, 444
Friedman, S. B., 421, 426
Friesen, W. V., 14, 15, 16, 18, 19, 20, 33, 49, 61, 62, 63, 64, 65, 66, 68, 72, 85, 86, 255, 327, 400
Frijda, N. H., 18, 28, 32, 57, 60, 63, 64, 65, 66, 73, 123, 198, 211, 217, 220, 228, 238, 258, 273, 295, 453
Fulcher, J. S., 61
Funkenstein, D. H., 129, 148, 162
Furedy, J. J., 134, 293, 407
Fuxe, E., 388

Gainotti, G., 400
Gal, R., 296
Galanter, E., 77, 266, 361, 364
Galin, D., 400
Gallistel, C. R., 361
Garber, J., 298
Garcia, J., 304
Gatchel, R. J., 160
Geen, R. G., 130, 444
Geer, J., 316
Geertz, H., 74, 216
Gellhorn, E., 158, 159, 160, 275, 388, 392
Gerdes, E. P., 223
Gergen, K. J., 447
Gergen, M. M., 447
Gibson, J. J., 186, 187, 205, 325

Giles, G., 159
Gilligan, S. G., 121
Glass, D. C., 293, 296, 302
Glazer, H. I., 397
Goffman, E., 405, 409
Goldschmidt, E. F., 127
Goldstein, J. B., 40, 153, 154
Goldstein, K., 45, 48
Goldwater, B. C., 139
Gollender, M., 395
Goltz, F., 380
Goodenough, F., 69
Goodman, S., 444
Goorney, A. B., 305
Gordon, S. L., 62, 74, 108, 247, 311, 446, 450
Gorsuch, R. L., 178
Graham, F. K., 127, 143, 165, 291
Graham, J. D. P., 130
Granet, M., 62, 412
Gratiolet, P., 10
Gray, J. A., 45, 87, 117, 208, 264, 266, 274, 279, 280, 286, 305, 348, 349, 359, 372, 377, 378, 379, 386, 393, 394, 395, 396, 399, 404, 415, 443
Gray, P., 24
Greenblatt, M., 127
Greenfield, N. S., 126
Gregory, J. C., 50, 51, 52, 286
Griffin, R. B., 348
Grings, W. W., 126, 272
Grinker, R. R., 295, 299, 422, 425
Grossen, N. E., 314
Grossman, S. P., 392
Groves, P. M., 302, 318, 319
Guernsey, M., 68
Gumenick, W. E., 293
Gunn, C. G., 126
Gur, R. C. J., 400

Haan, N., 422
Hackmiller, K. L., 226
Hager, J. C., 33, 61, 65, 234, 304, 400
Hager, J. L., 304
Hagman, E., 306
Hall, C. S., 378
Hall, G. S., 199, 311
Hall, K. R. L., 27
Hall, R. A., 348, 349
Hamburg, B. A., 69
Hamburg, D. A., 69, 149, 421, 426
Hammond, D. A., 131
Hammond, L. J., 266, 279, 280
Haner, C. F., 292
Harburg, E., 129, 130, 162
Hare, N., 304, 316
Hare, R. D., 170, 235, 305

Harlow, H. F., 12, 17, 69, 105, 273, 274, 276, 277, 349, 350, 376
Haroutunian, V., 222
Harrell, J. P., 130, 142, 175
Harris, F. R., 108
Harris, R. E., 307
Hart, J., 329
Harter, M. R., 156
Hartig, M., 444
Hassler, R., 385
Hawkins, D. R., 222
Heath, R. G., 385, 390, 395, 396
Hebb, D. O., 3, 109, 110, 113, 117, 196, 264, 265, 266, 269, 273, 274, 275, 282, 346, 350, 415, 416
Heider, F., 199
Henri, P., 159
Herd, J. A., 130
Herst, E. R., 305
Hess, E. H., 139
Hess, W. R., 92, 158, 382, 386, 392
Heymans, G., 377
Higgins, G. E., 226
Hilgard, E. R., 189, 416, 434, 435
Hinde, R. A., 351
Hite, S., 184
Hochberg, J., 276
Hochschild, A. R., 74, 247, 312, 405, 412, 449
Hoebel, G., 383
Hoffman, H. S., 272
Hoffman, M. L., 215, 355
Hohmann, G. W., 179, 225
Hokanson, J. E., 130, 142, 162, 296, 444
Hollon, S. D., 298
Holmes, F., 273, 313
Holmes, T. H., 154
Holtz, M., 93, 398
Hopkins, H. K., 348
Hoppe, F., 196
Horowitz, M. J., 97, 110, 175, 324, 415, 423, 427
Hotton, R. B., 292
Hull, C. L., 363
Hunsperger, R. W., 383
Hunt, H. F., 112, 147
Hunt, W. A., 11, 16, 126, 134, 221, 222
Hutchinson, R. R., 108
Hyman, R., 368

Ingvar, D. H., 131
Ira, G. H., 126
Irwin, F. W., 105
Isaacson, R. L., 379, 381, 384, 389, 393, 394
Isen, A. M., 122
Ison, J. R., 272

Izard, C. E., 20, 27, 60, 64, 65, 68, 72, 73, 85, 86, 182, 233, 234, 250, 257, 258

Jacobsen, C. F., 391
Jacquet, Y. F., 398
James, W., 125, 177, 190, 221, 225, 233
Janis, I. L., 97, 111, 121, 210, 290, 294, 295, 322, 419
Janisse, M. P., 139
Janke, W., 223
Jansen, J., 393
Jasnos, T. M., 226
Jefferson, J. W., 224
Jenkins, J. G., 40
Jensen, A., 111, 113
Jersild, A., 273, 313
Johannsen, O. E., 64
Johnson, E., 122, 123
Johnson, J. E., 270
Johnson, L. C., 319
Johnson, R. D., 447
Johnson, V. E., 127, 129, 130, 138, 159, 164, 295, 328, 446
Jones, H. E., 235
Jones, L. E., 398
Jones, M. C., 314
Jones, W. L., 126
Joseph, N., 224
Joslin, J., 275
Jost, H., 152
Jouvet, M., 387

Kaada, B. R., 384, 390, 393
Kafka, F., 254
Kahn, M., 162
Kahn, S., 438
Kahneman, D., 116, 121, 139
Kakolewski, J. W., 384
Kalbermatter, U., 15
Kamin, L. J., 97
Kamiya, J., 133, 164
Kanfer, F. H., 418, 424, 440, 442, 443, 444
Kanner, A. D., 266, 288
Kaplan, B., 184, 241, 243
Karabenick, S. A., 210
Karoly, P., 424, 440
Katz, D., 273
Katzoff, E. T., 142
Kazdin, A. E., 317, 321
Kellett, D. S., 294
Kemper, T. D., 203, 456
Kendon, A., 274
Kenny, A., 100, 243, 244
Kety, S. S., 397
Kiener, F., 15
Kierkegaard, S., 189
Kietz, G., 15, 42

Kimble, D. P., 393
King, A., 384
King, H. E., 385
King, S. H., 129
Kinsbourne, M., 399, 400
Kinsey, A. C., 129, 131
Klajner, F., 293, 407
Klapp, D., 450
Kleck, R., 23, 64, 234, 235, 242
Klein, D. F., 45, 274, 463
Kline, L. H., 40
Kline, L. W., 64
Kling, A., 127, 389
Klinger, E., 97, 292, 335, 337, 343, 344, 432
Klorman, R., 134, 301
Klüver, H., 389
Kobasa, S. C., 296, 438
Koch, B., 180
Kodama, M., 135
Koelling, R. A., 304
Köhler, W., 105, 186, 274
Koivumaki, J., 64
Konner, M., 275
Konrad, K. W., 376
Koolhaas, J. M., 383
Koriat, A., 206, 269, 319, 327, 423
Krause, M. S., 197
Krauss, R., 35, 42
Kreitler, H., 46, 289, 356
Kreitler, S., 46, 289, 356
Kreutzer, M. A., 68, 69
Kris, E., 356
Krout, M., 36
Kruk, M. R., 383

LaBarre, W., 62
Laborit, H., 297, 397
Labrum, A. H., 156, 163, 226
Lacey, B. C., 126, 127, 128, 157, 162, 165, 166
Lacey, J. I., 126, 127, 128, 157, 162, 165, 166
Lader, M. H., 156, 163, 169, 224, 225
Laferla, J. J., 93, 151
Lagerspetz, K., 377
Laird, J. D., 234
Lambert, W. W., 292
Landis, C., 11, 16, 65, 126, 134, 221
Lang, P. J., 309, 329
Lange, C. G., 125, 177
Langevin, R., 306
Langhoff, W., 416
Lanzetta, J. T., 64, 233, 234, 235, 242, 275, 355
Larsson, K., 383
Launier, R., 410

Lautch, H., 305
Laville, A., 153
Lawson, R., 279
Lazarus, A. A., 321
Lazarus, R. S., 5, 47, 89, 92, 112, 126, 135, 150, 156, 157, 178, 195, 204, 211, 266, 267, 268, 288, 290, 293, 294, 297, 298, 301, 319, 320, 325, 331, 403, 407, 410, 421, 422, 423, 427, 429, 433, 459
LeBeau, J., 395
Leeper, R. W., 109
Lefcourt, H. M., 297, 353
Lehmann, A., 128, 132, 141, 164, 177, 180
LeLordo, V. M., 272
LePage, A., 284
Leshner, A., 399
Leuba, J. C., 265
Levenson, R. W., 235
Leventhal, H., 95, 227, 233, 234, 235, 236, 269, 270, 271, 294, 299, 325, 399, 435
Levi, L., 146, 159, 164
Levine, S., 398
Levis, D. J., 304, 316
Lewin, K., 12, 189, 206
Lewinsohn, P. M., 163, 164
Lewis, H. B., 215, 286
Lhamon, W. I., 131, 141
Liddell, H., 293
Lief, H. J., 423
Lindeman, E., 110
Lindsley, D. B., 90, 116, 152, 170, 386
Lipps, Th., 358
Ljundberg, T., 396
Lloyd, E. L., 50
Loeb, C., 382
Loewenfeld, I. E., 139
Löfberg, I., 272
London, H., 127, 164
London, P., 439
Loofburrow, G. N., 158, 159, 392
Lorenz, K., 276, 308
Lorr, M., 178, 181, 183
Lowenstein, O., 139
Lubar, J. F., 393
Lubin, A., 319
Lubin, B., 178
Lueders, C. W., 136
Luria, A. R., 111, 140, 155, 163, 391
Lushene, R. E., 178
Lykken, D. T., 293, 407
Lynch, J. J., 286
Lynd, H. M., 286

McCandless, B., 301
McCaul, K. D., 235
McDougall, W., 72, 85, 101, 188
Mace, W., 234

McGeer, E. G., 381
McGeer, P. L., 381
McGhee, Ph. E., 286
McGinn, N. F., 128
McGuiness, D., 90, 171, 347, 386, 387, 388, 390, 391, 394, 397, 400, 443
McKeever, W., 400
MacLean, A. W., 319
MacLean, P. D., 379, 381, 393
MacMillan, J. W., 40
McNair, D. M., 378
McReynolds, P., 198, 211, 274, 295
Maddi, S. R., 438
Magoun, H. W., 386
Maguire, G. A., 319
Mahl, G. F., 111
Maier, N. R. F., 117
Mailer, N., 170
Makela, S., 149
Malatesta, C. Z., 69
Malmo, R. B., 40, 135, 153, 154
Malmstrom, E. J., 319
Malrieu, H. P., 18, 68, 69
Maltzman, I., 293
Mandel, J. J., 307, 314, 327, 328
Mandler, G., 10, 116, 125, 169, 177, 192, 228, 229, 230, 266, 282, 284, 286, 295, 334, 364
Mann, L., 111, 121, 419
Marañon, G., 146, 221
Mark, V. H., 385, 390, 408
Marks, I. M., 274, 286, 305, 315, 316
Marris, P., 278, 286, 350
Marshall, G. D., 222, 223
Marshall, J. F., 383
Marshall, S. L. A., 110
Marston, M. V., 107
Marston, W. M., 129
Martin, I., 126, 134
Martin, M., 306
Maslach, C., 222, 223
Mason, J. W., 147, 148, 149, 150, 151, 228, 421
Mason, R. F., 228
Masters, J. C., 292
Masters, W. M., 127, 129, 130, 138, 159, 164, 295, 328, 446
Matas, L., 48, 273
Matussek, P., 313
May, R., 306
Mechanic, D., 425
Mehrabian, A., 23
Meichenbaum, D., 299, 321, 440, 444
Melamed, B. G., 329
Meltzoff, A. N., 68
Melzack, R., 105, 271, 376
Mempel, E., 394

Menlove, F. L., 307
Menninger, K. A., 422
Meyer, H. D., 153
Meyer, J. S., 382
Meyer, L. B., 358
Michotte, A. E., 105, 211
Mickle, W. A., 390, 396
Millenson, J. R., 266, 279
Miller, G. A., 77, 266, 361, 364
Miller, N. E., 164, 292, 309, 315, 341
Miller, R. E., 274, 306, 307, 355
Miller, W. R., 296
Minsky, M., 350
Mir, D., 381
Mirsky, I. A., 274, 306, 307, 355
Mischel, W., 292, 298, 443, 444
Mitchell, S., 273
Modigliani, A., 24
Monat, A., 293, 407
Monrad-Krohn, G. H., 385
Monroe, R. R., 390, 396
Montague, E. K., 111
Monteiro, K. P., 121
Moore, M. K., 68
Mora, J. D., 132
Mordkoff, A. M., 156
Morgan, C. T., 362
Morgan, E., 55
Morgan, J. J. B., 21
Morgenthaler, W., 351, 413
Morris, D., 50, 276
Morrow, G. R., 156, 163, 226
Mountcastle, V. B., 392
Mowrer, O. H., 208, 209, 210, 266, 279, 280, 359
Moyer, K. H., 138, 383, 386
Mulder, G., 141
Munn, N. L., 3
Murphy, D. L., 348
Murphy, J. V., 274, 306, 307, 355
Murray, A. D., 108, 263, 275
Murray, E., 376
Murtaugh, T. T., 348, 378

Näätänen, E., 114, 149
Nadel, L., 394
Nafe, J. P., 180
Nakao, H., 395, 396
Napalkov, S. V., 301, 304
Nauta, W. J., 393
Neary, R. S., 348
Nebylitsyn, V. D., 349
Neil, E., 167
Neisser, U., 192, 433
Neumann, C., 131, 141
Newcomb, T. M., 446
Newman, A., 440

Nicholas, D. W., 453
Nieuwenhuyse, B., 226, 227, 228
Nisbett, R. E., 121, 192, 212, 226, 256, 270
Norman, D. A., 434
Notarius, C. I., 235
Nowlis, D. P., 164
Nowlis, V., 59, 178, 181, 182, 258

Obrist, P. A., 126, 127, 128, 129, 130, 147,
    158, 163, 166, 169
O'Connor, P. J., 305
Offenberg, L., 228
Öhman, A., 134, 272, 274, 275
O'Keefe, J., 394
Oken, D., 132
Older, H., 126
Olds, J., 395
O'Leary, K. D., 440
Oppenheim, B., 273
Opton, M., Jr., 126, 135, 157, 269, 301,
    320
Orr, S. P., 275, 355
Ortony, A., 204
Osgood, C. E., 32
Oster, H., 15, 68, 69, 73
O'Sullivan, M., 64
Otis, N. B., 301

Panksepp, J., 27, 87, 383, 384, 386
Papez, J. W., 394
Parin, P., 351, 413
Parkes, C. M., 97, 110, 119, 184, 193, 199,
    212, 231, 264, 286, 313, 351, 415, 420,
    422, 430, 431
Parlee, M. B., 398
Pastore, N., 198
Pátkai, P., 147, 159
Patterson, C. J., 444
Paul, G. L., 316
Pavlov, I. P., 318
Peiper, A., 11, 68
Pepitone, A., 446
Persky, H., 149
Pervin, L. A., 296
Pfaffman, C., 368
Pfeifer, R., 453
Piderit, Th., 11, 13, 21, 30, 56
Piët, S., 241, 246, 288, 298, 349, 419
Pittman, N. L., 297
Pittman, T. S., 297
Plessner, H., 50
Ploog, D., 384
Plutchik, R., 72, 85, 143, 182, 183, 222,
    258, 469
Poe, R. O., 150
Poeck, K., 54, 104, 385, 389
Poffenberger, A. T., 42

Poherecky, L. A., 397
Polt, J. M., 139
Poshivalov, V. P., 93, 398
Powell, G. E., 391, 395
Previn, D., 323
Pribram, D. K., 389
Pribram, K. H., 77, 90, 171, 236, 252, 266,
    347, 359, 361, 364, 370, 386, 387, 388,
    389, 390, 391, 392, 394, 397, 400, 443,
    465
Price, J. S., 344
Prins, P., 424, 440, 441
Proctor, J. D., 160
Proust, M., 292, 313, 324, 328, 428
Pylyshyn, Z., 468

Quanty, M. B., 130, 444

Rachman, S., 305, 306, 307, 322,
Ramsey, R., 315, 413
Rapaport, D., 121
Rapoport, A., 183
Rappaport, M., 348
Ray, A. A., 233
Rayner, R., 303, 304, 305
Razran, G., 145, 308
Rehwoldt, F., 132, 133
Reisenzein, R., 222, 223, 224, 225, 226
Rescorla, R. A., 303
Riccio, D. C., 222
Riechert, F., 385
Rinn, W. E., 385, 392, 400
Rinne, U. K., 149
Risberg, J., 131
Rissler, A., 147
Ritter, B., 317
Roberts, L. E., 145, 146
Roessler, R., 157
Rolls, E. T., 396
Roman, J., 126
Romaniuk, A., 383
Rombouts, H., 76, 248, 343
Rosch, E., 87
Rose, R. M., 150
Roseman, I., 202
Rosenkilde, C. E., 391
Rosenn, M., 293
Rosenthal, R., 64
Rosenthal, T. L., 305, 307
Rosenzweig, S., 198
Ross, L., 121, 212, 256
Rosvold, H. E., 383, 389, 390
Roth, K. A., 397
Rothbart, M. K., 51, 280
Rothbaum, F., 89, 97, 296, 298, 344, 432,
    439
Rotter, J. B., 211, 297

Rouchefoucauld, E. de, 215
Routtenberg, A., 381, 386, 387, 395
Rowe, D., 184, 200
Ruch, T. C., 379
Ruskin, A., 130
Russell, J. A., 34, 183, 184, 240

Sachar, E. J., 149
Sackett, G. P., 26, 274
Sackheim, H. A., 400
Safer, M. A., 399
Salter, A., 321
Samet, S., 368
Sartre, J. P., 36, 97, 119, 186, 189, 198, 230, 287
Schachter, J., 129, 130, 163, 164
Schachter, S., 3, 125, 177, 192, 222, 224, 226, 255, 351, 447, 448
Schaefer, C., 447
Schank, R. C., 83
Schänzle, J., 15, 21
Scheff, T., 450
Schein, E. H., 426
Scheler, M., 98, 196, 231
Scherer, K. R., 61, 64, 65, 203, 220, 311, 324
Schilder, P., 328
Schildkraut, J. J., 397
Schlosberg, H., 32, 169, 183, 184
Schmideberg, M., 295
Schneider, R. A., 129
Schneirla, T. C., 264, 265
Schoeck, M., 286
Schopenhauer, A., 209
Schreiner, L., 389
Schuette, D., 24
Schulze, R., 24
Schwartz, G. E., 129, 130, 132, 162, 163, 164
Schwartzbaum, J. S., 390
Scott, J. C., 129
Scott, J. P., 86, 107, 274, 376, 378
Scott, T. H., 105
Sears, R. R., 341
Seligman, M. E. P., 80, 212, 272, 275, 286, 293, 296, 302, 304, 315
Selye, H., 142, 149, 150, 174, 175
Sem-Jacobsen, C. W., 395
Sermat, V., 32
Shagass, C., 40, 154
Shand, A. F., 101, 102, 103, 334
Shaw, W. A., 40
Shea, T. M., 183
Sheffield, F. D., 292, 367
Shephard, J. F., 131
Shephard, M., 273
Sherrington, C. S., 382

Sherrod, D. R., 296, 297
Siegel, J., 348, 378
Silverman, A. J., 148
Silverman, R. E., 307
Simon, H. A., 280
Simonov, P. V., 267, 334, 340, 359, 372
Simons, R. C., 255, 327
Simpson, D. D., 159
Singer, J. E., 222, 293, 298, 302
Singh, B., 152
Sjöberg, L., 182
Skaggs, E. B., 132
Skinner, B. F., 403, 418
Sloman, A., 453
Smith, A. A., 40
Smith, C. A., 219, 258
Smith, I. R., 181, 183
Smith, L. G., 286
Smith, R., 126
Smith, R., 444
Smith, S. L., 398
Smith, W., 134
Smith, W. K., 394
Snow, D. A., 351
Snyder, D. R., 391
Snyder, F., 380, 397
Snyder, M., 122
Söderberg, U., 276
Sokolov, J. N., 131, 139, 165, 272, 318, 319
Solomon, R. C., 120, 203, 405
Solomon, R. L., 97, 229, 285, 292, 304, 315, 318
Sonneville, L. de, 181, 182, 217
Spangler, T. J., 352
Spear, P. J., 396
Speisman, J. C., 156, 423
Spence, J. F., 112, 113, 377
Spence, K. W., 111, 112, 113, 115, 377
Spencer, H., 34, 35, 47, 49, 51, 56, 97, 116
Spencer, W. A., 301, 318, 320
Spiegel, J. P., 295, 299, 422, 425
Spielberger, C. D., 178, 299, 342, 375
Spinoza, B., 178, 197, 214, 265, 370, 439
Spiro, R. J., 123
Spitz, R. A., 48, 277
Sroufe, L. A., 48, 51, 69, 196, 273, 280
Stampfl, T. G., 316
Staub, E., 294, 296
Stein, L., 396, 397
Steinman, B., 128, 129, 164
Stellar, E., 362, 368
Stendhal, H., 286, 343
Stener, F. B., 444
Stennett, R. G., 135
Stern, J. A., 177
Stern, R., 316
Stern, R. M., 164

Sternbach, R. A., 126, 132, 134, 156, 163, 164, 169
Stoller, R. J., 286
Stone, E. A., 396, 397
Storm, W. F., 156
Storms, M., 270
Stotland, E., 286
Strassman, H. D., 426
Straub, R. B., 224
Strehle, H., 15, 42
Stuart, R. B., 440
Styri, O. B., 395
Suess, W. M., 132
Suls, J., 448
Suomi, S. J., 12, 17, 69, 273, 274, 277, 301, 349, 350
Suter, J., 132, 133
Sutherland, N. S., 243

Tajfel, H., 272
Tavris, C., 112, 286
Teitelbaum, P., 383
Testa, T. J., 105, 272, 304
Thaler, M. B., 426
Thayer, R. E., 34, 181, 182, 288
Thompson, J., 69
Thompson, R. E., 301, 302, 318, 319, 320
Thorndike, R., 305
Thornton, D. R., 293
Tigerstedt, C., 128
Tinbergen, N., 308
Titchener, E. B., 176, 179, 243
Toates, F. M., 345, 361
Toda, M., 453
Tolman, E. C., 360
Tolson, W. W., 147
Tomita, M., 135
Tomkins, S. S., 27, 60, 72, 86, 201, 233, 264, 334, 372, 469
Tourangeau, R., 234, 235
Trap-Jensen, J., 147, 164
Tucker, D. M., 400
Tuddenham, R. D., 312
Tursky, B., 134, 270, 290, 291
Turtletaub, G., 316
Tversky, A., 121, 122, 123
Tyhurst, J. S., 110, 415
Tyrer, P. J., 163, 224, 225

Ungerstedt, U., 381, 396
Urban, I., 398
Ursin, H., 127, 128, 142, 146, 147, 149, 152, 292, 319, 384, 390

Vaillant, G. E., 422
Valenstein, E. S., 384, 392, 395
Valentine, C., 304

Valins, S., 224, 233
Van der Molen, M. W., 127
van Dis, H., 45, 383, 463
Van Gelder, D., 128
Van Heerden, J., 335
Van Hooff, J. A. R. A. M., 15, 16, 19, 26, 27, 28, 35, 37, 47, 48, 49, 50, 52, 69, 89, 277
Van Lawick-Goodall, J., 15, 16, 28, 69, 274, 406
Van Lindern, B., 225
Van Montfrans, G. A., 128
Van Olst, E. H., 134
Van Praag, H. M., 397
Venables, P. H., 126, 134, 170
Vine, I., 48, 277
Von Cranach, M., 15
von Holst, E., 382

Wachtel, P. L., 111, 116
Wallace, R., 152, 159
Walters, R. H., 108
Wapner, S., 329
Ward, A. A., Jr., 394
Warden, C. J., 341
Wasman, M., 382
Waters, E., 48, 51, 69, 196, 264, 273, 280
Watson, J. B., 262, 303, 304, 305
Weber, H., 21
Wegman, C., 453
Weiner, B., 192, 204, 227, 271, 285, 353
Weingartner, H., 122
Weinstein, J., 227
Weinstein, M. S., 306
Weisman, A. D., 402, 422, 427
Weiss, J. M., 160, 293, 298, 397
Welsh, J. D., 294
Wenger, M. A., 125, 129, 131, 146, 157, 158, 159, 161, 164
Wenzel, B. M., 229
Werner, H., 329
Whalen, R. E., 126
Wheeler, L., 224
Whimbey, A. E., 349
White, G. L., 99, 286
White, P. D., 117
White, Ph., 122
White, R. W., 298, 362
Whitey, S. B., 178
Wilbaut-Guillonard, T., 298
Wiersma, E., 377
Wilcoxon, L. A., 321
Wilensky, R., 83
Wilkins, W., 321
Williams, A. C., 40, 152
Williams, D., 396
Wilson, C. L., 170, 406

Wilson, D. W., 223, 296
Wilson, G. D., 134
Wilson, G. T., 316, 317, 321, 440
Wilson, T. D., 192
Wilson, W. P., 313
Wing, L., 163
Winters, L. C., 23
Wise, C. D., 396
Wise, R. A., 398
Wisner, A., 153
Wolf, S., 136, 138, 143, 163
Wolfe, M. M., 108
Wolff, C., 293
Wolff, C. T., 149, 150, 299, 426
Wolff, H. G., 136, 137, 138, 143, 154, 163
Wolff, P. H., 68
Wolpe, J., 316, 317, 320, 321
Wood, C. D., 390
Woodman, D. P., 148
Woodworth, R. S., 132, 169, 250, 382
Wortman, C. B., 296, 297, 353

Wundt, W., 11, 30, 176, 179, 257, 264, 346
Wynne, L. C., 97, 229, 304, 315, 318

Yates, A. J., 279
Yellin, A., 26
Yerkes, R. M., 112, 115
Young, G. A., 49
Young, L. B., 146
Young, P. T., 3, 16, 109, 180, 242, 264, 367, 368

Zacharko, A. M., 397
Zajonc, R. B., 189, 192, 214, 325, 331, 350
Zanchetti, A., 128
Zillmann, D., 93, 223
Zimbardo, P. G., 222, 223, 270, 286, 446, 447
Zuckerman, M., 129, 134, 178, 342, 347, 348, 349, 378
Zurcher, L. A., 351

Subject index

absence, component of, 200, 202, 208
ACTH, 148–50, 174, 398
Action Proposer, 455, 462
action readiness, 69–71, 239–40, 371, 469
  awareness of, 231, 463
  regulation of, 440–2
action tendency, 6, 69–73, 75–82, 85, 237–9, 371, 382, 457, 474
  definition of, 69
action theory of expression, 11
activated behavior, 33, 91, 92, 169
activating mechanisms, 386
activation, 32–5, 56, 90, 153, 284, 288, 386, 387, 388, 390, 467, 473
  concept of, 90–4
  level, 32
  manifestations, 34–5, 36
  modes, 57, 88, 457
  resources, 376, 467
active coping, 130, 147, 166
adaptive cost, 297, 302
adequacy reaction, 48
admiration, 84, 355
adrenaline (epinephrine), 146–89, 221
adrenocortical response, 148–50
adrenocorticotropic hormone (ACTH), 148–50, 174, 398
advance information, 293–5
AER, 348
aesthetic distance, 356
aesthetic emotions, 355–61
affective defense, 382, 386
affinitive behavior system, 28
affordance, 205, 325
agonistic, 88
alpha blocking, 152, 386
amazement, 18
ambiguity of experience, 354
amok, 107
amygdala, 381, 389
Analyzer, 455
anger, 74, 129, 148, 162, 217, 338, 429, 430

expressions of, 19, 26, 42, 162, 198
anguish, 243
anticipation, 292
antithesis, principle of, 29, 31, 56
anxiety, 45, 198, 243, 285, 305
anxiety conservation hypothesis, 317
apathy, 13, 97, 373, 426
appraisal, 194–5, 202, 268–9, 325, 390, 405, 420–1, 430, 432–6, 455, 464, 468
arousal, 90, 125, 155–8, 221, 346, 347, 386, 388
  concept of, 90, 168–71
  misattribution of, 223, 226
arousal jag, 51, 280, 346, 357
arousal–safety sequence, 51, 280, 287
arousal transfer, 223
arrogance, 89
assimilation, cognitive, 288, 346, 350, 358
attachment, 273, 308, 315, 339, 350–2
attention, expression of, 18, 21, 165
attentional activity, 38, 55, 90–4, 379, 384, 393, 466, 474
attentional capacity hypothesis, 116
attribution, 223, 226, 255, 320, 327
augmenting–reducing AER patterns, 348
autistic gestures, 35
autonomic arousal, 80, 155, 157, 160, 169, 171, 221, 286, 386
autonomic awareness, 221–6, 227, 229, 230
autonomic balance, 158
autonomic feedback, 177, 221, 224, 225
autonomic responses, 124, 143–5
availability heuristic, 121
average evoked response (AER), 348
aversion, 75, 213

basic emotions, 72–5, 86, 202, 229, 469
behavior intensity, 32–4
behavioral disturbance, 110, 409
behavioral inhibition system, 117, 393, 415
being-in-love, 76, 343
beta blockers, 224

biofeedback, 145, 443
blackboard control structure, 459
blood pressure, 128–32
bluffing, 27
blushing, 167–8
boredom, 39, 164
bound activation, 34, 288
brain stem, 379

catastrophe reaction, 45
catecholamine pathways, 380, 387
catecholamines, 146–8, 380
categorial viewpoint, 257
catharsis, 444
causal attribution, 210, 255, 270
caution, 45
central motive state, 362
central theory of emotion, 176
challenge, 200, 211, 287–9
challenge–mastery sequence, 280, 287, 289
cingulate cortex, 381, 394
civilization and emotion, 412–14
coding categories, 324–6, 374, 375, 457
cognitive dispositions or cognitive sets,
    374–6
cognitive penetrability, 468
cognitive processes, 194, 269, 308, 320,
    324–32, 468
cognitive theory of emotion, 177
coherence concerns, 350, 358
cold-pressor test, 269
collative variables, 272, 346
commitment, 342
communication and expression, 28, 55,
    60–2
Comparator, 455, 456
compassion, 355
competence, 193, 200, 288, 298, 320–2, 377
complex emotions, 72, 100
concentration, 21, 40, 42, 165
concern
    notion of, 80, 102, 277, 333–8, 359, 466
    satisfaction condition of, 336, 371–4
concern strength, 340
conditionability, 305
conditioned emotional response (CER),
    112, 378
conditioning, 105, 303
consciousness
    analysis of, 176, 187
    irreflexive, 187
    reflexive, 188
conspicuousness behavior, 27
constellations of stimuli, 277–83, 470
constructive reappraisal, 411, 437
contempt, 68, 72, 73, 89
context components, 204, 208–14

context evaluation, 206, 401, 455, 461
contrition, 201
control precedence, 78, 240, 459, 471–2
controllability, 199, 211, 293, 295–8, 352–3,
    438
coping, 96, 297
core components, 204, 205–8, 258
cortical arousal, 152, 169, 347, 386
corticosteroids, 148–50, 398
crying, 53, 385
cultural differences, 62, 312, 351, 412, 449
curiosity, 273, 280, 345–9, 364

deactivation, 39, 373
defenses, 419, 422
defensive appraisal, 420, 422, 426–32
    explanation of, 432–6
defensive exclusion, 432
defensive grin, 49
deindividuation, 446–7
delight, 83
demand character, 189, 194, 207
denial, 421–7, 429, 435
denial state, 110, 415
density of neural firing, 264
depersonalization, 214, 328, 416, 424
depressed mood, 39, 200, 397, 431
depth of emotion, 246
derived activation, 36
descriptive analysis, 184–7
desensitization, 318, 319
desirability component, 202, 207
desire, 75, 78, 83–5, 278, 282, 336, 362,
    460
desire strength, 341
despair, 279, 343
desynchronization of EEG, 152
detachment, 416, 423, 435
Diagnoser, 455, 456
diastolic blood pressure, 129
diencephalon, 380
difficulty, component of, 80, 173, 206,
    210, 287, 457, 478
diffuse discharge, principle of, 34, 50
dimensional analysis, 180
dimensional viewpoint, 183, 257
direct experience, 303, 307, 327
directional fractionation, 157
disappointment, 279, 287
discrete emotions, 257
disengagement from concerns, 342, 432
disgust, 11, 88, 163
disinterest, 13, 22, 39
displacement, 309, 442
display rules, 62, 405, 412, 449
dissociations between systems, 169
distancing, 437

distress, 75, 163, 273
distress calls, 53, 69, 275
dopamine, 380, 387, 396
dormant concerns, 336, 337, 363
drive, 93
dual control, 405, 474
dual principle of categorization, 73

EDR, 133–5
EEG, 152, 386
effectance motive, 365
effort system, 388, 394
ego component, 189, 214
ego–object fusion, 214
electrodermal response (EDR), 133–5
elements of consciousness, 179
elicited behaviors, 381–9
embarrassment, 24, 168
emblems, 61
emergency response, 128, 144, 155
EMG, 153
emotion
    and action readiness, 69–74
    and choice, 119
    and culture, 74, 107
    definition of, 1, 4, 71, 93, 172, 257, 466, 473
    and disturbance, 3, 109–11
    elicitation of, 263–5
    enhancement of, 401, 404
    functions of, 372–4, 475
    and memory, 121–2
    regulation of, 5
    significance of, 245–7, 299, 414, 430
emotion-focused coping, 410
emotion process, 453–9
emotion proper, 84, 257, 337, 474
emotion transformations, 429–32
emotional behavior, 2, 9ff
    characteristics of, 94–5
emotional experience, 3, 176ff, 463
    methods of study of, 178–86
emotional instability, 300, 377
emotional intensity, 32–4, 100, 226, 247, 290–5, 340
emotional object, 73, 187, 190
emotional phenomena, 1–3
emotional processing, 322
emotional qualities, 125, 161, 195, 227–9, 250
emotional responding, 46
emotional stimuli, 4, 263ff, 277ff, 285
emotions, definitions of, 72–5, 185, 281
empathic distress, 215, 274, 355
endorphins, 397
enjoyments, 83–5, 282, 460
epinephrine, 146–8, 221

ergotropic, 158, 392
Evaluator, 455, 457
excitement, 35, 43, 72, 76, 79, 90, 126, 127, 129, 132–3, 152, 169, 173, 180, 208, 227–8, 239, 257, 326, 474
exhaustion, 174, 302, 376
expectancies, 303, 320, 321
expectancy system, 384, 386
expectation strength, 291–2, 341
exploration, 345, 384
expression
    communication and, 28, 55–7, 60–2
    and cultural differences, 62
    functions of, 10–24
    principles of, 10, 29, 34, 55–7
    recognition of, 57, 63–9
    time course of, 41
    unlearned, 62–3, 67–9, 104
    vocal, 25, 64, 68
expressive behavior, 9–16
extinction, 314–19

Facial Action Coding System (FACS), 15, 65
facial expression, 15–24, 385, 400, 469
facial feedback theory, 233–9
facilitators, 283
familiarity, 213, 276, 349
fascination, 355
fatigue, 39, 174
fear, 16, 74, 163, 197, 216, 273, 429
fear expressions, 16, 31, 163
"feeling," 179, 183, 243–5, 251, 253, 360, 368, 371, 395, 399
feeling management, 253
feeling rules, 312, 412, 449
feelings, 251, 465
field actions, 12, 70
finality, 212
flooding, 315, 316, 319
flux, notion of, 47, 459
focality component, 213
frames, 350
free activation, 37, 373
freedom of action concern, 352, 364
frowning, 21–2
frustration, 198, 210, 279, 302, 352
frustration–aggression hypothesis, 198, 300, 340, 341
frustration effect, 114
function pleasure, 365
functional autonomy, 339
functionalist perspective, 75, 371, 475
fundamental distress, 284
fundamental emotions, 72f, 229

galvanic skin response (GSR), 133
gastrointestinal activity, 136, 160

gaze, gazing, 23
general adaptation syndrome (GAS), 174
generalization, stimulus, 308–9
gestures, 30, 61
globality component, 213
gonadal hormones, 151
grief, 23, 163, 196, 199, 212, 278, 343, 429, 430
GSR, 133
guilt feeling, 72, 99, 201, 430

habituation, 318–21
happiness, 164, 287
hardiness, 297, 438
hatred, 212
heart rate (HR), 126–32, 156, 165
hedonic asymmetry, laws of, 323–4, 369
hedonic concerns, 364–5, 366
hedonic quality, 179, 242–5, 367–9, 464
helplessness, 79
helplessness response, 53
hemiplegia, 225
hemispheric difference, 399
hippocampal, hippocampus, 381, 393
hope, 74, 280
hormonal response, 146–52
hyperesthetic–emotional syndrome, 175, 376
hypervigilance, 110
hypothalamus, 380, 382

I-fraction, 132
imageless thought, 179, 238, 250
imagery, role of, 298–9, 316, 329
immunosympathectomy, 229
implosion, 316
imprinting, 308, 338
impulse control, 440–5
impulses, analysis of, 75, 78, 472
impulsiveness, 43–4
impulsiveness trait, 348, 378, 444
inactivity, 39
incubation, 301, 315
individual response stereotypy, 157
information-processing approach, 75–6, 361, 453–63
inhibition, 44–6, 56, 57, 240, 241, 390, 391–5, 405–10, 414–18, 445
inhibitors, 283
inner control, 438
input format, 329, 467
input regulation, 418–20
insight, 104, 471
"intake-rejection" hypothesis, 165
intellectualization, 328, 423, 427, 435
intensity as stimulus, 264, 290–302
intention, 75, 80

intentional structures, 98, 240, 462, 465, 479
intentionality, concept of, 38
intentionality component, 91, 199, 210, 327
interactive expressions, 25f, 55
interest, 23, 24, 38, 42, 68, 88, 91, 134, 139, 170, 345, 386–9
interoceptive conditioning, 145
interruption, 266, 286, 365, 478
intimidating behavior, 26
intracranial self-stimulation (ICSS), 395
intrapsychic coping, 408, 410, 420–6, 437–9
introspection, 178, 179, 186–7
intrusion state, 110, 175, 427
intuitive links, 105, 471
inverted U-curve, 113, 265
irradiation principle (Spencer's), 35, 50, 51, 116
irrationality, 118–21, 327, 475
irreflexive experience, 186–93, 464
isolation, 424

James–Lange theory, 125, 162, 177, 190, 221–8, 233
jealousy, 72, 99, 431
joking, 419, 425, 437
joy, 27, 35–9, 200, 278, 288

Klüver–Bucy syndrome, 389

latah, 107
late injury, 313
latent concerns, 336, 337, 363
laughter, 28, 49–53, 55, 280, 385
Law of Intermittences, 328, 428
Law of Preponderance of Pleasure, 324
Law of Regret, 292, 323, 342
laws of hedonic asymmetry, 323–4, 369
levels of response, 95, 326
limbic system, 381
listlessness, 39
locus of control, 297, 353, 375
loneliness, 251, 362
love, 83, 212, 338, 343

manic state, 39
MAO inhibitors, 348, 378, 397
match–mismatch processes, 77, 265–7, 278–82, 346, 350, 361, 365, 368, 455, 467
match–mismatch theories, 265–7
"mental contents," 176, 186, 242
mental elements, 179
middle knowledge, 402, 427
mimiques, 30, 61
mirth, 164

modeling, 106, 316
modifiability component, 212
monitoring, 79, 239, 280, 370, 404, 459, 465
monoamines, 380, 396
mood, 59, 252, 289, 395
mood adjective checklists, 178–9, 181–4, 217
mood congruity effect, 121
mood-state-dependent retrieval, 121
motivation, 83, 267, 334, 335, 361–6, 369, 372, 460
"moved," 254, 357
movement scope, 32, 33
muscle tension, 40–1, 91, 153
"mussulman syndrome," 426

necessity, 439
neocortex, 381
neuronal model, 272, 318, 387
noradrenaline (norepinephrine), 146–8
norepinephrine, 146–8
nostalgia, 76
noting, 435
null states, 13, 71
numbness, 97, 415, 420, 423, 435

object components, 205, 214
object evaluation component, 212, 283
object fate component, 215
object of emotion, 73, 187, 190
objectivity component, 205
objectless emotions, 284
oblique eyebrows, 16, 23
observational learning, 106, 306
obstruction box technique, 341
openness component, 194, 210
opponent process theory, 285
optimal arousal level, 265, 346, 348
organ sensations, 177, 179
orienting, orientation response, 12, 131, 134, 152, 165, 272, 346
"ought," feature of, 199
outcome-controlled processes, 417–18

pain, 163
pain and pleasure, 78–9, 82, 243, 366–70, 471
palliation, 410, 411, 428
panic, 45, 210
"Papez circuit," 394
parasympathetic activity, 158–61
passions, 101, 231, 253, 338
passive avoidance, 417
passive coping, 147, 166
passivity, 80, 159, 240
perceptual cycle, 433

peripheral theory of emotion, 177, 239
persistence of emotions, 312–18
PGR, 133
physiological manifestations, 3, 124ff
piloerection, 140
pity, 215, 355
play face, 28, 50
play system, 37
pleasure, 78–9, 82, 164, 180, 243, 275, 366–70, 471
point of no return, 43, 91, 241
predictability, 293, 296
preparedness, 272, 274, 304
prepotent responses, 384
presence component, 208
pride, 89, 271
primary appraisal, 204, 401
primary coping, 96
primitive system, expression as, 31
problem-focused coping, 410, 426
profiles, situational meaning, 216
promise, 287
proprioceptive cues, 177, 179, 233
proximity seeking, 76, 274, 350, 358, 364
"pseudoaffective" response, 382
psychogalvanic response (PGR), 133
pupillary response, 138–9

qualia, 250, 463

reactance, 296, 297, 352, 353
reality, 206, 328–9
reappraisal, 411
recovery quotient, 142
reflection, 191, 243
reflexive control, 442
reflexive experience, 187, 191, 464
regulation, 5, 391, 401ff, 471
    definition of, 402
reinforcement, 107, 279, 335
relational activity, relational behavior, 12–13, 24–5, 55, 67
relaxation, 159
relevance component, 206
relevance evaluation, 206, 278, 401, 455
remorse, 201
repression, 428, 435
reptilian brain, 379
respiration, 132–3
response control, 442–6
reticular formation, 386
ritual, 449

sadness, 22, 163, 199
satisfaction condition, 336
SC, 133
secondary appraisal, 204, 401

secondary control, 97, 298, 320, 344, 432
secondary coping, 96
secondary gains, 108, 317
self as component, 189, 214
self-attribution, 178, 232
self-control, 241, 402, 410, 418, 437, 442–7
self-efficacy, 298, 321
self-evaluation, 245, 288
self-inoculation, 321
self-instructions, 424
self-monitoring, 442
self-perception theory, 178, 232
self-significance, 245
sensation seeking, 342, 347–9, 378
sense of expressions, 13–14
sensitivities, 361–3
sensitization, 300
sensory neglect, 383
sensory–tonic field theory, 329
sentimentality, 225, 352, 376
sentiments, 102, 253, 376
separation anxiety, 45, 274, 351
septal area, 381
sequential analysis, 15
seriousness component, 206, 291, 457
serotonin, 380, 396
set-point, 361–7, 369
sexual excitement, 129, 138, 164, 225, 407
sexual stimuli, 276, 294
sham rage, 380, 408
shame, 27, 73, 168, 271, 409
shyness, 17, 24, 44
significance of emotion, 245–7, 299, 414, 430
situation, notion of, 193, 268
situational meaning structure, 188–92, 193–4, 195–221, 455, 457, 459, 468
situational response stereotypy, 161
skin conductance level (SC), 133
smile, smiling, 28, 47–9, 55
social embedding, 247, 448–50
social norms, 311, 409
social regulation, 411, 445
social significance, 247
social support, 447
source concerns, 338–40, 344ff, 372
Spätschädigung, 313
species-specific behavior, 103
species-specific, defense reaction (SSDR), 106, 114
spinal cord lesions, 225
SSDR, 106, 114
staring, 19, 26, 274
startle pattern, 11, 16, 272
stimulus, notion of, 263, 267, 277, 456, 467

stimulus coding, 269, 271, 325, 435
stimulus evaluation checks, 203, 324, 325
stimulus intensity, 264, 301
stimulus processing, 324–30, 434–6, 468
stomach ulcers, 160
strangeness, 213, 272, 349
stress, 174, 296
stressors, 290
strong nervous system, 349
structural theory of emotion, 202, 203
submissive behavior, 27, 29, 89
summation, 300
surface concerns, 102, 338–40, 343, 466
surprise, 18
surrender, notion of, 14, 50, 54, 89, 357
sweating, 135
symbolic learning, 306
sympathetic arousal, 155–8, 161
systolic blood pressure, 129

tears, 54
temporal lobe, 384
tenderness, 83
tenseness, 40–1
tension release, 51–2, 91
testosterone, 151, 383, 398
thresholds, emotion, 299–300, 301, 457
time course, 41, 141
TOTE concept, 364
Totstellreflex, 44
trait anxiety, 342, 375, 378
transaction, notion of, 46, 268, 459
transferred expressions, 29–30
traumatic stimuli, 315, 415
trembling, 139
tremors, 153–5
triune brain, 379
trophotropic, 158, 392

uncertainty, 209, 280, 292
unconscious, 464
uncontrollability, 199, 211, 293, 295–8
unfamiliarity, 273, 349
unlearned stimuli, 271–7, 281
unobtrusiveness behavior, 27
urgency component, 173, 206, 291, 409, 457, 478
urinary response, 137

valence, 190, 207
values and emotions, 215, 311, 353
vicarious learning, 108, 306
visceral brain, 379

vitality, 80, 92, 231, 288
vocal emblems, 61
vocal expression, 25, 64, 68
volitional facial paralysis, 385
voodoo death, 215, 426

weeping, 53–5, 385

wild man, 107, 449
wonder, 18
work of grief, 97, 119, 322
work of worry, 97, 119, 294, 322
worry, 76
Wundt curve, 264, 346

Yerkes–Dodson law, 113, 115